Exam 70-680: Configuring Windows 7

OBJECTIVE	CHAPTER	LESSON
INSTALLING, UPGRADING, AND MIGRATING TO WINDOWS 7		
Perform a clean installation.	1	1
Upgrade to Windows 7 from previous versions of Windows.	1	2
Migrate user profiles.	1	3
DEPLOYING WINDOWS 7		
Capture a system image.	2	1
Prepare a system image for deployment.	3	1
Deploy a system image.	3	2
Configure a VHD.	2	2
CONFIGURING HARDWARE AND APPLICATIONS		
Configure devices.	4	1
Configure application compatibility.	5	1
Configure application restrictions.	5	2
Configure Internet Explorer.	12	2
CONFIGURING NETWORK CONNECTIVITY		
Configure IPv4 network settings.	6	1
Configure IPv6 network settings.	6	2
Configure networking settings.	6	3
Configure Windows Firewall.	7	1
Configure remote management.	7	2
CONFIGURING ACCESS TO RESOURCES		
Configure shared resources.	8	1
Configure file and folder access.	8	2
Configure user account control (UAC).	9	1
Configure authentication and authorization.	9	2
Configure BranchCache.	8	3
CONFIGURING MOBILE COMPUTING		
Configure BitLocker and BitLocker To Go.	11	1
Configure DirectAccess.	10	1
Configure mobility options.	11	2
Configure remote connections.	10	2
MONITORING AND MAINTAINING SYSTEMS THAT RUN WINDOWS 7		
Configure updates to Windows 7.	12	1
Manage disks.	4	2
Monitor systems.	13	1
Configure performance settings.	13	2
CONFIGURING BACKUP AND RECOVERY OPTIONS		
Configure backup.	14	1
Configure system recovery options.	14	2
Configure file recovery options.	14	3

Exam Objectives The exam objectives listed here are current as of this book's publication date. Exam objectives are subject to change at any time without prior notice and at Microsoft's sole discretion. Please visit the Microsoft Learning Web site for the most current listing of exam objectives: *http://www.microsoft.com/learning/en/us/exam .aspx?ID=70-680&locale=en-us#tub1*

MCTS Self-Paced Training Kit (Exam 70-680): Configuring Windows®7

Ian McLean
Orin Thomas

PUBLISHED BY
Microsoft Press
A Division of Microsoft Corporation
One Microsoft Way
Redmond, Washington 98052-6399

Library of Congress Control Number: 2009932326

Printed and bound in the United States of America.

2 3 4 5 6 7 8 9   WCT   4 3 2 1 0 9

Distributed in Canada by H.B. Fenn and Company Ltd.

A CIP catalogue record for this book is available from the British Library.

Microsoft Press books are available through booksellers and distributors worldwide. For further information about international editions, contact your local Microsoft Corporation office or contact Microsoft Press International directly at fax (425) 936-7329. Visit our Web site at www.microsoft.com/mspress. Send comments to tkinput@microsoft.com.

Acquisitions Editor: Ken Jones
Developmental Editor: Laura Sackerman
Project Editor: Rosemary Caperton
Editorial Production: Ashley Schneider, S4Carlisle Publishing Services
Technical Reviewer: Rozanne Whalen; Technical Review services provided by Content Master, a member of CM Group, Ltd.
Cover: Tom Draper Design

Body Part No. X16-10711

It's unusual to dedicate a book to one of its authors, but when Orin Thomas agreed to be my writing partner it was my lucky day. Orin is the most competent and capable professional I have ever come across. Not only can he do things, he can write about them too. He's my peer reviewer as well as my co-author and his reviews are both informative and ruthless, for which I'm eternally grateful. He is always ready and willing to step in with assistance if I am having any sort of problem. Orin, please keep tearing my text to shreds. By the way I'll do the same for you given the opportunity. I appreciate working with a true professional.

—IAN MCLEAN

To all of you who are beginning your certification journey, I hope that you find your journey as rewarding, as useful, and as fulfilling as I have found my own. Good luck on your Windows 7 exam!

—ORIN THOMAS

Contents at a Glance

Contents

What do you think of this book? We want to hear from you!

Microsoft is interested in hearing your feedback so we can continually improve our
books and learning resources for you. To participate in a brief online survey, please visit:

www.microsoft.com/learning/booksurvey/

Chapter 5   Managing Applications   255

Chapter 13 Monitoring and Performance   647

Acknowledgments

Writing a book is always a team effort, and we have the advantage of an excellent team working hard behind the scenes and, unlike the authors, never seeing their names on the front cover. We are grateful to Ken Jones, our acquisitions editor, for his continued faith in us whenever a new project comes along, to Laura Sackerman, our developmental editor, who guides us through the initial stages and helps us out with any problems regarding, for example, new templates, and to Heather Stafford, who performs a function close to our hearts—she draws up our contract.

Possibly the key person in the entire team is the project editor, who holds the whole team together. We had worked with the indefatigable and highly competent Rosemary Caperton before and were very pleased to work with her again. We were also pleased that Rozanne Whalen was available as our technical reviewer, and was there to point out any slips we made and to question our assumptions. Rozanne is unfailingly polite, which doesn't stop her being very sharp indeed.

Adherence to standards of layout and literacy is vital to the quality of a book and to the reader experience. We are grateful for the considerable contribution made by our copyeditor, Susan McClung; our editorial proofreader, Nicole Schlutt; our indexer, Maureen Johnson; and last but definitely not least, Ashley Schneider, the S4Carlisle project editor, who pulls it all together.

Few creatures are as antisocial as an author in mid-book, and we are both lucky to have understanding and supportive wives. So, many thanks, Oksana and Anne. You are an essential and much-valued part of the team.

—Orin and Ian

Introduction

This training kit is designed for IT professionals who operate in enterprise environments that use Windows 7 as a desktop operating system. You should have at least one year of experience in the IT field, as well as experience implementing and administering any Windows client operating system in a networked environment.

You should be able to install, deploy, and upgrade to Windows 7, including ensuring hardware and software compatibility. Additionally, you should be able to configure preinstallation and postinstallation system settings, Windows security features, network connectivity applications included with Windows 7, and mobile computing. You should also be able to maintain systems, including monitoring for and resolving performance and reliability issues and have a basic understanding of Windows PowerShell syntax.

By using this training kit, you will learn how to do the following:

- Install, upgrade, and migrate to Windows 7.
- Deploy Windows 7.
- Configure hardware and applications.
- Configure network connectivity.
- Configure access to resources.
- Configure mobile computing.
- Monitor and maintain systems that run Windows 7.
- Configure backup and recovery options.

> **MORE INFO** **FIND ADDITIONAL CONTENT ONLINE**
>
> As new or updated material that complements your book becomes available, it will be posted on the Microsoft Press Online Windows Server and Client Web site. The type of material you might find includes updates to book content, articles, links to companion content, errata, sample chapters, and more. This Web site will is available at *http://www.microsoft.com/learning/books/online/serverclient* and will be updated periodically.

Lab Setup Instructions

The exercises in this training kit require a minimum of two client computers or virtual machines running Windows 7 Enterprise or Ultimate editions. Instructions for configuring the first of these computers are given in Chapter 1, "Install, Migrate, or Upgrade to Windows 7." Instructions for configuring the second of these computers are given in Chapter 6, "Network Settings." You need an additional hard disk (internal or external), formatted using the NTFS file system, installed on the first of these computers.

You can obtain an evaluation version of Windows 7 Enterprise from the Microsoft Download Center at the following address: *http://technet.microsoft.com/en-us/evalcenter/default.aspx*.

All computers must be physically connected to the same network. We recommend that you use an isolated network that is not part of your production network to do the practices in this book. To minimize the time and expense of configuring physical computers, we recommend you use virtual machines. To run computers as virtual machines within Windows, you can use Hyper-V, Microsoft Virtual PC 2007, or third-party virtual machine software. To download Virtual PC 2007, visit *http://www.microsoft.com/windows/downloads/virtualpc/default.mspx*.

Hardware Requirements

You can complete almost all the practice exercises in this book using virtual machines rather than real hardware. The minimum and recommended hardware requirements for Windows 7 are listed in Table 1.

TABLE 1 Windows Server 2008 Minimum Hardware Requirements

HARDWARE COMPONENT	MINIMUM REQUIREMENTS	RECOMMENDED
Processor	1 GHz 32-bit (x86) or 64-bit (x64) processor	2 GHz or faster
RAM	1 GB	2 GB
Disk space	40 GB	60 GB
Graphics adapter	Supports DirectX 9 graphics Has a Windows Display Driver Model (WDDM) driver Pixel Shader 2.0 hardware 32 bits per pixel 128 MB graphics memory	As minimum requirement, but with 256 MB of graphics memory

If you intend to implement two virtual machines on the same computer (which is recommended), a higher specification will enhance your user experience. In particular, a computer with 4 GB RAM and 60 GB available disk space can host all the virtual machines specified for all the practice exercises in this book.

Using the DVD

The companion DVD included with this training kit contains the following:

- **Practice tests**   You can reinforce your understanding of how to configure Windows 7 by using electronic practice tests you customize to meet your needs from the pool of Lesson Review questions in this book. Or you can practice for the 70-680 certification exam by using tests created from a pool of 200 realistic exam questions, which give you many practice exams to ensure that you are prepared.

- **An eBook**   An electronic version (eBook) of this book is included for when you do not want to carry the printed book with you. The eBook is in Portable Document Format (PDF), and you can view it by using Adobe Acrobat or Adobe Reader.

- **Sample chapters**   Sample chapters from other Microsoft Press titles on Windows Server 2008. These chapters are in PDF format.

> **Digital Content for Digital Book Readers:** If you bought a digital-only edition of this book, you can enjoy select content from the print edition's companion DVD.
> Visit **http://go.microsoft.com/fwlink/?LinkId=163947** to get your downloadable content. This content is always up to date and available to all readers.

How to Install the Practice Tests

To install the practice test software from the companion DVD to your hard disk, do the following:

1. Insert the companion DVD into your DVD drive and accept the license agreement. A DVD menu appears.

> **NOTE   IF THE DVD MENU DOES NOT APPEAR**
>
> If the DVD menu or the license agreement does not appear, AutoRun might be disabled on your computer. Refer to the Readme.txt file on the DVD-ROM for alternate installation instructions.

2. Click Practice Tests and follow the instructions on the screen.

How to Use the Practice Tests

To start the practice test software, follow these steps:

1. Click Start, click All Programs, and then select Microsoft Press Training Kit Exam Prep. A window appears that shows all the Microsoft Press training kit exam prep suites installed on your computer.

2. Double-click the lesson review or practice test you want to use.

> **NOTE LESSON REVIEWS VERSUS PRACTICE TESTS**
>
> Select the (70-680) Windows 7, Configuring *lesson review* to use the questions from the "Lesson Review" sections of this book. Select (70-680) Windows 7, Configuring *practice test* to use a pool of 200 questions similar to those that appear on the 70-680 certification exam.

Lesson Review Options

When you start a lesson review, the Custom Mode dialog box appears so that you can configure your test. You can click OK to accept the defaults, or you can customize the number of questions you want, how the practice test software works, which exam objectives you want the questions to relate to, and whether you want your lesson review to be timed. If you are retaking a test, you can select whether you want to see all the questions again or only the questions you missed or did not answer.

After you click OK, your lesson review starts.

- **Article I**   To take the test, answer the questions and use the Next and Previous buttons to move from question to question.

- **Article II**   After you answer an individual question, if you want to see which answers are correct—along with an explanation of each correct answer—click Explanation.

- **Article III**   If you prefer to wait until the end of the test to see how you did, answer all the questions and then click Score Test. You will see a summary of the exam objectives you chose and the percentage of questions you got right, both overall and per objective. You can print a copy of your test, review your answers, or retake the test.

Practice Test Options

When you start a practice test, you choose whether to take the test in Certification Mode, Study Mode, or Custom Mode:

- **Certification Mode**   Closely resembles the experience of taking a certification exam. The test has a set number of questions. It is timed, and you cannot pause and restart the timer.

- **Study Mode**   Creates an untimed test during which you can review the correct answers and the explanations after you answer each question.

- **Custom Mode**   Gives you full control over the test options so that you can customize them as you like. In all modes, the user interface when you are taking the test is basically the same but with different options enabled or disabled depending on the mode. The main options are discussed in the previous section, "Lesson Review Options."

When you review your answer to an individual practice test question, a "References" section is provided that lists where in the training kit you can find the information that relates to that question and provides links to other sources of information. After you click Test Results to score your entire practice test, you can click the Learning Plan tab to see a list of references for every objective.

How to Uninstall the Practice Tests

To uninstall the practice test software for a training kit, use the Program And Features option in Control Panel.

Microsoft Certified Professional Program

The Microsoft certifications provide the best method to prove your command of current Microsoft products and technologies. The exams and corresponding certifications are developed to validate your mastery of critical competencies as you design and develop, or implement and support, solutions with Microsoft products and technologies. Computer professionals who become Microsoft-certified are recognized as experts and are sought after industry-wide. Certification brings a variety of benefits to the individual and to employers and organizations.

> **MORE INFO   ALL THE MICROSOFT CERTIFICATIONS**
>
> For a full list of Microsoft certifications, go to *http://www.microsoft.com/learning/mcp/ default.asp.*

Technical Support

Every effort has been made to ensure the accuracy of this book and the contents of the companion DVD. If you have comments, questions, or ideas regarding this book or the companion DVD, please send them to Microsoft Press:

E-mail
- tkinput@microsoft.com

For additional support information regarding this book and the DVD-ROM (including answers to commonly asked questions about installation and use), visit the Microsoft Press Technical Support Web site at *http://www.microsoft.com/learning/support/books/.* To connect directly to the Microsoft Knowledge Base and enter a query, visit *http://support.microsoft.com/search/.* For support information regarding Microsoft software, connect to *http://support.microsoft.com.*

Install, Migrate, or Upgrade to Windows 7

E xam 70-680, "Windows 7, Configuring," is suitable for information technology (IT) professionals with at least one year of experience working in a networked environment whose job role involves or will involve installing and supporting the Windows 7 client operating system. This first chapter focuses on installing Windows 7 through a clean installation, upgrade, or migration. As an experienced IT professional, you know that operating system installation is a critical starting point. The decisions that you make during the installation process have significant ramifications for how people will use that computer throughout its operational lifetime.

In this chapter, you will learn how to install Windows 7. You will learn the differences between the various Windows 7 editions, the operating system's hardware requirements; the different installation sources that you can use for operating system deployment; how to upgrade to Windows 7 from Windows Vista; and how to migrate user data to Windows 7 from Windows XP, Windows Vista, and other Windows 7 deployments.

Exam objectives in this chapter:

- Perform a clean installation.
- Upgrade to Windows 7 from previous versions of Windows.
- Migrate user profiles.

Lessons in this chapter:

Before You Begin

To complete the exercises in the practices in this chapter, you need the following:

- Access to hardware that meets the Windows 7 minimum requirements as outlined in the Introduction to this book.
- A copy of the Windows 7 Enterprise or Ultimate edition installation media or an evaluation version of Windows 7 Enterprise or Ultimate edition, which can be downloaded from Microsoft's Web site.
- To perform the practice exercise at the end of Lesson 2, you need to have access to a computer running Windows Vista that you can upgrade to Windows 7. You can use a virtual machine for this practice exercise.
- To perform the practice exercise at the end of lesson 3, you need to have access to a removable USB storage device that can store approximately 1 GB of data.

 REAL WORLD

Orin Thomas

As an experienced IT professional, people come to you for advice on computer-related subjects because you have knowledge and expertise that they lack. When a new operating system is released, people who trust you will want to know if you think they should start using it. They will want to know what features it has that make it different from what they are using now. They will want to know if their current hardware and software are compatible or if they will need a new computer. Although this book focuses on deploying and supporting Windows 7 in an organizational environment, many of the people that will seek out your advice will be family, friends, and coworkers. If you are to give them good advice, you need to know on what sort of hardware Windows 7 runs well and on what sort of hardware it runs poorly. You need to be able to evaluate whether hardware devices and software that they own work with Windows 7 or whether they are incompatible. Before they upgrade, they need to know that their 5-year-old multifunction printer and scanner do not work with Windows 7, rather than finding out after it is too late. When it comes to providing advice to people that trust you about important things, a best guess is not good enough.

Lesson 1: Installing Windows 7

If you get the installation of an operating system right, it makes supporting that operating system throughout its lifetime a great deal simpler. If you make an incorrect configuration decision when installing an operating system, and you do not find out about it until you have deployed the operating system to more than 100 computers in your organization, it will take significantly more time to rectify the problem. In this lesson, you learn about the minimum hardware requirements for Windows 7, the different editions, how to perform a fresh installation, and how to configure Windows 7 to dual-boot with other operating systems.

After this lesson, you will be able to:

- Identify Windows 7 hardware requirements.
- Configure Windows 7 as the sole operating system on a computer.
- Configure Windows 7 to dual-boot.
- Boot from installation media.
- Prepare for installation from USB, CD, network share, or Windows Deployment Services.

Estimated lesson time: 70 minutes

Windows 7 Editions

The Windows 7 operating system comes in multiple editions. You will sometimes see these editions referred to as Stock Keeping Units (SKUs). Microsoft targets specific editions at different usage scenarios, providing cheaper editions to customers who do not want all the features available in a more expensive edition. As an IT professional, your job may involve providing guidance to decision makers on which edition of Windows 7 should be purchased for the computers in your organization. You may also need to provide guidance to family and friends as to which edition of Windows 7 best meets their needs. There are six different Windows 7 editions:

- Starter
- Home Basic
- Home Premium
- Professional
- Enterprise
- Ultimate

Over the next few pages, you learn the primary differences between these editions.

Windows 7 Starter

Windows 7 Starter is available from retailers and on new computers installed by manufacturers. It does not support or include the Windows Aero user interface, DVD playback, Windows Media Center, IIS Web Server, or Internet connection sharing. You cannot join a computer with this edition of Windows to a domain. This edition does not support enterprise features such as Encrypting File System (EFS), AppLocker, DirectAccess, BitLocker, Remote Desktop Host, and BranchCache. This edition supports a maximum of one physical processor.

Windows 7 Home Basic

Windows 7 Home Basic is available only in emerging markets. It does not support or include the Windows Aero user interface, DVD playback, Windows Media Center, or IIS Web Server. You cannot join a computer with this edition of Windows 7 to a domain. This edition does not support enterprise features such as EFS, AppLocker, DirectAccess, BitLocker, Remote Desktop Host, and BranchCache. This edition supports a maximum of one physical processor. The x86 version supports a maximum of 4 GB of RAM, whereas the x64 version supports a maximum of 8 GB of RAM.

> **NOTE   MULTIPROCESSOR AND MULTICORE**
>
> Although some editions support only one physical processor, they do support an unlimited number of cores on that processor. For example, all editions of Windows 7 support quad-core CPUs.

Windows 7 Home Premium

Windows 7 Home Premium is available from retailers and on new computers installed by manufacturers. Unlike the Starter and Home Basic editions, the Home Premium edition supports the Windows Aero UI, DVD playback, Windows Media Center, Internet connection sharing, and the IIS Web Server. You cannot join this edition of Windows 7 to a domain, and it does not support enterprise features such as EFS, AppLocker, DirectAccess, BitLocker, Remote Desktop Host, and BranchCache. The x86 version of Windows 7 Home Premium supports a maximum of 4 GB of RAM, whereas the x64 version supports a maximum of 16 GB of RAM. Windows 7 Home Premium supports up to two physical processors.

Windows 7 Professional

Windows 7 Professional is available from retailers and on new computers installed by manufacturers. It supports all the features available in Windows Home Premium, but you can join computers with this operating system installed to a domain. It supports EFS and Remote Desktop Host but does not support enterprise features such as AppLocker, DirectAccess, BitLocker, and BranchCache. Windows 7 Professional supports up to two physical processors.

Windows 7 Enterprise and Ultimate Editions

The Windows 7 Enterprise and Ultimate editions are identical except for the fact that Windows 7 Enterprise is available only to Microsoft's volume licensing customers, and Windows 7 Ultimate is available from retailers and on new computers installed by manufacturers. The Enterprise and Ultimate editions support all the features available in other Windows 7 editions but also support all the enterprise features such as EFS, Remote Desktop Host, AppLocker, DirectAccess, BitLocker, BranchCache, and Boot from VHD. Windows 7 Enterprise and Ultimate editions support up to two physical processors.

EXAM TIP

Many of the Windows 7 features tested on the 70-680 exam are available only in the Enterprise and Ultimate editions of Windows 7.

Windows 7 Hardware Requirements

Operating systems work properly only when you install them on computers that meet the minimum hardware requirements. You should remember that these requirements are just for the operating system itself, but most people want to do more than just run an operating system: they also want to run applications. Applications require memory and storage space beyond that of the operating system minimum requirements. As someone who may be responsible for making recommendations about the specifications of computer hardware that your organization will purchase, you need to take into account the hardware requirements of the operating system and the applications that will run on it, not just the operating system itself. Windows 7 Starter and Windows 7 Home Basic have the following minimum hardware requirements:

- 1 GHz 32-bit (x86) or 64-bit (x64) processor
- 512 MB of system memory
- A 20-GB (x64) or 16-GB (x86) hard disk drive, traditional or Solid State Disk (SSD), with at least 15 GB of available space
- A graphics adapter that supports DirectX 9 graphics and 32 MB of graphics memory

Windows 7 Home Premium, Professional, Ultimate, and Enterprise editions have the following minimum hardware requirements:

- 1 GHz 32-bit (x86) or 64-bit (x64) processor
- 1 GB of system memory
- A 40-GB hard disk drive (traditional or SSD) with at least 15 GB of available space
- A graphics adapter that supports DirectX 9 graphics, has a Windows Display Driver Model (WDDM) driver, Pixel Shader 2.0 hardware, and 32 bits per pixel and a minimum of 128 MB graphics memory

Windows 7 supports two different processor architectures. The 32-bit version of Windows 7 is usually labeled as being x86. You should install the x86 version of Windows 7 on computers with older processors, such as the Pentium IV, as well as newer small form factor laptop computers, also known as *netbooks*. The main limitation of the x86 version of Windows 7 is that it does not support more than 4 GB of RAM. It is possible to install the x86 version of Windows 7 on computers that have x64 processors, but the operating system will be unable to utilize any RAM that the computer has beyond 4 GB. You can install the x64 version of Windows 7 only on computers that have x64-compatible processors. The x64 versions of Windows 7 Professional, Enterprise, and Ultimate editions support up to 128 GB of RAM. The x64 version of Windows 7 Home Basic edition supports 8 GB and the x64 edition of Home Premium supports a maximum of 16 GB.

 Quick Check

- What is the difference between Windows 7 Enterprise and Ultimate editions?

Quick Check Answer

- The difference is in the licensing arrangements. Windows 7 Enterprise can be used only by organizations that have enterprise licensing agreements with Microsoft. Windows 7 Ultimate uses a retail license.

Preparing the Windows 7 Installation Source

You can use several methods to install Windows 7. The most appropriate method depends on your individual circumstances. Although installing using a DVD-ROM is fine when you have only a couple of computers, you might want to consider alternate methods when you have to deploy Windows 7 to 20 computers or more. When considering which installation source to use, consider the following factors:

- Do you need to install Windows 7 on more than one computer?
- Does the computer or computers have DVD-ROM drives?
- Do you need to deploy a customized version of Windows 7?
- Do you want to automate the installation process?

Using a DVD as an Installation Source

If you purchase a boxed version of Windows 7 at a retail outlet, it will come with a DVD-ROM. Some enterprise customers also have access to a special section of Microsoft's Web site where they are able to download a DVD-ROM image of Windows 7 in International Organization for Standardization (ISO) format. You need to write this image to a DVD-ROM before it is possible to use it to install Windows 7.

To install Windows 7 from a DVD-ROM, boot from the DVD-ROM drive and follow the prompts. You may need to configure the computer's BIOS to support booting from

DVD-ROM. If a computer does not have a DVD-ROM drive attached, you can still install from DVD-ROM—you just need to acquire a USB DVD-ROM drive. In this case, it will be necessary to configure the computer's BIOS to boot from the USB device.

A DVD-ROM installation may suit your organization if you have a small number of computers to install Windows 7 on and you do not need to customize the operating system image.

Using a USB Drive as an Installation Source

Small form factor laptop computers, often called *netbook computers* or *netbooks*, are becoming increasingly popular. One drawback for the IT professional, however, is that these computers are so small that they often do not have an attached optical media drive. Although it is possible to purchase DVD drives that use USB connections to attach to netbook computers and perform an installation, more administrators are turning to cheap multi-gigabyte USB storage devices, sometimes called *flash drives*, as their preferred installation media of choice.

USB storage devices have several advantages over DVD-ROMs. With a USB storage device, you can modify the operating system image directly using tools such as Dism.exe. You can add extra drivers to the image stored on a USB storage device, something that is not possible to do to the installation image stored on a DVD-ROM. You will learn how to do this in Chapter 3, "Deploying System Images." Another advantage of USB flash devices is that they have faster read speeds than DVD-ROM drives, meaning that the time to transfer the operating system files to the target computer's hard disk is reduced.

A USB storage device needs to be 4 GB or larger if you want to use it as a Windows 7 installation source. This is because the x64 installation files are approximately 3.2 GB in size and the x86 installation files are approximately 2.5 GB in size. You use one architecture's installation files only when preparing a deployment from a USB storage device. The USB storage device should use the FAT32 file system.

To prepare a USB storage device as an installation source for Windows 7, perform the following steps:

1. Connect the USB storage device to a computer running Windows 7 or Windows Vista. Ensure that the storage device has no data stored on it that you want to keep (or that you have moved such data to another storage device) because this procedure removes all existing data.

2. Open an elevated command prompt and type **diskpart.**

3. At the DISKPART> prompt, type **list disk.** Identify which disk connected to the computer represents the USB storage device.

4. At the DISKPART> prompt, type **select disk X** where X is the number of the disk that you have identified as the USB storage device.

5. At the DISKPART> prompt, type **clean.** When the disk is clean, type **create partition primary.**

6. At the DISKPART> prompt, type **format fs=fat32 quick.** When the format is completed type **active** and then **exit.**

7. After you have completed these steps, copy all the files located on the Windows 7 installation DVD to the USB storage device.

8. Configure the BIOS computer on which you want to install Windows 7 to boot from the USB storage device. Attach the USB storage device and then reboot the computer to start installation.

There are several disadvantages to using USB storage devices as a Windows 7 installation source. Although they are reusable, USB storage devices are more expensive than DVD-ROMs. USB storage devices are also not suitable when you have to deploy Windows 7 to a large number of computers over a short amount of time because you need to attach a USB device to each computer to install Windows 7 on it. For example, if you wanted to deploy Windows 7 to 100 computers, you could configure 100 USB devices with the Windows 7 installation media and answer files for unattended installation, or you could configure one Windows Deployment Services (WDS) server and perform the installation over the network—a much more convenient option.

Using a Network Share as an Installation Source

As an alternative to DVD-ROMs or USB storage devices, you can host the Windows 7 installation files on a network share. To do this, you need to copy the contents of the Windows 7 installation media to a network share accessible to the clients on which you want to deploy Windows 7. To access a network share as an installation source from the client computer, you need to boot the client computer into the Windows Preintallation Environment (Windows PE) environment. The Windows PE environment is a minimally featured operating system that allows you to access diagnostic and maintenance tools as well as access network drives. Once you have successfully booted into the Windows PE environment, you can connect to the network share and begin the installation by running Setup.exe. You will learn about creating a bootable Windows PE DVD-ROM or USB device in Chapter 2, "Configuring System Images."

Because it is necessary to boot into Windows PE, using a network share as the installation source has several of the disadvantages of a DVD-ROM– and USB storage media–based installation. Even though you are using a network share to host the operating system installation files, you still need a DVD-ROM or USB storage device installed or attached to boot the computer. Network installations of this type are also slower than comparable installations from DVD-ROM or USB storage devices as the setup routine must transfer all operating system installation files across the network.

An advantage of using a network share as an installation source is that if you want to make changes to it, you can do so centrally. If you want to make a change to a USB source, you need to update each USB source. If you want to make a change to a DVD-ROM source, you must burn each DVD again. It will not be necessary to change the Windows PE media that you use to boot client computers when you update the central source. You can also use a network share as an installation source when your organization does not have an Active Directory Domain Services (AD DS) infrastructure or does not have servers running the Windows Server 2008 operating system.

Using Windows Deployment Services as an Installation Source

If you are going to perform more than a couple of operating system installations over the network, and you are using an AD DS network and Windows Server 2008, you should consider using Windows Deployment Services (WDS). WDS, a role that is available to a computer running Windows Server 2008, allows for the automatic deployment of operating system images. WDS uses multicast technology, which means that rather than transmitting a separate copy of the full operating system image across the network to each computer that you want to install Windows 7 on, WDS transmits the operating system once to all computers configured to receive it.

To access a WDS server, a computer must have a PXE-compliant network card or boot from a WDS discover image. When the computer boots from a PXE-compliant network card or discover image, the computer contacts the WDS server and can start the operating system installation process. Preparing the WDS server involves importing the installation image, Install.wim, from the Windows 7 installation media to the server. You do not copy the installation files across the network, as you do when you are preparing a network share or USB storage device.

You can also configure unattended installation files on the WDS server and modify the operating system images on the WDS server. You will learn more about the options for deploying customized Windows 7 images in Lesson 2 of Chapter 3.

> *MORE INFO* **WINDOWS DEPLOYMENT SERVICES**
>
> To learn more about WDS, consult the following Web page on Microsoft TechNet:
> *http://technet.microsoft.com/en-us/library/cc265612.aspx.*

EXAM TIP

Know which type of installation source you should use under specific circumstances.

Installing Windows 7

Installing Windows 7 is a relatively simple process. You start the setup process, either by booting from a DVD-ROM or USB storage device, connecting to a WDS server, or by booting into Windows PE, connecting to a network share, and running Setup.exe. The setup proceeds from there. You can perform a standard or an unattended installation. The differences between these are as follows:

- **Standard installation** During a standard installation, an administrator answers a series of questions that assist in configuring the Windows 7 deployment to the new computer. This type of installation is suitable when you are deploying Windows 7 to a small number of computers.

- **Unattended installation**   You can perform an unattended installation of Windows 7 by using an installation file called Unattend.xml. These installation files store answers to the questions asked by the Setup Wizard. When the Windows 7 installation process starts, Windows checks for attached USB storage devices that have this file in their root directory. Unattended installations are suitable when you need to deploy Windows 7 to a large number of computers because you do not have to interact with them manually, responding to prompts, as the installation progresses.

Clean Installations

A clean installation is one performed on a computer that does not currently have an operating system installed. This might be a brand-new computer arriving straight from the factory, or it might be an older computer with a brand-new hard disk drive on which you wish to install Windows 7. You can use any installation media to perform a clean installation. Although you perform a clean installation in the practice exercise at the end of this chapter, the next few pages will describe in detail some of the options and concepts that you encounter during the installation process.

The first page that you encounter when performing an installation asks you which language you wish to install, the time and currency format, and what keyboard or input method you are using for the installation. This selection is important, not only because installing Microsoft Windows in a foreign language can be a challenge if you do not understand that language, but because even keyboards from other English-speaking countries have layouts that differ from the standard layout of a U.S. keyboard. If you are installing Windows 7 for users that need access to multiple keyboard layouts, you can add these alternate layouts once the installation process has completed. Then the user can switch between them as necessary.

The next page, shown in Figure 1-1, is the Install Windows 7 page. From here, you can start the installation by clicking Install Now. You can also access some of the Windows 7 repair tools by clicking Repair Your Computer. You will learn more about the repair options in Chapter 14, "Recovery and Backup." Clicking the What To Know Before Installing Windows option provides you with general installation advice, such as ensuring that your computer needs to meet the minimum hardware requirements and that you should have your product key ready.

The next step is to review and accept the Windows 7 license terms. This is followed by choosing what type of installation you want to perform: Upgrade or Custom (Advanced). When you are performing a clean installation, you should select Custom (Advanced). Almost all installations of Windows 7 that you will perform will be of the Custom (Advanced) type rather than upgrades. You can initiate upgrade installations only from within Windows Vista or Windows 7. You learn more about upgrading to Windows 7 in Lesson 2.

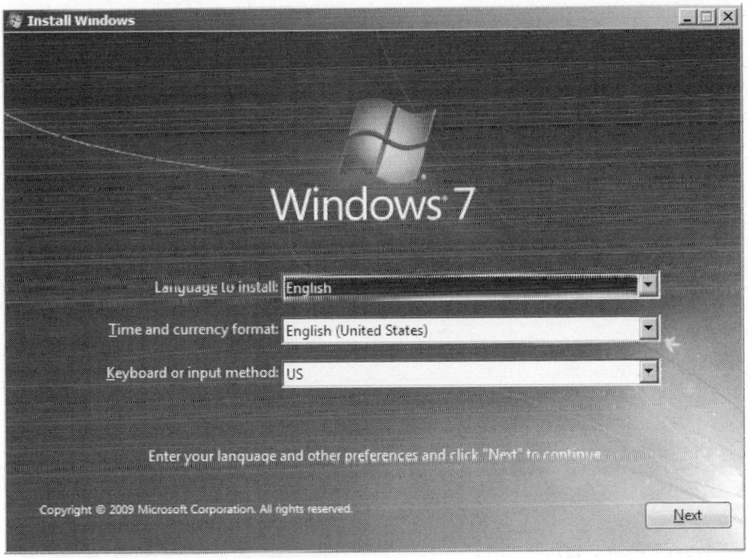

FIGURE 1-1 The Install Windows 7 page

The next step in the installation process is determining where the Windows 7 files will be stored. Windows 7 needs a minimum of 15 GB of free space, though you should generally allocate more than this amount. From this page, it is possible to partition an existing disk into smaller volumes. You can do this by clicking Drive Options (Advanced). The installation routine recognizes most Integrated Development Environment (IDE), Serial Advanced Technology Attachment (SATA), and Small Computer System Interface (SCSI) disk drives automatically. If your computer has special disk drive hardware, such as a redundant array of independent disks (RAID) array, it may be necessary to use the Load Driver option. It is necessary to use this option only if the disk that you want to install Windows on is not shown as a possible install location. If your disk is shown as an available option, Windows 7 has already loaded the appropriate drivers. Once you select the location where you want to install Windows 7, the Windows 7 installation process begins.

> **NOTE INSTALLING TO VHD**
>
> When performing a clean install of Windows 7 Enterprise and Ultimate editions, you have the additional option of installing to a virtual hard disk (VHD) file rather than directly to the volume. You will learn more about the steps required to do this in Chapter 2.

After the computer reboots, you need to specify a user name and a computer name. The user name you specify is the default administrator account for that computer. The account named Administrator, used in previous versions as the default administrative account, is disabled by default. It is possible to enable this account only by modifying Group Policy. Because the user name that you specify during setup is the default administrator account for that computer, organizations that are performing Windows 7 deployment need to come up with an account naming policy. Most organizations do not let the person that uses a computer run with full administrator privileges for security reasons. Having a consistent naming policy for the default administrator account also ensures that IT professionals do not have to guess what the name of the local administrator account is when they need to perform a local administrator logon. In organizational deployments, it is also necessary to have a consistent computer naming policy. Computer and user names cannot contain special characters, as shown in Figure 1-2.

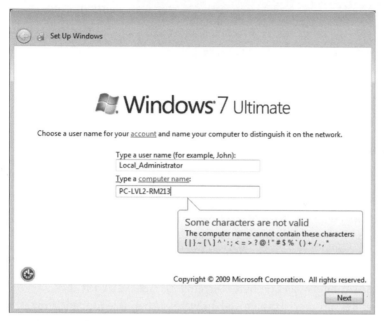

FIGURE 1-2 Local administrator and computer names

After you specify a user name and a computer name, it is necessary to enter a password and a password hint. Because this user account is the default administrative account for the computer running Windows 7, the password hint should not allow a reasonable person to guess the password. Password hints configured for local user accounts can be viewed by all users at the logon window, which can present a security risk.

The next step gives the option of entering your product key and configuring Windows to activate automatically after installation completes and you connect to the Internet. You should remember that you have 30 days in which to perform product activation and that you do not have to do it immediately after the installation process completes. Instead, you should use these 30 days to ensure that you are happy with the software and hardware configuration of the computer. You should not initiate product activation until you are happy with the software and hardware configuration.

If you enter a product key at this time, Windows 7 automatically selects the edition that corresponds to that key. If you do not enter a product key, you must select which edition of Windows 7 you are going to install on the computer. You should be careful here because you can use a product key only with its corresponding edition of Windows 7. If you choose to install Windows 7 Ultimate edition when you only have a product key for Windows 7 Home Premium, you either have to purchase an Ultimate edition key or reinstall Windows 7 again from the beginning.

Next, you will be presented with the Help Protect Your Computer And Improve Windows Automatically window, shown in Figure 1-3. When you are performing installations for computers in environments that do not have automatic update solutions, such as Windows Server Update Services (WSUS), you should select the Use Recommended Settings option. You should be aware, however, that if you select this option, the computer running Windows 7 uses an Internet connection to download important and recommended updates soon after you complete the installation process. This can have a significant impact on external bandwidth usage if you are deploying Windows 7 to a large number of computers. In those situations, you should consider deploying WSUS or a similar solution. It is also possible to add updates to the installation image before you deploy it. You will learn more about adding updates to Windows 7 installation images in Chapter 3. You will learn more about updating Windows 7 after it has been deployed in Chapter 12, "Windows Update and Windows Internet Explorer."

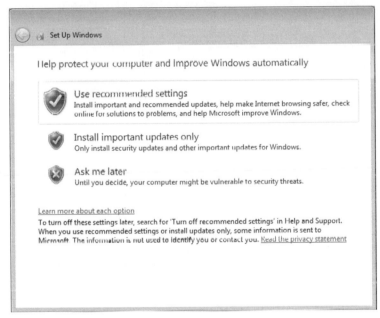

FIGURE 1-3 Configuring update settings

The next phase of the installation involves selecting the computer's time zone, whether the computer's clock should update for Daylight Savings Time automatically, and setting the time and the date. The computer presents its current time and date settings, which you can adjust. After the computer is connected to the network, it automatically corrects its time settings either based on that of a server on the local network (if it is a member of a Windows domain) or through a time server on the Internet (if it is not).

If the installation routine detects a network during installation, you specify whether the network is a Home Network, a Work Network, or a Public Network, as shown in Figure 1-4. The network type that you select determines what services are available from the computer running Windows 7 and what network locations the computer running Windows 7 can access, such as the Homegroup feature. If you select the Home Network setting, you select which libraries and devices you want to share with your Homegroup as well as being shown the Homegroup password. You will learn more about network locations in Chapter 6, "Network Settings."

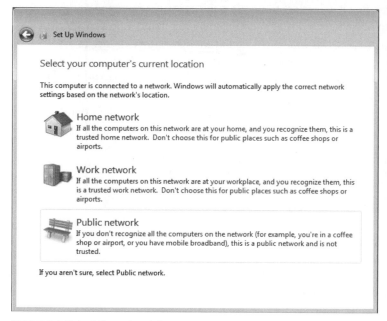

FIGURE 1-4 Select the network type

After you complete these steps, you are logged on to the Windows 7 installation with the local administrative account. It may be necessary, at this stage, to install extra device drivers manually for hardware whose drivers were not installed automatically during installation. You will learn more about configuring device drivers for Windows 7 in Chapter 4, "Managing Devices and Disks."

Dual-Boot Installations

Dual-boot installations allow you to have two or more operating systems installed on the same computer. For example, you can dual-boot between Windows XP and Windows 7 or between Windows Vista and Windows 7. When you configure a computer to dual-boot, you decide which operating system to run at boot time by selecting it from a menu, as shown in Figure 1-5.

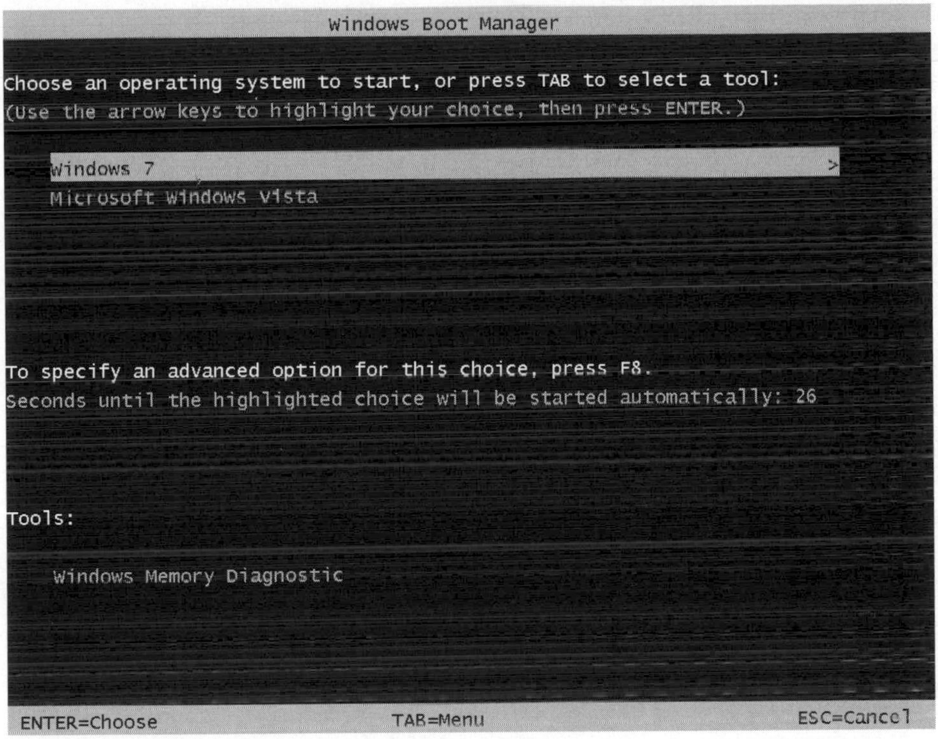

```
                        Windows Boot Manager

Choose an operating system to start, or press TAB to select a tool:
(Use the arrow keys to highlight your choice, then press ENTER.)

    Windows 7                                                        >
    Microsoft Windows Vista




To specify an advanced option for this choice, press F8.
Seconds until the highlighted choice will be started automatically: 26




Tools:

    Windows Memory Diagnostic




ENTER=Choose              TAB=Menu                      ESC=Cancel
```

FIGURE 1-5 Dual-boot operating system selection

Dual-booting is becoming less common now that virtualization applications, such as Microsoft Virtual PC 2007, allow you to run older operating systems when booted into newer operating systems. Today, dual-booting is most often required for hardware reasons. For example, if a computer meets the minimum memory requirement for Windows 7 but you still need to run programs that work only in Windows XP, you would consider a dual-boot configuration rather than a virtualization solution as the computer running Windows 7 would not have enough memory to run a virtualized instance of Windows XP. In this situation, you configure the computer to dual-boot so that the user can access both operating systems.

The key to configuring dual-booting is ensuring that each operating system has its own partition or hard disk drive. In the event that you do not have a spare partition or hard disk drive, Windows Vista and Windows 7 include a tool that allows you to resize a volume so you can create a new volume out of empty space on an existing volume. You can access this tool through the Disk Management console. To resize a volume, right-click it within the Disk Management console and then click Shrink Volume.

To dual-boot with Windows 7, you need to be able to create a new volume of at least 15 GB. Even if you have more free space available on the volume you want to shrink, you may not be able to create a volume of the appropriate size because Windows Vista may not be able to move some special types of data to a different place on the hard disk drive. Windows

XP does not have native tools with which you can shrink existing volumes, though it is possible to find products from third-party vendors that have this functionality.

When configuring a new computer to boot between multiple operating systems, it is also necessary to install operating systems in the order that they were released. For example, if you want to boot between Windows XP and Windows 7 on a new computer, you need to install Windows XP before you install Windows 7. If you install Windows XP after Windows 7, the Windows XP installation routine cannot recognize the Windows 7 operating system installation, and the computer only boots into Windows XP. It is possible to repair the computer from this point using Windows 7 startup repair so that it dual-boots, but the simplest course of action is just to install the operating systems in the order in which they were released by Microsoft.

To configure a computer to dual-boot with Windows 7, you can either boot from the Windows 7 installation media or run the installation routine from within the previous version of Windows. When presented with the choice of upgrading or performing a custom installation, shown in Figure 1-6, select the custom installation. If you select Upgrade from Windows XP, the installation routine terminates because it is not possible to upgrade Windows XP. If you select Upgrade from Windows Vista, an upgrade occurs and you cannot dual-boot. If you make this mistake, it is possible to perform a rollback to the original configuration up to the point where you successfully log on to the new Windows 7 installation.

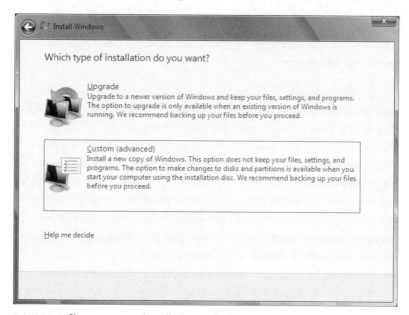

FIGURE 1-6 Choose custom installation to dual-boot.

The installation process when configuring a computer to dual-boot is the same as when you are performing a clean installation. The main issue is ensuring that you select the correct disk or volume when you reach the state where you specify where you want to install Windows 7. If you specify the volume or disk that hosts the operating system that you want to dual-boot with, you may end up wiping that volume and replacing it with a fresh installation of Windows 7. When the installation completes, you can dual-boot between operating systems and Windows 7 is the default operating system. You will learn about configuring the default operating system later in this lesson.

Dual-Boot and Virtual Hard Disks

An exception to the rule that you require a separate partition for each operating system if you want to dual-boot is booting from a VHD file. You can install and then boot Windows 7 Enterprise and Ultimate editions, as well as Windows Server 2008 R2, from VHD files. It is possible to boot from VHD only on computers that have a Windows 7 or Windows Server 2008 R2 boot environment. This means that you cannot dual-boot Windows XP or Windows Vista computers with Windows 7 installed on a VHD file, though it is possible to triple-boot with Windows 7 to VHD if you already have a computer that dual-boots between an earlier version of Windows and Windows 7. This is because a computer that you have configured to dual-boot to Windows 7 already has the Windows 7 boot environment present. You will learn how to install Windows 7 onto a VHD file in Chapter 2.

Configuring the Default Operating System

When you configure a computer to dual-boot, one of the operating systems is selected as the default. This means that the computer boots into this operating system by default unless the user intervenes to select the other operating system. To change the default operating system using the graphical user interface (GUI), perform the following steps:

1. From the Start menu, open the Control Panel. Select Small Icons from the View By drop-down list.

2. Click System and then click Advanced System Settings. This opens the System Properties dialog box.

3. On the Advanced tab, click Settings in the Startup And Recovery section. This opens the Startup And Recovery dialog box, shown in Figure 1-7.

4. From the Default Operating System drop-down list, select which operating system is booted by default.

To configure the default operating system using the Bcdedit.exe command-line utility, perform the following steps:

1. Open an administrative command prompt by right-clicking Command Prompt in the Accessories folder of the Start menu and choosing Run As Administrator. Click OK when prompted by the User Account Control dialog box.

2. Enter the command **bcdedit /enum** to view a list of the current boot menu entries, similar to what is displayed in Figure 1-8.

3. To change the default entry, use the command **bcdedit /default** and then list the identifier. In Figure 1-8, this would be {879f7be0-21e3-11de-b92d-d86aaca536b1}.

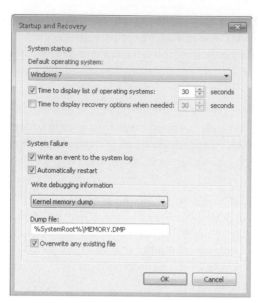

FIGURE 1-7 Selecting the default operating system

FIGURE 1-8 Using BCDedit to modify the boot menu

PRACTICE   Performing a Clean Installation

You perform a clean installation when you install an operating system on a computer that does not currently host one. The advantage of a clean installation is that you do not need to worry about preserving any data that may be already stored on the computer because the computer does not have any existing data. You perform this type of installation on computers that have just arrived from the vendor, or when you have replaced a computer's hard disk drive and have chosen not to restore the operating system from an existing backup.

EXERCISE   Windows 7 Installation

In this exercise, you install Windows 7 on a computer that does not have an existing operating system. Although the instructions assume that you are using a DVD-ROM installation source, you can also perform the installation by booting from a specially prepared USB storage device. Prior to beginning the exercise, ensure that the computer's BIOS is configured to boot from the appropriate device.

1. Insert the Windows 7 installation media into your computer's DVD-ROM drive and turn on the computer. You may be asked to press a key to boot from the DVD-ROM.

2. On the first page of the Install Windows wizard, shown in Figure 1-9, select which language you want to use for the installation, the time and currency format that you want to use, and your keyboard or input method. Click Next.

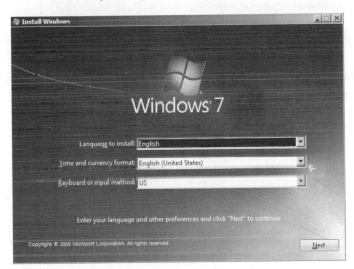

FIGURE 1-9 Select the installation language.

3. Click Install Now. Review the license terms and then check the I Accept The License Terms check box. Click Next.

4. On the Which Type Of Installation Do You Want? page, click Custom (Advanced). This allows you to install a new copy of Windows 7.

5. On the Where Do You Want To Install Windows? page, shown in Figure 1-10, select a disk that has at least 16 GB of free space and click Next. If no disk appears, you may need to load a driver for your disk by clicking the Load Driver item. Because this is a clean installation, the disks that appear in this dialog box should not host formatted volumes.

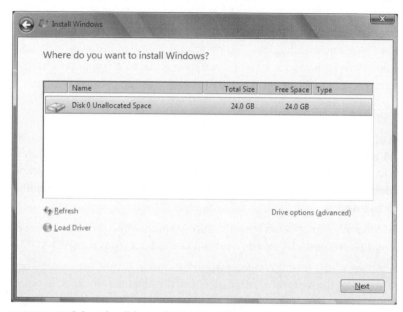

FIGURE 1-10 Select the disk on which to install.

6. The installation starts. This takes some time depending on the speed of the computer on which you are installing Windows 7. The computer reboots several times during the installation process.

7. When you are presented with the page shown in Figure 1-11, enter the user name Kim_Akers and the computer name Canberra and then click Next.

8. On the Set A Password For Your User Account page, enter the password **P@ssw0rd** twice. Enter the password hint as the page number of this page in the training kit. Click Next.

9. On the Type Your Product Key For Activation page, enter your product key, but clear the Automatically Activate Windows When I'm Online check box. Click Next.

10. On the Help Protect Your Computer And Improve Windows Automatically page, click Ask Me Later.

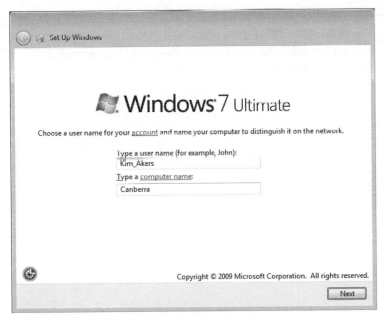

FIGURE 1-11 Enter the user and computer name.

11. On the Review Your Time And Date Settings page, shown in Figure 1-12, configure the time zone to that of your region, enable adjustment for Daylight Savings Time if your region uses it, and check the date and Time. Then click Next.

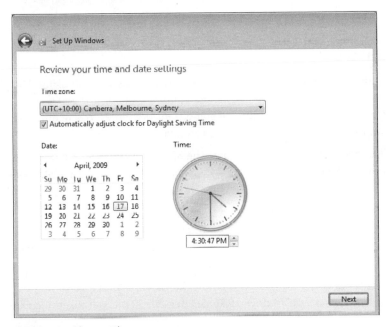

FIGURE 1-12 Time settings

12. On the Select Your Computer's Current Location page, click Home Network.

13. If you are presented with the Do You Want To Create A Homegroup? page, shown in Figure 1-13, select all libraries and then make a note of your Homegroup password. Click Next. After you perform this step, the installation is complete. Turn off the computer.

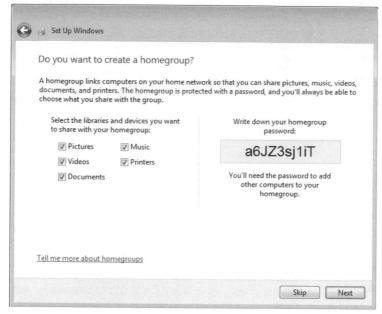

FIGURE 1-13 Create Homegroup

Lesson Summary

- Windows 7 comes in six different editions. Each edition has a different set of features. Only the Professional, Enterprise, and Ultimate editions can be configured to join a domain. Only the Enterprise and Ultimate editions include enterprise features such as BitLocker, AppLocker, DirectAccess, and BranchCache.

- Windows 7 comes in two different versions. The 32-bit version is also known as the x86 version. The 64-bit version is also known as the x64 version. The 32-bit versions support a maximum of 4 GB of RAM. The x64 versions support between 8 GB and 128 GB, depending on the edition.

- Windows 7 Home Basic and Starter editions require a 1 GHz x86 of x64 CPU, 512 MB of system memory, 20 GB HDD, and a 32-MB graphics adapter that supports DirectX9.

- Windows 7 Home Premium, Professional, Enterprise, and Ultimate editions require a 1 GHz x86 or x64 CPU, 1 GB of system memory, 20 GB HDD, and a 128-MB graphics adapter that supports a WDDM driver, Pixel Shader 2.0, 32 bits per pixel, and DirectX9 graphics.

- Windows 7 can be installed from a DVD-ROM, a USB storage device, a network share, or a WDS server. The DVD-ROM and USB storage devices should be used with a small number of computers. WDS with a large number of computers, and a network share in environments that do not support WDS.

- Windows 7 can be configured to dual-boot with Windows XP, Windows Vista, and Windows 7. You can only configure Windows 7 to boot from VHD if the computer has a Windows 7 or Windows Server 2008 R2 boot environment.

Lesson Review

You can use the following questions to test your knowledge of the information in Lesson 1, "Installing Windows 7." The questions are also available on the companion DVD if you prefer to review them in electronic form.

> **NOTE** **ANSWERS**
>
> Answers to these questions and explanations of why each answer choice is correct or incorrect are located in the "Answers" section at the end of the book.

1. Which utility can you use to prepare a USB storage device so that you can boot from it to install Windows 7 on a laptop computer that does not have a DVD-ROM drive?

    A. LoadState.exe

    B. ScanState.exe

    C. Diskpart

    D. Bcdedit

2. You want to deploy a new computer for software compatibility testing. This computer needs to be able to boot into the Windows 7, Windows XP, and Windows Vista operating systems. In which order should you install the operating systems to meet this objective without having to edit boot entries using Bcdedit?

    A. Windows 7, Windows XP, and then Windows Vista

    B. Windows Vista, Windows 7, and then Windows XP

    C. Windows XP, Windows 7, and then Windows Vista

    D. Windows XP, Windows Vista, and then Windows 7

3. Which of the following versions and editions of Windows 7 can you install to take advantage of the hardware resources on a computer that has 16 GB of RAM? (Choose all that apply.)

    A. Windows 7 Ultimate x86

    B. Windows 7 Professional x64

    C. Windows 7 Enterprise x86

    D. Windows 7 Home Premium x64

4. You want to use WDS to perform a network installation of Windows 7. Which of the following hardware devices must the computer have, assuming that you are not booting the computer from a WDS discover image?

    A. A DVD-ROM drive

    B. A PXE-compliant network adapter

    C. A USB 2.0 slot

    D. An HDMI port

5. What is the minimum number of volumes that a computer running Windows XP should have if you want to support dual-booting with Windows 7?

    A. 1

    B. 2

    C. 3

    D. 4

Lesson 2: Upgrading to Windows 7

Although most large organizations use system images to allow rapid deployment of an operating system, settings, and applications to new computers, most smaller organizations have a more haphazard approach to the management of desktop computers. Applications are often purchased and installed on an as-needed basis, and in many organizations, no two computers have exactly the same set of applications installed. This can make rolling out a new operating system challenging. If you perform clean installations for people, you need to make sure that you are able to install the unique set of applications that they had on their original computers. A large benefit of upgrading from one operating system to the next is that all user data and applications that were present on the previous operating system are present on the upgraded operating system. In this lesson, you learn about the conditions under which you an upgrade to Windows 7 while retaining all the applications and data that existed on the computer prior to the upgrade.

After this lesson, you will be able to:

- Upgrade to Windows 7 from Windows Vista.
- Migrate to Windows 7 from Windows XP.
- Upgrade from one edition of Windows 7 to another edition of Windows 7.

Estimated lesson time: 70 minutes

Upgrading from Windows 7 Editions

Sometimes it is necessary to upgrade from one edition of Windows 7 to another. For example, suppose that a small business has purchased several laptop computers that came with Windows 7 Home Basic installed, but they want to use the BitLocker feature and join the computers to the domain. Rather than just wiping the computers and installing another edition of Windows 7, it is possible to upgrade those computers to an edition of Windows 7 that supports the features the small business wants.

There are several advantages to performing an edition upgrade of Windows 7 rather than performing a clean install with another edition. The first advantage is that performing an intra-edition upgrade is cheaper than purchasing a brand-new operating system license. For example, upgrading to Windows 7 Ultimate from Windows 7 Home Basic is cheaper than purchasing a new Windows 7 Ultimate license. The second advantage is that you retain all applications and data that were already present on the existing computer.

As you learned in Lesson 1, each Windows 7 SKU is a superset of the one before it. Windows 7 Professional contains all the features present in Windows Home Premium as well as some additional features; and Windows 7 Ultimate contains all the features in Windows 7 Professional, as well as its own additional features.

Windows 7 allows you to upgrade from one edition to another so long as that edition has more features. For example, you can upgrade from Home Premium to Professional, Enterprise, or Ultimate editions, but you cannot upgrade from Ultimate to Home Premium or Professional editions.

Although it is possible to upgrade between editions of Windows 7, it is not possible to upgrade between versions of Windows 7. You cannot upgrade an x86 version to an x64 version, and you cannot upgrade an x64 version to an x86 version. For example, a developer in your organization has a computer with 4 GB of RAM and the x86 version of Windows 7 Enterprise installed. This particular developer does a lot of work testing application compatibility using virtual machines and needs more RAM. The x86 version of Windows 7 Enterprise supports a maximum of 4 GB of RAM. The x64 version of Windows 7 Enterprise supports up to 128 GB of RAM. However, it is not possible to upgrade the x86 version of Windows 7 Enterprise to the x64 version of Windows 7. It will be necessary to perform a wipe-and-load migration instead, backing up the developer's data and performing a clean installation of the x64 operating system before importing it onto the upgraded computer. Alternatively, you could configure the computer to dual-boot between an x86 and an x64 edition of Windows 7, something made even simpler with the boot from VHD functionality that is included with the Enterprise and Ultimate editions. It is still necessary to migrate data between the two operating systems however. Migration is covered in more detail in Lesson 3, "Managing User Profiles."

You can use either of the following two methods to perform an upgrade from one edition of Windows 7 to another:

- **Upgrade using the installation media** Upgrading using the media is similar to upgrading from Windows Vista. You obtain the product key for the edition you want to upgrade to and then start an upgrade using the Windows 7 installation media. This method is most appropriate for organizations where a large number of intra-edition upgrades is required.

- **Windows Anytime Upgrade** With Windows Anytime Upgrade, shown in Figure 1-14, you can purchase an upgrade to an application over the Internet and have the features unlocked automatically. This upgrade method is more suitable for home users and users in small businesses where a small number of intra-edition upgrades is required.

Upgrading from Windows Vista

You can upgrade computers running Windows Vista to Windows 7. When you upgrade from Windows Vista to Windows 7, all documents, settings, applications, and user accounts that existed on the computer running Windows Vista are available when the upgrade is finished. The advantage to an upgrade is that it allows you to keep the current application configuration. When you perform a migration, you need to reinstall the user's applications on the new computer. As mentioned previously, this can be problematic in organizations that are not careful about keeping track of which specific set of applications are installed on each user's computer.

FIGURE 1-14 Windows Anytime Upgrade

Prior to attempting to perform the upgrade from Windows Vista to Windows 7, you should run the Windows 7 Upgrade Advisor. The Windows 7 Upgrade Advisor is an application that you can download from Microsoft's Web site that will inform you if Windows 7 supports a computer running the current hardware and software configuration of Windows Vista. Prior to running the Windows 7 Upgrade Advisor, you should ensure that all hardware that you want to use with Windows 7, such as printers, scanners, and cameras, are connected to the computer. The Upgrade Advisor generates a report that informs you of which applications and devices are known to have problems with Windows 7. A similar compatability report is generated during the upgrade process, but the version created by the Windows 7 Upgrade Advisor is more likely to be up to date.

MORE INFO **WINDOWS 7 UPGRADE ADVISOR**

You can obtain the Windows 7 Upgrade Advisor from the following Web site: *http://www.microsoft.com/windows/windows-7/upgrade-advisor.aspx.*

NOTE **USE A SEARCH ENGINE**

Another way to determine whether a particular hardware device or application is compatible with Windows 7 is to use a search engine. It is likely that someone before you has attempted to use the set of hardware devices and applications that you are interested in with Windows 7. If they have had a problem with it, it is likely that they have posted information about it in a support forum, a blog, or somewhere else on the World Wide Web.

Windows Vista and Windows 7 have the same basic hardware requirements. This means that you should not have to upgrade the RAM or processor for your computer running Windows Vista to support Windows 7, though you need at least 10 extra gigabytes on the Windows Vista volume to perform the upgrade.

You should keep the following in mind prior to and during the upgrade from Windows Vista to Windows 7:

- Perform a full backup of the computer running Windows Vista prior to performing the installation. That way, if things go wrong, you can do a full restore back to Windows Vista.

- You must ensure that Windows Vista has Service Pack 1 or later installed before you can upgrade it to Windows 7.

- Ensure that you have the Windows 7 product key prior to the upgrade.

- You cannot upgrade between processor architectures. An x86 version of Windows Vista cannot be upgraded to an x64 version of Windows 7, and vice versa.

- You can upgrade only to an equivalent or higher edition of Windows 7. You can upgrade Windows Vista Home Premium to Windows 7 Home Premium, Professional, Enterprise, or Ultimate, but not to Windows 7 Starter. Windows 7 Professional is equivalent to Windows Vista Business.

- Ensure that there is at least 10 GB of free disk space on the Windows Vista volume prior to attempting the upgrade.

You will perform an upgrade from Windows Vista to Windows 7 in the practice exercise at the end of this lesson.

Rolling Back a Failed Upgrade

A Windows 7 upgrade automatically rolls back to Windows Vista if there is a failure during the installation process. You can also roll back to Windows Vista manually up until the point where a successful logon occurs. This means that if there is a problem with a hardware driver that prevents you from successfully logging on, you can go back to your existing Windows Vista installation. After you have performed a successful logon to Windows 7, however, it is not possible to return to Windows Vista without performing a clean installation of the operating system or a restore from backup.

 Quick Check

- Under which conditions is it not possible to upgrade from Windows Vista to Windows 7?

Quick Check Answer

- You cannot upgrade from an x86 version of Windows Vista to an x64 version of Windows 7, nor from an x64 version of Windows Vista to an x86 version of Windows 7. It is also not possible to upgrade from certain editions of Windows Vista to certain editions of Windows 7.

Migrating from Windows XP

It is not possible to upgrade directly from Windows XP to Windows 7. If you attempt an upgrade, you receive the message shown in Figure 1-15. Organizations that want to move users from computers running Windows XP to Windows 7 need to consider migration.

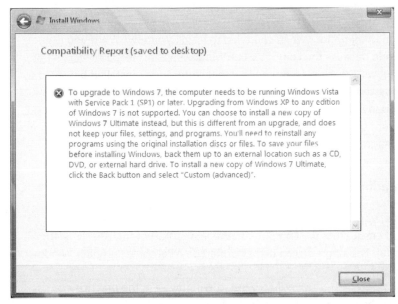

FIGURE 1-15 No upgrade from Windows XP to Windows 7

There are two basic migration scenarios for migrating user profile data: the *side-by-side migration* and the *wipe-and-load migration*. The version that you choose depends largely on the computer hardware of the source computer. If the source computer has sufficient hardware to support Windows 7, and you choose not to configure the computer to dual-boot, you perform a wipe-and-load migration. If the source computer's hardware is not sufficient to support Windows 7, you need to perform a side-by-side migration. You also need to perform a side-by-side migration if you are configuring the computers to dual-boot because that is the only way to get application data from the Windows XP partition to the Windows 7 partition.

Side-by-Side Migrations

You use *side-by-side migrations* when you need to move user data from one computer to another. Depending on the migration method you use, you may need to ensure that both computers are turned on during the migration. This is necessary when you use methods that directly transfer data from one computer to another, such as through a special cable or over the network. The advantage of a side-by-side migration is that all data remains on the source computer even after it is migrated to the destination computer. If something goes wrong with the migration, the user can still go back to the old computer.

Wipe-and-Load Migrations

Wipe-and-load migrations involve exporting user data from a machine to an external location, such as a USB storage device or network share, removing the existing operating system, performing a clean installation of Windows 7, and then importing the user data from the external location. Once you successfully complete the migration, you can delete the user data from the external location.

You use wipe-and-load migrations when you need to install Windows 7, but you cannot perform a direct upgrade because the computer has Windows XP installed or a version of Windows Vista or Windows 7 that uses a different architecture. For example, you wanted to change the operating system on a computer from Windows 7 Enterprise (x86) to Windows 7 Enterprise (x64). The disadvantage of a wipe-and-load migration is that the user cannot go back to their original configuration easily if something goes wrong during the migration. You will learn more about migrating data in Lesson 3.

PRACTICE   Upgrading to Windows 7

In this optional practice, you upgrade an existing computer running Windows Vista to Windows 7. You should ensure that the computer has at least 10 GB of free space for the upgrade to be successful. This upgrade can be performed on a computer running Windows Vista through virtualization software.

EXERCISE 1   Upgrading Windows Vista to Windows 7

Before starting this exercise, ensure that the version of Windows 7 that you will be upgrading to shares the same architecture as the version of Windows Vista that you are upgrading. For example, if you have an x86 version of Windows Vista, make sure that you have the installation media for the x86 version of Windows 7. Perform the following steps:

1. Log on to the computer running Windows Vista with a user account that is a member of the local Administrators group.

2. Access the Windows 7 installation source and double-click Setup.exe. When prompted by User Account Control, click Allow. This loads the Install Windows page. Click Install Now.

3. On the Get Important Updates For Installation page, click Do Not Get The Latest Updates For Installation.

4. On the licensing page, review the Windows 7 operating system license and then select the I Accept The License Terms check box. Click Next.

5. On the Which Type Of Installation Do You Want? page, click Upgrade. The installation routine performs a compatibility check and then begins upgrading Windows. Depending on the speed of the computer you are upgrading, this step may take time. The computer reboots several times during this process.

6. On the Type Your Product Key For Activation page, enter the Windows 7 product key
   as shown in Figure 1-16, clear the Automatically Activate Windows When I'm Online
   check box, and click Next.

FIGURE 1-16 Enter the product key.

7. On the Help Protect Your Computer And Improve Windows Automatically page, click
   Use Recommended Settings.

8. On the Review Your Time And Date Settings page, ensure that the time zone setting
   matches your locale and that the clock setting is accurate and then click Next.

9. On the Select Your Computer's Current Location page, click Home Network.

10. Log on to the upgraded computer running Windows 7 using the credentials that you
    used to log on to the computer running Windows Vista at the start of this exercise.

11. Turn off the upgraded computer running Windows 7.

Lesson Summary

- You can upgrade Windows Vista to Windows 7 only when the version of Windows 7 you are upgrading to shares the same architecture (x86 or x64) and is an equivalent or higher edition.
- You should run the Windows 7 Upgrade Advisor prior to attempting an upgrade to ensure that hardware and software installed on the computer running Windows Vista is compatible with Windows 7.
- You can upgrade from an edition of Windows 7 with fewer features to an edition with more features, but not from an edition that has more features to one that has fewer features.
- It is not possible to upgrade from Windows XP to Windows 7 at all.
- Side-by-side migrations involve moving data from one computer to another or from one partition to another in dual-boot scenarios.
- Wipe-and-load migrations involve moving user data off a computer, removing the existing operating system installation, replacing it with a new Windows 7 installation, and then importing the original user data.

Lesson Review

You can use the following questions to test your knowledge of the information in Lesson 2, "Upgrading to Windows 7." The questions are also available on the companion DVD if you prefer to review them in electronic form.

> **NOTE** **ANSWERS**
>
> Answers to these questions and explanations of why each answer choice is correct or incorrect are located in the "Answers" section at the end of the book.

1. To which of the following versions and editions of Windows 7 can you directly upgrade a computer running Windows Vista Enterprise (x86)?

   A. Windows 7 Home Professional (x86).

   B. Windows 7 Ultimate (x86)

   C. Windows 7 Ultimate (x64)

   D. Windows 7 Enterprise (x64)

2. In which of the following scenarios must you perform a migration rather than an upgrade? (Choose all that apply.)

   A. Windows XP Professional (x64) to Windows 7 Professional (x64)

   B. Windows Vista Business (x86) to Windows 7 Professional (x64)

   C. Windows Vista Enterprise (x64) to Windows 7 Enterprise (x64)

   D. Windows Vista Home Premium (x64) to Windows 7 Home Premium (x86)

3. A user has a home computer with a cable Internet connection and no other computers on his home network. Which of the following methods can this person use to upgrade from Windows 7 Home Premium to Windows 7 Ultimate?

   A. Sysprep

   B. Windows PE

   C. WDS

   D. Windows Anytime Upgrade

4. Which of the following tools can you use to determine if the applications installed on your computer running Windows Vista are known to have problems with Windows 7?

   A. Windows 7 Upgrade Advisor

   B. Sysprep

   C. USMT

   D. Windows PE

5. To which of the following editions and versions of Windows 7 can you upgrade a computer running Windows 7 Home Premium (x86)? (Choose all that apply.)

   A. Windows 7 Professional (x86)

   B. Windows 7 Professional (x64)

   C. Windows 7 Ultimate (x86)

   D. Windows 7 Enterprise (x64)

Lesson 3: Managing User Profiles

Unless you are performing a direct upgrade from Windows Vista to Windows 7 or one that uses roaming user profiles, any Windows 7 deployment requires that you have a plan for moving user profile data from the user's previous computer to the new computer. Getting user data such as e-mail messages and Web browser bookmarks properly transferred is as important to take into account when performing a Windows 7 deployment as getting the right hardware platform on which to run the operating system. If you cannot get all the users' data that was on their old computers on to their new computers, they may not be able to do their jobs. Users also feel less intimidated by a new operating system if all their old operating system preferences are in effect from the moment they first log on. The more comfortable users are with a new operating system, the more favorably they will look on the transition. In this lesson, you learn how to migrate user data from previous versions of Windows, or from an existing installation of Windows 7, to a new installation of Windows 7.

> **After this lesson, you will be able to:**
> - Migrate user profiles from one computer running Windows 7 to another.
> - Migrate user profiles from previous versions of Windows.
>
> **Estimated lesson time: 40 minutes**

Migrating User Profile Data

User data includes more than just documents from a word processor. User data includes things such as favorite Internet sites, customized application settings such as e-mail account data, desktop backgrounds, files, and folders. Unless you are using roaming user profiles in your organization, the computer that a person uses a computer is likely to have important data stored on that computer. Migrating a user from Windows XP or Windows Vista to Windows 7 successfully involves ensuring that all this important data makes the transition from a person's old computer to the new one.

You can view the list of user profiles stored on a computer running Windows 7 by opening System within Control Panel, clicking Advanced System Settings, and then clicking the Settings button in the User Profiles area of the Advanced System Settings tab. From this dialog box, shown in Figure 1-17, you can view the size of user profiles, delete user profiles stored on the computer, or change the user profile from a local profile to a roaming user profile.

A roaming user profile is a profile stored on a server that is accessible from any computer running Windows 7 on a network. Administrators implement roaming user profiles when people do not use a specific computer, but they might log on to any computer in the organization. Roaming user profiles also allow central backup of user data.

FIGURE 1-17 A list of user profiles

Windows Easy Transfer

Windows Easy Transfer is a utility that comes with Windows 7 that you can use to transfer user profile data from computers running Windows XP, Windows Vista, or Windows 7 to new computers running Windows 7. As Figure 1-18 shows, Windows Easy Transfer can be used to transfer user accounts, documents, music, pictures, e-mail, bookmarks, certificates, and other data.

FIGURE 1-18 The Windows Easy Transfer Welcome page

There are three separate methods that you can use to migrate data with Windows Easy Transfer. The method that is appropriate depends on the circumstances of the migration. To migrate profile data with Windows Easy Transfer, you can use any of the following:

- **Easy Transfer Cable**   This is a special cable with USB connectors that you can acquire from hardware vendors. You connect one end to the source computer and the other to the destination computer. Both computers are turned on during the migration, and Windows Easy Transfer runs on both computers at the same time. You can perform only a side-by-side migration using this method.

- **Network**   To use the network migration method, you must have two computers running Windows Easy Transfer connected to the same local area network. Both computers are turned on during the migration, and Windows Easy Transfer runs on both computers at the same time. You can perform only a side-by-side migration using this method. When performing a network migration, you configure a password on the source computer that you have to enter on the destination computer.

- **External Hard Disk or USB Flash Drive**   You can specify an attached external hard disk or USB flash drive. It is also possible to specify an internal hard disk drive or network share when using this method. You can perform a side-by-side migration as well as a wipe-and-restore migration using this method. You protect your data by entering a password on the source computer that you must again enter before importing the data on the destination computer.

Installing Windows Easy Transfer

Unless the source computer is running Windows 7, you will need to install the Windows Easy Transfer application. This includes source computers running Windows Vista. Although Windows Vista comes with an earlier version of the Windows Easy Transfer software, you should use the updated Windows 7 version when transferring data to Windows 7 computers. To install Windows Easy Transfer on the source computer, perform the following steps:

1. Run Windows Easy Transfer on the destination computer and select the transfer method that you are going to use.

2. Select the This Is My New Computer option. If you have chosen the Easy Transfer Cable or Network options, go to step 3. Otherwise, click No when prompted as to whether Windows Easy Transfer has already saved your files.

3. On the Do You Need To Install Windows Easy Transfer On Your Old Computer? page, shown in Figure 1-19, select I Need To Install It Now.

4. On the How Do You Want To Install Windows Easy Transfer On Your Old Computer? page, select either USB Flash Drive or External Hard Disk or Shared Network Folder. The Windows Easy Transfer application installation file will be copied to this location and you will then be able to install the application on the source computer.

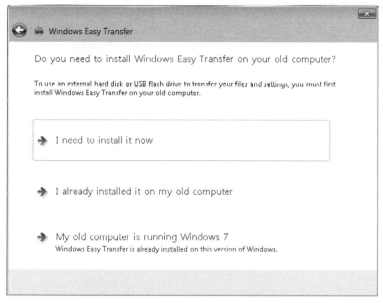

FIGURE 1-19 Prepare Windows Easy Transfer installation files.

Windows Easy Transfer Migration

After you have set up Windows Easy Transfer on the source computer, you are ready to perform migration. If you want to migrate only a single user account, you can log on with that account to perform the transfer. If you want to migrate all accounts on the computer, you need to log on with a user account that has local administrator privileges. To do this, start Windows Easy Transfer, select the transfer method, and then, on the Which Computer Are You Using Now? page, select This Is My Old Computer. If you are using the External Hard Disk or USB storage device method, Windows Easy Transfer will then perform a migration check and provide an estimate of the size of the data you can transfer to the new computer on the source computer. If you are using the Network or Easy Transfer Cable method, you will select items for migration on the destination computer.

When selecting items for migration, you can accept the default values or customize what to migrate for each user account and all shared items. To customize, click Customize under each user account. This will allow you to select whether you want to transfer each user's Documents, Music, Pictures, Videos, Program Settings, Windows Settings, and Other Items. If you want to be more specific, you can click Advanced, which brings up the Modify Your Selections dialog box shown in Figure 1-20. This dialog box allows you to select which accounts to migrate, as well as which files and folders Windows Easy Transfer will migrate to the new machine.

By selecting Advanced, you can determine what you want to do with the user accounts being migrated from the source computer to the destination computer. You have the option of mapping a user account on the old computer to a specific user account on the new computer or

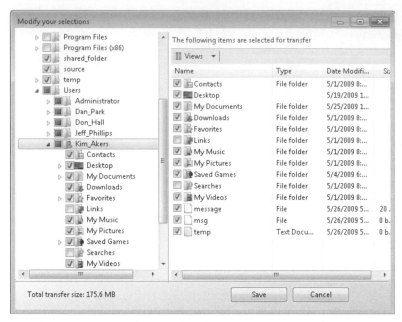

FIGURE 1-20 Customizing data transferred by Windows Easy Transfer

you can have Windows Easy Transfer create a new account as shown in Figure 1-21. If you select the Create A New Account option, you will need to specify a password for the new account. If you do not choose to use Advanced, Windows Easy Transfer will create new accounts on the computer running Windows 7 with the old account names but will assign a blank password that needs to be changed when the user associated with that account first tries to log on.

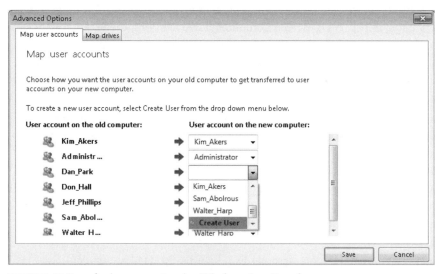

FIGURE 1-21 Transferring accounts using Windows Easy Transfer

The first step to take when running Windows Easy Transfer on the destination computer is to specify the transfer method that you are going to use and that this is your new computer. Depending on which method you are using, one of the following will happen:

- If you are using the external hard disk or USB flash drive method, you will be asked to specify the location of the Easy Transfer file and to enter a password to open it.

- If you are using the network method, you will need to enter the Windows Easy Transfer key before the transfer will begin. The source computer displays this key. You will then go through the process of selecting what to transfer that was described previously.

- If you are using the Easy Transfer Cable method, the wizard will attempt to detect the cable and then will initiate the transfer. You will then go through the process of selecting what to transfer as described earlier.

You will use Windows Easy Transfer to perform a migration in the practice exercise at the end of the lesson.

 Quick Check

- Which Windows Easy Transfer method should you use when you want to perform a wipe-and-load migration?

Quick Check Answer

- The only Windows Easy Transfer method that supports wipe-and-load migrations is the External Hard Disk or USB flash drive method.

User State Migration Tool

USMT 4.0 is a command-line utility that allows you to automate the process of user profile migration. The USMT is part of the Windows Automated Installation Kit (WAIK) and is a better tool for performing a large number of profile migrations than Windows Easy Transfer. The USMT can write data to a removable USB storage device or a network share but cannot perform a direct side-by-side migration over the network from the source to the destination computer. The USMT does not support user profile migration using the Windows Easy Transfer cable. USMT migration occurs in two phases, exporting profile data from the source computer using ScanState and importing profile data on the destination computer using LoadState.

USMT 4.0 allows you to capture user accounts, user files, and operating system and application settings. The USMT tool also migrates access control lists (ACLs) for files and folders, ensuring that permissions set on the source computer are retained on the destination computer. You can use USMT to migrate profile data to computers running Windows 7 from computers running Windows XP, Windows Vista, and Windows 7. You can also use the USMT to migrate data from computers running Windows 7 to Windows Vista. You cannot use USMT to migrate mapped network drives, local printers, device drivers, passwords, shared folder permissions, and Internet connection sharing settings.

Unlike Windows Easy Transfer, where you select the particular items you want to migrate when you are running the application, with USMT, you configure a set of migration rules prior to the migration that specify what data to export from the source computer.

There are four different .xml migration files used with the USMT:

- **MigApp.xml**   This file contains rules about migrating application settings. These include Accessibility settings, dial-up connections, favorites, folder options, fonts, group membership, Open Database Connectivity (ODBC) settings, Microsoft Office Outlook Express mailbox files, mouse and keyboard settings, phone and modem options, Remote Access Service (RAS) connection phone book files, regional options, remote access, screen-saver settings, taskbar settings, and wallpaper settings.

- **MigUser.xml**   This file contains rules about user profiles and user data. The default settings for this file migrate all data in My Documents, My Video, My Music, My Pictures, desktop files, Start Menu, Quick Launch settings, favorites, Shared Documents, Shared Video, Shared Music, Shared desktop files, Shared Pictures, Shared Start menu, and Shared Favorites. This file also contains rules that ensure that all the following file types are migrated from fixed volumes: .qdf, .qsd, .qel, .qph, .doc, .dot, .rtf, .mcw, .wps, .scd, .wri, .wpd, .xl*, .csv, .iqy, .dqy, .oqy, .rqy, .wk*, .wq1, .slk, .dif, .ppt*, .pps*, .pot*, .sh3, .ch3, .pre, .ppa, .txt, .pst, .one*, .mpp, .vsd, .vl*, .or6, .accdb, .mdb, .pub, .xla, .xlb and .xls. The asterisk (*) represents zero or more characters.
- **MigDocs.xml**   This file contains information on the location of user documents.
- **Config.xml**   This file is different from the other migration files as it is used to exclude features from the migration. You can create and modify the Config.xml file using ScanState.exe with the */genconfig* option.

It is also possible to create custom XML files to be used with the migration. For example, you can create a custom XML file that reroutes folders, specific file types, or specific files. You would use rerouting if you wanted to move all the files of one type, such as .avi files, that may have been stored in different places on the source computer to a specific folder on the destination computer.

ScanState

You run ScanState on the source computer during the migration. You must run ScanState. exe on computers running Windows Vista and Windows 7 from an administrative command prompt. When running ScanState on a source computer that has Windows XP installed, you need to run it as a user that is a member of the local administrators group.

The following command creates an encrypted store named Mystore on the file share named Migration on the file server named Fileserver that uses the encryption key Mykey:

```
scanstate \\fileserver\migration\mystore /i:migapp.xml /i:miguser.xml /o /config:config.xml
/encrypt /key:"mykey"
```

Running ScanState and LoadState with the */v:13* option creates a detailed log file. You should use this option if you are having problems migrating data.

LoadState

LoadState is run on the destination computer. You should install all applications that were on the source computer on the destination before you run LoadState. You must run Loadstate. exe on computers running Windows Vista and Windows 7 from an administrative command prompt.

To load profile data from an encrypted store named Mystore that is stored on a share named Migration on a file server named Fileserver and which is encrypted with the encryption key Mykey, use this command:

```
loadstate \\fileserver\migration\mystore /i:migapp.xml /i:miguser.xml /decrypt
/key:"mykey"
```

Migration Store Types

When planning a migration using USMT, you need to decide where you are going to store migrated data that is generated by ScanState on the source computer and required by LoadState on the destination computer. USMT supports three types of migration stores:

- **Uncompressed** Uncompressed migration stores use a hierarchy of folders that mirror the user profile data being migrated. You can navigate an uncompressed migration store using Windows Explorer. This creates a duplicate of the backed-up files in another location.

- **Compressed** A compressed migration store is a single image file that contains all data being migrated. The image file can be encrypted and password-protected. It is not possible to navigate to this file using Windows Explorer.

- **Hard-link** Hard-link migration stores are used in wipe-and-load scenarios only. The hard-link migration store is stored on the local computer while the old operating system is removed and the new operating system is installed. Use the /hardlink option with ScanState to create a hard-link migration store. Hard linking does not create a duplicate of the migrated data and hence uses less space than the uncompressed or compressed stores when those are used on the volume being migrated. Hard-link migrations require only 250 MB of free space on the volume being migrated, regardless of the amount of profile data being migrated.

ScanState with the /p option allows you to estimate the size of the migration store prior to performing a migration. All migrations require a minimum of 250 MB of free space on the volume being migrated.

> **MORE INFO** **MIGRATION STORE TYPES**
>
> To learn more about USMT migration store types, consult the following article on Microsoft TechNet: *http://technet.microsoft.com/en-us/library/dd560795.aspx.*

Performing Offline Migrations

You can use USMT to perform offline migrations. Offline migrations involve booting the computer into a Windows PE environment that includes the USMT files and then running ScanState against the installation of Windows on the computer's hard disk drive. You must still run the LoadState feature of the migration from within Windows 7. You cannot run LoadState when booted into a Windows PE environment.

> **NOTE** **SCANSTATE AND UPGRADES**
>
> You can also run ScanState in offline mode against the Windows.old directory that is generated when you perform an upgrade from Windows Vista.

An advantage of offline migrations is that the person performing the migration does not need administrator access to the computer on which they are performing the migration. You cannot perform an offline migration on a computer where BitLocker is. It is necessary to temporarily suspend BitLocker to allow USMT access to the files to be migrated.

MORE INFO **OFFLINE MIGRATIONS**

To learn more about performing offline migrations with USMT, consult the following page on Microsoft TechNet: *http://technet.microsoft.com/en-us/library/dd560758.aspx.*

PRACTICE **Migrating User Data**

When it is not possible to perform a direct upgrade from one version of Windows to another, it is necessary to perform a migration. It can also be necessary to perform a migration if you need to move user data from one computer running Windows 7 to another. There are two tools which you can use to migrate user profile data reliably from one computer to another: USMT and Windows Easy Transfer.

EXERCISE 1 Migrating User Data Using Windows Easy Transfer

In this exercise, you will create a user account and data; use the Windows Easy Transfer tool to export that data to a USB device; remove the user data from the computer; and then migrate the user account back using Windows Easy Transfer to simulate migrating the user to another computer running Windows 7.

1. Log on to computer Canberra with the Kim_Akers user account you created in the exercise at the end of Lesson 1.

2. Click Start, Control Panel. Under User Accounts And Family Safety, click Add Or Remove User Accounts.

3. In Manage Accounts, click Create A New Account. Enter the account name as **Don_Hall** and make the account a Standard User.

4. In Manage Accounts, click the Don_Hall account and then click Create A Password. Enter the password **P@ssw0rd** twice. In the password hint text box, type the page number of this page in the training kit. Click **Create Password** and then close the Control Panel.

5. Click Start. Click the arrow next to Shut Down, and then click Switch User. Log on using the Don_Hall user account.

6. When you are logged on to computer Canberra with the Don_Hall user account, right-click the desktop and then click New, Text Document. Name the text document **Migration_Test.txt.** Open the file and type **Migration_Test.** Close and save the document.

7. Log off the Don_Hall user account and then log back on with the Kim_Akers user account.

8. Connect the USB storage device that you will use to store Windows Easy Transfer data to the computer.

9. Click Start. In the Search Programs and Files text box, type **Windows Easy Transfer** and then press Enter.

10. On the Welcome To Windows Easy Transfer page, click Next. On the What Do You Want To Use To Transfer Items To Your New Computer? page, click An External Hard Disk Or USB Flash Drive.

11. On the Which Computer Are You Using Now? page, click This Is My Old Computer.

12. Windows Easy Transfer then performs a check of what information can be transferred. On the Choose What To Transfer From This Computer page, ensure that only the Don_Hall user account is selected as shown in Figure 1-22. You do not need to migrate Kim_Akers or Shared Items in this exercise. Click Next.

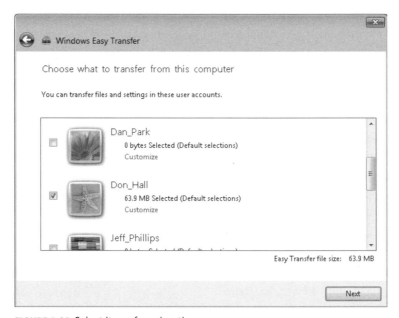

FIGURE 1-22 Select items for migration.

13. On the Save Your Files And Settings For Transfer page, enter the password **P@ssw0rd** twice and then click Save.

14. In the Save Your Easy Transfer file dialog box, specify the USB storage device that you connected to the computer in step 8 and then click Save. When the data has been saved to the USB storage device, click Next twice and then click Close.

15. Click Start, right-click the Computer item, and then choose Properties. Click Advanced System Settings. In the System Properties dialog box, click the Settings button in the User Profiles area to bring up the User Profiles dialog box shown in Figure 1-23.

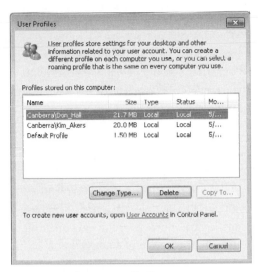

FIGURE 1-23 The user profile list

16. Click on the Canberra\Don_Hall profile and then click Delete. When prompted to confirm the deletion of the profile, click Yes. Click OK twice to close the User Profiles and System Properties dialog boxes.

17. Click Start, Control Panel. Under User Accounts And Family Safety, click Add Or Remove User Accounts.

18. Select the Don_Hall user account and then click Delete The Account. On the Do You Want To Keep Don_Hall's Files? page, click Delete Files. Click Delete Account and close the Control Panel.

19. Log out and verify that it is not possible to log on to the computer Canberra with the Don_Hall user account.

20. Log on using the Kim_Akers user account.

21. Click Start. In the Search Programs and Files text box, type **Windows Easy Transfer** and then press Enter. On the Windows Easy Transfer Welcome page, click Next.

22. On the What Do You Want To Use To Transfer Items To Your New Computer? page, click An External Hard Disk Or USB Flash Drive.

23. On the Which Computer Are You Using Now? page, click This Is My New Computer.

24. On the Has Windows Easy Transfer Already Saved Your Files To An External Hard Disk Or USB Flash Drive? page, click Yes, Open The File.

25. Navigate to the location on the USB storage device where you saved the Windows Easy Transfer migration data in step 14, select the file named Windows Easy Transfer – Items From Old Computer and then click Open. Enter the password **P@ssw0rd.**

26. On the Choose What To Transfer To This Computer page, ensure that only the Don_ Hall user account is selected and then click Transfer. Click Close to dismiss the Windows Easy Transfer Wizard.

27. Log off and then log on with the Don_Hall user account. It will be necessary to enter a new password for the account. Use the password **P@ssword.** When you log on, verify that the file named Migration_Test.txt is present on the desktop.

Lesson Summary

- Windows Easy Transfer can be used to migrate user profile data from computers running Windows XP, Windows Vista, and Windows 7 to computers running Windows 7.
- Windows Easy Transfer can migrate data using a Windows Easy Transfer cable or directly from source computer to destination computer over the network, or it can store migration data on a removable USB storage device or a network share.
- USMT 4.0, which is available through the WAIK, is used when it is necessary to migrate profile data on a large number of computers. USMT can be used to perform an offline migration.
- ScanState is run on the source computer. LoadState is run on the destination computer.
- USMT uses XML configuration files such as MigApp.xml, MigUser.xml, MigDocs.xml, and Config.xml to control which data is migrated from the source computer to the destination computer.
- An offline migration can be performed by booting into Windows PE and running ScanState.

Lesson Review

You can use the following questions to test your knowledge of the information in Lesson 3, "Managing User Profiles." The questions are also available on the companion DVD if you prefer to review them in electronic form.

> **NOTE ANSWERS**
>
> Answers to these questions and explanations of why each answer choice is correct or incorrect are located in the "Answers" section at the end of the book.

1. Which of the following operating systems support an offline migration using USMT?
   A. Windows 2000 Professional
   B. Windows XP Professional
   C. Windows Vista
   D. Windows 7

2. Which of the following utilities can you use to transfer user encryption certificates from a computer running Windows XP Professional to Windows 7 Professional? (Choose all that apply.)

    A. File Settings and Transfer Wizard

    B. USMT

    C. Windows Easy Transfer

    D. Robocopy.exe

3. Which XML file is used with ScanState to specify information about user profile data that should be migrated?

    A. MigDocs.xml

    B. MigUser.xml

    C. MigApp.xml

    D. Config.xml

4. Which of the following must you download from Microsoft's Web site to obtain USMT 4.0?

    A. Windows Anytime Upgrade

    B. Windows Upgrade Advisor

    C. WAIK

    D. Microsoft Application Compatibility Toolkit

5. Which of the following types of USMT migration store types minimizes hard disk space used when performing a wipe-and-load migration?

    A. Uncompressed

    B. Compressed

    C. Hard-link

Chapter Review

To further practice and reinforce the skills you learned in this chapter, you can perform the following tasks:

- Review the chapter summary.
- Review the list of key terms introduced in this chapter.
- Complete the case scenarios. These scenarios set up real-world situations involving the topics of this chapter and ask you to create a solution.
- Complete the suggested practices.
- Take a practice test.

Chapter Summary

- Windows 7 requires a 1 GHz x86 or x64 processor, 512 MB of RAM for the Starter or Home Basic editions, and 1 GB of RAM for other editions. To support the Aero UI, Windows 7 requires a graphics card with 128 MB RAM.
- Windows 7 can be dual-booted with Windows XP and Windows Vista. A computer requires multiple partitions to support dual-boot.
- Windows 7 can be installed from DVD-ROM, USB storage device, network share, or WDS.
- The Upgrade Advisor can inform you of which hardware and software attached to your computer running Windows Vista is compatible with Windows 7.
- You can only upgrade from an x86 version of Windows Vista to an x86 version of Windows 7. You can only upgrade from an x64 version of Windows 7.
- You cannot upgrade directly from Windows XP to Windows 7. You can only upgrade from Windows Vista to Windows 7.
- Windows Easy Transfer allows migration of user profile data from computers running Windows XP and Windows Vista to computers running Windows 7. It is suitable for when a small number of computers need to be migrated.
- USMT is a command-line tool that allows migrating of user profile data from computers running Windows XP and Windows Vista to computers running Windows 7. It is suitable when a large number of computers need to be migrated.

Key Terms

Do you know what these key terms mean? You can check your answers by looking up the terms in the glossary at the end of the book.

- **dual-boot**
- **Netbook**

- side-by-side migration
- wipe-and-load migration

Case Scenarios

In the following case scenarios, you will apply what you've learned about the topics covered in this chapter. You can find answers to these questions in the "Answers" section at the end of this book.

Case Scenario 1: Installing Windows 7 at Contoso

You work for Contoso, Ltd. The company has a head office and two branch office locations. The company has just purchased 50 small form factor laptops on which you want to deploy Windows 7. A total of 40 of these computers will be deployed at the head office site, with 5 deployed to each of the branch office sites. The small computers do not include DVD-ROM drives, but they do have PXE-compliant network adapters and USB ports. You have tested the default version of Windows PE available with the WAIK and found that it is not compatible with the network adapters on these computers. Contoso, Ltd has a volume license agreement with Microsoft. All servers at Contoso, Ltd have the Windows Server 2008 operating system installed. You would like to ensure that the computers' hard disks are protected with encryption so that data is protected in case they are lost. Considering these facts, answer the following questions:

1. Which installation media or source could you use to deploy Windows 7 in the head office?

2. Which installation media or source could you use to deploy Windows 7 in the branch offices?

3. Which edition of Windows 7 should you deploy to the computers?

Case Scenario 2: Migrating User Data at Fabrikam

You are in charge of supporting client operating systems at Fabrikam. In the head office, you have 20 users that have computers running Windows 7 Enterprise (x86). You will be increasing the amount of RAM in these computers from 4 GB to 16 GB and need to upgrade the operating system to Windows 7 Enterprise (x64). After the upgrade is complete, users should not be able to boot into the x86 version of Windows 7. You have 10 users at a branch office who currently have computers running Windows XP Professional that are more than 5 years old. These computers each have only 256 MB of RAM. You do not have any Windows Easy Transfer cables and do not want to store branch office user profile data on network drives or on USB storage devices. You will replace these computers with 10 new computers running Windows 7 Professional. Considering these facts, answer the following questions:

1.   What sort of migration should you perform at the branch office, side-by-side or wipe-and-load?

2.   What sort of migration should you perform at the head office, side-by-side or wipe-and-load?

3.   Which technology and method would you use to perform the migrations in the branch office?

Suggested Practices

To help you master the exam objectives presented in this chapter, complete the following tasks.

Perform a Clean Installation

As an alternative to performing a clean installation of Windows 7 on a computer that does not have an existing operating system installed, consider configuring a computer to dual-boot between an existing operating system and Windows 7.

- Configure a computer running Windows XP or Windows Vista to dual-boot with Windows 7. Ensure that you have a separate partition that has more than 15 GB of space available.

Upgrade to Windows 7 from a Previous Version of Windows

The Windows 7 Upgrade Advisor is a tool that allows you to determine whether the applications and hardware on a computer running Windows Vista are compatible with Windows 7.

- Download the Windows 7 Upgrade Advisor onto a computer running Windows Vista. Run the upgrade advisor to determine if any of the hardware or applications used with the computer running Windows Vista are incompatible with Windows 7.

Migrate User Profiles

The USMT is a fully featured and complex user profile migration tool. Like Windows Easy Transfer, you can use the USMT to migrate user profiles from computers running Windows XP, Windows Vista, and Windows 7 to computers running Windows 7.

- Create a new user account on the computer running Windows 7 named Canberra. Log in and create an example document.

Take a Practice Test

The practice tests on this book's companion DVD offer many options. For example, you can test yourself on just one exam objective, or you can test yourself on all the 70-680 certification exam content. You can set up the test so that it closely simulates the experience of taking a certification exam, or you can set it up in study mode so that you can look at the correct answers and explanations after you answer each question.

> **MORE INFO**   **PRACTICE TESTS**
>
> For details about all the practice test options available, see the section entitled "How to Use the Practice Tests," in the Introduction to this book.

CHAPTER 2

Configuring System Images

As a network professional in an enterprise environment, you have probably configured a reference computer, created an image, and used a distribution server to apply that image to your client computers. You should be familiar with the Sysprep tool and how you can remove hardware-specific information from an image. This chapter looks at recent developments and enhancements to the various tools you use in configuring *system images* (disk image files that include an operating system) and in particular the use of file-based Windows Image (WIM) images and the ImageX tool.

In previous Microsoft operating systems, the use of *virtual hard disks (VHDs)* containing system images was limited to virtualization and the facility was used with Hyper-V, Microsoft Virtual Server, and Microsoft Virtual PC software when implementing virtual machines. In Windows 7, this has been extended and you can create and use VHDs on hardware PCs that are not virtual machines. In Windows 7 Enterprise and Ultimate editions, you can boot from VHD, back up an entire system disk to VHD, and install a system image to VHD. This new operating system feature enables you to recover quickly from a catastrophic system disk failure and provides failover protection without needing to implement disk array systems.

This chapter looks at how you capture a system image and prepare it for distribution to other computers. It also looks at how to configure a VHD to hold a system image and how to enable a computer running Windows 7 Enterprise or Ultimate to boot from a VHD containing a system image. The chapter covers the various tools and methods you use to prepare system images for capture and to manage VHD files.

EXAM TIP
The use of native VHDs on non-virtual computers is a new feature in Windows 7 and is likely to be tested in the 70-680 examination.

Exam objectives in this chapter:

- Capture a system image.
- Configure a VHD.

Lessons in this chapter:

Before You Begin

To complete the exercises in the practices in this chapter, you need to have done the following:

- Installed Windows 7 on a stand-alone client PC as described in Chapter 1, "Install, Migrate, or Upgrade to Windows 7." You need Internet access to complete the exercises.
- Implemented a second hard disk on this computer to host the VHD you create (this is an option). You can use an internal disk if one is available, or an external hard disk such as a USB device. You should have at least 20 GB free space on this hard disk. This is not essential because you can create a VHD on the C: drive, but it makes your practice exercises more realistic.
- You need a USB flash drive (UFD) with 4 GB free memory.

 REAL WORLD

Ian McLean

Setting up large numbers of computers has become much easier than it was 10 or even 5 years ago.

I recall going from computer to computer, booting each with a floppy disk that implemented a subset of MS-DOS that permitted network access and file transfer (and very little else). Installation files and answer files were then downloaded to each client computer (often from a single and creakingly slow CD-ROM) and the operating system was installed. In those days, "hands-free" installation was a bit of a joke. I recall going around to several hundred computers in the middle of the night agreeing to licensing terms and conditions.

Installing from captured images posed other difficulties. You typically needed to capture an image for each computer because of security ID (SID) considerations. This was OK for teaching networks where you could have images for each course, but it's not the way to install a few hundred new computers. Sysprep was one of the more welcome utilities when it was first introduced. Also, if you captured an image with time-critical information (for example passwords) and applied it at a later date you could hit trouble. I recall installing a computer as the domain controller for a Microsoft Official Course from an image and finding 1,000 passwords had expired. Also, if you imaged a computer and installed that image later, the security updates that had been issued in the meantime were not applied, leaving the computer vulnerable.

Now client computers can be installed from image files on a distribution server (much faster than downloading and running installation files). Images can be generalized with SIDs and computer names removed. You can add security updates, language packs, and applications to an image before you distribute it, and keep images up to date.

Administrators don't have easy lives. Nevertheless, I think it's a bit easier now than it used to be. Learn about the best ways to install large numbers of client computers. It will make one aspect of your job considerably less arduous. It won't do you any harm in your examinations, either!

Lesson 1: Capturing System Images

This lesson discusses how you prepare a system image for automated or manual capture and the use of Windows Image (WIM) files. It discusses the Windows Automated Installation Kit (Windows AIK), the Windows Preinstallation Environment (Windows PE), and the Sysprep command-line tool.

The lesson briefly discusses the Microsoft Deployment Toolkit (MDT) 2010 and the Deployment Image Servicing and Management (DISM) tool. However, Chapter 3, "Deploying System Images," describes in detail how you use DISM to amend system images and how you load and install MDT and use it to deploy a system image.

After this lesson, you will be able to:

- Download and use the Windows AIK. In particular, use the ImageX and Oscdimg tools to create system images and Windows System Image Manager (Windows SIM) to create an answer file that enables hands-free installation of a WIM image.

- Create a Windows PE boot disk, boot to Windows PE, and image a Windows 7 installation.

- Use the Sysprep utility to prepare a reference computer for imaging and understand the Windows Setup configuration passes.

- Understand the functions of the MDT tool and know that you can use Deployment Workbench to access MDT documentation and to access a checklist of tasks you must complete before deploying an operating system. Chapter 3 describes this tool in detail.

Estimated lesson time: 50 minutes

Installing and Using the Windows Automated Installation Toolkit

The *Windows Automated Installation Kit (Windows AIK)* is a collection of tools and documentation designed to help you deploy Microsoft Windows operating system images to target computers or to a VHD. You can use the Windows AIK to automate Windows 7 installations, capture Windows system images with ImageX, configure and modify images using DISM, create Windows PE images, and migrate user profiles and data with the User State Migration Tool (USMT).

The Windows AIK consists of a number of tools that enable you to configure various deployment options. Depending upon your requirements, you will use some or all of the resources available in the Windows AIK.

To install the Windows AIK, you first download the ISO image, burn it to a DVD-ROM, and then install from the DVD-ROM. At the time of this writing, you can download the Windows

AIK International Organization for Standardization (ISO) image by accessing
http://technet.microsoft.com/en-us/library/dd349343.aspx and clicking the appropriate link.

Installing the Windows AIK from a DVD-ROM

You create an installation DVD-ROM by burning the downloaded ISO image to DVD-ROM.
Right-click the ISO image file and click Burn Disk Image. To install Windows AIK from
DVD-ROM, perform the following steps:

1. Insert the DVD-ROM. On the Welcome screen, click Windows AIK Setup.

2. On the Setup Wizard Welcome page, click Next.

3. Select the I Agree check box to accept the license terms. Click Next.

4. Click Next to accept the defaults on the Select Installation Folder page (unless you
    want to change the installation folder).

5. Click Next to start installation. The installation can take some time.

6. Click Close to exit.

   When the Windows AIK is installed, you can access the Windows AIK from the All Programs
menu. This gives you access to the Windows AIK documentation; the Deployment Tools
command prompt, which offers command-line utilities that implement ImageX; DISM; the
Oscdimg tool (for creating ISO images); and Windows SIM.

 Quick Check

   ■ Which Windows AIK tool do you use to create an answer file that enables
     hands-free installation of a WIM image?

Quick Check Answer

   ■ Windows SIM

Windows AIK Tools

Table 2-1 lists the tools included with the Windows AIK.

TABLE 2-1 Tools Included in the Windows AIK

TOOL	DESCRIPTION
Windows SIM	Opens Windows images, creates answer files, and manages distribution shares and configuration sets.
ImageX	Captures, creates, modifies, and applies Windows images.
DISM	Applies updates, drivers, and language packs to a Windows image. DISM is available in all installations of Windows 7.

TOOL	DESCRIPTION
Windows PE tools	The Windows AIK includes several tools used to build and configure Windows PE environments.
USMT	Used to migrate user data from a previous version of Windows to Windows 7. USMT is installed as part of the Windows AIK in the %PROGRAMFILES%\Windows AIK\Tools\USMT directory.
Oscdimg	Creates ISO images.

MORE INFO   USMT

For more information about USMT, see the User State Migration Tool User's Guide. When you install Windows AIK and USMT, you can find this guide at %PROGRAMFILES%\Windows AIK\Docs\Usmt.chmz.

Using the Windows Preinstallation Environment

The Windows Preinstallation Environment (*WinPE* version 3.0—commonly known as *Windows PE*) is a lightweight version of Windows 7 that is primarily used for the deployment of client computers. It is intended as a 32-bit or 64-bit replacement for MS-DOS during the installation phase of Windows 7 and can be booted via the Preboot Execution Environment (PXE), DVD-ROM, UFD, VHD, or hard disk. Windows PE is available free via the Windows AIK.

Originally, Windows PE was used as a preinstallation platform for deploying Windows operating systems. It has developed into a platform that lets you deploy workstations and servers in the enterprise environment and as a recovery platform to run 32-bit or 64-bit recovery tools such as the Windows Recovery Environment (Windows RE).

Typically you use the *copype.cmd* script in the C:\Program Files\Windows AIK\Tools\PETools subdirectory to create a local Windows PE build directory. You then use the Oscdimg Windows AIK tool in the same subdirectory to create an ISO image of Windows PE 3.0. You use this image to create a bootable DVD-ROM. You can then boot from the DVD-ROM into the preinstallation environment and use the ImageX tool to capture a WIM image. You do this in the practice exercises at the end of this lesson.

Creating a Reference Image

Later in this chapter, you will see how to use the Windows AIK ImageX tool and the Windows PE environment to prepare a WIM image of a computer running Windows 7 Enterprise or Ultimate and place that image on a bootable VHD on the same computer so you can boot the image from the VHD. This gives you failover protection for that specific computer and a form of backup. You do this in the practices in this lesson and Lesson 2 of this chapter.

However, in the enterprise environment, you are more likely to be concerned with installing Windows 7, on a reference computer and generating an image of that reference computer that can be installed on a large number of client computers on your network. Chapter 3 discusses adding the current operating system security updates, basic applications, and language packs to a captured image.

You need to generalize a reference image, removing hardware-specific information (such as the reference computer's SID), and generate an installation answer file and scripts to automate the installation.

Typically, in addition to the reference computer whose image you intend to build and capture, you require a technician computer that runs the tools you use to generalize and capture the image, for example the Windows AIK tools. The technician computer does not need to be running Windows 7—it could, for example, be a Windows Vista or Windows XP client.

The procedure for installing the Windows AIK on the technician computer is described in the previous section. To configure a reference computer and capture an image suitable for distribution to your client computers, you perform the following steps:

1. Build an answer file to automate the installation of Windows 7 on the reference computer (this is an option).

2. Validate and save your settings.

3. Configure a reference installation.

4. Create a bootable Windows PE optical disk or UFD that also contains the ImageX Windows AIK tool.

5. Capture the installation onto a network share.

6. Deploy the image from a network share.

> **NOTE USING AN ANSWER FILE**
>
> It is not compulsory to create an answer file, although this is the method recommended in Microsoft documentation. If you choose, you can install the reference computer manually.

Building an Answer File

The first step in creating a custom installation on your reference computer is (optionally) to build an answer file on your technician computer that you use to configure Windows settings during installation. You can, for example, configure the default Windows Internet Explorer settings, networking configuration, and other customizations. The answer file should contain all the settings required for an unattended installation so you are not prompted with user interface pages during installation. However, if you choose, you can build a reference computer using the traditional "click and type" installation method.

You use the Windows SIM utility in Windows AIK on your technician computer to create an answer file that includes basic Windows Setup configuration and minimum Windows Welcome customizations. In this example, the answer file does not import any special drivers, applications, or packages. You will study more advanced answer files in Chapter 3.

To create an answer file, you copy a Windows image (WIM) file to your technician computer and then use the Windows SIM tool. To create an answer file that will enable you to install Windows 7 on your reference computer using the WIM file on the installation DVD-ROM, perform the following procedure:

1. Create a folder on your technician computer called C:\Myimages.

2. Insert the Windows 7 product DVD into your technician computer.

3. Navigate to the \Sources directory on your DVD-ROM drive and copy the Install.wim file from the Windows product DVD to C:\Myimages.

4. Click Start, All Programs, Microsoft Windows AIK, and then Windows System Image Manager. This opens Windows SIM.

5. On the Windows SIM File menu, right-click Select A Windows Image Or Catalog File and choose Select Windows Image, as shown in Figure 2-1.

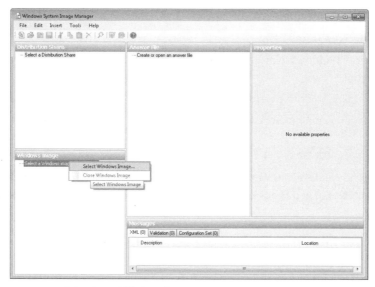

FIGURE 2-1 Selecting a Windows image

6. In the Select A Windows Image dialog box, navigate to C:\Myimages and then click Open.

7. You are prompted to select an image. Choose Install.wim and click Open. Select the image you want to install (for example, Windows 7 Ultimate) in the Select An Image dialog box and click OK.

8. If you are prompted to create a catalog file, click Yes. If prompted, click Yes again to allow the program to run. It can take some time to create a catalog file.

9. On the File menu, choose New Answer File. An empty (untitled) answer file appears in the Answer File pane, as shown in Figure 2-2.

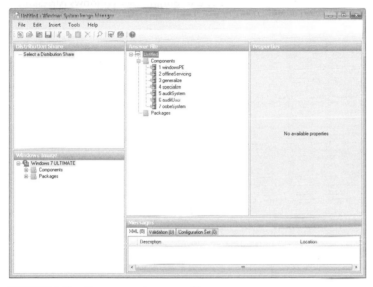

FIGURE 2-2 Creating an empty answer file

10. In the Windows SIM Windows Image pane, expand the Components node to display available feature settings.

11. On the expanded list of features, add features to your answer file by right-clicking each feature and then selecting the appropriate configuration pass. Table 2-2 shows a basic set of features and their associated configuration passes. Select a configuration pass, as shown in Figure 2-3.

TABLE 2-2 Specifying Features and Their Associated Configuration Passes

FEATURE	CONFIGURATION PASS
x86_Microsoft-Windows-Deployment_6-1.<build>_neutral	**oobeSystem**
x86_Microsoft-Windows International Core-WinPE_6-1.<build>_neutral	**windowsPE**
x86_Microsoft-Windows-Setup_6-1.<build>_neutral	**windowsPE**
x86_Microsoft-Windows-Shell-Setup_6-1.<build>_neutral	**oobeSystem**

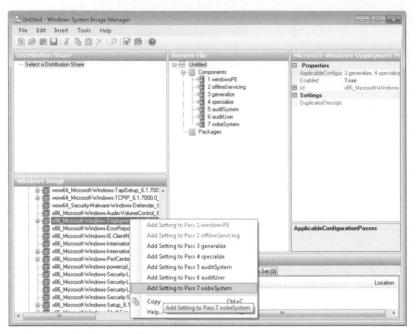

FIGURE 2-3 Selecting a configuration pass

12. Under Settings, select the appropriate setting and, in the right column, enter the appropriate value. Typical values are shown in Table 2-3 (for example, the table shows entries for the English-US Locale). Figure 2-4 shows the Windows SIM dialog box

TABLE 2-3 Adding Component Values

CONFIGURATION PASS	FEATURE	VALUE
WindowsPE	x86_Microsoft-Windows-International-Core-WinPE_6-1.<build>_neutral	InputLocale = en-US SystemLocale = en-US UILanguage = en-US UserLocale = en-US
WindowsPE	x86_Microsoft-Windows-Setup_6-1.<build>_neutral	EnableFirewall = true EnableNetwork = true LogPath = <path to log files> Restart = Restart UseConfigurationSet = true

CONFIGURATION PASS	FEATURE	VALUE
oobeSystem	x86_Microsoft-Windows-Deployment_6-1.<build>_neutral	Id = x86_Microsoft-Windows-Deployment__neutral_<guid>_nonSxS
oobeSystem	x86_Microsoft-Windows-Shell-Setup_6-1.<build>_neutral	BluetoothTaskbarIconEnabled = true
		DisableAutoDaylightTimeSet = false
		DoNotCleanTaskBar = true
		RegisteredOrganization = Microsoft
		RegisteredOwner = Microsoft
		ShowWindowsLive = true
		StartPanelOff = true
		TimeZone = EST

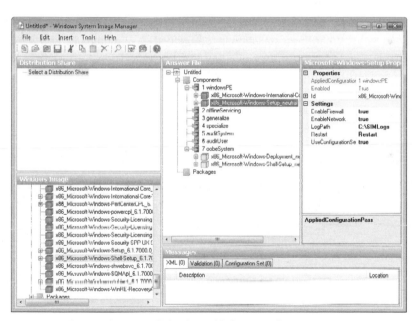

FIGURE 2-4 The Windows SIM dialog box with feature values

13. If you want, you can expand the feature and alter further sets of feature values from their defaults. Figure 2-5 shows this option.

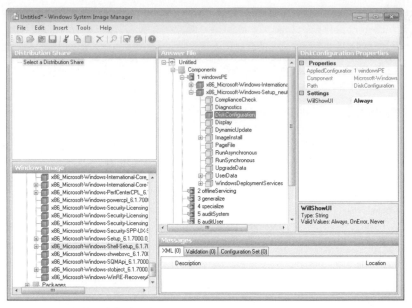

FIGURE 2-5 Altering default values

These settings define a basic unattended installation in which no user input is required during Windows Setup. When the installation is complete, the computer will reboot to audit mode. This enables you to boot quickly to the desktop, install additional applications and device drivers, and test the installation. Windows Welcome does not run in audit mode, but it will run the next time the computer restarts if you run the *sysprep /oobe* command. Windows Welcome, also called Machine OOBE, prompts the user to read the Microsoft Software License Terms and to configure the computer.

> **MORE INFO** **AUDIT MODE AND SYSPREP**
>
> For more information about audit mode, see *http://technet.microsoft.com/en-us/library/cc722413.aspx*. For more information about the Sysprep utility, see *http://technet.microsoft.com/en-us/library/cc766049.aspx*.

Validating and Saving Settings

To validate the settings in your answer file and save them to a file on removable media, perform the following procedure:

1. Click Tools in Windows SIM and then choose Validate Answer File.

2. Warnings that state that default settings have not been changed will not prevent the file from being validated or saved. If error messages or other warnings appear in the Messages pane, you need to check your settings.

3. If an error occurs, double-click the error message in the Messages pane to navigate to the incorrect setting. Change the setting to fix the error, and then validate again by choosing Tools, Validate Answer File. Repeat this step until the answer file validates.

4. On the File menu, choose Save Answer File. Save the answer file as Autounattend.xml. Figure 2-6 shows a portion of an Autounattend.xml file.

FIGURE 2-6 An Autounattend.xml file

5. Copy the Autounattend.xml file to the root directory of a removable storage device (such as a UFD). You now have a basic answer file that automates Windows Setup.

MORE INFO **BUILDING ANSWER FILES**

For more information about building answer files, see *http://technet.microsoft.com/en-us/library/cc748874.aspx*. This is a Windows Vista link, but the information also applies to Windows 7.

Building a Reference Installation

You configure your reference computer with a customized installation of Windows 7 that you then duplicate onto one or more destination computers. You can create a reference installation by using the Windows product DVD and (optionally) the answer file you created in the previous section. To install your reference computer using an answer file, perform the following procedure:

1. Turn on the reference computer. Insert the Windows 7 product DVD and the UFD containing the answer file (Autounattend.xml) that you created in the previous section. Note that the use of an answer file is optional, although it is the method Microsoft recommends. If you prefer, you can install Windows 7 manually from the installation DVD-ROM.

2. Restart the computer by pressing CTRL+ALT+DEL. You may have to override the boot order to boot from the CD/DVD-ROM disk. If so, select the appropriate function key to override the boot order during initial boot. Windows Setup (Setup.exe) starts automatically and searches the root directory of all removable media for an answer file called Autounattend.xml.

3. After Setup finishes, you can validate that all customizations were applied. For example, if you included the optional Microsoft-Windows-IE-InternetExplorer feature and set the Home_Page setting in your answer file, you can verify these settings by opening Internet Explorer.

> **NOTE INSTALLING A SMALL NUMBER OF CLIENT COMPUTERS**
>
> If you want to install only a very small number of client computers, say five or less, you can simply repeat the installation using the DVD-ROM installation disk and the Autounattend.xml file on each computer in turn. However, for a larger number of computers, it is more efficient to create a WIM image and distribute it. To do this, the reference computer needs to be prepared for the end user.

4. To prepare the reference computer for the user, you use the Sysprep utility with the */generalize* option to remove hardware-specific information from the Windows installation and the */oobe* option to configure the computer to boot to Windows Welcome upon the next restart. Open an elevated command prompt on the reference computer and run the following command:

c:\windows\system32\sysprep\sysprep.exe /oobe /generalize /shutdown

Sysprep prepares the image for capture by cleaning up various user-specific and computer-specific settings, as well as log files. The reference installation now is complete and ready to be imaged.

> **CAUTION OUT-OF-BOX DEVICE DRIVERS**
>
> When you run the *sysprep /generalize* command, out-of-box device drivers are removed from the Windows image. If you add out-of-box device drivers during installation and you intend to capture the Windows image that includes these drivers, set the PersistAllDeviceInstalls setting of the Microsoft-Windows-PnpSysprep feature to True in the answer file.

Creating a Bootable Windows PE Medium

In this step, you create a bootable Windows PE CD-ROM or DVD-ROM disk by using the Copype.cmd script. Windows PE enables you to start a computer for the purposes of deployment and recovery by booting directly into memory. You can remove the Windows PE media after the computer boots. After you have booted into Windows PE, you can use the ImageX tool to capture, modify, and apply file-based disk images.

To create a bootable Windows PE CD-ROM or DVD-ROM disk and install the ImageX
Windows AIK tool on that disk, perform the following procedure:

1. On your technician computer, create a local Windows PE build directory. Open an
    elevated command prompt and enter the following commands:

    ```
    cd C:\Program Files\Windows AIK\Tools\PETools\
    copype.cmd <architecture> <destination>
    ```

    Here *<architecture>* can be x86, amd64, or ia64, and *<destination>* is a path to the
    local directory. For example, to create a Windows PE build directory winpe_86 on an
    x86 computer, you enter the following command:

    ```
    copype.cmd x86 C:\winpe_x86
    ```

2. Copy ImageX into the Iso subdirectory of your Windows PE build directory. On an x86
    computer, you enter the following command:

    ```
    copy "C:\program files\Windows AIK\Tools\x86\imagex.exe" C:\winpe_x86\iso\
    ```

3. Optionally, create a configuration file called Wimscript.ini by using a text editor such as
    Windows Notepad. The configuration file instructs the ImageX tool to exclude certain
    files during the capture operation (for example, Pagefile.sys or all .zip files). Figure 2-7
    shows a Wimscript.ini file.

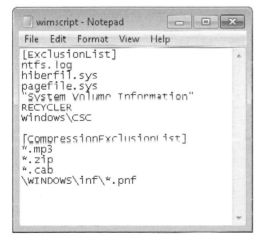

FIGURE 2-7 A Wimscript.ini file

4. Save the configuration file to the Iso subdirectory of the Windows PE build directory. The ImageX tool will recognize a Wimscript.ini file in the same location.

5. Create an image (.iso) file by using the Oscdimg tool. For example, on an x86 computer you would click All Programs, Microsoft Windows AIK, open the Deployment Tools Command Prompt, and enter the following:

   oscdimg -n –bc:\winpe_x86\etfsboot.com Cc:\winpe_x86\ISO c:\winpe_x86\winpe_x86.iso

> **MORE INFO   ETFSBOOT.COM**
>
> This specifies the location of the El Torito boot sector file. For more information, see *http://technet.microsoft.com/en-us/library/cc749036.aspx*. Note also there is no space between the *–b* flag and C:\Winpe_x86\Etfsboot.com.

6. Burn the image (Winpe_x86.iso) to a CD-ROM or DVD-ROM disk. Windows AIK does not include CD/DVD-ROM burning software. Use trusted third-party software to burn the image to optical media. You now have a bootable Windows PE optical disk containing the ImageX tool.

Capturing the Installation onto a Network Share

You can capture an image of your reference computer by using Windows PE and the ImageX tool. Then you store that image on a network share. Alternatively, on a computer running Windows 7 Enterprise or Ultimate edition, you can store the image on a VHD and make that VHD bootable, as described in the practice in Lesson 2, later in this chapter.

To capture the installation image you have created on your reference computer to a network share, perform the following procedure:

1. Insert your Windows PE media into your reference computer and restart the computer. As before, you may have to override the boot order to boot from the CD/DVD-ROM drive. If so, select the appropriate function key to override the boot order during initial boot.

2. Windows PE starts and opens a command-prompt window. Use the ImageX tool located on your Windows PE media to capture an image of your reference computer installation. For example, if your optical drive is drive E:, your installation is on drive C:, and you want to capture the image on drive D:, you would enter:

   ```
   e:\imagex.exe /capture C: d:\installationimage.wim "my Win7 Install" /compress
   fast /verify
   ```

3. Copy the image to a network location. For example, enter:

```
net use y: \\network_share\images
copy d:\myimage.wim y:
```

4. If necessary, provide network credentials for appropriate network access. Your image is now on volume Y:.

Deploying from a Network Share

After you have imaged your reference installation, you can deploy the image onto new hardware (one or more destination computers). This section describes how you would do this manually. Chapter 3 discusses MDT 2010 and the automatic installation of multiple client computers.

To deploy an image from a network share, you use the Diskpart tool to format the hard drive of a destination computer. Then you copy the image from the network share. Perform the following procedure:

1. On your destination computer, insert your Windows PE media and restart the computer by pressing the CTRL+ALT+DEL keys. Windows PE opens a command-prompt window.

2. Format the hard drive to reflect the disk configuration requirements by using the Diskpart tool from the Windows PE command-prompt window. To do this, open an elevated command prompt.

3. Enter **diskpart.**

4. Enter **select disk 0.**

5. Enter **clean.**

6. Enter **create partition primary size=100.**

7. Enter **select partition 1.**

8. Enter **format fs=ntfs label="system".**

9. Enter **assign letter=c.**

10. Enter **active.**

> **NOTE SYSTEM PARTITION**
>
> Steps 6 through 9 create a 100-MB system partition. This is not strictly necessary because the Windows 7 installation routine creates a system partition automatically on installation if one has not been created already. However, Microsoft recommends creating this partition before installation.

11. Enter **create partition primary.**

12. Enter **select partition 2.**

13. Enter **format fs=ntfs label="Windows".**

14. Enter **assign letter=d.**

15. Enter **exit.**

> **NOTE CREATING A SCRIPT**
>
> You can create a script with this information in a text file and store in the same location as your image. To run the script from a Windows PE command-prompt window, enter diskpart /s <*scriptname*>.txt, where <*scriptname*> is the name of the text file that includes the Diskpart commands. Figure 2-8 shows a typical script file named DiskConfigurationFormat.txt.

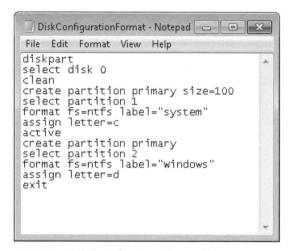

```
diskpart
select disk 0
clean
create partition primary size=100
select partition 1
format fs=ntfs label="system"
assign letter=c
active
create partition primary
select partition 2
format fs=ntfs label="windows"
assign letter=d
exit
```

FIGURE 2-8 A disk configuration format file

16. Copy the image from the network share to your local hard drive. For example, at an elevated command prompt, type:

```
net use y: \\network_share\images
copy y:\installationimage.wim d:
```

17. If necessary, provide network credentials for appropriate access.

18. Apply the image to the hard drive by using the ImageX tool located on the Windows PE media. For example, at an elevated command prompt, enter:

```
e:\imagex.exe /apply d:\myimage.wim 1 C:
```

19. Use BCDboot to initialize the Boot Configuration Data (BCD) store and copy boot environment files to the system partition. For example, at a command prompt, type:

```
d:\windows\system32\bcdboot d:\windows
```

Your custom image is now deployed onto your destination computer. The computer is ready for customer delivery. Repeat this procedure for each additional computer that you configure.

NOTE   CROSS-ARCHITECTURE TOOLS

Both ImageX (x86) and Windows PE (x86) and are cross-architecture tools. You can capture both 32-bit and 64-bit images using these utilities.

EXAM TIP

Know the functions of a Wimscript.ini, disk configuration format, and Autounattend. xml file. Know how these files are created, how they are accessed, and when you would use them.

Windows Imaging Format

You can use the ImageX Windows AIK tool to create a WIM file that images a reference computer. Unlike ISO files, which are used to contain images of operating systems and toolkits across an intranet or the Internet, WIM is a file-based disk image format that contains a set of files and associated file system metadata. However, unlike sector-based formats (such as ISO) used for CD-ROM and DVD-ROM images, WIM is file-based, which means that the smallest unit of information in a WIM image is a file. A file-based image is hardware-independent and provides unique single-instance storage of a file that can be referenced multiple times in the file system tree.

The files are stored inside a single WIM database. The resource cost of reading or writing many thousands of individual files on a local disk is reduced by hardware- and software-based disk caching and sequential data reads and writes. WIM images are deployed to an existing volume or partition because the toolset does not create low-level disk structures, nor does it format them. Instead, the Microsoft command-line tool Diskpart is used to create and format volumes on the target computer.

WIM files can contain multiple disk images, which are referenced either by a numerical index or a unique name. Because WIM uses single-instance storage, information common to more than one image is stored only once. Thus, as more images are added, each typically takes up less disk space than did the first image. A WIM can be split (or spanned) into multiple parts. Spanned WIM image parts have a .swm extension.

A WIM image can also be mounted as a new volume under Windows with a drive letter associated with it to facilitate easier extraction or updating of its contents. The WimFltr.sys device driver needs to be loaded before a WIM image can be mounted using ImageX.

The Wimgapi.dll dynamic link library provides a set of public application programming interfaces (APIs) for manipulating WIMs. A number of third-party applications include the capability to read or write WIM files. You can make WIM images bootable by using the ImageX tool, this time with the */boot* switch.

 Quick Check

1. What file can you create, if you want, to instruct the ImageX tool to exclude specified files and folders when capturing a system image?

2. How does ImageX detect this file?

Quick Check Answer

1. The Wimscript.ini file.

2. You save the file in the same folder as the ImageX tool (Imagex.exe), and ImageX detects it automatically.

Distributing an Image to Many Computers

This section describes how you capture a WIM image from a reference computer and distribute it manually to one or more destination computers. However, if you have a large number of destination computers, manual distribution would be tedious and time consuming. To avoid this, you need an automated method of simultaneously distributing an image to many computers on your network.

Chapter 1 introduced Windows Deployment Services (WDS). This is suitable for destination computers that boot from PXE. If you want to use WDS to distribute an image to a non-PXE computer, you need to boot that computer into a WDS capture image. WDS images are discussed later in this lesson.

Windows 7 introduces MDT 2010, which is a powerful tool for distributing system images to multiple destination computers. Chapter 3 discusses MDT 2010 in some detail, but it is appropriate to introduce the tool briefly in this chapter.

Using MDT 2010

MDT 2010 is the Microsoft solution accelerator for operating system and application deployment and offers flexible driver management, optimized transaction processing, and access to distribution shares from any location. You can use the MDT on imaging and deployment servers to implement the automatic deployment of Windows 7 (for example) on client computers. It is possible to run MDT 2010 on a client running Windows 7, but in practice it would typically run from a distribution server running Windows Server 2008.

The MDT provides detailed guidance and job aids and offers a common deployment console that contains unified tools and processes that you can use for client and server deployment. The toolkit offers standardized desktop and server images, along with improved security and ongoing configuration management.

The Lite Touch Installation (LTI) method lets you distribute images with a small degree of user intervention and can be used when no other distribution tools are in place. Most of the new features in MDT 2010 are related to LTI.

The Zero Touch Installation (ZTI) method requires no user intervention but requires that Microsoft System Center Configuration Manager (SCCM) 2007 with the Operating System Deployment Feature Pack is available on the network. This method also requires other software utilities, such as Microsoft SQL Server.

> **NOTE SYSTEM MANAGEMENT SERVER (SMS) 2003**
>
> MTD 2010 ZTI does not work with SMS 2003.

When you have installed MDT 2010, you can start Deployment Workbench from the Microsoft Deployment Toolkit program suite. This gives you access to the following items:

- **Information Center** This lets you access MDT 2010 documentation.
- **Distribution Share** This gives you a checklist of tasks you need to perform before you can deploy an operating system. You can also create a distribution share directory.
- **Task Sequences** This provides a list of task sequences in the details pane and enables you to create and configure a task sequence.
- **Deploy** You can expand this item to see the Deployment Points and Database items. You can configure deployment points and the MDT database.

> **MORE INFO MDT 2010**
>
> To download MDT documentation files (without necessarily installing the software), go to https://connect.microsoft.com/site/sitehome.aspx?SiteID=14 and click Download.

WDS Images

WDS provides a PXE-booted version of Windows PE. A WDS image is contained in a WIM file and is booted over the network into a RAMDisk. The installation then proceeds under Windows PE.

WDS integrates into Active Directory Domain Services (AD DS), but the PXE server can also run without AD DS if required. WDS can be initiated from Windows PE booted from something other than PXE, such as a CD/DVD-ROM or UFD.

The process of capturing a WIM image into a WDS server is similar to the use of ImageX and Sysprep except that the last step involves booting into the WDS capture image. This is a Windows PE image that helps you capture a client system to the WDS server.

WDS is relatively lightweight compared to other image deployment methods such as MDT and provides a method that can be faster than an optical media-based installation of Windows.

You use WDS images to deploy system files to client computers. A number of image files exist; for example, you use a capture image to create an install image. You should be familiar with the following image types:

- Install
- Boot
- Capture
- Discover

An install image is an operating system image that you deploy to the client computer. Typically, this is a WIM file.

A boot image is a Windows PE image into which you boot a client before you install the WIM image file. To install Windows 7, you first boot the computer into the boot image, and then you select the install image to install. Unless you are using a reference computer and adding applications to the image, you should use the standard boot image that is included on the Windows 7 installation media (Install.wim). Capture and discover images are types of boot images.

A capture image is a type of boot image into which you boot a client computer to capture the operating system as a WIM install image file. You create a capture image before you create a custom install image. A capture image contains Windows PE and the Windows Deployment Services Image Capture Wizard. When you boot a computer (after preparing it with Sysprep) into a capture image, the wizard creates an install image of the computer and saves it as a WIM file. Then you can upload the image to the WDS server or copy it to bootable media (for example, DVD-ROM).

A discover image is a type of boot image that you can use to install Windows 7 (or another Windows operating system) on a computer that is not PXE-enabled. When you boot a computer into a discover image, the WDS client locates a valid WDS server, and then you can choose the install image you want to install. A discover image enables a computer to locate a WDS server and use it to install an image.

Using the Deployment Image Servicing and Management Tool

Windows 7 introduces the DISM command-line tool. Chapter 3 discusses this tool in some detail, so it is introduced only briefly here. You can use DISM to service a Windows image or to prepare a Windows PE image. DISM replaces Package Manager (Pkgmgr.exe), PEimg, and Intlcfg in Windows Vista, and includes new features to improve the experience for offline servicing.

You can use DISM to perform the following actions:

- Prepare a Windows PE image.
- Enable or disable Windows features within an image.
- Upgrade a Windows image to a different edition.
- Add, remove, and enumerate packages.
- Add, remove, and enumerate drivers.
- Apply changes based on the offline servicing section of an unattended answer file.
- Configure international settings.
- Implement powerful logging features.
- Service operating systems such as Windows Vista with SP1 and Windows Server 2008.
- Service a 32-bit image from a 64-bit host and service a 64-bit image from a 32-bit host.
- Service all platforms (32-bit, 64-bit, and Itanium).
- Use existing Package Manager scripts.

DISM Command-Line Options

To service a Windows image offline, you must apply or mount it. WIM images can be mounted using the WIM commands within DISM, or applied and then recaptured using ImageX. You can also use the WIM commands to list the indexes or verify the architecture for the image you are mounting. After you update the image, you must dismount it and then either commit or discard the changes you have made.

Table 2-4 lists and describes the *dism* command options that you can use to mount, dismount, and query WIM files, as well as their associated flags. These options and flags are not case-sensitive.

TABLE 2-4 DISM Command Options

OPTION	DESCRIPTION	FLAGS
/mount-wim	Mounts the WIM file to the specified directory so that it is available for servicing. The optional */readonly* flag sets the mounted image with read-only permissions. Example: dism /mount-wim /wimfile:C:\practice\myimages\install.wim /index:1 /mountdir:C:\practice\offline /readonly	/wimfile:*<path_to_image.wim>* /index:*<image_index>* /name:*<image_name>* /mountdir:*<path_to_mount_directory>* /readonly
/commit-wim	Applies the changes you have made to the mounted image. The image remains mounted until the */dismount* option is used. Example: dism /commit-wim /mountdir:C:\practice\offline	/mountdir:*<path_to_mount_directory>*
/unmount-wim	Dismounts the WIM file and either commits or discards the changes that were made while the image was mounted. Example: dism /unmount-wim /mountdir:C:\practice\offline /commit	/mountdir:*<path_to_mount_directory>*{/commit | /discard}
/remount-wim	Recovers an orphaned WIM mount directory. Example: dism /remount-wim /mountdir:*<path_to_mount_directory>*	/mountdir:*<path_to_mount_directory>*
/cleanup-wim	Deletes all the resources associated with a mounted WIM image that has been abandoned. This command does not dismount currently mounted images, nor does it delete images that can be remounted. Example: dism /cleanup-wim	None
/get-wiminfo	Displays information about the images within the WIM. When used with the */index* option, information about the specified image is displayed. Example: dism /get-wimInfo /wimfile:C:\practice\offline\install.wim /index:1	/wimfile:*<path_to_image.wim>* /index:*<Image_index>* /name:*<Image_name>*

OPTION	DESCRIPTION	FLAGS
/get-mountedwiminfo	Lists the images that are currently mounted and information about the mounted image such as read/write permissions, mount location, mounted file path, mounted image index. Example: dism /get-mountedwimInfo	/name:<image_name> /mountdir:<path_to_mount_directory> /readonly

DISM Syntax

DISM commands have a base syntax that is very similar from command to command. After you mount your Windows image, you can specify DISM options, the servicing command that will update your image, and the location of the mounted image. You can use only one servicing command per command line. If you are servicing a running computer, you can use the /online option instead of specifying the location of the mounted Windows image.

The syntax for DISM is as follows:

```
DISM.exe [/image:<path_to_image> | /online} [dism_options] {servicing_command}
[<servicing_argument>]
```

EXAM TIP

You use DISM to manipulate existing images. You cannot use the tool to capture new operating system images.

Using Sysprep to Prepare a Windows 7 Installation

You use the Sysprep command-line tool to prepare an installation of Windows for imaging or delivery to a user. *Sysprep /generalize* and *sysprep /oobe* were mentioned earlier in this lesson. Sysprep is a powerful tool that includes the Sysprep executable (Sysprep.exe) located in the %WINDIR%\System32\Sysprep directory. Sysprep.exe first verifies that Sysprep can run. You can run Sysprep only as an administrator, and only one instance of Sysprep can run at any given time. Also, the version of Sysprep differs with each version of Windows. Sysprep must run on the version of Windows with which it was installed.

Sysprep.exe calls other executable files that prepare the Windows installation. The Sysprep process initializes logging and parses any command-line arguments provided. If no command-line arguments are provided, the Sysprep window appears. This lets you specify Sysprep actions. Sysprep processes these actions and calls the appropriate .dll and executable files. It adds the actions to the log file.

When all tasks are processed, Sysprep either shuts down and restarts the system, or exits.

Sysprep Command-Line Options

If you have experience with Windows Vista, you will find the *sysprep* command-line options for Windows 7 very similar. These are described in Table 2-5.

TABLE 2-5 Sysprep Command-Line Options

OPTION	DESCRIPTION
/audit	Restarts the computer in Audit mode rather than Windows Welcome mode. Audit mode lets you add additional drivers or applications to Windows 7. You can also test an installation of Windows 7 and verify its integrity before it is sent to a user. If you specify an unattended Windows setup file, the Windows Setup /audit mode runs the auditSystem and auditUser configuration passes.
/generalize	Prepares the Windows installation to be imaged. If you specify this option, all unique system information is removed from the Windows installation. The SID is reset, system restore points are cleared, and event logs are deleted. The next time the computer starts, the specialize configuration pass runs. A new SID is created, and the clock for Windows activation resets (unless the clock has already been reset three times).
/oobe	Restarts the computer in Windows Welcome mode. Windows Welcome enables users to customize their Windows 7 operating system, create user accounts, and name the computer. Any settings in the *oobeSystem* configuration pass in an answer file are processed immediately before Windows Welcome starts.
/reboot	Restarts the computer. You can use this option to audit the computer and to verify that the first-run experience operates correctly.
/shutdown	Shuts down the computer after Sysprep completes.
/quiet	Runs Sysprep without displaying on-screen confirmation messages. You can use this option if you want to automate Sysprep.
/quit	Closes Sysprep after the specified commands complete.
/unattend: answerfile	Applies settings in an answer file to Windows during unattended installation. The variable *answerfile* specifies the path and file name of the answer file.

If you do not specify a command-line option, Sysprep presents you with the graphical user interface (GUI) shown in Figure 2-9. This lets you specify a system cleanup action, choose the *generalize* option, and specify a *shutdown* option.

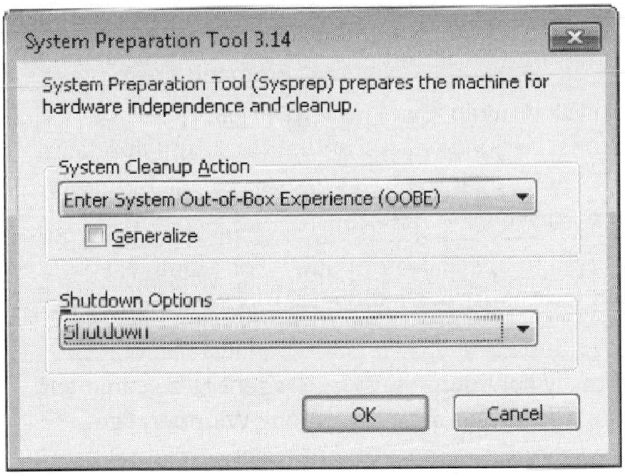

FIGURE 2-9 The Sysprep GUI

MORE INFO   **AUDIT MODE**

For more information about Audit mode, see *http://technet.microsoft.com/en-us/library/cc722413.aspx.*

If you intend to transfer a Windows 7 image to a different computer, you need to run *sysprep /generalize* even if the computer has the same hardware configuration. The *sysprep /generalize* command removes unique information from your Windows 7 installation. This enables you to reuse your image on different computers. The next time you boot the Windows 7 image the specialize configuration pass runs. During this pass, many feature actions are processed automatically when you boot a Windows 7 image on a new computer.

All methods of moving a Windows 7 image to a new computer, such as through imaging or hard disk duplication, must be prepared with the *sysprep /generalize* command. You cannot move or copy a Windows 7 image to a different computer without running *sysprep /generalize*.

Configuration Passes

Configuration passes are phases of Windows Setup during which you apply settings to an unattended installation answer file. Table 2-6 describes the different configuration passes.

TABLE 2-6 Configuration Passes

CONFIGURATION PASS	DESCRIPTION
windowsPE	Configures Windows PE options and basic Windows Setup options. These options can include setting the product key and configuring a disk. You can use this configuration pass to add drivers to the Windows PE driver store and to reflect boot-critical drivers required by Windows PE if you require that drivers for Windows PE access the local hard disk drive or a network.

CONFIGURATION PASS	DESCRIPTION
offlineServicing	Applies updates to a Windows image. Also applies packages, including software fixes, language packs, and other security updates. During this pass, you can add drivers to a Windows image before that image is installed during Windows Setup.
specialize	Creates and applies system-specific information. For example, you can configure network settings, international settings, and domain information.
generalize	Enables you to minimally configure the *sysprep /generalize* command and other Windows settings that must persist on your reference image. The *sysprep /generalize* command removes system-specific information from the image, for example the unique SID and other hardware-specific settings. The generalize pass runs only if you run the *sysprep /generalize* command.
auditSystem	Processes unattended Setup settings while Windows is running in system context before a user logs onto the computer in Audit mode. The *auditSystem* pass runs only if you boot to Audit mode.
auditUser	Processes unattended Setup settings after a user logs onto the computer in Audit mode. The auditUser pass runs only if you boot to Audit mode.
oobeSystem	Applies settings to Windows before Windows Welcome starts.

EXAM TIP

Know the Sysprep command-line options and the Windows Setup configuration passes, and also know when the configuration passes run; for example, *generalize* runs if you run the *sysprep /generalize* command, and *auditUser* and *auditSystem* run if you boot to Audit mode. Remember that you can use several Sysprep switches in the same command. For example, to generalize an image and specify the boot-up mode you could enter **C:\windows\system32\sysprep\Sysprep.exe /oobe /generalize /shutdown.** Also, know how to boot to Audit mode (Ctrl+Shift+F3), as described later in this lesson.

Sysprep Answer Files

You can use a Sysprep answer file to configure unattended Setup settings. Not all configuration passes run during Windows Setup—some are available only when you run Sysprep.exe. For example, the *generalize, auditSystem,* and *auditUser* passes are available only if you run Sysprep.exe. If you add settings to your answer file in these configuration passes, you need to run Sysprep.exe to apply the settings.

To apply settings in the *auditSystem* and *auditUser* passes, you use the *sysprep /audit* command to boot to Audit mode. To apply settings in the *generalize* pass, you use the *sysprep /generalize* command to generalize the Windows image.

If you install Windows using an answer file (for example, Autounattend.xml), that answer file is cached. When subsequent configuration passes run, settings in the answer file are applied to the system. Because the answer file is cached, settings in the cached answer file are applied when you run Sysprep.exe. If you want to use the settings in a different answer file, you can specify a separate answer file by using the *sysprep /unattend:filename* option. You need to ensure your answer file is a .xml file but is not named Autounattend.xml.

You can use the Answer File pane in Windows SIM to create this file and you can edit it with a text editor such as Microsoft Notepad. Some experienced administrators use a text editor rather than Windows SIM to create answer files.

MORE INFO   CREATING AN ANSWER FILE WITH WINDOWS SIM

For step-by-step instructions that enable you to create an unattended answer file, see *http://technet.microsoft.com/en-us/library/dd349348.aspx*.

NOTE   PERSISTING PLUG AND PLAY DEVICE DRIVERS DURING THE GENERALIZE PASS

You can persist device drivers when you run the *sysprep /generalize* command by specifying the PersistentAllDeviceInstalls setting in the Microsoft-Windows-PnPSysprep feature. During the *specialize* pass, Plug and Play scans the computer for devices and installs device drivers for the detected devices. By default, these device drivers are removed from the system when you generalize the system. If you set PersistAllDeviceInstalls to True in an answer file, Sysprep does not remove the detected device drivers.

You can view the status of RunSynchronous commands that run during *auditUser* in Audit mode. The AuditUI window displays the status for commands and provides visual progress to indicate that an installation is continuing and not suspended and a visual indication of when and where failures occur.

If there are RunSynchronous commands in the answer file in the *auditUser* configuration pass, a list of the commands are displayed in the AudiUI window in the order specified by RunSynchronous/RunSynchronousCommand/Order.

All RunSynchronous commands are processed in order. If the command succeeds, then its related list item is annotated with a green checkmark. If the command fails, then its related list item is annotated with a red cross. If a reboot is requested, the AuditUI is redisplayed after the boot, but only unprocessed list items are shown.

If the list of items in the AuditUI exceeds the height of the display, then the list is clipped to the display and does not scroll. As a result, some items might not be visible.

Resetting Windows 7 Activation

When you install Windows 7 with a single license product key, you have a 30-day period during which you must activate the Windows installation. If you do not activate Windows within this 30-day period, Windows enters Reduced Functionality Mode (RFM). This prevents you from logging on to the computer until Windows 7 is activated.

When you run the *sysprep /generalize* command, the activation clock automatically resets. You can use the *sysprep /generalize* command to reset Windows a maximum of three times. After the third time you run the *sysprep /generalize* command, the activation clock can no longer be reset.

You can bypass resetting the activation clock by using the SkipRearm setting in the Microsoft-Windows-Security-Licensing-SLC feature. You can set the value of SkipRearm to 1 in the *sysprep /generalize* command, which enables you to run the Sysprep utility without resetting the activation clock.

> **MORE INFO**   **MICROSOFT-WINDOWS-SECURITY-LICENSING-SLC**
>
> For more information about the Microsoft-Windows-Security-Licensing-SLC feature, see *http://technet.microsoft.com/en-us/library/cc766403.aspx*. This is a Microsoft Vista link, but it is also applicable to Windows 7.

For volume licenses, activation clock reset behavior is different depending on the type of license. Activation can be reset an unlimited number of times for activated Key Management Service (KMS) clients. For non-activated KMS clients, the activation clock can be reset only up to three times, the same as a single license.

Microsoft recommends KMS clients to use the *sysprep /generalize* command where the value of the SkipRearm setting is equal to 1. After capturing this image, use the *sysprep /generalize* command, where the value of the SkipRearm setting is equal to 0.

Microsoft recommends Multiple Activation Keys (MAK) clients to install the MAK immediately before running *sysprep* the last time before delivering a client computer to a user.

For OEM Activation licenses, you do not typically require activation. OEM Activation is available only to royalty OEMs.

Most users can manage activation after receiving their clients running Windows 7. However, if you prefer, you can activate the software on behalf of your users. After activation, most users do not need to activate their installation again.

To activate Windows on a client computer, use the unique Product Key from the certificate of authenticity (COA) label that is affixed to the specific computer, and activate the computer on behalf of the user. Run the *sysprep /oobe* command to prepare the computer for delivery to the user.

Booting to Audit Mode or Windows Welcome

When Windows 7 boots, the computer can start in the following modes:

- **Windows Welcome**   By default, all Windows installations boot to Windows Welcome first. Windows Welcome is also called Machine OOBE. It is the first user experience and enables users to customize their Windows installation. Users can create user accounts, read and accept the Microsoft Software License Terms, and choose language and time zones. The *oobeSystem* configuration pass runs immediately before Windows Welcome starts.

- **Audit mode**   Audit mode enables enterprise organizations to customize their Windows images. Audit mode does not require Windows Welcome settings to be applied. Bypassing Windows Welcome lets you access the desktop quicker to perform the required customizations. You can, for example, add additional device drivers, install applications, and test installation validity. Settings in an unattended answer file in the *auditSystem* and *auditUser* configuration passes are processed in Audit mode.

If you are running in Audit mode, run the *sysprep /oobe* command to configure the installation to boot to Windows Welcome. By default Windows Welcome starts after installation completes. However, you can skip Windows Welcome and boot directly to Audit mode by pressing Ctrl+Shift+F3 at the first Windows Welcome screen.

For unattended installation, you can configure Windows to boot to Audit mode by using the Microsoft-Windows-Deployment | Reseal setting in an answer file.

> **MORE INFO   AUDIT MODE**
>
> For more information about Audit mode, see *http://technet.microsoft.com/en-us/library/cc722413.aspx*. This is a Windows Vista link, but the information also applies to Windows 7.

> **MORE INFO   DETECTING THE STATE OF A WINDOWS IMAGE**
>
> You can identify the state of a Windows image, such as whether it will boot to Audit mode, Windows Welcome, or if the image is still in the process of installation. For more information, see *http://technet.microsoft.com/en-us/library/cc721913.aspx*. This is a Windows Vista link, but the information also applies to Windows 7.

Sysprep Log Files

Sysprep logs Windows Setup actions in different directories depending on the configuration pass. Because the *generalize* pass deletes some Windows Setup log files, Sysprep logs generalize actions outside the standard Windows Setup log files. Table 2-7 shows the log file locations that Sysprep uses.

TABLE 2-7 Sysprep Log File Locations

ITEM	LOG PATH
Generalize pass	%WINDIR%\System32\Sysprep\Panther
Specialize pass	%WINDIR%\Panther\
Unattended Windows setup actions	%WINDIR%\Panther\Unattendgc

PRACTICE **Creating a WIM Image**

In this practice, you install the Windows AIK. You then create a Windows PE boot disk and boot the computer into Windows PE. This enables you to use the ImageX tool in the Windows AIK to create a WIM image of the computer.

EXERCISE 1   Installing the Windows AIK and Creating a Windows PE Boot DVD

In this exercise, you download the ISO image in Windows AIK and create an installation DVD. You then install the Windows AIK. Instructions for doing this were given in the section entitled "Installing and Using the Windows Automated Installation Toolkit," earlier in this lesson. You create a Windows PE build directory and copy ImageX into it. You use the Oscdimg tool to create an ISO image of Windows PE. You burn this image onto optical media (CD-ROM or DVD) that you can use to boot the computer. You need to be connected to the Internet to perform this exercise.

1. Log on to the Canberra computer using the Kim_Akers account.
2. Download the appropriate ISO image, burn this to optical media, and install the Windows AIK.
3. In Accessories in the All Programs menu, right-click Command Prompt and choose Run As Administrator. If prompted, click Yes to permit the program to run.
4. In the Command Prompt window, enter **cd C:\Program Files\Windows AIK\Tools\ PETools\.**
5. At the C:\Program Files\Windows AIK\Tools\PETools> prompt, enter **copype.cmd x86 c:\winpe_x86.** This exercise is written for a 32-bit computer and the Windows PE build directory is Winpe_x86. If you are using an amd64 or ia64 computer, amend the entry accordingly. Figure 2-10 shows the output from this command.
6. To copy ImageX into the Windows PE build directory, enter **copy "c:\program files\ Windows AIK\Tools\x86\imagex.exe" c:\winpe_x86\iso.**
7. To create an image (.iso) file by using the Oscdimg tool, click Microsoft Windows AIK in All Programs and then click Deployment Tools Command Prompt.

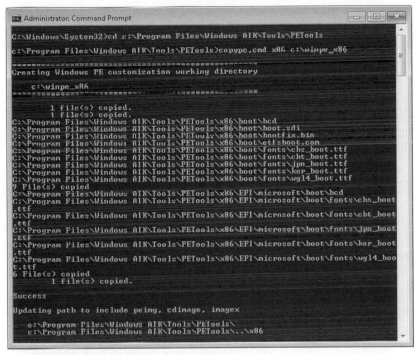

FIGURE 2-10 Creating the Windows PE build directory

8. To create the ISO image, enter **oscdimg -n c:\winpe_x86\ISO c:\winpe_x86\winpe_x86.iso -n -bc:\winpe_x86\etfsboot.com**. Figure 2-11 shows the output from this command. Note that there is no space between the *–b* flag and *c:\winpe_x86\etfsboot.com*.

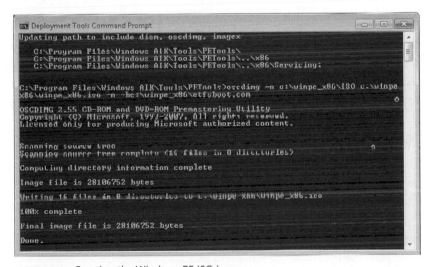

FIGURE 2-11 Creating the Windows PE ISO image

9. The ISO image is in C:\Winpe_x86 and is named Winpe_x86.iso. However, the Windows AIK toolset currently does not include an image-burning utility, and Microsoft advises the use of reputable third-party software to create the Windows PE boot disk from this ISO image.

EXERCISE 2 Creating a WIM Image of the Canberra Computer

In this exercise, you boot the Canberra computer from the optical Windows boot disk that contains ImageX, which you created in Exercise 1. You then create a WIM image of the Windows 7 installation and (optionally) save it to a network share.

1. If necessary, log on to the Canberra computer using the Kim_Akers account.

2. On the Canberra computer, insert the Windows PE medium and restart the computer.

> *NOTE* **CHANGING THE BIOS BOOT ORDER**
>
> To boot from the optical drive, you may have to override the BIOS boot order. During initial boot, select the appropriate function key.

3. Windows PE starts and opens a command-prompt window.

4. To capture an image of the reference installation by using the ImageX tool located on your Windows PE medium, enter **e:\imagex.exe /capture c: d:\images\ myimage.wim "Canberra Win7 Install" /compress fast /verify**. This command uses ImageX on the CD/DVD-ROM drive E: to capture the image of the system disk C: to the folder images on the second hard disk D:. If your volume assignments are different, amend the command accordingly. The command takes a considerable time to complete and lists folders (such as the recycle bin) that are not included in the image by default.

5. Enter **exit** and remove your Windows PE boot disk. The computer boots into Windows 7.

6. Check that the file Myimage.wim exists on the D: drive (or wherever you chose to put it).

7. Optionally, if you want to share the image across a network, create a network share, (for example, \\Canberra\Images) and map it to a network drive (such as Y:) and then copy the WIM file to this share.

Lesson Summary

- The Windows AIK introduced in Windows 7 offers various tools for creating system images. These include Windows SIM, ImageX, Oscdimg, DISM, USMT, and several Windows PE tools.

- You use Windows SIM to create an unattend answer file that you can in turn use with a WIM image to install a reference computer. You use Sysprep to prepare the image and then boot the reference computer into Windows PE and use the ImageX tool to capture the image in a WIM file.

- WIM images are file-based and can be installed on a VHD or placed on a network share for distribution. You can store several images in the same WIM file.
- You use the Sysprep command-line tool to prepare an installation of Windows for imaging or delivery to a user. In particular, you can generalize an image and remove specific information such as the SID.

Lesson Review

You can use the following questions to test your knowledge of the information in Lesson 1, "Capturing System Images." The questions are also available on the companion DVD if you prefer to review them in electronic form.

> **NOTE   ANSWERS**
>
> Answers to these questions and explanations of why each answer choice is correct or incorrect are located in the "Answers" section at the end of the book.

1. You are creating a WIM system image of a Windows 7 installation on a reference computer. What operating system should you boot to, and what Windows AIK tool should you use?

   A. Boot to Windows 7 and use ImageX.

   B. Boot to Windows 7 and use Windows SIM.

   C. Boot to Windows 7 and use DISM.

   D. Boot to Windows PE and use ImageX.

   E. Boot to Windows PE and use Windows SIM.

   F. Boot to Windows PE and use DISM.

2. You are creating an unattend answer file for automatic Windows 7 installation. What can you use to do this? (Choose all that apply.)

   A. The Windows SIM tool in Windows AIK

   B. The DISM tool in Windows AIK

   C. The Deployment Workbench MDT tool

   D. Sysprep.exe

   E. Microsoft Notepad

3. You want to prepare a reference computer and capture its Windows 7 image for distribution to several destination computers. You intend to use your own client running Windows 7 as the technician computer. Which of the following tasks must you perform to achieve your goal? (Choose all that apply.)

   A. Install the Windows AIK on your technician computer (if not already installed).

   B. Use Windows SIM to create an Autounattend.xml answer file and save this to the root directory of a UFD.

C. Install your chosen edition of Windows 7 on the reference computer.

D. Install MDT 2010 on your technician computer (if not already installed).

E. Create a WDS capture image.

F. Create a bootable Windows PE optical disk or UFD (if one does not already exist).

G. Use the ImageX tool to capture a systems image of the reference computer.

H. Use the Sysprep tool to prepare the reference computer for imaging.

4. You are using the Sysprep tool to prepare a Windows 7 installation to be imaged. Which command-line option removes all unique system information from the installation?

    A. */audit*

    B. */oobe*

    C. */generalize*

    D. */unattend*

5. Which Windows Setup configuration pass applies settings to Windows 7 before Windows Welcome starts?

    A. *oobeSystem*

    B. *auditSystem*

    C. *specialize*

    D. *offlineServicing*

Lesson 2: Managing Virtual Hard Disk Files

This lesson discusses how to create native VHD files on a computer running Windows 7 and how to deploy, mount, attach, detach, and delete these files using tools such as Diskpart. It discusses bootable VHD files and the use of the BCDEdit tool.

The lesson looks at how you use Windows Image to Virtual Hard Disk (WIM2VHD) command-line tool to create VHD images from a Windows 7 installation source or from an image in a custom WIM file. It describes how you use the Offline Virtual Machine Servicing Tool to update the image on a VHD that is normally offline, and how you use the tools provided by WDS to manage images and export them to client computers and to virtual machines and VHDs that are online.

After this lesson, you will be able to:

- Create, mount, attach, and deploy VHD files and create a bootable VHD.
- Use the Diskpart, BCDEdit, and Disk Management tools.
- Use WIM2VHD to create VHD images from a WIM file.
- Describe the Offline Virtual Machine Servicing Tool and the GUI and command-line tools provided by WDS.

Estimated lesson time: 45 minutes

Using Native VHDs in Windows 7

The VHD format specifies a VHD encapsulated in a single file, capable of hosting native file systems and supporting standard disk operations. VHD files are used by Hyper-V, Virtual Server, and Virtual PC for virtual disks connected to a virtual machine. The VHD file format is used by Microsoft Data Protection Manager, Windows Server Backup, client computer backup (Vista and Windows 7 Enterprise and Ultimate), and other Microsoft and non-Microsoft solutions.

In Windows 7 Enterprise or Ultimate, you can use a native VHD to host the running operating system without any other parent operating system or virtual machine. Windows 7 disk management tools, such as Diskpart and Disk Management, can be used to create a VHD file. You can deploy a Windows 7 WIM image to a VHD and the VHD file can be copied to multiple systems. Windows Boot Manager can be configured for a native boot of the VHD Windows image.

Although virtual machines are widely used, many enterprise environments operate on physical machines. For example, you might need to run tests on a physical machine to access a specific hardware device. As an enterprise administrator, you probably need to maintain images based on both the WIM format for physical machines and the VHD format for virtual machines. A common image format supporting both physical and virtual machines provides flexibility in image deployment and simplifies the process of image management.

In Windows 7, native support for the VHD format means that VHD files can be created and modified without installing the Hyper-V Server role. VHD files can be attached using the Disk Management tool, and the Windows image inside the VHD is available for servicing. The Windows Deployment tools in the Windows AIK (specifically ImageX and DISM) can be used to create a Windows image to be stored on VHD, and to apply updates to the system image in the VHD file (available in Windows 7 Ultimate and Enterprise editions only).

A native boot of Windows 7 from a VHD file requires the Windows 7 boot environment. The Windows 7 boot environment is initialized during a full operating system installation and includes the Windows Boot Manager and Boot Configuration Data (BCD).

> **MORE INFO   RECOMMENDATIONS AND LIMITATIONS**
>
> For more information about recommendations and limitations for VHDs, see
> *http://technet.microsoft.com/en-us/library/dd440865.aspx.*

> **NOTE   EDITION LIMITATIONS**
>
> Only Windows 7 Enterprise and Windows 7 Ultimate can be booted when installed on a VHD. This was said before but is worth remembering.

Creating a Native VHD

Windows 7 provides native support for VHD. Previously, VHD files were used in virtualization platforms, such as Hyper-V, Virtual Server, and Virtual PC, and this facility is still available. However, in Windows 7, you can also create native VHDs on non-virtual computers.

You will find step-by-step instructions in the practice later in this lesson that enable you to create a native VHD and attach and detach the VHD file. However, the high-level procedure is as follows.

To create a native VHD, you right-click My Computer and click Manage to open Computer Management. You then select Disk Management, You can then right-click Disk Management and click Create VHD. This opens the Create And Attach Virtual Hard Disk dialog box. You select the location where you want to create the VHD file (first making sure you have sufficient free space).

Typically, you place the VHD on a second internal or external hard disk (although this is not essential). You then specify the VHD size and format settings. Microsoft recommends the default Fixed Size setting, but you can select Dynamic Expanding if you do not want to allocate the disk space. Fixed Size gives better performance and is more suitable in a production environment.

When you click OK, a newly attached (mounted) VHD is created. To initialize the disk, right-click the icon beside the disk designation and click Initialize Disk. This opens the Initialize

Disk dialog box. You select the partition and click OK. Typically, you do not need to change the default settings. The status of the disk then changes to Online.

You create a new simple volume on a VHD by right-clicking Unallocated and selecting New Simple Volume. This starts the New Simple Volume Wizard. You specify size, file system, and drive letter; label the drive; and click Finish to create the VHD.

Attaching and Detaching a VHD

You can also use the Disk Management tool to attach a VHD so you can use it and to detach it so you can change its properties or delete it. In Computer Management, you click Disk Management and then right-click Disk Management and click Attach VHD. This opens the Attach Virtual Hard Disk dialog box. Click OK to attach the existing VHD. If you do not want to change the VHD contents (for example, if you have installed an operating system on it), you can select the Read-Only check box.

To detach a VHD, you click the icon beside the disk designation and click Detach VHD. A Detach Virtual Hard Disk message appears. Click on OK to detach the VHD. If you want to delete the VHD permanently after it is detached, you can select the Delete The Virtual Hard Disk File After Deleting The Disk check box.

Using the Diskpart Utility to Create and Attach a VHD

You can use the Diskpart command-line utility to create and attach a VHD by performing the following steps:

1. On the Accessories menu, right-click Command Prompt and choose Run As Administrator. If necessary, click Yes to allow the program to run.

2. Enter **diskpart**.

3. Enter **create vdisk file=c:\win7\myothervhd.vhd maximum=20000**. This creates a VHD file called Myothervhd Win7 with a maximum size of 20 GB in a folder called Win7 on the C: drive. You can also create a VHD on a second internal hard disk or on a USB external hard disk formatted with the NTFS filing system.

4. Enter **select vdisk file=c:\win7\myothervhd.vhd**.

5. Enter **attach vdisk**.

6. Enter **create partition primary**.

7. Enter **assign letter=v**.

8. Enter **format quick label=Windows7**.

9. Enter **exit**.

This creates the VHD file *C:\Win7\Myothervhd.vhd* as a primary partition. Figure 2-12 shows the Diskpart commands to create and attach a new VHD. Figure 2-13 shows the newly attached disk in Disk Management with drive letter V:.

FIGURE 2-12 Creating and attaching a VHD

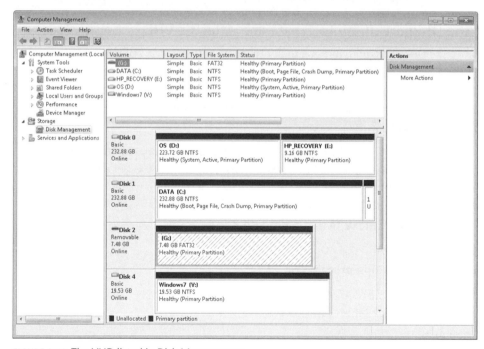

FIGURE 2-13 The VHD listed in Disk Management

Booting from VHD

The ability to boot from VHD (available in Windows 7 Ultimate and Enterprise editions only) is one of the more significant new features introduced by Windows 7. You can boot the machine as if it were running from the primary hard disk, and your operating system recognizes all the hardware available in your system. This lets you run multiple operating systems on the same computer without the performance issues sometimes encountered in virtual PCs. You can create multiple VHDs with multiple operating systems installed on them.

Previously in this lesson, you saw how to create a new VHD and attach it using Disk Management or the Diskpart utility. If you choose to install the Windows 7 operating system from the installation DVD-ROM, you require the Install.wim file from that optical device. You also need the ImageX utility (Imagex.exe). If you have installed the Windows AIK, as instructed in Lesson 1, you will find this file at C:\Program Files\Windows AIK\Tools\\x86.

You can also copy a WIM system image that you created for your computer (as described in Lesson 1) to a VHD on that computer. You do this in the practice later in this lesson.

Adding a Boot Entry for a VHD File

When you have created a VHD and installed a system image on it, you can use the BCDEdit tool Bcdedit.exe to add a boot entry for the VHD file in your computer running Windows 7. A step-by-step procedure to do this is given in the practice later in this lesson. The high-level procedure is as follows:

Open the elevated command prompt with Administrator privileges and enter a command similar to the following:

bcdedit /copy {current} /d "Your New VHD Description"

This returns the GUID of the loader object. You use this value to replace the variable *<guid>* in the following commands:

bcdedit /set <guid> device vhd=[driveletter:]\<directory>\<vhd filename>
bcdedit /set <guid> osdevice vhd=[driveletter:]\<directory>\<vhd filename>

BCDEdit locates the VHD file and Bootmgr locates the partition containing the VHD File to boot from. Finally, you enter the command:

bcdedit /set <guid> detecthal on

Detecthal is used to force Windows 7 to automatically detect the Hardware Abstraction Layer (HAL). The following command tests if your boot entry is successfully created:

bcdedit /v

If you want to delete an existing VHD entry from the Boot menu, you use the following command:

bcdedit /delete <guid> /cleanup

This deletes the specified operating system entry from the store and removes the entry from the display order.

When you restart your computer after successfully completing this procedure, you should see an additional entry in the Boot menu along with the default Windows 7 operating system.

> **MORE INFO**   **BCDEdit**
>
> For more information about BCDEdit, go to *http://msdn.microsoft.com/en-us/library/aa906217.aspx,* expand BCD Boot Options Reference, and click the links in the navigation pane.

EXAM TIP

You can use Bcdedit.exe to enable a VHD file as a boot option, but you cannot use the tool to create VHD files.

Using the Windows Image to Virtual Hard Disk Tool

You can use the WIM2VHD command-line tool to create VHD images from any Windows 7 installation source or from an image in a custom WIM file. WIM2VHD creates VHDs that boot directly to the Out-of-Box Experience (OOBE). You can also automate the OOBE configuration by supplying your own Unattend.xml file.

You need a client computer running Windows 7 that has the Windows AIK installed, and an operating system image in a WIM file. You also need to have created a native VHD on that computer.

The WIM2VHD tool runs from the Cscript command. The syntax is as follows:

cscript wim2vhd.wsf. /wim:<wimPath> /sku:<sku> [/vhd:<vhdPath>] [/size:<vhdSizeInMb>] [/disktype:<dynamic|fixed>] [/unattend:<unattendxmlPath>] [/qfe:<qfe1,.,qfen>] [/hyperv:<true|false>] [/ref:<ref1,.,refn] [/dbg:<args>] [/passthru:<physicaldrive>])

WIM2VHD Parameters

Table 2-8 describes the parameters of the WIM2VHD tool.

TABLE 2-8 WIM2VHD Parameters

PARAMETER	DESCRIPTION
/wim:<wimPath>	This is the path of the WIM file you use when creating the VHD.
/sku:<skuName>|<skuIndex>	The Stock-Keeping Unit (SKU) identifies the operating system to use when creating the VHD (for example, "HomePremium"). You can also specify a number that you obtain by using ImageX to analyze the relevant WIM file.

PARAMETER	DESCRIPTION
/vhd:<vhdPath> (optional)	This defines the path and the name of the VHD to be created. If a file with this name already exists, it will be overwritten. If no VHD is specified, a VHD will be created in the current folder.
/size:<vhdSizeInMb> (optional)	For Fixed disks, this is the size in megabytes of the VHD that will be created. For Dynamic disks, this is the maximum size in megabytes to which the VHD can grow if additional space is required. If you do not specify this parameter, a default value of 40 GB is used.
/disktype:<dynamic|fixed> (optional)	This specifies what kind of VHD should be created, dynamic or fixed. A Fixed disk allocates all of the necessary disk space for the VHD upon creation. A Dynamic disk only allocates the space required by files in the VHD at any given time and will grow as more space is required. The default value is Dynamic.
/unattend:<unattendxmlpath> (optional)	This specifies the path to an Unattend.xml file that is used to automate the OOBE portion of Windows setup the first time the VHD is booted.
/qfe:<qfe1,..qfen> (optional)	This is a comma-separated list of Quick Fix Engineering (QFE) or hotfix patches to apply to the VHD after the WIM is implemented.
/ref:<ref1,..refn> (optional)	This is a comma-separated list of WIM "pieces" (split files) to apply to the VHD. A WIM "piece" is the result of a split WIM, and typically has a .swm file extension. The first piece of the split WIM should be specified with the /wim switch. Subsequent pieces should be specified (in order) with /ref.
/dbg:<protocol>,<port/ channel/target>[,<baudrate>]. (optional)	This configures debugging in the OS on the VHD.

You can use your own custom WIM files in this process. However, be careful. Although Microsoft supports the underlying process, as documented in the Windows AIK, WIM2VHD is not supported at this time.

You can copy files manually into the VHD, but there is no mechanism to do this with WIM2VHD.

WIM2VHD Examples

To create a Windows 7 Ultimate VHD with an automated setup answer file Unattend.xml, open an elevated command prompt and enter:

```
cscript wim2vhd.wsf /win:x:\mysources\install.wim /sku: ultimate
/unattend:C:\answer_files\unattend.xml
```

You need to adjust the location of the WIM file and the answer file to your own specifications.

To apply the first image in a custom WIM in the folder C:\Mystuff to a VHD named Mycustom.vhd when you have analyzed the WIM file with ImageX and know the SKU is designated as 1 within the WIM, open an elevated command prompt and enter:

cscript wim2vhd.wsf /wim:C:\mystuff\custom.wim /sku:1 /VHD:C:\mycustom.vhd

> **MORE INFO**   **VIM2VHD**
>
> For more information about VIM2VHD, see *http://code.msdn.microsoft.com/wim2vhd*.

Using the Offline Virtual Machine Servicing Tool to Update a VHD

The Offline Virtual Machine Servicing Tool 2.0.1 is a solution accelerator (as is MDT 2010). In addition to the appropriate installation files, a *solution accelerator* provides automated tools and additional guidance files. You can install the tool on a server running Windows Server 2008 or Windows Server 2003 SP2, where it works with Microsoft System Center Virtual Machine Manager (SCVMM) 2007 or SCVMM 2008 to maintain offline virtual machines and VHDs.

If your server is on the same network as a client running Windows 7 Enterprise or Ultimate edition, on which you have configured a bootable VHD, you can use the tool to update the VHD content when the VHD is typically offline. If your computer running Windows 7 is not normally booted from the VHD, the offline VHD does not receive operating system updates. The tool provides a way to keep the VHD up to date so that booting from the VHD does not introduce vulnerabilities into your computer.

The Offline Virtual Machine Servicing Tool can be configured to boot the client computer from the VHD just long enough for the VHD to receive updates from either SCCM 2007 or Windows Server Update Services (WSUS). As soon as the VHD's operating system is up to date, the tool reboots the client computer from its default boot disk.

The Offline Virtual Machine Servicing Tool solution accelerator includes the following features:

- Brief Overview
- OfflineVMServicing_x64.msi installation file
- OfflineVMServicing_x86.msi installation file
- Offline Virtual Machine Servicing Tool Getting Started Guide
- Offline_VM_Servicing_Tool_2.0_Release_Notes
- Offline_Virtual_Machine_Servicing_Tool_Help

The tool uses a servicing job that you schedule using Windows Task Scheduler on the server to manage the update operation. The servicing job boots the client computer from the

VHD, triggers the appropriate software update cycle using SCCM or WSUS, and then reboots the client computer from its default boot disk.

Installing the Offline Virtual Machine Servicing Tool

You cannot install the Offline Virtual Machine Servicing Tool until you have first installed SCVMM (although you can download and study the associated documentation). A beta version of SCVMM 2008 is currently available at *http://www.microsoft.com/systemcenter/ scvmm/downloadbeta.mspx*. You can download SCVMM documentation from the same source. Note that the Offline Virtual Machine Servicing Tool and SCVMM are server tools. You cannot install them on a computer running Windows 7.

You can download the Offline Virtual Machine Servicing Tool installation files and associated documentation directly from *http://www.microsoft.com/downloads/ details.aspx?FamilyID=8408ecf5-7afe-47ec-a697-eb433027df73&DisplayLanq=en*. However, it is probably easier to access *http://technet.microsoft.com/en-us/library/cc501231.aspx* and click the link at the end of the Web page. All the files are downloaded as a single compressed file that you expand into a folder that you have created on the server for this purpose. It is a good idea to read the release notes and the Getting Started Guide and become familiar with them before running the appropriate installation file.

The SCVMM Administrative Console

SCVMM provides a management solution for the virtualized data center that helps enable centralized management of IT infrastructure, increased server utilization, and dynamic resource optimization across multiple virtualization platforms. It works with the Offline Virtual Machine Servicing Tool to ensure virtual machines and VHDs are kept up to date. SCVMM delivers the following features:

- It manages virtual machines running on Windows Server 2008 Hyper-V and Microsoft Hyper-V Server.
- It provides virtualization support for virtual machines running on Virtual Server and VMware ESX Server.
- It offers end-to-end support for consolidating physical servers onto a virtual infrastructure.
- It provides performance and resource optimization (PRO) for dynamic management of virtual infrastructure.
- It implements placement of virtual workloads on the best suited physical host servers.
- It provides a complete library to manage all the building blocks of the virtual data center centrally.

The SCVMM Administrator Console, shown in Figure 2-14, is built upon a Windows PowerShell command-line interface. Any action in the Administrator Console can be performed through the Windows PowerShell command line, and each wizard in the user interface shows the associated command-line actions. The Administrator Console integrates with System Center Operations Manager 2007 to provide insight into the physical environment as well as the virtual environment.

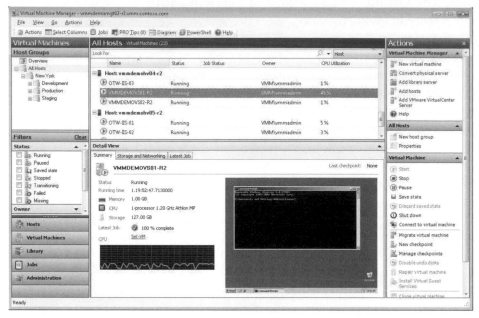

FIGURE 2-14 The SCVMM Administrator Console

Deploying to an Online VHD Using Windows Deployment Services

WDS enables you to deploy Windows 7 Enterprise or Ultimate remotely to bootable VHDs on client computers. Lesson 1 of this chapter briefly discussed WDS images. You can download the WDS documentation (including a Getting Started Guide, Deployment Guide, and WDSUTIL command-line syntax) at *http://www.microsoft.com/downloads/details.aspx?display lang=en&FamilyID=3cb929bc-af77-48d2-9b51-48268cd235fe*. You can download a step-by-step guide at *http://www.microsoft.com/downloads/details.aspx?familyid=14CA18B1-B433-4F62-8586-B0A2096460EB&displaylang=en*.

To use WDS to distribute Windows 7 images, you should install it on a server running Windows Server 2008 or Windows Server 2008 R2. WDS is a server role and you can install it by using the Initial Configuration Wizard, Server Manager, or the ServerManagerCmd command-line utility.

> **MORE INFO**   **WDS INSTALLATION REQUIREMENTS**
>
> For more information about the requirements for installing and using WDS, see *http://technet.microsoft.com/en-us/library/cc771670(WS.10).aspx*.

WDS reduces the complexity of deployments and the costs associated with manual installation. It enables you to perform network-based installation of Windows operating systems, including Windows 7, to destination computers, online virtual machines, and online VHDs. WDS uses standard Windows Server 2008 setup technologies, including Windows PE, WIM files, and image-based setup.

WDS provides the Windows Deployment Services MMC snap-in GUI tool and the WDSUTIL command-line tool. The console enables you to perform almost all deployment tasks, although you cannot use it to pre-stage client computers. You can, however, use it to set the Auto-Add policy and approve or reject pending computers.

You can use the WDSUTIL command-line tool to perform all deployment tasks. WDSUTIL also enables you to script common tasks and run the required commands from simple batch files, because no WDSUTIL command requires an interactive user session.

> *MORE INFO* **CONFIGURING YOUR DEPLOYMENT**
>
> For more information about configuring a deployment using WDS,
> see *http://technet.microsoft.com/en-us/library/cc732529(WS.10).aspx.*

> *MORE INFO* **WDS DEPLOYMENT SCENARIOS**
>
> For a description of scenarios in which you would use WDS, see *http://technet.microsoft.com/
> en-us/library/cc770667.aspx.*

 Quick Check

1. What management tools are provided by WDS?
2. Which of these tools can you use to pre-stage a client computer?

Quick Check Answers

1. The Windows Deployment Services MMC snap-in GUI tool and the WDSUTIL command-line tool
2. The WDSUTIL command-line tool

Using WDS Images

WDS uses a split WIM image method in which file resources are shared across each image group and the metadata of each image resides in a separate image file. The WDS image store creates a split media set consisting of two files:

- A minimal WIM file that contains only the definition of the image
- A Res.rwm file that contains all the file resources for all images in the image group. The data within Res.rwm is single-instanced and compressed.

At this juncture, it is probably helpful to briefly restate the difference between an install image and a boot image. Install images are the operating system images that you deploy to the client computer on internal disks, bootable external disks, and bootable VHDs. Boot images are the images that you boot a client computer into to perform an operating system installation. Boot images contain Windows PE and the WDS client Setup.exe with its supporting files for WDS. You can use the standard boot images that are included on the Windows 7 or Windows Server 2008 R2 media without modification.

> **MORE INFO   WDS DOCUMENTATION**
>
> You can download WDS documentation (including a step-by-step guide) at *http://www.microsoft.com/downloads/details.aspx?displaylang=en&FamilyID=3cb929bc-af77-48d2-9b51-48268cd235fe*. You might need to supply your Microsoft Passport. This is a Windows Server 2008 link because WDS is a server role and cannot be installed on a client computer.

When you install the WDS server role on your deployment server, you also install the WDSUTIL command-line tool. You can create boot images from the WIM file on an appropriate operating system installation disk by using the Windows Deployment Services MMC snap-in or WDSUTIL.

Creating a Capture Image

To use the Windows Deployment Services MMC snap-in to create a capture image, perform the following procedure on your WDS server:

1. In the Windows Deployment Services MMC snap-in, expand the Boot Images node.
2. Right-click the image to use it as a capture image (typically the \Sources\Boot.wim file from the installation media).
3. Click Create Capture Boot Image.
4. Type a name, description, and location where you want to save a local copy of the file. You specify a location so that if there is a network issue when you deploy the capture image, you have a local copy.
5. Follow the instructions in the wizard. When it completes, click Finish.
6. Right-click the boot image folder.
7. Click Add Boot Image.
8. Select the new capture image and then click Next.
9. Follow the instructions in the Image Capture Wizard.

To use WDSUTIL to create a capture image, perform the following procedure:

1. Open an elevated command prompt.
2. Enter **WDSUTIL /New-CaptureImage /Image:<*source boot image name*> /Architecture:{x86|ia64|x64} /DestinationImage /FilePath:<*file path*>**, where <*file path*> is the path and name for the capture image.

Adding a Boot Image

To use the Windows Deployment Services MMC snap-in to add a boot image to the WDS image store, perform the following procedure on your WDS server:

1. Right-click the Boot Images node and then click Add Boot Image.
2. Enter the path to the boot image or browse to the image file, and then click Next. Typically, you use the standard boot image that is included on the Windows Server operating system installation media without modification.
3. Enter an image name and description, and then click Next.
4. Review your choices, and then click Next.

To use WDSUTIL to add a boot image, perform the following procedure:

1. Open an elevated command prompt.
2. Enter **WDSUTIL /Verbose /Progress /Add-Image /ImageFile:<*path*>** **/ImageType:Boot**, where <*path*> is a full path to the image file.

Creating a Discover Image

To use the Windows Deployment Services MMC snap-in to create a discover image, perform the following procedure on your WDS server:

1. In the Windows Deployment Services MMC snap-in, expand the Boot Images node.
2. Right click the image you want to use as a discover image. Typically, this is the Boot. wim file from the \Sources directory of the operating system installation DVD.
3. Click Create Discover Boot Image.
4. Follow the instructions in the Image Capture Wizard. When it completes, click Finish.

To use WDSUTIL to create a discover image, perform the following procedure:

1. Open an elevated command prompt.
2. Enter **WDSUTIL /New-DiscoverImage /Image:<*name*>** **/Architecture:{x86|x64|ia64} /DestinationImage /FilePath:<*path and name* *to new file*>**. To specify which server the discover image connects to, append **/WDSServer:<*server name or IP*>**.

Adding an Install Image

To use the Windows Deployment Services MMC snap-in to add an install image to the WDS image store, perform the following procedure on your WDS server:

1. Right-click the image group in the MMC console and click Add Install Image
2. Select an image group.
3. Select the file to add.
4. Proceed through the rest of the wizard.

To use WDSUTIL to add an install image, perform the following procedure:

1. Open an elevated command prompt.

2. If you need to create an image group, enter **WDSUTIL /Add-ImageGroup /ImageGroup:<*image group name*>**.

3. Enter **WDSUTIL /Verbose /Progress /Add-Image /ImageFile:<*path to .wim file*> /ImageType:Install**.

If more than one image group exists on the server, append **/ImageGroup:<*image group name*>** to specify to which group the image should be added. If you want to skip the integrity check before adding the image, append **/SkipVerify** to the command in step 3.

Exporting an Image

When you export a boot image, WDS copies the file to the specified destination. When you export an install image, WDS combines the metadata in the Install.wim file with the resources in the Res.rwm file into a single WIM file at the specified destination.

To use the Windows Deployment Services MMC snap-in to export a boot or install image from your server to a hard disk or bootable VHD on a client computer, perform the following procedure on your WDS server:

1. Right-click a boot or install image and click Export Image.

2. In the dialog box, choose a file name and network path to which to export the image.

To use WDSUTIL to export a boot or install image from your server to a hard disk or bootable VHD on a client computer, perform the following procedure:

1. Open an elevated command prompt.

2. To export a boot image, enter **WDSUTIL /Verbose /Progress /Export-Image /Image:<*name*> /ImageType:Boot /Architecture:{x86|x64|ia64} /DestinationImage /Filepath:<*path and file name*>**.

3. To export an install image, enter **WDSUTIL /Verbose /Progress /Export-Image /Image:<*name*> /ImageType:Install /ImageGroup:<*image group name*> /DestinationImage /Filepath:<*path and file name*>**.

You can append **/Name:<*name*>** or **/Description:<*description*>** to the command if you want to set these metadata fields on the image. To determine behavior when the image specified in **/DestinationImage** already exists, append **/Overwrite:{Yes|No|Append}**. Yes overwrites the image, No causes an error, and Append (available for install images only) appends the new image to the existing WIM file.

Updating an Image

To use the Windows Deployment Services MMC snap-in to replace an image on the server with an updated version, perform the following procedure on your WDS server:

1. Right-click a boot or install image, and then click Replace Image.

2. Browse to the updated image.

3. Complete the wizard.

To use WDSUTIL to replace an image on the server with an updated version, perform the following procedure:

1. Open an elevated command prompt.

2. To replace a boot image, enter **WDSUTIL /Verbose /Progress /Replace-Image /Image:<*name*> /ImageType:Boot /Architecture:{x86|x64|ia64} /ReplacementImage/ImageFile:<*path*>**.

3. To replace an install image, enter **WDSUTIL /Verbose /Progress /Replace-Image /Image:<*name*> /ImageType:Install /ImageGroup:<*image group name*> /ReplacementImage /ImageFile:<*path*>**.

These procedures add the new image to the image store and remove the old one. You can then export the new image to destination computers, online virtual machines, or online VHDs.

EXAM TIP

You can update WIM images on rewritable media, place them in a WDS image store, and export them to the appropriate destination computers, online virtual machines, and online VHDs. However, if you want to "wake" offline virtual machines or VHDs on a scheduled basis so they can receive updates from WSUS (for example), you need to use the Offline Machine Servicing Tool described previously in this lesson.

MORE INFO **MANAGING IMAGES WITH WDS**

For more information about how you can use WDS to manage images, including how to set and display image attributes, how to remove an image and add and remove an image group, and how display information about all images in an image group, see *http://technet.microsoft.com/en-us/library/cc732961.aspx*.

Pre-staging Client Computers

You can use WDS to link physical computers to computer account objects in AD DS servers. This is called pre-staging the client. Pre-staged clients are also called *known computers*. You can then configure properties on the computer account to control the installation for the client. For example, you can configure the network boot program and the unattend answer file that the client should receive, as well as the server from which the client should download the network boot program. You do not pre-stage a VHD, but rather the client computer that boots from that VHD.

If you use WDS as part of the image installation process, a client computer is joined to a domain by default. You can disable this functionality using the Client tab of the server's Properties page.

You can use the WDSUTIL tool or the Active Directory Users And Computers snap-in to pre-stage client computers before deploying an image. You can also enable the Auto-Add policy. If you enable this policy and approve the installation for an unknown client, the installation proceeds and a computer account is created in AD DS for that client. The WDSUTIL command to pre-stage a computer is WDSUTIL /Add-Device /Device:<*name*> /ID:<*ID*>.

When the Auto-Add policy is enabled, administrative approval is required before clients that are not pre-staged can have an image installed. To enable this policy, open an elevated command prompt and enter **WDSUTIL /Set-Server /AutoAddPolicy /Policy:AdminApproval.** You can also enable the policy using the PXE Response settings tab of the server's Properties page.

> *MORE INFO* **USING THE ACTIVE DIRECTORY USERS AND COMPUTERS SNAP-IN TO PRE-STAGE CLIENT COMPUTERS**
>
> For more information about using the Active Directory Users And Computers snap-in to pre-stage client computers, see *http://technet.microsoft.com/en-us/library/ cc754289(WS.10).aspx.*

Pre-staging clients adds an additional layer of security. You can configure WDS to answer only to pre-staged clients, ensuring that clients that are not pre-staged are not able to boot from the network. If you pre-stage clients, you can control the following:

- The computer account name and location within AD DS
- Which PXE server should service the client
- Which network boot program (NBP) the client should receive
- What boot image a client receives and what WDS client unattend answer file the client will use

Pre-staging allows multiple PXE servers to service the same network segment by restricting the server to answer only a particular set of clients. Note that the pre-staged client must be in the same forest as the WDS server.

The Auto-Add policy applies only when the WDS server is set to answer all clients and WDS does not find a pre-staged computer account for a booting computer. In all other cases, this policy will not take effect. This policy does not pertain to computers that use Extensible Firmware Interface (EFI).

> *MORE INFO* **PRE-STAGING CLIENT COMPUTERS**
>
> For more information about pre-staging client computers, see *http://technet.microsoft.com/ en-us/library/cc770832(WS.10).aspx.*

Creating a Bootable VHD

In this practice, you use the Computer Management tool to create a VHD. You then add the VHD to the Boot menu so that your computer can boot from it. You need to have completed the practice exercises in Lesson 1 before attempting this practice.

EXERCISE 1 Creating a VHD

To use Computer Management to create a VHD, perform the following procedure:

1. Log on to the Canberra computer with the Kim_Akers account.

2. Create a folder called VHDs on the C: drive. If you prefer to use an external USB disk drive, adjust your drive letter accordingly, but first ensure that the external drive is formatted with the NTFS file system.

3. On the Start menu, right-click Computer and choose Manage. If prompted, click Yes to allow the program to run.

4. Select Disk Management.

5. Right-click Disk Management and choose Create VHD, as shown in Figure 2-15.

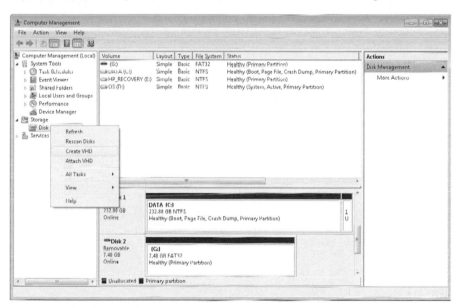

FIGURE 2-15 Creating a VHD

6. Complete the Create And Attach Virtual Hard Disk Drive dialog box, as shown in Figure 2-16. Click OK. If necessary, close the AutoPlay dialog box.

FIGURE 2-16 Specifying VHD file size, file name, and location

7. In Disk Management, right-click the icon beside the disk designation, as shown in Figure 2-17, and choose Initialize Disk. The VHD appears in the Disk Management pane. (Note: It can take some time for this to happen.)

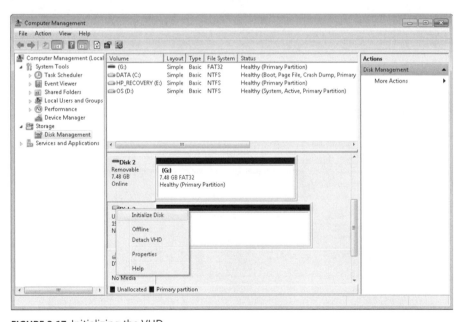

FIGURE 2-17 Initializing the VHD

8. Ensure MBR (Master Boot Record) is selected and click OK. The status of the disk changes to Online.

9. On the newly created disk, right-click Unallocated and select New Simple Volume. This starts the New Simple Volume Wizard. Click Next.

10. Click Next to accept the volume size defaults.

11. In the Assign Drive Letter Or Path dialog box, select W and then click Next.

12. In the Format Partition dialog box, give the volume a label (such as MyVHD), as shown in Figure 2-18. Ensure that Perform A Quick Format is selected. Click Next.

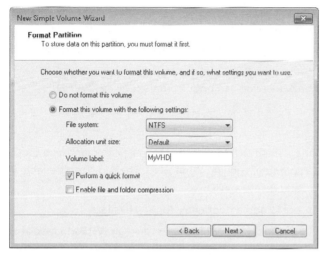

FIGURE 2-18 The Format Partition dialog box

13. Click Finish.

EXERCISE 2 Adding a VHD to the Boot Menu

To add the VHD that you have created to the Boot menu, perform the following procedure:

1. If necessary, log on to the Canberra computer with the Kim_Akers account.

2. Open an elevated command prompt and enter **bcdedit /copy {current} /d "MyVHD"**. As shown in Figure 2-19, this returns the GUID of the loader object. You use this value to replace the variable *<guid>* in the next steps in this procedure. The GUID that you detect will be different from that shown in Figure 2-19.

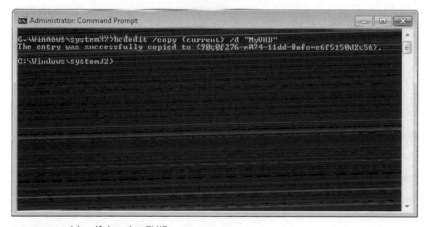

FIGURE 2-19 Identifying the GUID

3. Enter **bcdedit /set <*guid*> device vhd=partition w:**.

4. Enter **bcdedit /set <*guid*> osdevice vhd=C:\vhds\myvhd.vhd**.

5. To force Windows 7 to automatically detect the HAL, enter **bcdedit /vbcdedit /set <*guid*> detecthal on**.

6. To test if your boot entry has been successfully created, enter **bcdedit /v**.

7. Copy the WIM image file Myimage.wim that you created in Lesson 1 to the bootable W: drive.

8. Reboot the computer. Check that you can boot from the device MyVHD.

Lesson Summary

- You can use the Disk Management GUI tool or the Diskpart command-line tool to create a native VHD on a computer running Windows 7. The same tools enable you to attach, mount, detach, and delete a VHD.

- You can use the BCDEdit tool to add a boot entry for a VHD file.

- The WIM2VHD command-line tool uses WIM images to create VHDs that boot directly to the OOBE.

- You can use the Offline Virtual Machine Servicing Tool to implement a scheduled update of the image on bootable VHDs that are normally offline. WDS provides tools that let you deploy images to client computers and to virtual machines and VHDs that are online.

Lesson Review

You can use the following questions to test your knowledge of the information in Lesson 2, "Managing Virtual Hard Disk Files." The questions are also available on the companion DVD if you prefer to review them in electronic form.

> **NOTE ANSWERS**
>
> Answers to these questions and explanations of why each answer choice is correct or incorrect are located in the "Answers" section at the end of the book.

1. You want to create a 20-GB native VHD called Systemvhd in a folder called Windows 7 on an external USB hard disk with the drive designation G:. Which command do you use?

   A. **create vdisk file=g:\windows7\systemvhd maximum=20000**

   B. **create vdisk file=g:\windows7\systemvhd.vhd maximum=20000**

   C. **create vdisk file=g:\windows7\systemvhd.vhd maximum=20**

   D. **create vdisk file=g:\windows7\systemvhd maximum=20**

2. You have used the ImageX tool to install a WIM system image on a VHD and added a boot entry for that VHD using the BCDEdit tool. The bootable VHD has been designated with the drive letter W:. The variable *<guid>* is replaced by the GUID of the VHD. What command can you use to verify that your boot entry is created successfully?

   A. **bcdedit /set <guid> detecthal on**

   B. **bcdedit /delete <guid> /cleanup**

   C. **bcdedit /v**

   D. **bcdedit /copy {current} /d "My New VHD"**

3. You want add an install image to the image store on a WDS server. You want to use the source image file Install.wim in the C:/Myimages folder. Which command do you use?

   A. **WDSUTIL /Verbose /Progress /Replace-Image /Image:myimage.wim/ ImageType:Install /ImageGroup:<myimagegroup> /ReplacementImage /ImageFile:C:\myimages/oldimage**

   B. **WDSUTIL /Set-Server /AutoAddPolicy /Policy:AdminApproval**

   C. **WDSUTIL /New-DiscoverImage /Image:myimage.wim /Architecture:x86 /DestinationImage /FilePath C:/myimages/install.wim**

   D. **WDSUTIL /Verbose /Progress /Add-Image /ImageFile:C:/myimages/ install.wim /ImageType:Install**

4. You administer a network in which all the client computers run Windows 7 Ultimate. You have created bootable VHDs on all your clients to provide failover protection. However, because the VHDs are normally offline, the images they hold do not receive all the latest security updates. You want to boot the clients from their VHDs automatically every Saturday at 11:30 P.M. just long enough for them to receive updates from your WSUS server. What tool do you use to do this?

   A. Offline Virtual Machine Servicing Tool

   B. SCVMM

   C. Windows Deployment Services MMC snap-in

   D. WDSUTIL

Chapter Review

To further practice and reinforce the skills you learned in this chapter, you can perform the following tasks:

- Review the chapter summary.
- Review the list of key terms introduced in this chapter.
- Complete the case scenarios. These scenarios set up real-world situations involving the topics of this chapter and ask you to create a solution.
- Complete the suggested practices.
- Take a practice test.

Chapter Summary

- Windows 7 operating systems support native VHDs, and you can make a VHD containing a WIM image (in Ultimate and Enterprise editions only) bootable by using the BCDEdit tool.
- You need to install the Windows AIK before you can create or deploy WIM image files. Windows AIK tools include Windows SIM, ImageX, Oscdimg, DISM, USMT, and Windows PE tools.
- You can use the Diskpart and Disk Management tools to create, attach, and initialize VHDs. You can use the Sysprep tool to generalize an image and remove computer-specific information.
- The WDS provides tools that allow you to create and manage images for online deployment. The Offline Virtual Machine Servicing Tool works with SCVMM on a server running Windows to schedule updates of images on offline VHDs.

Key Terms

Do you know what these key terms mean? You can check your answers by looking up the terms in the glossary at the end of the book.

- **solution accelerator**
- **system image**
- **Virtual Hard Disk (VHD)**
- **Windows Automated Installation Toolkit (Windows AIK)**
- **Windows Preinstallation Environment (Windows PE)**

Case Scenarios

In the following case scenarios, you apply what you've learned about configuring system images. You can find answers to these questions in the "Answers" section at the end of this book.

Case Scenario 1: Generating a System Image

You are an enterprise administrator at a large computer software organization. You want to install Windows 7 Ultimate automatically on any new client computers in your organization. You also need to transfer user data from computers running Windows Vista Ultimate to computers running Windows 7 Ultimate. Your company has recently developed a graphics toolkit, and you want to distribute an installation image over the Internet that will enable customers to generate an installation DVD-ROM. Answer the following questions:

1. What type of image file should you generate to install Windows 7 Ultimate and what tool do you use to do this?

2. What type of image file should you generate to distribute the graphics toolkit over the Internet, and what tool do you use to do this?

3. What Windows AIK tool can you use to transfer user data from computers running Windows Vista Ultimate to computers running Windows 7 Ultimate?

Case Scenario 2: Working with VHDs

You have set up a test network to investigate the Windows 7 operating systems. You have two client computers on your network. One runs Windows 7 Ultimate and the other runs Windows 7 Home Premium. Answer the following questions:

1. You want to create VHDs on your client computers and create a WIM file using each of the computers as reference computers. You want to install the reference WIM files on to VHDs on both clients and boot each computer into an operating system from the VHD. On which of your client computers can you do this?

2. You add three more client computers to your test network and want to install Windows 7 Ultimate on all of them. You use the computer running Windows 7 Ultimate on your network as a reference computer. What Sysprep utility do you need to run before you create a WIM image file on your reference computer and install the image on the additional clients?

Suggested Practices

To help you master the exam objectives presented in this chapter, complete the following tasks.

Use Windows SIM and Sysprep

In this practice, you create an answer file. Optionally, you use this answer file to install Windows 7 on a reference computer and then use the Sysprep tool to generalize the installation before capturing it as a WIM image. It is a bad idea to use the Canberra computer for this because you need it set up for other lessons in this book, so Practices 2 and 3 are optional. You should do them if you have another client computer that you can use for this purpose.

- **Practice 1**   Practice using Windows SIM to generate a number of answer files. You will find step-by-step instructions at *http://technet.microsoft.com/en-us/library/dd349348.aspx*.

- **Practice 3**   Install Windows 7 on a reference computer using one of the answer files you generated. Again, refer to the URL given in the first practice.

- **Practice 2**   Run *sysprep /generalize* to remove hardware-specific information from the reference computer and generate a WIM image of the reference computer. As before, refer to the URL given in the first practice.

Work with VHDs

Complete Practice 1. Practice 2 is optional.

- **Practice 1**   Create, mount, attach, detach, and delete VHDs. Use both Disk Management and Diskpart to do this. It becomes quite easy with a bit of practice. Also practice installing WIM images on VHDs and using BCDEdit to create bootable VHDs.

- **Practice 2**   Create and configure a virtual server running Windows Server 2008 or Windows Server 2008 R2. Install the Offline Virtual Machine Servicing Tool and SCVMM. Create a scheduled task that boots your client running Windows 7 from its bootable VHD.

Take a Practice Test

The practice tests on this book's companion DVD offer many options. For example, you can test yourself on just one exam objective, or you can test yourself on all the 70-680 certification exam content. You can set up the test so that it closely simulates the experience of taking a certification exam, or you can set it up in study mode so that you can look at the correct answers and explanations after you answer each question.

> **MORE INFO**   **PRACTICE TESTS**
>
> For details about all the practice test options available, see the section entitled "How to Use the Practice Tests," in the Introduction to this book.

CHAPTER 3

Deploying System Images

This chapter discusses the management, manipulation, and deployment of system images. You *deploy* an image when you install it on one or more target computers. It looks at how you mount a system image so it can be updated and altered, how you then commit these changes to the original image, and how you distribute that image to a number—often a large number—of client computers. In the context of system images, you *mount* an image by expanding it into a folder so you can obtain information about it and add or remove features such as drivers, updates, and language packs.

Microsoft provides a range of tools for image manipulation and deployment, some of which are specific to Windows 7 images, whereas others are more general. Some tools manipulate images, others deploy them, and some tools do both. It is your job as a network administrator to choose the best tools for your current and future needs and configure them so that they work efficiently and go on working efficiently.

If your users are sitting at computers with operating systems, drivers, and applications that are up to date and as invulnerable as you can make them to Internet (and intranet) attacks they will be less unhappy. If you can bring one computer or 100 computers into full operation quickly, efficiently, and without error, then your boss will be less unhappy. (We all know, of course, that neither users nor bosses are ever happy.)

Exam objectives in this chapter:

- Prepare a system image for deployment.
- Deploy a system image.

Lessons in this chapter:

Before You Begin

To complete the exercises in the practices in this chapter you need to have done the following:

- Installed the Windows 7 operating system on a stand-alone client PC, as described in Chapter 1, "Install, Migrate, or Upgrade to Windows 7." You need Internet access to complete the exercises.

- Completed all the practice exercises in Chapter 2, "Configuring System Images." In particular, you need to have installed the Windows Automated Installation Kit (Windows AIK) and deployed an offline image of the Canberra computer on a bootable virtual hard disk (VHD).

 REAL WORLD

Ian McLean

Each of the tools you use for network and system administration has its own set of features and enables you to perform specific tasks. Where people sometimes get upset and confused is if there is overlap. For example, you can use Windows Deployment Services (WDS) or the Microsoft Deployment Toolkit (MDT) 2010 to deploy Windows 7 images to client computers. However, MDT 2010 allows you to specify a set of configuration tasks that should be run on a computer after an image has been deployed to it through WDS, whereas WDS cannot run configuration tasks on a client after the image has been deployed.

You use ImageX to create an image of a computer running Windows 7 while it is booted to Windows Preinstallation Environment (Windows PE) and you use the Deployment Image Servicing and Management (DISM) tool to manipulate that image after it has been created. However, you can use ImageX or DISM to mount an image so you can work with it offline.

So, you are entitled to ask, which tool do I use and, more to the point in this book, what tool will the examination ask about? The simple answer is to use the most recently introduced tool when there is a choice. For example, ImageX has been around for some time, whereas DISM was introduced fairly recently; however, ImageX has new features in the latest edition of the Windows AIK.

Traditionally, examinations ask more questions about new features of an operatingsystem and new tools that are introduced to carry out tasks on the new operating system than they do about features that are unchanged from the previous operating system and tools that, however worthy, have been around for a while. This is simply a statement of fact and any conclusions you draw from it are your own.

However, as a professional administrator rather than merely an examination candidate, what tool do you choose to do your job? That's up to you. My advice is if you've been using DISM frequently in the recent past and have got into the rhythm of typing in DISM commands, use that tool if you are given the choice. Otherwise, my preferred tool when I'm mounting an image is ImageX. The commands are shorter (important when you're as slow a typist as I am), I find the command completes sooner, and if something does go wrong, ImageX usually gives a more detailed explanation. That, however, is only my opinion, with which you are absolutely entitled to disagree.

As a professional, use your best judgment. As an examination candidate, know what all the tools do, what a tool does that no other tool can do, what a tool does that is unique to the new operating system or that you haven't been able to do before, and what jobs can be done equally well by two or more tools.

Good luck.

Lesson 1: Managing a System Image Before Deployment

Sometimes when you have created a master reference image for deploying to other computers, you might find that you need to amend it. You night need to add a new driver, change settings, and support multiple languages. Even a fairly minor change, such as enabling a feature currently disabled in the image, can generate a considerable workload if it needs to be done after the image has been distributed to several hundred computers.

Typically, it involves less administrative effort if you make these changes without deploying the image and recapturing it. If your requirement is to add security updates, then it is certainly preferable to apply the security patches offline—otherwise, you are deploying an insecure image. If you service the image offline, you do not need to run the Sysprep tool and therefore do not need to use a rearm parameter. Finally, you might want to apply an amended Autounattend.xml file for unattended install or an additional Unattend.xml file that automates post-installation tasks such as installing mission-critical applications. Unattend.xml files are discussed in the section entitled "Unattended Servicing Command-Line Options," later in this chapter.

This lesson discusses how you use Windows AIK tools such as ImageX and DISM to mount a system image and how you use DISM to manage the image, insert packages, insert updates, enable and disable features, manage international settings, manage language packs, and associate unattend answer files.

> **After this lesson, you will be able to:**
> - Mount an offline image for servicing.
> - Use DISM to manage and manipulate the image.
> - Associate one or more answer files with the image.
> - Commit and unmount the image.
>
> **Estimated lesson time: 50 minutes**

Using DISM WIM Commands and Mounting an Image

Chapter 2 introduced the Windows 7 DISM command-line tool. DISM enables you to service offline images, mount and dismount Windows Imaging format (WIM) files, and customize Windows PE boot images. The DISM tool replaces many of the tools in previous versions of the Windows AIK, including Package Manager (Pkgmgr.exe), the International Settings Configuration Tool (Intlcfg.exe), and the Windows PE command-line tool (PEimg.exe).

Microsoft has designed the DISM tool to manage WIM images. Also, DISM is backward-compatible with Vista tools, such as Pkgmgr.exe, Intlcfg.exe, and PEimg.exe, so scripts that you developed and tested for Vista should work unamended in Windows 7.

Chapter 2 also introduced the ImageX tool, which you used to create a WIM image file.
Typically you can use either DISM or Image X to mount WIM files. DISM is the recommended
Windows AIK tool for managing and manipulating offline images. It allows you to install and
configure operating system updates, packages, and drivers on an offline system image. You
can use DISM to modify Windows PE images offline and to change the language, locale,
fonts, and input settings on a Windows image.

The commands that DISM offers for image management depend upon the type of image
you want to manage. You access DISM by clicking All Programs on the Start menu, clicking
Microsoft Windows AIK, right-clicking Deployment Tools Command Prompt, and choosing
Run As Administrator. You might need to click Yes to allow the program to run. Entering
dism in the elevated Deployment Tools Command Prompt window generates a list of DISM
commands. Figure 3-1 shows commands specific to WIM images.

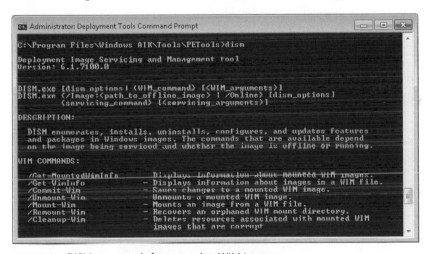

FIGURE 3-1 DISM commands for managing WIM images

For example, to get information about Myimage.wim, the WIM file that you created in
Chapter 2 and installed on a bootable VHD with the drive letter W:, you enter the following
command:

```
dism /get-wiminfo /wimfile:w:\myimage.wim
```

The output from this command is shown in Figure 3-2. If this command cannot find the image, open Computer Management and attach the VHD. It is the file Myvhd.vhd in the VHDs folder. If you did not create a VHD, you should find the same file in the D:\Images folder (or whatever destination you specified in the practice session in Chapter 2). If the file Myimages. wim does not exist at all, copy the file Install.wim from your installation DVD-ROM to D:\Images and use it instead.

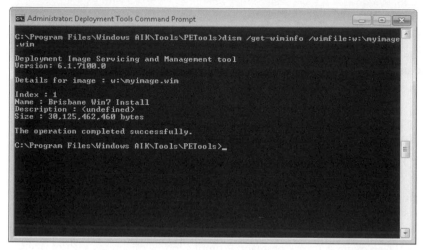

FIGURE 3-2 Using the /Get-WimInfo and /Wimfile switches

However, if you want more detailed information about the image, you can use the ImageX tool as follows:

```
imagex /info w:\myimage.wim
```

Part of the output from this command is shown in Figure 3-3. The file contains only one image with the index number 1. (If you are using the Install.wim image, you need to discover the index number for the Windows 7 Ultimate image—typically 5.)

FIGURE 3-3 Detailed information about a WIM image

Mounting WIM Images

If you want to manage an image, you first need to mount it. To mount the W:\Myimage.wim image on (for example) the C:\MountedImages folder, you enter the following command in the elevated Deployment Tools command prompt:

```
dism /mount-wim /wimfile:w:\myimage.wim /index:1 /mountdir:c:\mymountedimages
```

The *index* flag in this command indicates the image that you want to mount. You can have several images (for example, several editions of Windows 7) within a single WIM file.

You can add the *readonly* flag to this command if you want the image to be read-only. Alternatively, you can use the ImageX tool from the same console by entering the following command:

```
imagex /mountrw w:\myimage.wim 1 c:\mountedimages
```

If you want to try out both commands, you need to create and use another destination folder for the second command (for example, C:\Othermount). The destination folder must initially contain no files. Alternatively, you can delete the mounted image in the C:\MountedImages folder and regenerate the mounted image. You cannot use Windows Explorer to delete a mounted image but must instead unmount it by using the following ImageX command:

```
imagex /unmount c:\mountedimages
```

You can also use DISM to unmount a mounted WIM file by entering a command similar to the following:

```
dism /unmount-wim c:\mountedimages
```

You use these commands in the practice session later in this lesson.

> **NOTE** **MOUNTING THE INSTALL.WIM FILE ON THE INSTALLATION DVD-ROM**
>
> You can mount the Install.wim file on the installation DVD-ROM, but this enables you to create only a read-only image, and you need to specify the *readonly* flag if you execute a DISM command. If you want to create an image that you can manipulate, you need first to copy Install.wim to rewritable media and ensure that the Read Only file attribute is not set.

Getting Information About Mounted WIM Images

You can get information about all mounted WIM files on your computer by entering the following command:

```
dism /get-mountedwiminfo
```

The output from this command is shown in Figure 3-4.

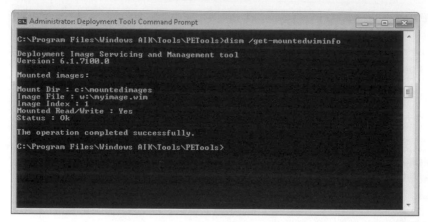

FIGURE 3-4 Mounted WIM files on the computer

If you are working with files from a mounted image, it is good practice to create a temporary scratch directory in which you can place these files. You need first to create a folder to hold the files (for example, C:\Working Files). You then enter the following command:

```
dism /image:c:\mountedimages /scratchdir:c:\workingfiles
```

When you have created a mounted Read/Write image, you can amend and update existing files and add applications and drivers. You can specify edition and international settings and add language packs. These operations are described later in this lesson. You can save (or *commit*) any amendments you make to the offline image by using a command similar to the following:

```
dism /commit-wim /mountdir:c:\mountedimages.
```

This command can take a considerable time to complete. In this example, it saves any changes you have made to the mounted image in C:\MountedImages to the source image W:\Myimage.wim. The command does not unmount the image and you have the option of further amending and saving the image. Figure 3-5 shows the output from this command.

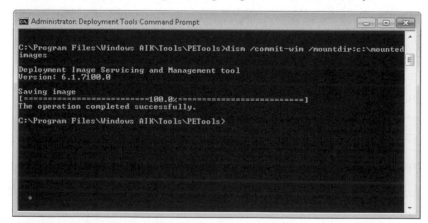

FIGURE 3-5 Saving an amended mounted WIM image

Files in a mounted WIM image could become corrupt and you would not want to save such files back to the source image. It is also possible that a mounted image could become orphaned because of changes in directory structure. You can remove corrupt files from all mounted images on the computer with the following command:

```
dism /cleanup-wim
```

Figure 3-6 shows that all writable volumes are scanned for corrupt files.

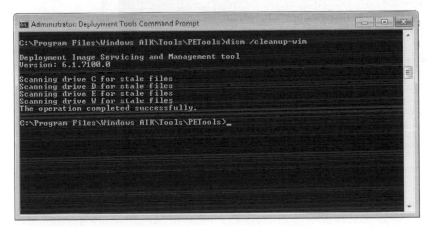

FIGURE 3-6 Scanning for corrupt files

You can retrieve and remount orphaned images by entering a command similar to the following:

```
dism /remount-wim /mountdir:c:\mountedimages
```

EXAM TIP

Distinguish between /cleanup-wim, which removes corrupt files, /remount-wim, which retrieves and remounts orphaned images, and /cleanup-image. This last option is typically used with the /RevertPendingActions parameter to attempt a system recovery if you experience a boot failure. This operation reverts all pending actions from the previous servicing operations because these actions might be the cause of the boot failure. Note that /RevertPendingActions is not supported on a running operating system or a Windows PE or Windows Recovery Environment (Windows RE) image.

Working with an Online Image

In addition to mounting and manipulating an offline image, you can work with the operating system image that is currently online. For example, the following command lists all the out of box drivers that are currently installed:

```
dism /online /get-drivers
```

Figure 3-7 shows some of the output from this command. If you want to list all drivers rather than all out-of-box drivers, append /all to the command.

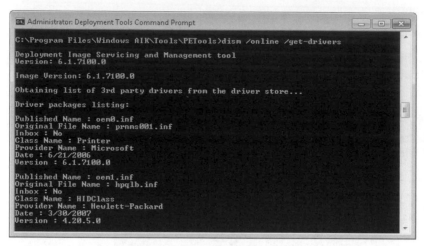

FIGURE 3-7 Listing drivers in the online system image

In general, you get information from an online image rather than amend or manipulate it. For example, a command such as *dism /online /get-currentedition*, which returns the edition of the operating system, could be used in a batch file where the action implemented depends upon the Windows 7 edition. Table 3-1 shows parameters that can be used with the */Online* option.

TABLE 3-1 Parameters That Can Be Used Online

PARAMETER	DESCRIPTION
/Get-CurrentEdition	Displays the edition of the online image
/Get-StagedEditions	Displays a list of Microsoft Windows editions that can be removed from an image
/Get-TargetEditions	Displays a list of Windows editions to which the online image could be upgraded
/Get-DriverInfo	Displays information about a specific driver
/Get-Drivers	Displays information about all out-of-box drivers
/Get-Intl	Displays information about the international settings and languages
/Get-Packages	Displays information about all packages in the online image
/Get-PackageInfo	Displays information about a specific package
/Get-Features	Displays information about all features in the online image
/Get-FeatureInfo	Displays information about a specific feature

Any parameter that can be used online can also be used offline by specifying a mounted WIM image with the *image* switch. For example, the following command lists all the drivers in the image mounted in the folder C:\MountedImages:

```
dism /image:c:\mountedimages /get-drivers /all
```

Table 3-2 lists the information retrieval parameters that you can use with an offline mounted image but not with an online image.

TABLE 3-2 Parameters That Cannot Be Used with an Offline Image

PARAMETER	DESCRIPTION
/Get-AppPatchInfo	Displays information about installed Windows Installer patch files (MSP patches)
/Get-AppPatches	Displays information about all applied MSP patches for all installed applications
/Get-AppInfo	Displays information about a specific installed Windows Installer (MSI) application
/Get-Apps	Displays information about all installed MSI applications

Servicing Drivers, Applications, Patches, Packages, and Features

You can use driver servicing commands on an offline mounted image to add and remove drivers based on the .inf file format. You can specify a directory where the driver .inf files are located, or you can point to a driver by specifying the name of the .inf file.

On an online running operating system, you can only enumerate drivers and obtain driver details. The commands and options to list drivers and obtain driver information were discussed in the previous section of this lesson. DISM can manage only .inf file drivers. Windows Installer (MSI) and other driver package types (such as .exe files) are not supported.

The following driver servicing options are available for an offline image:

```
dism /image:path_to_ image_directory [/get-drivers | /get-driverinfo | /add-driver |
/remove-driver]
```

For example, if you wanted to add the driver Mydriver.inf that you have downloaded and stored in the folder C:\Newdrivers, you would use a command similar to the following:

```
dism /image:c:\mountedimages /add-driver:c:\newdrivers\mydriver.inf
```

Figure 3-8 shows the output from this command.

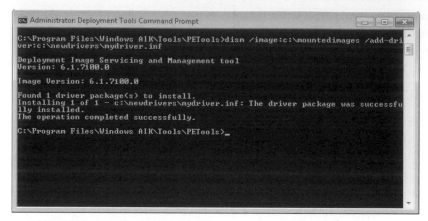

FIGURE 3-8 Adding a driver to an image

When you are adding a new driver, you should store it in a convenient location. In this case, you can specify the file name and path directly after the Add-Drivers option and do not need the */driver* parameter. However, if you want to add several drivers that are in the same folder you would enter a command similar to the following:

```
dism /image:c:\mountedimages /add-driver /driver:c:\newdrivers
```

If you want to add all the drivers in two or more folders, you can use the */driver* parameter as many times as you require; for example:

```
dism /image:c:\mountedimages /add-driver /driver:c:\printdrivers /driver:d\nicdrivers.
```

If you want to add all the drivers in a folder and its subfolders you can use the */recurse* option. For example:

```
dism /image:c:\mountedimages /add-driver /driver:c:\newdrivers /recurse
```

Figure 3-9 shows the output from this command.

FIGURE 3-9 Using the */recurse* option

On x64-based computers running Windows 7, drivers must have a digital signature. However, you might want to install an unsigned driver for test purposes. In this case you can use the */forceunsigned* parameter to override this requirement.

You can use the */remove-drivers* option to remove third-party drivers from an offline image. You cannot remove default drivers with the *dism* command. When you add third-party drivers, they are named *oem0.inf, oem1.inf*, and so on. You must specify the published name, but fortunately, the */get-drivers* parameter lists both the published name and the original name. If you have installed a lot of third-party drivers and are having difficulty finding the new name of the driver you want to remove, you can direct the output from a *dism* command that uses the */get-drivers* parameter to a text file and search this file for the original name. When you have identified the driver's published name, such as *oem10.inf*, you can then remove it using a command similar to the following:

```
dism /image:c:\mountedimages /remove-driver /driver:oem10.inf
```

Servicing Applications and Application Patches

You can use application servicing command-line options applied to a offline image to check the applicability of Windows Installer application patches and to query the offline image for information about installed Windows Installer applications (.msi files) and application patches (.msp files).

None of the application servicing commands can be applied to online images, although if an image is online, it can receive updates from, for example, Windows Server Update Services (WSUS) or Microsoft Update. If you are administering an enterprise network, you should consider the Offline Virtual Machine Servicing Tool and System Center Virtual Machine Manager, which were discussed in Chapter 2.

DISM offers the following options are available to list Windows Installer (.msi) applications and .msp application patches, and to check the applicability of an application patch on an offline system image:

```
dism /image:path_to_directory [/check-apppatch | /get-apppatchinfo: | /get-apppatches |
/get-appinfo | /get-apps]
```

When managing applications and patches, your first step should be to discover what application patches and applications exist and are applicable to the image. For example, in an image mounted directly from an Install.wim file copied from the installation media, it is likely that no applicable patches or applications exist. To obtain information about application patches (MSI files) applicable to a mounted image, you would use a command similar to the following:

```
dism /image:c:\mountedimages /get-apppatches
```

If you know the product code globally unique identifier (GUID) of a Windows Installer application, you can use the */productcode* parameter to display all the application patches in the specified application. You would use a command similar to the following:

```
dism /image:c:\mountedimages /get-apppatches /productcode:{GUID}
```

If you want to display information about specific .msp patches applicable to the offline image, you can use the */check-apppatch* parameter. You use */patchlocation* to specify the path to the MSP patch file. You can specify multiple patch files by using */patchlocation* more than once in the command. For example, to display information about two patch files, 30880d0. msp and 8c82a.msp (both in C:\Windows\Installer) in the mounted image, you would enter the following command:

```
dism /image:c:\mountedimages /check-apppatch
/patchlocation:c:\windows\installer\30880d0.msp
/patchlocation:c:\windows\installer\8c82a.msp
```

If you need detailed information about all installed MSP patches applicable to the offline image, you would enter a command similar to the following:

```
dism /image:c:\mountedimages /get-apppatchinfo
```

 Quick Check

- You want to add all the drivers in the folder C:\Orinsnewdrivers and its subfolders to the mounted offline image in D:\Orinsimage. What command would you use?

Quick Check Answer

- dism /image:d:\orinsimage /add-driver /driver:d:\orinsimage /recurse

You can use the */get-apppatches* option described earlier in this section to find the patch code GUID and the product code GUID specific to a patch. You can also use the */get-apps* option described here to list all product code GUIDs for an installed Windows Installer application. You can filter the information returned by the */get-apppatchinfo* parameter either by the patch code GUID or the product code GUID, or by both, for example:

```
dism /image:c:\mountedimages /get-apppatchinfo /patchcode:{patch_code_GUID}
/productcode:{product_code_GUID}
```

In addition to obtaining information about applicable application patches, you typically need to obtain information about the MSI applications. The */get-apps* parameter lists the MSI applications installed on the mounted image and you can use it to determine each application's GUID; for example:

```
dism /image:c:\mountedimages /get-apps
```

You can then obtain more detailed information about installed applications by using the */get-appinfo* parameter. Optionally you can filter this information by specifying the product code GUID for the application in which you are interested; for example:

```
dism /image:c:\mountedimages /get-appinfo /ProductCode:{product_code_GUID}
```

If you do not specify a product code GUID, the */get-appinfo* parameter returns detailed information about all installed MSI applications.

Adding Applications to an Image

The */check-apppatch, /get-apppatchinfo, /get-apppatches, /get-appinfo,* and */get-apps* DISM options obtain information about Windows Installer applications and installed patches on an offline mounted image. The next section describes how you add cabinet (.cab) or Windows Update Stand-alone Installer (.msu) files to an image and, in particular, install security patches to offline-mounted images. You can also enable and disable Windows features, but you cannot add features or any other type of executable files, such as .exe, .bat, .com, or .vbs files. The DISM command does not have an */add-apps* option.

If you want to add a mission-critical application to the image for distribution, you can install that application on your reference computer before you image it. If, however, you want to add an application to an already existing offline image, the DISM tool does not do this. Instead, you should use the Add Application Wizard provided by MDT 2010, which is discussed in Lesson 2, "Deploying System Images."

You can also use DISM to associate an image with an Unattend.xml answer file. Such a file automates installation of the image but also automates post-installation tasks, for example, connecting to a file server and installing applications or configuring settings. This approach, where applications and settings are applied after installation rather than included in the image, is known as "thin image" and is described in Lesson 2 of this chapter.

Servicing Operating System Packages

One of the problems you have with system images either held for distribution to a number of computers or installed on a bootable VHD of a single client computer for failover purposes is that you need to keep the image up to date, particularly with security updates and fixes. Otherwise, if you boot with the new image, the computer is vulnerable to known security threats.

In the case of a single client computer where you have captured a system image as described in Chapter 2 and installed this to bootable VHD, you have several options. The most straightforward way, if possibly not the fastest, is to boot the computer from its VHD, go immediately to Microsoft Update, and install any critical or recommended packages. You can do this manually or, in an enterprise, by using the Offline Virtual Machine Servicing Tool on a server that has Microsoft System Center Virtual Machine Manager (SCVMM) installed. The disadvantage is that computers are brought online without the latest security updates and are vulnerable, if only for a short time.

You can also re-image your client computer on a regular basis and install the new image on to the VHD. This involves booting the computer to Windows PE and is a time-consuming process, especially when carried out on a regular basis. It has the advantage that the new image contains any software applications and user files that have been added to the computer since the last image capture and provides a form of backup.

If you have created an image for distribution to significant numbers of new computers, you can ensure your reference computer (as defined in Chapter 1) is kept fully up to date and create a fresh image whenever you want to configure a batch of client computers. You can also use MDT 2010 to manipulate images, as described in Lesson 2 of this chapter.

However, possibly the quickest and easiest way to manipulate images and install packages is to use DISM. DISM enables you to list Windows packages installed on a mounted offline image, get information about them, add and remove packages, and manipulate Windows features on a mounted offline image. You can also use DISM with an online operating system to perform the same operations, although if you want to ensure that an online image has all its critical and recommended updates installed, it is easier to use Microsoft Update or WSUS.

✔ **Quick Check**

- You want to display information about two patch files, Mypatch.msp and Otherpatch.msp, both in C:\Windows\Patches, in an image mounted in D:\Myimages\Mountedimage1. What command would you use?

Quick Check Answer

- `dism /image:d:\myimages\mountedimagei /check-apppatch`
  `/patchlocation:c:\windows\patches\mypatch.msp`
  `/patchlocation:c:\windows\patches\otherpatch.msp`

You can use DISM package-servicing commands with an offline-mounted image to install, remove, or update Windows packages provided as cabinet (.cab) or Windows Update Stand-alone Installer (.msu) files. Microsoft uses packages to distribute software updates, service packs, and language packs, and packages can also contain Windows features (optional features for the core operating system). You can use package-servicing commands to enable or disable Windows features both on an offline-mounted image and on a running Windows installation.

You can identify a package in your online image and install it on your mounted offline image. You can also disable and re-enable a feature.

For an offline image, you can use the following operating system package-servicing options:

```
dism /image:path_to_ image_directory [/get-packages | /get-packageinfo | /add-package |
/remove-package ] [/get-features | /get-featureinfo | /enable-feature | /disable-feature ]
```

For an online (running) operating system, you can use the following operating system package-servicing options:

```
dism /online [/Get-Packages | /Get-PackageInfo | /Add-Package | /Remove-Package]
[/Get-Features | /Get-FeatureInfo | /Enable-Feature | /Disable-Feature]
```

If you want to compare an online operating system with an offline-mounted image, you need to first list the packages and features installed in both images. You would enter commands similar to the following:

```
dism /online /get-packages > c:\onlinepackages.txt
dism /image:c:\mountedimages /get-packages > c:\offlinepackages.txt
dism /online /get-features > c:\onlinefeatures.txt
dism /image:c:\mountedimages /get-features > c:\offlinefeatures.txt
```

It is a good idea to redirect the output of each of these commands to a text file. This enables you to compare lists easily. Also, the names of some packages can be long and complex, and it is useful to be able to copy them and paste them into the command line.

> **NOTE** **FEATURE NAMES ARE CASE-SENSITIVE**
>
> DISM commands are not case-sensitive. However, feature names are.

Suppose, for example, you wanted to find out more about the file *Package_for_KB970419~31bf3856ad364e35~x86~~6.1.1.0*. You would enter a command similar to the following:

```
dism /online /get-packageinfo
/packagename:Package_for_KB970419~31bf3856ad364e35~x86~~6.1.1.0
```

The output of this command is shown in Figure 3-10.

You cannot use the */get-packageinfo* option to get information about .msu files and you can specify only .cab files.

Suppose that you have downloaded or created a file called Mypackage.cab and placed it in a folder called C:\Mypackages. If you decide you need to insert this package into the offline mounted image, you would enter a command similar to the following:

```
dism /image:c:\mountedimages /add-package /packagepath:c:\mypackages\mypackage.cab
```

DISM checks the applicability of each package. If the package is not applicable to the specified image, DISM generates an error message. If you want the command to process without checking the applicability of each package, you can append the */ignorecheck* parameter.

```
Administrator: Deployment Tools Command Prompt                              [ - ] [ □ ] [ X ]

C:\Program Files\Windows AIK\Tools\PETools>dism /online /get-packageinfo /packag
ename:Package_for_KB970419~31bf3856ad364e35~x86~~6.1.1.0

Deployment Image Servicing and Management tool
Version: 6.1.7100.0

Image Version: 6.1.7100.0

Package information:

Package Identity : Package_for_KB970419~31bf3856ad364e35~x86~~6.1.1.0
Applicable : Yes
Copyright : Microsoft Corporation
Company : Microsoft Corporation
Creation Time :
Description : Fix for KB970419
Install Client : WindowsUpdateAgent
Install Package Name : update.mum
Install Time :
Last Update Time :
Name : default
Product Name : Package_for_KB970419
Product Version :
Release Type : Update
Restart Required : Possible
Support Information : http://support.microsoft.com/?kbid=970419
State : Not Present

Custom Properties:

<No custom properties found>

Features listing for package : Package_for_KB970419~31bf3856ad364e35~x86~~6.1.1.
0

<No features found for this package>

The operation completed successfully.

C:\Program Files\Windows AIK\Tools\PETools>
```

FIGURE 3-10 Information about an online package

You cannot remove an .msu file you have added to an image, but you can remove a .cab file by using the */remove-package* option. You can use the */get-packages* option to discover the package name as it is listed in the image and then use the */packagename* parameter in the command to identify it. Alternatively, you can use the */packagepath* parameter and specify the path to the source package you added; for example:

```
dism /image:c:\mountedimages /remove-package /packagepath:c:\mypackages\mypackage.cab
```

EXAM TIP

Remember that when you change an offline-mounted image by adding a package, removing a package, and so on you need to save the changes to the original source image by using the DISM */commit-wim* option.

The DISM options to manipulate and manage features are very similar to those that you use to work with packages. For example, to get information about the feature Chess in a running operating system, you would use the following command:

```
dism /online /get-featureinfo /featurename:Chess
```

If you want, you can use the */packagename* and */packagepath* parameters to find a specific feature in a package. You can enable or disable a specific feature in an image by using the */enable-feature* and */disable-feature* options, for example:

```
dism /image:c:\mountedimages /disable-feature /featurename:Minesweeper
```

Package Installation Considerations

When you install a package in an offline image, the package state becomes "install pending," and the package is installed when the image is booted and pending online actions are processed. If subsequent actions are requested, they cannot be processed until the previous pending online actions complete. If a package is in the "installed pending" state and you stage the package, the package state is set to "uninstall pending" because the package must be uninstalled before it can be staged.

Some packages require other packages to be installed first. If there are dependency requirements, you should use an answer file to install the necessary packages. By passing an answer file to DISM, you can install multiple packages in the correct order. Microsoft recommends the use of an answer file for installing multiple packages. Packages are installed in the order that they are listed in the command line, which in turn can be generated in an answer file.

When you use DISM to list the feature packages in a Windows PE image, the packages will always be listed as pending even when the servicing operation was successful. This is by design, and you do not need to take any further action.

Configuring International Settings in an Image

You can use the DISM tool to manage international settings in a Windows 7 (or a Windows PE) image. You can also query existing settings in an offline or an online image.

You can use the following international servicing options on an offline-mounted image:

```
dism /image:path_to_offline_image_directory [/get-intl] [/set-uilang |
/set-uilangfallback | /set-syslocale | /Set-UserLocale | /Set-InputLocale | /Set-AllIntl
| /Set-Timezone | /Set-SKUIntlDefaults | /Set-LayeredDriver] [/Gen-Langini |
/Set-SetupUILang | /Distribution]
```

You can use the following command on a running operating system:

```
dism /online /get-intl
```

This is the only international servicing option you can apply to a running operating system. Its output is shown in Figure 3-11.

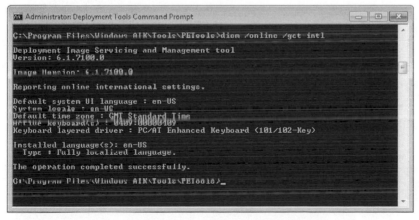

FIGURE 3-11 International settings for an online operating system

If you use the /get-intl option with an offline-mounted image and specify the /distribution parameter, information about international settings and languages in the distribution share is displayed. Lesson 2 of this chapter discusses the distribution share.

If the language specified by *the /set-uilang* option is not installed in the Windows image, the command will fail. A fallback default language is required only when the language specified by the /set-uilang option is a partially localized language (for example, Ukrainian or Arabic).

The /set-syslocale option sets the language for non-Unicode programs (also called the system locale) and the font settings. You specify the name of the language and locale to set as the default language, for example, en-US. The /set-userlocale option configures a per-user setting that determines the default sort order and the default settings for formatting dates, times, currency, and numbers (for example, fr-FR).

 **Quick Check**

- You want more information about the package *Package_for_KB654321~ 22cf8952ad824e22~x86~~6.1.0.0* in a WIM image currently mounted in the folder C:\MountedImages. What command would you use?

Quick Check Answer

- dism /image:c:\mountedimages /get-packageinfo /packagename:Package_for_KB654321~22cf8952ad824e22~x86~~6.1.0.0

The /set-inputlocale option sets the input locale and keyboard layout. For example, if you specify en-US as the local name, the option also sets the default keyboard layout defined for this locale. If you want to activate multiple keyboards in a single image, you can specify more than one keyboard layout by using semicolons as separators. The first value specifies the default keyboard. For example if you want to include the U.S. and U.K. keyboards in an image and use the U.K. layout as a default, you would enter a command similar to the following:

```
dism /image:c:\mountedimages /set-inputlocale:0409:00000409;0410:00010410
```

Figure 3-12 shows the output from this command.

FIGURE 3-12 Specifying multiple keyboard layouts

If your image needs to include a keyboard driver for Japanese or Korean keyboards, you can use the /set-layereddriver option. This option takes an argument of 1 through 6 as follows:

1. PC/AT Enhanced Keyboard (101/102-Key)

2. Korean PC/AT 101-Key Compatible Keyboard/MS Natural Keyboard (Type 1)

3. Korean PC/AT 101-Key Compatible Keyboard/MS Natural Keyboard (Type 2)

4. Korean PC/AT 101-Key Compatible Keyboard/MS Natural Keyboard (Type 3)

5. Korean Keyboard (103/106 Key)

6. Japanese Keyboard (106/109 Key)

You can use the /set-allintl option to set the user interface (UI) language, system locale, user locale, and input locale to the same value, for example, en-US. If you use the /set-allintl option with any of the options that specify the individual language or locales, the individual settings take precedence.

You can also use the /set-skuintldefaults option to set an image's default system UI language, language for non-Unicode programs, standards and formats language, input locale, keyboard layout, and time zone values to the Windows 7 default value specified by a language name argument, such as en-US. Note that the /set-skuintldefaults option does not change the keyboard driver for Japanese and Korean keyboards. You use the /set-layereddriver option to specify this.

You can use the /set-timezone option to specify the default time zone. If you use this option, DISM verifies that the specified time-zone string is valid for the image. The name of the time zone must exactly match the name of the time zone settings in the registry in the HKLM\SOFTWARE\Microsoft\Windows NT\CurrentVersion\TimeZones\ registry key. If you add a custom time zone to your computer, you can specify that custom time-zone string.

> **NOTE** **THE Tzutil COMMAND-LINE TOOL**
>
> On a computer running Windows 7, you can use the Tzutil command-line tool to list the time zone for that computer. The Tzutil tool is installed by default on Windows 7 and is not part of the Windows AIK.

Managing Windows Editions

Windows 7 edition packages for each potential target edition are staged within a Windows 7 Install.wim image on Windows 7 installation media. This is referred to as an edition-family image. Because the target editions are staged, you can service a single mounted image and apply the updates as appropriate to each edition in the image. This reduces the number of images you have to manage. However, it could increase the factory time or user time spent in the specialize configuration pass.

You can use the Windows edition-servicing commands to change one edition of Windows 7 to a higher edition within the same edition family. When you upgrade an offline image, you do not require a product key. If you change an online image to a higher edition, you can add the product key using one of the following methods:

- Enter the product key during the out-of-box experience (OOBE) pass.
- Use an unattended answer file to enter the product key during the specialize configuration pass.
- Use DISM and the Windows edition-servicing command-line option */set-productkey* after you configure the edition offline.

You can use the following edition-servicing options on an offline image to list editions or to change a Windows image to a higher edition:

```
dism /image:path_to_ image_directory [/get-currentedition | /get-targeteditions |
/set-edition | /set-productkey]
```

On a running Windows 7 operating system, the following edition-servicing options are available:

```
dism /online [/get-currentedition | /get-targeteditions]
```

Because this book is written for the Windows 7 installation image and product code on the installation media supplied, you will not be able to upgrade the mounted image you generated and placed on a bootable VHD and then subsequently mounted. The following commands entered on the online image or the installed image that you mount in the practice session exercises later in this lesson identify the online and mounted image Windows 7 editions:

```
dism /online /get-currentedition
dism /image:c:\mountedimages / get-currentedition
```

Similarly you cannot upgrade your current edition to a target edition. As shown in Figure 3-13, the following command should tell you just that:

```
dism /online /get-targeteditions
```

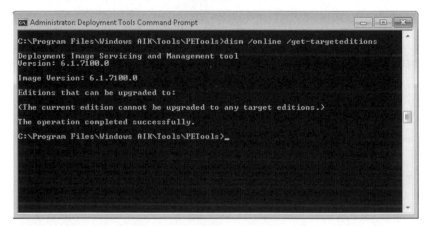

FIGURE 3-13 No target editions are available.

If a target edition is available, you can use the /set-edition option without the /productkey option to change an offline Windows image to a higher edition. Use /get-targeteditions to discover the edition ID. To change a running operating system to a higher edition, you can use the /set-edition option with the /productkey option, as in the following command:

```
dism /online /set-edition:Ultimate /productkey:12345-67890-12345-67890-12345
```

Servicing Windows PE Images

You can mount a Windows PE image and add or remove packages, drivers, and language packs in the same way as you would for any other Windows 7 image. DISM also provides options specific to a Windows PE image. You can use these options to prepare the Windows PE environment, enable profiling, list packages, and prepare the Windows PE image for deployment.

For example, if you use DISM or ImageX to mount a Windows PE image in the folder C:\MountedPEImage, the options specific to Windows PE are as follows:

```
dism /image:c:\mountedpeimage [/get-pesettings | /get-profiling | /get-scratchspace |
/get-targetpath | /set-scratchspace: | /set-targetpath : | /enable-profiling |
/disable-profiling | /apply-profiles path_to_myprofile.txt]
```

> **NOTE DISM WINDOWS PE OPTIONS APPLY ONLY TO OFFLINE-MOUNTED IMAGES**
> You cannot use DISM Windows PE options to manage an online, running version of Windows PE. You must specify a mounted Windows PE image using the /image: path_to_image_directory option.

You can obtain a list of PE settings in a mounted Windows PE image by entering a command similar to the following:

```
dism /image:c:\mountedpeimage /get-pesettings
```

You can discover whether the Windows PE profiling tool is enabled or disabled by entering a command similar to the following:

```
dism /image:c:\mountedpeimage /get-profiling
```

If you need to find out the amount of writeable space available on a Windows PE system volume when booted in RAMdisk mode, known as the Windows PE system volume scratch space, you can enter a command similar to the following:

```
dism /image:c:\mountedpeimage /get-scratchspace
```

Similarly, if you need to know the path to the root of the Windows PE image at boot time, known as the target path, you can enter a command similar to the following:

```
dism /image:c:\mountedpeimage /get-targetpath
```

You can set the scratch space and the target path by using commands similar to the following:

```
dism /image:c:\mountedpeimage /set-scratchspace:256
dism /image:c:\mountedpeimage /set-targetpath:D:\WinPEboot
```

Scratch space is specified in megabytes. Valid values are 32, 64, 128, 256, and 512. In hard disk boot scenarios, the target path defines the location of the Windows PE image on the disk. The path must be at least 3 characters and no longer than 32 characters. It must have a volume designation (C:\, D:\, and so on) and it must not contain any blank spaces.

File logging (or profiling) lets you create your own profiles in Windows PE 3.0 or later. By default, profiling is disabled. You can enable it, or disable it if previously enabled, by entering commands similar to the following:

```
dism /image:c:\mountedpeimage /enable-profiling
dism /image:c:\mountedpeimage /disable-profiling
```

When you create one or more profiles, each is stored in its own folder and identified in the file Profile.txt. You can remove any files from a Windows PE image that are not part of the custom profiles and check the custom profile against the core profile to ensure that custom application files and boot-critical files are not deleted, by entering a command similar to the following:

```
dism /image:c:\mountedpeimage /apply-profiles:c:\peprofiles\profile01\profile.txt,
c:\peprofiles\profile02\profile.txt
```

The paths to one or more profile.txt files are included in the command as a comma-separated list.

 Quick Check

1. You want to obtain a list of PE settings in a mounted Windows PE image in the folder C:\Mypeimage. What command do you enter in the elevated Deployment Tools command prompt?

2. You need to determine the amount of Windows PE system volume scratch space available on a Windows PE system volume in a mounted Windows PE image in the folder C:\Mypeimage when booted in RAMdisk mode. What command do you enter in the elevated Deployment Tools command prompt?

Quick Check Answers

1. `dism /image:c:\mypeimage /get-pesettings`

2. `dism /image:c:\ mypeimage /get-targetpath`

Unattended Servicing Command-Line Options

You can use DISM to apply an Unattend.xml answer file to an image. Typically, you would use this feature when you are installing multiple packages to the image. As stated previously in this lesson, some packages require other packages to be installed first. Microsoft recommends that the best way of ensuring the correct installation order is to use an answer file. If you use DISM to apply an Unattend.xml answer file to an image, the unattended settings in the offline Servicing configuration pass (previously described in Chapter 2) are applied to the Windows image.

The following servicing options are available to apply an Unattend.xml answer file to a offline Windows image:

```
dism /image:path_to_ image_directory /apply-unattend:path_to_unattend.xml
```

The following command applies an Unattend.xml answer file to a running operating system:

```
dism /online /apply-unattend:path_to_unattend.xml
```

For example, if the Unattend.xml file is located in C:\Windows\Panther, you can apply it to an offline-mounted image in C:\Mountedimages by entering the following command:

```
dism /image:c:\mountedimages /apply-unattend:c:\windows\panther\unattend.xml
```

Figure 3-14 shows the output from this command. It tells you the answer file has been applied but gives no additional information.

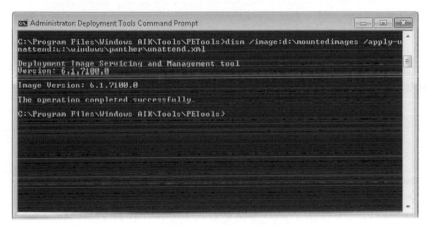

FIGURE 3-14 Applying an answer file to an offline-mounted image

Using Answer Files with Windows Images

The ability to associate an Unattend.xml answer file to an image provides a powerful tool to implement and configure image deployment, and to determine actions that can be taken if deployment fails or after deployment succeeds.

As discussed in Chapter 2, an answer file is an Extensible Markup Language (XML) file that contains setting definitions and values to use during Windows Setup. You specify Setup options in an answer file, including how to partition disks, the location of the Windows image to install, the product key to apply, and other custom Windows Setup settings. You can also specify values such as names of user accounts, display settings, and Windows Internet Explorer favorites. The answer file is typically called Autounattend.xml and is created using Windows System Image Manager (Windows SIM), as described in Chapter 2. If you want to add an additional answer file to install applications or specify the order in which packages are installed, you would typically use the file name Unattend.xml. When Windows SIM opens a Windows image file or catalog file, all of the configurable features and packages inside that image are displayed in the Windows Image pane. You can then add features and settings to the answer file.

 Quick Check

- Your offline-mounted WIMimage file is in C:\Images\Mounted. An unattend answer file that you want to associate with this image has the file path C:\Answerfiles\Unattend\Unattend.hml. What command associates the answer file with the image?

Quick Check Answer

- `dism /image:c:\images\mounted /apply-unattend:c:\answerfiles\unattend\unattend.hml`

Chapter 2 described how Windows SIM displays the properties and settings of a selected feature or package in its Properties pane. You can manage the feature settings for each configuration pass in this Properties pane. In the case of packages, editable Windows feature selections are displayed. Settings that are not available for each feature or package appear dimmed. Settings that have been edited appear in bold. Feature settings let you configure the aspects of each feature in a Windows 7 installation during unattended setup. For example, the Internet Explorer feature setting Home_Page can be configured to open to a particular URL by configuring the default value of the setting.

Feature properties are nonconfigurable attributes of the feature. Feature properties display differently when the feature is added to the currently open answer file. Feature IDs uniquely identify the feature of the operating system to which the settings belong. The ID contains the name, version, architecture, and so on for the feature selected in the Windows Image pane or Answer File pane. For example, the Language ID specifies the language code and the Name ID specifies the name of the feature or package. Package properties are nonconfigurable package attributes. For example, the ID Attribute package property specifies the identifier for the package in the following format: ProcessorArchitecture_Version_Language_PublicKeyToken_VersionScope.

Package settings are configurable attributes of a package placed in the Answer File pane, where you can edit them; for example, the Action package setting defines the action to be performed on the package. Possible actions are Install, Configure, Remove, or Stage.

Settings are sometimes organized into groups called list items. List items specify one or more values for a list item type. A list item type may include one or more feature settings. For example, you can create multiple favorites links by using the Favorite Item setting for Internet Explorer. Each list item must have a unique identifier, which is known as the key for that specific list item. If you use Windows SIM to manage list items, this enables you to add or delete a list item or modify its properties.

You can extend this concept to automate post-installation tasks. You can edit the answer file with a text editor in addition to Windows SIM. For example, if you are accustomed to writing batch files to automate application installation, you can add the same code to an answer file. Windows SIM creates a binary catalog file that lists all the settings in a Windows image.

You can create code manually or use Windows SIM to create a distribution that contains third-party drivers, applications, and Microsoft packages such as security bulletins. To create a distribution share, you must first create a distribution-share folder manually or by using Windows SIM. A *distribution share* is a shared Windows folder that contains the following subfolders:

- OEM folders
- Packages
- Out-of-box drivers
- LangPacks

Creating Answer Files

Microsoft recommends the use of Windows SIM to create unattend answer files, although you can also edit and create such files with a text editor such as Microsoft Notepad. If you use a manually authored answer file, you must validate the answer file in Windows SIM to verify that the answer file works. Answer files from Windows XP, Windows Server 2008, or Windows Vista do not work in Windows 7.

In general, it is best to expand to the lowest level of a feature and select only those elements that you intend to set. If you want to accept a default value, there is no need to include the element unless it is a required element. When creating answer files, you need to understand what happens during each configuration pass. Chapter 2 described configuration passes.

> **MORE INFO   CONFIGURATION PASSES**
>
> For more information about how configuration passes work, see *http://technet.microsoft.com/en-us/library/dd744341(WS.10).aspx*.

When adding data, such as additional drivers or applications, take care that you do not overwrite Windows System files. Overwriting system files can corrupt your computer's operating system.

> **MORE INFO   ADDING APPLICATIONS, DRIVERS, PACKAGES, FILES, AND FOLDERS**
>
> For more information about adding applications, drivers, packages, files, and folders, see *http://technet.microsoft.com/en-us/library/dd744568(WS.10).aspx.*

Using Multiple Answer Files

You can use multiple second answer files (Unattend.xml) to create different custom images. For example, you could create a generic answer file that is used for each of your systems and then apply a second answer file during audit mode for changing disk configurations, drivers, or applications. To do this, you would use the Sysprep command (described in Chapter 2) with the */unattend:answerfile* option. You can run this command manually during audit mode or you can add a custom command.

> **MORE INFO   ADDING CUSTOM COMMANDS AND SCRIPTS**
>
> For more information about adding custom commands and scripts, see *http://technet.microsoft .com/en-us/library/dd744393(WS.10).aspx.*

PRACTICE   Mounting an Offline Image and Installing Language Packs

In this practice, you use both ImageX and DISM to mount an image. You also practice unmounting an image. You then apply language packs to a mounted image.

EXERCISE 1   Mounting, Unmounting, and Remounting an Image

In this exercise, you use the ImageX tool to mount the system image Myimage.wim that you installed on the VHD to which you allocated drive letter W:. You mount the image in the folder C:\Mountedimages. You then unmount the folder. Finally, you use DISM to mount the image to the folder D:\Mountedimages. Note that it is not essential to create a different folder to hold the second mounted image. However, if you do not, it is a good idea to delete and re-create the original folder because DISM sometimes returns an error even though the image has been unmounted from the folder. Proceed as follows:

1. Log on to the Canberra computer with the Kim_Akers account.

2. Create a folder called C:\MountedImages. If this folder already exists, ensure that it is empty.

3. On the Start menu, right-click Computer and choose Manage. Select Disk Management. If the W: disk does not appear in the Volume list, right-click Computer

Management and choose Attach VHD. Navigate to the Myvhd.vhd file in the C:\VHDs folder, as shown in Figure 3-15, and click OK. Drive W: should then appear. If necessary, close the AutoPlay dialog box.

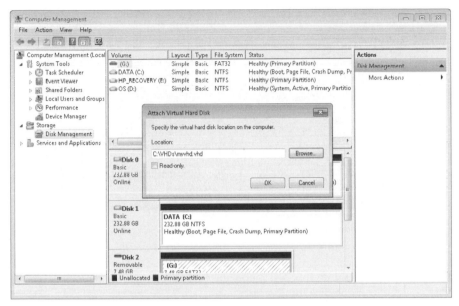

FIGURE 3-15 Attach the VHD if it does not appear in Computer Management.

4. On the Start menu, click All Programs, click Microsoft Windows AIK, right-click Deployment Tools Command Prompt, and choose Run As Administrator.

5. In the Deployment Tools command prompt, enter the command: **imagex /mountrw w:\myimage.wim 1 c:\mountedimages.** Figure 3-16 shows the output from this command.

FIGURE 3-16 Using ImageX to mount a WIM image

6. If you want, you can unmount the image and then use the DISM tool to mount it in a different folder. To unmount the tool, enter the command: **imagex /unmount c:\mountedimages.** Figure 3-17 shows the output from this command.

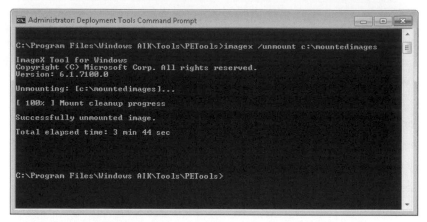

FIGURE 3-17 Unmounting an image

7. Create a folder called D:\MountedImages. If you do not have a second hard disk, you can use the C:\MountedImages folder, but you might need to delete and re-create it if DISM returns an error.

8. Mount the image with the DISM tool by entering the command: **dism /mount-wim /wimfile:w:\myimage.wim /index:1 /mountdir:d:\mymountedimages.**

9. Test the image is mounted correctly by entering the command **dism /get-mountedwiminfo.** The output from this command is shown in Figure 3-18. Note that the mounted image folder is not the same as that shown in Figure 3-4 earlier in this lesson.

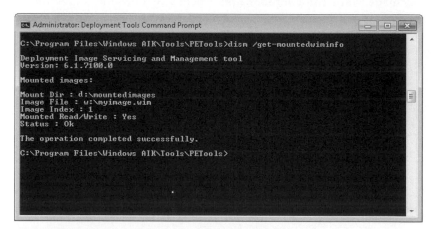

FIGURE 3-18 An image mounted in D:\Mountedimages

EXERCISE 2 Applying a Language Pack to a Mounted Image

In this exercise, you apply the en-US language pack to your mounted image. You might do this if, for example, you already had an image with the lp_fr FR language pack installed and wanted to be able to configure international settings and distribute the image to both French-speaking and English-speaking areas. Note that you can apply multiple language packs only to Windows 7 Ultimate or Enterprise images. You should consider this a generic procedure because it is the way you would apply all packages that are distributed as cabinet (.cab) files. You need to have completed Exercise 1 before attempting this exercise. Proceed as follows:

1. If necessary, log on to the Canberra computer with the Kim_Akers account.

2. If it does not already exist, create a folder called C:\Mypackages.

3. Navigate to C:\Program Files\Windows AIK\Tools\PETools\x86\WinPE_FPs\en-us.

4. Copy the lp_en-us cabinet file and save it in the C:\Mypackages folder.

5. Create a directory C:\Scratch. This will be used as the Scratch directory.

6. On the Start menu, click All Programs, click Microsoft Windows AIK, right-click Deployment Tools Command Prompt, and choose Run As Administrator.

7. Enter **dism /image:d:\mountedimages /scratchdir:c:\scratch /add-package /packagepath:c:\mypackages\lp_en-us.cab.** Figure 3-19 shows the output from this command.

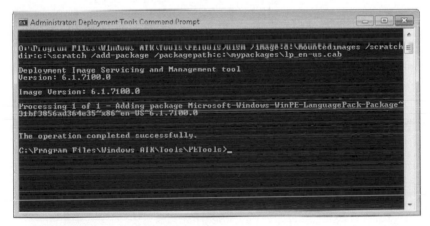

FIGURE 3-19 Adding a language pack

8. To commit your changes to the source image, enter: **dism /commit-wim /mountdir:d:\mountedimages.** If you want, unmount the image.

Lesson Summary

- You need to mount a writeable system image (WIM) file in a folder to service it. You can use the DISM or ImageX Windows AIK tools to mount an image.

- Very limited servicing options are available for an online running operating system, although you can use the DISM tool to discover information about the online image.

- You can use the DISM tool to add packages, drivers, and updates to a mounted image. You can obtain information about Windows Installer applications, application packages, and Windows features. You can disable and enable Windows features and display and configure international settings and Windows editions. You can apply unattended answer files to an image to implement hands-free installation and post-installation tasks. Finally, you can save the changes to the mounted image to the source image and unmount the image.

- You can use the DISM tool to mount and service Windows PE images.

Lesson Review

You can use the following questions to test your knowledge of the information in Lesson 1, "Managing a System Image Before Deployment." The questions are also available on the companion DVD if you prefer to review them in electronic form.

> **NOTE   ANSWERS**
>
> Answers to these questions and explanations of why each answer choice is correct or incorrect are located in the "Answers" section at the end of the book.

1. You have copied the system image Install.wim file from your Windows 7 installation media to the folder C:\Images. You have mounted the image with index value 5 (Windows 7 Ultimate) to the folder D:\Mount. You want to add third-party drivers that you have stored in C:\Drivers\Printer and C:\Drivers\Scanner to the mounted image. Which of the following DISM commands would you use? (Choose all that apply.)

   A. `dism /image:c:\images /add-driver /driver:c:\drivers /recurse`

   B. `dism /image:d:\mount /add-driver /driver:c:\drivers /recurse`

   C. `dism /image:c:\images /add-driver /driver:c:\drivers\printer /driver:c:\drivers\scanner`

   D. `dism /image:d:\mount /add-driver /driver:c:\drivers\printer /driver:c:\drivers\scanner`

2. You need to find out the amount of writeable space available on a Windows PE system volume when booted in RAMdisk mode. The PE image is mounted in the folder D:\PEMount. What command would you use?

   A. `dism /image:d:\pemount /get-scratchspace`

   B. `dism /image: d:\pemount /get-targetpath`

   C. `dism /image: d:\pemount /get-profiling`

   D. `dism /image: d:\pemount /enable-profiling`

3. Which of the following DISM options can you run against an online, running operating system?

   A. */set-syslocale*

   B. */set-userlocale*

   C. */set-inputlocale*

   D. */get-intl*

4. You have created an answer file called Unattend.xml in the C:\Textfiles\Answer folder. You want to apply it to an image mounted in the C:\Mount folder. What command would you use?

   A. `dism /image:c:\textfiles\answer /apply-unattend:c:\ mount \unattend.xml`

   B. `dism /image:c:\mount /apply-unattend:c:\textfiles\answer\unattend.xml`

   C. `dism /image:c:\mount /apply:c:\textfiles\answer\unattend.xml`

   D. `dism /image:c:\mount /apply-answer:c:\textfiles\answer\unattend.xml`

5. You want to obtain detailed information about all the Windows Installer (.msi) applications installed in the WIM image mounted in the C:\Mount folder. What command do you use?

   A. `dism /online /get-packageinfo`

   B. `dism /image:c:\mount /get-featureinfo`

   C. `dism /image:c:\mount /get-appinfo`

   D. `dism /image:c:\mount /get-apppatchinfo`

Lesson 2: Deploying Images

Deploying images to large numbers of computers is a vital task in the enterprise environment. If 100 new client computers are purchased, you want to be able to deploy your current operating system, drivers, language packs, and so on with no errors and little or no user intervention. If a new user joins and a single client workstation is purchased, you want to be able to connect it to the network and have the appropriate image efficiently deployed.

Unfortunately, however, nothing stays the same, and few things go out of date more quickly than system images. A new driver is released, and a new edition of the software that your organization relies on arrives. New updates seem to appear daily (although they tend to show up mostly on Tuesdays). Some of them are important security updates and if you deploy your image without them, your clients are at risk. The company introduces additional hardware, and it is not Plug and Play.

This lesson looks at how you deploy images over a network, how you deal with image updates, and how you deploy to clients, some of which can boot automatically on to the network and some cannot. It discusses the tools you have available to perform this important administrative function efficiently.

After this lesson, you will be able to:

- Use MDT to add updates, applications, and language packs to a disk image online and offline and keep WIM image files up to date.
- Create a deployment share to hold deployment images. Add deployment points and task sequences.
- Know the server tools such as WDS and SCCM 2007 that work with MDT 2010 or independently to deploy system images.
- Know the requirements for Lite Touch Installation (LTI) and Zero Touch Installation (ZTI).

Estimated lesson time: 50 minutes

Using the Microsoft Deployment Toolkit

Chapter 2 briefly introduced the Microsoft Windows Deployment Toolkit (MDT) 2010. This toolkit is the Microsoft solution accelerator for operating system and application deployment and presents a number of new features, including flexible driver management, optimized transaction processing, and access to distribution shares from any location. In an enterprise environment, you would use the MDT on imaging and deployment servers to implement the automatic deployment of Windows 7 (for example) on client computers.

MDT 2010 unifies the tools and processes that you need for both desktop and server deployment into a deployment console. It features a fourth-generation deployment accelerator that integrates with Microsoft deployment technologies to create a single path for image creation and automated installation. In other words, it makes the creation and deployment of a system image a lot easier. Microsoft states that MDT provides detailed guidance and job aids for every organized role involved with large-scale deployment projects. It offers unified tools and processes that you use for desktop and server deployment in a common deployment console and that reduce deployment time. The toolkit offers standardized desktop and server images, along with improved security and ongoing configuration management.

You can use MDT 2010 with the LTI method or it can be completely automated using ZTI. ZTI uses the Microsoft System Center Configuration Manager (SCCM) 2007 with the Operating System Deployment Feature Pack and also requires that a server running Microsoft SQL Server 2005 or SQL Server 2008 is available on the network. You can use LTI when software distribution tools are not in place to deploy to non–pre-execution environment (PXE)–compliant clients, although you need to use it with WDS to deploy to PXE-compliant clients. Although you install MDT 2010 on your Canberra computer in this lesson so you can investigate its features, it would be typically used on a deployment server with the WDS server role installed. Whatever deployment method you use, MDT 2010 requires that the Windows AIK is installed.

> **NOTE SYSTEMS MANAGEMENT SERVER**
>
> Unlike the previous MDT version (MDT 2008 Update 1), MDT 2010 cannot use Microsoft Systems Management Server (SMS) 2003 to implement ZTI.

Microsoft offers MDT 2010 in two versions to support Solution Accelerator feature installation on x64 or x86 hosts. The Quick Start Guide for Lite Touch Installation guide for MDT 2010 is available as a separate download for those who want to evaluate MDT 2010 quickly by viewing step-by-step instructions for using it to install Windows 7.

New Features in MDT 2010

MDT 2010 offers a number of new features that are supported for LTI-based deployment. ZTI-based deployment using SCCM 2007 was introduced fairly recently (by MDT 2008 Update 1) and is mostly unaltered except that ZTI can no longer be implemented by using SMS 2003.

The MDT 2010 includes the following new features:

- Support for Windows 7
- Support for Windows Server 2008 R2
- Support for Windows AIK version 2.0
- Support for Windows User State Migration Toolkit (USMT) version 4.0. Specifically, the following new features of USMT 4.0 are supported in LTI-based deployments:
  - Support for USMT 4.0 hardlink migration
  - Support for USMT 4.0 shadow copy
- Support for the DISM tool

- Support for Windows PE version 3.0

- Support for the Boot Configuration Data (BCD) management tool and the BCDEdit command-line utility

- Support for Windows 7 default disk partition configuration. In MDT 2010, the disk partition configuration for Windows 7 places the operating system on Disk 0, Partition 2, and the system partition on Disk 0, Partition 1.

> **MORE INFO**   **NEW MDT 2010 FEATURES**
>
> For more information about the new features MDT 2010 introduces, download the file What's New in MDT 2010 Guide.docx, as described in the practice later in this lesson, or use Deployment Workbench to access the Information Center.

MDT Program Folders

When you install MDT 2010, you create a number of subfolders in the MDT 2010 program folder %Sysvol%\Program Files\Microsoft Deployment Toolkit\ (typically C:\Program Files\ Microsoft Deployment Toolkit\). Table 3-3 describes these subfolders.

TABLE 3-3 MDT 2010 Program Folders

SUBFOLDER	DESCRIPTION
Bin	Holds the Deployment Workbench MMC snap-in and supporting files.
Control	Holds configuration data for Deployment Workbench. Typically, this folder is empty directly after installation.
Documentation	Holds documentation and job aids such as a splash screen for MDT 2010.
Downloads	Holds a feature list for features that Deployment Workbench downloads.
Management Pack	Holds management pack files, for example Microsoft.Deployment. Management.Pack.xml.
Samples	Holds sample task sequence scripts (for example, ZTICache.vbs) and Windows PE desktop background graphics.
SCCM	Holds task sequence templates and automation objects used during SCCM integration; for example, Deploy_SCCM_Scripts.vbs.
Scripts	Holds scripts that Deployment Workbench uses; for example ComponentCheck_scripts.vbs.
Templates	Holds template files that Deployment Workbench uses.

Using Deployment Workbench

When you have installed MDT 2010, you can start Deployment Workbench from the Microsoft Deployment Toolkit program suite. You will be using this tool extensively in this lesson to deploy a Windows 7 system image. This section gives an overview of the features the tool offers. Deployment Workbench gives you access to the following items:

- **Information Center** This lets you access MDT 2010 documentation, including the latest news about MDT 2010 and the features you require to use it.

- **Distribution Share** This gives you a checklist of tasks you need to perform to deploy an operating system image, as shown in Figure 3-20. You also use this tool to create a distribution directory, which is the second task on the list. You installed the Windows AIK in Chapter 2.

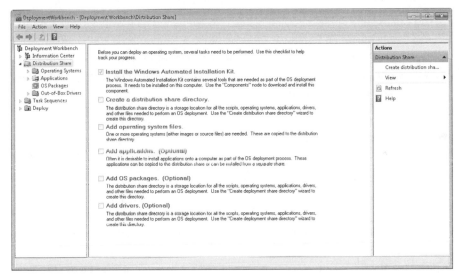

FIGURE 3-20 Task checklist

- **Task Sequences** This provides a list of task sequences in the details pane. To create a task sequence, right-click Task Sequences and then click New. To configure a task sequence, right-click it in the details pane and then click Properties.

- **Deploy** You can expand this item to see the Deployment Points and Database items. Click Deployment Points to see a list of deployment points in the details pane. To create a deployment point, right-click Deployment Points, and then click New. To configure a deployment point, right-click a deployment point in the details pane, and then click Properties. Click Database to edit the database.

> **CAUTION** **OPEN ONLY A SINGLE INSTANCE OF DEPLOYMENT WORKBENCH**
>
> Microsoft recommends that you open only a single instance of Deployment Workbench. Opening two or more instances can result in unpredictable behavior.

Choosing an Image Strategy

If you are distributing an image across an enterprise environment, your aim should be to create a standard configuration that is based on a common image for each version of an operating system. Organizations want to apply a common image to any computer in any region at any time, and then customize that image quickly to provide services to users.

Most organizations build and maintain many images. However, you can reduce the number of different images by making disciplined hardware purchases and by using advanced scripting techniques. You can utilize the software distribution infrastructure necessary to deploy applications and to keep your images updated.

You can use one of the following image types depending on whether you want to install only operating systems to large numbers of computers, whether you want to deploy applications, language packs, and other files at the same time as operating systems, or whether you are deploying an image to a VHD on a single computer for backup and failover purposes:

- Thick image
- Thin image
- Hybrid image

Thick images contain core applications, language packs, and other files in addition to the operating system. When you create a disk image that contains core applications and language packs, you need only a single step to deploy the disk image and core applications to the target computer, with language support for all target locales. Also, thick images can be less costly to develop, because they frequently do not require advanced scripting technique. You can use MDT 2010 to build thick images with little or no scripting. If you use thick images, core applications and language packs are available on first start.

The disadvantage of thick images is that updating a thick image with a new version of an application or language pack requires rebuilding, retesting, and redistributing the image. If thick images are built that include core applications and language packs, you need to install the core applications and language packs during the disk imaging process. You use thick images when you employ WIM files for backup and failover on bootable VHDs on individual computers running Windows 7 Enterprise or Ultimate.

A thin image carries a much lower cost to maintain and store. It contains few (if any) core applications or language packs. Applications and language packs are installed separately from the disk image. If you need to mitigate the network transfer time, you can use trickle-down technology such as Background Intelligent Transfer Service (BITS). Many software distribution infrastructures provide this facility.

The main disadvantage of thin images is that they can be more complex to develop. Deploying applications and language packs outside the disk image requires scripting and a software distribution infrastructure. If you use thin images, core applications and language packs are not available on first start. In some scenarios, this is regarded as a security risk.

If you choose to build thin images that do not include applications or language packs, your organization should have a systems management infrastructure such as SCCM 2007 in place to deploy applications and language packs. You should use this infrastructure to deploy applications and language packs after installing the thin image.

Hybrid images mix thin- and thick-image strategies. In a hybrid image, the disk image is configured to install applications and language packs on first run but automatically installs the applications and language packs from a network source. Hybrid images present most of the advantages of thin images, but they are not complex to develop and do not require a software distribution infrastructure. They do, however, require longer installation times.

You can choose to build a one-off thick image from a thin image by building a reference thin image. Then, you can add core applications and language packs, capture them, test them, and distribute a thick image based on the thin image. However, be wary of applications that are not compatible with the disk imaging process.

Hybrid images store applications and language packs on the network but include the commands to install them when you deploy the disk image. This process differs from installing the applications and language packs in the disk image because the image deployment process installations that would typically occur during the disk imaging process is deferred.

Managing and Distributing Images with MDT 2010

When you create an image on a distribution share using the MDT 2010 utility, you often need to add updates, language packs, and applications. You can do this both offline and online with the MDT 2010 tool.

Although you are unlikely to use a computer running a Windows 7 client operating system as a distribution server in an enterprise environment, you nevertheless can install the MDT 2010 tool and use it to create a deployment share, deployment points, and task sequences. You can use MDT 2010 running on a machine running Windows 7 on a small test network to install client operating systems. You might possibly also do this in a small workgroup environment, although Microsoft recommends the use of a server running Windows Server 2008 Foundation for this purpose.

MDT 2010 is a mechanism for managing and distributing WIM images. If you want to configure a Windows 7 operating system on a large number of client computers, you can obtain a WIM image (Install.wim) from the installation media. Depending on the type of computers in the environment and the hardware they contain, you may need to add device drivers from hardware vendors to make the system fully functional. You also need to add updates to the image.

You can distribute the operating system image to client computers using either the LTI or the ZTI method. The latter method requires that you have SCCM 2007 along with SQL Server 2005 or SQL Server 2008 available on your network.

As described in Chapter 2, you can install Windows 7 on a reference computer, together with any software you want to include as part of the image, and use the Sysprep tool to prepare the computer for imaging. You can then boot into Windows PE and use the ImageX Windows AIK tool to generate a WIM image file that you can place in the MDT distribution share.

> **NOTE TWO TYPES OF REFERENCE COMPUTER**
>
> If you are using a thin-image approach and using Deployment Workbench to add updates, drivers, packages, language packs, and applications to an operating system image copied from installation media, you should always deploy the resulting image to a single client computer and test it thoroughly before deploying to a number of clients. The single client computer used for testing is often termed the *reference computer*. Distinguish between a reference computer that you install and configure manually and test before you capture its image (as described in Chapter 2) and a reference computer that you install from an image that you have configured in MDT 2010 for testing purposes.

 Quick Check
  - You have installed Windows AIK and MDT 2010. What additional software tools do you require to implement ZTI?

Quick Check Answer
  - SCCM 2007 and SQL Server.

Creating a Distribution Share

Your first step in using MDT 2010 to deploy a system image is to create a distribution share to hold that image. You do this in the practice later in this lesson, but a high-level procedure is described here. The distribution share contains all the information and settings that MDT 2010 uses. To create a new distribution share, carry out the following procedure:

1. Open Deployment Workbench, right-click Distribution Share, and click Create Distribution Share Directory.

2. In the Specify Directory page of the Create Distribution Share Wizard, click Create A New Distribution Share.

3. Type the location for the distribution share on the local system in the Path For New Distribution Share Directory text box, and then click Finish.

You can use Deployment Workbench to configure the distribution share to implement the following tasks:

- Add, remove, and configure operating systems.
- Add, remove, and configure applications.
- Add, remove, and configure operating system packages, including updates and language packs.
- Add, remove, and configure out-of-box device drivers.

The source files for these tasks are stored in the distribution share folder and are associated with task sequences during the configuration process. Deployment Workbench stores metadata about operating systems, applications, operating system packages, and out-of-box device drivers in the distribution share's Control subfolder.

Adding an Operating System Image

If you have created a custom image either by imaging a reference computer, as described in Chapter 2, or by imaging a client workstation running Windows 7 Enterprise or Ultimate to place that image on bootable VHD for failover, you can add that operating system image to the distribution share on a computer running MDT 2010. This is typically a thick-image approach because your reference image will contain updates, applications, drivers, and packages (including language packs). You can also add WDS images from WDS servers to the distribution share.

However, possibly the most typical scenario is that you add an image and all its associated installation files from installation media. You do this in the practice later in this lesson. Typically, this gives you flexibility because a single Install.wim file can contain images for several Windows 7 editions. It is a thin-image approach because images on the installation media will not include any third-party drivers, Windows Installer files, mission-critical applications, or additional language packs. Most significantly, critical security packs issued since the installation image was created will not be present. Applying such images to multiple client computers and bringing these computers online represents a security risk unless at least critical security updates are added to the image before deployment.

To deploy images using MDT 2010, you need to specify the source directory in which the WIM file resides. The New OS Wizard moves the file to the distribution share. To add an operating system image to the distribution share, perform the following high-level procedure:

1. In the Deployment Workbench console tree, expand Distribution Share, right-click Operating Systems, and click New (or click Operating Systems and click New in the Actions Pane). This starts the New OS Wizard.

2. On the OS Type page, select the type of image (custom, installation files, or WDS) that you want to add.

3. Select an image source and then specify a target folder that is a subfolder of the distribution share. In the case of custom images, you have the option of moving the files to the distribution share instead of copying them.

Adding Device Drivers

After the operating system has been added to Deployment Workbench, add any required device drivers. During operating system deployment, these drivers are added to Windows PE and the target computers and deployed with Windows 7. The New Driver Wizard in Deployment Workbench copies the device driver files to the distribution share. The high-level procedure for adding out-of-box (third-party) device drivers is as follows:

1. In Deployment Workbench, expand Distribution Share, click Out Of Box Drivers, and click New in the Actions pane.

2. In the New Driver Wizard, browse or type the path to the folder in which the drivers you want to add are stored. Figure 3-21 shows a path to a folder that holds drivers on the Canberra computer, but in practice, you would create a folder to hold specific third-party drivers that you want to install.

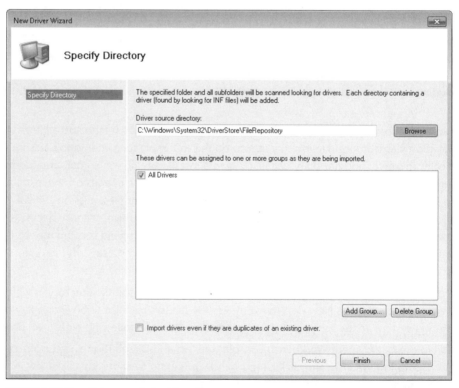

FIGURE 3-21 Specifying a path to driver files

3. Click Add Group and add a driver group, for example, Windows 7. Take a note of the name of this group—you need this information to create bootable LTI media.

4. Select the check box for the new driver group.

5. If you want, you can select Import Drivers Even If They Are Duplicates Of An Existing Driver.

6. Click Install.

The out-of-box device drivers install in subfolders of the C:\Distribution\Out-Of-Box Drivers folder.

Configuring Task Sequences

You use task sequences to add updates, language packs and other packages, and applications to an image. You also specify a task sequence that binds operating system source files with a configuration. The system source files include the following:

- **Operating system**   You can choose an operating system or custom image to use for the build.

- **Unattended Setup answer file (Unattend.xml or Autounattend.xml)**   You can create an answer file that describes how to install and configure Windows 7 on the target computer. For example, the answer file can contain a product key, organization name, and information necessary to join the computer to a domain. Chapter 2 described how you use Windows SIM to create unattended answer files.

- **Task sequence**   Each build has a default task sequence for hands-free installation.

Creating and Editing a Task Sequence

The Task Sequencer runs the task sequence in the order specified. Each task in the sequence is a step, and steps can be organized into groups and subgroups. When creating a task sequence in Deployment Workbench, the tool creates a default task sequence. You can edit tasks and groups. You can also import task sequences created by other software packages, for example, SCCM 2007.

Task sequences contain the following item types:

- **Tasks**   Within a task sequence, tasks are commands that the Task Sequencer runs during the sequence, such as partitioning the disk, capturing user state, and installing the operating system. In the default task sequence, most tasks are commands that run scripts.

- **Groups**   The task sequence can be organized into groups, which are folders that contain subgroups and tasks. For example, the default task sequence puts tasks in groups by phase and deployment type. Tasks and groups (including the groups and tasks they contain) can be filtered based on specified conditions. Groups are useful for filtering because an entire collection of tasks can be run based upon a condition such as the deployment phase or type of deployment.

You create task sequences by using the Task Sequence Editor in Deployment Workbench. Each sequence consists of a series of steps designed to complete a specific task. Task sequences can operate across a computer restart and typically are configured to automate tasks on a computer without user intervention. Task sequence steps can be added to a task sequence group, which help keep similar task sequence steps together for better organization and error control.

Task sequence steps can use utilities and scripts provided with MDT 2010 or written as custom solutions for a particular task. You use the Task Sequence Editor to specify the task sequence groups, task sequence steps, and the valid properties and options to use to configure each part of the image preparation and deployment process. You need to provide the following information for each task sequence group and step:

- **Name** Names the task sequence group or step
- **Description** Describes the purpose of the task sequence group or step and provides information regarding its customization
- **Properties** Specifies the configuration properties for the task sequence group or step and defines how the task is performed
- **Options** Indicates the configuration options that can be specified for the task sequence group or step, when the task is performed, and successful exit conditions

> **NOTE** **ADDITIONAL TASK SEQUENCE STEP TYPES**
>
> Additional task sequence step types and conditional statements typically are available if you configure task sequences using SCCM 2007.

The high-level procedure to create a task sequence using MDT 2010 is as follows:

1. In Deployment Workbench, select Task Sequences and then click New in the Actions pane. In the General Settings page of the New Task Sequence Wizard, specify the Task Sequence ID and Task Sequence name. If you want, add comments.

2. On the Select Template page, select a task sequence template from the list shown in Figure 3-22.

3. On the Select OS page, select an operating system to be associated with the task sequence. Your choice is limited to the operating systems contained in the WIM image that you added to the deployment share.

4. You can specify the product key on the Specify Product Key page, or you can choose to provide this information at the time of deployment.

5. On the OS Settings page, provide your full name, your organization, and your organization's Internet Explorer home page.

6. At this point, you can choose to supply and confirm an administrator password on the Admin Password page or to supply this information later at deployment time.

7. Click Finish to create the task sequence. The task sequence appears in Deployment Workbench, as shown in Figure 3-23.

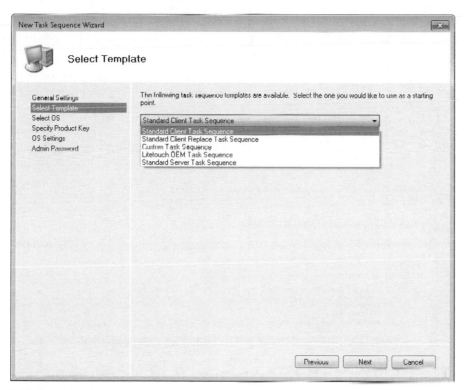

FIGURE 3-22 Available templates

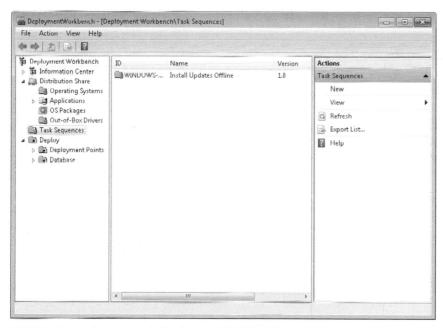

FIGURE 3-23 A task sequence in Deployment Workbench

8. To edit the task sequence, right-click it and choose Properties. On the General tab, you can change settings such as the sequence name. You can also specify to which client operating system the task sequence can be applied, as shown in Figure 3-24.

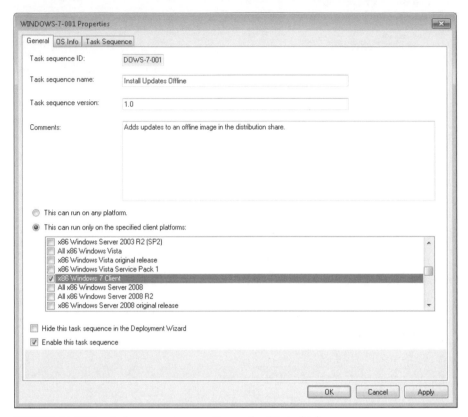

FIGURE 3-24 Editing task sequence properties on the General tab

9. The Task Sequence tab for a new task sequence shows the template chosen for that task sequence. Figure 3-25 shows the Standard Client Task Sequence template. You can edit this (typically by deleting unwanted tasks) so your new task sequence carries out the required tasks. The Options tab on the Task Sequence tab lets you disable the step, set a Continue On Error condition, or, in some cases, specify a Success Code.

> **MORE INFO**   **TASK SEQUENCE EDITOR**
>
> For more information about the Task Sequence Editor, see *Operating System Deployment: Task Sequence Editor* at *http://technet.microsoft.com/en-us/library/bb680396.aspx.*

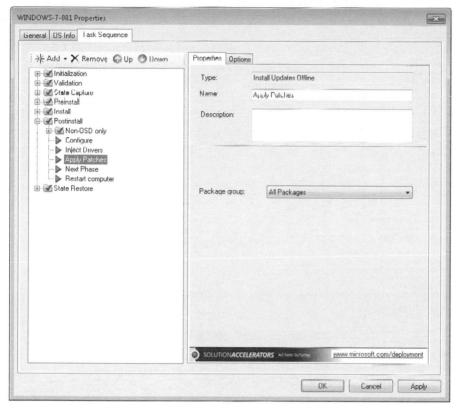

FIGURE 3-25 The Standard Client Task Sequence template

Creating a Task Sequence to Deploy Windows 7 to VHD

Sometimes you might want to deploy a Windows 7 image to boot from VHD on your client computers. You might have users whose computers currently run Windows Vista and who want to have the option of a dual boot so they can try Windows 7 before committing to it. One option is to create virtual machines running Windows 7 on the client computers. Doing this through centralized deployment, however, is not straightforward.

A second alternative is to use MDT 2010 to deploy Windows 7 to a bootable VHD on each client computer. Users can then choose to boot into Windows Vista or boot from VHD into Windows 7. This is an attractive option for client computers that have only a single hard disk because it avoids having to repartition the drive for Windows 7 while keeping the original operating systems intact.

By default, MDT 2010 deploys Windows 7 to Disk 0 Partition 1. To change this behavior so that MDT 2010 deploys to a VHD and leaves the existing operating system intact, you need to create a standard Task Sequence that installs Windows 7 and then modify it as follows:

1. In the Task Sequence tab of the Task Sequence Properties box, expand Preinstall, Expand New Computer Only, and click Format And Partition Disk.

2. Disable this step, as shown in Figure 3-26.

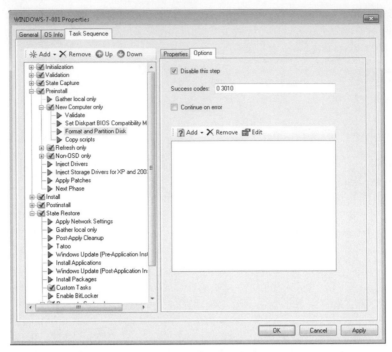

FIGURE 3-26 Disabling the Format And Partition Disk step

3. Click Add, click General, and click Set Task Sequence Variable. Configure the Task Sequence Variable BootVHDLocation, as shown in Figure 3-27.

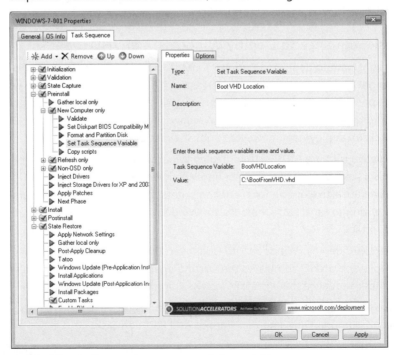

FIGURE 3-27 Configuring the BootVHDLocation variable

4. Click Add, click General, and click Set Run Command Live. Configure the Task Sequence Variable BootVHDSize, as shown in Figure 3-28. Ensure that there is enough space on the drive (20 GB) because the VHD may grow to this size.

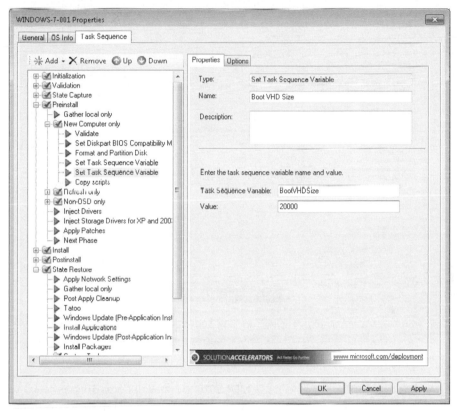

FIGURE 3-28 Configuring the size of the VHD

5. Click Add, click General, and click Set Task Sequence Variable. Name the variable Set Up VHD. Insert the Run Command Line step cscript.exe "%SCRIPTROOT%\ZTIDiskPartVHD .wsf", as shown in Figure 3-29.

6. Click Apply.

Using this Task Sequence, Windows 7 is deployed to a VHD rather than to an internal hard disk.

Adding Updates

When developing an image, you should ensure that all critical security updates are included in the image. You can use different approaches to perform these updates. Microsoft recommends that if possible, you should add updates offline. The following options are available (provided a distribution share exists):

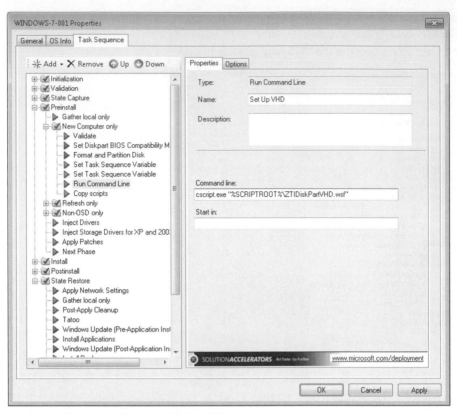

FIGURE 3-29 Inserting a Run command

- **Add updates offline**   You can use MDT 2010 to install updates offline using a task sequence. In the Deployment Workbench Task Sequence Editor, select the Install Updates Offline task. This option is available only if SCCM 2007 is available on your network.

- **Add updates online**   You can use MDT 2010 to install updates online using a task sequence. In the Deployment Workbench Task Sequence Editor, select the Install Updates Online task. As with the previous option, SCCM 2007 needs to be available on your network.

- **Add updates to the master image**   You can download security updates from the Microsoft Update Web site, and then install them as part of the image build process if you are applying a custom image. Additional updates can be added by placing the downloaded updates in the distribution share. You can add updates to an installation image copied from installation media by downloading them from the Microsoft Update Catalog at *http://catalog.update.microsoft.com/v7/site/Home.aspx* and adding them to a distribution share. Figure 3-30 shows the Microsoft Update Catalog home page.

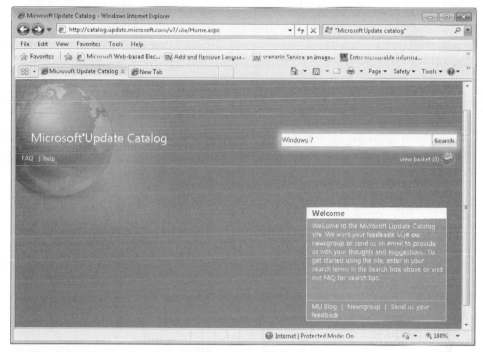

FIGURE 3-30 The Microsoft Update Catalog home page

- **Add updates using WSUS or SCCM 2007** You can use WSUS or SCCM 2007 to install the security updates after deployment. Depending on the configuration, it might take an hour or more before all updates are applied. Including the SCCM client in the image and setting it to communicate with a specific SCCM site can result in all computers built from the image communicating with only that site.

- **Slipstream updates to the installation source** You can download security updates from the Microsoft Update Catalog and integrate them into the Windows installation source before beginning the unattended build process. This protects the image from known security exploits, but integrating the security updates requires administrative effort.

Keeping an Offline File on a VHD Up to Date

You can use the Offline Virtual Machine Servicing Tool, discussed in Chapter 2, to keep offline VHD files that contain installations of Windows 7 up to date with service packs and software updates. The Offline Virtual Machine Servicing Tool can update a large number of offline virtual machines or VHDs according to their individual needs. The tool works with SCVMM 2007 or SCVMM 2008, in addition to WSUS 3.0, SCCM 2007, or Configuration Manager 2007 R2.

The tool uses the concept of "servicing jobs" to manage the update operations based on lists of existing virtual machines stored in SCVVM. A servicing job runs Windows PowerShell scripts to work with virtual machines and VHDs. The servicing job deploys a virtual machine to a host and starts it or boots a computer that holds an image installed to implement failover from that image, triggers the software update cycle, and closes down the updated device. The Offline Virtual Machine Servicing Tool then either shuts down the virtual machine or boots the computer that has the VHD installed from its normal boot image.

To use the tool, you configure virtual machine (or VHD) groups and create and schedule servicing jobs. You can schedule jobs to run immediately, or to run during low-traffic maintenance windows. You can also schedule servicing jobs to recur at regular intervals. The disadvantage of the Offline Virtual Machine Servicing Tool is that a virtual machine or physical machine with a bootable VHD is brought online in an insecure state, if only for a short time while the image is updated.

> **MORE INFO** **OFFLINE VIRTUAL MACHINE SERVICING TOOL AND SCVMM**
>
> For more information about the Offline Virtual Machine Servicing Tool, see *http://technet .microsoft.com/en-us/library/cc501231.aspx*. For more information about SCVMM 2008, go to *http://technet.microsoft.com/en-us/library/cc668737.aspx* and access the links on the navigation pane.

Adding Language Packs

Language packs create a multilingual Windows environment. Windows operating systems are language-neutral, and language and locale resources are added through language packs (lp.cab files). By adding one or more language packs to Windows 7, these languages can be activated when installing the operating system. As a result, the same Windows 7 image can be deployed to regions with different language and locale settings, reducing development and deployment time.

You can add language packs offline or online using MDT 2010 and SCCM 2007. In the Deployment Workbench Task Sequence Editor select the Install Language Packs Offline or Install Language Packs Online task. You are presented with a list of language packs to add. If SCCM 2007 is not available, you can add language packs with a custom task sequence by choosing a template that contains the Add Packages step.

Adding Applications

If you are using a reference computer, you can install applications on that computer and then create an image. Take care that you do not violate licensing conditions if you then install the image on other computers.

You can also add applications to an existing image build by adding them to the distribution share. Deployment Workbench can install the application from its original network location, or it can copy the application source files to the distribution share. In either case, you can specify the commands for installing the application when adding it to the distribution share. Applications can also be installed as SCCM 2007 packages for ZTI deployments. After you have added an application to the distribution share, it can be installed in one of the following ways:

- **Add it to the task sequence** Application installations added to the task sequence occur when MDT 2010 executes the task sequence on the target computer. Typically, for a third-party OEM application, you would choose the LiteTouch OEM Task Sequence template and specify the Copy CD to Local Hard Disk For OEM Pre-Installation step.

- **Use The New Application Wizard** You access this wizard by expanding Distribution Share, right-clicking Applications, and clicking New in the Actions pane. Figure 3-31 shows the Application Type page of the New Application Wizard. In this wizard, you specify the application name and publisher, the source directory for the application files, whether you want to move or copy these files, the name of the destination directory, and the command-line command used to install the application.

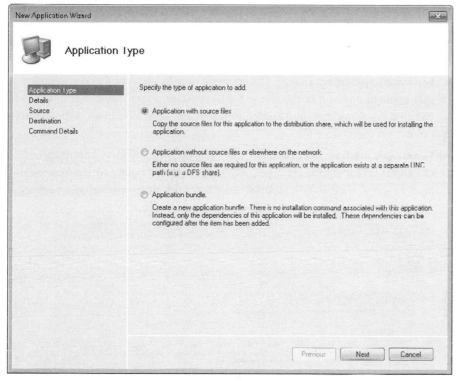

FIGURE 3-31 The New Application Wizard

CAUTION DO NOT ALLOW AN APPLICATION TO RESTART THE COMPUTER

If you are using MDT 2010, do not allow an application to restart the computer. MDT 2010 must control restarts, or the task sequence will fail. You can use the command-line property *reboot=reallysuppress* to prevent applications from restarting.

EXAM TIP

You cannot add an application to an image using DISM. You can, however, add an application to an image build in a distribution share in MDT 2010.

Configuring Deployment Points

A distribution share contains the files necessary to install and configure a build on a target computer. A deployment point defines a subset of those files and how to connect to them. For example, the distribution share might contain several operating systems and applications. A deployment point defines which of those files to distribute and how to access them.

To create a deployment point, you click Deployment Points in Deployment Workbench and then click New in the Actions pane. The Choose Type page of the New Deployment Point Wizard, shown in Figure 3-32, lets you choose one of the following deployment point types:

- **Lab or single-server deployment point**   This enables you to use the distribution share to deploy task sequences.

- **Separate Deployment share**   This creates a new local or remote deployment share that contains a subset of the files in the distribution share. You can choose the images, device drivers, updates, and applications that are replicated to this type of deployment point.

- **Removable media**   This creates directories and (optionally) an International Organization for Standardization (ISO) image that can be installed on removable media such as DVD-ROM, universal serial bus (USB) disk, or USB flash memory so you can perform stand-alone, network-disconnected deployments.

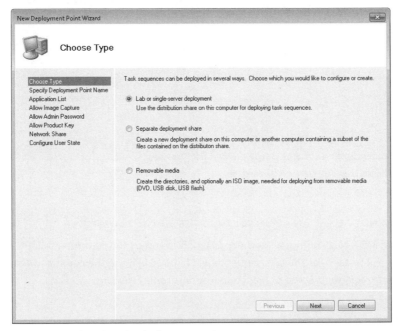

FIGURE 3-32 Choosing the deployment point type

WIM image files and ISO Windows PE image files are created for each deployment point. Client computers connect to the deployment point and the installation begins. During the deployment process, you can choose which build to install from the deployment point.

After you have chosen the type of deployment point, you can specify the deployment point name. Next, you can specify whether to allow users to select additional applications. This control applies in an upgrade scenario where users are typically prompted to install additional applications, but you may want to prevent this because of compatibility considerations.

Typically, if you are deploying a new computer (bare metal deployment) into a workgroup, the deployment wizard asks if an image should be captured. If this is not required, you can configure the deployment point to block this prompt. You can also specify whether users should be prompted for a local administrator password. In a typical scenario, it is considered insecure to permit users to know local administrator passwords. You can also decide whether to prompt users for an installation or activation product key.

The wizard then prompts you for a network share. You need to supply the name of the computer that hosts the distribution share, the share name, and the share path. Finally, you are prompted to configure the user state, which is the location in which information about the user and user settings are stored. By default, this location is determined automatically. Figure 3-33 shows the available options.

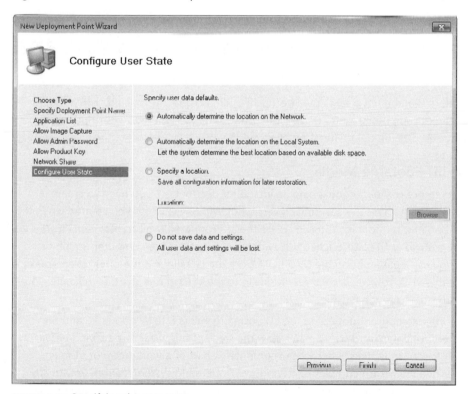

FIGURE 3-33 Specifying the user state

When you have completed the configuration, click Finish to create the deployment point.

> **NOTE   CONFIGURING A DEPLOYMENT DATABASE**
>
> You can use the New DB Wizard in Deployment Workbench to configure a deployment database. To do this, you need a server running SQL Server 2005 or SQL Server 2008 on your network. This functionality is used when MDT 2010 works with SCCM 2007.

Configuring Windows PE Options

After creating your deployment point, you need to configure its Windows PE configuration options. Assuming you have configured a LAB deployment point, you do this in Deployment Workbench as follows:

1. In the Deployment Workbench console tree, expand Deploy and select Deployment Point.
2. In the details pane, click LAB.
3. In the actions pane, click Properties.
4. In the LAB Properties dialog box, on the Windows PE tab, in the Driver group, select the device driver group you created earlier in the deployment process (for example, Windows 7) and then click OK.
5. In the details pane, right-click LAB and choose Update.

This updates the deployment point and creates a Windows PE directory. All the MDT 2010 configuration files are updated, and Deployment Workbench generates a customized version of Windows PE that is used to initiate the LTI deployment process.

Deployment Workbench creates the LiteTouchPE_x86.iso and LiteTouchPE_x86.wim files (for 32-bit target computers) in the C:\Distribution\Boot folder (where C:\Distribution is the shared folder used as the deployment point share).

Creating LTI Bootable Media

To boot a reference computer and create an image for distribution, you need to create bootable media containing the customized version of Windows PE that you created when the deployment point was updated. You can create the appropriate LTI bootable media from the LiteTouchPE_x86.iso or the LiteTouchPE_x86.wim file. If the reference computer is a physical computer, you can create a bootable DVD ROM from the ISO file. If it is a physical computer with a bootable VHD, you can copy the WIM file in to the VHD. If it is a virtual machine, you can start it directly from the ISO file.

The reference computer boots from the LTI bootable media into Windows PE and the Windows Deployment Wizard starts. You follow the steps of this wizard, specifying details such as your logon credentials, whether the computer is part of a workgroup or domain, and so on. When the wizard completes, a Windows 7 operating system, complete with any additions and amendments you made to the original installation image, is installed on the reference machine.

You need to test the reference computer thoroughly. When you are satisfied that the installation is satisfactory, you can create an image as described in Chapter 2 and deploy it with either MDT or WDS.

If your target computers are not PXE-compliant, you boot them from the LTI bootable media. Microsoft recommends that you do not do this for PXE client computers but instead use WDS with MDT 2010 to deploy these computers through LTI. WDS is listed as required software to enable MDT 2010 to implement LTI, but only if you are deploying PXE-compliant computers.

Deploying Images with WDS

Chapter 2 discussed WDS and WDS images. WDS is installed as a server role and deploys images to multiple computers. An advantage of using WDS is that it uses multicast transmissions. As a result, an operating system image needs to be transferred across the network only once to be deployed to multiple computers.

EXAM TIP

Although WDS is a server role, the topic is prominent in the 70-680 examination objectives, and it is likely to be tested.

Installing and Configuring WDS

You install WDS as a server role on a server running Windows Server 2008 or Windows Server 2008 R2 that is a member of an Active Directory Domain Services (AD DS) domain. Because WDS deploys to clients that are PXE-compliant, you must have a Dynamic Host Configuration Protocol (DHCP) server on your network. You also require a Domain Name System (DNS) server and your WDS deployment server requires an NTFS file system volume for its image store. You must be a member of the Local Administrators group on the server. To use WDS to deploy images, you need to select the Deployment Server option when installing the server role.

After you install the server role, you must configure the server, add a boot image, and add an install image. The server will then be ready to deploy images to target computers.

The high-level procedure to configure the WDS server role is as follows:

1. Open the Windows Deployment Services console from the Administrative Tools menu. If there is no server listed in the Servers node, right-click the node and choose Add Server to add the local server.

2. In the left pane of the Windows Deployment Services console, expand the server list.

3. Right-click the local server, and then choose Configure Server.

4. Follow the instructions in the wizard.

5. When the configuration completes, clear the Add Images To Windows Deployment Services Now check box and then click Finish.

6. If you want to modify any of the settings of the server, right-click the server in the console, and choose Properties.

Adding Boot and Install Images

After you have configured the server, you need to add images. These images include a *boot image* (the bootable environment that you initially boot a target computer into), and one or more *install images* (the images that you deploy). Initially you add the default boot image (Boot.wim) included on the Windows Server or Windows 7 installation DVD-ROM. The Boot.wim file contains Windows PE and the WDS client. The high-level procedure to add the default boot image is as follows:

1. In the left pane of the Windows Deployment Services console, right-click the Boot Images node, and then choose Add Boot Image.

2. Select the default boot image (Boot.wim) in the \Sources folder on the Windows Server installation DVD-ROM.

3. Click Open and then click Next.

4. Follow the instructions in the wizard to add the image.

Install images are the operating system images that you deploy to the client computer. For Windows 7, you can also use the Install.wim file from the Windows 7 installation DVD, or you can create your own install image from a reference computer running Windows 7. WDS can use a capture image to capture the image of a reference computer. The high-level procedure to add the default install image from a Windows 7 installation DVD-ROM (Install.wim) is as follows:

1. In the Windows Deployment Services console, right-click the Install Images node and choose Add Install Image.

2. Specify an image group name and click Next.

3. Select the default install image (Install.wim) in the \Sources folder on the Windows 7 DVD-ROM and click Open.

4. If you do not want to add all the images in Install.wim on the DVD-ROM, clear the check boxes for the images that you do not want to add. Add only the images for which you have licenses.

5. Follow the instructions in the wizard.

Deploying an Install Image

You can now deploy the install image directly to PXE-compliant target computers. In practice, you would not install the image from the DVD-ROM directly to a number of target computers, which would make these computers vulnerable to known security threats.

You could update the image with security patches, drivers, language packs, and so on with a tool such as DISM, or you could use WDS with MDT 2010, which can add security patches, language packs, and applications. Even then, you would deploy to only one reference computer and test it carefully before deploying it across the enterprise. If you make any changes to your reference computer, you can use a capture image to capture the amended settings on the reference computer.

The high-level procedure to deploy an install image to a PXE-compliant target computer is as follows:

1. Configure the BIOS of the target computer to enable PXE booting, and set the boot order so that it is booting from the network first.

2. Restart the computer, and when prompted, press F12 to start the network boot.

3. If you have more than one boot image on the WDS server, you are presented with a boot menu on the client. Select the appropriate boot image.

4. Follow the instructions in the Windows Deployment Services user interface.

When the installation is complete, the target computer restarts and Setup continues.

Creating a Discover Image

If you need to deploy a Windows 7 operating system to a computer that is not PXE-compliant, you should create a discover image and save it to bootable media such as a DVD-ROM or bootable USB flash drive. Booting the target computer from the discover image enables it to locate a WDS server, which then deploys the install image to the computer. You can configure discover images to target a specific WDS server. If you have multiple WDS servers in your environment, you can create a discover image for each one.

You can create a discover image from the Boot.wim file on the Windows Server 2008 or Windows 7 installation DVD-ROM. You cannot use the Windows PE file (WinPE.wim) from Windows AIK to create a discover image. Note, however, that Windows AIK needs to be installed on the WDS server to create the bootable media that contains the discover image. The high-level procedure to create a discover image and install it on bootable media is as follows:

1. In the Windows Deployment Services console, expand the Boot images node.

2. Right-click the image that you want to use as a discover image. This must be the Boot. wim file from the Windows Server or Windows 7 DVD-ROM.

3. Click Create Discover Boot Image.

4. Follow the instructions in the wizard, and when it is completed, click Finish.

5. To create media that contains the discover image, click Microsoft Windows AIK in the All Programs menu and then download and install the Windows AIK (*http://www.microsoft.com/downloads/details.aspx?FamilyId=94BB6E34-D890-4932-81A5-5B50C657DE08&displaylang=en*).

6. Click Start, click All Programs, and then click Windows PE Tools Command Prompt.

7. To create a Windows PE build environment, enter the following:

```
copype architecture c:\winpe
```

8. To copy the discover image that you created, enter the following:

```
copy /y c:\imagename.wim c:\winpe\iso\sources
```

9. To change back to the PETools folder, enter the following:

```
cd c:\program files\windows aik\tools\petools
```

10. To create the bootable .iso image, enter the following:

```
oscdimg -n -bc:\winpe\iso\boot\etfsboot.com c:\winpe\iso c:\imagename.iso
```

11. Create a bootable DVD-ROM or USB flash drive from the ISO image. If you transfer the image to a Windows 7 (or Windows Vista) client, double-clicking the image does this for you. Otherwise, use reputable third-party software.

Creating a Capture Image

Capture images are boot images into which you boot a client computer to capture its operating system in a WIM file. You create a capture image, run Sysprep on the reference computer, restart the reference computer, press F12 (or use a discover image if the reference computer is not PXE-compliant), select the capture image which should now appear on the boot menu, capture the reference computer image as a WIM image, and upload it to the WDS server.

Note that you can capture a system image using the ImageX tool in the Windows AIK and install it on the WDS server, but a capture image automates the process. Typically, you create a capture image from Boot.wim. The high-level procedure to do this is as follows:

1. In the Windows Deployment Services console, expand the Boot Images node.

2. Right-click the image you want to use as a capture image (typically, Boot.wim).

3. Choose Create Capture Boot Image.

4. Type a name, a description, and the location where you want to save a local copy of the file. You specify this location in case there is a network problem when you deploy the capture image.

5. Follow the instructions in the wizard, and when it is complete, click Finish.

6. Right-click the boot image folder.

7. Choose Add Boot Image.

8. Select the new capture image, and then click Next.

9. Follow the instructions in the wizard.

WDS Images

In the previous sections, we looked at how WDS creates install, boot, capture, and discover images. However, it is valuable at this juncture to briefly summarize the purpose of these images. WDS installs an install image (typically a WIM file) to its target computers. It cannot manipulate this file by adding drivers, language packs, and applications (for example) to its distribution share as can MDT 2010, but you can manipulate the WIM image with DISM before you distribute it with WDS. You can also deploy the WDS image to a reference computer, test and amend it online if necessary, ensure it is up to date, generalize it using Sysprep, and then use a capture image to create an install image on the WDS server.

WDS works by first booting the target computers with a boot image. This enables the deployment of the install image to the target computers.

WDS can also capture an image on a reference computer and install it to multiple target computers. To do this, the reference computer boots from a special type of boot image called a capture image. A capture image contains Windows PE and the Windows Deployment Services Image Capture Wizard. When the reference computer boots from a capture image (after you prepare it with Sysprep), the wizard creates an install image of the computer and saves it as a WIM file. This then becomes the install image that WDS deploys to the target computers after booting them with a standard boot image.

Typically WDS works with PXE-enabled computers. PXE enables computers to boot from the network to a state that allows you to select a WDS boot image. If the target computers are not PXE-enabled, WDS can deploy an operating system provided the computers are first booted with a discover image. When you boot a computer into a discover image, the WDS client locates a valid WDS server, and you can choose the image you want to deploy.

> **NOTE WDS AND STANDARD WINDOWS PE IMAGES**
>
> The WDS discover image contains a Windows PE image and WDS client software. You should not boot into Windows PE from a Windows PE boot disk (for example) to attempt to access a WDS server. You should not attempt to boot to Windows PE or from a discover image if your target computer is PXE-compliant.

Booting a Target Computer Manually

If a computer is not PXE-compliant and you need to boot it manually using a discover image, you can use optical media or other removable media, such as a USB hard disk or USB flash memory. You can use the BCDEdit and BCDBoot tools to create bootable media. Chapter 2 discussed the BCDEdit tool and used it to mark a VHD as bootable. You can use the same procedure for USB devices.

BCDboot is a Windows AIK tool that you can use to set up a system partition or to repair the boot environment located on the system partition. The tool creates a system partition by copying a small set of boot environment files from an installed Windows image. BCDboot also creates a BCD store on the system partition with a new boot entry that enables you to boot to the installed Windows image. You can run BCDboot from Windows PE. If you have not installed the Windows AIK, you still have access to BCDboot in the Windows\System32 directory. The tool is also available in the Windows OEM Preinstallation Kit (OPK).

Specific BCD settings can be defined in the BCD-Template file. The tool also copies the most recent versions of boot-environment files from the operating system image Windows\Boot folder and Windows\System32 folder to the default system partition identified by the firmware. You can create this partition by using a partitioning tool such as DiskPart.

When a computer has been booted into Windows PE and an image is installed, you use BCDBoot to initialize the BCDstore and copy boot environment files to the system partition. This allows the computer to boot normally when it is restarted without Windows PE.

Using the WDSUTIL Tool

WDS provides a GUI tool and a command-line tool. You can perform most deployment tasks using the Windows Deployment Services console in the Microsoft Management Console (MMC), including setting the Auto-Add policy and approving or rejecting pending computers. However, if you want to prestage client computers, you need to use the WDSUTIL command-line tool.

For example, you can use the WDSUTIL */add* construct to add images or image groups, or to prestage computers. The following command prestages the computer Aberdeen with a MAC address 00-13-E8-64-46-01:

```
WDSUTIL /Add-Device /Device:Computer1 /ID: 00-13-E8-64-46-01
```

The following command adds a boot image to the WDS server. The image is called Myboot.wim and is stored on C:\MybootImages.

```
WDSUTIL /Add-Image /ImageFile:"C:\mybootimages\myboot.wim" /ImageType:Boot
```

You can use the WDSUTIL tool to carry out the following tasks:

- Configure a WDS server for initial use.
- Start and stop all services on the WDS server.
- Update serve files on the RemoteInstall share.
- Revert changes made during server initialization.
- Create new capture and discover images, as well as multicast transmissions and namespaces.
- Add images and image groups and prestage computers.
- Approve or reject computers that are pending administrator approval.
- Copy an image within the image store.
- Export an image from the image store to a .wim file.
- Replace a boot or installation image with a new version of that image.
- Remove images, image groups, multicast transmissions, and namespaces.

- Convert an existing Remote Installation Preparation (RIPrep) image to a Windows Image (.wim) file.
- Delete computers that are in the Auto-Add Device Database, which stores information about the computers on the server.
- Disable or enable all services for WDS.
- Disconnect a client from a multicast transmission.
- Set properties and attributes of a specified object.
- Retrieve properties and attributes of a specified object.
- Display the progress status while a command is being executed.

> **MORE INFO** **WDSUTIL**
>
> For more information about WDSUTIL, including syntax and code examples, see *http://technet.microsoft.com/en-us/library/cc771206.aspx.*

> **MORE INFO** **WDS**
>
> For more information about WDS, go to *http://www.microsoft.com/downloads/details .aspx?displaylang=en&FamilyID=3cb929bc-af77-48d2-9b51-48268cd235fe* and download the WDS documentation files.

Using SCCM 2007

SCCM 2007 (ConfigMgr) is Windows Server 2003 or Windows Server 2008 software that implements change and configuration management for Microsoft platforms. It enables you to perform tasks such as the following:

- Deploying operating systems, software applications, and software updates
- Metering software usage
- Assessing variation from desired configurations
- Taking hardware and software inventory
- Remotely administering computers

SCCM 2007 collects information in a SQL Server database that you can configure, using tools such as MDT 2010. This allows queries and reports to consolidate information throughout the organization. SCCM 2007 can manage a wide range of Microsoft operating systems, including client platforms, server platforms, and mobile devices. It works with MDT 2010 to implement ZTI.

SCCM 2007 collects hardware and software inventories, distributes and installs software applications and software updates such as security fixes. It works with Windows Server 2008 Network Policy Server (NPS) to restrict computers from accessing the network if they do not meet specified requirements, such as having security updates installed. SCCM 2007 determines what a desired configuration should be for one or more computers, and monitors adherence to that configuration. It controls computers remotely to provide troubleshooting support.

 Quick Check

- What command-line utility enables you to prestage target computers for system image deployment?

Quick Check Answer

- WDSUTIL

SCCM Clients and Sites

After you have installed your central SCCM 2007 site, you can add clients and resources to the site. These are added by using one of the available SCCM discovery methods, which search your network to find resources that you can use with SCCM. You must discover computers on your network before you can install the Configuration Manager client software that allows you to deliver such items as packages and updates to those clients. Discovery methods include:

- Heartbeat Discovery
- Network Discovery
- Active Directory User Discovery
- Active Directory System Group Discovery
- Active Directory Security Group Discovery
- Active Directory System Discovery

MORE INFO **SCCM CLIENT DISCOVERY**

In-depth discussion of client discovery is beyond the scope of the 70-680 examination and this book. If you want to learn more out of professional interest, see *http://msdn.microsoft .com/en-us/library/cc143989.aspx.*

When it has discovered clients, SCCM 2007 installs client software on the Windows-based computers it manages. Configuration Manager 2007 client software can be installed on desktop computers, servers, portable computers such as laptops, mobile devices running Windows Mobile or Windows CE, and devices running Windows XP Embedded (for example, automated teller machines).

You can use SCCM 2007 to group clients into sites. SCCM sites group clients into manageable units with similar requirements for feature sets, bandwidth, connectivity, language, and security. SCCM 2007 sites can match your AD DS sites or be totally independent of them. Clients can move between sites or be managed from remote locations such as home offices.

Clients communicate with site systems hosting site system roles. Site systems communicate with the site server and with the site database. If there are multiple sites connected in a hierarchy, the sites communicate with their parent, child, or, sometimes, grandchild sites. SCCM 2007 uses boundaries to determine when clients and site systems are in the site and outside the site. Boundaries can be IP subnets, IP address ranges, IPv6 prefixes, and AD DS sites. Two sites should never share the same boundaries.

When SCCM 2007 features within the same site communicate with each other, they use either server message block (SMB), Hypertext Transfer Protocol (HTTP), or Hypertext Protocol Secure (HTTPS), depending on various site configuration choices you make. Because all these communications are unmanaged, it is a good idea to make sure these site elements have fast communication channels.

SCCM 2007 Task Sequence Editor

SCCM 2007 uses task sequences in a similar way to MDT 2010, and you can export and import task sequences between the tools. The SCCM 2007 Task Sequence Editor creates and modifies task sequences that are organized into groups of task sequence steps. Depending on whether the Install An Existing Image package or the Build A Reference Operating System Image package is selected in the New Task Sequence Wizard, the task sequence contains a set of baseline task sequence groups and steps. If the Create A New Custom Task Sequence is selected in the New Task Sequence Wizard, an empty task sequence is created.

The Task Sequence Editor displays the task sequence groups and steps in the tree view on the left side of the editor window in a manner similar to the MDT 2010 Task Sequence Editor. When you select a task sequence group or step, its properties are displayed next to the tree view with tabs that you can select to configure settings. Task sequence groups and steps can be nested within other task sequence groups.

Task sequence steps are grouped into general, disk, user state, images, drivers, and settings. General SCCM task sequence steps include the following:

- **Run Command Line** This task sequence step can run any command line. The task sequence action can be run in a standard operating system or Windows PE.

- **Install Software** This task sequence step specifies an SCCM 2007 package and program to install as part of the task sequence. The installation will begin immediately without waiting for a policy polling interval. The Install Software task sequence step runs only in a standard operating system such as Windows 7 and will not run in Windows PE.

- **Install Software Updates** This task sequence step installs software updates on a target computer. When this task sequence step runs, the target computer is evaluated for applicable software updates. In particular, the step installs only software updates that are targeted to collections of which the computer is currently a member. The Install Software Updates task sequence step runs only in a standard operating system such as Windows 7 and will not run in Windows PE.

- **Join Domain or Workgroup**   This task sequence action adds a target computer to a workgroup or domain. The Join Domain or Workgroup task sequence step runs only in a standard operating system such as Windows 7 and does not run in Windows PE.

- **Connect to Network Folder**   This task sequence action creates a connection to a shared network folder. The Connect to Network Folder task sequence step runs only in a standard operating system such as Windows 7 and does not run in Windows PE.

- **Restart Computer**   This task sequence step restarts the computer running the task sequence. After the restart, the computer automatically continues with the next step in the task sequence. The Restart Computer task sequence action can be run in either a standard operating system or Windows PE.

- **Set Task Sequence Variable**   This task sequence step sets the value of a task sequence variable to be used with the task sequence. Task sequence actions read task sequence variables, which specify the behavior of those actions.

> **MORE INFO**   **TASK SEQUENCE ACTIONS AND VARIABLES**
>
> For more information about task sequence actions, see *http://technet.microsoft.com/en-us/library/bb632625.aspx*. For more information about task sequence variables, see *http://technet.microsoft.com/en-us/library/bb632442.aspx*.

Disk steps, user state steps, image steps, driver steps, and setting steps let you configure the following on SCCM clients:

- Disk steps
  - Format and partition disk
  - Convert disk to dynamic
  - Enable and disable BitLocker
- User state steps
  - Request state store
  - Release state store
  - Capture user state
  - Restore user state
- Image steps
  - Apply operating system
  - Apply data image
  - Install deployment tools
  - Prepare ConfigMgr client for capture
  - Prepare Windows for capture
  - Capture operating system image

- Driver steps
  - Auto-apply drivers
  - Apply driver package
  - Setting steps
  - Capture network settings
  - Capture Windows settings
  - Apply network settings
  - Apply Windows settings

Integrating SCCM 2007 and MDT 2010

SCCM 2007 and MDT 2010 can be integrated in the Configuration Manager console on a distribution server to implement tasks such as installing language packs. However, possibly the most typical reason for integrating the two tools is that it enables you to implement ZTI. You need to install MDT 2010 on each computer running the Configuration Manager console. The SCCM 2007 Integration option can then be implemented, and data can be specified for MDT 2010 packages.

Before you can use the SCCM integration features of MDT 2010, you need to run the Configure Configuration Manager 2007 Integration script. This script copies the appropriate SCCM integration files to *Configuration Manager 2007_root* (where *Configuration Manager 2007_root* is the folder in which SCCM is installed). The script also adds Windows Management Instrumentation (WMI) classes for the new MDT 2010 custom actions. The classes are added by compiling a new Managed Object Format (.mof) file that contains the new class definitions. The .mof file is the mechanism by which information about WMI classes is entered into the WMI Repository.

Before you run the Configure Configuration Manager 2007 Integration script, ensure the Configuration Manager console is closed. The high-level procedure to run this script is as follows:

1. On the All Programs menu, click Microsoft Deployment Toolkit and then choose Configure ConfigMgr 2007 Integration. Figure 3-34 shows the Configure ConfigMgr Options page (as yet unconfigured).

2. In the Site Server Name dialog box, type the name of the SCCM 2007 server on which you want to implement MDT 2010 integration and then click OK.

3. In the Site Code dialog box, type the SCCM site code that installs MDT 2010 integration and then click Finish.

You can now manage your deployment using the features and utilities provided by MDT 2010 with SCCM features such as client discovery and client integration methods to provide a fully automated deployment that requires no user intervention.

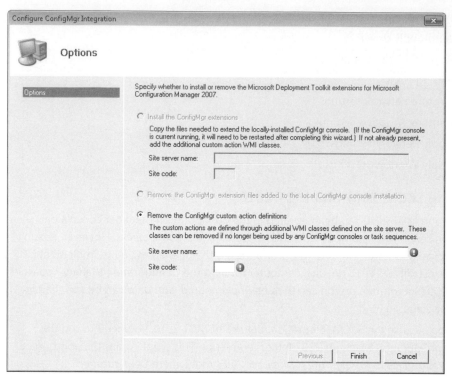

FIGURE 3-34 The Configure ConfigMgr Options page

MORE INFO **SCCM 2007 AND SOFTWARE UPDATE INSTALLATION**

For more information about using SCCM 2007 and the built-in ConfigMgr Install Software Updates task sequence, see *http://technet.microsoft.com/en-us/library/bb632402.aspx*.

Installing an Image Manually

Sometimes you do not want to use sophisticated deployment tools such as MDT 2010, SCCM 2007, or WDS. Suppose, for example, you have installed a computer running Windows 7 on your small office/home office (SOHO) network, generalized the installation using Sysprep, and created a bootable Windows PE DVD-ROM disk (or bootable USB hard disk or flash memory) by using the Copype.cmd script.

You have copied the ImageX tool into the Iso subdirectory on the Windows PE media, booted your computer into Windows PE, and used ImageX to create a WIM image of your computer installation. You have booted into the Windows PE environment and used ImageX to capture an image of your computer. You have copied the resulting WIM file on to your Windows PE media (and you might have used DISM to add additional drivers if you wanted).

You now want to apply this customized image to the hard disks of two new computers you have purchased without operating systems. You boot each computer in turn from the Windows

PE media and use ImageX to install the image. Your final step, to make the image bootable, is to use BCDboot from Windows PE to initialize the BCD store and copy boot environment files to the system partition. When you reboot each new computer, it will boot into Windows 7 and will have the same settings configured and applications installed as your original computer. Take care you are not violating any licensing conditions.

PRACTICE   **Downloading, Installing, and Configuring MDT 2010**

In this practice, you download the MDT 2010 installation and documentation files and then install the toolkit. You use the Deployment Workbench tool to create a Distribution Share and install an image.

> **NOTE**   **THE MDT 2010 INTERFACE**
>
> At the time of this writing, MDT 2010 is in beta. Therefore, its eventual interface might vary from what you see in this book.

EXERCISE 1   Downloading the MDT 2010 Installation Files and Documentation

In this exercise, you download the MDT and its associated documentation by accessing *https://connect.microsoft.com/site/sitehome.aspx?SiteID=14*. You probably first need to supply your Microsoft password credentials. You have the option of downloading the following files:

- MicrosoftDeploymentToolkit_x64.msi
- MicrosoftDeploymentToolkit_x86.msi
- Quick Start Guide for Lite Touch Installation.docx
- Release Notes.docx
- What's New in MDT 2010 Guide.docx

You can download and install the version suitable for your operating system—this book assumes the 32-bt (x86) version. You need no additional software to run the MDT on Windows 7, although if you choose to use the MDT in conjunction with SCCM 2007 on a deployment server, you need to install the relevant software and additional software such as SQL Server.

To download MDT 2010 and its associated documentation, proceed as follows:

1. Log on to the Canberra computer with the Kim_Akers account.
2. Create a folder to hold the downloaded files; for example, C:\Windows 7\MDT 2010 Files. Also create a folder to hold documentation, such as C:\Windows 7\MDT 2010 Documentation.
3. Open Internet Explorer and access *https://connect.microsoft.com/site/sitehome .aspx?SiteID=14*. If asked, supply your Microsoft Password details.
4. Click Microsoft Deployment Toolkit 2010.
5. Under Microsoft Deployment Toolkit (MDT) 2010, click Download.

6. Specify the files that you want to download and the Download Location Nearest You, as shown in Figure 3-35. Click Download.

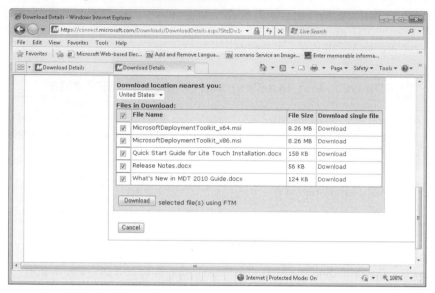

FIGURE 3-35 Selecting files to download

7. If necessary, click Allow to open Web content. Also, if prompted, right-click the Address Bar and install the required ActiveX control.

8. Ensure that the files received will be placed in the folder C:\Windows 7\MDT 2010 Files. If not, browse to that folder.

9. Click Transfer. Microsoft File Transfer Manager transfers the files. Figure 3-36 shows the transfer. Click Close when the transfer completes.

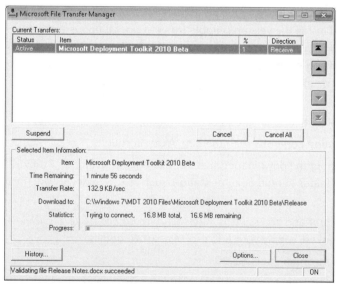

FIGURE 3-36 Microsoft File Transfer Manager transfers the files.

10. Access C:\Windows 7\MDT 2010 Files. Check that all the specified files have been downloaded to the subfolder folder Microsoft Deployment Toolkit 2010 Beta.

EXERCISE 2   Accessing the MDT 2010 Documentation

Microsoft recommends that you read the MDT 2010 documentation before installing the tool. To access this documentation, proceed as follows:

1. If necessary, log on to the Canberra computer with the Kim_Akers account.

2. Access the folder C:\Windows 7\MDT 2010 Files. Open the Microsoft Deployment Toolkit 2010 Beta folder.

3. Double-click Quick Start Guide For Lite Touch Installation.docx and save the file to C:\Windows 7\MDT 2010 Documentation.

4. Double-click Release Notes.docx and save the file to the same location.

5. Double-click What's New In MDT 2010 Guide .docx and save the file to the same location.

6. Read the downloaded documents carefully before you attempt Exercise 3 in this practice session.

EXERCISE 3   Installing MDT 2010

In this exercise, you install MDT 2010. This exercise assumes that you have installed the x86 version of Windows 7 Ultimate. If you have installed a 64-bit operating system, install the x64 version of MDT 2010 instead. To install MDT 2010, proceed as follows:

1. If necessary, log on to the Canberra computer with the Kim_Akers account.

2. Right-click the file MicrosoftDeploymentToolkit_x86.msi, which you downloaded in Exercise 1 and choose Install.

3. On the Welcome page, click Next.

4. On the End-User License Agreement page, review the license agreement. If you agree with the terms, select I Accept The Terms In The License Agreement, and then click Next.

5. On the Custom Setup page, shown in Figure 3-37, choose the features to install and the destination folder for the installation, and then click Next. The features are as follows:

   - **Documents** This feature installs the guidance and job aids. By default, this feature is installed in C:\Program Files\Microsoft Deployment Toolkit\ Documentation. The prerequisites for installing this feature and using Deployment Workbench to view the documentation are Microsoft .NET Framework version 2.0 and MMC version 3.0, both of which are implemented in Windows 7.

   - **Tools and templates** This feature installs the wizards and template deployment files, such as Unattend.xml. By default, this feature is installed in C:\Program Files\Microsoft Deployment Toolkit.

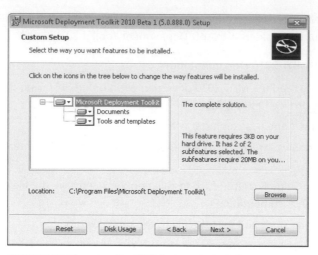

FIGURE 3-37 Choosing the MDT features to install

6. If you want to change a feature's state, click the feature, and then choose a state. To change the destination folder, click Microsoft Deployment Toolkit, and then click Browse. In the Change Current Destination Folder dialog box, specify the new destination folder and then click OK.

7. Ensure Microsoft Development Toolkit is selected, as shown previously in Figure 3-37, and click Install. If prompted, click Yes to allow the program to continue.

8. When installation completes, click Finish.

EXERCISE 4 Creating a Distribution Share

In this exercise, you create a distribution share. You must have installed MDT 2010 before you attempt this exercise. To create a distribution share, proceed as follows:

1. If necessary, log on to the Canberra computer with the Kim_Akers account.

2. On the Start menu, click All Programs. Click Microsoft Deployment Toolkit and then choose Deployment Workbench. If necessary, click Yes to allow the program to make changes to your computer.

3. In Deployment Workbench, right-click Distribution Share and then choose Create Distribution Share Directory.

4. On the Specify Directory page of the Create Distribution Share Wizard, click Create A New Distribution Share.

5. Type **C:\Downloads** in the Path For New Distribution Share Directory text box, as shown in Figure 3-38, and then click Finish.

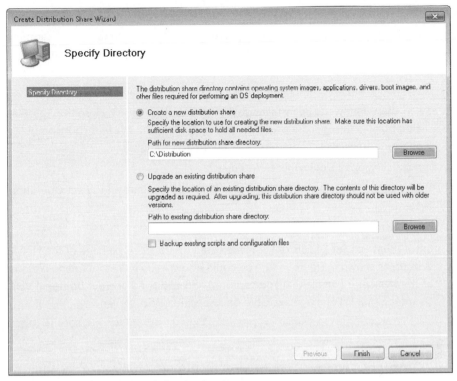

FIGURE 3-38 Specifying the path for the distribution share

6. Navigate to C:\Downloads and check that the folder is populated by subfolders, as shown in Figure 3-39. Some of these folders (such as Applications) are initially empty; others (such as Tools) are not.

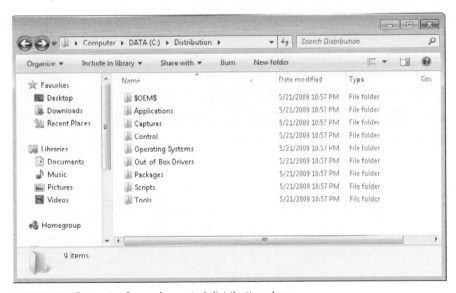

FIGURE 3-39 Contents of a newly created distribution share

EXERCISE 5 Install an Image on the Distribution Share

In this exercise, you install the Windows 7 source files on the Windows 7 Installation media in the distribution share that you created in the previous exercise. To install this image, proceed as follows:

1. If necessary, log on to the Canberra computer with the Kim_Akers account.

2. Insert the Windows 7 x86 installation DVD-ROM. If necessary, close the AutoPlay dialog box. As this exercise is written, the DVD-ROM drive is F:. If your computer uses a different drive letter, amend the procedure accordingly.

3. If necessary, open Deployment Workbench.

4. Under Deployment Workbench, expand Distribution Share and select Operating Systems.

5. In the Action pane, click New.

6. Ensure that Full Set Of Source Files is selected on the OS Type page of the New OS Wizard, as shown in Figure 3-40. You could also specify a Custom Image file, such as the Myimage.wim file that you captured and deployed on your bootable VHD in Chapter 2 or a WDS image available on a specified WDS server.

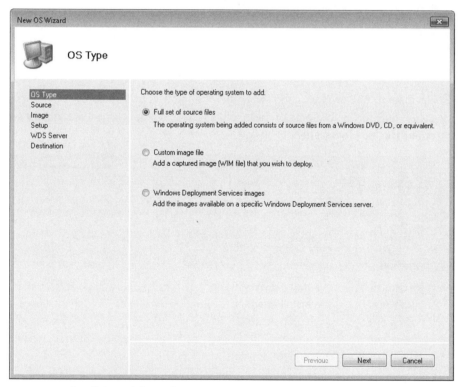

FIGURE 3-40 Specifying a full set of source files

7. Click Next.

8. On the Source page, type **F:** in the Source Directory text box. Click Next.

9. Ensure that Windows 7 x86 is entered in the Destination Directory Name text box and click Finish.

10. The copy operation takes some time. When it is complete, ensure that the appropriate operating system images have been placed in the distribution share, as shown in Figure 3-41.

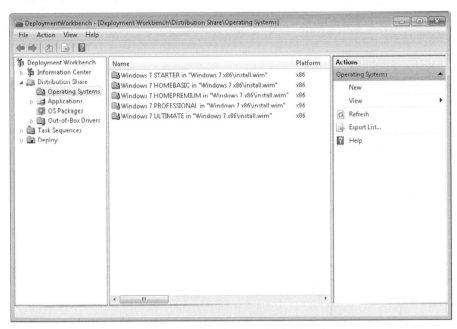

FIGURE 3-41 Operating system images placed in the distribution share

Lesson Summary

- MDT 2010 enables you to manage and manipulate disk images and to create a distribution share to distribute an operating system image to other computers on your network. You need to install Windows AIK before you can create or deploy WIM image files.

- WDS uses boot images that enable PXE-compliant computers to boot from the network and obtain an install image. If a computer is not PXE-compliant, you can boot it from a discover image on bootable media and WDS can then deploy an install image to it. Discover images enable you to boot a reference computer and transfer its system image to WDS, which can then deploy it to other computers.

- MDT 2010 can work with WDS in an LTI scenario. To implement ZTI, MDT 2010 requires that SCCM 2007 and SQL Server are available on the network. MDT 2010 requires that Windows AIK is installed.

Lesson Review

You can use the following questions to test your knowledge of the information in Lesson 2, "Deploying Images." The questions are also available on the companion DVD if you prefer to review them in electronic form.

> **NOTE ANSWERS**
>
> Answers to these questions and explanations of why each answer choice is correct or incorrect are located in the "Answers" section at the end of the book.

1. You want to ensure that offline VHD files that contain installations of Windows 7 are kept up to date with service packs and software updates. Which tool should you use?

    A. MDT 2010

    B. Offline Virtual Machine Servicing Tool

    C. BCDEdit

    D. Configuration Manager 2007 R2

2. You want to deploy a WIM image file captured from a reference computer running Windows 7. You need to specify the source directory in which the WIM file resides, specify whether Setup or Sysprep files are required, and then move the file to the distribution share. What tool lets you do this?

    A. The Windows Deployment Services Image Capture Wizard, which is contained in a WDS capture image

    B. The New Task Sequence Wizard, which you can access from the SCCM 2007 Task Sequence Editor

    C. The Create Distribution Share Wizard, which you can access from the Deployment Workbench console

    D. The New OS Wizard, which you can access from the MDT 2010 Deployment Workbench console

3. WDS creates install, boot, discover, and capture images. Which of these do you need to install on bootable removable media?

    A. Install

    B. Boot (standard boot image)

    C. Discover

    D. Capture

4. Which of the following are required if WDS is to be installed and to deploy images? (Choose all that apply.)

    A. AD DS

    B. MDT 2010

C. SQL Server

D. SCCM 2007

E. DHCP

F. DNS

5. You have created a bootable DVD-ROM containing a Windows PE image, the ImageX tool, and a Windows 7 Ultimate Edition WIM image that you have captured from a workstation on your SOHO network. You have used ImageX to install the image on another computer. What tool do you use to configure that computer to boot from the image?

A. BCDboot

B. DISM

C. BCDEdit

D. ImageX

Chapter Review

To further practice and reinforce the skills you learned in this chapter, you can perform the following tasks:

- Review the chapter summary.
- Review the list of key terms introduced in this chapter.
- Complete the case scenarios. These scenarios set up real-world situations involving the topics of this chapter and ask you to create a solution.
- Complete the suggested practices.
- Take a practice test.

Chapter Summary

- You can use DISM or Image X to mount and unmount a system image. DISM adds packages, drivers, and updates to a mounted image and obtains information about online and offline-mounted system images. You can also use DISM to mount and service Windows PE images.
- MDT 2010 enables you to manage and manipulate disk images and to deploy them to target computers through a distribution share. Windows AIK needs to be installed before you can use MDT 2010 to deploy images.
- WDS creates a boot menu that you can use from a PXE-compliant computer booted from the network to install a system image to that computer. If a target computer is not PXE-compliant, you can boot it from a discover image to access the boot menu. A capture image is a type of boot image and appears on the boot menu. If you boot a reference computer from a capture image, you can capture its system image and copy it to a WDS server, which can in turn deploy it to other target computers.
- You need MDT 2010 (and Windows AIK), along with SCCM 2007 and SQL Server, to implement ZTI. You can implement LTI on PXE-compliant computers by using MDT 2010 and WDS.

Key Terms

Do you know what these key terms mean? You can check your answers by looking up the terms in the glossary at the end of the book.

- **Boot image**
- **Commit**
- **Deploy**
- **Distribution share**

- **Install image**
- **Mount**

Case Scenarios

In the following case scenarios, you apply what you've learned about deploying system images. You can find answers to these questions in the "Answers" section at the end of this book.

Case Scenario 1: Deploying an Image with More Than One Language Pack

Don Hall, a systems administrator at Litware, Inc., has created a primary deployment image for Litware's client computers running Windows 7. He discovers that he needs to apply an update, add a new driver, change settings, and support multiple languages. He wants to make these changes without deploying the image and recapturing it. He also knows that if he services the image offline, he is not required to run the Sysprep tool and therefore does not need to use a rearm.

Litware is a relatively small organization with two locations. However, these two locations are in different countries. Don has created a single master image so that he does not have to maintain several variations. This image contains both the language packs that Litware requires. Don needs to apply updates to the single image and ensure that all the updates are applied to each language in the image. Before he deploys the image, he uses offline servicing to remove the unnecessary language pack. He needs to service only Litware's WIN image. There is no requirement to service a Windows PE image.

Don intends to use the DISM tool to mount and service the offline image and then unmount the image and commit his changes. He also wants to use DISM to create a report about the state of the drivers, applications, language settings, and packages that are installed.

1. What does Don need to carry out these tasks?
2. What is the first thing Don needs to do with the master image?
3. What tasks does Don carry out using the DISM tool?

Case Scenario 2: Deploying an Image to 100 Client Computers

You are a network administrator at Northwind Traders. Your company is expanding its Detroit operation from a small branch office to a major facility, and you are tasked with deploying 100 client computers. The server infrastructure has already been upgraded. Detroit is part of the Northwind Traders AD DS domain, and DHCP and DNS servers are available on the Detroit subnet. The WDS server role has been installed and configured on a member server running Windows Server 2008 R2 and a standard boot image has been created.

You have been given a workstation running Windows 7 Enterprise that was previously used by a staff member that has left the company. All personal files and non-mission-critical applications have been stripped from the computer. Your boss wants all the new client computers to be installed "just like that one." The target computers are new machines and easily meet the recommended Windows 7 Enterprise specifications. They are PXE-compliant.

1. What do you need to do to the workstation you have been given before you can use it as a reference computer?
2. What do you need to create in WDS to enable you to obtain an image from the reference computer?
3. How do you go about deploying the target computers?

Suggested Practices

To help you master the exam objectives presented in this chapter, complete the following tasks.

Manage and Manipulate a System Image

Perform this practice exercise when logged on to the Canberra computer with the Kim_Akers user account.

- Use the DISM tool. Like all command-line tools, it might seem daunting to use at first, but it becomes familiar with practice. Mount the image on your bootable VHD, use all the Get options to obtain information, and then try all the configuration options. Commit your amendments to the image, boot from the VHD, and see the result of your changes.

Become Familiar with the Deployment Tools

Perform the first practice exercise when logged on to the Canberra computer with the Kim_ Akers user account. The second and third exercises are optional.

- **Practice 1**   MDT is already installed on your Canberra computer. Use the tool to install an operating system image, install drivers, install updates, install language packs, and install applications. Create and edit task sequences and associate answer files with the image.
- **Practice 2**   Create a virtual PC running Windows 7. Deploy the system image that you created in MDT and observe the results.
- **Practice 3**   Create a virtual server running Windows Server 2008. Install the AD DS server role and configure DHCP and DNS. Install the WDS role and practice using the Windows Deployment Services console and the WDSUTIL command-line tool.

Take a Practice Test

The practice tests on this book's companion DVD offer many options. For example, you can test yourself on just one exam objective, or you can test yourself on all the 70-680 certification exam content. You can set up the test so that it closely simulates the experience of taking a certification exam, or you can set it up in study mode so that you can look at the correct answers and explanations after you answer each question.

> **MORE INFO   PRACTICE TESTS**
>
> For details about all the practice test options available, see the section entitled "How to Use the Practice Tests," in the Introduction to this book.

CHAPTER 4

Managing Devices and Disks

This chapter discusses two topics that are close to the heart of the typical user. User experience depends heavily on how well peripherals and devices work. It is your job to ensure that the best device drivers available are installed on your organization's client computers. The best drivers are not always the most recent, and you need to ensure that the latest device drivers downloaded from an update site (typically Windows Update) are compatible with your hardware before you deploy them to your network clients.

If the hard disk on a client machine is badly fragmented, has faults, or has too little free space, or if you have not configured your disk systems for optimal performance or fault tolerance, the quality of the user experience deteriorates rapidly. You can manage disks using both graphical user interface (GUI) and command-line tools to ensure optimal disk performance. If your client computers have more than one hard disk, you need to ensure that their disk arrays are correctly configured.

This chapter looks at tools and techniques for managing devices and device drivers, and for managing disks.

Exam objectives in this chapter:
- Configure devices.
- Manage disks.

Lessons in this chapter:

Before You Begin

To complete the exercises in the practices in this chapter, you need to have done the following:

- Installed Windows 7 on a stand-alone client PC as described in Chapter 1, "Install, Migrate, or Upgrade to Windows 7." You need Internet access to complete the exercises. You also need a universal serial bus (USB) flash memory device to complete the practice exercises in Lesson 2.

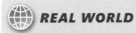

REAL WORLD

Ian McLean

Users do not typically concern themselves with the internal workings of their computers. Even the small percentage of users who know what a motherboard is seldom think about what it does. Your users are much more concerned about devices. Does the keyboard work correctly, or do they get a quotation mark when they press the @ key? Is the screen sharp, clear, and easy to read, and is the screen resolution what they want it to be? Do pointing devices work? Is disk access slow? Did the USB flash memory lose an important file, and can anyone else read the data on the flash memory device that the CEO left on an airplane? The list is endless.

Both administrators and help-desk staff spend a lot of time dealing with peripherals. If a motherboard goes down, you replace it, but you can spend hours messing around with devices that users want to plug into their computers or with configuring printers that work, but not quite in the way a user expects them to. A high percentage of the updates that you apply will be updated drivers, and sometimes a new driver will not work as well as the old one did, or will clash with other drivers on a computer. How often have you heard, "My computer plug-in thingy's stopped working—it's not been right since you messed around with it"?

Part of your job is dealing with high-level technical problems on serious equipment such as domain controllers and servers running Microsoft SQL Server and Microsoft Exchange Server, but you also need to spend time on devices, device drivers, printers, and these "pesky" peripherals. The whole of your job, after all, is keeping your users contented.

Lesson 1: Managing Device Drivers and Devices

In this lesson, you learn how to identify the driver that controls a peripheral device and check that it is working properly. You discover how to update, disable, and uninstall a device driver; and how to roll back to the previously installed driver if a recently installed driver does not work (for example, if it causes STOP errors). You learn about signed drivers, conflicts between drivers, configuring driver settings, and resolving device driver problems. In particular, you use the Device Manager console, which is the tool that Windows 7 provides to manage devices and device drivers.

After this lesson, you will be able to:

- Install Plug and Play (PnP) and non-PnP hardware
- Update, disable, uninstall, and roll back a device driver
- Prestage a device driver and permit standard users to install devices in a device install type
- Configure driver updates from the Windows Update Web site
- Troubleshoot device driver problems

Estimated lesson time: 50 minutes

Using Device Manager to View Device Information

A device driver is a software package (typically an .exe file installed by an .inf file) that enables Windows 7 to communicate with a specific hardware device. Before Windows 7 can use new hardware, a device driver for that hardware must be installed. If the device is Plug and Play (PnP), the driver should install automatically, but you might need to install updated drivers subsequently as these are released and downloaded. If the driver does not install automatically, you need to install it. You can use Device Manager to install and update drivers for hardware devices, change the hardware settings for those devices, and troubleshoot problems.

You can use Device Manager to perform the following tasks:

- Identify the device drivers that are loaded for each device and obtain information about each device driver.
- Determine whether the hardware on your computer and its associated device driver are working properly.
- View devices based on their type, by their connection to the computer, or by the resources they use.
- Enable, disable, and uninstall devices.
- Change hardware configuration settings.
- Install updated device drivers.

- Roll back to the previous version of a driver.
- Change advanced settings and properties for devices.
- Show hidden devices.

Typically, you use Device Manager to check the status of your hardware and to update device drivers on a client computer. You can also use the diagnostic features in Device Manager to resolve device conflicts and change resource settings, although resources are allocated automatically by the system during hardware setup and you seldom need to (or are able to) change resource settings.

> **NOTE DEVICE MANAGER WORKS IN READ-ONLY MODE ON A REMOTE COMPUTER**
>
> You can use Device Manager to manage devices and drivers only on a local computer. On a remote computer, Device Manager works in read-only mode, enabling you to view but not to change that computer's hardware configuration.

Opening Device Manager

You can open Device Manager on a computer running Windows 7 while logged on with any account. However, by default, only administrators can make changes to devices and install, uninstall, and roll back drivers.

You can open Device Manager in the following ways:

- In Control Panel, click Hardware And Sound. Click Device Manager under Devices And Printers.
- Click Start, right-click Computer, and choose Manage. Click Device Manager in the Computer Management tree pane.
- Open an elevated command prompt and enter **mmc devmgmt.msc.** Note that if you do not run the command prompt as administrator, Device Manager opens as read-only.

You can open Device Manager on a remote computer. Open Computer Management and choose Connect To Another Computer on the Action menu. Either type in the name of the remote computer or click Browse and select it. Click OK. You can now use Device Manager to view devices and device settings on the remote computer. You cannot, however, change any settings or install, uninstall, or roll back drivers.

Whatever method you use, Device Manager opens as shown in Figure 4-1. If you use Computer Management, you will also see the Computer Management tree pane on the left side.

> **NOTE OPENING DEVICE MANAGER**
>
> The practice exercises later in this lesson ask you to open Device Manager. It makes no difference which method you use. You will not be required to open Device Manager on a remote computer.

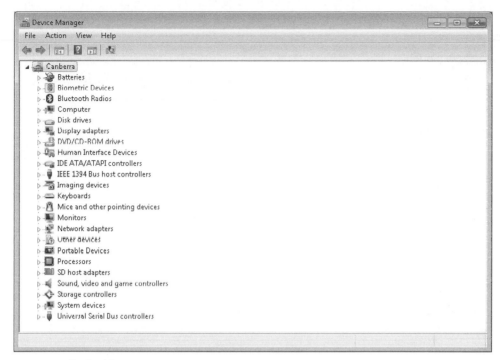

FIGURE 4-1 Device Manager

Viewing Device Information

You can use Device Manager to view device status and details (including hidden devices), to view USB power and bandwidth allocations for a device, and to view device driver information.

To view the status of a device, double-click the type of device you want to view (keyboards, monitors, network devices, and so on), and then right-click the appropriate device and choose Properties. On the General tab of the Properties dialog box, the Device Status area displays whether the device is working properly. If the device is working, a driver is installed and Windows 7 is able to communicate with it. Figure 4-2 shows the status of a network adapter.

If the device is experiencing a problem, the type of problem is displayed. You might also see a problem code and number and a suggested solution. If the Check For Solutions button is available, you can submit a Windows Error Report to Microsoft.

On the Power Management tab, you can configure settings such as whether the device can be disabled to save power and, depending on the type of device, whether the device is permitted to wake the computer (optionally in network adapters by using a magic packet). A magic packet is a standard Wake-Up on LAN frame that targets a specific network interface and enables remote access to a computer that is in a power-saving state.

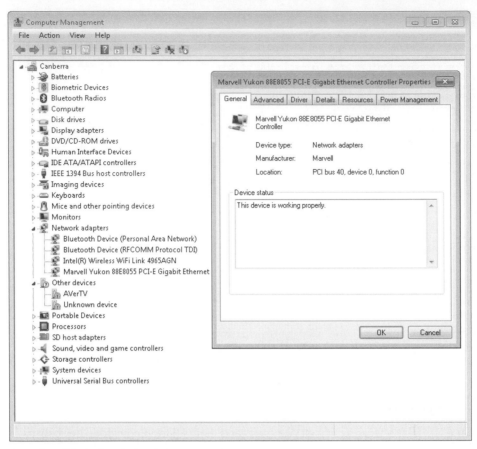

FIGURE 4-2 Displaying device status

The Resources tab gives details of memory range, interrupt request (IRQ), and input/output range resources that the device requires. The Advanced tab, shown in Figure 4-3, gives you access to a number of configurable settings that vary depending on the device for which you are viewing the Properties dialog box. The Details tab, shown in Figure 4-4, accesses an even larger number of properties. You can click any property and observe its value. The Drivers tab is discussed later in this lesson.

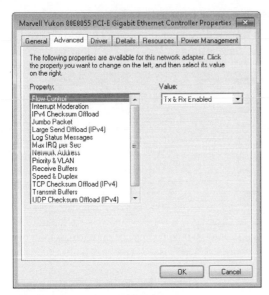

FIGURE 4-3 Advanced settings

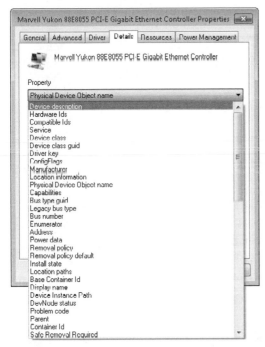

FIGURE 4-4 Property details

By default, devices are displayed in groups by their device type. Alternatively, you can view them based on how they are connected to the computer, such as the bus they are plugged into. You can also view resources by the type of device that uses the resource or by allocated connection type. Access the Device Manager View menu to specify one of these views.

You can also use the View menu to view hidden devices. Typically, a hidden device is one that is not currently attached but whose driver is installed, such as older devices and devices that are no longer installed. Figure 4-5 shows this View setting.

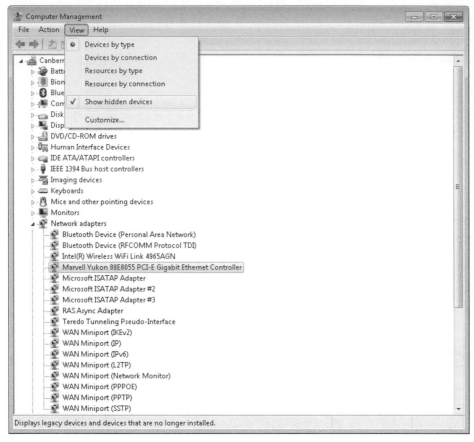

FIGURE 4-5 Viewing hidden devices

Viewing Power Allocation for a USB Hub

USB hubs can be self-powered or bus-powered. A self-powered hub has its own power supply, whereas a bus-powered hub draws its power from the USB to which it is connected. Devices requiring a lot of power, such as cameras, should be plugged into self-powered hubs.

You can check the power allocations for a USB hub to detect situations in which too many devices are using the hub. In Device Manager double-click Universal Serial Bus Controllers, right-click the USB Root Hub, and choose Properties. On the Power tab, you can view the power required by each device in the Attached Devices list. Note that USB Root Hub appears in Universal Serial Bus Controllers only if you have one or more USB hubs attached to your computer. Some USB devices (for example, modems) might not appear because they do not report bandwidth requirements to the operating system.

Viewing Bandwidth Allocations for a USB Host Controller

Each USB controller has a fixed amount of bandwidth that all attached devices share. If you suspect a USB controller requires more bandwidth, you can confirm this by viewing the bandwidth allocations currently being used by each device. In Device Manager, double-click Universal Serial Bus Controllers, right-click the Host Controller for your system, and choose Properties. On the Advanced tab, in the Bandwidth-Consuming Devices list, view the bandwidth used by each device.

Viewing Device Driver Information

To view details about the device drivers that are running on your computer, navigate to the device whose driver you are investigating, right-click the device, and choose Properties. On the Driver tab, you can click Update Driver to update the driver, Uninstall to remove it, and Disable to disable the device. If the driver replaced a previously installed driver, the Roll Back Driver button is also enabled. To obtain details about the driver, click Driver Details. The Driver File Details dialog box appears as shown in Figure 4-6, with a list of the individual files that make up the driver, file version information, and digital signature information.

FIGURE 4-6 Driver details

Installing Devices and Managing Device Drivers

PnP specifications define how a computer detects and configures newly added hardware and automatically installs the device driver. Windows 7 supports PnP so that when a user plugs in a hardware device, the operating system searches for an appropriate device driver package, automatically configuring it to work without interfering with other devices. This makes the installation straightforward.

However, users cannot be permitted to plug any device they please into their work computers. Device driver software runs as if it is a part of the operating system with unrestricted access to the entire computer, and only authorized device drivers can be permitted.

When a user inserts a device, Windows 7 detects the new hardware and the Plug and Play service identifies the device and searches the driver store for a driver package that matches the device. If a suitable driver is found, the device is considered to be authorized and the Plug and Play service copies the driver file (or files) from the driver store to its operational location, typically C:\Windows\Sysrem32\Drivers. The Plug and Play Service configures the registry and starts the newly installed driver.

Installing Device Drivers from Windows Update

By default, updated device drivers uploaded to Windows Update are downloaded and installed automatically on a client computer. You can amend this behavior through the Device Installation Settings dialog box, shown in Figure 4-7. The most straightforward method of accessing this dialog box is to type **device installation** in the Search text box on the Start menu and click Change Device Installation Settings.

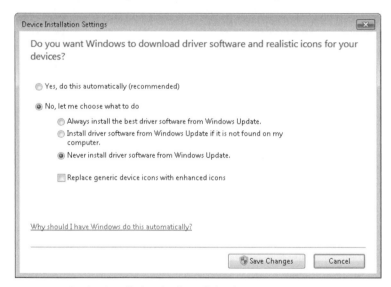

FIGURE 4-7 Device Installation Settings dialog box

The default setting is Yes, Do This Automatically (Recommended). However, if you want to ensure that only device drivers you have tested are installed on the computers running Windows 7 in your organization, you can select Never Install Driver Software From Windows Update.

If you choose Always Install The Best Driver Software From Windows Update, Windows 7 will determine automatically whether a new driver is superior to one already installed. However, you will not be able to test the new driver before installation. Similarly, if you select Only Install

Driver Software From Windows Update If It Is Not Found On My Computer, you will not be able to test the new drivers before they are installed. In an enterprise environment, particularly if software is distributed through Windows Server Update Services (WSUS), driver updates from the Windows Update site are disabled and the site is removed from the search path.

Staging a Device Driver

If the device driver does not exist in the driver store, then an administrator needs to approve the device. This process is known as *staging*. You can configure a computer Group Policy so that ordinary users can approve the installation of a device in a specific device setup class, and you can stage a specific device driver so ordinary users can install that device. However, it would be most unwise to do this for all devices. You learn how to configure Group Policy to allow non administrators to install specific devices and device setup classes in the practice session later in this lesson.

Windows 7 starts the staging process by searching for a matching driver package in folders specified by the DevicePath registry entry. You learn how to configure Windows 7 to search additional folders for device drivers in the practice session later in this lesson. If a suitable driver is not found, Windows 7 searches the Windows Update Web site. Finally, the user is prompted to insert installation media.

If a driver is found, the operating system checks that the user has permission to place the driver package in the driver store. The user must have administrator credentials or computer policy must be set to allow standard users to install the identified device. Windows 7 then checks that the driver package has a valid digital signature. If the driver package is unsigned or signed by a certificate not found in the Trusted Publishers store, Windows 7 prompts the user for confirmation. If the driver is approved by an authorized user, the operating system places a copy of the driver package in the driver store and installation continues.

Windows performs all the required security checks during staging, including the verification of administrator rights and the validation of digital signatures. After a driver package has been successfully staged, any user that logs on to that computer can install the drivers in the driver store by simply plugging in the appropriate device. There are no prompts, and no special permissions are required.

 Quick Check

- You have four devices plugged into an unpowered USB hub. You have a powered hub with an empty slot and decide you could improve hardware performance by transferring one device from the first hub to the second. How to you determine which of the devices on the unpowered hub consumes the most power?

Quick Check Answer

- Double-click Universal Serial Bus Controllers, in Device Manager. Right-click the unpowered USB hub and choose Properties. On the Power tab, view the power required by each device in the Attached Devices list.

Installing a Non-PnP Device

If a device is non-PnP (for example an older device), your logged-in account needs to have administrator credentials for you to install it. If the device comes with installation media, Microsoft recommends you insert that media and use the installation software it contains. Typically, you do this before you plug in the device.

Otherwise, open Device Manager, right-click the computer name at the root of the tree in the details pane, and click Add Legacy Hardware. This starts the Add Hardware Wizard shown in Figure 4-8.

FIGURE 4-8 The Add Hardware Wizard

The wizard lets you choose whether to scan and search for hardware or to install hardware you manually select from a list. If you choose the former option, the device needs to be attached to the computer. The procedure is the same as for staging PnP hardware that has not been preauthorized.

If you choose to select hardware from a list, you are presented with a list of device types. If you opt to select All Devices, you can select a device by manufacturer as shown in Figure 4-9. If you have the driver (but not necessarily the driver installation package) on removable media or in a folder on your hard disk, you can click Have Disk.

When a driver has been chosen, the wizard installs your hardware. If there are problems with the hardware (for example, you get a Code 10 error—the device cannot start), these are listed in the final page of the wizard.

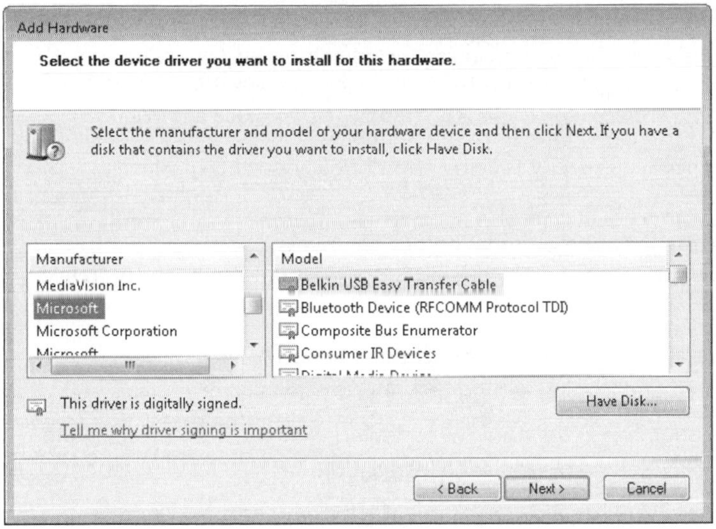

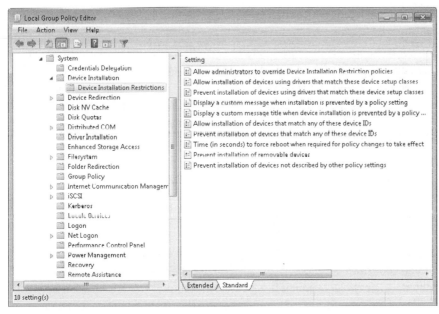

FIGURE 4-9 Selecting a device driver

Configuring Device Installation Policies

In the practice later in this lesson, you use Local Group Policy Editor to permit non-administrators to install devices of a specified device setup class. You can also configure other device installation policies using the same tool. In Local Group Policy Editor, expand Computer Configuration; expand Administrative Templates, System, Device Installation; and click Device Installation Restrictions. In the right pane, click Standard to view the Standard tab. This tab contains a list of policies, as shown in Figure 4-10.

FIGURE 4-10 Device installation restriction policies

You can use these policies to perform the following actions:

- Permit members of the Administrators group to install and update the drivers for any device, regardless of other policy settings.

- Enable Windows 7 to install or update device drivers whose device setup class globally unique identifiers (GUIDs) you specify, unless another policy setting specifically prevents installation.

- Prevent Windows 7 from installing or updating device drivers whose device setup class GUIDs you specify. This policy overrides any other policy that permits update or installation.

- Display a custom message to users in the notification balloon when a device installation is attempted and a policy setting prevents the installation.

- Display a custom message title in the notification balloon when a device installation is attempted and a policy setting prevents the installation.

- Specify a list of PnP hardware IDs and compatible IDs for devices that Windows is allowed to install. Other policy settings that prevent device installation take precedence over this policy.

- Specify a list of PnP hardware IDs and compatible IDs for devices that Windows is prevented from installing. This policy overrides any other policy that permits installation.

- Set the amount of time (in seconds) that the system will wait to reboot to enforce a change in device installation restriction policies.

- Prevent Windows 7 from installing removable devices. This policy setting takes precedence over any other policy setting that allows Windows 7 to install a removable device.

- Prevent the installation of devices that are not specifically described by any other policy setting.

You can open Local Group Policy Editor by entering **gpedit.msc** in the Start search box. It is highly recommended that you double-click each of the policies in Device Installation Restrictions (and in Device Installation) in turn and obtain more details about each. Investigating the policies in Local Group Policy Editor is one of the suggested practices at the end of this chapter.

Working with Device Drivers

You saw previously that installing a hardware device involved locating the device driver installation files and installing the driver. Once the driver is installed, you can update it (by installing a replacement driver), uninstall it, disable it, and enable it. If you have updated a driver and find that the updated driver does not work as well as the previous driver, you can roll back to the driver that was installed before the update.

If an updated device driver is distributed through Windows Update, it is typically installed automatically if you choose to download it. Usually you use the Update Driver functionality if a new or updated device driver becomes available from a vendor some time before it is published to Windows Update. To get the latest version of the driver and test it on your reference computer running Windows 7, you need to download the driver files from the vendor's Web site and then manually update the driver.

When you update a driver, the process is similar to the way a driver is installed when new hardware is added to the computer. If the driver is already authorized and in the driver store, or if an administrator it has staged it, the update process, once started, proceeds automatically without user intervention. Otherwise, you can allow Windows 7 to search for drivers for the hardware device or you can specify a folder address manually as described in the previous section, "Installing a PnP Device." If a driver can be found that is more recent than that already installed, the administrator is prompted to approve the driver.

You can start the driver update process in Device Manager in two ways:

- Right-click the device and choose Update Driver Software.
- Double-click the device. On the Driver tab, click Update Driver.

You can install a new driver or one that has been updated. If, however, you consider the current driver installation might be corrupt, updating a driver will not by itself reinstall the current driver. In this case, you need to uninstall the driver and then go through the process of installing it again. As with updating a driver, you can either right-click the device in Device Manager and choose Uninstall, or you can double-click the device and click Uninstall on the Driver tab. The Driver tab is shown in Figure 4-11.

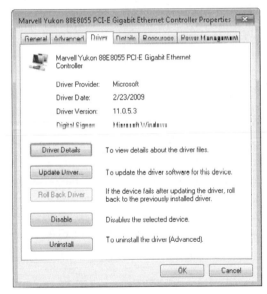

FIGURE 4-11 The Driver tab

Sometimes, rather than uninstalling and reinstalling a driver, you can solve problems by disabling it. If you have a driver conflict, you probably need to disable one of the drivers or stop it if it is a non-PnP device.

You cannot roll back a driver by right-clicking the device in Device Manager. You need to access the device's Driver tab. Unless a previous driver has been installed, the Roll Back

Driver control is disabled. In general, you roll back a driver if you have updated a device driver but the new driver does not work as well as the previous one or causes conflicts with other drivers. In this case, the previous driver should still be in the driver store and the process should take place without user prompts (other than clicking Yes to confirm).

If you are investigating problems with a driver, or if you have any other reason for wanting to know more about it, you can click Driver Details on the Driver tab. Driver details for a network adapter driver are shown in Figure 4-12.

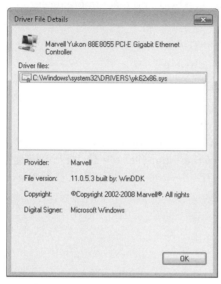

FIGURE 4-12 Driver details

Driver details indicate where the working driver file is stored. Note that this is not the driver store, which is a protected area. It also tells you the file name and type. Working driver files operate as if they are part of the operating system and typically have a .sys extension. Driver installation files have an .inf extension. Driver details include the provider (typically third party), the file version, the Digital Signer (typically Microsoft), and copyright information. It can often be useful to know a file version if you are having problems with a driver and are looking for information on the Internet, such as on Microsoft blogs. You might see a message along the lines of, "Version 10.0.5.3 has this problem. Uninstall it and install version 10.0.5.2."

Resolving Driver Conflicts

Driver conflicts are much less common than they used to be. It was common 15 years ago that you connected a printer and your mouse stopped working. Almost all modern hardware is PnP. The operating system controls installation, and conflicts typically are avoided. However, no system is perfect, and a conflict could still occur.

Typically a conflict occurs when two devices require the same resources, particularly when their interrupt or input/output (I/O) requirements clash. You can determine resource usage on the Resources tab of the device Properties dialog box, as shown in Figure 4-13. In most device drivers, Use Automatic Settings is selected and Change Settings is disabled.

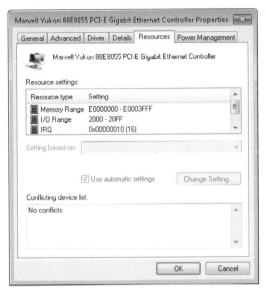

FIGURE 4-13 The Resources tab

Conflicts between PnP devices are unusual and can be solved temporarily by disabling one of the devices. Updating the driver (if an update is available) or uninstalling and reinstalling the hardware will probably solve the conflict.

Figure 4-14 illustrates a conflict situation in which a non-PnP device uses resources also used by the motherboard. If a conflict involves a non-PnP device, you may need to stop this device to resolve the problem.

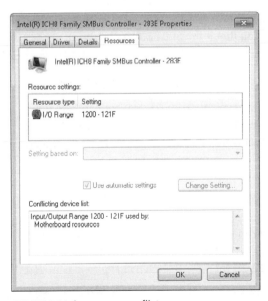

FIGURE 4-14 A resource conflict

To stop a non-PnP device, perform the following procedure:

1. Open Device Manager.

2. On the View menu, choose Show Hidden Devices.

3. Double-click Non-Plug and Play Drivers, right-click the device you want to stop, and choose Properties.

4. On the Driver tab shown in Figure 4-15, click Stop and then click OK.

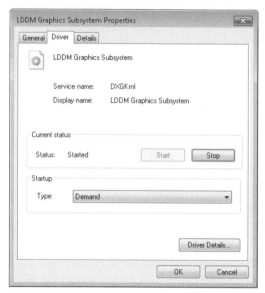

FIGURE 4-15 The Driver tab for a non-PNP device

The procedure to restart a device is identical except you click Start instead of Stop. You can also change the Startup Type on this tab. Note that if the Start button on the Driver tab is unavailable, the driver is already loaded.

Using the System Information Tool to Identify Resource Conflicts

If you suspect that a device driver is working incorrectly because of resource conflicts, you can view the I/O and IRQ requirements of each device by using the System Information (Msinfo32) tool. Using a single tool is more convenient than accessing the Resources tab of each individual device. You start the Msinfo32 tool by entering **msinfo32** in the Start search box, the Run command box, or the command prompt. You do not need to open an elevated command prompt to run Msinfo32. The tool provides general system information, as shown in Figure 4-16.

When you expand Hardware Resources, you can view the Memory, I/O, and IRQ resources used by every device on the computer. However, arguably the most useful information for resolving conflicts is obtained by selecting Conflicts/Sharing, as shown in Figure 4-17. If you are having problems with a particular device, you can search for the device by specifying it in the Find What: box, determining what devices it shares resources with, and identifying possible conflicts.

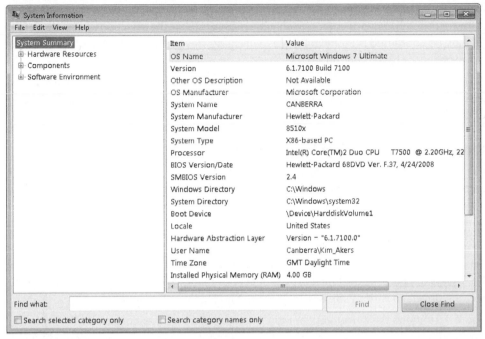

FIGURE 4-16 MSinfo32 displays general system information.

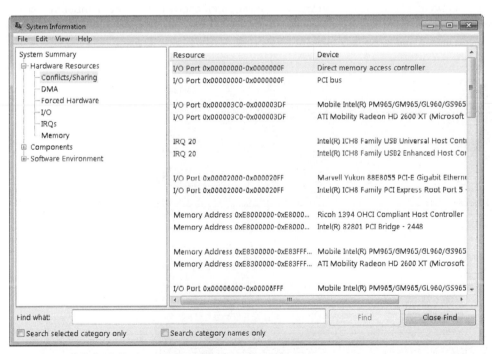

FIGURE 4-17 MSinfo32 displays conflicts/sharing information.

You can access information about specific devices (CD-ROM, sound device, display, and so on) by expanding Components. Arguably the most useful of the selections available as far as diagnosis is concerned is Problem Devices, which lists devices that cannot start, have no drivers installed, or have other problems.

When you expand Software Environment, you can click System Drivers. This displays a list of kernel drivers, and you can determine whether a driver has started. You can use the Find What: box to find a driver by its file name or description.

Testing Drivers with Driver Verifier Monitor

Not all driver problems are due to conflicts. Sometimes devices do not work properly or STOP errors occur, but no conflict information is shown and disabling other drivers does not resolve the problems. As with any software installation, you can use Reliability Monitor to determine when the installation occurred and whether reliability was affected adversely, but this tool does not diagnose device driver problems specifically.

Windows 7 provides the Driver Verifier Monitor command-line tool, which lets you monitor device drivers to detect illegal function calls or actions that might corrupt the system. It can subject the drivers to various stresses and tests to find incorrect behavior.

Figure 4-18 shows the Driver Verifier Monitor tool and the *verifier* command. The */volatile* flag lets you start verification of any driver without rebooting, even if Driver Verifier Monitor is not already running, and you can start the verification of a driver that is already loaded. These improvements, introduced in Windows Vista, significantly reduce the number of reboots required. This saves time and lets you use Driver Verifier Monitor to monitor a driver while you attach and remove devices.

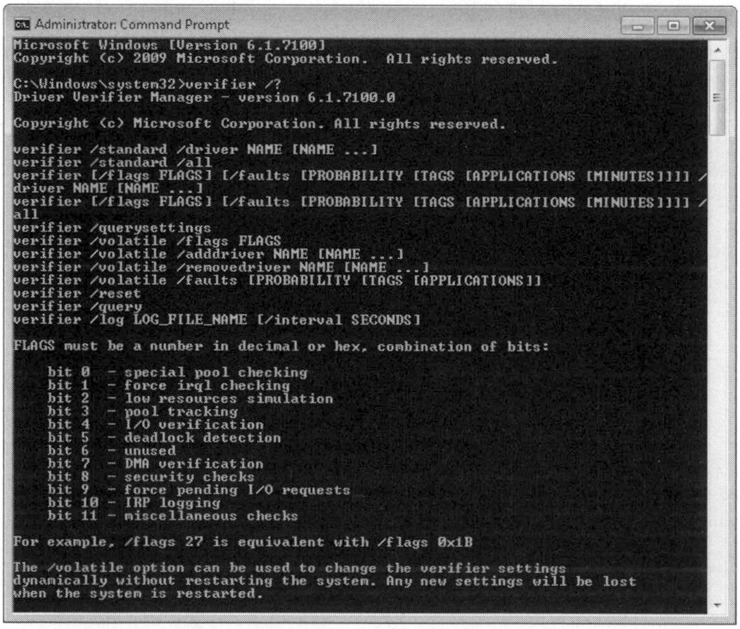

FIGURE 4-18 The Driver Verifier Monitor tool

You can query settings and add and remove drivers, but the main functionality is provided by the /faults flag that lets you inject stress tests of configurable severity to determine whether the driver is working properly in all situations. You can, for example, simulate a low-resources situation or a wait situation that returns an unexpected result. You can monitor resource usage (pool allocation) and keep a record of the number of faults injected into a system.

Driver Verifier Monitor is primarily a stress tool that, for example, informs you that a device driver will fail if disk or memory usage is above a certain limit. You can use more general tools, such as Performance Monitor and Task Manager, to monitor resource usage and diagnose low-resource situations.

> **MORE INFO   DRIVER VERIFIER MONITOR**
>
> For more information about Driver Verifier Monitor, download the white paper "Driver Verifier in Windows Vista," at *http://www.microsoft.com/whdc/devtools/tools/vistaverifier.mspx*. This document describes the use of the tool in Windows Vista, but the information also is relevant to Windows 7.

Driver Signing and Digital Certificates

Digital signatures allow administrators and users who are installing Windows-based software to know whether a legitimate publisher has provided the software package. Administrator privilege is required to install unsigned kernel-mode features such as device drivers. Drivers must be signed by certificates that Windows 7 trusts. Certificates that identify trusted signatories are stored in the Trusted Publishers certificate store.

As an administrator, you can authorize the installation of a driver that is unsigned or is not in the *Trusted Publisher store*. Provided you are installing the driver on a test computer to evaluate it rather than distributing it to a large number of client computers, this is a valid thing to do. Many drivers come from reputable sources (for example, the device manufacturer) but have not yet gone through the validation process that results in a digital signature. Even some Microsoft drivers are unsigned.

When you or other administrators are installing drivers, authorization is not typically a problem. However, you might have a driver that you want ordinary users to install. Even if you stage the driver, users cannot install it because only administrators can approve installation of a driver that does not have a valid signature.

You can obtain a self-signed certificate that is valid within your organization only from a certificate authority (CA) server running Windows Server and Certificate Services. The certificate is not trusted by other organizations where no trust relationship exists. Even within your organization, Microsoft recommends that you use this procedure only on a test network and that only drivers with valid signatures are installed in the production environment.

If you want to sign a device driver so that it can be used by other organizations, you need a certificate issued by a trusted external CA such as VeriSign. This is much more difficult to obtain.

To enable non-administrators to install a driver that does not have a trusted signature, you need to sign the device driver package with a digital certificate, and then place that certificate on client computers so that users do not have to determine whether a device driver or its publisher is "trusted."

You then need to stage the device driver package in the protected driver store of a client computer (as described previously in this lesson) so that a standard user can install the package without requiring administrator rights.

Typically, you would use Group Policy to deploy the certificate to client computers. Group Policy allows you to have the certificate automatically installed to all managed computers in a domain, organizational unit, or site.

A digital signature guarantees that a package came from its claimed source (authenticity) and it is 100 percent intact and unmodified (integrity). A digital certificate identifies an organization, and it is trustworthy because it can be checked electronically by a CA.

The high-level procedure to sign a device driver is as follows:

1. Create a digital certificate for signing. You do this on the Certificates console on the Certificate Server (CA). You can also use the MakeCert utility.

2. Add the certificate to the Trusted Root CA Certification Authorities store. This is a copy-and-paste operation that you perform in the Certificates Console, from which you can access the Trusted Root CA Certification Authorities store.

3. Add the certificate to the Trusted Publishers store. You can do this also in the Certificates snap-in.

4. Sign the device driver package with the certificate. To do this, you prepare the driver package .inf file, create a catalog file for the driver package, and sign the catalog file by using the Signtool utility.

EXAM TIP

The procedure to sign a device driver digitally has been deliberately given as a high-level procedure. You typically would do this in a domain, organizational unit, or site. The examination is most unlikely to test this procedure in any detail. It is sufficient to know that it is possible and to know why you would do it.

NOTE   DISABLE DRIVER SIGNATURE ENFORCEMENT

If you want to test new drivers that are being developed by your organization but do not want to sign these drivers every time they are revised, you can restart your computer, press F8 during reboot, and select Disable Driver Signature Enforcement. This permits you to run unsigned drivers until the computer is again rebooted. This workaround is particularly useful in 64-bit versions of Windows 7, where unsigned drivers cannot by default be installed even if you supply administrator credentials.

MORE INFO   **DISABLE DRIVER SIGNATURE ENFORCEMENT**

For more information about the Disable Driver Signature Enforcement function, see *http://msdn.microsoft.com/en-us/library/aa906338.aspx*.

Checking Digital Signatures with the DirectX Diagnostic Tool

You can use the DirectX Diagnostic (DXdiag) tool to troubleshoot DirectX-related issues. One of these issues is whether a device driver for a DirectX device (for example your video driver) has passed Microsoft's Windows Hardware Quality Labs (WHQL) testing regimen and has been digitally signed. You start the DXdiag tool by entering **dxdiag** in the Start search box, the Run command box, or the command prompt. You do not need to open an elevated command prompt to run DXdiag.

When DXdiag starts, it displays the System tab. This provides system information and specifies the version of DirectX that is installed on your computer. The first time you use the tool, select the Check For WHQL Digital Signatures check box, as shown in Figure 4-19. This option remains selected if you close and reopen the tool, so the tool will check for digital signatures each time you run it.

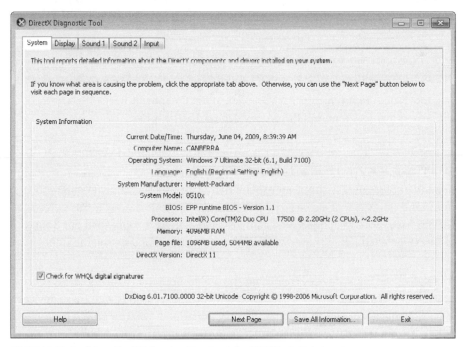

FIGURE 4-19 Enabling the DXdiag tool to check for WHQL digital signatures

The Display tab provides details about your display hardware and driver. It also lists available memory for your video hardware and tells you if your video driver has passed the WHQL testing regime. As shown in Figure 4-20, you can check whether WHQL Logo'd is set to Yes or No.

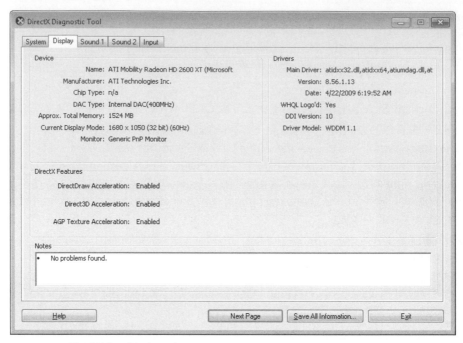

FIGURE 4-20 The DXdiag Display tab

> **NOTE** **YOUR HARDWARE MIGHT HAVE MORE AVAILABLE MEMORY THAN IS INDICATED**
>
> The *Dxdiag* tool cannot report memory that is in use at the time that it starts. Therefore, you might see less memory reported than your video card actually has.

If DXdiag detects a problem with your display settings, a warning message appears in the Notes box. Otherwise, the box displays No Problems Found.

The Sound tab displays details about your sound hardware and device driver and reports any problems in the Notes box. It also tells you whether WHQL Logo'd is set to Yes or No for that driver. If you have more than one sound card installed, you have more than one Sound tab. Default Device on each tab indicates whether the device described on the tab is the default.

The Input tab lists the input devices connected to your computer and related devices classified as USB devices and PS/2 devices. It reports any problems it finds with these devices but does not list the device drivers or say whether they are signed. You can obtain this information by accessing the devices in Device Manager.

Checking Digital Signatures with the File Signature Verification Tool

The Dxdiag tool identifies problems with DirectX hardware and tells you whether that hardware has passed the WHQL testing regimen and has been signed digitally. However, it does not test the device drivers that are not associated with DirectX devices. To scan your computer and identify any unsigned drivers, you should use the File Signature Verification (Sigverif) tool.

You start the Sigverif tool by entering **sigverif** in the Start search box, the Run command box, or the command prompt. You do not need to open an elevated command prompt to run Sigverif. The Sigverif tool is shown in Figure 4-21.

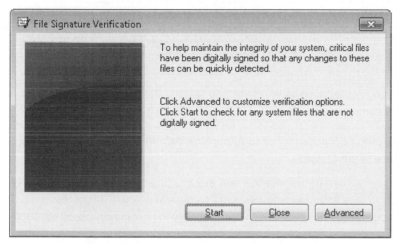

FIGURE 4-21 The Sigverif tool

You start the scan by clicking Start. Clicking Advanced lets you configure logging before a scan and view the log file when a scan is complete. Figure 4-22 shows the Sigverif log. Even if no unsigned device drivers are detected, Sigverif provides a useful method for listing every device driver on your computer.

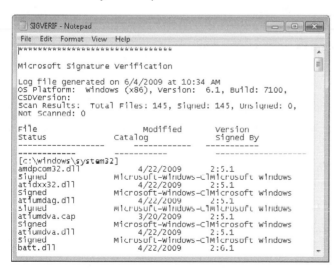

FIGURE 4-22 The Sigverif log

PRACTICE Configuring Computer Policy and Driver Search

By default, only local administrators can install devices on a computer unless these devices are authorized and their drivers are in the driver store. You can configure computer policy on a computer running Windows 7 to permit ordinary users to install devices from specific device setup classes. You can also permit these users to stage drivers on the computer.

These procedures would be suitable if you had a small number of client computers in a workgroup. In an enterprise environment, you would perform the configurations in Group Policy Editor on a domain controller and apply them to client computers. However, the procedure would be similar to that described here.

You also configure a computer running Windows 7 to search other directories for drivers that are not in the driver store.

EXERCISE 1 Configuring Computer Policy to Allow Non-Administrators to Install Specific Device Setup Classes

This exercise permits a non-administrative user to install any imaging device (such as a webcam) that has a signed driver on the Canberra computer. You first determine the GUID of the Imaging Devices setup class and then configure computer policy to permit non-administrators to install this class of device. The exercise requires that at least one device of that setup class is installed on your computer. If not, use another setup class. You need to know the procedure—the actual device setup class you choose is not important. To permit non-administrators to install a specific type of hardware device, perform the following procedure:

1. Log on to the Canberra computer with the Kim_Akers account.

2. If the Don Hall non-administrator (ordinary user) account does not already exist, create it.

3. Open Device Manager.

4. Expand Imaging Devices in the Device Manager tree. Select a device (such as a webcam).

5. Right-click the device and choose Properties.

6. On the Details tab, in the Property list, click Device Class Guid, as shown in Figure 4-23.

7. The GUID is displayed, as shown in Figure 4-24. Right-click the GUID and choose Copy. Paste the GUID into Microsoft Notepad so you do not lose it.

8. Click Start. Enter **mmc gpedit.msc** in the Start Search box and press Enter. This starts Local Group Policy Object Editor.

9. In Local Group Policy Object Editor, under Local Computer Policy, double-click Computer Configuration, double-click Administrative Templates, double-click System, and select Driver Installation.

FIGURE 4-23 Determining a device class GUID

FIGURE 4-24 Monitor device type GUID

10. In the details pane, double-click Allow Non-Administrators To Install Drivers For These Device Setup Classes, as shown in Figure 4-25.

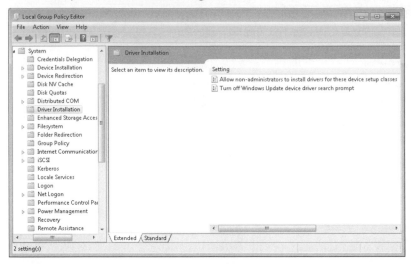

FIGURE 4-25 Accessing the Allow Non-Administrators To Install Drivers For These Device Setup Classes policy

11. In the Allow Non-Administrators To Install Drivers For These Device Setup Classes dialog box, shown in Figure 4-26, select Enabled.

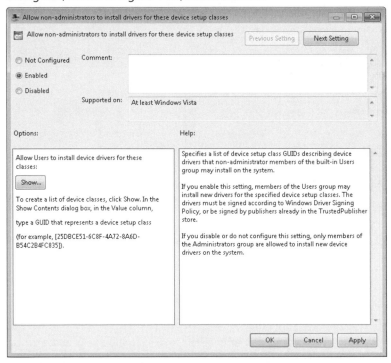

FIGURE 4-26 Enabling the Allow Non-Administrators To Install Drivers For These Device Setup Classes policy

12. Click Show.

13. In the Show Contents dialog box, select the text box under Value to highlight it, double-click the text box, and paste the GUID you copied earlier (including the curly braces). The Show Contents box should be similar to Figure 4-27.

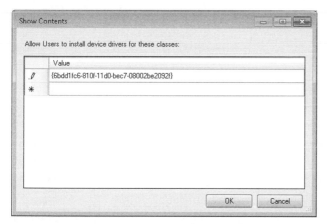

FIGURE 4-27 Pasting the GUID into the Show Contents dialog box

14. Click OK to close the Show Contents dialog box.

15. Click OK to close the Allow Non-Administrators To Install Drivers For These Device Setup Classes dialog box. Local Group Policy Editor shows the policy is Enabled.

16. If you want, stage the driver for a reputable third-party imaging device. Then log on to the Canberra computer as Don Hall and install the device. Staging a driver is described in Exercise 2.

> **NOTE   DRIVERS MUST BE SIGNED OR APPROVED BY AN ADMINISTRATOR**
>
> The device driver package must be signed in accordance with computer policy. If the certificate for the driver is not in the Trusted Publishers certificate store, then the user is prompted to accept the unverified certificate during the installation process. If the device driver does not have a valid digital signature, it is not installed unless an administrator approves its installation.

EXERCISE 2   Staging a Device Driver in the Driver Store

If you have permitted non-administrators to install devices in a device setup class, you can also enable them to install a specific device in this class automatically, as if it was a PnP device. To do this, you stage the driver for that device in the driver store.

The driver store is a protected area that contains device driver packages that have been approved for installation on the computer. After a device driver package is in the driver store, a non-administrative user on the computer can install its device without needing elevated user permissions. To stage a driver package in the driver store, perform the following procedure:

1. If necessary, log on to the Canberra computer with the Kim_Akers account.

2. Copy a driver from media supplied with a reputable third-party device to a folder on your hard disk, for example C:\Newdrivers. For copyright reasons, the driver used in this exercise has been renamed Mydriver.inf.

3. Open an elevated command prompt. If necessary, click Yes to clear the UAC dialog box.

4. Enter **pnputil –a c:\newdrivers\mydriver.inf** (amend this instruction if your path and file name are different).

5. If the driver package is not signed or is signed by a certificate that is not currently in the Trusted Publishers certificate store, the Windows Security dialog box appears, asking you to confirm whether the driver should be installed. View the details of the message to determine the problem with the driver's signature. If you are sure that the driver package is valid, click Install to finish the staging operation.

6. When staging is complete, the PnPUtil tool reports a published name (*oem*<number> *.inf*) that Windows 7 assigns to this package in the driver store. You need to reference this name if you want to delete the driver package from the store later. If you need to determine the published name for a driver package, enter **pnputil.exe -e** and search for the driver you need.

> **MORE INFO**   **THE PnPUtil TOOL**
>
> For more information about the PnPUtil tool, see *http://technet.microsoft.com/en-us/ library/cc732408.aspx*.

EXERCISE 3   Configuring Windows 7 to Search Additional Folders for Device Drivers

When a new device is connected to a computer, Windows 7 checks the driver store to determine if an appropriate driver package is staged. If not, it checks several locations to find a driver package to place in the driver store. These locations are:

- The folders specified in the DevicePath registry setting.

- The Windows Update Web site. Note that you can prohibit this Internet search in Local Group Policy Object Editor by navigating to Open Local Computer Policy/ Computer Configuration/Administrative Templates/System/Internet Communication Management/Internet Communication Settings and configuring the Turn Off Windows Update Device Driver Searching setting.

- A file path (typically to removable media) is provided by the user.

To modify the list of folders that Device Manager searches for a driver package, perform the following procedure:

1. If necessary, log on to the Canberra computer with the Kim_Akers account.

2. Click Start. Enter **regedit** in the Start Search box. If necessary, click Yes to clear the UAC dialog box.

3. Navigate to the following registry key:

   HKEY_LOCAL_MACHINE/Software/Microsoft/Windows/CurrentVersion

4. In the Details pane, double-click DevicePath.

5. Add additional folder paths to the setting, separating each folder path with a semicolon as shown in Figure 4-28. Ensure that you do not delete %Systemroot%\Inf from the setting.

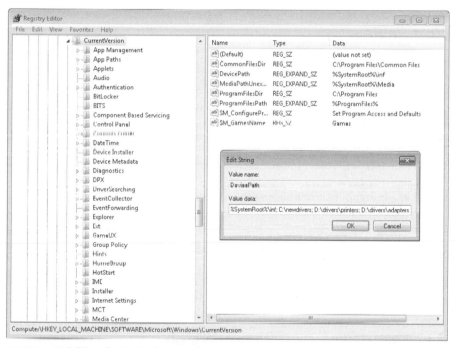

FIGURE 4-28 Editing the DevicePath setting

> *NOTE* **DEVICEPATH SUBFOLDERS**
>
> If the folders listed in the DevicePath registry entry contain other subfolders, the subfolders will also be included in the search. For example, including C:\ as one of the paths causes Windows to search the entire drive (which could take some time).

Lesson Summary

- A non-administrator can install PnP devices with valid digital signatures linked to certificates in the Trusted Publishers store. If the device driver is not in the device driver store, or if it is unsigned, or if the signature is not trusted, administrator credentials are required to install the device.

- An administrator can prestage a device by placing its driver in the device driver store. If the device driver is unsigned, the administrator can sign it with a certificate obtained from an internal CA to allow it to be installed by standard users within an organization.

- You can prevent drivers downloading from Windows Update and automatically installing. You can also remove Windows Update from the device driver search path. You can disable or stop drivers to diagnose driver problems. If a new driver is giving you problems, you can roll back to a previous driver.

Lesson Review

You can use the following questions to test your knowledge of the information in Lesson 1, "Managing Device Drivers and Devices." The questions are also available on the companion DVD if you prefer to review them in electronic form.

> **NOTE ANSWERS**
>
> Answers to these questions and explanations of why each answer choice is correct or incorrect are located in the "Answers" section at the end of the book.

1. A user without administrator privileges attaches a device to a computer running Windows 7. Which of the following needs to be true for the device to be installed? (Choose all that apply.)

   A. The device driver must have a valid digital signature.

   B. The device driver must be stored in the Trusted Publishers store.

   C. The device driver must be stored in the device driver store.

   D. The device must connect through a USB port.

   E. The device driver must be signed by Microsoft.

2. You have four devices connected to a USB hub and none of them are working satisfactorily. You suspect one of the devices requires more bandwidth and should not be connected through a hub. How do you discover the bandwidth requirements of the devices?

   A. In Device Manager, double-click Universal Serial Bus Controllers, right-click the Host Controller for your system, and choose Properties. Access the Power tab.

   B. In Device Manager, double-click Universal Serial Bus Controllers, right-click the Host Controller for your system, and choose Properties. Access the Advanced tab.

   C. In Device Manager, double-click Human Interface Devices, and right-click each instance of USB Input Device in turn. For each device, access the Details tab.

D. In Device Manager, double-click IEEE 1394 Bus Host Controllers, and right-click each device in turn. For each device, access the Resources tab.

3. You want ordinary users to install a device. The device driver has a valid digital signature that uses a certificate that is in the Trusted Publishers store. How do you ensure that non-administrators can install the device? (Choose all that apply; each answer forms part of the solution.)

   A. In Device Manager, double-click the device type, right-click the device, and click Properties. On the Details tab, determine the device class GUID. In Local Group Policy Management, enable the Allow Non-Administrators To Install Drivers For These Device Setup Classes policy and associate it with the GUID.

   B. Access the registry key HKEY_LOCAL_MACHINE/Software/Microsoft/Windows/ Current Version and double-click DevicePath In the Details pane. Add the C: drive to the device path.

   C. Stage the device driver by copying it to the Trusted Publishers store.

   D. Stage the device driver by copying it to the device driver store.

4. You want to prevent Windows 7 from searching Windows Update for a device driver when no driver is available in the device driver store. How do you do this?

   A. In the Device Installation Settings dialog box, clear Yes Do This Automatically (Recommended) and select No Let Me Choose What To Do and Never Install Driver Software From Windows Update. Click Select Changes.

   B. In Local Group Policy Object Editor, navigate to Open Local Computer Policy/Computer Configuration/Administrative Templates/System/Internet Communication Management/Internet Communication Settings and configure the Turn Off Windows Update Device Driver Searching setting.

   C. Access the registry key HKEY_LOCAL_MACHINE/Software/Microsoft/Windows/ Current Version and double-click DevicePath in the Details pane. Remove Windows Update from the device path.

   D. In the Device Installation Settings dialog box, clear Yes Do This Automatically (Recommended) and select No Let Me Choose What To Do and Always Install The Best Driver Software From Windows Update. Click Select Changes.

5. You suspect that a device listed under Non-Plug And Play Drivers in Device Manager is causing problems. How do you immediately stop the device to investigate?

   A. Open the device Properties dialog box in Device Manager. On the Driver tab, click Stop.

   B. Open the device Properties dialog box in Device Manager. On the Driver tab, change the Startup Type to Disabled.

   C. Open the device Properties dialog box in Device Manager. On the Driver tab, click Disable.

   D. Open the device Properties dialog box in Device Manager. On the Driver tab, click Uninstall.

Lesson 2: Managing Disks

Windows 7 offers a considerable number of disk management options. You can automatically clean unnecessary and unwanted files from your disks and reduce data access times by regular *defragmentation*, so files are stored on contiguous areas of the disk.

You can work with basic and dynamic disks and convert between dynamic disks, GUID Partition Table (GPT) partition style disks, and Master Boot Record (MBR) disks. You can extend and shrink volumes and work with spanned or striped partitions. Windows 7 introduces options with regard to USB external disks and USB flash memory not previously available. You can install system partitions on removable USB media and boot from it.

If you have multiple drives (or spindles) you can implement *redundant array of inexpensive disks (RAID)* systems to improve performance, provide data protection, or both. You can implement striping, mirroring, or striping with parity. You can shrink or extend volumes without needing to use third-party tools.

After this lesson, you will be able to:

- Perform disk cleanup and defragmentation.
- Manage disks with the Diskpart and Disk Management tools.
- Manage removable media.
- Manage disk volumes and partitions, including RAID volumes.

Estimated lesson time: 50 minutes

Disk Maintenance

Before we consider the options Windows 7 offers to manipulate and manage disks, we should first consider basic principles. Any disk system works better if it is not clogged with unnecessary files and if files are contiguous and not stored in fragments in different physical areas on the disk surface. Therefore, you can almost always improve performance by carrying out a disk cleanup and by defragmenting your disks on a regular basis.

Using Disk Cleanup

Disk Cleanup removes unneeded files, such as files that you downloaded to install programs, temporary Internet files, files in the Recycle Bin, offline Web pages, hibernation files, setup log files, temporary files, and thumbnails. The Disk Cleanup dialog box, shown in Figure 4-29, lets you specify the files to be removed from the disk you select. Downloaded Program Files, Temporary Internet Files, and Thumbnails are selected by default. The easiest way to access the tool is to type **disk cleanup** in the Start search box.

You can obtain details about any of the selections by clicking the item. Selecting the check box beside an item marks the relevant files for deletion. You can click View Files to get more details about the files before deciding whether or not to remove them.

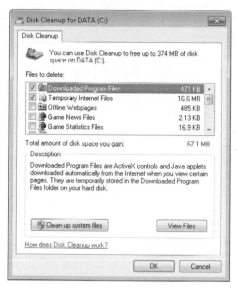

FIGURE 4-29 Disk Cleanup

When you select the various types of file you want to delete and click OK, a Disk Cleanup dialog box asks you to confirm if you want to delete the files permanently. When you click Delete Files, the files are deleted.

A standard, non-administrative user can use Disk Cleanup to delete files. If, however, you want to clean up the system files by clicking the Clean Up System Files control, you need to be logged on as an administrator or supply administrator credentials. In this case, the system cleanup happens automatically. The Disk Cleanup tool displays with the Clean Up System Files control removed, and you can access the More Options tab shown in Figure 4-30 to perform additional cleanup operations.

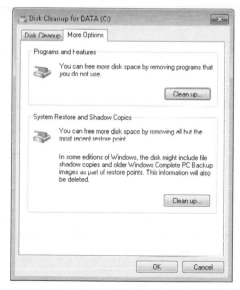

FIGURE 4-30 The Disk Cleanup More Options tab

Defragmenting Disks

You can defragment internal and external hard disks, USB flash memory devices, and virtual hard disks (VHDs). If your disk or storage device is fragmented, it can slow your computer. Disk Defragmenter rearranges fragmented data so your disks and drives can work more efficiently. Typically, Disk Defragmenter runs on a schedule, but you can also analyze and defragment your disks and drives manually.

The tool displays the disks and storage devices on the computer that can be defragmented. To obtain the current fragmentation level and determine if a disk needs to be defragmented, select the disk and click Analyze Disk. You need to be logged on with an administrator account or to supply administrator credentials to analyze (and to defragment) a disk. If the analysis shows a fragmentation level of 10 percent or more, defragment the disk by clicking Defragment Disk.

Disk defragmentation might take from several minutes to a few hours to finish, depending on the size and degree of fragmentation of the hard disk. You can continue to use your computer during the defragmentation process.

You can also schedule regular disk defragmentation by clicking Configure Schedule. The Disk Defragmenter Modify Schedule dialog box is shown in Figure 4-31. By default, disks are defragmented weekly at 1:00 AM on Wednesdays. You can change this in the pull-down menu boxes. By default, all disks are defragmented, and any new disks that are added are also defragmented. You can change this by clicking Select Disks.

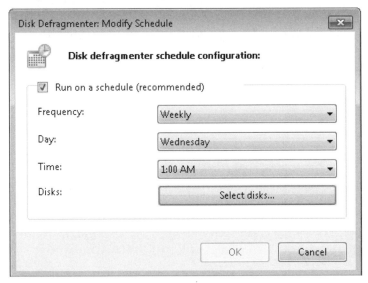

FIGURE 4-31 Scheduling disk defragmentation

You cannot set more than one schedule on a computer for disk defragmentation by using the Disk Defragmentation tool. If a disk is excluded from the schedule, it is not defragmented unless you do so manually. If a disk is in exclusive use by another program, or if a disk is formatted using a file system other than NTFS, it cannot be defragmented. Network locations cannot be defragmented.

A disk can become fragmented very quickly if it is used heavily and data is written to it frequently. Figure 4-32 (also used in the Practice Test Questions CD-ROM) shows just such a situation. Drive C: has become very highly fragmented in only six days and is already slowing the operation of the computer. The quick fix is to defragment the disk manually, but it will become fragmented again quickly. The solution is to alter the schedule and defragment more often.

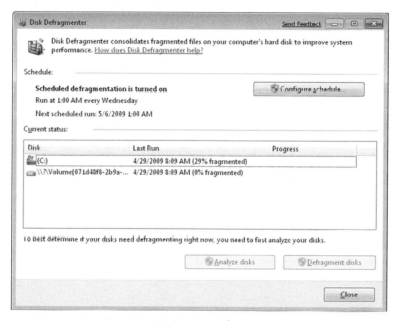

FIGURE 4-32 A high degree of disk fragmentation

You can also defragment a disk by using the command-line defragmentation tool Defrag from an elevated command prompt. Defrag has the following syntax:

```
Defrag <volume> | /C | /E <volumes> [/A | /X | /T] [/H] [/M] [/U] [/V]
```

EXAM TIP

The Defrag syntax has changed from Windows Vista. Traditionally, examiners have tended to test things that have changed.

The defrag options are as follows:

- *<volume>*   The drive letter or mount point of the volume to defragment.
- */C*   Defragment all local volumes on the computer.
- */E*   Defragment all local volumes on the computer except those specified.

- **/A** Display a fragmentation analysis report for the specified volume without defragmenting it. An analysis report tells you the volume size, available free space, total fragmented space, and the largest free space extent. It also tells you whether you need to defragment the volume.

- **/X** Perform free space consolidation. This is useful if you need to shrink a volume. It can also reduce fragmentation of future files.

- **/T** Track an operation already in progress on the specified volume.

- **/H** Run the operation at normal priority, instead of the default low priority. Specify this option if a computer is not busy doing something else.

- **/M** Defragment multiple volumes simultaneously, in parallel. This is used on computers that access multiple disks simultaneously, such as those using Small Computer System Interface (SCSI)– or Serial Advanced Technology Attachment (SATA)–based disks, rather than disks with an Integrated Development Environment (IDE) interface.

- **/U** Print the progress of the operation on the screen.

- **/V** Verbose mode. Provides additional detail and statistics.

For example, the command *defrag /c /h /u* defragments all the defragmentable disks and storage devices on a computer and shows the progress on the Command Prompt screen. The command provides a pre-defragmentation report for each disk or device, provides details of the defragmentation passes, automatically performs free space consolidation, and provides a post-defragmentation report. It runs at normal priority so it completes more quickly, but you should avoid using the */H* switch if you are carrying out other operations at the same time.

> **NOTE   DEFRAG OUTPUT**
>
> The command defrag */c /h /u* produces output too detailed to capture in a figure in this book. If you want to see it, try this on your computer instead.

Checking a Hard Disk for Errors

If a disk you expect to see in Disk Defragmenter is not there, it might be experiencing errors. You can solve computer problems and improve computer performance by checking your hard disk for errors, many of which Windows 7 can fix automatically. To check a hard disk for errors, perform the following procedure:

1. On the Start menu, choose Computer.
2. Right-click the hard disk you want to check and choose Properties.
3. On the Tools tab, under Error-Checking, click Check Now.

4. To repair detected problems automatically, select the Automatically Fix File System Errors check box. If you do not select this check box, the disk check reports problems but does not fix them.

5. To perform a thorough disk check, select the Scan For And Attempt Recovery Of Bad Sectors check box. The scan then attempts to find and repair physical errors on the hard disk itself. Note, however, that this can take considerable time. Figure 4-33 shows the Check Disk dialog box with both options selected.

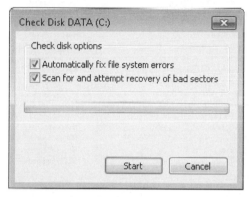

FIGURE 4-33 Scanning for file errors and physical errors

6. Click Start.

7. If you selected Automatically Fix File System Errors and specified a disk that is in use (for example, the partition that contains Windows), you are prompted to reschedule the disk check for the next time you restart your computer. In this case, ensure that your work is saved and all windows are closed and then restart your computer.

Setting Disk Policies with Local Group Policy Editor

Removable media is convenient, but it can also pose a security threat. Confidential company data saved to a USB flash memory device can easily be lost or stolen, as can data downloaded to an MP3 player or cell phone. If the computer can burn CD-ROMs or DVD-ROMs, these can also be mislaid (they make very convenient bookmarks and get lost in libraries).

As an alternative to protecting your data with BitLocker, you can prohibit users from writing data to removable media. You can also prevent users from downloading data and running software stored on removable media, which could contain malware.

On a stand-alone client computer, you can do this through Local Group Policy Editor. In an enterprise, you would edit domain Group Policy at a domain controller and apply it to all clients in the domain. In Local Group Policy Editor, expand Computer Configuration and then expand Administrative Templates. You next expand System and click Removable Storage Access. The policies that you can configure are shown in Figure 4-34. Note that "WPD devices" refers to cell phones, media players, auxiliary displays, CE devices, and so on.

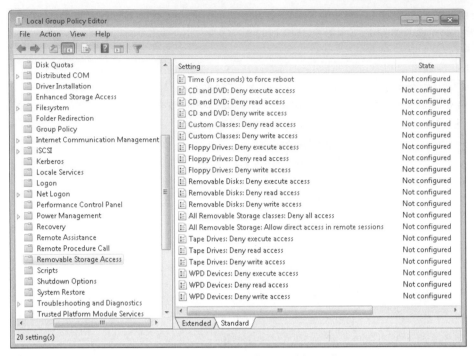

FIGURE 4-34 Configurable policies control the use of removable media.

You can enable, disable, or otherwise configure the following policies:

■ Time (In Seconds) To Force Reboot

■ CD And DVD: Deny Execute, Read, or Write Access

■ Custom Classes: Deny Read or Write Access

■ Floppy Drives: Deny Execute, Read, or Write Access

■ Removable Disks: Deny Execute, Read, or Write Access

■ All Removable Storage Classes: Deny All Access

■ All Removable Storage: Allow Direct Access In Remote Sessions

■ Tape Drives: Deny Execute, Read, or Write Access

■ WPD Devices: Deny Execute, Read, or Write Access

Most of these policies are self-explanatory. If you enable the Time (In Seconds) To Force Reboot policy, for example, you need to specify the amount of time that you want the system to wait until a reboot. If you disable or do not configure this setting, the system does not force a reboot and any access right policies you configure do not take effect until the system is restarted. Configuring the Custom Classes access rights policies lets you specify removable storage classes by entering the class GUID.

The Removable Disks policies do not apply to CD-ROMs, DVD-ROMs, or floppy disks and typically are used to control access to USB flash memory, portable media players, and cellular phones. However, if you enable the All Removable Storage Classes: Deny All Access policy, this denies execute, read, and write permission to all types of removable media and overwrites any other configured removable media access rights policies. If you enable the All Removable Storage: Allow Direct Access policy in remote sessions, remote users can access removable storage devices in remote sessions.

Detailed step-by step instructions to disable downloads to USB flash memory are given in the practice later in this lesson.

Changing Disk Type and Partition Style

Chapter 2, "Configuring System Images," introduced the Disk Management tool and discussed the new features of the tools that let you create, attach, mount, detach, and delete a VHD file. In addition to these new features, you can use Disk Management to convert disks from basic to dynamic (and less typically, from basic to dynamic) and change the partition style. Windows 7 also provides the Diskpart command-line tool for disk management.

> **NOTE FDISK**
>
> **Windows 7 does not support the Fdisk tool that was used for disk management in earlier versions of Windows.**

You need Administrator or Backup Operator credentials to perform most Disk Management tasks. You can use the tool for managing hard disks and the volumes or partitions that they contain. You can initialize disks, create volumes, and format volumes with the FAT, FAT32, or NTFS file systems. Disk Management lets you perform disk-related tasks without needing to restart the system and most configuration changes take effect immediately.

Working with Partitions

Disk Management enables you to extend and shrink partitions directly from the interface. When you right click a volume in the Disk Management console, you can choose whether to create a basic, spanned, or striped partition directly from the menu. If you add more than four partitions to a basic disk, you are prompted to convert the disk to dynamic or to the GPT partition style.

Disk Management allows you to change disks between various types and partition styles. However, some of the operations are irreversible (unless you reformat the drive). You should consider carefully the disk type and partition style that is most appropriate for your application. You can convert between the following partition styles:

- MBR can be converted to GPT if there are no volumes on the disk.
- MBR can be converted to dynamic, but the disk may become unbootable.
- GPT can be converted to MBR if there are no volumes on the disk.
- GPT can be converted to dynamic, but the disk may become unbootable.
- Dynamic can be converted to MBR if there are no volumes on the disk.
- Dynamic can be converted to GBT if there are no volumes on the disk.

If you add a disk to a computer, it appears as Not Initialized. Before you can use a disk, you must first initialize it. If you start Disk Management after adding a disk, the Initialize Disk Wizard appears. You can also right-click an uninitialized disk and click Initialize Disk. The disk is initialized as a basic disk and you can select whether to use the MBR or GPT partition style.

One advantage of GPT disks is that you can have more than four partitions on each disk. GPT is also required for disks larger than 2 TB. You can change a basic disk from MBR to GPT partition style so long as the disk does not contain any partitions or volumes. You first need to back up the data on the MBR disk so you can restore it after the conversion.

You can use Disk Management to remove any volumes or partitions on the disk you want to convert, and then to implement the conversion. Right-click each volume in turn, and then click Delete Volume. When there are no volumes or partitions on the disk, right-click it and click Convert To GPT Disk.

> **NOTE   REMOVABLE MEDIA**
>
> You cannot use the GPT partition style on removable media.

To use the Diskpart command-line utility to change a disk from MBR to GPT partition style, perform the following procedure:

1. Back up the data on the basic MBR disk that you want to convert.
2. Open an elevated command prompt and enter **diskpart.**
3. At the DISKPART> prompt, enter **list volume**. Note all the volume numbers.
4. For each volume listed, at the DISKPART> prompt, enter **select volume <*volumenumber*>.**
5. For each volume, at the DISKPART> prompt, enter **delete volume.**
6. At the DISKPART> prompt, enter **list disk.** Note the disk number of the disk that you want to convert.
7. At the DISKPART> prompt, enter **select disk <*disknumber*>.**
8. At the DISKPART> prompt, enter **convert gpt.**

You can also use both Disk Manager and the Diskpart utility to convert a GPT disk to an MBR disk. The procedure is almost identical to converting an MBR disk to a GPT disk. You must back up all data and then delete all volumes. In Disk Manager, you right-click the disk and click Convert To MBR Disk. If you are using Diskpart, you enter the Diskpart command **convert mbr** as the final command.

Using Basic and Dynamic Disks

Basic disks use the original MS-DOS-style MBR partition tables to store primary and logical disk partitioning information. Dynamic disks use a private region of the disk to maintain a Logical Disk Manager (LDM) database. The LDM database contains volume types, offsets, memberships, and drive letters of each volume. The LDM database is also replicated, so each dynamic disk knows about every other dynamic disk configuration. This feature makes dynamic disks more reliable and recoverable than basic disks.

If you move dynamic disks between computers, however, you might not be able to move the dynamic disks back to the original host. If you need to move dynamic disks, move all the dynamic disks from a computer at the same time, and make sure that they are all online and running on the destination computer before you try to import them. The disk group name and the identity of the primary disk group of the host system is always retained if a dynamic disk is present. If there are no dynamic disks already on the destination computer, that computer ends up with the same disk group name as the source computer when the disks are moved to it and you cannot then move the disks back to the source computer.

Microsoft recommends that before you convert basic disks to dynamic disks, you should determine whether you require the features provided by dynamic disks, for example spanned volumes, striped volumes, mirrored volumes, or RAID-5 volumes. If you do not intend to use these features, it may be best to use basic disks. You can change a basic disk into a dynamic disk using either Disk Management or the Diskpart command-line utility.

> **CAUTION** **CONVERTING DISKS**
>
> Before you convert disks, close any programs that are running on those disks.

 Quick Check

- What partition type enables you to have more than four partitions on each disk?

Quick Check Answer

- GPT

To convert a basic disk to a dynamic disk by using Disk Management, right-click the disk you want to convert and click Convert To Dynamic Disk.

To convert a basic disk to a dynamic disk by using Diskpart, you first select the disk you want to convert and then, at the DISKPART> prompt, enter **convert dynamic.** You do this in the practice later in this lesson.

Once converted, a dynamic disk does not contain basic volumes. When you convert a basic disk to a dynamic disk, any existing partitions or logical drives on the basic disk become simple volumes on the dynamic disk. After you convert a basic disk to a dynamic disk, you cannot change the dynamic volumes back to partitions. Instead, you must delete all dynamic volumes on the disk and then convert the dynamic disk to a basic disk. If you want to keep your data, you must first back it up or move it to another volume.

Converting a dynamic disk back to a basic disk is a much less common procedure and can have serious implications (for example, the requirement to back up data and delete all dynamic volumes). You can change a dynamic disk back into a basic disk using either Disk Management or the Diskpart command-line utility.

To use Disk Management, you must first back up all volumes on the disk you want to convert. Then, in Disk Management, right-click each volume and click Delete Volume on each of them. When all volumes on the disk have been deleted, right-click the disk and then click Convert To Basic Disk. A dynamic disk must not have any volumes nor contain any data if you want to change it back to a basic disk. Figure 4-35 shows the Disk Management controls for converting an MBR disk to a GPT disk and for converting a basic disk to a dynamic disk.

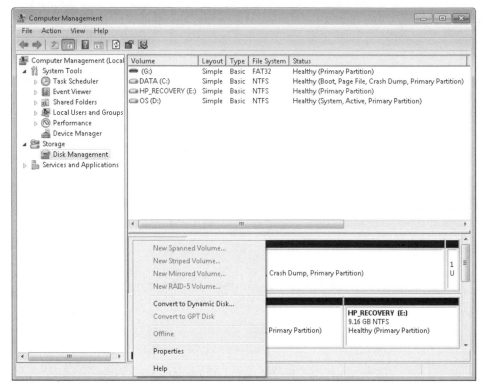

FIGURE 4-35 Controls for converting MBR and basic disks

To change a dynamic disk back to a basic disk using the Diskpart utility, perform the following procedure:

1. Back up all volumes on the disk you want to convert.

2. Open an elevated command prompt and enter **diskpart.**

3. At the DISKPART> prompt, enter **list disk.** Note the number of the disk you want to convert.

4. At the DISKPART> prompt, enter **select disk *<disknumber>*.**

5. At the DISKPART> prompt, enter **detail disk *<disknumber>*.**

6. For each volume on the disk, at the DISKPART> prompt, enter **select volume= *<volumenumber>*** and then enter **delete volume.**

7. At the DISKPART> prompt, enter **select disk *<disknumber>*.**

8. At the DISKPART> prompt, enter **convert basic.**

Moving Disks to Another Computer

Before you move disks to another computer, you should use Disk Management to make sure the status of the volumes on the disks is Healthy. If the status is not Healthy, you should repair the volumes before you move the disks. To verify the volume status, check the Status column in the Disk Management console.

Your next step is to uninstall the disks you want to move. In the Computer Management Navigation pane (the left pane), open Device Manager. In the device list, double-click Disk Drives. Right-click each of the disks you want to uninstall in turn and then click Uninstall. In the Confirm Device Removal dialog box, click OK.

If the disks that you want to move are dynamic disks, right-click the disks that you want to move in Disk Management, and then click Remove Disk.

After you have removed dynamic disks, or if you are moving basic disks, you can disconnect the disk drives physically. If the disks are external, you can now unplug them from the computer. If they are internal, turn off the computer and then remove the disks.

If the disks are external, plug them into the destination computer. If the disks are internal, make sure the computer is turned off and then install the disks in that computer. Start the destination computer and follow the instructions on the Found New Hardware dialog box.

On the destination computer, open Disk Management, click Action, and then click Rescan Disks. Right-click any disk marked Foreign, click Import Foreign Disks, and then follow the on-screen instructions.

When you move basic volumes to another computer, they receive the next available drive letter on that computer. Dynamic volumes retain the drive letter they had on the previous computer. If a dynamic volume did not have a drive letter on the previous computer, it does not receive a drive letter when moved to another computer. If the drive letter is already used on the computer where it is moved, a volume receives the next available drive letter. If an administrator has used the *mountvol /n* or the *diskpart automount* command to prevent new volumes from being added to the system, volumes moved from another computer are not mounted and do not receive a drive letter. To use the volume, you must mount it manually and assign it a drive letter using Disk Management or the *diskpart* and *mountvol* commands.

If you are moving spanned, striped, mirrored, or RAID-5 volumes, move all disks containing the volume at once. Otherwise, the volumes on the disks cannot be brought online and are not accessible except to delete them.

You can move multiple disks from different computers to a single destination computer by installing the disks, opening Disk Management, right-clicking any of the new disks, and then clicking Import Foreign Disks. When importing multiple disks from different computers, always import all of the disks from one computer at a time.

Disk Management displays the condition of the volumes on the disks before they are imported. Review this information carefully, because it can indicate what will happen to each volume on these disks once the disks have been imported.

Reactivating a Missing or Offline Dynamic Disk

A dynamic disk may become Missing when it is corrupted, powered down, or disconnected. It may become Offline if it is corrupted or intermittently unavailable, or if you attempt to import a foreign (dynamic) disk and the import fails. An error icon appears on the Offline disk. Only dynamic disks display the Missing or Offline status and can be reactivated. You reactivate a dynamic disk by right-clicking it in Disk Management and clicking Reactivate Disk.

You can also use the Diskpart utility. As in previous procedures, you list the disks and identify the disk number of the disk you need to reactivate. You select the disk by its disk number and enter the *online* command at the DISKPART> prompt.

You may instead choose to remove a missing dynamic disk. You first delete all volumes on the missing disk using either Disk Management or the Diskpart utility. In Disk Management you then right-click the disk and click Remove. If you are using Diskpart, you list the disks to discover the disk number, select the disk by its number, and enter the *delete disk* command at the DISKPART> prompt.

Managing Disk Volumes

Windows 7 enables you to expand and contract volumes without data loss and without requiring a reboot. You can create simple volumes, spanned volumes, striped volumes, mirrored volumes, and striped volumes with parity on dynamic disks. You can also create simple volumes on basic disks. The options to use unallocated portions of the disk to create volumes are shown in Figure 4-36.

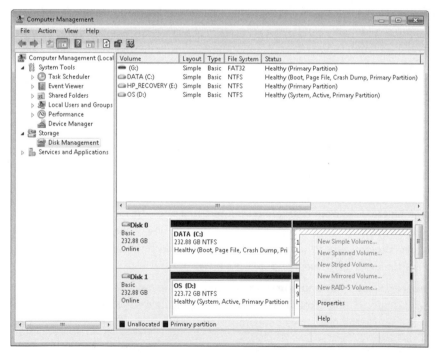

FIGURE 4-36 Volume options

Creating a Simple Volume

In Windows 7 (and Windows Vista), simple volumes can include both partitions on basic disks and simple volumes on dynamic disks. If all your requirements can be met by a simple volume, Microsoft recommends that you use a basic disk.

To create a simple volume using Disk Management, perform the following procedure:

1. Open Disk Management.
2. Right-click an unallocated space on your chosen disks and choose New Simple Volume. This starts the New Simple Volume Wizard.
3. On the Specify Volume Size page, enter the size in megabytes of the volume you want to create. The default is the maximum space available on the disk.
4. On the Assign Drive Letter Or Path page, assign a drive letter or a mount point.
5. On the Format Partition page, choose the formatting options.
6. On the Summary page, read the information provided. If this is satisfactory, click Finish.

This procedure creates simple volumes on dynamic disks and primary partitions on basic GPT disks. For basic MBR disks, the first three volumes created will be primary partitions. The fourth simple volume on a basic MBR disk is created as an extended partition and a logical drive. Further simple volumes on the basic MBR disk are logical drives.

If you create a simple volume using the Diskpart tool, you need to decide whether the disk on which you intend to create the volume is a dynamic or basic disk. Using Diskpart, you must create a partition on a basic disk and a volume on a dynamic disk. To create a simple volume on a dynamic disk, enter a command with the following syntax at the DISKPART> prompt:

```
create volume simple [size=<n>] [disk=<n>]
```

Creating a Spanned Volume

A spanned volume uses the free space on more than one physical hard disk to create a volume. The portions of disk used to create the volume do not need to be the same size and can include more than one portion of free space on a single disk. A spanned volume increases the risk of failure, leading to data loss. The failure of any disk involved in the spanned volume makes the entire volume unavailable.

Spanned volumes offer no significant performance benefit. To achieve a speed benefit with multiple disks, you must use striping, such as that provided by RAID arrays (for example, RAID-0 or RAID-5). The advantage of a spanned volume is that the portions of disk space need not be the same size and more than one of them can be on the same disk. RAID arrays are discussed later in this lesson.

You create a spanned volume on dynamic disks. To create a spanned volume using Disk Management, perform the following procedure:

1. Open Disk Management.
2. Right-click a free-space segment that you want to include in the spanned volume and then select New Spanned Volume from the shortcut menu. The New Spanned Volume Wizard starts.

3. On the Select Disks page, select the disks you want to include and then click Add to add them to the spanned volume. Select each disk in the Selected column and specify the amount of space to use on that disk for the spanned volume.

4. On the Assign Drive Letter Or Path page, the default is to assign the next available drive letter to the new volume. You can also mount the volume on an empty NTFS folder on an existing volume.

5. On the Format Volume page, choose the formatting options for the new volume. Windows 7 supports only NTFS formatting from the Disk Management snap-in. To format with FAT or FAT32, you need to use the Diskpart tool.

6. On the Summary page, read the information provided. If this is satisfactory, click Finish.

To create a spanned volume using Diskpart, you need to make sure that the disks to be used are converted to dynamic. Then you create a simple volume on the first disk of the spanned volume, extend the volume to the second disk, and then add any additional disks involved in the span. Finally, you assign the volume to a drive letter or mount point.

The Diskpart routine to create a spanned volume depends on whether the disk selected is basic or dynamic. On a basic disk, you can create a spanned volume only if you have free space on the same disk as the selected volume and contiguous to it. You then enter a command with the syntax extend [size=<n>]. If you omit the size parameter, the spanned disk is as large as the available unallocated space permits. If you have a dynamic disk with a simple or spanned volume, this can be spanned on to a second disk that has unallocated space. After you select a volume you use a command with the syntax extend [size=<n>] [disk=<n>]. If the disk parameter is omitted, the spanned volume is created on the same disk as the selected volume. If the size parameter is omitted, the spanned volume is as large as the amount of unallocated space allows.

Creating a Striped Volume (RAID-0)

A striped volume uses the free space on more than one physical hard disk to create the volume. It enables the operating system to write across all disks in small blocks, or stripes, distributing the load across the disks in the volume. Data is written to a stripe on the first disk, the next block of data is written to a stripe on the next disk, and so on. The data can be split into stripe-sized blocks and written to all the disks in the stripe set simultaneously. A striped (RAID-0) volume requires at least two disks.

When data is read from the volume, it can be accessed simultaneously on all the disks in the volume. RAID-0 therefore significantly improves both read and write performance. The portions of disk used to create the volume need to be the same size; the size of the smallest free space included in the striped volume is the determinant. A striped volume is not fault-tolerant. If one disk fails, the entire volume fails.

You create a striped volume on dynamic disks. To create a striped volume using Disk Management, perform the following procedure:

1. Open Disk Management.

2. Right-click a free-space segment that you want to include in the striped volume and click New Striped Volume. The New Striped Volume Wizard opens.

3. On the Select Disks page, select from the available disks and then click Add to add the disks to the striped volume. Specify the amount of space to use on the disks for the striped volume.

4. On the Assign Drive Letter Or Path page, the default is to assign the next available drive letter to the new volume. You can also mount the volume on an empty NTFS folder on an existing volume.

5. On the Format Volume page of the New Striped Volume Wizard, choose the formatting options for the new volume. Windows 7 supports only NTFS formatting from the Disk Management snap-in. To format with FAT or FAT32, you need to use Diskpart.

6. On the Summary page, read the information provided. If this is satisfactory, click Finish.

To create a striped volume on a dynamic disk, enter a command with the following syntax at the DISKPART> prompt:

```
create volume stripe [size=<n>] disk=<n>[,n[,..]]
```

The total size of the stripe volume is the size multiplied by the number of disks.

Creating a Mirrored Volume (RAID-1)

A mirrored or RAID-1 volume provides availability and fault tolerance but does not improve performance. It uses two disks (or two portions on separate disks) that are the same size. Any changes made to the first disk of a mirror set are also made to its mirror disk. If the first disk fails, the mirror is broken and the second disk is used until the first is repaired or replaced. The mirror is then re-created, and the information on the working disk is mirrored on the repaired disk. The disadvantage of RAID-1 is that you need (for example) two 200-GB disks to hold 200 GB of data. The advantage is that you can mirror a system disk containing your operating system.

You create a mirrored volume using a very similar procedure to the one that creates a striped volume, except that you right-click the first disk of your mirror and click New Mirrored Volume to start the appropriate wizard. You then select the second disk. The second disk needs to have a portion of unallocated space that is at least as large as the disk you want to mirror. The drive letter for a mirrored volume is the same as the drive letter of the first disk.

You can also use the Diskpart tool to create a mirrored volume. At the DISKPART> prompt you first use the *select disk* command to select the first disk. You then enter a command with the syntax add disk=<n> to specify the mirror disk.

Creating a Striped Volume with Parity (RAID-5)

A striped volume with parity offers high availability, failover protection, and performance improvement. It requires at least three disks, or equally sized portions of unallocated space on at least three separate disks. The volume is striped in a similar way to RAID-0, but on each disk, some of the capacity is used to store parity information, which is compressed information about the contents of the other disks in the set.

Thus, if a disk fails, the data it contained is stored on the other disks in the set, although there is a performance degradation because the parity information needs to be decompressed whenever it is accessed. If a replacement disk is installed, its contents can be regenerated from the parity information on the other disks.

Read performance in a RAID-5 (assuming that all disks are working) is enhanced because data can be read from all the disks in the set simultaneously. Although data can also be written to disks simultaneously, this is balanced by the need to generate and write parity information whenever a write occurs. RAID-5 offers an improvement in write performance, but this is less significant than the improvement in read performance.

Parity information uses disk space equivalent to a single disk in the RAID-5 set. Thus, if you have three disks, each 200 GB in size, you have 400 GB of useable capacity. If you have four disks, each 200 GB in size, you have 600 GB of useable capacity, and so on.

A RAID-5 volume cannot hold system information and cannot store your operating system. Typically, you use RAID-5 to store data because it provides disaster protection and improved performance. You use RAID-1 to mirror your operating system so you can still boot if a disk fails. You can use RAID-0 to store data and this improves both read and write performance significantly, but you should be aware that RAID-0 offers no fault tolerance whatsoever.

> **NOTE HARDWARE RAID**
>
> Windows 7 offers software implementations of RAID-0, RAID-1, and RAID-5 that require no additional hardware. You can purchase hardware RAID systems that offer advantages (at a price). For example, some hardware RAID-5 systems can store system files. You can also purchase other RAID systems; for example, RAID-10 implements two sets of striped (RAID-0) volumes which are then mirrored (RAID-1). This provides both significant performance gains and fault protection.

EXAM TIP

The 70-680 examination is likely to test you on software implementations of RAID in Windows 7. It is unlikely to test you on hardware RAID systems supplied by external manufacturers.

You create a striped volume with parity using a very similar procedure to that which creates a striped volume, except that you right-click the first disk with unallocated space and click New RAID-5 Volume to start the appropriate wizard. You then select the remaining disks in the set and specify the size of the volume. By default, the equal portion of unallocated space on each disk used to create the volume is equal to the portion of unallocated space on the volume with the least amount of that resource. Thus, if the first disk selected has 100 GB of unallocated space, the second 150 GB of unallocated space, and the third 200 GB of unallocated space, a 300-GB RAID-5 volume with 200 GB of usable storage is created by default.

As with a RAID-0 volume, you then specify the drive letter or mount point and the formatting option.

You can also use the Diskpart tool to create a RAID-5 volume. At the DISKPART> prompt, you enter a command with the following syntax:

```
create volume raid [size=<n>] disk=<n>[,n[,..]]
```

Resizing a Volume

Windows 7 enables you to expand and shrink simple volumes and spanned volumes, but striped volumes are fixed in size. To change the size of a striped volume, you need to delete and re-create it.

To shrink a volume using Disk Management, perform the following procedure:

1. Open the Disk Management console.

2. Right-click the volume you want to shrink and click Shrink Volume. Disk Management queries the volume to discover the maximum available shrink space. This can take some time.

3. The Shrink dialog box, displayed in Figure 4-37, shows the maximum amount (in megabytes) that you can shrink the volume. Specify the amount which you want to shrink the volume and click Shrink. The shrink process proceeds without further prompting.

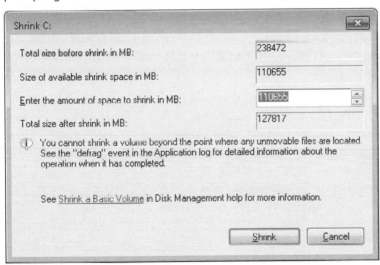

FIGURE 4-37 The Shrink dialog box

You can also use the Diskpart tool to list the volumes available for shrinking and to shrink a selected volume. The procedure to do this is as follows:

1. Open an elevated command prompt.

2. Enter **diskpart.**

3. At the DISKPART> prompt, enter **list volume.**

4. Select the volume you want to shrink; for example, enter **select volume 2.**

5. To find out the maximum amount by which you can shrink the volume, enter **shrink querymax.**

6. To shrink the selected volume, enter a command of the form **shrink desired=<n>**, where <n> is the size in megabytes by which you want to shrink the volume. Figure 4-38 shows this procedure.

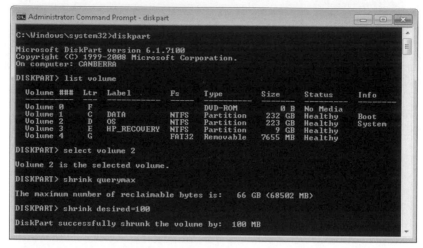

FIGURE 4-38 Using Diskpart to shrink a volume

The procedures to extend a volume are similar. In Disk Management, you right-click the volume you want to extend, click Extend Volume, and complete the Extend Volume Wizard. If you are using Diskpart, you select a volume and enter a command with the following syntax:

```
extend [size=<n>] [disk=<n>]
```

Deleting a Volume

You can delete a volume from either the Disk Management snap-in or the command line. Deleting a volume permanently erases the data stored on the volume.

In the Disk Management console, right-click the volume and then click Delete Volume. From the DISKPART> prompt, list the volumes with the *list volume* command, select the volume (for example, *select volume 3*), and enter the *delete volume* command.

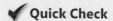 **Quick Check**

- You have selected a volume using the Diskpart tool. What command tells you the maximum amount by which you can shrink it?

Quick Check Answer

- *shrink querymax*

MORE INFO **DISKPART**

For more information about the Diskpart command-line tool, see *http://support.microsoft.com/kb/300415.*

Configuring Access Policy and Converting a Disk

In this practice, you use the Local Group Policy Editor to configure a computer policy that denies write access to USB flash memory devices. You then use the Diskpart command-line utility to convert a basic disk to dynamic.

EXERCISE 1 Configuring Write Access to USB Flash Memory Devices

In this exercise, you disable write access to USB flash memory devices. You then remove this configuration setting.

1. Ensure you have a USB flash memory device connected to your computer.
2. Log on to the Canberra computer with the Kim_Akers account.
3. Click Start, and in the Start Search box, enter **gpedit.msc.** This opens the Local Group Policy Editor.
4. In the left pane of the Local Group Policy Editor, expand Computer Configuration and then expand Administrative Templates.
5. Expand System and click Removable Storage Access.
6. Click Standard to select the Standard tab on the right pane. You see a screen similar to Figure 4-34.
7. In the right pane, double-click Removable Disks: Deny Write Access.
8. Select Enabled, as shown in Figure 4-39. Click OK.

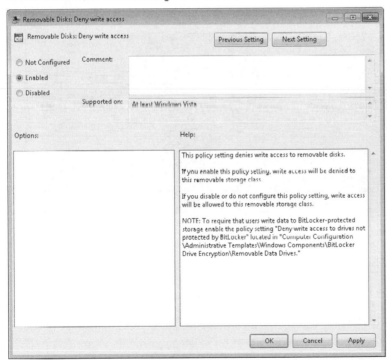

FIGURE 4-39 Enabling the Removable Disks: Deny Write Access policy

9. Check that you can no longer write to the USB flash memory device. You might have to remove the device and reinsert it to see it in the Computer console.

10. In the Local Group Policy Editor, double-click Removable Disks: Deny Write Access.

11. Select Not Configured. Click OK.

12. Check that you can now write to the USB flash memory device. As before, you might have to remove the device and reinsert it to see it in the Computer console.

EXERCISE 2   Converting a Basic Disk to Dynamic

Converting a basic disk to dynamic is typically a safe procedure that does not affect the information on the disk. Nevertheless, before you attempt this procedure, it is a good idea to back up any important files on the disk. If you have two disks on your computer, choose the disk that does not contain your operating system.

1. If necessary, log on to the Canberra computer with the Kim_Akers account.

2. On the All Programs/Accessories menu, right-click Command Prompt and click Run As Administrator. If necessary, click OK to close the UAC dialog box.

3. Enter **diskpart.**

4. At the DISKPART> prompt, enter **list disk** and note the number of the disk you want to convert.

5. At the DISKPART> prompt, enter **select disk <*disknumber*>**. Your screen should look similar to Figure 4-40.

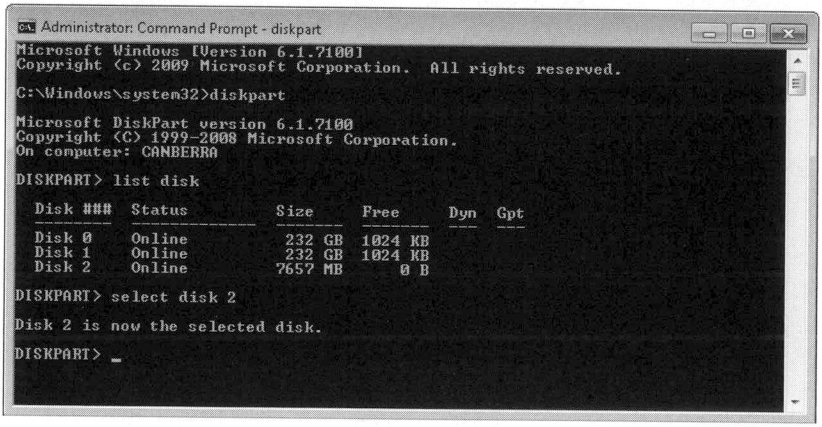

FIGURE 4-40 Selecting a disk to convert

6. At the DISKPART> prompt, enter **convert dynamic.**

Lesson Summary

- You can use the Disk Management console or the Diskpart command-line tool to manage disks, partitions, and volumes on a computer running Windows 7.
- You can use Group Policy to control access to removable devices.

- Windows 7 supports basic disks, dynamic disks, the MBR partition type, and the GPT partition type and allows you to convert from one to the other.
- Windows 7 offers software RAID-0, RAID-1, and RAID-5 volumes. You can also create simple and spanned volumes. You can shrink or expand a volume without needing to use third-party tools.

Lesson Review

You can use the following questions to test your knowledge of the information in Lesson 2, "Managing Disks." The questions are also available on the companion DVD if you prefer to review them in electronic form.

NOTE ANSWERS

Answers to these questions and explanations of why each answer choice is correct or incorrect are located in the "Answers" section at the end of the book.

1. Which Diskpart command converts an MBR disk to a GPT disk?

   A. *convert gpt*

   B. *convert mbr*

   C. *convert basic*

   D. *convert dynamic*

2. You require fault tolerance for your operating system so that your computer running Windows 7 Home Premium can still boot up if a disk fails. You have two disks and unallocated space on your second disk. What do you do?

   A. Create a VHD and install an image of your computer on the VHD. Use BCDEdit to make the VHD bootable.

   B. Create a RAID-0 volume.

   C. Create a RAID-1 volume.

   D. Create a RAID-5 volume.

3. You want to prohibit read, write, and execute access to all types of external storage devices. What computer policy setting do you enable?

   A. All Removable Storage: Allow Direct Access In Remote Sessions

   B. All Removable Storage Classes: Deny All Access

   C. Removable Disks: Deny Read Access

   D. Removable Disks: Deny Write Access

4. You are using the Diskpart tool to create a RAID-0 volume from unallocated space on Disks 1, 2, and 3. You want the volume to be as large as possible. What command do you enter?

   A. `create volume stripe size=0 disk=1,2,3`

   B. `create volume stripe disk=1,2,3`

C. `create volume raid size=0 disk=1,2,3`

D. `create volume raid disk=1,2,3`

5. You are moving a dynamic volume from the Canberra computer running Windows 7 to the Aberdeen computer running Windows 7. The disk had been allocated drive letter H: on Canberra. Drives C:, D:, and E: already exist on Aberdeen. You have not configured Aberdeen to prevent new volumes from being added to the system. What drive letter is allocated to the disk on Aberdeen?

A. The disk is not mounted, and no drive letter is allocated.

B. F:

C. G:

D. H:

Chapter Review

To further practice and reinforce the skills you learned in this chapter, you can perform the following tasks:

- Review the chapter summary.
- Review the list of key terms introduced in this chapter.
- Complete the case scenarios. These scenarios set up real-word situations involving the topics of this chapter and ask you to create a solution.
- Complete the suggested practices.
- Take a practice test.

Chapter Summary

- If a device is not PnP, you need to supply administrator credentials to install it. You can prestage a device driver and (if necessary) digitally sign it so non-administrators can install it.
- You can prevent drivers downloading from Windows Update and installing automatically. You can also remove the Windows Update site from the search path for device drivers not in the device driver store. You can update, disable (or stop), uninstall, or roll back device drivers.
- Windows 7 enables you to manage disks, partitions, and volumes and to control access to removable devices. You can convert one disk type to another and one partition type to another. You can shrink or expand volumes.
- Windows 7 supports single, spanned, RAID-0, RAID 1, and RAID-5 volumes.

Key Terms

Do you know what these key terms mean? You can check your answers by looking up the terms in the glossary at the end of the book.

- **defragmentation**
- **driver store**
- **staging**
- **Redundant Array of Independent Disks (RAID)**
- **Trusted Publisher store**

Case Scenarios

In the following case scenarios, you apply what you've learned about deploying system images. You can find answers to these questions in the "Answers" section at the end of this book.

Case Scenario 1: Enforcing a Driver Signing Policy

You are a senior systems administrator at the A. Datum Corporation. A. Datum's written company policy states that only drivers that have been through the WHQL evaluation process and have been digitally signed by Microsoft should be installed on the production network. You have a test network completely separate from the production network on which you test software, including currently unsigned device drivers. You suspect that one of your assistants has installed an unsigned driver on a computer on the production network and as a result, the video card on that computer is not working properly.

Answer the following questions:

1. How do you check the DirectX video card and discover whether the driver is not WHQL-approved and if there are any other problems?

2. How do you check there are no other unsigned drivers installed on the computer?

3. If the problem is not the driver, what tool can you use to determine if there is a resource clash with other hardware?

4. The unsigned driver in question worked fine on your test network. You want to test it again more thoroughly under stress conditions, such as low resources. What tool can you use to do this?

Case Scenario 2: Managing Disks

You have configured a computer running Windows 7 Enterprise and added three hard disks. Drive 0 is the original disk. It holds the operating system on the C: drive. It is a 200-GB disk and has no unallocated space. Drive 1 is a 200-GB drive, Drive 2 is a 400-GB drive, and Drive 3 is a 200-GB drive. Currently, all space on Disks 1, 2, and 3 is unallocated. You want to ensure fault tolerance for both your operating system and your data. You also want to reduce the time taken to access data.

Answer the following questions:

1. What type of volume would you create to hold your operating system, and on which disks would you create it?

2. What type of volume would you create to hold your data, and on which disks would you create it?

3. Given the answer to question 2, what would be the size of the usable data storage on your data volume?

Suggested Practices

To help you master the exam objectives presented in this chapter, complete the following tasks.

Investigate the Group Policies Available for Managing Device Installation

- **Practice 1** Investigate the available policies in the Local Group Policy Editor. Double-clicking any policy enables you to read a detailed description. In particular, browse to Computer Management, Administrative Templates, System, and investigate the policies under Removable Storage Access, Driver Installation, Device Installation, and Device Installation Restrictions.

Use the Driver Verifier Monitor Tool

- **Practice 1** Use the Driver Verifier Monitor to test a chosen driver under stress conditions. If you intend to install a third-party device that is not PnP, use the Driver Verifier Monitor to test the driver the manufacturer provides.

Use Diskpart

- **Practice 1** The Diskpart tool is widely used for disk management. Use the tool until you are familiar with its parameters and processes, such as selecting (focusing) on a disk or volume before carrying out operations on it. Look at how you would create scripts using the tool and the use of the *noerr* parameter.

Take a Practice Test

The practice tests on this book's companion DVD offer many options. For example, you can test yourself on just one exam objective, or you can test yourself on all the 70-680 certification exam content. You can set up the test so that it closely simulates the experience of taking a certification exam, or you can set it up in study mode so that you can look at the correct answers and explanations after you answer each question.

> ***MORE INFO*** **PRACTICE TESTS**
>
> For details about all the practice test options available, see the section entitled "How to Use the Practice Tests," in the Introduction to this book.

CHAPTER 5

Managing Applications

One of the most important aspects of migrating to a new operating system is ensuring that all of the business-critical applications that functioned on the previous operating system function on computers running the new operating system. Organizations are understandably unwilling to migrate to a new operating system if it means that they will be unable to run the applications necessary to perform their important business activities. Compatibility is a big issue with the adoption of Windows 7 because many organizations will be migrating from Windows XP. Applications designed to run on Windows XP sometimes do not run on Windows 7 because of compatibility problems. Windows 7 includes several application compatibility features that allow administrators to configure the operating system in such a way so that these older applications can be run, which allows organizations that rely on these older applications to move their computers to Windows 7.

Just as it is important to ensure that critical business applications function on a new operating system, it is also important to block users from executing unauthorized applications that may disrupt a business environment. There can be many reasons for only allowing a list of authorized applications to execute on a computer. These reasons range from securing your environment against malware to ensuring that users are not distracted by productivity-sapping diversionary applications. Allowing only authorized applications to execute automatically stops the execution of unauthorized applications, such as malware, games, and file sharing programs.

In this chapter, you learn what steps you can take to resolve application compatibility issues, from configuring the built-in Windows 7 compatibility modes to using the Windows XP Mode virtualization option. You also learn how to use AppLocker and Software Restriction Policies to limit which applications that users can execute on the computers running Windows 7 in your organization.

Exam objectives in this chapter:

- Configure application compatibility.
- Configure application restrictions.

Lessons in this chapter:

Before You Begin

To complete the exercises in the practices in this chapter, you need to have done the following:

- Install the Windows 7 operating system on a stand-alone client PC, as described in Chapter 1, "Install, Migrate, or Upgrade to Windows 7."

- Download Process Explorer from Microsoft's Web site. You can find Process Explorer by navigating to *http://technet.microsoft.com/en-us/sysinternals/bb896653.aspx*.

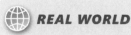 **REAL WORLD**

Orin Thomas

Software Restriction Policies are one of those things that are a great idea in theory but rather time consuming to implement in practice. The theory is that you can use Software Restriction Policies to enforce an allow list of applications that you let run on the computers that are in your organization. If the application is not on the list, it cannot execute. In practice, this means figuring out precisely which executable files on your computer you are going to allow. This is not a simple process because there are a lot of applications hidden in the Windows folder that are essential to the operation of the computer. The strongest sort of Software Restriction Policy is the hash rule, which uses a digital fingerprint for file identification. To use hash rules, you need to generate manually a separate digital fingerprint for every executable file on your allow list. Needless to say, this takes even longer than coming up with the list itself. To complicate matters further, every time you update your software with a patch, you need to recalculate the hash values for all executable files modified by the update process. This is because the original digital fingerprint no longer matches the updated files. The process of generating an allow list and then going out to calculate and recalculate hash values is one that even the most enthusiastic security administrators find a little tedious. It results in a very secure environment, but it takes a lot of effort to maintain that security. AppLocker, which debuts in Windows 7 and Windows Server 2008 R2, greatly reduces the workload involved in creating an application allow list. There are wizards that automate the process of creating hash rules. There are also improved publisher rules that give you the ability to allow-list a particular application and all later versions of that application. You can build a reference system and then automatically generate rules for every executable file on it. Needless to say, this improvement allows the great idea in theory to become a great idea in practice.

Lesson 1: Application Compatibility

There are significant differences between Windows 7 and earlier Microsoft Windows client operating systems. Improvements in the way that the operating system handles application security, with features such as Data Execution Protection and Mandatory Integrity Control, mean that applications that were able to perform certain functions in earlier versions of Windows are unable to perform the same functions when run on the Windows 7 platform. As already mentioned, this can cause problems for administrators trying to migrate organizations from earlier Windows client operating systems to Windows 7. In this lesson, you learn about the steps that you can take to resolve application compatibility problems that stop important applications that worked on one version of Windows from functioning properly on the Windows 7 platform.

After this lesson, you will be able to:

- Configure compatibility modes for applications by editing their properties.
- Configure compatibility fixes using the Application Compatibility Toolkit (ACT)
- Locate Windows Internet Explorer compatibility issues using the Internet Explorer Compatibility Test Tool.

Estimated lesson time: 40 minutes

Configuring Compatibility Options

Although many applications that work on Windows XP work without a problem on Windows 7, a small, but significant, number of mission-critical applications do not. There are several steps that you can take to configure these applications to run on Windows 7, ranging from simply letting the Program Compatibility troubleshooter automatically select compatibility settings to running the application in Windows XP Mode, a fully virtualized operating system environment. The important thing to realize is that there will be a way to get an incompatible application to work on a computer running Windows 7, but that it may take some time and effort to find.

The Program Compatibility Troubleshooter

The Program Compatibility troubleshooter, shown in Figure 5-1, is a tool that automatically attempts to configure application compatibility settings based on a set of tests that it performs on an application. This is the simplest method of resolving compatibility problems because the problem is fixed automatically by the operating system. After the Program Compatibility troubleshooter has determined the solution to the compatibility problem, that solution is remembered and the application functions without causing problems in the future.

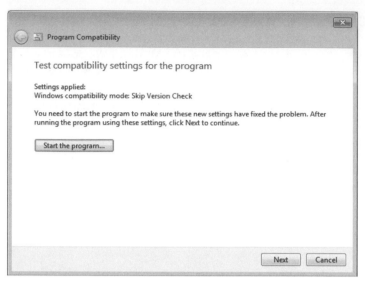

FIGURE 5-1 Program Compatibility troubleshooter

The Program Compatibility troubleshooter works only with executable files. You can start it by right-clicking a problematic application shortcut or file and then clicking Troubleshoot Compatibility. You cannot use the Program Compatibility troubleshooter to troubleshoot the installation of an installation file that is in .MSI format. The Program Compatibility troubleshooter solves the most common compatibility problems. If the Program Compatibility troubleshooter does not resolve the compatibility problem that you are having, it will be necessary to move on to the next method: manually specifying a built-in compatibility mode.

Built-in Compatibility Modes and Options

Windows 7 includes several built-in compatibility modes that allow you to configure an application to execute using settings that partially replicate the environment of previous operating systems. Although these compatibility modes replicate previous operating systems in some respects, an application that functioned on one of these operating systems does not always function when you configure it to use a corresponding compatibility mode. You can configure compatibility modes for applications by editing the application's properties and navigating to the Compatibility tab on the Properties dialog box, as shown in Figure 5-2.

You can use the drop-down menu to select from one of the following compatibility modes:

- Windows 95
- Windows 98 / Windows Me
- Windows NT 4.0 (Service Pack 5)
- Windows 2000
- Windows XP (Service Pack 2)

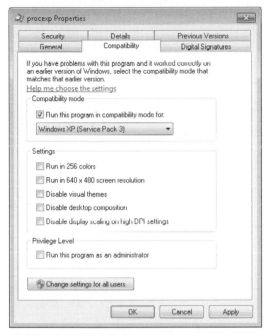

FIGURE 5-2 Available compatibility modes

- Windows XP (Service Pack 3)
- Windows Server 2003 (Service Pack 1)
- Windows Vista
- Windows Vista (Service Pack 1)
- Windows Vista (Service Pack 2)

Windows 7 also supports other compatibility options, which are available on the same tab. These options include:

- **Run In 256 Colors**   This option allows you to run applications designed to run with a limited color pallet to display correctly.

- **Run In 640 x 480 Screen Resolution**   This option allows applications that are designed to run in low resolution and do not support higher resolutions to display properly.

- **Disable Visual Themes**   Visual themes can cause display problems with the menus and buttons in some applications. Enabling this setting can resolve those problems.

- **Disable Desktop Composition**   Enabling this setting disables features of the Aero user interface (UI) such as transparency while the application is active.

- **Disable Display Scaling On High DPI Images**   Enabling this option turns off automatic resizing of applications if large-scale fonts are being used. This setting should be enabled if large-scale fonts adversely impact on application appearance.

- **Run This Program As An Administrator**   Some older programs that require administrative privileges are not able to prompt for elevation, which would normally result in a user being presented with a User Account Control dialog box. Enabling this option runs the program as an Administrator. This means that only users that have administrative privileges on the computer are able to execute this program.
- **Change Settings For All Users**   By default, when you configure compatibility options, they only apply to the currently logged on user. You can click the Change Settings For All Users button to configure compatibility settings for all users of the computer.

When the Program Compatibility troubleshooter runs, it tries to use these options to get the application to work. If the troubleshooter is unsuccessful, you may have success manually adjusting these options. You cannot configure the compatibility options of applications that are included with the Windows operating system. In the event that you are unable to configure these compatibility options to get the application to work, you can use the ACT to create a custom application compatibility mode that is more specifically tailored for the application you are trying to run.

 Quick Check

- Which compatibility option should you enable for a program that needs administrative privileges but that triggers a User Account Control prompt?

Quick Check Answer

- You should enable the Run This Program As An Administrator option because this allows the application to run using elevated privileges. The user is presented with a User Account Control prompt prior to elevated privileges being granted.

The Application Compatibility Toolkit

The Application Compatibility Toolkit (ACT) is a collection of tools that allows you to resolve application compatibility issues. You can use the ACT to determine whether existing applications are compatible with Windows 7 before deploying the new operating system.

The ACT contains the following components:

- Application Compatibility Manager
- Compatibility Administrator
- Internet Explorer Compatibility Test Tool
- Setup Analysis Tool
- Standard User Analyzer

You learn more about each of these tools in the rest of this lesson.

Application Compatibility Manager

The Application Compatibility Manager, shown in Figure 5-3, allows you to configure, collect, and analyze compatibility data so you can resolve issues prior to deploying Windows 7 in your organization. The Application Compatibility Manager interfaces with a Microsoft SQL Server database that stores all the collected compatibility telemetry. You can use the Application Compatibility Manager to create and deploy data-collection packages. Data-collection packages gather data about hardware, software, and device information for a group of specified client computers. This data is forwarded through Application Compatibility Manager to the SQL Server database, which must be present on your network if you want to use this tool. By analyzing the contents of the database, you can understand what compatibility issues are likely to be experienced given the current application deployment within your organization.

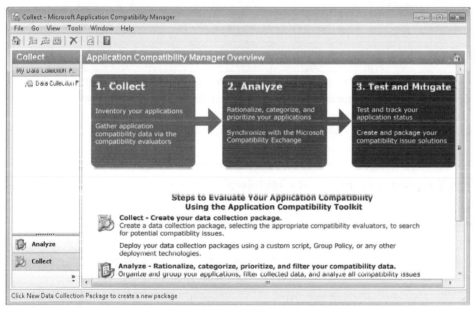

FIGURE 5-3 Application Compatibility Manager

Compatibility Administrator

The Compatibility Administrator, shown in Figure 5-4, allows you to resolve a large number of application compatibility issues that might occur when you attempt to deploy an existing application on Windows 7. The Compatibility Administrator provides a collection of individual compatibility fixes and compatibility modes that can resolve problems with existing software. A large number of existing applications already have compatibility fixes that allow them to run on the Windows 7 platform, and you should check here first to see if a solution has already been developed for the application that you are interested in.

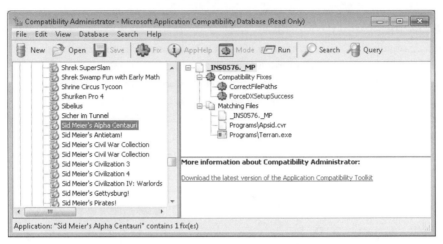

FIGURE 5-4 Compatibility Administrator showing an existing fix

If no solution exists within the database, you can also create your own compatibility fixes, compatibility modes, and compatibility databases that can help resolve application compatibility issues. A *compatibility fix*, also known as a *shim*, is a piece of software that intercepts application programming interface (API) calls from applications, modifying them so that Windows 7 provides a similar response as a previous version of Windows did. A *compatibility mode* is a group of compatibility fixes.

Internet Explorer Compatibility Test Tool

The Internet Explorer Compatibility test tool, shown in Figure 5-5, allows you to test existing Web sites to determine if they have compatibility problems that adversely influence how they will display on Internet Explorer 8, the version of Internet Explorer that ships with Windows 7. As many organizations have business-critical Web applications on their intranet, it is as important to resolve compatibility issues with Web applications as it is to resolve compatibility issues with more traditional applications. To use Internet Explorer Compatibility Test Tool, open the tool from the Developer And Tester Tools menu the Microsoft Application Compatibility Toolkit folder on the Start menu, click Enable, and then open Internet Explorer. A message appears informing you that compatibility evaluation logging is enabled. Visit the Web sites and Web applications that you need to test. As you visit each site, the test tool records potential compatibility issues.

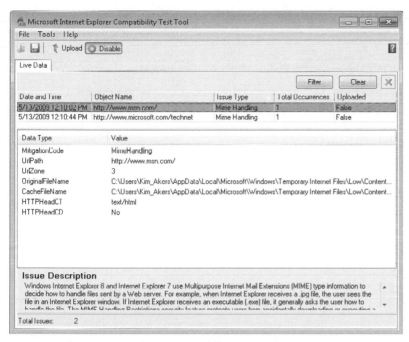

FIGURE 5-5 The Internet Explorer Compatibility Test Tool

Setup Analysis Tool

The Setup Analysis Tool monitors the actions taken by application installers and can detect the following compatibility issues:

- Installation of kernel mode drivers
- Installation of 16-bit components
- Installation of Graphical Identification and Authentication dynamic-link libraries (DLLs)
- Modification of files or registry keys that are guarded by Windows Resource Protection (WRP)

To perform an analysis, open the Setup Analysis Tool and type in the location of the setup file that you want to analyze. The Setup Analysis Tool runs the setup command and profiles the installation procedure to determine what issues might exist.

Standard User Analyzer

The Standard User Analyzer, shown in Figure 5-6, allows you to test applications to determine if they might have compatibility issues caused by User Account Control. The Standard User Analyzer provides data about problematic files and APIs, registry keys, .ini files, tokens, privileges, namespaces, processes, and other related items that the application uses that might cause problems when running on a computer with Windows 7 installed. To use the Standard User Analyzer, start the tool, specify the target application, and then click Launch.

The application attempts to start, and the Standard User Analyzer profiles how it interacts with the Windows 7 environment.

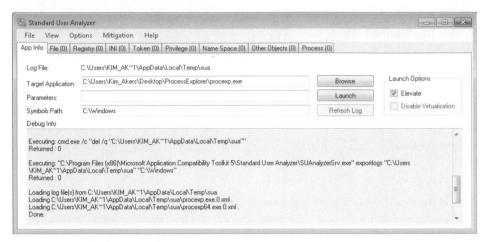

FIGURE 5-6 Standard User Analyzer

MORE INFO **ACT**

For more information about the ACT, consult the following *TechNet Magazine* article: *http://technet.microsoft.com/en-us/magazine/dd797545.aspx.*

Application Compatibility Diagnostics Policies

There are six application compatibility related group policies that influence how Windows 7 responds when it encounters an application compatibility problem. These policies are located in the Computer Configuration\Administrative Templates\System\Troubleshooting and Diagnostics\Application Compatibility Diagnostics node of a Group Policy Object (GPO). These policies are shown in Figure 5-7.

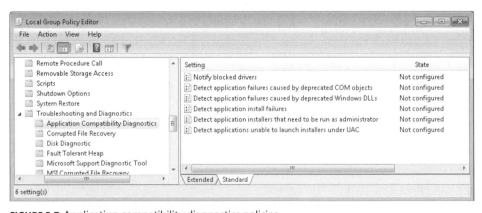

FIGURE 5-7 Application compatibility diagnostics policies

The policies have the following functions:

- **Notify Blocked Drivers**   When enabled, Windows notifies the user when a driver is blocked due to compatibility issues.

- **Detect Application Failures Caused By Deprecated COM Objects**   When enabled, Windows notifies the user if a program attempts to create a COM object that is not supported by Windows 7.

- **Detect Application Failures Caused By Deprecated Windows DLLs**   When enabled, Windows notifies the user if a program tries to load Windows DLLs that are not supported by Windows 7.

- **Detect Application Install Failures**   When enabled, application installer failures are detected and the user is presented with the option to restart the installation process using application compatibility mode.

- **Detect Application Installers That Need To Be Run As Administrator**   When enabled, application installations that fail because they need to be run as an administrator can be restarted with the Run As Administrator option.

- **Detect Applications Unable To Launch Installers Under UAC**   This setting is similar to the previous one except that instead of running as an administrator, the user receives a User Account Control prompt to elevate privileges when the installation of an application fails.

If you do not configure these policies, the default Windows 7 setting is to notify the user that the failure has occurred and, in some instances, to start the Program Compatibility Troubleshooter. In environments where users are not able to resolve application compatibility issues by themselves, administrators often disable these notifications because there is little reason to notify a user of the reason for the failure if the user is unable to resolve the problem causing the failure.

Windows XP Mode for Windows 7

Windows XP Mode is a downloadable compatibility option that is available for the Professional, Enterprise, and Ultimate editions of Windows 7. Windows XP Mode uses the latest version of Microsoft Virtual PC to allow you to run an installation of Windows XP virtually under Windows 7. The difference between Windows XP Mode and other operating system virtualization solutions is that all applications that you install on the Windows XP Mode client will be available automatically on the Windows 7 host computer. For example, if you install Microsoft Office 2000 on the Windows XP Mode client, the shortcuts for the Office 2000 applications become available on the Windows 7 Start menu. When you run an application, it starts in its own separate window as any other application does. From the perspective of the user, this means that applications appear as though they are executing directly within Windows 7.

Windows XP Mode requires a processor that supports hardware virtualization using either the AMD-V or Intel VT options. Most processors have this option disabled by default; to enable it, you must do so from the computer's BIOS. After the setting has been configured, it is necessary to turn the computer off completely. The setting is not enabled if you perform a warm reboot after configuring BIOS. As 256 MB of RAM must be allocated to the Windows XP Mode client, the computer running Windows 7 on which you deploy Windows XP Mode requires a minimum of 2 GB of RAM, which is more than the 1 GB of RAM Windows 7 hardware requirement.

To install applications that are not compatible with Windows 7, you must start the Windows XP Mode client from the Windows Virtual PC folder of the Start menu. After you have installed the application, you can then start it from the Virtual Windows XP Applications folder of the Start menu. You can also copy items from this folder to the desktop or to the Taskbar to start them directly as you would any other program installed on a computer running Windows 7. When you start an application installed on Virtual XP directly from the Start menu in Windows 7, the Virtual Windows XP operating system is shut down, as shown in Figure 5-8.

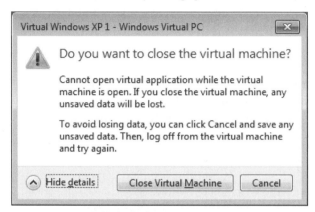

FIGURE 5-8 Virtual XP shut down to run application

Windows XP Mode provides an x86 version of Windows XP Professional SP3. Windows Virtual PC does not support x64 virtual clients, which means that you cannot use Windows XP Mode or Virtual PC as a compatibility solution for x64 applications. Because the application is not executing natively within Windows 7, there will be some performance overhead to using an application through Windows XP Mode.

You should consider Windows XP Mode as a compatibility option of last resort. This is because it requires significantly more system resources to use than the built-in or custom compatibility modes. Another drawback to Windows XP Mode is that it requires administrators to manage and maintain the Windows XP virtual client as they would any other client desktop computer in their organization. This means that you need to keep the Windows XP virtual client up to date with updates even though the people using the computer will not be accessing the Windows XP operating system directly.

EXAM TIP

An application that functions well on a computer that has Windows XP SP3 installed, but which does not run normally on Windows 7, might run without a problem if you configure it to use the Windows XP SP3 compatibility mode.

In this practice, you investigate Windows 7 compatibility options for an application that you have downloaded from the Internet.

EXERCISE Configuring Compatibility Options for Process Explorer

In this exercise, you explore the compatibility options for an application and verify that an application is digitally signed. Although Process Explorer functions without problems in Windows 7, you need to obtain an application that is not included with Windows 7 to configure compatibility options. It is not possible to configure compatibility options for an application that is included within Windows 7, such as Calc.exe or Solitaire.exe.

1. If you are not logged on already, log on to computer Canberra using the Kim_Akers user account. If you have not already downloaded the file ProcessExplorer.zip to the desktop from Microsoft's Web site, do so now.

2. Right-click ProcessExplorer.zip and then choose Extract All. This opens the Extract Compressed (Zipped) Folders Wizard. Accept the default folder location and settings and then click Extract.

3. Right-click the Procexp.exe application and then choose Properties. Click the Digital Signatures, select Microsoft Corporation, and then click Details. Verify that the application is digitally signed by Microsoft, as shown in Figure 5-9. Click OK to close the Digital Signature Details dialog box.

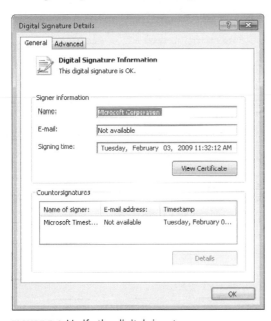

FIGURE 5-9 Verify the digital signature

4. Click the Compatibility tab. Under Compatibility Mode, select the Run This Program In Compatibility Mode For check box and use the drop-down menu to select Windows Vista (Service Pack 2).

5. Select the Disable Desktop Composition check box and then select the Run This program As An Administrator check box, as shown in Figure 5-10. Click OK.

FIGURE 5-10 Configuring application compatibility

6. Double-click procexp.exe. You should be confronted by a User Account Control dialog box that warns you that the following program may make changes to your computer, the program name, and the origin of the file, as shown in Figure 5-11. Click Yes.

FIGURE 5-11 User Account Control prompt for Process Explorer

7. In the Process Explorer License Agreement dialog box, click Agree. Process Explorer does not execute with these compatibility settings. Click Close The Program.

8. Right-click Procexp.exe and choose Properties. Click the Compatibility tab and then clear the Run This Program In Compatibility Mode, Disable Desktop Composition, and Run This Program As An Administrator check boxes. Click OK.

9. Double-click Procexp.exe. Click Run if prompted by the Open File–Security Warning dialog box.

10. Verify that the application executes properly and then close the application.

Lesson Summary

- You can run the Program Compatibility troubleshooter to diagnose common application compatibility issues.
- Windows 7 has several compatibility modes that allow the majority of existing software to execute on it.
- The ACT contains several tools that allow you to analyze potential compatibility problems prior to deploying Windows 7 in your organization.
- You can use the Compatibility Administrator to search for existing compatibility fixes and compatibility modes that have already been developed for popular applications.
- You can use the Internet Explorer Compatibility Test Tool to check existing Web sites and applications for compatibility problems that might exist when Internet Explorer 8 is used as a browser.
- Windows XP Mode allows you to run applications through a virtualized instance of Windows XP that runs on Windows 7 Professional, Ultimate, or Enterprise edition.

Lesson Review

You can use the following questions to test your knowledge of the information in Lesson 1, "Application Compatibility." The questions are also available on the companion DVD if you prefer to review them in electronic form.

> **NOTE ANSWERS**
>
> Answers to these questions and explanations of why each answer choice is correct or incorrect are located in the "Answers" section at the end of the book.

1. You are planning to migrate all the computers in your organization to Windows 7 Professional. Your organization has several applications that are installed on computers running Windows XP Professional. You are unable to install these applications on computers running Windows 7 due to compatibility problems. You are unable to configure a custom compatibility mode to support these applications using the ACT.

Which of the following solutions could you implement to deploy these mission-critical applications on the computers running Windows 7?

   A. Install the Window XP Mode feature. Install the application under Windows XP.

   B. Create a custom compatibility fix for the application using the ACT.

   C. Create a shim for the application using the ACT.

   D. Configure the application installer to run in Windows XP Professional SP2 compatibility mode.

2. Which of the following compatibility modes would you configure for an application that works on computers running Microsoft Windows 2000 Professional but does not work on computers running Windows XP?

   A. Windows 98 / Windows Me

   B. Windows NT 4.0 (Service Pack 5)

   C. Windows XP (Service Pack 2)

   D. Windows 2000

3. Which of the following file types does the Windows 7 Program Compatibility troubleshooter application work with?

   A. .cab files

   B. .exe files

   C. .msi files

   D. .zip files

4. An application used by the administrators in your organization is not configured to prompt for elevation when it is run. Which of the following compatibility options could you configure for the application to ensure that users with administrative privileges are always prompted when they execute the application?

   A. Configure the application to run in Windows XP (Service Pack 3) compatibility mode.

   B. Enable the Run In 256 Colors compatibility option.

   C. Enable the Run This Program As An Administrator compatibility option.

   D. Enable the Disable Desktop Composition compatibility option.

5. Your organization's internal Web site was designed several years ago, when all client computers were running Windows XP and Microsoft Internet Explorer 6. You want to verify that your organization's internal Web site displays correctly when you migrate all users to computers running Windows 7. Which of the following tools can you use to accomplish this goal?

   A. Internet Explorer Administration Kit (IEAK)

   B. Application Compatibility Toolkit (ACT)

   C. Windows Automated Installation Kit (Windows AIK)

   D. Microsoft Deployment Toolkit (MDT)

Lesson 2: Managing AppLocker and Software Restriction Policies

Occasionally it might be necessary to limit the applications that users can run on a computer. You might want to block a specific application from running, or you might want to ensure that only applications that are on an approved list function on your organization's network. There are two different technologies that you can use with computers running Windows 7 to restrict the execution of applications: AppLocker and Software Restriction Policies. You manage AppLocker and Software Restriction Policies through Group Policy. You can use these technologies to restrict programs, installation files, scripts, and even DLL libraries. In this lesson, you learn the differences between the two technologies and the situations in which you would choose to deploy one technology over the other.

> **After this lesson, you will be able to:**
> - Configure Software Restriction Policies to restrict the execution of applications.
> - Configure AppLocker policies to restrict the execution of applications, installers, and scripts.
>
> **Estimated lesson time: 50 minutes**

Software Restriction Policies

Software Restriction Policies is a technology available to clients running Windows 7 that is available in Windows XP, Windows Vista, Windows Server 2003, and Windows Server 2008. You manage Software Restriction Policies through Group Policy. You can find Software Restriction Policies in the Computer Configuration\Windows Settings\Security Settings\ Software Restriction Policies node of a group policy. When you use Software Restriction Policies, you use the Unrestricted setting to allow an application to execute and the Disallowed setting to block an application from executing.

> **NOTE CONTROLLING APPLICATIONS THROUGH PERMISSIONS**
> Although it is possible to restrict the execution of an application on the basis of NTFS permissions, configuring the NTFS permissions for a large number of applications on a large number of computers requires significant administrative effort.

You can achieve many of the same application restriction objectives with Software Restriction Policies that you can with AppLocker policies. The advantage of Software Restriction Policies over AppLocker policies is that Software Restriction Policies can apply to computers running Windows XP and Windows Vista, as well as to computers running Windows 7 editions that do not support AppLocker. The disadvantage of Software Restriction Policies is that all rules must be created manually because there are no built-in wizards to simplify the process of rule creation. You learn more about AppLocker policies later in this lesson.

Software Restriction Policies are applied in a particular order, with the more explicit rule types overriding more general rule types. The order of precedence from most specific (hash) to least specific (default) is as follows:

1. Hash rules

2. Certificate rules

3. Path rules

4. Zone rules

5. Default rules

If two conflicting rules with different security levels are established for the same program, the most specific rule takes precedence. For example, a hash rule that sets a particular application to Unrestricted overrides a path rule that sets a particular application to Disallowed. This is different from AppLocker policies, which do not use precedence rules and where a block in any rule type always overrides any allow rule.

> **NOTE** **APPLOCKER OVERRIDES SOFTWARE RESTRICTION POLICIES**
>
> In environments that use both Software Restriction Policies and AppLocker, AppLocker policies take precedence. If you have an AppLocker policy that specifically allows an application that is blocked by a Software Restriction Policy, the application executes.

Security Levels and Default Rules

The Security Levels node allows you to set the Software Restriction Policies default rule. The default rule applies when no other Software Restriction Policy matches an application. You can enable only one default rule at a time. The three default rules, shown in Figure 5-12, are:

- **Disallowed**   When this rule is set, users are unable to execute an application if the application is not allowed by an existing Software Restriction Policy.

- **Basic User**   When this rule is set, users are able to execute applications so long as those applications do not require administrative access rights. Users are able to access applications that require administrative access rights only if a rule has been created that covers that application.

- **Unrestricted**   When this rule is set as the default rule, a user is able to execute an application unless an existing Software Restriction Policy blocks that application.

If you are working on an allow list of applications, you would configure the disallowed default rule. This ensures that any application that is not specifically allowed cannot run. If you just want to block a couple of troublesome applications but do not want to go to the trouble of creating a rule for all the applications used in your environment, you should set the Unrestricted default rule. This allows any application to run unless you explicitly block it.

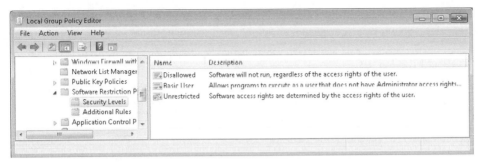

FIGURE 5-12 Software Restriction Policy security levels

Enforcement

You can use the Enforcement Properties policy, shown in Figure 5-13, to specify whether Software Restriction Policies to all software files except libraries, such as DLLs, or all software files, including DLLs. If the default level is set to Disallowed and you configure the enforcement policies to apply to all software files, you need to configure rules for all the DLL files used by a program to use that program. Microsoft recommends that you do not include DLLs unless you are managing computers in a highly secure environment. This is primarily because managing rules for DLLs adds significantly to the amount of work that an administrator has to undertake to maintain Software Restriction Policies successfully

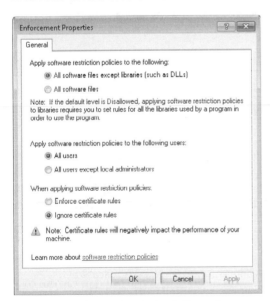

FIGURE 5-13 Software Restriction Policy enforcement

You can use the Enforcement policy to apply Software Restriction Policies to all users or all users except for members of the local administrators group. You can also use this policy to specify whether certificate rules will be enforced or ignored. The drawback to enforcing certificate rules is that it can degrade a computer's performance significantly.

Designated File Types

The Designated File Types policy, shown in Figure 5-14, allows you to determine which file extensions should be recognized as executable files and hence fall under the influence of Software Restriction Policies. Using the Add and Remove buttons, administrators modify the list of application extensions that are managed by Software Restriction Policies. Although an administrator is able to modify this list, she cannot remove the standard executable extensions, such as .com, .exe, and .vbs. These extensions are always recognized as executable.

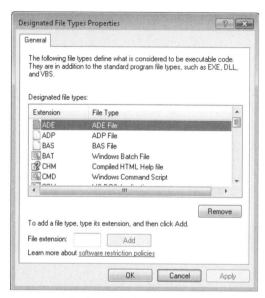

FIGURE 5-14 Designated File Types

Path Rules

Path rules, shown in Figure 5-15, allow you to specify a file, folder, or registry key as the target of a Software Restriction Policy. The more specific a path rule is, the higher its precedence. For example, if you have a path rule that sets the file C:\Program files\Application\App.exe to Unrestricted and one that sets the folder C:\Program files\Application to Disallowed, the more specific rule takes precedence and the application can execute. Wildcards can be used in path rules, so it is possible to have a path rule that specifies C:\Program files\Application\ *.exe. Wildcard rules are less specific than rules that use a file's full path.

The drawback of path rules is that they rely on files and folders remaining in place. For example, if you created a path rule to block the application C:\Apps\Filesharing.exe, an attacker could execute the same application by moving it to another directory or renaming it something other than Filesharing.exe. Path rules work only when the file and folder permissions of the underlying operating system do not allow files to be moved and renamed.

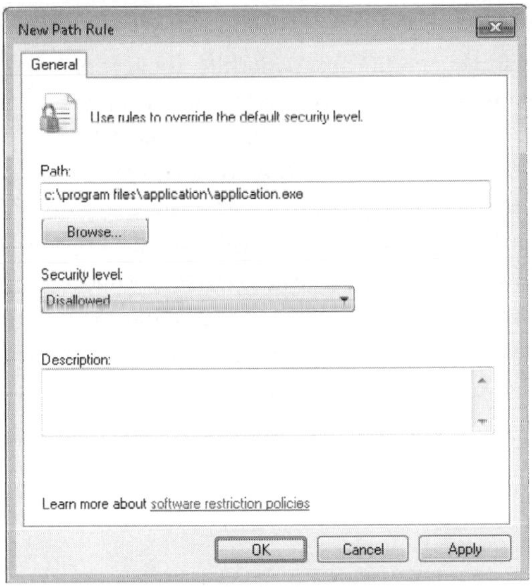

FIGURE 5-15 Software Restriction Policy path rule

Hash Rules

Hash rules, shown in Figure 5-16, work through the generation of a digital fingerprint that identifies a file based on its binary characteristics. This means that a file that you create a hash rule for will be identifiable regardless of the name assigned to it or the location from which you access it. Hash rules work on any file and do not require the file to have a digital signature. The drawback of hash rules is that you need to create them on a per-file basis. You cannot create hash rules automatically for Software Restriction Policies; you must generate each rule manually. You must also modify hash rules each time that you apply a software update to an application that is the subject of a hash rule. Software updates modify the binary properties of the file, which means that the modified file does not match the original digital fingerprint.

FIGURE 5-16 Hash rule for Minesweeper

Certificate Rules

Certificate rules use a code-signed software publisher's certificate to identify applications signed by that publisher. Certificate rules allow multiple applications to be the target of a single rule that is as secure as a hash rule. It is not necessary to modify a certificate rule in the event that a software update is released by the vendor because the updated application will still be signed using the vendor's signing certificate. To configure a certificate rule, you need to obtain a certificate from the vendor. Certificate rules impose a performance burden on computers on which they are applied because the certificate's validity must be checked before the application can execute. Another disadvantage of certificate rules is that they apply to all applications from a vendor. If you want to allow only 1 application from a vendor to execute but the vendor has 20 applications available, you are better off using a different type of Software Restriction Policy because otherwise users can execute any of those other 20 applications.

Network Zone Rule

Internet zone rules apply only to Windows Installer (.msi) packages obtained using Internet Explorer. Zone rules do not apply to non-.msi applications, such as .exe files, obtained using Internet Explorer. Zone rules function by differentiating installer packages based on the site from which they were downloaded. Possible locations include Internet, Intranet, Restricted Sites, Trusted Sites, and My Computer.

> **MORE INFO** **SOFTWARE RESTRICTION POLICIES**
>
> To learn more about Software Restriction Policies, consult the following Web site on Microsoft TechNet: *http://technet.microsoft.com/en-us/library/cc782792(WS.10).aspx*.

 Quick Check

- What is the advantage of using a hash rule over a path rule?

Quick Check Answer

- Hash rules are like digital fingerprints that identify a unique file. A path rule only works based on a file name and path, which means that malware can be inserted into locations covered by path rules and executed.

AppLocker Application Control Policies

AppLocker is a feature new to Windows 7 that is available only in the Enterprise and Ultimate editions of the product. *AppLocker policies* are conceptually similar to Software Restriction Policies, though AppLocker policies have several advantages, such as the ability to be applied to specific user or group accounts and the ability to apply to all future versions of a product. As you learned earlier in this chapter, hash rules apply only to a specific version of an application and must be recalculated whenever you apply software updates to that application. AppLocker policies are located in the Computer Configuration\Windows Settings\ Security Settings\Application Control Policies node of a standard Windows 7 or Windows Server 2008 R2 GPO.

AppLocker relies upon the Application Identity Service being active. When you install Windows 7, the startup type of this service is set to Manual. When testing AppLocker, you should keep the startup type as Manual in case you configure rules incorrectly. In that event, you can just reboot the computer and the AppLocker rules will no longer be in effect. Only when you are sure that your policies are applied correctly should you set the startup type of the Application Identity Service to Automatic. You should take great care in testing AppLocker rules because it is possible to lock down a computer running Windows 7 to such an extent that the computer becomes unusable. AppLocker policies are sometimes called *application control policies*.

Default Rules

Default rules are a set of rules that can be created automatically and which allow access to default Windows and program files. Default rules are necessary because AppLocker has a built-in fallback block rule that restricts the execution of any application that is not subject to an Allow rule. This means that when you enable AppLocker, you cannot execute any application, script, or installer that does not fall under an Allow rule. There are different default rules for each rule type. The default rules for each rule type are general and can be tailored by administrators specifically for their environments. For example, the default executable rules are path rules. Security-minded administrators might replace the default rules with publisher or hash rules because these are more secure.

You can create the default rules by right-clicking the Executable Rules, Windows Installer Rules, or Script Rules node, and then clicking Create Default Rules. The default executable rules are shown in Figure 5-17.

FIGURE 5-17 Default executable rules

Rules That Block

You can configure AppLocker rules to allow or block applications. Explicitly defined Block rules override any Allow rule, no matter how that rule is defined. This is different from how Software Restriction Policies work, where one rule type can override another. The fallback Block rule, mentioned earlier in this lesson, does not override any rules. The fallback Block rule just restricts the execution of any application that has not been allowed specifically. You need to add a Block rule only if another AppLocker rule allows an application, installer, or script to be executed. For example, suppose that you want to allow everyone in your organization to use an application named Alpha.exe except members of the Accounting group. You would need to create two rules. The first rule would allow everyone to run Alpha. exe. The second rule would block members of the Accounting group from running Alpha.exe. Although AppLocker rules include exceptions, you cannot apply exceptions on the basis of group membership.

You can use explicitly defined Block rules to stop the execution of applications that are enabled through the default rules. For example, the default rules allow the application Solitaire.exe to be executed on a computer running Windows 7. You can block Solitaire from executing by creating an explicit Block rule. You could also block Solitaire from executing by configuring an exception to the default rules. Exceptions are covered later in this lesson.

Executable Rules

Executable rules apply to files that have .exe and .com file extensions. AppLocker policies are primarily about executable files, and it is likely that the majority of the AppLocker policies that you work with in your organizational environment will involve executable rules. The default executable rules are path rules that allow everyone to execute all applications in the Program Files folder and the Windows folder. The default rules also allow members of the administrators group to execute applications in any location on the computer. It is necessary to use the default executable rules, or rules that mirror their functionality, because Windows does not function properly unless certain applications, covered by these default rules, are allowed to execute. When you create a rule, the scope of the rule is set to Everyone, as shown in Figure 5-18, even though there is not a local group named Everyone. If you choose to modify the rule, you can select a specific security group or user account.

Windows Installer Rules

Windows Installer rules cover files with .msi and .msp file extensions. You can use installer rules to block or allow the installation of software on computers. The default Windows Installer rules allow the Everyone group to use digitally signed Windows Installer files, all Windows Installer Files in the %Systemdrive%\Windows\Installer directory and allow members of the local administrators group to run any .msi or .msp file. The default rules allow the installation of software and software updates through Group Policy.

It is important to remember that even if an AppLocker rule allows everyone to access a particular installer file, they still need the relevant administrative permissions to install software on the computer. Installer rules are most useful when your organization has portable computers running Windows 7 that require you to give users local administrator access. After removing the default rule that allows local administrators to use any installer, you can restrict which installer files the local administrator can access. In this scenario, you also have to restrict access to the Local Group Policy Editor, or else the local administrator could modify this policy setting.

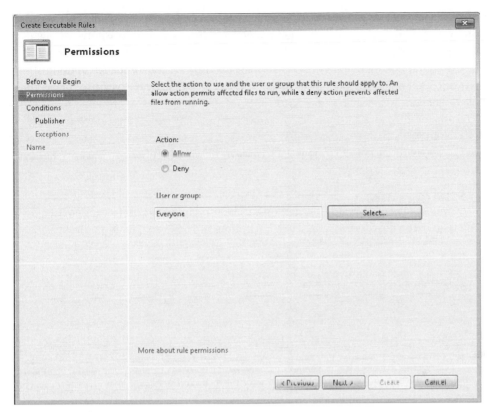

FIGURE 5-18 Default rule scope

Script Rules

Script rules cover files with the .ps1, .bat, .cmd, .vbs, and .js file extensions. Although it is possible to use publisher rules with scripts, most scripts are created on an ad-hoc basis by administrators and are rarely digitally signed. You should use hash rules with scripts that are rarely modified and path rules with directories containing scripts that are regularly updated. If you use path rules, you should ensure that the permissions on the folders hosting the scripts are configured so that nefarious scripts cannot be placed in this folder. The default script rules allow the execution of all scripts located in the Program Files and Windows folders. The default script rules also allow members of the built-in administrators group to execute scripts in any location.

DLL Rules

DLL rules cover files known as libraries, which have the .dll and .ocx file extensions. Libraries support the execution of applications. DLL rules are not enabled by default when you enable AppLocker. DLL rules provide a maximum level of security but also involve performance drawbacks. You need to create a DLL rule for each DLL that is used by the applications on your client running Windows 7. Although creating rules is made easier by the ability to generate rules automatically, users experience a performance reduction as AppLocker needs to check each DLL that an application loads each time it is loaded. To enable DLL rules, right-click the Computer Configuration\Windows Settings\Security Settings\Application Control Policies\AppLocker node in Group Policy, select the Advanced tab, and check the Enable The DLL Rule Collection, as shown in Figure 5-19.

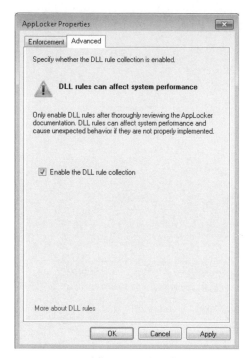

FIGURE 5-19 Enabling DLL rule collection

Publisher Rules

Publisher rules in AppLocker work on the basis of the code-signing certificate used by the file's publisher. Unlike a Software Restriction Policy certificate rule, it is not necessary to obtain a certificate to use a publisher rule because the details of the digital signature are extracted from a reference application file. If a file has no digital signature, you cannot restrict or allow it using AppLocker publisher rules.

Publisher rules allow you more flexibility than hash rules because you can specify not only a specific version of a file but also all future versions of that file. This means that you do not have to re-create publisher rules each time you apply a software update because the existing rule remains valid. You can also allow only a specific version of a file by setting the Exactly option, as shown in Figure 5-20.

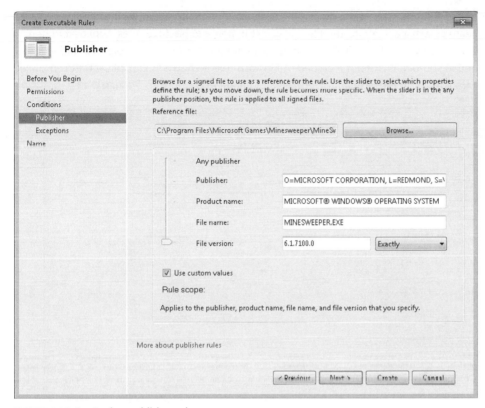

FIGURE 5-20 AppLocker publisher rule

Using the slider, you can also vary the scope of the publishing rule so that it applies to a specific file name signed by the publisher, a specific product signed by the publisher, any product signed by the publisher, or any product signed by any publisher. This last setting does not apply to any application, only to applications digitally signed by publishers. If you applied an Allow rule that had the slider set to Any Publisher, then all applications signed by publishers could be executed, but applications that were not signed would not fall under the scope of the rule.

Hash Rules

Hash rules in AppLocker function in the same basic way that they do in Software Restriction Policies. Hash rules allow you to identify a specific binary file that is not digitally signed by creating a digital fingerprint of that file. This fingerprint is known as a *file hash*. File hashes in AppLocker are more manageable than file hashes in Software Restriction Policies because you can use the Rule Creation wizard to automate the creation of file hashes for all files in a specific location. As mentioned earlier, the drawback to hash rules is that it is necessary to re-create file hashes each time a software update is applied because software updates can modify the properties of the file, so the hash file digital fingerprint no longer matches it. To create a hash, navigate to the file and select it. It is also possible to browse to a folder and create hashes of all files within that immediate folder. When you browse to a folder, files contained in subfolders are not included. A file hash rule is shown in Figure 5-21. Because file hashes are specific to individual files, you cannot create exceptions to file hash rules.

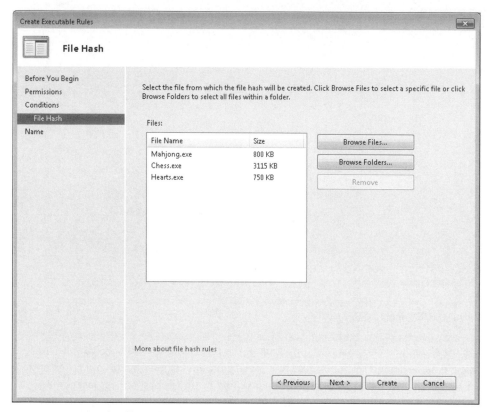

FIGURE 5-21 AppLocker file hash rule

Path Rules

AppLocker path rules work in a similar way to Software Restriction Policy path rules that you learned about earlier in this lesson. Path rules let you specify a folder, in which case the path rule applies to the entire contents of the folder, including subfolders, and the path to a specific file. The advantage of path rules is that they are easy to create. The disadvantage of path rules is that they are the least secure form of AppLocker rules. An attacker can subvert a path rule if they copy an executable file into a folder covered by a path rule or overwrite a file that is specified by a path rule. Path rules are only as effective as the file and folder permissions applied on the computer. An AppLocker path rule is shown in Figure 5-22.

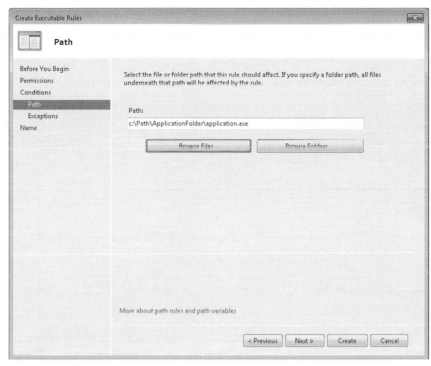

FIGURE 5-22 AppLocker path rule

Creating Rules Automatically

A significant advantage of AppLocker over Software Restriction Policies is the ability to generate rules automatically. To configure rules for AppLocker, you can right-click either the Executable Rules, Windows Installer Rules, or Script Rules node and then click Automatically Generate Rules. You are asked to specify a directory for the wizard to scan. Your options, shown in Figure 5-23, enable you to have Windows automatically generate publisher rules for files that are digitally signed and give you the option of creating a hash rule or a path rule if a file is not signed. Alternatively, you can create a file hash rule for all files of the type you are configuring. The Automatically Generate Rules wizard scans a folder and all folders that it contains when generating rules.

Configuring Exceptions

Exceptions allow specific applications to be exempt from more general rules. For example, you could create a publisher rule that allows all versions of a Contoso application named Alpha but then use an exemption to block the execution of version 42 of application Alpha. You can use any method to specify an exception, and the method you choose does not depend on the type of rule that you are creating. For example, as Figure 5-24 shows, you can create a publisher rule that allows all applications published by Microsoft to execute on a computer, but you also can configure a file hash exemption for Solitaire.exe. Of course, this example rule would work only if the default path rule for the Program Files folder is not created. You can create exemptions for Block rules as well as Allow rules.

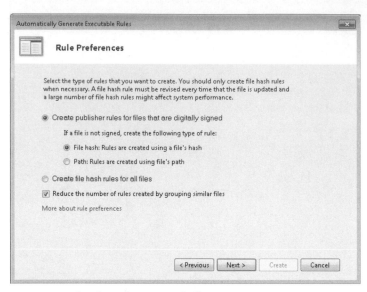

FIGURE 5-23 Creating rules automatically

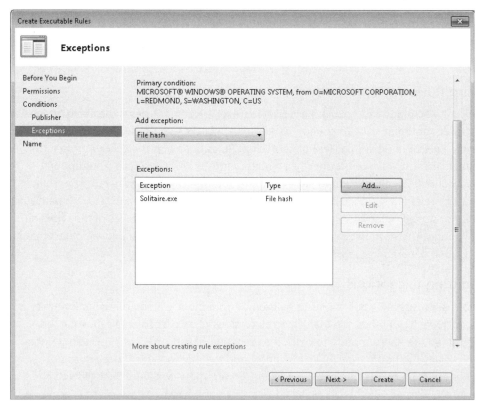

FIGURE 5-24 Configuring an exemption

AppLocker Auditing

As AppLocker can have a significant impact on the way that applications function in your organization's environment, it is often prudent to audit the way that AppLocker functions prior to fully enforcing AppLocker policies. This allows you to verify which applications are affected by AppLocker without actually blocking those applications from executing. To configure AppLocker to audit rules rather than enforce them, configure each AppLocker rule type to be audited only, as shown in Figure 5-25.

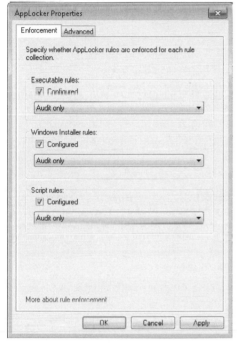

FIGURE 5-25 Configuring AppLocker auditing

AppLocker audit events are written to the AppLocker event log, which is found in Event Viewer in the Applications and Service Logs\Microsoft\Windows node. Each event in the AppLocker log contains detailed information about:

- The rule name
- The SID of the targeted user or group
- Which file the rule affects and its path.
- Whether the file is allowed or blocked
- The rule type (publisher, path or file hash)

You will learn more about auditing in Chapter 8, "Branch Cache and Resource Sharing."

EXAM TIP

Understand why one user might be able to execute an application and another user is unable to execute the same application.

PRACTICE Restricting Applications

In this practice, you use two different methods to restrict the execution of applications: Software Restriction Policies and AppLocker. Software Restriction Policies are used to restrict the execution of applications on computers running Windows XP, Windows Vista, and Windows 7. AppLocker is a feature that is new to Windows 7 and is available only in the Ultimate and Enterprise editions of the product.

EXERCISE 1 Configuring a Software Restriction Policy

In this exercise, you create a Software Restriction Policy hash rule to block the execution of the Windows calculator application. To complete this exercise, perform the following steps:

1. Log on to computer Canberra using the Kim_Akers user account.

2. Click Start, type **Calculator,** and then press Enter. Verify that the Calculator application starts and then close it.

3. Click Start and then type **gpedit.msc** and press Enter. This opens the Local Group Policy Editor console.

4. Navigate to the Computer Configuration\Windows Settings\Security Settings node.

5. Select and then right-click the Software Restriction Policies node. Choose New Software Restriction Policies.

6. Right-click the Additional Rules node and then choose New Hash Rule. This will open the New Hash Rule dialog box. Click Browse. Navigate to the \Windows\System32 folder.

7. In the Open dialog box, type **calc.exe** in the File Name text box and then click Open. Ensure that the Security Level is set to Disallowed, as shown in Figure 5-26, and then click OK.

8. Close the Local Group Policy Editor and then reboot the computer. Log back on using the Kim_Akers user account.

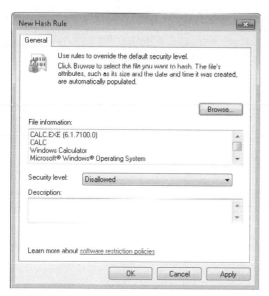

FIGURE 5-26 Creating a hash rule

9. Click Start, type **Calculator,** and then press Enter. You should get the message shown in Figure 5-27.

FIGURE 5-27 Calculator application blocked by policy

10. Click Start, type **gpedit.msc,** and then press Enter. This opens the Local Group Policy Editor console. Navigate to the Computer Configuration\Windows Settings\Security Settings\Software Restriction Policies\Additional Rules node and then delete the policy for Calc.exe.

11. Close the Local Group Policy Editor console and then reboot the computer. Log on as Kim_Akers and verify that you can again open the Calculator application.

EXERCISE 2 Configuring AppLocker

In this exercise, you configure an AppLocker policy to block the Solitaire application.
To complete the exercise, perform the following steps:

1. If you are not already logged on to computer Canberra, log on as Kim_Akers.

2. Click Start, type **Solitaire,** and then press Enter. Verify that the Solitaire application opens. Close Solitaire.

3. Click Start, type **services.msc,** and then press Enter. This opens the Services console.

4. Double-click the Application Identity service. Set the Startup Type to Automatic, as shown in Figure 5-28, click Start, and then click OK. Close the Services console.

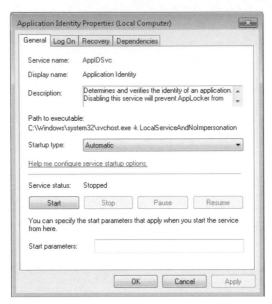

FIGURE 5-28 Configuring the startup properties of the Application Identity service

5. Click Start, type **gpedit.msc,** and press Enter. This opens the Local Group Policy Editor console.

6. Navigate to the Computer Configuration\Windows Settings\Security Settings\ Application Control Policies node and then select the AppLocker item.

7. Right-click Executable Rules and then choose Create New Rule. On the Before You Begin page of the Create Executable Rules wizard, click Next.

8. On the Permissions page, select Deny and then click Next.

9. On the Conditions page, select Publisher and then click Next.

10. On the Publisher page, click Browse. Navigate to the \Program Files\Microsoft Games\ Solitaire folder and then double-click Solitaire.exe.

11. On the Publisher page, select the Use Custom Values check box, and then verify that the settings match those shown in Figure 5-29. Click Create.

12. When prompted to create the default rules, click Yes.

13. Close the Local Group Policy Editor console, turn off the computer, and then restart it.

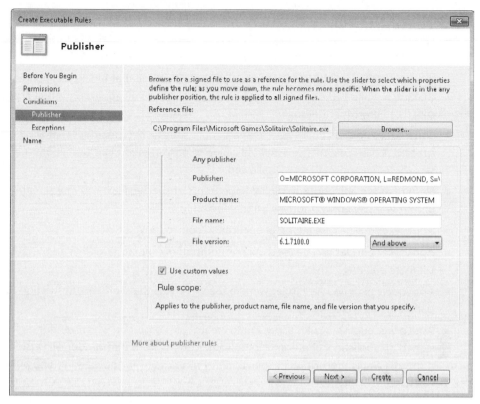

FIGURE 5-29 A rule blocking the Solitaire application

14. Log on with the Kim_Akers user account and attempt to access the Solitaire application. You should receive a message informing you that it has been blocked by policy, as shown in Figure 5-30.

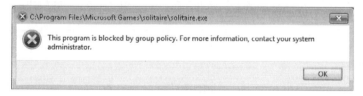

FIGURE 5-30 Solitaire blocked by policy

15. Click Start, type **services.msc,** and then press Enter. This opens the Services console.

16. Double-click the Application Identity service. Set the Startup Type to Disabled. Close the Services console.

Lesson Summary

- Software Restriction Policies can be used on computers running Windows XP, Windows Vista, Windows Server 2003, Windows Server 2008, and Windows 7.

- You can choose a Software Restriction Policy default rule that blocks all applications that are not allowed or choose a default rule that allows all applications that are not subject to any other rules.

- Software Restriction Policy rules that are more specific override rules that are less specific. A hash rule that sets an application to unrestricted overrides a path rule that sets the same application to Disallowed.

- Hash rules are analogous to digital fingerprints of specific files. You must create a new hash rule if you apply a software update to a file.

- AppLocker policies are a type of application control policy.

- AppLocker policies can be used only on computers running Windows 7 Enterprise and Ultimate editions.

- AppLocker path and hash rules work in the same way that Software Restriction Policy path and hash rules work.

- AppLocker publisher rules allow you to create rules based on which vendor digitally signed an application. You can allow all applications from that vendor, all versions of a specific application, or just a specific version of a specific application using publisher rules.

- Some AppLocker rule types allow exceptions. Exceptions allow you to exempt a specific application from the scope of a general AppLocker rule.

- An AppLocker block rule always overrides an AppLocker allow rule. The fallback rule for AppLocker blocks the execution of any application not explicitly allowed by another rule.

- AppLocker overrides Software Restriction Policies when both are applied to the same computer.

Lesson Review

You can use the following questions to test your knowledge of the information in Lesson 2, "Managing AppLocker and Software Restriction Policies." The questions are also available on the companion DVD if you prefer to review them in electronic form.

> **NOTE ANSWERS**
>
> Answers to these questions and explanations of why each answer choice is correct or incorrect are located in the "Answers" section at the end of the book.

1. Your organization has 50 computers running Windows Vista Enterprise and 40 computers running Windows 7 Professional. You want to stop users from accessing the Solitaire game application. Which of the following strategies should you pursue to accomplish this goal?

   A. Use AppLocker to create a publisher rule to block Solitaire.exe.

   B. Use AppLocker to create a hash rule to block Solitaire.exe.

   C. Use AppLocker to create a path rule to block Solitaire.exe.

   D. Use Software Restriction Policies to create a path rule to block Solitarie.exe.

2. What type of AppLocker rule should you create to block all applications that are created by a specific software vendor?

   A. Publisher rules

   B. Path rules

   C. Hash rules

3. You want to configure a set of AppLocker rules to block the execution of application software that is not digitally signed by the software vendor. You want to test that these rules work before enforcing them. Which of the following settings should you configure to accomplish this goal? (Choose all that apply; each answer forms part of a complete solution.)

   A. Create AppLocker publisher rules.

   B. Create AppLocker hash rules.

   C. Configure AppLocker enforcement to audit executable rules.

   D. Configure AppLocker enforcement to audit Windows Installer rules.

4. Your organization has a mix of computers running Windows 7 Ultimate and Windows 7 Professional. Each group of computers is located in a separate organizational unit (OU) in your Windows Server 2008 R2 Active Directory Domain Services environment. You have configured AppLocker policies to block application execution to the OU hosting the Windows 7 Ultimate computer accounts. You have configured Software Restriction Policy rules and applied them to the OU hosting the Windows 7 Professional accounts. The Software Restriction Policy rules block the required applications. The applications blocked by the AppLocker policies function normally—that is, they are not blocked. Which of the following steps should you take to ensure that the AppLocker policies function properly?

   A. Configure Group Policy to set the Application Management service to start automatically. Apply this policy to the OU hosting the computer accounts of the computers running Windows 7 Ultimate.

   B. Configure Group Policy to set the Application Management service to start automatically. Apply this policy to the OU hosting the computer accounts of the computers running Windows 7 Professional.

C. Configure Group Policy to set the Application Identity service to start automatically. Apply this policy to the OU hosting the computer accounts of the computers running Windows 7 Ultimate.

D. Configure Group Policy to set the Application Identity service to start automatically. Apply this policy to the OU hosting the computer accounts of the computers running Windows 7 Professional.

5. You have configured AppLocker policies to allow the execution of specific applications only. If an AppLocker policy hasn't been created for it, an application cannot execute. After a recent software update, users are unable to execute one of the applications for which you have configured a rule. Other applications function normally. This application is not signed digitally by the software vendor. Which of the following strategies should you pursue to ensure that the application is able to execute on the computers running Windows 7?

A. Create a new hash rule for the application.

B. Create a new publishing rule for the application.

C. Ensure that you enable the Application Identity service on the computers running Windows 7.

D. Ensure that you enable the Application Management service on the computers running Windows 7.

Chapter Review

To further practice and reinforce the skills you learned in this chapter, you can perform the following tasks:

- Review the chapter summary.
- Review the list of key terms introduced in this chapter.
- Complete the case scenarios. These scenarios set up real-world situations involving the topics of this chapter and ask you to create a solution.
- Complete the suggested practices.
- Take a practice test.

Chapter Summary

- You can use built-in compatibility modes to allow applications designed for previous versions of Windows to run on Windows 7. If one of the existing compatibility modes does not resolve the compatibility issues, you can use the ACT to search a large database of existing application specific fixes and modes.
- Windows XP Mode is a fully virtualized instance of Windows XP that can be run on a client running Windows 7 Professional, Ultimate, or Enterprise edition as a way of resolving compatibility problems that you are unable to solve using compatibility modes or the ACT.
- Software Restriction Policies can be used on all versions of Windows and allow you to create rules based on a file hash, software path, publisher certificate, or network zone. Software Restriction Policies are applied from the most specific rules to the least specific. Rules that are more specific override rules that are less specific.
- AppLocker policies can only be used on computers running Windows 7 Enterprise and Ultimate editions. AppLocker policies can be applied on the basis of publisher identity, file hash, or software path. AppLocker includes wizards that automatically generate rules. AppLocker block rules override all other AppLocker rules.

Key Terms

Do you know what these key terms mean? You can check your answers by looking up the terms in the glossary at the end of the book.

- **AppLocker policy**
- **compatibility fix**
- **compatibility mode**
- **hash rule**

- **path rule**
- **publisher rule**
- **Software Restriction Policy**

Case Scenarios

In the following case scenarios, you apply what you've learned about subjects of this chapter. You can find answers to these questions in the "Answers" section at the end of this book.

Case Scenario 1: Configuring Application Compatibility at Fabrikam

You are in the process of planning a migration of your organization's desktop computers from Windows XP to Windows 7. At the moment, you are investigating application compatibility issues. You are primarily concerned with three applications named Alpha, Beta, and Gamma. After investigation, you have found that application Alpha does not run on computers running Windows 7 Enterprise but that it does run without problems on computers that have Windows XP Professional SP3 installed. Application Beta runs only on computers with Windows 7 installed when you right-click the desktop shortcut for it and then click Run As Administrator. Application Gamma was created when your organization had a small team of developers. The application does not function under the existing Windows 7 compatibility modes, and your organization now lacks the expertise to revise the original source code so that the application functions properly when installed on computers running Windows 7. With these facts in mind, answer the following questions.

Questions

1. What steps should you take to get application Alpha to execute?
2. What steps should you take to enable the execution of application Beta by just clicking on its shortcut?
3. What tool can you use to configure custom compatibility options for application Gamma?

Case Scenario 2: Restricting Applications at Contoso

You are responsible for configuring computers running Windows 7 Enterprise at Contoso's Antarctic Research facility. In-house developers created a data collection and analysis application used at the facility. This application communicates with instruments that measure temperature variations in the ice fields that surround the Contoso outpost. The in-house developers did not digitally sign this application. As the application interacts with delicate scientific instruments, only members of the Scientists group should be able to execute the data collection application. You want to create a single rule to manage the execution of this application. With this information in mind, answer the following questions.

Questions

1. What type of rule would you create for the data collection application?

2. How can you ensure that only members of the Scientists group can execute the data collection application and other users cannot?

3. What steps would the in-house developers need to take to allow you to create a publisher rule for this application?

Suggested Practices

To help you master the exam objectives presented in this chapter, complete the following tasks.

Configure Application Compatibility

In this set of practices, you configure application compatibility. Use your favorite search engine to locate and download an evaluation version of an application that works on a previous version of Windows, such as Windows XP, but which does not work when running Windows 7.

- **Practice 1**   Edit the properties of an application and configure the Windows 7 compatibility modes to get the application to function when running Windows 7.

- **Practice 2**   Edit the properties on an application and configure the Windows 7 compatibility modes to disable the Aero UI when the application is executing.

Configure Application Restrictions

In this set of practices, you configure application restrictions. It requires that you have downloaded the Process Explorer application to the desktop of your computer running Windows 7. You can obtain this application from the Web site at *http://technet.microsoft .com/en-us/sysinternals/bb896653.aspx*. You need to enable the Application Identity service temporarily to complete these practices. Remember to disable the service when you complete these exercises, or else you may experience problems executing other applications in later chapters.

- **Practice 1**   Use the Local Group Policy Editor to configure an AppLocker path rule to block the execution of the Process Explorer application that you downloaded for the exercises at the end of Lesson 1. After rebooting the computer, verify that the application is blocked by the path rule. When you have done this, create a copy of the executable file in another location. Attempt to execute the application in its new location.

- **Practice 2**   Use the Local Group Policy Editor to create a publisher rule to block the execution of the Process Explorer application. After rebooting the computer, verify that the Process Explorer application does not execute. Copy the application file to another location. Verify that the Process Explorer application does not execute in the new location.

Take a Practice Test

The practice tests on this book's companion DVD offer many options. For example, you can test yourself on just one exam objective, or you can test yourself on all the 70-680 certification exam content. You can set up the test so that it closely simulates the experience of taking a certification exam, or you can set it up in study mode so that you can look at the correct answers and explanations after you answer each question.

> **MORE INFO   PRACTICE TESTS**
>
> For details about all the practice test options available, see the section entitled "How to Use the Practice Tests," in the Introduction to this book.

CHAPTER 6

Network Settings

This chapter discusses networks and how you locate computers and other devices within networks. It looks at Internet Protocol version 4 (IPv4), a robust, reliable protocol that has implemented routing and delivered packets to hosts on subnets for many years. It also discusses the various types of IPv4 address and the services on which IPv4 relies.

Internet Protocol version 6 (IPv6) is the successor to IPv4, and the chapter explains why IPv4 might no longer be adequate to cope with modern intranetworks, in particular the Internet. It describes the various types of IPv6 addresses and their functions, as well as address types that implement the transition from IPv4 to IPv6.

Traditionally, most networks used wired connections, but wireless networking is now much more common, particularly with the increase in mobile communication and working from home. The chapter looks at how you set up both wired and wireless networks and troubleshoot connectivity problems.

Finally, the chapter considers the new Windows 7 feature of location-aware printing that enables mobile users to move between networks without needing to re-specify their default printer.

Exam objectives in this chapter:
- Configure IPv4 network settings.
- Configure IPv6 network settings.
- Configure networking settings.

Lessons in this chapter:

Before You Begin

To complete the exercises in the practices in this chapter, you need to have done the following:

- Installed the Windows 7 operating system on a stand-alone client PC as described in Chapter 1, "Install, Migrate, or Upgrade to Windows 7." You need Internet access to complete the exercises.

- Installed Windows 7 on a second PC. The procedure is the same as for installing the first PC, and the user name and password are the same (Kim_Akers and P@ssw0rd). The computer name is Aberdeen. As with the installation of the Canberra computer, accept the installation defaults (unless you are not U.S.-based, in which case select the appropriate keyboard and time zone). It is highly recommended that you create the Aberdeen computer as a virtual machine (VM). You can do this by using Hyper-V or by downloading Microsoft Virtual PC 2007 at *http://www.microsoft.com/downloadS/details.aspx?FamilyID=04d26402-3199-48a3-afa2-2dc0b40a73b6&displaylang=en*.

- If you have two physical computers that are not connected to the same network by any other method, you need to connect their Ethernet ports with a crossover cable or by using an Ethernet switch.

- You will need a wireless connection on the Canberra computer and a wireless access point (WAP) connected via a cable modem to the Internet to complete the optional exercise in Lesson 1. You need a wireless adapter on each computer to complete the exercise in Lesson 3, "Network Configuration," later in this chapter.

 REAL WORLD

Ian McLean

I've just read it in a Microsoft magazine, so it must be correct—we're running out of IPv4 addresses.

As one of those who was crying wolf very loudly indeed in 1999, I can't say I'm surprised; in fact I am surprised it has taken so long. The use of Network Address Translation (NAT) and private addressing, of Classless Inter-Domain Routing (CIDR), and Variable-Length Subnet Mask (VLSM), and the claw-back of allocated but unused addresses were at best a temporary fix. They were never a solution. We were using up a limited resource. We could slow the process, but we could not halt it. So what's the solution?

In a word (or to be pedantic an acronym): IPv6.

There's a huge amount of money invested in the IPv4 Internet and it's not about to go away. As a professional, you need to know about IPv4 and how to configure and work with it, and you will for some time yet. However, where there are now islands of IPv6 Internet among seas of IPv4 Internet, IPv6 is growing, and eventually IPv4 will become the islands, and they'll get smaller all the time.

So don't ignore IPv4, but the time has come to add IPv6 to your skills base. After all, it's hardly new. The IPv6 Internet has been around since the last millennium. You don't need to subnet or supernet it, and a device can have several IPv6 addresses for different functions. There is quite an incredible (literally) number of available addresses. I'm told the resource is almost infinite. Forgive me, but wasn't that what they said about IPv4 address space in 1985?

So learn IPv6. If I were you, I'd do so quickly. The human race is never more ingenious than when it sets its mind to using up a seemingly infinite resource. I may be getting on a bit, but I have bets with several of my colleagues that IPv8 will be around before I'm finally laid to rest.

What hasn't occurred to them is—how are they going to collect their winnings?

Lesson 1: Configuring IPv4

As an IT professional with at least one year's experience, you will have come across IPv4 addresses, subnet masks, and default gateways. You know that in the enterprise environment, Dynamic Host Configuration Protocol (DHCP) servers configure IPv4 settings automatically and Domain Name System (DNS) servers resolve computer names to IPv4 addresses.

You might have configured a small test network with static IPv4 addresses, although even the smallest of modern networks tend to obtain configuration from a cable modem or a WAP, which in turn is configured by an Internet service provider (ISP). You might have set up Internet Connection Sharing in which client computers access the Internet through, and obtain their configuration from, another client computer.

You have probably come across Automatic Private Internet Protocol (APIPA) addresses that start with 168.254 when debugging connectivity because computers that fail to get their IPv4 configuration addresses from DHCP typically configure themselves using APIPA instead—so an APIPA address can be a symptom of DHCP failure or loss of connectivity, although it is also a valid way of configuring isolated networks that do not communicate with any other network, including the Internet.

However, you might not have been involved in network design or have subnetted a network. Subnetting is not as common these days, when private networks and NAT give you a large number of addresses you can use. It was much more common in the days when all addresses were public and administrators had to use very limited allocations. Nevertheless, subnetting remains a useful skill and subnet masks are likely to be tested in the 70-680 examination.

In this lesson, you look at the tools available for manipulating IPv4 addresses and subnet masks and implementing IPv4 network connectivity. The lesson considers the Network And Sharing Center, the Netstat and Netsh command-line tools, Windows Network Diagnostics, how you connecting a computer to a network, how you configure name resolution, the function of APIPA, how you set up a connection for a network, how you set up network locations, and how you resolve connectivity issues.

Before you look at all the tools for manipulating and configuring IPv4, you first need to understand what the addresses and subnet masks mean. You will learn the significance of addresses such as 10.0.0.21, 207.46.197.32, and 169.254.22.10. You will learn why 255.255.255.128, 255.255.225.0, 225.255.254.0, and 255.255.252.0 are valid subnet masks, whereas 255.255.253.0 is not. You will learn what effect changing the value of the subnet mask has on the potential size of your network and why APIPA addresses do not have default gateways.

This chapter starts with an introduction to IPv4, in particular IPv4 addresses, subnet masks, and default gateways. It continues with the practical aspects of configuring and managing a network.

After this lesson, you will be able to:

- Explain the functions of an IPv4 address, a subnet mask, and a default gateway, and interpret the dotted decimal format.
- Connect workstations to a wired network and set up Internet Connection Sharing (ICS) on that network.
- Manage connections for wired networks.

Estimated lesson time: 50 minutes

Introduction to IPv4 Addressing

IPv4 controls packet sorting and delivery. Each incoming or outgoing IPv4 packet, or datagram, includes the source IPv4 address of the sender and the destination IPv4 address of the recipient. IPv4 is responsible for routing. If information is being passed to another device within a subnet, the packet is sent to the appropriate internal IPv4 address. If the packet is sent to a destination that is not on the local subnet (for example, when you are accessing the Internet), IPv4 examines the destination address, compares it to a route table, and decides what action to take.

You can view the IPv4 configuration on a computer by opening the Command Prompt window. You can access this either by selecting Accessories and then Command Prompt on the All Programs menu, or by entering **cmd** in the Run box. If you need to change a configuration rather than to merely examine it, you need to open an elevated command prompt.

The Ipconfig command-line tool displays a computer's IPv4 settings (and IPv6 settings). Figure 6-1 shows the output of the *Ipconfig* command on a computer connected wirelessly through a WAP to the Internet and internally to a private wired network that is configured through APIPA. For more detail enter **ipconfig /all.**

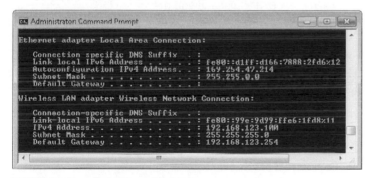

FIGURE 6-1 *Ipconfig* command output

The IPv4 address identifies the computer and the subnet that the computer is on. An IPv4 address must be unique within a network. Here the private address is unique within the internal network (the number 10 at the start of the address indicates that the address is private). If an IPv4 address is a public address on the Internet, it needs to be unique throughout the Internet. We look at public and private addresses later in this lesson.

There is nothing magical about the IPv4 address. It is simply a number in a very large range of numbers. It is expressed in a format called *dotted decimal notation* because that provides a convenient way of working with it. An IPv4 address is a number defined by 32 binary digits (bits), where each bit is a 1 or a 0. Consider this binary number:

00001010 00010000 00001010 10001111

The spaces are meaningless. They only make the number easier to read.

The decimal value of this number is 168,823,439. In hexadecimal, it is 0A100A8F. Neither of these ways of expressing the number is memorable or convenient.

> **NOTE   BINARY AND HEXADECIMAL NOTATION**
>
> You do not need to be a mathematician or an expert in binary notation to understand IPv4 addressing, but you do need a basic knowledge. To learn more, you can search for "the binary system" (for example) on the Internet, but possibly the best way to become familiar with binary and hexadecimal is to use the scientific calculator supplied by Windows 7. For example, enable binary (Bin) and type in **11111111**. Enable decimal (Dec) and then hexadecimal (Hex), and ensure that you get 255 and FF, respectively. The same calculator is available in the 70-680 examination.

Binary digits are generally divided into groups of eight, called *octets* (an electronics engineer would call them bytes). So let us group this number into four octets and put a dot between each because dots are easier to see than spaces.

00001010.00010000.00001010.10001111

Convert the binary number in each octet to decimal and you get:

10.16.10.143

Binary, decimal, hexadecimal, and dotted decimal are all ways of expressing a number. The number uniquely identifies the computer (or other network feature) within a network and the specifically identifiable network (or subnet) that it is on.

A network is divided into one or more subnets. Small networks—for example, a test network—might consist of only a single subnet. Subnets are connected to other subnets by a router (for example, a WAP, a Microsoft server configured as a router, or a hardware device such as a Cisco or 3Com router). Each subnet has its own subnet address within the network and its own gateway or router connection. In large networks, some subnets can connect to more than one router. You can also regard the connection through a modem to an ISP as a subnet, and this subnet in turn connects to the Internet through a router at the ISP.

So what identifies the computer and what identifies the subnet? To discover this, we need to look at the next value, the subnet mask. Subnet masks are most peculiar numbers. They represent binary numbers that consist of all ones followed by all zeros. For example:

255.255.255.0 is the binary number 11111111 11111111 11111111 00000000.

The actual value of this number is irrelevant. What matters is the number of ones and zeros. A one says that the corresponding bit in the IPv4 address is a network address bit. A zero says that the corresponding bit in the IPv4 address is a computer or host address bit.

In the example given, the last 8 bits of the subnet mask are all zero. So the host address is the final octet of the subnet address, or 143. The network address of the subnet is 10.16.10.0. Because hosts are defined by a single octet in this example, the 10.16.10.0 subnet contains 254 host addresses. The first IPv4 address in the subnet is 10.16.10.1. The last is 10.16.10.254. The number 10.16.10.0 identifies the subnet and is called the *subnet address*. The number 10.16.10.255 is called the *broadcast address* and is used when a packet needs to be sent to every host on a subnet.

Subnetting and Supernetting

You can split a subnet into smaller subnets by adding ones to the end of the ones in the subnet mask. If you have two (or more) suitable contiguous subnets, you can merge them into a single subnet by changing one or more ones at the end of the ones in the subnet masks to zeros. These techniques are known as *subnetting* and *supernetting*, respectively.

If an organization has a significant number of computers on its network (say over 100—this number varies depending on the type, volume, and pattern of traffic on the network—or if it has several geographic locations, the organization probably creates several subnets. If a subnet contains too many computers and other devices, it tends to slow down because there is a greater chance of two computers trying to put data onto the network simultaneously and causing a collision. Dividing a network into several subnets reduces the likelihood of such collisions.

At the router that connects to the Internet, however, the organization uses supernetting to combine (or summarize) the subnets so that they can be defined with a single network address that will be translated to a public address on the Internet. Public addresses and address translation are discussed later in this lesson.

> **MORE INFO** **SUBNETTING AND SUPERNETTING**
>
> For more information about supernetting and subnetting, and about CIDR and VLSM technologies, see *http://support.microsoft.com/kb/164015*.

> **NOTE** **CIDR NOTATION**
>
> Because the subnet mask 255.255.255.0 consists of 24 ones followed by 8 zeros, you can also write it as /24. A subnet with a network address 192.168.0.0 and a subnet mask 255.255.255.0 (for example) is then designated 192.168.0.0/24. This is sometimes called *CIDR notation*. A subnet mask with 25 ones followed by 7 zeros is a /25 subnet mask. In dotted decimal, this would be 255.255.255.128.

The final value shown in Figure 6-1 is the *default gateway*. This is the IPv4 address of the router connection on the same subnet as the IPv4 address of the host computer. If an IPv4 packet has a destination address of a different subnet, it is routed through other subnets via the router until it finds the destination it is looking for. If you browse to a Web site, for example, you need to send data to the Web server for that site, which has an IPv4 address somewhere on the Internet.

Put simply, some packets need to get out of your subnet and go to another network (for example, the Internet). Your computer sends these packets to a routing device. This can be a hardware router, a server that is configured as a router, or the computer or wireless router through which the other computers in a small office/home office (SOHO) network access the Internet. The default gateway is the address within the subnet of the routing device (which has at least one more IPv4 address on another subnet). It is where outgoing packets leave the subnet. It is also where incoming packets from other networks enter the subnet.

 Quick Check

1. What is the binary number 00001010 11110000 10101010 01000000 in dotted decimal notation?

2. Are the IPv4 addresses 192.168.1.200 and 192.168.1.24 on the same subnet? Both have a subnet mask of 255.255.255.0.

3. Is 10.0.0.130 a valid IPv4 address on the 10.0.0.0/25 subnet?

Quick Check Answers

1. 10.240.170.64.

2. The subnet mask specifies that the final octet holds the host address. Therefore the first three octets hold the subnet's network address. In both cases, this is 192.168.1.0, so the computers are on the same subnet.

3. No. The /25 subnet mask specifies 25 ones and therefore 32 − 25 = 7 zeros. Zeros denote host address. Therefore, the host address is from 0000001 to 1111110 binary (0000000 is the network address and 111111 the broadcast address). In decimal, this is 1 to 126. So the valid IPv4 addresses on the network are 10.0.0.1 to 10.0.0.126. 10.0.0.130 is not in this range and therefore is not valid on this subnet. It is an address on another subnet (for example, 10.0.0.128/25).

Network Services

IPv4 configuration and operation relies on a number of network services. In an enterprise environment, these services (apart from APIPA) are implemented on servers. However, on a small network, DHCP and DNS services can be provided by a client running ICS or by a WAP. Services associated with IPv4 include the following:

- **DHCP** Assigns IPv4 addresses to hosts that are set to receive their configurations automatically. It assigns IPv4 addresses from one or more scopes and handles IPv4 address leasing and renewal. Exclusion ranges can be defined for non-DHCP-enabled hosts, and static assignments can be made to specific media access control (MAC) addresses. DHCP can also specify the IPv4 address of the default gateway(s) and DNS server(s).

- **DNS** Resolves both local host names and fully qualified domain names (FQDNs)—for example, *http://www.contoso.internal*—to IPv4 addresses (and vice versa). A local DNS server can perform this function on its own subnet. For example, if you enter **ping canberra** in the Command Prompt window, DNS resolves the computer name Canberra to its IPv4 address. DNS also works over the Internet to resolve the FQDNs of remote Web sites to their IPv4 addresses. DNS provides a connection-specific DNS suffix for e-mail addresses. If you had an e-mail server (for example, a server running Microsoft Exchange Server) on your network, the connection-specific DNS suffix would be the section of the e-mail address after the @ symbol (for example, don.hall@tailspintoys.com). The Dynamic Domain Name Service (DDNS) uses the concept of a dynamic database and enables dynamic updates.

> **MORE INFO** **INTERNAL VS. EXTERNAL RESOLUTION**
>
> If you need to resolve a computer name on your internal network to an IPv4 address (for example, if you entered **ping canberra** in the Command Prompt window), then the DNS service on your WAP or ICS computer will provide the IPv4 address that corresponds to the computer name. If, on the other hand, you needed to resolve an FQDN on the Internet (for example if you entered **http://www.contoso.com** in your browser), then that FQDN is resolved over the Internet. FQDNs are resolved over the Internet using a DNS server hierarchy and an iterative process. It is unlikely that the 70-680 examination will test your knowledge of iterative DNS queries. However, if you want to know more about this topic out of professional interest, see *http://technet. microsoft.com/en-us/library/cc775637.aspx*.

- **APIPA** Configures an internal private network when DHCP is not provided. If you have a network with no connection to any other network and you want the computers on that network to see one another, you can connect them by using an Ethernet switch and allow them to configure themselves without requiring DHCP services. APIPA configures a computer's IPv4 settings with an IPv4 address in the range 169.254.0.1 through 169.254.255.254 and a subnet mask of 255.255.0.0. APIPA does not configure a default gateway because an APIPA-configured network does not send IPv4 packets to, or receive them from, any other network.

- **NAT** Allows many devices on a private network to gain access to the Internet through one public IPv4 address. NAT translates between private IPv4 addresses used internally in a local network and public addresses used on the Internet. When you send a request to the Internet—for example, by typing a Uniform Resource Locator

(URL) into a browser—the information that the request returns (the Web page) needs to find its way back to your computer, which has an internal IPv4 address on your local area network (LAN). Typically, your ISP allocates only one public IPv4 address that all the computers on your LAN share when accessing the Internet. NAT deals with this situation and ensures that IPv4 packets from the Internet reach the correct LAN destinations.

> **MORE INFO** **NETWORK ADDRESS TRANSLATION**
>
> For more information about NAT, see *http://technet.microsoft.com/en-us/library/cc739385.aspx*.

Public and Private IPv4 Addresses

Every device on the Internet has its own unique public IPv4 address that is shared with no other device (a LAN also has at least one IPv4 address that is unique on the Internet). For example, if you type a URL such as **http://www.adatum.com** into your Web browser, the FQDN *www.adatum.com* identifies a Web server that has a public IPv4 address—for example, 207.46.197.32.

Any organization that has an Internet presence is allocated one or more public IPv4 addresses that that organization and only that organization can use. The Internet Assigned Numbers Authority (IANA) issues and controls public IPv4 addresses through various agencies—for example, the United Kingdom Education and Research Network (UKERNA). In the case of a SOHO network, the ISP allocates one public IPv4 address from a range that IANA or one of its agencies has allocated to the ISP.

Most organizations do not have enough public IPv4 addresses to allocate one to every device on their networks. Also, issuing public IPv4 addresses to computers in an organization's network has security implications. Instead, organizations use private IPv4 addresses for their internal networks and use NAT to translate these addresses to a public address or addresses for Internet access.

Private IPv4 addresses should never be used on the Internet, and typically a router on the Internet ignores private IPv4 addresses. An organization can use whatever private IPv4 address range it chooses without requiring permission from IANA. Because private IPv4 addresses are internal to an organization, many organizations can use the same range of IPv4 addresses without causing IPv4 conflicts. Most computers on internal networks do not need a unique public address but instead share a single public address that identifies their LAN and that NAT translates to their private addresses. Only devices on a LAN that have an Internet presence—for example, Web servers, e-mail servers, and DNS servers—require a unique public address mapped through NAT to their internal private address.

IANA has reserved the following three blocks of IPv4 address space for private networks:

- 10.0.0.0/8 (10.0.0.1 through 10.255.255.254)
- 172.16.0.0/12 (172.16.0.1 through 172.31.255.254)
- 192.168.0.0/16 (192.168.0.1 through 192.168.255.255)

In addition, the APIPA range 169.254.0.0/16 (169.254.0.1 through 169.254.255.254) is also considered private because these addresses should never appear on the Internet. However, you should use this range only for automatic IPv4 address allocation through APIPA in an isolated subnet. You should not use this range in private networks that configure their devices though DHCP or manual (static) configuration and use NAT to implement Internet access.

Most organizations use only a small subsection of the private address space. For example, the 10.0.0.0/8 network contains more than 16 million host addresses, and very few organizations need that many. A commercial company with two private subnets might, for example, use 10.0.10.0/24 (10.0.10.1 through 10.0.10.254) and 10.0.20.0/24 (10.0.20.1 through 10.0.20.254) for these subnets. ICS uses the 192.168.0.0/24 address range (192.168.0.1 through 192.168.0.254), and most WAPs also use this range of addresses.

> **NOTE PRIVATE NETWORKS—THE DEFINITIVE DOCUMENT**
>
> The accurate definition of a private network is a network that uses RFC 1918 IPv4 address space. As you progress in your career as a network administrator, you will refer more and more frequently to RFCs like RFC 1918. To view this RFC, see *http://tools.ietf.org/html/rfc1918*.

Connecting to a Network

If you are setting up a wired test or SOHO network from scratch, you likely start with a single computer connected to your modem (either wired or wirelessly via a WAP), which in turn provides a connection to the Internet. Typically, most networks are connected to the Internet, either directly or through other networks. If your network is completely isolated, with no connections to either the Internet or other LANs, then it is usually sufficient to let it configure itself through APIPA.

More commonly, you are adding a computer to an existing network (for example, a SOHO network or a small test network). In this case, a DHCP service typically already exists on the network, possibly on a computer configured to provide ICS, or (in the case of a wireless network) from a WAP. When you connect to the Internet, your ISP automatically configures your dial-up or cable modem connection. If you set up ICS, then the computer on your network that directly accesses your modem automatically configures all the other computers on its subnet.

> **MORE INFO INTERNET CONNECTION SHARING**
>
> For more information about ICS and an excellent illustrative diagram, see *http://windowshelp .microsoft.com/Windows/en-US/Help/bfd3bd31-82f0-4b9c-9cde-fb92bc2b14771033.mspx*. This is a Windows Vista article, but it works for Windows 7 if you substitute "Change Adapter Settings" for "Manage Network Settings."

Typically, client computers on a network are set to receive their IP configurations automatically. However, if the computer you are adding is an ICS client, you need to access Network And Sharing Center, click Internet Options, click LAN Settings on the Connections tab, and clear the Automatically Select Connections check box in the Local Area Network (LAN) Settings dialog box. You configure an ICS computer and an ICS client in a practice exercise later in this lesson.

You can check if a computer is configured and get IPv4 configurations automatically by opening the Network And Sharing Center. You do this by opening Control Panel, clicking Network And Internet, and then clicking Network And Sharing Center. In the Network And Sharing Center, click Change Adapter Settings. Right-click the local area connection that connects to your test network (typically, Local Area Connection) and choose Properties. The Local Area Connection Properties dialog box appears, as shown in Figure 6-2. Note that the names of the antivirus supplier and the Ethernet controller manufacturer have been obscured for legal reasons.

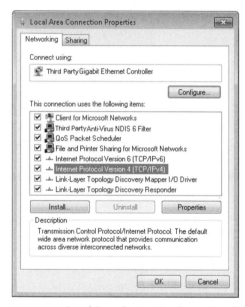

FIGURE 6-2 Local Area Connection Properties dialog box

In this dialog box, you can select Internet Protocol Version 4 (TCP/IPv4) and click Properties. Unless you have chosen manual configuration by selecting Use The Following IP Address, you should see that IPv4 is set up for automatic configuration, as shown in Figure 6-3. If you click the Alternate Configuration tab, you see that APIPA is used by default if DHCP information is not available.

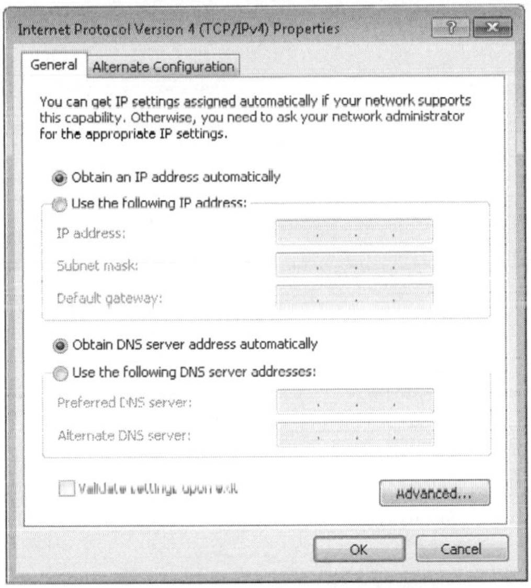

FIGURE 6-3 Automatic IPv4 configuration

Lesson 3 discusses the various configurations and combinations of wired and wireless computers, modems, and WAPs you can use to set up a SOHO or a small test network. Setting up a production network is a much more complex procedure involving the use of multiple firewalls, peripheral zones, NAT servers, and so on. It is unlikely that the 70-680 examination will ask you about setting up a fully secured production network in the enterprise. In this lesson, we connect the Canberra and Aberdeen computers on a private wired network and (optionally) connect the Canberra computer wirelessly to a WAP that accesses the Internet through a cable modem (or uses a composite device that is both a WAP and a cable modem) and configuring ICS on that computer.

To connect wirelessly to a WAP (if this is necessary), open the Network And Sharing Center (shown in Figure 6-4) and click Connect To A Network. You can select a network from the list of those available. You can also specify that the computer should always connect to this network when it is in range.

> **NOTE UNCONFIGURED WAPS**
>
> Figure 6-4 shows the Canberra computer connected to an as-yet-unconfigured WAP. Unconfigured WAPs are typically called Default, have a password of admin, and allow a client computer to connect to them. This WAP is currently unconfigured because WAP configuration is discussed in Lesson 3. Always configure your WAP; failure to do so is a major security risk.

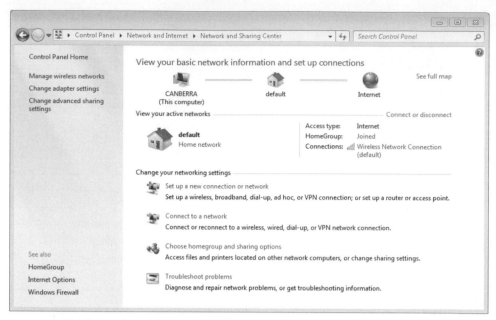

FIGURE 6-4 The Network And Sharing Center

Setting an IPv4 configuration

In the Internet Protocol Version 4 (TCP/IPv4) Properties dialog box shown in Figure 6-3, you can select Use The Following IP Address and type in a static IPv4 address, a subnet mask, and a default gateway. You can also select Use The Following DNS Server Address and type in the IPv4 address of a DNS server and an alternate DNS server the client can use if the first is unavailable. Clicking Advanced lets you add more DNS servers. You can also add the IPv4 addresses of one or more Windows Internet Naming Service (WINS) server if you need NetBIOS name resolution.

However, many administrators prefer to use the Netsh command-line tool from an elevated command prompt. For example, if you want to configure the Local Area Connection interface with an IPv4 address 10.0.0.11, a subnet mask 255.255.255.0, and a default gateway 10.0.0.11, you enter the following command:

```
netsh interface ipv4 set address "local area connection" static 10.0.0.11 255.255.255.0
10.0.0.11
```

If you also wanted to set the DNS server address as 10.0.0.11, you enter the following command:

```
netsh interface ipv4 set dnsservers "local area connection" static 10.0.0.11
```

If you wanted the interface to obtain its IPv4 configuration automatically (dynamically), you enter the following commands:

```
netsh interface ipv4 set address name="local area connection" source=dhcp
netsh interface ipv4 set dnsservers name="local area connection" source=dhcp
```

You use both the Internet Protocol Version 4 (TCP/IPv4) Properties dialog box and the *Netsh* command to configure an interface in the practice later in this lesson.

> **NOTE NETSH SYNTAX**
>
> For backward compatibility, you can use *netsh interface ip* in place of *netsh interface ipv4*. For IPv6 *Netsh* commands, you must specify IPv6. Note also for static settings, the interface name is simply *local area connection*. The syntax *name="local area connection"* is acceptable but not necessary. For dynamic configuration you need to use *name="local area connection"*.

Troubleshooting Network Connectivity

As an IT professional, one of the most common problems you encounter is computers not being able to connect to one another, to other internal networks within your organization, or to the Internet. In this section, you look at general troubleshooting tools that help you debug network connectivity, as well as the Windows Network Diagnostics tool.

Basic Troubleshooting

Connection problems can have many possible causes. In wired networks, a cable could be faulty or might not be connecting properly to its socket. Interfaces that should get their IP configurations dynamically could be set with a static configuration. Where two or more interfaces form a network bridge, one or more interfaces could have been removed from the bridge. In the enterprise environment, a DHCP or DNS server, or even a domain controller, might have developed a fault (although there is typically a failover mechanism in this situation). A firewall might be misconfigured.

On a small network, ICS might be set up incorrectly or not set up at all. A third-party WAP could have been added to a wired network so that wireless computers can connect, but the computer previously configured to provide ICS might not be reconfigured to obtain its configuration from the WAP. A WAP, network adapter, or modem could be faulty. Your ISP could be suffering an outage. Newly installed software might have changed your connection properties. The list is practically endless.

First principles always apply. Start with the network and ensure that no cables have been pulled out or are halfway out and causing unreliable connections. Make sure all the appropriate light-emitting diodes (LEDs) on the modem, WAP, and network interfaces are lit when they should be lit and flickering when they should be flickering. If a device shows no sign of life, check that its power supply is connected to a power socket and to the device. Check out any illuminated red LEDs. A red light does not always indicate a fault, but red frequently signifies danger.

If you are having problems with wireless connections, try switching the WAP off. You should then power down any computers that connect to the WAP through Ethernet cables and possibly your wireless computers as well. Wait a few minutes, switch the WAP back on, and restart the computers. If you suspect the modem, switch off the modem, the WAP, and all network computers and then turn them on again in that order. Check the WAP settings.

Checking Computer to Computer Connectivity

Before you start to use the tools Windows 7 provides to check computer-to-computer connectivity, make sure the computer you are trying to connect to is switched on. In a wired network, make sure it is plugged into the network. If you are using ICS, make sure the ICS computer is switched on and running, otherwise none of the other computers will connect to the Internet. If the computers on your network get their IPv4 configurations from a third-party WAP, make sure the WAP is switched on and connected to the modem.

For a computer running Windows 7 to connect to other computers on a LAN, Network Discovery needs to be enabled on both the source and destination computers. Network Discovery is enabled by default, but if you are having problems accessing other computers, check this setting by clicking Change Advanced Sharing Settings in the Network And Sharing Center. Figure 6-5 shows the Advanced Sharing Settings dialog box.

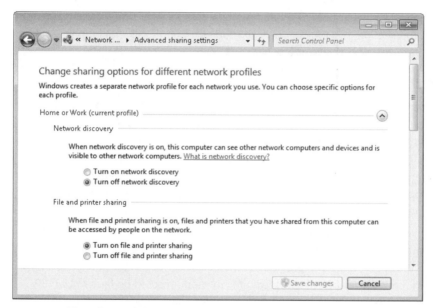

FIGURE 6-5 The Advanced Sharing Settings dialog box

If a network connection is suffering intermittent problems, it is sometimes sufficient to disable and then enable the network connector device driver. If this does not help, the device driver might be corrupt or out of date, or it might recently have been replaced by a new driver that is causing compatibility problems. Chapter 4, "Managing Devices and Disks," gives more details about updating, uninstalling, rolling back, and troubleshooting drivers.

Troubleshooting IP Configuration

Command-line tools for troubleshooting IP configuration have been around for some time and are well known. The *Ping* tool is still widely used, although more firewalls block Internet Control Message Protocol (ICMP) echo requests than used to be the case. However, even if you cannot get past a firewall on your organization's network, *Ping* is still useful. You can check that the IPv4 protocol is working on a computer by entering **ping 127.0.0.1.** You can then ping the IPv4 address of the computer. You can find out what this is by using the Ipconfig tool. If your computer has more than one interface combined in a network bridge, you can ping the IPv4 address of the network bridge. When you have established that you can ping your computer using an IPv4 address, you can test that DNS is working internally on your network (assuming you are connected to a DNS server, a WAP, or have ICS configured on your network) by pinging your computer name—for example, entering **ping canberra.** Note that if DNS is not implemented on your system, *ping canberra* still works because the IPv6 link-local address resolves automatically.

MORE INFO **NETWORK BRIDGES**

For more information about network bridges, see *http://technet.microsoft.com/en-us/library/cc781097.aspx.* Although this is a fairly old article (concerning Windows Server 2003), it gives a clear explanation and some excellent diagrams. For a more recent article (although not about Windows 7), see *http://technet.microsoft.com/en-us/library/cc748895.aspx.* This also gives information about ICS.

You can also use the Ipconfig tool for troubleshooting. Entering **ipconfig /all** gives you configuration information for all interfaces. Figure 6-6 shows the output from an *ipconfig /all* command. The computer whose configuration is shown here is a wireless-enabled laptop used on a small test network. It obtains its configuration through DHCP from a third-party WAP with an IPv4 address 192.168.123.254. The WAP also provides internal DNS services. However, the resolution of FQDNs such as *www.contoso.com* is provided by the ISP's DNS server with the public IPv4 address 194.168.4.100.

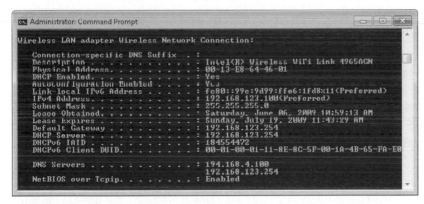

FIGURE 6-6 *Ipconfig /all* output for a wireless-enabled laptop on a test network

When you are debugging connection problems by using the *Ipconfig /all* command, look out for an address in the APIPA range 169.254.0.1 through 169.254.255.254. If your computer is not on a completely isolated network and receives its configuration through DHCP, an APIPA address indicates a connection error.

If you can ping your computer by name and IPv4 address, you can then ping other workstations on your network by IPv4 address and computer name. Finally, you should check that you can ping your default gateway from all the computers in your network. On a small network, you can then test connectivity to your ISP by pinging the ISP's DNS server. On an enterprise network, you can ping DNS servers and domain controllers (typically the same servers), and computers on other subnets.

If you cannot ping a computer on your network to test connectivity, make sure your internal firewalls are not blocking ICMP. If the problem still exists with the firewalls reconfigured or disabled (please remember to enable them afterward), use Ipconfig on the computer you cannot reach to check its IP settings.

> **✔ Quick Check**
>
>   - You have purchased a secondhand computer and are connecting it to a hybrid network that obtains its configuration from DHCP provided by a third-party WAP. The computer is not wireless-enabled, so you plug it into the Ethernet switch on the WAP and switch it on. It cannot access the Internet. You use the Ipconfig tool and discover that the computer has an IP address of 10.1.10.231. You know the WAP is working properly and the Ethernet connection is okay. What should you check next?
>
> **Quick Check Answer**
>
>   - Check that the computer is set to receive its IPv4 configuration dynamically. It has not been reconfigured by DHCP on the WAP and its previous owner has probably configured it statically with the 10.1.10.231 address. You need to reconfigure the computer to receive its IPv4 settings dynamically.

If you want to reconfigure IP settings on a client computer on your network, you can reboot the client. If this is not convenient, the commands *ipconfig /release* and *ipconfig /renew* release the old configuration and obtain a new one. (In theory, *ipconfig /renew* should be sufficient, but it is safer to use both commands.) Sometimes when you renew a computer's configuration, it does not immediately register its new settings in DNS and you cannot ping it by computer name. In this case, *ipconfig /registerdns* forces registration. Note that you need to enter these commands in an elevated command prompt.

If you try to ping a computer by name or access a Web site from a client workstation and DNS cannot resolve the computer name or URL, then information that resolution has failed is stored (cached) in the workstation. If you try to do the same thing again, the source computer does not attempt to obtain name resolution but instead uses the cached information and again fails the request. This is known as *negative caching*. However, name resolution might have failed because of a temporary glitch in the internal or external DNS service. Even though DNS is now working, the computer name or FQDN is not resolved to an IPv4 address because of the cached information. The problem disappears in 30 minutes or so because the workstation's DNS resolver cache is regularly cleared. However, if you do not want to wait this long, you can solve the problem immediately by entering the **ipconfig /flushdns** command to flush the DNS cache.

If you want to trace the route of an IP packet through an internetwork (a series of networks or hops), you can use the Tracert tool to list the path the packet took and the delays encountered at each hop; for example, *tracert 194.168.4.100.* You can use the *Tracert* tool to trace the path to a Web site; for example, *tracert –d www.contoso.com.* The *–d* flag prevents the tool from resolving IPv4 addresses to host names, which significantly reduces the time the command takes to complete. The *Pathping* tool (for example, *pathping www.contoso.com*) traces a route in much the same way as the *Tracert* tool but gives more detailed statistics about each hop.

Using the Windows Network Diagnostics Tool

There has never been a substitute for good basic fault-finding. However, after you have gone through the basic checks, Windows 7 provides automated assistance with the Windows Network Diagnostics tool.

You can access the automated Windows Network Diagnostics tool if you fail to connect to a Web site on the Internet. The Web page that appears in your browser gives you a direct link to the tool when you click Diagnose Connection Problems, as shown in Figure 6-7.

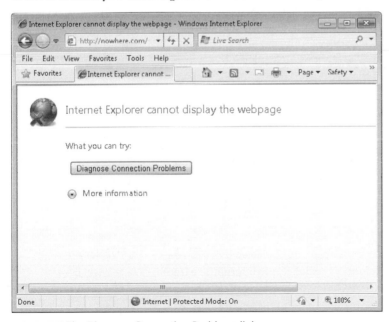

FIGURE 6-7 The Diagnose Connection Problems link

You can also access the Windows Network Diagnostics tool by clicking Change Adapter Settings in Network And Sharing Center, right-clicking the interface that is having problems, and choosing Diagnose. You can also access the tool from Network And Sharing Center if you click the red X that denotes you have a problem connecting your computer to your network or your network to the Internet. Whatever way you access the tool, it performs a diagnosis automatically and (if possible) comes up with one or more suggested solutions. In Figure 6-8, you can see that the administrator has failed to follow first principles and has not checked that the Ethernet cable is plugged in.

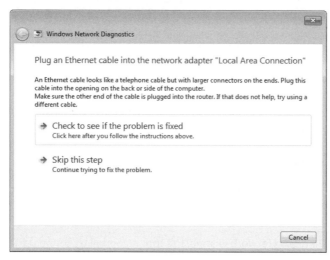

FIGURE 6-8 Failure diagnosis

Additional diagnostic options are available when you click Troubleshoot Problems in Network And Sharing Center, as shown in Figure 6-9. However, most of these tools simply provide another method of accessing Windows Network Diagnostics.

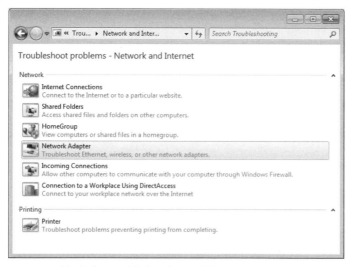

FIGURE 6-9 Tools for troubleshooting problems

Configuring Network Settings in Windows Firewall

Chapter 7, "Windows Firewall and Remote Management," discusses firewalls and firewall configuration in detail. This chapter therefore provides only a brief introduction and discusses firewall settings only insofar as they affect network connectivity and your ability to test and troubleshoot this connectivity. The defaults in Windows Firewall and Windows Firewall with Advanced Security (WFAS) are sensible, and often you can solve problems by restoring these defaults.

Windows Firewall is enabled by default in Windows 7. It blocks all incoming traffic other than traffic that meets the criteria defined in the exceptions. You can configure an exception by allowing a program to send information back and forth through the firewall—sometimes called *unblocking*. You can also allow a program through the firewall by opening one or more ports. Windows Firewall allows Core Networking Components by default in both public and private networks. As shown in Figure 6-10, the Core Networking firewall rules are required for reliable IPv4 and IPv6 connectivity. However, these rules do not allow ICMPv4 or ICMPv6 Echo Requests; hence, the firewall blocks *Ping* commands.

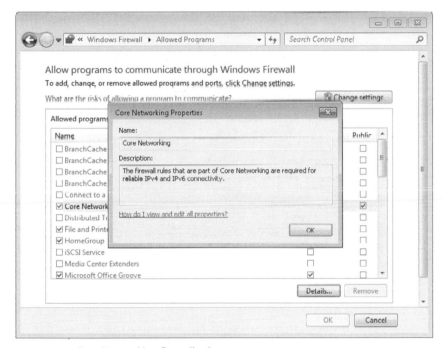

FIGURE 6-10 Core Networking firewall rules

You access Windows Firewall by clicking System And Security in Control Panel and then clicking Windows Firewall. In the left pane, you can choose to turn the firewall on or off and change the notification settings. You can also click Advanced Settings to access WFAS.

Figure 6-11 illustrates the Core Networking Inbound Rules in WFAS. The Outbound Rules that allow Core Networking and File And Printer Sharing are displayed in Figure 6-12. These

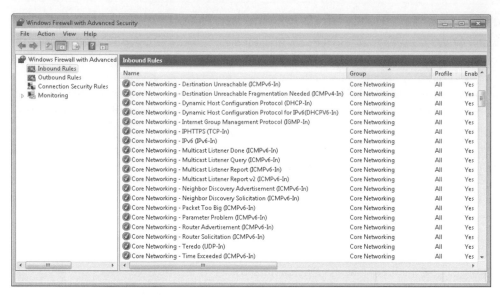

FIGURE 6-11 WFAS Inbound Rules

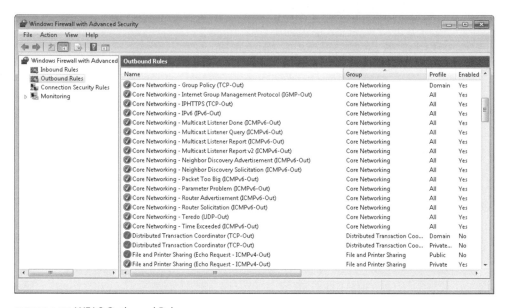

FIGURE 6-12 WFAS Outbound Rules

rules allow specific traffic that lets Windows 7 carry out these functions but do not permit the use of the *Ping* tool.

If you are having connectivity problems and disabling Windows Firewall solves them, look at your firewall settings. In some cases, restoring the defaults solves your immediate problems, but this is a simplistic approach. The settings were changed for a reason. You need to investigate further. Chapter 7 gives you the tools to do so.

For example, restoring the defaults does not permit you to use Ping to test continuity on your network, and it would not be a good idea to disable firewalls on all the computers on your subnet. Instead, you need to add rules that enable ICMPv4 and ICMPv6 packets to pass through your firewall:

To permit ICMPv4 and enable you to ping other computers by their IPv4 addresses, enter the following in an elevated command prompt on all computers on your network:

```
netsh advfirewall firewall add rule name="ICMPv4" protocol=icmpv4:any,any dir=in
action=allow
```

To permit ICMPv6 and enable you to ping other computers by their IPv6 addresses, enter the following in an elevated command prompt on all computers on your network:

```
netsh advfirewall firewall add rule name="ICMPv6" protocol=icmpv6:any,any dir=in
action=allow
```

 **Quick Check**

- How do you restore the default firewall settings?

Quick Check Answer

- In Control Panel, click System and Security. Click Windows Firewall. In the left pane, click Restore Defaults.

 EXAM TIP

Remember that in Windows 7, you cannot ping other computers on your network by default.

Accessing Network Statistics

If you are debugging performance issues as opposed to troubleshooting a total connectivity failure, you need information about the various protocols that implement network connectivity. The *Netstat* command-line tool displays active connections, the ports on which the computer is listening, Ethernet statistics, the IP routing table, and IPv4 and IPv6 statistics. Used without parameters, the command displays active connections, as shown in Figure 6-13.

```
Administrator: Command Prompt

C:\Windows\system32>netstat

Active Connections

  Proto  Local Address          Foreign Address        State
  TCP    127.0.0.1:9080         Canberra:53307         ESTABLISHED
  TCP    127.0.0.1:53307        Canberra:9080          ESTABLISHED
  TCP    192.168.123.100:2492   blugro1relay:2492      ESTABLISHED
  TCP    192.168.123.100:2492   blugro2relay:2492      ESTABLISHED
  TCP    192.168.123.100:52568  OFFICE:microsoft-ds    ESTABLISHED
  TCP    192.168.123.100:52630  SERVER:microsoft-ds    ESTABLISHED

C:\Windows\system32>
```

FIGURE 6-13 The *Netstat* command displays active connections.

The syntax of the *Netstat* command is as follows:

```
netstat [-a] [-e] [-n] [-o] [-p Protocol] [-r] [-s] [Interval]
```

The parameters implement the following functions:

- **-a**   Displays all active connections and the Transmission Control Protocol (TCP) and User Datagram Protocol (UDP) ports on which the computer is listening.

- **-e**   Displays Ethernet statistics, such as the number of bytes and packets sent and received. This parameter can be combined with *-s*.

- **-n**   Displays active connections. Addresses and port numbers are expressed numerically and no attempt is made to determine names.

- **-o**   Displays active connections and includes the process ID (PID) for each connection. You can find the application based on the PID on the Processes tab in Windows Task Manager. This parameter can be combined with *-a*, *-n*, and *-p*.

- **-p protocol**   Shows connections for the protocol specified by the protocol variable, which can be *tcp, udp, tcpv6,* or *udpv6*. If this parameter is used with *-s* to display statistics by protocol, which can be *tcp, udp, icmp, ip, tcpv6, udpv6, icmpv6,* or *ipv6*.

- **-s**   Displays statistics by protocol. By default, statistics are shown for the TCP, UDP, ICMPv4, ICMPv6, IPv4, and IPv6 protocols. The *-p* parameter can be used to specify a set of protocols.

- **-r**   Displays the contents of the IP routing table. This is equivalent to the *route print* command.

- ***interval***   Displays the selected information periodically. The number of seconds between each display is defined by the interval parameter. If this parameter is omitted, *Netstat* prints the selected information only once.

Netstat provides statistics for the following:

- The name of the protocol (TCP or UDP)

- The IP address of the local computer and the port number being used

- The IP address and port number of the remote computer

- The state of a TCP connection

> **MORE INFO   TCP CONNECTION STATES**
>
> For more information about the states of a TCP connection, see *http://support.microsoft.com/kb/137984*. This article was written some time ago but remains relevant to Windows 7.

For example, to display both the Ethernet statistics and the statistics for all protocols, enter the following command:

```
netstat -e -s
```

To display the TCP statistics for the IPv4 protocol, enter the following command:

```
netstat -s -p tcp
```

Figure 6-14 shows the TCP statistics for the IPv4 protocol on the Canberra computer.

FIGURE 6-14 TCP protocol statistics for IPv4

Configuring IPv4 Network Connectivity and Setting Up ICS

In this practice, you configure the Canberra and Aberdeen computers with static IPv4 addresses, configure the firewalls on both computers to allow *Ping* commands, and test connectivity. You then reconfigure the computers to obtain their IPv4 configuration automatically and set up ICS in Canberra so both computers can access the Internet through Canberra's wireless link.

EXERCISE 1 Configuring IPv4 Connectivity

This exercise assumes that Canberra and Aberdeen are configured to obtain their IPv4 configurations automatically (the default). If they are both physical computers, they need to be connected on the same Ethernet network either by a switch or hub or by a crossover Ethernet cable. To configure IPv4 connectivity, proceed as follows:

1. Log on to the Canberra computer using the Kim_Akers account.
2. Open an elevated command prompt.
3. To allow ICMPv4 traffic through the Canberra firewall, enter **netsh advfirewall firewall add rule name="ICMPv4" protocol=icmpv4:any,any dir=in action=allow.**
4. To configure static IPv4 configuration, enter **netsh interface ipv4 set address "local area connection" static 10.0.0.11 255.255.255.0 10.0.0.1.** Currently, there is no DNS service on your private network, so there is no point configuring a DNS setting. Note that if you are using virtual machines, the connection to your private wired network may have a name other than Local Area Connection.
5. Enter **ipconfig.** Your screen should look similar to Figure 6-15.
6. Remaining logged on to the Canberra computer, log on to the Aberdeen computer using the Kim_Akers account.

FIGURE 6-15 Static configuration of the Canberra computer

7. Open an elevated command prompt.

8. To allow ICMPv4 traffic through the Aberdeen firewall, enter **netsh advfirewall firewall add rule name="ICMPv4" protocol=icmpv4:any,any dir=in action=allow.**

9. Open Network And Sharing Center. Click Change Adapter Settings.

10. Right-click the Ethernet adapter Local Area Connection and choose Properties.

11. Click Internet Protocol Version 4 (TCP/IPv4) and click Properties.

12. Configure the connection as shown in Figure 6-16.

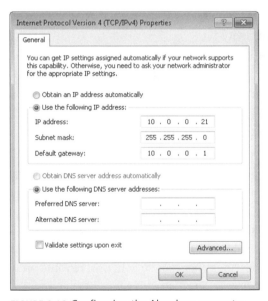

FIGURE 6-16 Configuring the Aberdeen computer

13. Click OK. Click Close.

14. In the elevated command prompt, enter **ipconfig.** Your screen should look similar to Figure 6-17.

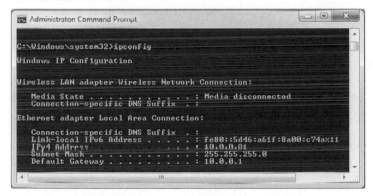

FIGURE 6-17 Static configuration of the Aberdeen computer

15. Enter **ping 10.0.0.11.** Your screen should look similar to Figure 6-18.

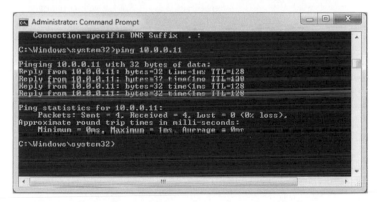

FIGURE 6-18 Pinging the Canberra computer from the Aberdeen computer

16. On the Canberra computer, enter **ping 10.0.0.21.** Check that you have two-way connectivity.

17. Restore dynamic IPv4 configuration on both the Canberra and Aberdeen computers.

EXERCISE 2   Configuring ICS on the Canberra Computer

In this exercise, you install ICS on the Canberra computer. This enables Internet access on Aberdeen and ensures that Canberra can supply DNS and DHCP services on the network. The exercise requires that Canberra can access the Internet wirelessly and is therefore optional. If you also have a wireless adapter on the Aberdeen computer, ensure that this is disabled. Ensure that both Aberdeen and Canberra are configured to obtain IPv4 settings automatically.

1. If necessary, log on to the Canberra computer using the Kim_Akers account.

2. Open Network And Sharing Center. Click Change Adapter Settings.

3. Right-click the wireless adapter Wireless Network Connection and choose Properties.

4. Click the Sharing tab.

5. Select the Allow Other Network Users To Connect Through This Computer's Internet Connection check box, as shown in Figure 6-19. Click OK.

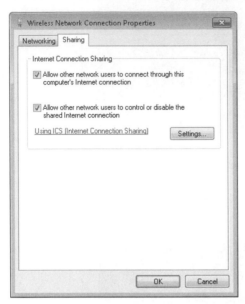

FIGURE 6-19 Allowing other computers to use the Canberra Internet connection

6. If necessary, log on to the Aberdeen computer using the Kim_Akers account.

7. Open Network And Sharing Center. Click Internet Options.

8. Click the Connections tab and ensure that Never Dial A Connection is selected.

9. Click LAN Settings.

10. In the Local Area Network (LAN) Settings dialog box, under Automatic Configuration, clear the Automatically Detect Settings and Use Automatic Configuration Script check boxes.

11. Under Proxy Server, clear the Use A Proxy Server For Your LAN check box. The LAN Settings dialog box should look similar to Figure 6-20. Click OK.

12. Click OK to close the Internet Properties dialog box.

13. Open Windows Internet Explorer. You should have Internet connectivity. If not, run Windows Network Diagnostics.

14. Open an elevated command prompt (if necessary). Enter **ping canberra.** You now have a DNS service and can resolve computer names to IPv4 addresses.

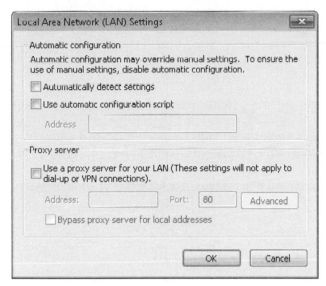

FIGURE 6-20 The LAN Settings dialog box on an ICS client computer

Lesson Summary

- IPv4 is responsible for ensuring that a packet sent across an IPv4 network reaches its destination. DHCP automatically configures computers on a network with their IPv4 configurations. DNS resolves a host name or FQDN to an IP address.

- An IPv4 address identifies a computer (or other network device) on a subnet. A subnet mask defines the range of IP addresses on a subnet.

- A wired small network that contains more than one computer typically implements Transmission Control Protocol/Internet Protocol (TCP/IP) configuration through ICS. Computers and other devices on a wireless or hybrid small network obtain their configurations from the WAP.

- You use the Network And Sharing Center to view computers and devices on a network, connect to a network, set up a connection or network, and manage network connections. You can also use the *Netsh interface ipv4* command to manage IPv4 networks.

- You can access the Windows Network Diagnostics tool from the Network And Sharing Center to troubleshoot a faulty network connection. If you fail to connect to a Web site, you can access the same tool by clicking Diagnose Connection Problems.

- You can use the *Ping, Tracert,* and *Pathping* commands to troubleshoot network connectivity. The *Netstat* command returns network protocol statistics.

Lesson Review

You can use the following questions to test your knowledge of the information in Lesson 1, "Configuring IPv4." The questions are also available on the companion DVD if you prefer to review them in electronic form.

> **NOTE** **ANSWERS**
>
> Answers to these questions and explanations of why each answer choice is correct or incorrect are located in the "Answers" section at the end of the book.

1. Which command-line command displays the IP configuration of a computer's interfaces?

   A. *Ping*

   B. *Tracert*

   C. *Ipconfig*

   D. *Netstat*

2. Which of the following methods can you use to display the properties of a LAN connection? (Choose all that apply.)

   A. In the Network And Sharing Center, click Internet Options. On the Connections tab of the Internet Properties dialog box, click LAN Settings.

   B. In the Network And Sharing Center, click Change Adapter Settings. Right-click the LAN connection and choose Status. In the Local Area Connection Status dialog box, click Properties.

   C. In the Network And Sharing Center, click Change Adapter Settings. Right-click the LAN connection and choose Properties.

   D. In the Network And Sharing Center, click Change Adapter Settings. Double-click the LAN connection. In the Local Area Connection Status dialog box, click Properties.

3. You are configuring static IPv4 addresses for two computers, Perth and Brisbane, on an isolated private wired subnet. You configure Perth with the IPv4 address 172.16.10. 140 and the subnet mask 255.255.255.0. You configure Brisbane with the IPv4 address 172.16.10. 210 and the subnet mask 255.255.255.0. You enter **ping 172.16.10.140** on Brisbane, but the command times out. Similarly, entering **ping 172.16.0.210** on Perth fails to locate the Brisbane computer's IPv4 address. What is the likely reason for this lack of connectivity?

   A. DNS service is not available on the subnet.

   B. The computers should have different subnet masks.

   C. You have not specified a default gateway.

   D. You need to permit ICMPv4 traffic through the firewalls of both computers.

4. You have created the statically configured wired subnet 10.0.10.128/25. Currently the only device on the subnet is a router with the IPv4 address 10.0.10.129. You plug a computer into an Ethernet port on the subnet. What command configures the computer correctly on the subnet?

   A. `netsh interface ipv4 set address "local area connection" static 10.0.10.162 255.255.255.0 10.0.10.129`

   B. `netsh interface ipv4 set address "local area connection" static 10.0.0.162 255.255.255.128 10.0.10.129`

   C. `netsh interface ipv4 set address name="local area connection" dhcp`

   D. `netsh interface ipv4 set address name="local area connection" static 10.0.10.16 255.255.255.128 10.0.10.129`

5. You want to examine the contents of both the IPv4 and the IPv6 route table. What command do you use? (Choose all that apply.)

   A. `netsh interface ipv4 show route`

   B. `tracert -d`

   C. `route print`

   D. `netstat -r`

   E. `netstat -a`

Lesson 2: Configuring IPv6

As a network professional, you have likely worked with IPv4. You might be less familiar with the IPv6 infrastructure and the types of IPv6 address. As IPv6 usage increases, you need to be aware of IPv4-to-IPv6 transition strategy and IPv4 and IPv6 interoperability, particularly the use of Teredo addresses. This lesson looks at how you configure name resolution for unicast and multicast addresses and how you configure a network connection and connect network locations. It discusses how you resolve connectivity issues.

> **After this lesson, you will be able to:**
> - Identify the various types of IPv6 addresses and explain their use.
> - Describe the advantages of IPv6 and how these are achieved.
> - Identify IPv6 addresses that can be routed on the IPv4 Internet.
> - Implement IPv4 and IPv6 interoperability.
> - Troubleshoot IPv6 connectivity.
>
> **Estimated lesson time: 55 minutes**

Analyzing the IPv6 Address Structure

IPv4 and IPv6 addresses can be readily distinguished. An IPv4 address uses 32 bits, resulting in an address space of just over 4 billion. An IPv6 address uses 128 bits, resulting in an address space of 2^{128}, or 340,282,366,920,938,463,463,374,607,431,768,211,456—a number too large to comprehend. This represents $6.5*2^{23}$ or 54,525,952 addresses for every square meter of the earth's surface. In practice, the IPv6 address space allows for multiple levels of subnetting and address allocation between the Internet backbone and individual subnets within an organization. The vastly increased address space available allows us to allocate not one but several unique IPv6 addresses to a network entity, with each address being used for a different purpose.

IPv6 provides addresses that are equivalent to IPv4 address types and others that are unique to IPv6. A node can have several IPv6 addresses, each of which has its own unique purpose. This section describes the IPv6 address syntax and the various classes of IPv6 address.

IPv6 Address Syntax

The IPv6 128-bit address is divided at 16-bit boundaries, and each 16-bit block is converted to a 4-digit hexadecimal number. Colons are used as separators. This representation is called *colon-hexadecimal*.

Global unicast IPv6 addresses are equivalent to IPv4 public unicast addresses. To illustrate IPv6 address syntax, consider the following IPv6 global unicast address:

21cd:0053:0000:0000:03ad:003f:af37:8d62

IPv6 representation can be simplified by removing the leading zeros within each 16-bit block. However, each block must have at least a single digit. With leading-zero suppression, the address representation becomes:

21cd:53:0:0:3ad:3f:af37:8d62

A contiguous sequence of 16-bit blocks set to 0 in the colon-hexadecimal format can be compressed to ::. Thus, the previous example address could be written:

21cd:53::3ad:3f:af37:8d62

> **NOTE IPv6 ABBREVIATION**
>
> **You cannot use :: twice in the same address.**

Some types of addresses contain long sequences of zeros and thus provide good examples of when to use this notation. For example, the multicast address ff05:0:0:0:0:0:0:2 can be compressed to ff05::2.

IPv6 Address Prefixes

The prefix is the part of the address that indicates either the bits that have fixed values or the network identifier bits. IPv6 prefixes are expressed in the same way as CIDR IPv4 notation, or slash notation. For example, 21cd:53::/64 is the subnet on which the address 21cd:53::23ad:3f:af37:8d62 is located. In this case, the first 64 bits of the address are the network prefix. An IPv6 subnet prefix (or subnet ID) is assigned to a single link. Multiple subnet IDs can be assigned to the same link. This technique is called *multinetting*.

> **NOTE IPv6 DOES NOT USE DOTTED DECIMAL NOTATION IN SUBNET MASKS**
>
> Only prefix length notation is supported in IPv6. IPv4 dotted decimal subnet mask representation (such as 255.255.255.0) has no direct equivalent.

IPv6 Address Types

The three types of IPv6 address are as follows:

- **Unicast** Identifies a single interface within the scope of the unicast address type. Packets addressed to a unicast address are delivered to a single interface. RFC 2373 allows multiple interfaces to use the same address, provided that these interfaces appear as a single interface to the IPv6 implementation on the host. This accommodates load-balancing systems.

- **Multicast** Identifies multiple interfaces. Packets addressed to a multicast address are delivered to all interfaces that are identified by the address.

- **Anycast** Identifies multiple interfaces. Packets addressed to an anycast address are delivered to the nearest interface identified by the address. The nearest interface is the closest in terms of routing distance, or number of hops. An anycast address is used for one-to-many communication, with delivery to a single interface.

IPv6 Unicast Addresses

IPv6 supports the following types of unicast address:

- Global
- Link-local
- Site-local
- Special

Global Unicast Addresses

Global unicast addresses are the IPv6 equivalent of IPv4 public addresses and are globally routable and reachable on the IPv6 Internet. These addresses can be aggregated to produce an efficient routing infrastructure and are therefore sometimes known as aggregatable global unicast addresses. A global unicast address is unique across the entire IPv6 Internet. (The region over which an IP address is unique is called the *scope* of the address.)

The Format Prefix (FP) of a global unicast address is held in the three most significant bits, which are always 001. In other words, in theory, they start with 2 or 3—but in practice, they always start with 2. The internal structure of the address is beyond the scope of the 70-680 examination and this book, but you should know that the section of the address that defines the host (the final 64 bits) is either derived from the 48-bit hardware media access control (MAC) address of the network adapter card or is assigned directly to that network adapter card. Put simply, the interface identity is provided by the network adapter hardware.

Link-Local Addresses

Link-local IPv6 addresses are equivalent to IPv4 addresses allocated through APIPA. You can identify a link-local address by an FP of 1111 1110 10, which is followed by 54 zeros (link-local addresses always begin with *fe8*). Nodes use link-local addresses when communicating with neighboring nodes on the same link. The scope of a link-local address is the local link. A link-local address is always automatically configured, even if no other unicast address is allocated.

Site-Local Addresses

Site-local IPv6 addresses are equivalent to the IPv4 private addresses. Private intranets that do not have a direct, routed connection to the IPv6 Internet can use site-local addresses without conflicting with global unicast addresses. The scope of a site-local address is the site (or organization internetwork). Site-local addresses begin with *fec0*.

Site-local addresses can be allocated by using stateful address configuration, such as from a DHCPv6 scope. A host uses stateful address configuration when it receives router advertisement messages that do not include address prefixes. A host will also use a stateful address configuration protocol when no routers are present on the local link.

Site-local addresses can also be configured through stateless address configuration. This is based on router advertisement messages that include stateless address prefixes and require that hosts do not use a stateful address configuration protocol.

Alternatively, address configuration can use a combination of stateless and stateful configuration. This occurs when router advertisement message include stateless address prefixes but require that hosts use a stateful address configuration protocol.

Figure 6-21 shows a global unicast and a link-local address associated with a Teredo tunnel. You can work out for yourself which is which. Teredo is discussed later in this lesson.

FIGURE 6-21 A global unicast and a link-local address

Link-Local and Site-Local Addresses

You can implement IPv6 connectivity between hosts on an isolated subnet by using link-local addresses. However, you cannot assign link-local addresses to router interfaces (default gateways) and you cannot route from one subnet to another if only link-local addresses are used. DNS servers cannot use only link-local addresses. If you use link-local addresses, you need to specify their interface IDs—that is the number after the % symbol at the end of the address. Link-local addresses are not dynamically registered in Windows DDNS.

For these reasons, site-local addresses are typically used on the subnets of a private network to implement IPv6 connectivity over the network. If every device on the network has its own global address (a stated aim of IPv6 implementation), you can also use global addresses to route between internal subnets, to peripheral zones, and to the Internet.

Special Addresses

Two special IPv6 addresses exist—the unspecified address and the loopback address. The unspecified address 0:0:0:0:0:0:0:0 (or ::) is used to indicate the absence of an address and is equivalent to the IPv4 unspecified address 0.0.0.0. It is typically used as a source address for packets attempting to verify whether a tentative address is unique. It is never assigned to an interface or used as a destination address. The loopback address 0:0:0:0:0:0:0:1 (or ::1) is used to identify a loopback interface and is equivalent to the IPv4 loopback address 127.0.0.1.

IPv6 Multicast Addresses

IPv6 multicast addresses enable an IPv6 packet to be sent to a number of hosts, all of which have the same multicast address. They have an FP of 11111111 (they always start with *ff*).

 Quick Check

- **What type of address is fec0:0:0:eadf::1ff?**

Quick Check Answer

- Unicast site-local

IPv6 Anycast Addresses

An anycast address is assigned to multiple interfaces. Packets sent to an anycast address are forwarded by the routing infrastructure to the nearest of these interfaces. The routing infrastructure must be aware of the interfaces that are assigned anycast addresses and their distance in terms of routing metrics. Currently, anycast addresses are used only as destination addresses and are assigned only to routers.

 EXAM TIP

A global unicast address is the IPv6 equivalent of an IPv4 public unicast address, and it typically starts with a 2. A link-local IPv6 address is equivalent to an IPv4 APIPA address and it starts with *fe8*. A site-local IPv6 address is equivalent to an IPv4 private address and it starts with *fec0*. The special IPv6 addresses :: and ::1 are equivalent to the IPv4 addresses 0.0.0.0 and 127.0.0.1. Multicast IPv6 addresses start with *ff*. Anycast addresses are assigned only to routers and are beyond the scope of the 70-680 examination.

The Advantages of IPv6

IPv6 was designed to overcome the limitations of IPv4. The main advantages that IPv6 has over its predecessor are as follows:

- **Increased address space** IPv6 provides sufficient addresses for every device that needs to have a unique public IPv6 address. In addition, the 64-bit host portion (interface ID) of an IPv6 address can be automatically generated from the network adapter hardware.

- **Automatic Address Configuration** Typically IPv4 is configured either manually or by using DHCP. Automatic configuration (autoconfiguration) through APIPA is available for isolated subnets that are not routed to other networks. IPv6 deals with the need for simpler and more automatic address configuration by supporting both stateful and stateless address configuration.

- **Network level security** Communication over the Internet requires encryption to protect data from being viewed or modified in transit. Internet Protocol Security (IPSec) provides this facility and IPv6 makes IPSec mandatory.

- **Real-time data delivery** Quality of Service (QoS) exists in IPv4, and bandwidth can be guaranteed for real-time traffic over a network, but not when an IPv4 packet's payload is encrypted. Payload identification is included in the Flow Label field of the IPv6 header, so payload encryption does not affect QoS operation.

- **Routing table size** On the IPv6 Internet, backbone routers have greatly reduced routing tables that use route aggregation, which permits a number of contiguous address blocks to be combined and summarized as a larger address block.

- **Header size and extension headers** IPv4 and IPv6 headers are not compatible, and a host or router must use both IPv4 and IPv6 implementations to recognize and process both header formats. Therefore, the IPv6 header was designed to be as small as was practical. Nonessential and optional fields are moved to extension headers placed after the IPv6 header.

- **Removal of broadcast traffic** IPv4 relies on ARP broadcasts to resolve the MAC addresses of the network adapters. The IPv6 Neighbor Discovery (ND) protocol uses a series of ICMPv6 messages. ND replaces ARP broadcasts, ICMPv4 Router Discovery, and ICMPv4 Redirect messages with efficient multicast and unicast ND messages.

✔ **Quick Check**

1. How many bits are in an IPv4 address?
2. How many bits are in an IPv6 address?

Quick Check Answers

1. 32
2. 128

Address Resolution in IPv6

The ND protocol resolves IPv6 addresses to MAC addresses. This is typically a straightforward process. For example, in unicast global IPv6 addresses the 64-bit host portion of the IPv6 address is derived from the MAC address of the network adapter in the first place.

The resolution of host names to IPv6 addresses is accomplished through DNS (apart from link-local addresses that are not stored by DNS and resolve automatically). The procedure is the same as for IPv4 address resolution with the computer name and IPv6 address pair being stored in a AAAA (quad-A) DNS resource record, which is equivalent to an A or host record for IPv4. Reverse DNS lookup that returns a computer name for an IPv6 address is implemented by a pointer (PTR) DNS resource record that is referred to the IPv6 reverse lookup zone (or tree) *ipv6.arpa,* which is the equivalent of the *in-addr.arpa* reverse lookup zone in IPv4.

Creating an *ipv6.arpa* reverse lookup zone is a complex procedure that involves splitting the IPv6 address into 4-bit nibbles and entering these in reverse order. This is beyond the scope of the 70-680 examination.

In peer-to-peer environments where DNS is not available (for example, ad hoc networks), the Peer Name Resolution Protocol (PNRP) provides dynamic name registration and name resolution. PNRP can apply peer names to the machine or to individual applications and services on the machine. A peer name resolution includes an address, port, and possibly an extended payload. Peer names can be published as secured (protected) or unsecured (unprotected). PNRP uses public key cryptography to protect secure peer names against spoofing.

> *MORE INFO*   **PEER NAME RESOLUTION PROTOCOL**
>
> For more information about PNRP, see *http://msdn.microsoft.com/en-us/library/ bb968779.aspx.*

Implementing IPv4-to-IPv6 Compatibility

In addition to the various types of addresses described earlier in this lesson, IPv6 provides the following types of compatibility addresses to aid migration from IPv4 to IPv6 and to implement transition technologies.

IPv4-Compatible Address

The IPv4-compatible address 0:0:0:0:0:0:*w.x.y.z* (or ::*w.x.y.z*) is used by dual-stack nodes that are communicating with IPv6 over an IPv4 infrastructure. The last four octets (*w.x.y.z*) represent the dotted decimal representation of an IPv4 address. When the IPv4-compatible address is used as an IPv6 destination, the IPv6 traffic is automatically encapsulated with an IPv4 header and sent to the destination using the IPv4 infrastructure.

IPv4-Mapped Address

The IPv4-mapped address 0:0:0:0:0:ffff:*w.x.y.z* (or ::ffff:*w.x.y.z*) is used to represent an IPv4-only node to an IPv6 node and hence to map IPv4 devices that are not compatible with IPv6 into the IPv6 address space.

6to4 Address

A 6to4 address enables IPv6 packets to be transmitted over an IPv4 network (generally the IPv4 Internet) without the need to configure explicit tunnels. 6to4 hosts can communicate with hosts on the IPv6 Internet. A 6to4 address is typically used when a user wants to connect to the IPv6 Internet using their existing IPv4 connection. It takes the form 2002:<*first two bytes of the IPv4 address*>:<*second two bytes of the IPv4 address*>::/16.

To use a 6to4 address, you do not need to configure or support IPv6 on any nearby networking devices relative to the host. As a result, 6to4 is relevant during the initial phases of deployment to full, native IPv6 connectivity. It is intended only as a transition mechanism and is not meant to be used permanently. It does not facilitate interoperation between IPv4-only hosts and IPv6-only hosts.

Teredo Address

A Teredo address consists of a 32-bit Teredo prefix. In Windows 7 (and in Windows Vista and Windows Server 2008), this is 2001::/32. The prefix is followed by the IPv4 (32-bit) public address of the Teredo server that assisted in the configuration of the address. The next 16 bits are reserved for Teredo flags. Currently, only the highest-ordered flag bit is defined. This is the cone flag and is set when the NAT connected to the Internet is a cone NAT

> **NOTE   TEREDO IN WINDOWS XP AND WINDOWS SERVER 2003**
>
> In Windows XP and Windows Server 2003, the Teredo prefix was originally 3ffe:831f::/32. Computers running Windows XP and Windows Server 2003 use the 2001::/32 Teredo prefix when updated with Microsoft Security Bulletin MS06-064.

The next 16 bits store an obscured version of the external UDP port that corresponds to all Teredo traffic for the Teredo client interface. When a Teredo client sends its initial packet to a Teredo server, NAT maps the source UDP port of the packet to a different, external UDP port. All Teredo traffic for the host interface uses the same external, mapped UDP port. The value representing this external port is masked or obscured by exclusive ORing (XORing) it with 0xffff. Obscuring the external port prevents NATs from translating it within the payload of packets that are being forwarded.

The final 32 bits store an obscured version of the external IPv4 address that corresponds to all Teredo traffic for the Teredo client interface. The external address is obscured by XORing the external address with 0xffffffff. As with the UDP port, this prevents NATs from translating the external IPv4 address within the payload of packets that are being forwarded.

The external address is obscured by XORing the external address with 0xffffffff. For example, the obscured version of the public IPv4 address 131.107.0.1 in colon-hexadecimal format is 7c94:fffe. (131.107.0.1 equals 0x836b0001, and 0x836b0001 XOR 0xffffffff equals 0x7c94fffe.) Obscuring the external address prevents NATs from translating it within the payload of the packets that are being forwarded.

For example, Northwind Traders currently implements the following IPv4 private networks at its headquarters and branch offices:

- Headquarters: 10.0.100.0 /24
- Branch1: 10.0.0.0 /24
- Branch2: 10.0.10.0 /24
- Branch3: 10.0.20.0 /24

The company wants to establish IPv6 communication between Teredo clients and other Teredo clients, and between Teredo clients and IPv6-only hosts. The presence of Teredo servers on the IPv4 Internet enables this communication to take place. A Teredo server is an IPv6/IPv4 node connected to both the IPv4 Internet and the IPv6 Internet that supports a Teredo tunneling interface. The Teredo addresses of the Northwind Traders networks depend on a number of factors, such as the port and type of NAT server used, but they could, for example, be the following:

- Headquarters: 2001::ce49:7601:e866:efff:f5ff:9bfe through 2001::0a0a:64fe:e866:efff: f5ff:9b01
- Branch 1: 2001:: ce49:7601:e866:efff:f5ff:fffe through 2001::0a0a:0afe:e866:efff: f5ff:ff01
- Branch 2: 2001:: ce49:7601:e866:efff:f5ff:f5fe through 2001::0a0a:14fe:e866:efff:f5ff:f501
- Branch 3: 2001:: ce49:7601:e866:efff:f5ff:ebfe through 2001::0a0a:1efe:e866:efff:f5ff:ebfe

Note that, for example, 10.0.100.1 is the equivalent of 0a00:6401, and 0a00:6401 XORed with ffff:ffff is f5ff:9bfe.

EXAM TIP

The 70-680 examination objectives specifically mention Teredo addresses, which are supported by Microsoft. However the examination is unlikely to ask you to generate a Teredo address. You might, however, be asked to identify such an address and work out its included IPv4 address. Fortunately you have access to a scientific calculator during the examination. You are more likely to be asked to identify a Teredo or a 6to4 address. Both are public addresses. A Teredo address starts with 2001; a 6to4 address starts with 2002.

NOTE **TEREDO**

For more information about Teredo, see *http://www.ietf.org/rfc/rfc4380.txt* and *http://www.microsoft.com/technet/network/ipv6/teredo.mspx.*

Cone NATs

Cone NATs can be full cone, restricted cone, or port-restricted cone. In a full-cone NAT, all requests from the same internal IP address and port are mapped to the same external IP address and port and any external host can send a packet to the internal host by sending a packet to the mapped external address.

In a restricted-cone NAT, all requests from the same internal IP address and port are mapped to the same external IP address and port but an external host can send a packet to the internal host only if the internal host had previously sent a packet to the external host.

In a port-restricted-cone NAT, the restriction includes port numbers. An external host with a specified IP address and source port can send a packet to an internal host only if the internal host had previously sent a packet to that IP address and port.

Intra-Site Automatic Tunneling Addressing Protocol (ISATAP) Address

IPv6 can use an Intra-Site Automatic Tunneling Addressing Protocol (ISATAP) address to communicate between two nodes over an IPv4 intranet. An ISATAP address starts with a 64-bit unicast link-local, site-local, global, or 6to4 global prefix. The next 32 bits are the ISATAP identifier 0:5efe. The final 32 bits hold the IPv4 address in either dotted decimal or hexadecimal notation. An ISATAP address can incorporate either a public or a private IPv4 address. To identify an ISATAP address look for 5efe followed by an IP address in either dotted decimal or hexadecimal format.

Implementing IPv6-to-IPv4 Compatibility

You can implement IPv6-to-IPv4 compatibility by using the IPv6 tools *Netsh interface ipv6 6to4*, *Netsh interface ipv6 isatap*, and *Netsh interface ipv6 add v6v4tunnel*. For example, to create an IPv6-in-IPv4 tunnel between the local address 10.0.0.11 and the remote address 192.168.123.116 on an interface named Remote, you would enter **netsh interface ipv6 add v6v4tunnel "Remote" 10.0.0.11 192.168.123.116.**

> *NOTE* **TRANSITION TECHNOLOGIES**
>
> The various methods of implementing IPv6-to-IPv4 compatibility are known as *transition technologies*.

> *NOTE* **6TO4CFG**
>
> Windows 7 does not support the *6to4cfg* tool.

Configuring IPv6 Connectivity

Windows Server 2008 provides tools that let you configure IPv6 interfaces and check IPv6 connectivity and routing. Tools also exist that implement and check IPv4-to-IPv6 compatibility.

In Windows 7 the standard command-line tools such as *Ping, Ipconfig, Pathping, Tracert, Netstat,* and *Route* have full IPv6 functionality. For example, Figure 6-22 shows the *Ping* command used to check a link-local IPv6 address on the Canberra computer. The IPv6 address on your computer is different. Note that if you were pinging from one host to another using link-local addresses, you would also need to include the interface ID (for example, *ping fe80::d1ff:d166:7888:2fd6%12*). Interface IDs are discussed later in this lesson. Note also that this command works because you are pinging a link-local address in the same computer. To ping between computers you need to allow ICMPv6 traffic though each computer's firewall.

FIGURE 6-22 Pinging an IPv6 link-local address

> **NOTE** **Ping6**
>
> The *Ping6* command-line tool is not supported in Windows 7.

Tools specific to IPv6 are provided in the *Netsh* command structure. For example, the *netsh interface ipv6 show neighbors* command shows the IPv6 interfaces of all hosts on the local subnet. You use this command in the practice later in this lesson, after you have configured IPv6 connectivity on a subnet.

Verifying IPv6 Configuration and Connectivity

If you are troubleshooting connectivity problems or merely want to check your configuration, arguably the most useful tool—and certainly one of the most used—is Ipconfig. If you enter **ipconfig /all,** this displays both IPv4 and IPv6 configuration. The output from this tool was shown in Figure 6-6.

If you want to display the configuration of only the IPv6 interfaces on the local computer, you can enter **netsh interface ipv6 show address.** Figure 6-23 shows the output of this command run on the Canberra computer. Note the % character followed by a number after each IPv6 address. This is the interface ID, which identifies the interface that is configured with the IPv6 address.

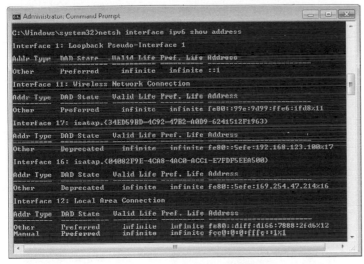

FIGURE 6-23 Displaying IPv6 addresses and interface IDs

NOTE **NETWORK CONNECTION DETAILS INFORMATION BOX**

You can also find the IPv6 address of an interface by accessing the Network Connection Details information box. The procedure to do this is described in Lesson 3 and the information box is shown in Figure 6-38 in that lesson. However, the Network Connection Details Information box does not show the interface ID.

If you are administering an enterprise network with a number of sites, you also need to know site IDs. You can obtain a site ID by entering the command **netsh interface ipv6 show address level=verbose.** Part of the output from this command is shown in Figure 6-24.

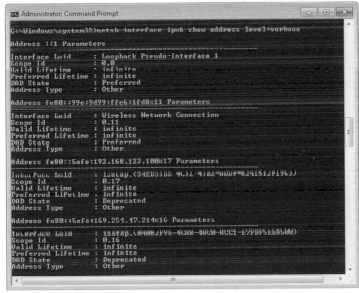

FIGURE 6-24 Displaying IPv6 addresses and site IDs

Configuring IPv6 Interfaces

Typically, most IPv6 addresses are configured through autoconfiguration or DHCPv6. However, if you need to manually configure an IPv6 address, you can use the *Netsh interface ipv6 set address* command, as in this example: `netsh interface ipv6 set address "local area connection" fec0:0:0:ffee::2`. You need to run the command prompt as an administrator to use this command. In Windows 7, you can also manually configure IPv6 addresses from the properties of the Internet Protocol Version 6 (TCP/IPv6) GUI. Figure 6-25 shows this configuration.

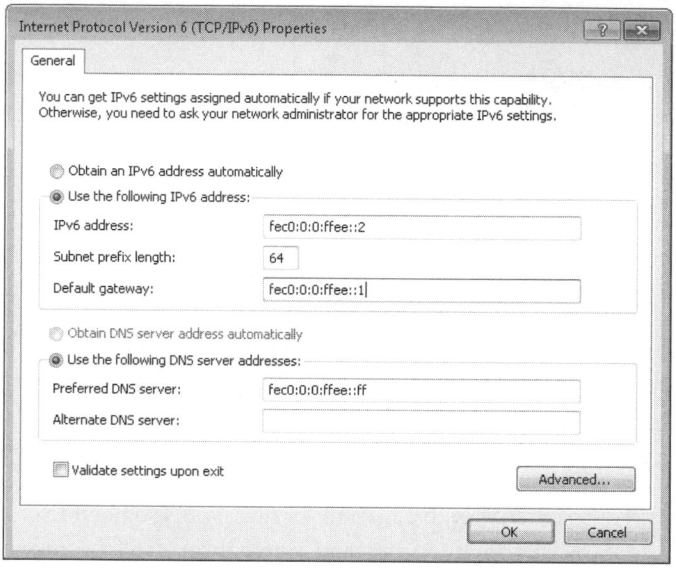

FIGURE 6-25 Configuring an IPv6 address through a GUI

The advantage of using the TCP/IPv6 GUI is that you can specify the IPv6 addresses of one or more DNS servers in addition to specifying the interface address. If, however, you choose to use Command Line Interface (CLI) commands, the command to add IPv6 addresses of DNS servers is *Netsh interface ipv6 add dnsserver*, as in this example: `netsh interface ipv6 add dnsserver "local area connection" fec0:0:0:ffee::ff`. The command to add a default gateway is *Netsh interface ipv6 add route* followed by the metric (the order of preference if there are multiple routes), as in this example: `netsh interface ipv6 add route ::/0 "local area connection" fec0:0:0:ffee::1`.

To change the properties of IPv6 interfaces (but not their configuration), use the *Netsh interface ipv6 set interface* command, as in this example: `netsh interface ipv6 set interface "local area connection" forwarding=enabled`. You need to run the command prompt as an administrator to use any *Netsh* configuration commands.

> **MORE INFO** Netsh
>
> Netsh is an exceptionally powerful and versatile utility that enables you to carry out a very large number of configuration tasks through a command-line interface. For more information, see *http://technet.microsoft.com/en-us/library/cc785383.aspx*.

 Quick Check

- What *Netsh* command lists site IDs?

Quick Check Answer

- netsh interface ipv6 show address level=verbose

Verifying IPv6 Connectivity

To verify connectivity on a local network, your first step should be to flush the neighbor cache, which stores recently resolved link-layer addresses and might give a false result if you are checking changes that involve address resolution. You can check the contents of the neighbor cache by entering **netsh interface ipv6 show neighbors.** Entering **netsh interface ipv6 delete neighbors** flushes the cache. You need to run the command prompt as an administrator to use these commands.

You can test connectivity to a local host on your subnet and to your default gateway by using the *Ping* command. Note that Windows Firewall blocks *Ping* commands by default and you need to allow ICMPv6 packets through the firewalls of both computers before one can ping the other by its IPv4 address. You can add the interface ID to the IPv6 interface address to ensure that the address is configured on the correct interface. Figure 6-22 shows a *Ping* command using an IPv6 address and an interface ID.

To check connectivity to a host on a remote network, your first task should be to check and clear the destination cache, which stores next-hop IPv6 addresses for destinations. You can display the current contents of the destination cache by entering **netsh interface ipv6 show destinationcache.** To flush the destination cache, **enter netsh interface ipv6 delete destinationcache.** As before, these commands need administrator credentials.

Your next step is to check connectivity to the default router interface on your local subnet. This is your default gateway. You can identify the IPv6 address of your default router interface by using the *Ipconfig, Netsh interface ipv6 show routes*, or *Route print* command. You can also specify the zone ID, which is the interface ID for the default gateway on the interface on which you want the ICMPv6 Echo Request messages to be sent. When you have ensured that you can reach the default gateway on your local subnet, ping the remote host by its IPv6 address. Note that you cannot ping a remote host (or a router interface) by its link-local IPv6 address because link-local addresses are not routable.

If you can connect to the default gateway but cannot reach the remote destination address, trace the route to the remote destination by using the *Tracert –d* command followed by the destination IPv6 address. The *–d* command-line switch prevents the Tracert tool from performing a DNS reverse query on router interfaces in the routing path. This speeds up the display of the routing path. If you want more information about the routers in the path, and particularly if you want to verify router reliability, use the *Pathping -d* command, again followed by the destination IPv6 address.

>  **Quick Check**
>
> - What *Netsh* command could you use to identify the IPv6 address of your default router interface?
>
> **Quick Check Answer**
>
> - netsh interface ipv6 show route

Troubleshooting Connectivity

If you cannot connect to a remote host, you first need to check the various hardware connections (wired and wireless) in your organization and ensure that all network devices are up and running. If these basic checks do not find the problem, the Internet Protocol Security (IPSec) configuration might not be properly configured, or firewall problems (such as incorrectly configured packet filters) might exist.

You can use the IP Security Policies Management console, shown in Figure 6-26, to check and configure IPSec policies and the Windows Firewall With Advanced Security console (shown previously in Figures 6-11 and 6-12 in Lesson 1) to check and configure IPv6-based packet filters.

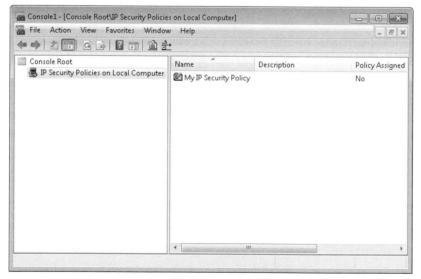

FIGURE 6-26 The IP Security Policies Management console

> **NOTE** **IPSec6**
>
> The IPSec6 tool is not implemented in Windows 7.

You might be unable to reach a local or remote destination because of incorrect or missing routes in the local IPv6 routing table. You can use the *Route print, Netstat –r,* or *Netsh interface ipv6 show route* command to view the local IPv6 routing table and verify that you have a route corresponding to your local subnet and to your default gateway. Note that the *Netstat –r* and *Route print* commands display both IPv4 and IPv6 routing tables.

PRACTICE   Configuring IPv6 Connectivity

In this practice, you configure a static site-local IPv6 configuration on the Canberra computer running Windows 7. You then configure a static site-local IPv6 configuration on the Aberdeen computer running Windows 7 and test IPv6 connectivity.

EXERCISE 1   Configuring IPv6 on the Canberra Computer

In this exercise, you configure IPv6 on the Canberra computer.

1. Log on to the Canberra computer with the Kim_Akers account.
2. To permit ICMPv6 traffic to pass through the Canberra firewall, open an elevated command prompt and enter **netsh advfirewall firewall add rule name="ICMPv6" protocol=icmpv6:any,any dir=in action=allow.**
3. Open Network And Sharing Center and click Change Adapter Settings.
4. Right-click the network connection to your private network and choose Properties.
5. Select Internet Protocol Version 6 (TCP/IPv6) and click Properties.
6. Configure a static site-local IPv6 address, fec0:0:0:fffe::1.
7. Click the box beside Subnet Prefix Length. The value 64 is entered automatically. The Properties dialog box should look similar to Figure 6-27.

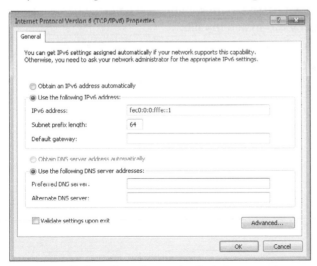

FIGURE 6-27 IPv6 configuration on the Canberra computer

8. Click OK. Close the Local Area Connections Properties dialog box.

9. Close Network And Sharing Center.

10. In the elevated command prompt, enter **ping fec0:0:0:fffe::1.** Your screen should look similar to Figure 6-28.

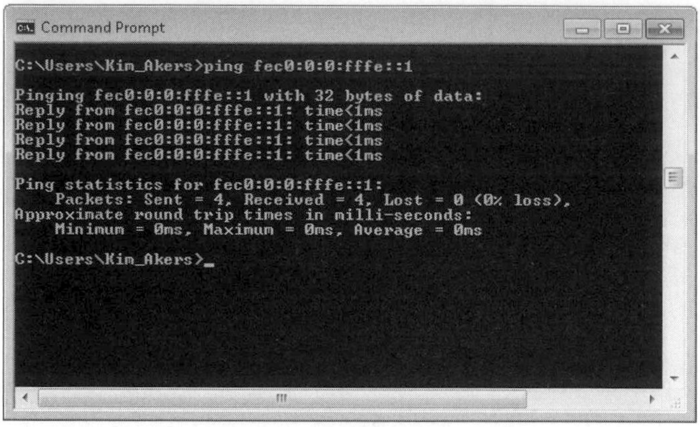

FIGURE 6-28 Pinging a site-local IPv6 address

EXERCISE 2 Configuring the Aberdeen Computer and Testing IPv6 Connectivity

In this exercise, you configure IPv6 site-local addresses on the Aberdeen computer and test connectivity. You need to have configured the IPv6 settings on the Canberra computer before you start this exercise. If Aberdeen is a virtual machine, the designation of the Ethernet adapter that connects to your private network may be something other than "local area connection." If so, adjust the commands accordingly.

1. Log on to the Aberdeen computer with the Kim_Akers account.

2. To permit ICMPv6 traffic to pass through the Aberdeen firewall, open an elevated command prompt and enter **netsh advfirewall firewall add rule name="ICMPv6" protocol=icmpv6:any,any dir=in action=allow.**

3. To configure static IPv6 configuration, enter **netsh interface ipv6 set address "local area connection" fec0:0:0:fffe::a.**

4. Enter **ping fec0:0:0:fffe::a** to test your IPv6 configuration.

5. If necessary, log on to the Canberra computer using the Kim_Akers account and open an elevated command prompt.

6. Enter **ping fec0:0:0:fffe::a.** You should get the response shown in Figure 6-29.

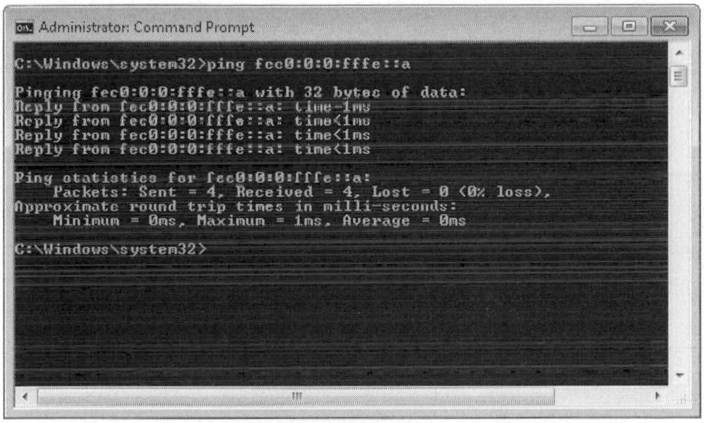

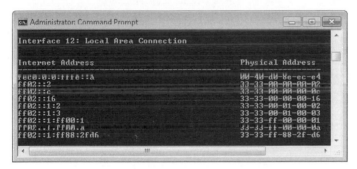

FIGURE 6-29 Pinging the Aberdeen computer from Canberra

7. Enter **netsh interface ipv6 show neighbors.** Figure 6-30 shows the *fec0:0:0:fffe::a* interface as a neighbor on the same subnet as the Canberra computer.

FIGURE 6-30 Showing the Canberra computer neighbors

Lesson Summary

- IPv6 supports unicast, multicast, and anycast addresses. Unicast addresses can be global, site-local, link-local, or special.

- IPv6 is fully supported in Windows 7 and addresses problems such as lack of address space that are associated with IPv4.

- IPv6 is designed to be backward-compatible, and you can specify IPV4-compatible addresses such as Teredo and 6to4 addresses.

- Tools to configure and troubleshoot IPv6 include *Ping, Ipconfig, Tracert, Pathping,* and *Netsh.*

- You can configure IPv6 by using the TCP/IPv6 Properties GUI. You can also use *Netsh interface ipv6* commands to configure IPv6 settings.

Lesson Review

You can use the following questions to test your knowledge of the information in Lesson 2, "Configuring IPv6." The questions are also available on the companion DVD if you prefer to review them in electronic form.

> **NOTE ANSWERS**
>
> Answers to these questions and explanations of why each answer choice is correct or incorrect are located in the "Answers" section at the end of the book.

1. What type of unicast IPv6 address would you typically use on the subnets of a private network to implement IPv6 connectivity over the subnet?

   A. Site-local address

   B. Link-local address

   C. Special address

   D. Anycast address

2. You are analyzing the configuration of an IPv6 network. Which of the following addresses can be used across the IPv6 Internet and is the equivalent of an IPv4 unicast public address?

   A. fec0:0:0:0:fffe::1

   B. 21cd:53::3ad:3f:af37:8d62

   C. fe80:d1ff:d166:7888:2fd6

   D. ::1

3. You are using Network Monitor to analyze traffic on an IPv6 network. You want to examine the protocol that uses ICMPv6 messages to manage the interaction of neighboring nodes and resolves IPv6 addresses to hardware (MAC) addresses. What protocol do you examine?

   A. ARP

   B. DNS

   C. DHCPv6

   D. ND

4. You are examining transition technologies on a network and want to identify the IPv4-to-IPv6 compatibility addresses being used. Which of the following is a Teredo address?

   A. 2001::0a0a:1efe:e866:efff:f5ff:ebfe

   B. 2002:c058:6301::

   C. fe80::5efe:0a00:028f

   D. fec0:0:0:0:fffe::1

5. You are examining a DNS forward lookup zone to investigate problems with name resolution. What type of resource record enables DNS to resolve a host name to an IPv6 address?

   A. PTR

   B. A

   C. AAAA

   D. Host

Lesson 3: Network Configuration

As an IT professional, you mainly are involved with setting up and administering production networks that contain domain controllers, file servers, DNS servers, DHCP servers, servers running Exchange Server, servers running Microsoft SQL Server, and so on. However, large organizations often have small networks set up for specific purposes (for example, test networks) and you might have to set up a workgroup that uses ICS or configure wireless connectivity.

This lesson discusses how you set up and add devices to both a wired and a wireless network but it concentrates mainly on wireless networks. It shows how you configure security settings on a client, manage preferred wireless networks, configure wireless network adapters, and troubleshoot connectivity issues specific to wireless adapters. The chapter also covers security settings on a WAP and how you configure location-aware printing.

After this lesson, you will be able to:

- Connect workstations to a wired network.
- Add a device to a wireless network.
- Manage connections for both wired and wireless networks.
- Manage preferred wireless networks.
- Configure security settings on a third-party WAP.
- Configure location-aware printing.

Estimated lesson time: 50 minutes

Connecting to a Network

Lesson 1 described how you would go about setting up a small wired network where one computer connects directly to a cable or dial-up modem and obtains its IPv4 configuration from the modem, which in turn is configured by the ISP. Typically, that computer is configured to provide ICS, and other clients you connect to the network obtain their configurations automatically from the ICS computer. Figure 6-31 shows this configuration.

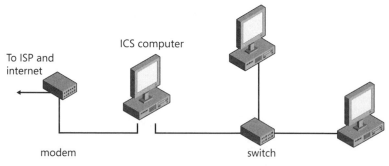

FIGURE 6-31 A wired small network

In a wireless small network, you typically connect your wireless WAP to your cable or dial-up modem. The other devices on your network, such as computers or printers, then connect to the WAP. In this case, the computers on the network all connect to the Internet through the WAP, which is configured by default to provide IP configuration. Figure 6-32 shows this configuration. If you are setting this up from scratch and your ISP is not providing a modem, you can purchase a combined modem and WAP.

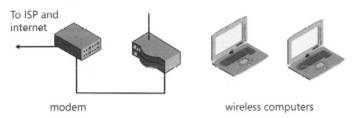

To ISP and
internet

modem   wireless computers

FIGURE 6-32 A wireless small network

You can also implement a hybrid network. In this case, the WAP is typically connected to the modem as before, and computers in fixed locations are connected using wired connections to Ethernet ports on the WAP. Most WAPs have several Ethernet ports in addition to the wide area network (WAN) port that connects to the modem. You can wire the fixed computers directly to the ports on the WAP, or you can connect them by using an Ethernet switch and connect the switch to the WAP. Wireless-enabled devices connect directly to the WAP, and both wired and wireless devices are on the same network and obtain their IP configuration from the WAP, which provides DHCP and internal DNS services. Figure 6-33 shows this configuration.

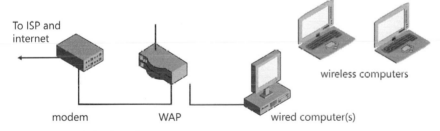

To ISP and
internet

         wireless computers

modem   WAP   wired computer(s)

FIGURE 6-33 A hybrid small network

The WAP forwards any packets that need to go to the Internet (for example, browser requests) through the modem to your ISP, which provides DNS resolution across the Internet. Typically, you configure a WAP by accessing a Web page interface. Refer to the manufacturer's documentation for details.

MORE INFO **EXTERNAL RESOLUTION**

It is unlikely that the 70-680 examination will test your knowledge of how DNS works over the Internet. However, if you want to learn more out of professional interest, see *http://technet.microsoft.com/en-us/library/cc775637.aspx*.

If you have two or more wireless computers in close proximity (no more than 30 feet apart), you can set up an ad hoc network that lets you access shared resources on the computers on the network (provided the sharing permissions permit access). An ad hoc network requires no central WAP and does not need IPv4 configuration because it uses IPv6. Ad hoc networks are discussed in more detail later in this lesson, and you set up an ad hoc network in a practice exercise.

Setting Up a Network Connection

The first computer you install on a wired SOHO or test network will likely be connected to a modem through a universal serial bus (USB) or Ethernet connection. It will also have an Ethernet connection to enable computers and other devices to connect to it through a switch. Your ISP will give you instructions about how to establish an Internet connection and will provide a user name and password.

To connect to the Internet, you open Network And Sharing Center, click Set Up New A Connection Or Network, select Connect To The Internet, and click Next. You then select the method you are using to connect, such as broadband point-to-point protocol over Ethernet (PPPOe), and enter the name and password that your ISP provided, as shown in Figure 6-34. If you select Allow Other People To Use This Connection and you are not logged in with an administrator account, you are prompted for credentials.

FIGURE 6-34 Providing information from your ISP

You can get details about the sharing and discovery settings, and change a setting if required, by clicking the Change Advanced Sharing Settings. The Advanced Sharing Settings dialog box is shown in Figure 6-35. You can specify the settings for a public profile or a private (home or work) profile by clicking the arrow to the right of the current profile. For each profile, you can configure the following:

- Network discovery
- File and printer sharing
- Public folder sharing
- Media streaming
- File sharing connections (encryption strength)
- Password protected sharing
- Homegroup connections

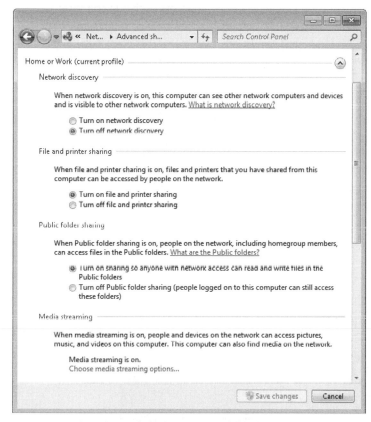

FIGURE 6-35 The Advanced Sharing Settings dialog box

Typically, other computers on a small wired network connect to the Internet through the first computer that you configure on the network. To enable this to happen, you need to configure ICS on that computer. You configured an ICS computer and an ICS client in Exercise 2, "Configuring ICS on the Canberra Computer," in Lesson 1.

When you enable ICS, your LAN connection is configured with a new static IP address (192.168.0.1) and other settings (for example, subnet mask, default gateway, and DNS server address). The static address (192 168.0.1) is used as the default gateway for the subnet. If you connect other computers to your network before you enable ICS, you might need to change their TCP/IP settings, typically by rebooting. As a general rule, it is preferable to add other computers to your network after you have configured ICS.

To add a computer to a wired network on which ICS is configured, you connect it to the network and turn it on. In Network And Sharing Center, you click Internet Options and, on the Connections tab, you click LAN Settings and clear the Automatically Detect Settings check box. Provided that the computer's network adapter is set to receive its configuration automatically, and the computer's name is not the same as that of another computer already on the network, the computer joins the network and receives its configuration through ICS. If you have changed the default workgroup name (WORKGROUP) on your network, you also need to change this setting on any computer you add.

Adding a computer through a wired connection to a hybrid network is even more straightforward than adding it to a fully wired network. You simply plug it in and turn it on. By default, it should be configured to obtain its IP settings automatically. In this case, however, it obtains them from the WAP.

Adding a Wireless Computer to a Network

If you have a wireless-enabled computer, you can click the network icon on your toolbar at the bottom right section of your screen. This displays all wireless networks within range, and you can double-click the network to which you want to connect. Alternatively, you can open Network And Sharing Center and click Connect To A Network. To view and change your connection status, you can click Connect or Disconnect beside View Your Active Networks in Network And Sharing Center. This again presents you with a list of the wireless networks within range.

You can also connect a computer to a wireless network through the command line. The following command shows the available wireless interfaces:

```
netsh wlan show interfaces
```

The output from this command for a computer with only one interface available is shown in Figure 6-36.

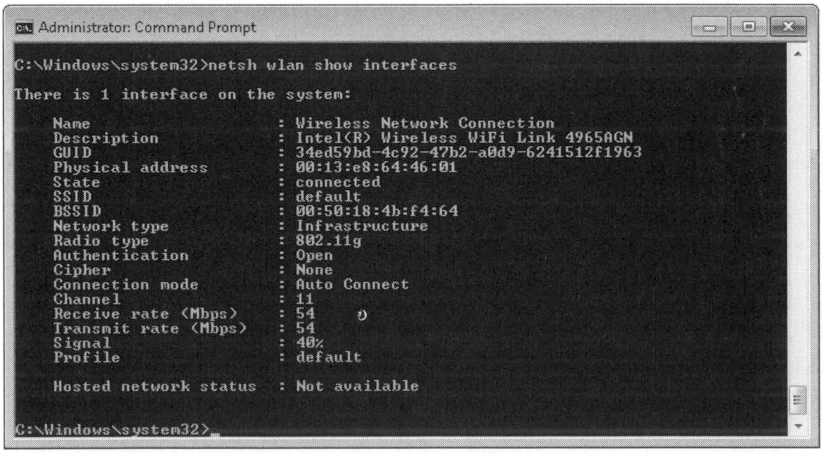

FIGURE 6-36 Wireless interface on the Canberra computer

To connect to the wireless network displayed in Figure 6-36, you enter the following command:

```
netsh wlan connect name=default
```

If there is more than one wireless network on the same profile, you also need to specify the service set identifier (SSID) of the network to which you want to connect. For example, if you created an ad hoc network called MyOtherNet and want to connect to it, you enter the following command:

netsh wlan connect name=default ssid=myothernet

If you issue a command to connect to a wireless network and your computer is already connected to another wireless network, it disconnects from its current network and connects to the network that you specify. If you want to disconnect from a network without connecting to another one and you have only one network adapter on your computer, you enter the following command:

netsh wlan disconnect

If you have more than one wireless interface on your system, you can specify the interface that you want to disconnect by entering a command similar to the following:

netsh wlan disconnect interface="Wireless Network Connection"

To disconnect from all interfaces, you enter the following command:

netsh wlan disconnect interface=*

The *Netsh wlan* utility is both versatile and powerful. As with all command-line utilities, the best way of becoming familiar with it is to use it and experiment with it. This is one of the suggested practices at the end of this chapter. Figure 6-37 shows the commands available for the *Netsh wlan* utility.

FIGURE 6-37 *Netsh wlan* utility commands

You can configure wireless connection behavior by clicking Change Adapter Settings in Network And Sharing Center, right-clicking your wireless adapter, and clicking Status. Clicking Details on the Status dialog box displays the adapter configuration, as shown in Figure 6-38.

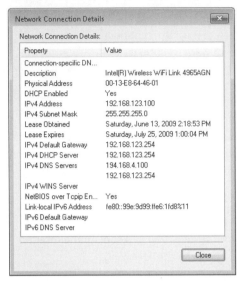

FIGURE 6-38 Wireless adapter configuration

Clicking Wireless Properties in the adapter's Status dialog box opens the Wireless Network Properties dialog box for the wireless network to which you are currently connected, as shown in Figure 6-39. You can configure your computer to always connect to the currently connected network if it is in range, or to connect to a more preferred network when available. You can configure a WAP so that it does not broadcast its name or SSID. This enhances security because the network does not appear on the list of wireless networks in range and you need to connect to it manually. You can configure your computer (and hence, other computers on your network) to connect to a network that is in range but is not broadcasting its SSID. You can copy this and other settings to a USB flash drive that you then use to configure other computers to connect to your wireless network.

If you select the Connect To A More Preferred Network If Available, automatic switching is enabled, which can be a useful feature in a large organization that requires more than one wireless network to cover its floor space. Suppose, for example, a doctor is moving from ward to ward in a hospital and is using a laptop computer. She does not want to manually connect to another wireless network whenever she gets out of the range of the one to which she is currently connected. Automatic switching accomplishes this seamlessly, without user intervention.

However, automatic switching can cause problems if two networks overlap. This is discussed in the section entitled "Troubleshooting Wireless Networks," later in this lesson.

FIGURE 6-39 Configuring connection properties

You can add additional wireless-enabled computers to your network by inserting the USB flash drive and clicking Wireless Network Setup Wizard in the AutoPlay dialog box. Alternatively, you can manually add a wireless computer running Windows 7 to your network by clicking Connect To A Network on Network And Sharing Center and using the same procedure that you followed when connecting the first computer.

> **NOTE   NETWORK SECURITY KEY**
>
> By default, a WAP is set to permit open access by any wireless-enabled computer within its range. You can configure both authentication and encryption type on the Security tab of the Wireless Network Properties dialog box. Configuring security settings on a third-party WAP is discussed later in this lesson.

✔ Quick Check

- You are adding a new computer to a wired network that connects to the Internet through a cable modem attached to one of your computers by a USB cable. The new computer is configured to obtain its IP configuration automatically. When you switch the new computer on, it is configured with an IP address, a subnet mask, and IP addresses for its default gateway and DNS server. Where does it get this information?

Quick Check Answer

- From the computer attached to the modem, which is configured to run ICS.

To connect to a wireless network that does not broadcast its SSID, you need to know details such as the network name and security type. In Network And Sharing Center, you click Set Up A Connection Or Network, click Manually Connect To A Wireless Network, and click Next. You are prompted for the network name and security type and (if appropriate) encryption type and security key. Alternatively, you can open an elevated command prompt and enter a command with the following syntax:

```
netsh wlan connect name=<profile_name> ssid-<network_ssid> [interface=<interface_name>]
```

To add a wireless device other than a computer to a network, you need to follow the manufacturer's instructions in the information that came with the device. You might be able to add the device using a USB flash drive. If the device is a printer, you might need to enable printer sharing so that other computers on the network can use it. If you want to add a Bluetooth enabled device to your network, you need a Bluetooth network adapter.

> **MORE INFO** **BLUETOOTH**
>
> For more information about Bluetooth, access *http://bluetooth.com/Bluetooth/Technology/* and follow the links.

> **NOTE** **VIRTUAL PRIVATE NETWORKS**
>
> You can also connect to a virtual private network (VPN) by clicking Connect To A Network in Network And Sharing Center. Chapter 10, "DirectAccess and VPN Connections," discusses VPNs in detail.

Managing Preferred Wireless Networks

If you have a wireless-enabled mobile computer such as a laptop, you can take it to various locations and connect to whatever wireless networks are available at any location. You can see the available networks by opening Network And Sharing Center and clicking Connect To A Network. You can also click the Wireless icon on the Toolbar at the bottom right section of your screen. You can then right-click a network and click Connect. Available networks are listed in the Manage Wireless Networks dialog box.

If you do not see the network to which you want to connect, you can click Set Up A New Connection Or Network in Network And Sharing Center. You can select from a list of available options (for example, Connect To The Internet) and manually search for and connect to a network. You can also create a new network connection.

Some networks require a network security key or passphrase. To connect to a secure network that you do not administer, you need to ask the network administrator or the service provider for the key or passphrase.

If you have previously connected to various wireless networks, the list of these networks is referred to as your *preferred list*. The wireless networks on your preferred list are your preferred wireless networks. You can click Manage Wireless Networks in the Network And Sharing Center and view saved wireless networks. You can change the order in which your computer attempts to connect to preferred networks by dragging the networks up or down in the list. You can also change preferences for the network by right-clicking the network and selecting Properties.

Suppose, for example, that a doctor works in a large hospital. On the first floor, she can connect to the wireless networks Wards_10_to_14 and Wards_15_to_19. On the second floor, she can connect to the wireless networks Wards_20_to_24 and Wards_25_to_29. There is shielding between the floors, and she cannot connect to a network if she is not on the appropriate floor. She knows that the networks Wards_10_to_14 and Wards_20_to_24 have high bandwidth, and she wants to connect to them by preference of whatever ward she is in. If she cannot connect to her first choice of network, she wants to connect to her second choice.

The doctor has previously been connected to all four networks (not at the same time), and they are on her preferred list. Note that a network can be on a preferred list even if it is not currently in range. The doctor needs to make sure that the network Wards_10_to_14 is above the network Wards_15_to_19 and that the network Wards_20_to_24 is above the network Wards_25_to_29 in her preferred network list. It makes no difference whether the first-floor wards are above the second-floor wards in the list or the other way round.

On the first floor, the second-floor networks cannot be reached. The doctor's computer connects to the network Wards_10_to_14 if it is available. If not, it connects to the network Wards_15_to_19. On the second floor, the first-floor networks cannot be reached. The doctor's computer connects to the network Wards_20_to_24 if it is available. If not, it connects to the network Wards_25_to_29.

Setting Internal Wireless Adapter Security

Later in this lesson, you will learn how to configure security settings on a third-party WAP. You should also configure compatible security in a wireless network adapter. By default, a WAP is set to permit open access by any wireless-enabled computer within its range. However, it can be configured to restrict access to authenticated connections and to use a specified encryption standard. You can configure both authentication and encryption for a wireless network adapter on the Security tab of the Wireless Network Properties dialog box, shown in Figure 6-40. The figure shows the choice of security type. The Encryption Type is either None or Wired Equivalent Privacy (WEP).

FIGURE 6-40 The Security tab of the Wireless Network Properties dialog box

The following authentication types are available:

- No authentication (open)
- Shared (a shared secret passkey)
- Wi-Fi Protected Access (WPA)-Personal
- WPA2-Personal
- WPA-Enterprise
- WPA2-Enterprise
- 802.1X

WPA and WPA2 indicate compliance with the security protocol created by the Wi-Fi Alliance to secure wireless computer networks. WPA2 enhances WPA, which in turn addresses weaknesses in the previous system, WEP. WPA was intended as an intermediate measure to take the place of WEP while an IEEE 802.11i standard was prepared. 802.1X provides port-based authentication, which involves communications between a supplicant (a client computer), an authenticator (a wired Ethernet switch or WAP), and an authentication server (typically a Remote Authentication Dial In User Service, or RADIUS, server).

The WPA2 certification mark indicates compliance with an advanced protocol that implements the full 802.11 standard, and it is mandatory for all new wireless routers that bear the Wi-Fi trademark. This advanced protocol does not work with some older network cards, and WPA is still supported in Microsoft operating systems, including Windows 7. The main difference between WPA and WPA2 is that WPA2 uses Advanced Encryption Standard (AES). AES has its own mechanism for dynamic key generation and is resistant to statistical analysis of the cipher text.

Pre-shared key (PSK) mode is also known as Personal mode and is designed for SOHO networks that do not require the complexity of an 802.1X authentication server and do not contain a certificate authority (CA) server. Each wireless network device encrypts the network traffic using a 256-bit key. This key may be entered either as a string of 64 hexadecimal digits, or as a passphrase of 8 to 63 printable ASCII characters. Both WPA-Personal and WPA-2 Personal modes are supported in Windows 7.

WPA-Enterprise and WPA2-Enterprise authenticate through the Extensible Authentication Protocol (EAP) and require computer security certificates rather than PSKs. The following EAP types are included in the certification program:

- EAP-TLS
- EAP-TTLS/MSCHAPv2
- PEAPv0/EAP-MSCHAPv2
- PEAPv1/EAP-GTC
- EAP-SIM

> **MORE INFO** EAP
>
> For more information about EAP, see *http://technet.microsoft.com/en-us/network/bb643147.aspx*.

The authentication type you choose to configure on your network adapter needs to be supported by the networks to which you want to connect and by your network hardware. For example:

- If you have a RADIUS server on your network to act as an authentication server and you want the highest possible level of security, you would choose 802.1X.
- If you want to use AES and to use computer certificates rather than a PSK, you would choose WPA2-Enterprise.
- If your network router does not support the AES standard but you want to use computer certificates, you would choose WPA-Enterprise.
- If you have a small network that is not in a domain and cannot access a CA server, but you install a modern WAP that supports AES, you would use WPA2-Personal (with a PSK).
- If you have a small network that is not in a domain and cannot access a CA server and your WAP does not support AES, you would use WPA-Personal.
- Shared uses a shared passkey but offers no other protection. You would choose this if no other method was available.
- By default, an unconfigured WAP has no authentication. An unconfigured WAP is a security risk and it is most unwise and unprofessional to leave it in that condition.

If no authentication is configured, anyone can connect a computer to your network. If no encryption exists, someone with a protocol sniffer can intercept and read confidential data.

> **MORE INFO**   **WEP AND WPA**
>
> For more information about WEP and WPA, see *http://www.ezlan.net/wpa_wep.html*. This is not a TechNet site, but it is maintained by a Microsoft Most Valued Professional (MVP).

Using an Ad Hoc Network

You can set up a temporary wireless network, or ad hoc network, between two or more computers running Windows 7 (or between computers running Windows 7 and Windows Vista) provided they are all within 30 feet (9 meters) of each other. A WAP is not required to set up an ad hoc network. This enables users to share folders and other resources without needing to connect to an organizational network.

Suppose, for example, that you were holding a meeting with representatives from another company and you wanted to share information (such as product specifications) with them but did not want to grant them access to your company network. Or suppose that you were holding a meeting in a hotel room and did not want to share confidential information through the hotel's network. In these and similar cases, you can easily and quickly set up an ad hoc network by doing the following procedure.

On the first computer on the network, you open Network And Sharing Center and click Set Up A New Connection Or Network. You then choose the option Set Up A Wireless Ad Hoc (Computer To Computer) Network. You give the network a name and (if you want) set up a security key so that users joining the network need to supply a password. For WEP, this can be 5 case-sensitive characters, 13 case-sensitive characters, 10 hexadecimal case-insensitive characters, or 26 hexadecimal case-insensitive characters, depending on security considerations. (If you choose WPA-2 Personal, you can insist on a 64-character password, but by the time everyone has typed it in correctly, the meeting would probably be over.)

Other users join the ad hoc network as they would any other wireless network. You can choose to save the network settings if you want to set up an ad hoc network with the same configuration sometime in the future, but typically an ad hoc network is transient and is torn down when the last member leaves. Ad hoc networks use IPv6 and do not require IPv4 connectivity. You set up and join an ad hoc network in a practice exercise later in this lesson.

One use for an ad hoc network is if you connect to the Internet through, for example, an internal cellular modem or a high-speed dial-up modem that uses a mobile phone network. This type of connection (unlike Internet access through a WAP and cable modem) cannot be accessed simultaneously by several computers. In this case you can set up an ad hoc network and share your Internet connection through ICS so that friends with wireless laptops can access the Internet when they visit you.

Wireless Network Technologies

Advantages of wireless networks include mobility and easy physical installation (you do not need to run cables under the floor). Disadvantages include a slower connection (typically) than a wired network and interference from other wireless devices, such as cordless phones.

Currently there are (arguably) four types of wireless network technologies in common use:

- **802.11b** Up to 11 megabits per second (Mbps); good signal range; low cost. This technology allows fewer simultaneous users than the other options and uses the 2.4-gigahertz (GHz) frequency. This frequency is prone to interference from microwave ovens, cordless phones, and other appliances.

- **802.11a** Up to 54 Mbps; more simultaneous users than 802.11b, but a smaller signal range; expensive. This option provides a fast transmission speed and uses the 5-GHz frequency, which limits interference from other devices. However, its signal is more easily obstructed by walls and other obstacles and it is not compatible with 802.11b network adapters, routers, and access points.

- **802.11g** Up to 54 Mbps (under optimal conditions); more simultaneous users than 802.11b; very good signal range; not easily obstructed. This option is compatible with 802.11b network adapters, routers, and access points, but it uses the 2.4-GHz frequency and has the same interference problems as 802.11b. It is also more expensive than 802.11b.

- **802.11n** Still in draft format, although this situation may have changed by the time you read this book. However, a number of vendors are manufacturing equipment using the current draft 802.11n standard. Most 802.11n devices are compatible with 802.11b and 802.11g. 802.11n builds on previous 802.11 standards by adding multiple-input, multiple-output (MIMO), which uses multiple transmitter and receiver antennas to improve the system performance.

802.11b is adequate for most home and many small-office applications. If, however, your network carries a high volume of streaming media (video or music) traffic, or if interference is a major problem, you might consider 802.11a. If you already have 802.11b devices on your network but require high-speed transmission between specified network points, you might consider 802.11g. Most modern WAPs available from computer equipment retailers now are 802.11g.

If you have more than one wireless network adapter in your computer, or if your adapter uses more than one standard, you can specify which adapter or standard to use for each network connection.

EXAM TIP

Several 802.11 standards exist in addition to 802.11a, 802.11b, and 802.11c. However, the standards described in this lesson are those in common use. If you see any other standard (for example, 802.11d) given as a possible answer in the examination, that answer is almost certainly wrong.

Managing Network Connections

You can view a list of all the connection interfaces (wired and wireless) on a computer by opening Network And Sharing Center and clicking Change Adapter Settings. You can right-click any network connection and select Status. If you click Details on the Local Area Connection Status dialog box, you access the Network Connection Details information box. This was shown in Figure 6-38 earlier in this lesson.

On a small wired network with ICS enabled, a workstation typically has an address on the 192.168.0.0/24 network with its default gateway 192.168.0.1. A WAP is typically not configured with the 192.168.0.1 address but might instead have, for example, the IP address 192.168.123.254. Whatever the settings on your network are, you should take note of them when everything is working correctly. This information is invaluable if something goes wrong.

> **NOTE CHANGING NETWORK SETTINGS**
>
> Rather than accept the default ICS settings, many administrators prefer to change them, for example by using the 10.0.10.0/24 network for wired computers and the 192.168.123.0/24 subnet for wireless ones. However, changing default ICS settings is not in the objectives for the 70-680 examination.

When you right-click an adapter and click Properties, this accesses the Local Area Connections Properties dialog box. From this dialog box, you can enable or disable the items shown, or install more items (client services, server services, or protocols) by clicking Install.

Typically, the Local Area Connection Status dialog box for both wired and wireless connections) might contain the following items:

- **Client for Microsoft Networks**   Enables the computer to access resources on a Microsoft network.
- **Quality of Service (QoS) Packet Scheduler**   Provides traffic control. This can be significant if you have high-bandwidth traffic, such as video streaming, on your network.
- **File and Printer Sharing for Microsoft Networks**   Enables other computers to access resources on your computer in a Microsoft network (and other networks).
- **Internet Protocol Version 6 (TCP/IPv6)**   Permits IPv6 configuration.
- **Internet Protocol Version 4 (TCP/IPv4)**   Permits IPv4 configuration.
- **Link-layer Topology Discovery Mapper I/O Driver**   Discovers and locates other computers, devices, and network infrastructure features on the network, and determines network bandwidth.
- **Link-layer Topology Discovery Responder**   Allows a computer to be discovered and located on the network.

If an item is configurable, selecting the item activates the Properties button, which you can click to configure the item's properties. You can also configure the adapter itself (for example, updating the driver) by clicking Configure in the Local Area Connections Properties dialog box.

Take note of the items that have been installed and enabled on your computer while it is working correctly. It is probable that all the other computers on a network that you are administering have similar settings (apart from their IP addresses). It is a good idea to check this, possibly by using Remote Desktop. You might not change these settings very often, but if something goes wrong, you can find out what the original settings were.

 Quick Check

- From which dialog box can you add a new protocol, server service, or client service?

Quick Check Answer

- The Local Area Connections Properties dialog box

You can also right-click a connection in the Network Connections dialog box and select Diagnose. This starts Windows Network Diagnosis, as discussed in Lesson 1 of this chapter.

If you have more than one network connection, you can create a network bridge by selecting two or more connections (click each connection in turn while holding down the Ctrl key), and then right-clicking and selecting Bridge Connections. If you are not logged in as an administrator, you are asked to supply credentials.

A network bridge is software or hardware that connects two or more networks so that they can communicate. If you are managing a network that has different types of networks (for example, wired and wireless), you would typically use a bridge when you want to exchange information or share files among all the computers on those networks. If you use the network bridge software built into Windows 7, you do not need to buy additional hardware.

Troubleshooting Wireless Networks

Lesson 1 discussed basic troubleshooting and resolving connectivity issues. However, connectivity problems exist that are unique to wireless networks and you need to be aware of them and know how to resolve them.

Preventing Your Computer from Switching Between WAPs

When you, or users you support, move around with a mobile wireless-enabled computer, the computer can switch automatically from one wireless network to another to stay connected. This is normal behavior if automatic switching is enabled. Automatic switching is used, for example, in business premises, hospitals, or academic institutions that are too large to be covered by a single network.

However, problems can occur when the same location is within range of several wireless networks and a computer tries to switch among these access points even though the user has not moved his location. This can cause temporary interruptions to the user's connection, or the computer might lose the connection entirely.

With 802.11b or 802.11g routers and access points, the maximum range is up to 150 feet (46 meters) indoors and 300 feet (92 meters) outdoors. With 802.11a routers and access points, the maximum range is 50 feet (15 meters) indoors and 100 feet (30 meters) outdoors. These ranges are for optimal conditions with no interference. If a wireless-enabled computer is (for example) on a desktop that is 50 feet distant from one WAP and 70 feet away from another, problems can occur. You can ask the user to move (usually impractical) or turn off automatic switching in one or both of the network profiles.

You do this by clearing the Connect To A More Preferred Network If Available check box on the network's Wireless Network Properties dialog box, shown earlier in Figure 6-39. You can do this for one or both of the overlapping networks. This action results in a user needing to detect and manually connect to the network she wants to use rather than having the computer attempting to connect to both networks.

> *WARNING* **DISABLING AUTOMATIC SWITCHING IS NOT ALWAYS A GOOD IDEA**
>
> You can disable automatic switching between preferred networks to solve the problems that occur when a user is working in an overlap area. However, be very cautious about doing this as a matter of course. A doctor working in a hospital does not want to manually connect to another WAP point when she moves from one ward to another. A teacher does not want to change his settings when moving between classes. Always ensure that your users understand the disadvantages of this "fix."

Reducing Interference

To reduce interference from devices such as mobile phones and microwave ovens, you can change the channel that your WAP uses. Some channels are less prone to interference than others. To configure a third-party WAP, you follow the manufacturer's instructions. However, you can configure most third-party WAPs through a Web interface from any computer on the network.

If, for example, your WAP has an IPv4 address of 192.168.123.154, then entering **http://192.168.123.254** should access configuration controls similar to those shown in Figure 6-41. This figure shows the basic setup page for an unidentified third-party WAP with default settings. Whatever the equivalent control looks like on your network, you can log in and change the channel settings. A number of factors determine which channel gives you the least interference, such as your location and the type of devices that are causing interference. You need to experiment with channel settings until you find the best one.

802.11b and 802.11g use the 2.4-GHz frequency. Microwave ovens and cordless phones also use this frequency. 802.11a uses the 5-GHz frequency. Some cordless phones also use this frequency. If these devices cause interference between a computer and the network it is connected to, the computer might try to switch to another nearby network. It is often impractical to ask your friends not to phone or your neighbors not to use their microwaves while you are browsing the Internet. The solution here is to change the WAP settings to use

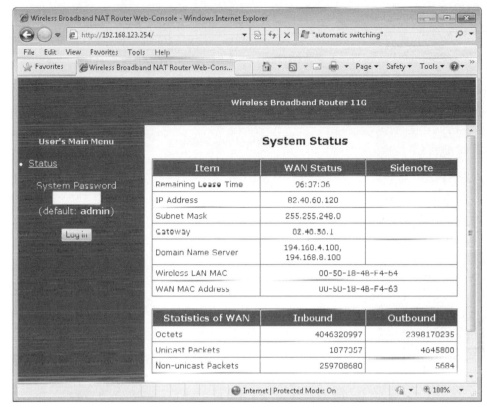

FIGURE 6-41 A typical third-party WAP configuration interface

a different wireless channel or to configure the channel to be selected automatically if it is set to a fixed channel number. In the United States and Canada, you can use channels 1, 6, and 11. Check the manufacturer's information that came with your WAP for instructions about how to set the wireless signal channel.

Networks with the Same Service Set Identifier (SSID)

The SSID is the identity of your wireless network. If a network on your list of preferred wireless networks has the same SSID as another network that is in range of your computer, Windows might try to switch between the two WAPs because it considers them to be the same network. Typically, the default SSID of a WAP is named Default. If several people set up wireless networks (for example, in an apartment block or in a building that contains a number of small business offices) and none of them change the default, then problems can occur. In this case, the solution is to give each WAP a unique SSID.

Figure 6-42 shows the wireless setup page for a third-party WAP with default settings. This page lets you specify the channel and change the SSID.

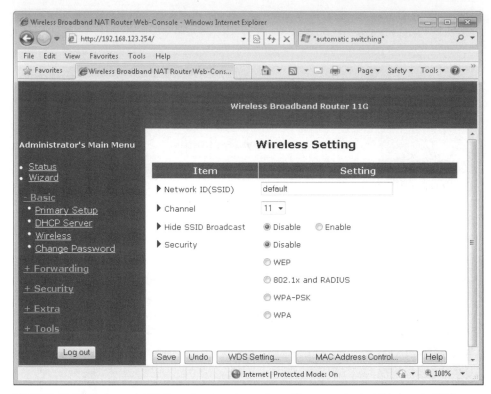

FIGURE 6-42 SSID, channel, SSID broadcast, and security settings on a typical third-party WAP

You should always secure a wireless network by changing the SSID and configuring other security settings, as described later in this lesson. If you do not secure your wireless network, a thief no longer needs to break into your home. He or she can sit in an automobile outside your front gate, turn on a wireless-enabled laptop, steal your passwords, and empty your bank account. If you are configuring a wireless network for your company and do not secure it, your company could be out of business, and you could be out of a job.

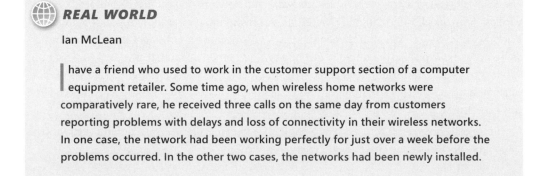

REAL WORLD

Ian McLean

I have a friend who used to work in the customer support section of a computer equipment retailer. Some time ago, when wireless home networks were comparatively rare, he received three calls on the same day from customers reporting problems with delays and loss of connectivity in their wireless networks. In one case, the network had been working perfectly for just over a week before the problems occurred. In the other two cases, the networks had been newly installed.

My friend took the precaution of checking the addresses of the customers. They all lived in the same apartment block. Apparently one of them had set up a wireless network and had been so impressed with it that he had invited his immediate neighbors in to have a look at it. They too had been impressed, and as a result they purchased exactly the same equipment—with exactly the same defaults.

Configuring Wireless Network Security

Many wireless connection problems are related to security. The precise steps involved in setting up security depend on the type of WAP you have installed on your network. This section discusses the settings available in most WAPs and ways in which you can increase wireless network security. You can take the following steps to increase security in your own or your employer's wireless network:

- **Change the default SSID**   Typically, you do this so that nearby networks with default settings do not interfere with your wireless network. Changing a SSID also improves network security because hackers who see a network with a default SSID deduce that it is a poorly configured network, so they are more likely to attack it.

- **Turn on WPA or WEP encryption**   All wireless equipment supports some form of encryption that scrambles messages sent over wireless networks so they cannot be easily read if they are intercepted. You should choose the strongest form of encryption that works with your wireless network. However, all wireless devices on your LAN must share the identical encryption settings. Therefore, you need to find the most secure setting that you can configure on both your WAP and your wireless adapters. You configure authentication and encryption settings on your wireless adapters by using the Security tab of the network's Wireless Network Properties dialog box, as described earlier in this lesson.

- **Change default administrator passwords**   The Web page interface that allows you to configure a third-party WAP usually presents you with a logon dialog box that requires at least a password (typically *admin*) and sometimes a user name. The default settings are well known to hackers. Change them.

- **Enable MAC address filtering**   This is regarded as a fairly complex configuration because MAC addresses—48-bit hexadecimal numbers—look daunting. Many administrators believe they need to go around all their network devices, enter the ipconfig /all command, write down the MAC addresses, and then type this information into the WAP configuration Web site interface. In fact, this time-consuming operation is not necessary. ARP resolves IP addresses to MAC addresses and caches the results. So all you need to do is sit at a single station on your network, ping all the network devices (firewalls permitting), and then capture the contents of the ARP cache into a text file from which you can copy and paste them into the WAP interface. Unless you require that other laptops should be able to use a wireless network (in a hotel, for example) you should configure MAC filtering to help secure your network.

- **Disable SSID broadcast**   A WAP typically broadcasts its SSID at regular intervals. This feature is designed for businesses and mobile hot spots where wireless clients might come and go. In a home network and many small office networks, this feature is unnecessary and increases the likelihood that a hacker will try to log on. If you know the settings on your WAP, you can connect to it either through Network And Sharing Center or by a *Netsh* command, as described earlier in this lesson.

- **Do not auto-connect to open wireless networks**   Connecting to an unsecured wireless network exposes a computer to security risks. Some network adapters have a setting that prohibits this. This is a setting specific to the adapter, not to Windows 7. Windows Live One-Care, if installed, increases browser and firewall security if a computer connects to an unsecured network.

- **Enable firewalls**   Ensure that Windows Firewall is enabled on wireless computers. If the WAP has a built-in firewall, check that this firewall is enabled.

- **Position the WAP centrally**   Wireless signals normally reach to the exterior of a home or office, but you should minimize the outdoor leakage as much as possible. Position the WAP near the center of the building. Do not put it on your front windowsill.

- **Turn off the network during extended periods of nonuse**   It is often impractical to turn a WAP off frequently, but consider doing so during extended period's offline (for example during holiday closures).

- **Consider assigning static IP addresses to wireless clients**   DHCP makes setup easy and comparatively error-free. However, network attackers can obtain valid IP addresses from a network's DHCP pool. Most WAPs let you disable DHCP. You can then assign private static IP addresses to all your network devices. This increases security, but static setup is inconvenient and error-prone. You should consider this option only in networks where security is a highly critical consideration or in networks where your WAP appears to have problems configuring (for example) external DNS settings through DHCP.

Windows 7 Printing Enhancements

Windows 7 introduces location-aware printing, printer driver isolation, configurable default spooler security settings, and an improved point-and-print experience for users. These enhancements build upon the features introduced by Windows Vista and are fully supported in Windows 7, such as high-fidelity print output, improved print performance, greater manageability of printers and print servers, integrated support for the new XML Paper Specification (XPS), and the Windows Color System.

On a Windows 7 computer you can take advantage of integrated support for the new XML Paper Specification (XPS) that describes the content and appearance of paginated documents. The XPS document printing capability supports vector-based graphics that can be scaled up to a high degree without creating jagged or pixilated text. An XPS document is created by default when you print from any application running on Windows 7, and you can print this document without re-rendering to an XPS-capable printer by using Microsoft XPS Document Writer. You can view XPS documents in Internet Explorer by using the Microsoft XPS Viewer.

By default, Windows 7 renders print jobs on the client instead of the print server. This can significantly reduce print processing times when printing to XPS-capable printers. Client-side rendering (CSR) also works on non-XPS printers, reduces the CPU and memory load on print servers, and can reduce network traffic. XPS documents render an image once and reuse the rendered image on multiple pages of a print job.

The Print Management MMC snap-in has been enhanced to allow administrators to configure default security settings for print servers and printer driver isolation settings. Custom filter capabilities have also been extended with additional filter criteria to make filtering more powerful.

The Network Printer Installation Wizard is easier to use than the Add Printer Wizard (which is still available in Windows 7) and has new capabilities, making it easier for users to connect to remote printers and to local printers that are not Plug and Play. Standard users can install printers without requiring administrative privileges.

Improved Color Facilities

The new Windows Color System (WCS) provides a richer color-printing experience and supports wide-gamut printers (that is, inkjet printers that use more than four ink colors). To improve print quality on an installed printer, carry out the following procedure:

1. On the Start menu, click Devices And Printers.

2. Double-click a printer. You can see what is printing; change the name, security settings, and other properties of your printer; or change color, layout, and paper settings.

3. Double-click Adjust Print Options. The Advanced tab of the Printer Preferences dialog box, shown in Figure 6-43, lets you specify color settings and enhance print quality and gray scale. The Icons at the top right of the tab let you specify duplex printing (if available), set a watermark, specify page settings, and set device options.

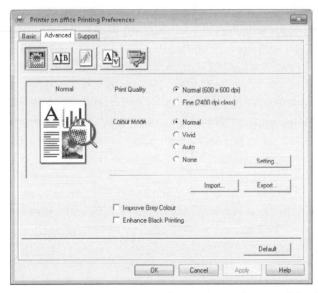

FIGURE 6-43 The Advanced tab of the Printer Preferences dialog box

Location-Aware Printing

Windows Vista enables you to assign printers based on location by using Group Policy and linking Group Policy Objects to sites in Active Directory Domain Services (AD DS). When mobile users move to a different site, Group Policy updates their printer connections for the new location, and when the users return to their primary site, their original default printers are restored.

Windows 7 extends this idea and introduces location-aware printing. This allows mobile computer (for example, laptop) users to set a different default printer for each configured network location. Note, however, that location-aware printing is not the same as assigning printers based on their AD DS site.

Microsoft introduced location-aware printing in response to the increasing importance of mobile computers in enterprises. A typical scenario is as follows:

- Don Hall, an employee of the A. Datum Corporation is issued with a company laptop for use in the office and at home. While at work, he connects to a laser printer via the Add Printer Wizard. The printer is automatically set as the default for the A. Datum Corporation network.

- On returning home, Don adds a Plug-and-Play USB inkjet printer. The printer is automatically set as the default for his home network. However, when Don goes back to work the following day and connects to his corporate network, the A. Datum Corporation laser printer is automatically set as his default printer. When he returns home, connects to his home network, and plugs in his inkjet printer, the inkjet printer is once again the default.

- Whenever Don is at work, his work printer is his default printer, and whenever he is at home, his home printer is his default printer. Don does not need to specify a new default printer every time he switches networks, as in previous versions of Windows. He does not need to set up or configure anything as he moves from network to network.

When location-aware printing is available on a computer running Windows 7, an additional control named Manage Default Printers is displayed on the toolbar of the Devices and Printers dialog box. By clicking this control, you open the Manage Default Printers dialog box, shown in Figure 6-44, in which you can configure default printers for each connected network.

When Change My Default Printer When I Change Networks is selected, you can choose each network in turn by clicking the Select Network drop-down box. You can then choose a printer as the default for this network from the Select Printer drop-down box. If a user installs a printer on a network and selects it as the default, these settings are automatically configured in the Manage Default Printers dialog box. You can disable location-aware printing by selecting Always Use The Same Printer As My Default Printer in the Manage Default Printers dialog box.

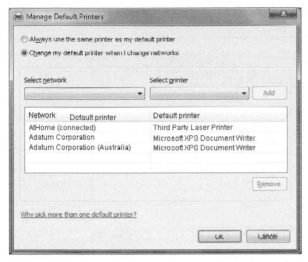

FIGURE 6-44 The Manage Default Printers dialog box

Creating an Ad Hoc Network

In this practice, you create an ad hoc network linking the Aberdeen and Canberra computers. This requires that both computers have wireless adapters and is therefore an optional exercise.

EXERCISE Creating an Ad Hoc Network

In this exercise, you create an ad hoc network while logged on to the Aberdeen computer with the Kim_Akers administrator-level account. You then log on to the Canberra computer with a standard (nonadministrative) account and join the ad hoc network. You created standard accounts earlier in this book—for example the Don Hall account you created in Chapter 4. If you do not have a standard account on Canberra, create one before you start the exercise.

To create an ad hoc network, proceed as follows:

1. Disconnect the Ethernet connection between the two computers and ensure that both computers have their wireless adapters switched on.

2. Log on to the Aberdeen computer with the Kim_Akers account.

3. Create a folder called Test on the Aberdeen computer.

4. Right-click the Test folder and choose Properties.

5. On the Sharing tab, click Advanced Sharing and share the folder. Ensure that the Everyone group has Read permission.

6. Open Network And Sharing Center.

7. Click Set Up A New Connection Or Network.

8. Select Set Up A Wireless Ad Hoc (Computer To Computer) Network, as shown in Figure 6-45. Click Next.

FIGURE 6-45 Selecting the Set Up A Wireless Ad Hoc (Computer To Computer) Network option

9. Click Next to clear the Set Up A Wireless Ad Hoc Network message box.

10. Specify a Network Name called **MyAdHoc,** specify WEP as the Security Type, and enter **P@ss1** as the Security Key, as shown in Figure 6-46. Click Next.

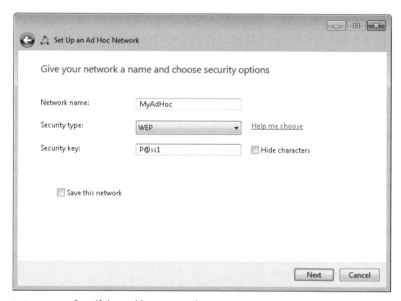

FIGURE 6-46 Specifying ad hoc network parameters

11. Click Close.

12. In Network And Sharing Center, click Connect to a Network. The MyAdHoc network displays with the message Waiting For Users.

13. Log on to the Canberra computer with a nonadministrative account.

14. Click the Wireless Network icon at the bottom left section of your screen.

15. Right-click MyAdHoc and click Connect.

16. Enter the security key (**P@ss1**).

17. In the Search box on the Start menu, enter **\\Aberdeen.** Check that you can see the shared Test folder.

18. Click the Wireless Network icon at the bottom left section of your screen.

19. Right-click MyAdHoc and click Disconnect. If the Canberra computer was previously connected to another network, reconnect it.

20. On the Aberdeen computer, disconnect from the MyAdHoc network. Check that the network is no longer listed on either computer.

Lesson Summary

- Problems with wireless connectivity can occur if a computer is within range of two preferred networks or two networks that have the same SSID. Interference from domestic devices can also cause problems. You can change the channel that a WAP uses to reduce interference.

- Using an unsecured wireless network can create significant security risks. If you configure a wireless network, always ensure that it is secure.

- You can connect to a wireless network, manage wireless networks, and enable or disable a wireless adapter through the Network And Sharing Center. You can also use the *Netsh wlan* command-line utility to mange wireless networks.

- Windows 7 configures the default printer that you specify on a particular network to be the default whenever you connect to that network. Thus, when you switch networks, you seamlessly shift default printers. You can configure location-aware printing and specify default printers for specific networks.

Lesson Review

You can use the following questions to test your knowledge of the information in Lesson 3, "Network Configuration." The questions are also available on the companion DVD if you prefer to review them in electronic form.

NOTE **ANSWERS**

Answers to these questions and explanations of why each answer choice is correct or incorrect are located in the "Answers" section at the end of the book.

1. One of the users whom you support uses a wireless laptop in the office and also takes it with her on business trips. She reports that when she uses the laptop in the lounge area of a hotel in which she frequently stays, she experiences delays and connection problems. She has no problems when using the laptop in her hotel room or when she returns to the office. What should you do to help solve the problem?

   A. Change the SSID of your office network.

   B. Advise the user to change the order in which her laptop attempts to access preferred networks.

   C. Disable network switching on one or both of the preferred networks that the user connects to in order to access the Internet from her hotel.

   D. Update the device driver for the user's wireless LAN adapter.

2. You want to ensure that only certain designated wireless laptops can connect to your network. What do you need to enable?

   A. MAC address control

   B. IPv4 address control

   C. WEP

   D. WPA

3. You are having problems with a connection and want to run the Windows Network Diagnostics tool. How can you access this tool? (Choose all that apply.)

   A. On the Accessories menu, select System Tools.

   B. On the Administrative Tools menu, select Task Scheduler. Schedule the Windows Network Diagnostic tool to start immediately.

   C. In the Network And Sharing Center, click the red X that indicates a failed connection.

   D. Access the Local Area Connections Properties dialog box and click Configure. On the General tab, click Repair.

   E. On the message returned by the browser when it cannot access a Web page, click Diagnose Connection Problems.

   F. Open the Network Connections dialog box by selecting Manage Network Connections on the Network And Sharing Center. Right-click a connection and click Diagnose.

4. Don Hall has set up a wireless network at home. He is pleased with the ease with which he set up her third-party WAP by clicking a single button in the Web interface. However, his next door neighbor tells him that she can access his network from her home computer. What should Don do?

   A. Enable Windows Firewall

   B. Change the security settings of his WAP

   C. Change the channel his WAP uses

   D. Implement ICS

5. Sam Abolrous hot-desks at the A. Datum Corporation. When he is working at a desk on the third floor, he wants all his print jobs to go to the printer LaserF3. When he is working at a desk on the second floor, he wants all his print jobs to go to the printer LaserF2. The third floor of the A. Datum building is covered by the wireless network Adatum3. The second floor of the A. Datum building is covered by the wireless network Adatum2. There is shielding between the floors, and the Adatum2 network cannot be accessed from the third floor. Similarly, the Adatum3 network cannot be accessed from the second floor. How do you configure location-aware printing on Sam's laptop running Windows 7 Enterprise?

   A. Select Always Use The Same Printer As My Default Printer. From the Printers drop-down list select LaserF2.

   B. Select Always Use The Same Printer As My Default Printer. From the Printers drop-down list, select LaserF3.

   C. Select Change My Default Printer When I Change Networks. Select LaserF2 as the default printer for the Adatum3 network. Select LaserF3 as the default printer for the Adatum2 network.

   D. Select Change My Default Printer When I Change Networks. Select LaserF2 as the default printer for the Adatum2 network. Select LaserF3 as the default printer for the Adatum3 network.

Chapter Review

To further practice and reinforce the skills you learned in this chapter, you can perform the following tasks:

- Review the chapter summary.
- Review the list of key terms introduced in this chapter.
- Complete the case scenarios. These scenarios set up real-world situations involving the topics of this chapter and ask you to create a solution.
- Complete the suggested practices.
- Take a practice test.

Chapter Summary

- IPv4 routes packets within a subnet and over an intranetwork. IPv6 performs the same functions as IPv4 but also addresses the problems associated with the earlier protocol, such as lack of address space.
- You use Network And Sharing Center and *Netsh* commands to configure networks and network connections, and connect to networks. You can access Windows Network Diagnostics by using Network And Sharing Center.
- Network command-line diagnostic tools include *Ping, Tracert, Pathping,* and *Netstat.* Windows Network Diagnostics can solve many network problems automatically.
- Windows 7 offers an enhanced printing experience, including location-aware printing.

Key Terms

Do you know what these key terms mean? You can check your answers by looking up the terms in the glossary at the end of the book.

- **default gateway**
- **global address**
- **IP address**
- **IP packet**
- **preferred wireless network**
- **public address**
- **subnet**
- **subnet mask**

Case Scenarios

In the following case scenarios, you apply what you've learned about network settings. You can find answers to these questions in the "Answers" section at the end of this book.

Case Scenario 1: Implementing IPv4 Connectivity

Your friend runs a small business from home. Until recently, he used a single computer running Windows 7 and connected directly to his cable modem to access the Internet. His business has expanded, and now he uses three computers. He has connected them with an Ethernet hub and connects to his modem through a USB cable.

Answer the following questions:

1. Your friend calls you and reports that the computer connected to the modem can access the Internet, but the others cannot. What do you advise?

2. He calls you for more advice. He has purchased a wireless computer and a WAP. He wants to know how he can use this computer on his network while still using his three desktop computers that have only wired connections. What do you advise?

Case Scenario 2: Implementing IPv6 Connectivity

You are a network administrator at Blue Sky Airlines. Your corporate network consists of two subnets with contiguous private IPv4 networks configured as virtual local area networks (VLANs) connected to a layer-3 switch. Blue Sky Airlines accesses its ISP and the Internet through a dual-homed server running Microsoft Internet Security and Acceleration (ISA) that provides NAT and firewall services and connects through a peripheral zone to a hardware firewall and, hence, to its ISP. All user workstations run Windows 7 Enterprise. The company wants to implement IPv6 connectivity. All the network hardware supports IPv6, as does the ISP.

Answer the following questions:

1. What options are available for the type of unicast address used on the subnets?

2. You know your clients running Windows 7 have IPv6 enabled by default. Your site-local addresses are allocated through stateful configuration (by DHCPv6), but on entering **ipconfig /all** on a client computer, you see the address 2001:: ce49:7601:e866:efff:f5ff:ebfe. What type of address is this, and what is its function?

Case Scenario 3: Using Laptop Computers Running Windows 7 on Wireless Networks

You are a network administrator at Margie's Travel. You are planning to upgrade all client computers to laptops running Windows 7 Enterprise. All clients will connect wirelessly, and employees are expected to have wireless networks at home and to work from home and in the office.

Answer the following questions:

1. A senior staff member is concerned that she needs to switch her default printer from the printer that she uses in the office to a wireless network inkjet printer that she uses at home. What do you advise her?

2. The same employee intends to replace her home printer with a newer model. She asks you to grant her account local administrator privileges so she can install the new printer. What do you tell her?

3. The main office at Margie's Travel has two wireless networks. Employees can typically move between one area of the office to another without losing connectivity. However, one employee complains of poor service when she is seated at her desk, though she has no problem if she moves to another part of the building. How do you solve this problem?

Suggested Practices

To help you master the exam objectives presented in this chapter, complete the following tasks.

Configure IPv4

- **Practice 1** You can do a lot with the versatile and powerful Network And Sharing Center. Investigate all its functions thoroughly and become familiar with its screens, wizards, and dialog boxes.

- **Practice 2** Become familiar with all the switches available with *Ping, Tracert, Ipconfig, Pathping,* and *Netstat*. Use the command-line help (for example, **ping /?**).

- **Practice 3** Create some problems on your interfaces (for example, by unplugging Ethernet cables and misconfiguring adapters). Use the Windows Network Diagnostic tool to find these problems.

- **Practice 4** Use the help function in the Command Prompt console to investigate the *Netsh interface ipv4 set, Netsh interface ipv4 add,* and *Netsh interface ipv4 show* commands. Also, investigate the *Netsh dhcp* commands.

Configure IPv6

- **Practice 1** You should be able to look at an IPv6 address and tell whether it is global, link-local, site-local, or multicast. Teredo, 6to4, and ISATAP addresses are slightly more difficult to identify but you can become proficient at this with practice. Look at lists of addresses. The *Ipconfig /all* utility is a good place to start.

- **Practice 2** Use the help function in the Command Prompt console to investigate the *Netsh interface ipv6 set, Netsh interface ipv6 add,* and *Netsh interface ipv6 show* commands.

Configure Networks

- **Practice 1** Although you might not use every function that a third-party WAP configuration Web interface dialog box provides, make sure you know what wireless access settings are available. Become familiar with the configuration pages (or tabs) on your interface and with the manufacturer's documentation.

- **Practice 2** Use the Command Prompt help function to learn the syntax of the *Netsh wlan add, Netsh wlan connect, Netsh wlan delete, Netsh wlan disconnect, Netsh wlan dump, Netsh wlan export, Netsh wlan refresh, Netsh wlan reportissues, Netsh wlan set, Netsh wlan show, Netsh wlan start,* and *Netsh wlan stop* commands. Use these commands to manage wireless networks.

- **Practice 3** Windows 7 offers improvements in print quality and enhanced print management. Investigate the facilities available from the Devices And Printers dialog box.

Take a Practice Test

The practice tests on this book's companion DVD offer many options. For example, you can test yourself on just one exam objective, or you can test yourself on all the 70-680 certification exam content. You can set up the test so that it closely simulates the experience of taking a certification exam, or you can set it up in study mode so that you can look at the correct answers and explanations after you answer each question.

> **MORE INFO** **PRACTICE TESTS**
>
> For details about all the practice test options available, see the section entitled "How to Use the Practice Tests," in the Introduction to this book.

CHAPTER 7

Windows Firewall and Remote Management

F irewalls are important. From the moment that your computer connects to a public
network, automated scanners probe Its network Interfaces looking for weaknesses to
exploit. Today's computer user is much more likely to access a publically accessible Wi-Fi
network, either in a coffee shop or in an airport lounge. When you connect to the free Wi-Fi
network at the coffee shop, you do not know if someone sitting a couple of tables away
is running a port scanner looking for vulnerabilities in your computer's security. You need
a firewall all the time, not just when connected to a public network. You need it active when
you are connected to your corporate network because you cannot be sure if a member
of the sales team, who takes her laptop with her wherever she goes, might have had her
machine compromised when she was not being careful. If a compromised computer
connects to a network where other clients do not have firewalls enabled, it will not be long
until that infected computer compromises all the unprotected computers on the network..

As IT departments are asked to do more with less, support staffs have less time to
perform on-site visits to resolve customer technical issues. It is increasingly necessary to be
able to resolve as many client maintenance issues as you can remotely from the helpdesk
rather than having to visit each computer that is the subject of a support ticket. Windows 7
makes this easier. Not only do clients running Windows 7 support Remote Desktop and
Windows Remote Assistance, it is now possible to run Windows PowerShell scripts and
command-line utilities against properly configured clients, giving support staff even more
options when it comes to resolving maintenance issues.

Exam objectives in this chapter:
- Configure Windows Firewall.
- Configure Remote Management.

Lessons in this chapter:

Before You Begin

To complete the exercises in the practices in this chapter, you need to have done the following:

- Installed Windows 7 on a stand-alone client PC named Canberra, as described in Chapter 1, "Install, Migrate, or Upgrade to Windows 7."

- Installed Windows 7 on a stand-alone client PC named Aberdeen, as described in Chapter 6, "Network Settings."

 REAL WORLD

Orin Thomas

It is probably a good thing that remote management technologies were still in their infancy back when I was doing first-level support. Back when I was working Helpdesk at an Australian university, I had to do a lot of walking across a very large campus to assist people with computer problems in far-flung departments. So even though I had to walk past the donut shop on my way out to visit a broken computer, I felt better about it because at least I was out in the air getting some exercise. If I was back in that job today and had the plethora of remote assistance technologies built into Windows 7 available, it would have been less necessary to leave my desk. Rather than having to walk from my office to the Department of Social Work to assist someone because "the mail-merge thingy won't go in the doodad," I would be able to use Remote Assistance to see exactly what that person could see on the screen and guide him through the process. I could have performed many maintenance tasks using Remote Desktop or Windows PowerShell rather than having to go from office to office applying updates and resolving configuration settings manually. If today's remote management technologies had existed back then, I would rarely have left my desk and would not have gotten any exercise at all.

Lesson 1: Managing Windows Firewall

The firewall that ships with Windows 7 is designed to keep your computer safe. It will help keep your computer safe when it is connected to the protected network in the office or the less-safe public WiFi networks of coffee shops and airport lounges. In this lesson, you learn the differences between Windows Firewall and Windows Firewall with Advanced Security. You also learn about *connection security rules,* which you can use to limit your computer's network communication so that it occurs only with other computers that have proven their identity.

> **After this lesson, you will be able to:**
> - Configure rules for multiple profiles.
> - Allow or deny applications.
> - Create profile network-profile-specific rules.
> - Configure notifications.
> - Configure authenticated exceptions.
>
> **Estimated lesson time: 40 minutes**

Windows Firewall

Firewalls restrict network traffic based on a collection of configurable rules. Another name for these rules is *exceptions*. When traffic reaches a network interface protected by a firewall, the firewall analyzes it, either discarding the traffic or allowing it to pass on the basis of the rules that have been applied to the firewall. Windows 7 uses two firewalls that work together: Windows Firewall and the Windows Firewall with Advanced Security (WFAS). The primary difference between these firewalls relates to the complexity of the rules that can be configured for them. Windows Firewall uses simple rules that directly relate to a program or service. WFAS allows for more complicated rules that filter traffic on the basis of port, protocol, address, and authentication. WFAS will be covered in more detail later in this lesson.

When thinking about how firewall rules work, remember that unless a rule exists that explicitly allows a particular form of traffic, the firewall will drop that traffic. In general, you must explicitly allow traffic to pass across a firewall, though there will be some occasions when you need to configure a deny rule. You will learn about deny rules later in this lesson. Windows Firewall and WFAS ship a minimum number of default rules that allow you to interact with networks. This means that although you are able to browse the Web without having to configure a firewall rule, if you try to use an application to interact with the network that is not covered by a default rule, such as File Transfer Protocol (FTP), you receive a warning. This behavior is different to earlier versions of Microsoft Windows, such as Windows XP, where the firewall blocked only incoming traffic and did not block outgoing traffic. The firewall in Windows 7 blocks most outbound traffic by default. When a program is blocked for the first time, you are notified by the firewall, as shown in Figure 7-1, allowing you to configure an exception that allows traffic of this type in the future.

FIGURE 7-1 Most outbound traffic is blocked but generates a warning.

The Windows 7 firewall uses a feature known as full stealth. Stealth blocks external hosts from performing Operating System (OS) fingerprinting. OS fingerprinting is a technique where an attacker determines what operating system a host is running by sending special traffic to the host's external network interface. After an attacker knows what operating system a host is using, they can target OS-specific exploits at the host. You cannot disable the stealth feature of Windows 7.

Boot time filtering, another feature of Windows 7, ensures that Windows Firewall is working from the instant the network interfaces become active. In previous operating systems, such as Windows XP, the firewall, either built into Windows or from a third-party vendor, would become operational only once the startup process was complete. This left a small but important period where a network interface would be active but not protected by a firewall. Boot time filtering closes this window of opportunity.

To understand the operation of Windows Firewall, you need to be familiar with some core networking concepts. If you have a lot of experience with networks, you may want to skip ahead to the next section because you are already familiar with them. These core concepts are:

- **Protocol** In terms of Windows Firewall, you need to consider only three protocols, Transmission Control Protocol (TCP), User Datagram Protocol (UDP), and Internet Control Message Protocol (ICMP). TCP is more reliable and is used for the majority of Internet traffic. UDP is used for broadcast and multicast data, as well as the sort of traffic associated with online games. You use ICMP primarily for diagnostic purposes.

- **Port** A port is an identification number that is contained within the header of a TCP or UDP datagram. Ports are used to map network traffic to specific services or programs running on a computer. For example, port 80 is reserved for World Wide Web traffic and port 25 is reserved for the transmission of e-mail across the Internet.

- **IPSec (Internet Protocol Security)** IPSec is a method of securing network traffic by encrypting it and signing it. The encryption ensures that an attacker cannot read captured traffic. The signature allows the recipient of the traffic to validate the sender's identity.

- **Network address** Each host on a network has a network address. You can configure firewalls to treat traffic differently based on the destination network of outgoing or the origin network of incoming traffic.

- **Inbound traffic** Inbound traffic is network data that originates from the external host and is addressed to your client running Windows 7.

- **Outbound traffic** Outbound traffic is traffic that your client running Windows 7 sends to external hosts over the network.

- **Network interface** A network interface can be a physical local area network (LAN) connection, a wireless connection, a modem connection, or a virtual private network (VPN) connection.

Network Location Awareness

Network Location Awareness (NLA) is a feature through which Windows 7 assigns a network profile based on the properties of a network connection. As you can see in Figure 7-2, Windows 7 uses three network profiles, Domain Networks, Home Or Work (Private) Networks, and Public Networks. When you connect to a new network, Windows 7 queries you with a dialog box asking you whether the network is a Home network, a Work network, or a Public network. Windows 7 remembers the designation that you assign to the network and associates it with the properties of the network so that that designation will be applied the next time you connect the computer to that network. You can change the designation of a network using the Network and Sharing center. You learned about changing Network designations in Chapter 6. NLA assigns the Domain network profile when you log on to an Active Directory Domain Services (AD DS) domain.

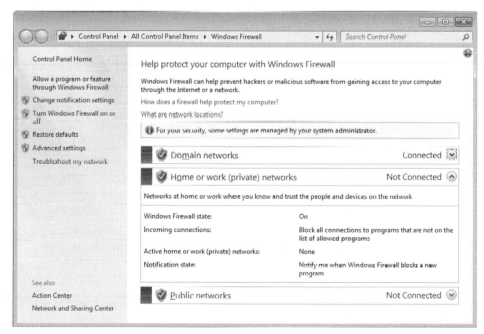

FIGURE 7-2 Windows Firewall in Control Panel

Network profiles are important because you can use them to apply different collections of firewall rules based on which network profile is active. Figure 7-3 shows that the Windows Virtual PC rule is active in the Domain and Home/Work (Private) profiles but not in the Public profile. A significant difference between Windows Vista and Windows 7 is that in Windows 7, profiles apply on a per-network interface basis. This means that if you have one network adapter connected to the Internet and another connected to your office LAN, different sets of rules apply for each connection. The firewall in Windows Vista chooses the most restrictive network profile when a computer has connections to different network types and applies the most restrictive set of rules to all interfaces.

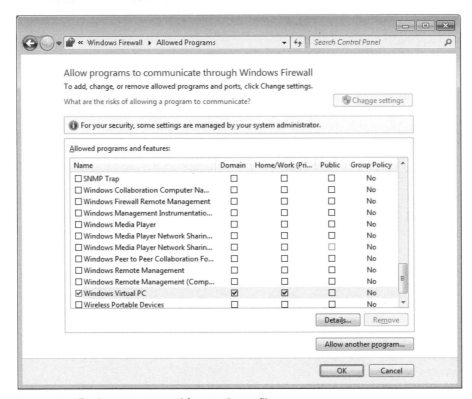

FIGURE 7-3 Allowing programs and features by profile

As shown in Figure 7-4, you can selectively enable Windows Firewall for each network profile. You can also specify whether you want notifications to appear to the logged-on user when Windows Firewall blocks a new program and whether you want all incoming connections blocked, including those for which there are existing firewall rules. Users are only able to create rules to deal with the traffic that they have been notified about if they have local administrator privileges.

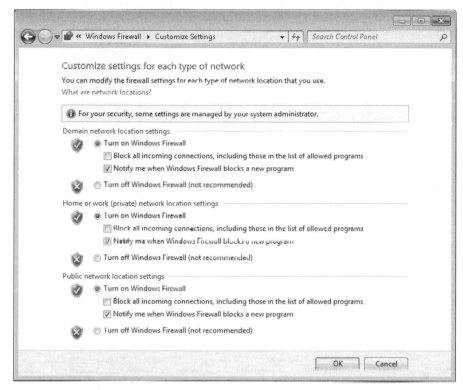

FIGURE 7-4 Enabling Windows Firewall selectively

The primary reason why you might want to disable Windows Firewall for all profiles is if you have a firewall product from another vendor and you want that vendor's firewall to protect your computer rather than having Windows Firewall perform that function. It is important to note that you should not disable Windows Firewall just because there is another firewall, such as a small office/home office (SOHO) router or hardware firewall, between your client running Windows 7 and the Internet. It is possible that malware has infected another computer on your local network. Good security practice is to treat all networks as potentially hostile.

Allowing Programs Through Windows Firewall

Windows Firewall allows you to configure exceptions based on programs. This differs from Windows Vista where Windows Firewall would allow you to configure exceptions based on port address. You can still create rules based on port address; you just have to do it using WFAS, covered later in this lesson. You can also allow specific Windows 7 features, such as Windows Virtual PC, through Windows Firewall. Feature rules become available when you enable the feature using the Programs And Features item in Control Panel. To add a rule for a feature or program, click Allow A Program Or Feature Through Windows Firewall item in the Windows Firewall section of Control Panel. The dialog box, displayed earlier in Figure 7-3, shows a list of currently installed features and any programs for which rules have been created as well as the profiles for which rules concerning those programs and features are enabled.

To modify the settings on this page, you need to click the Change Settings item. Only users that are members of the local Administrators group, or who have been delegated the appropriate privileges are able to modify Windows Firewall settings. If a program that you want to create a rule for is not present on this list, click Allow Another Program. This opens the Add A Program dialog box, shown in Figure 7-5. If the program that you want to create a rule for is not listed, click Browse to add it. Use the Network Location Types button to specify the network profiles in which the rule should be active.

FIGURE 7-5 Adding a program exception

> **NOTE RESET FIREWALL TO DEFAULT CONFIGURATION**
>
> You can reset Windows Firewall and WFAS to their out-of-the-box configuration by running the command **netsh advfirewall reset** from an elevated command prompt. You can also reset Windows Firewall and WFAS by clicking on Restore Defaults in the Windows Firewall control panel.

✔ Quick Check

- On what basis can you create rules for Windows Firewall (as opposed to WFAS)?

Quick Check Answer

- You can create rules for Windows Firewall only for programs and Windows 7 features. You cannot create rules for Windows Firewall based on port address or service.

Windows Firewall with Advanced Security

Windows Firewall with Advanced Security (WFAS) allows you to create nuanced firewall rules. For most users, the options available with Windows Firewall will be enough to keep their computers secure. If you are a more advanced user, however, you can use WFAS to:

- Configure inbound and outbound rules. Windows Firewall does not allow you to create rules based on whether traffic is inbound or outbound.
- Configure rules that apply based on protocol type and port address.
- Configure rules that apply based on traffic that addresses specific services, rather than just specific applications.
- Limit the scope of rules so that they apply based on traffic's source or destination address.
- Configure rules that allow traffic only if it is authenticated.
- Configure connection security rules.

You can access the WFAS console either by typing **Windows Firewall with Advanced Security** into the Search Programs And Files text box on the Start menu or by clicking the Advanced Settings item in the Windows Firewall control panel. The WFAS console displays which network profiles are currently active. As is the case with Windows Firewall, different collections of rules apply depending on which profile is active for a particular network adapter. For example, Figure 7-6 shows that the Domain Profile and Public Profile are active. In this case, it is because the computer on which this screen shot was taken is connected to a domain network through its wireless network adapter and to the Internet through a universal serial bus (USB) cellular modem. You could enable a rule that allows traffic on port 80 for the Domain Profile but not enable it for the Public Profile. This would mean that hosts contacting this computer through the wireless network adapter would be able to access a Web server hosted on the computer, whereas hosts attempting to access the same Web server through the USB cellular modem's Internet connection are blocked.

Creating WFAS Rules

The process for configuring inbound rules and outbound rules is essentially the same: In the WFAS console, select the node that represents the type of rule that you want to create and then click New Rule. This opens the New Inbound (or Outbound) Rule Wizard. The first page, shown in Figure 7-7, allows you to specify the type of rule that you are going to create. You can select between a program, port, predefined, or custom rule. The program and predefined rules are similar to what you can create using Windows Firewall. A custom rule allows you to configure a rule based on criteria not covered by any of the other options. You would create a custom rule if you wanted a rule that applied to a particular service rather than a program or port. You can also use a custom rule if you want to create a rule that involves both a specific program and a set of ports. For example, if you wanted to allow communication to a specific program on a certain port but not other ports, you would create a custom rule.

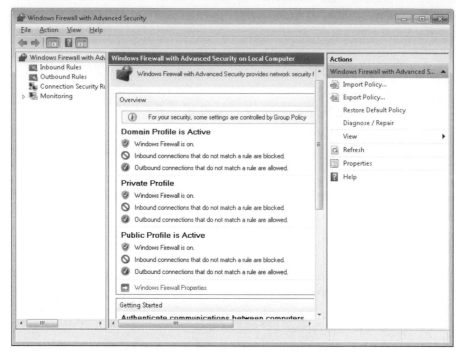

FIGURE 7-6 Multiple active network profiles in the WFAS console

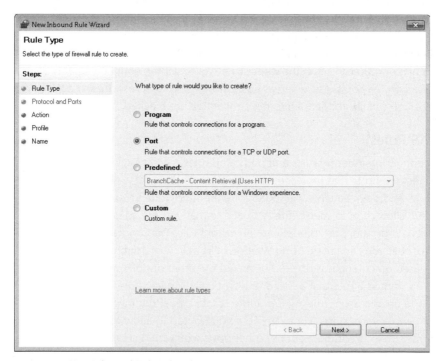

FIGURE 7-7 New Inbound Rule Wizard

If you decide to create a program rule, you then need to specify a program for which the rule applies. If you choose a port rule, you must choose whether the rule applies to the TCP or the UDP protocol. You must also specify port numbers. In the next step, you specify what action to take when the firewall encounters traffic that meets the rule conditions. The options are as follows:

- **Allow the connection**   WFAS allows the connection if the traffic meets the rule conditions.

- **Block the connection**   WFAS blocks the connection if the traffic meets the rule conditions.

- **Allow the connection if it is secure**   WFAS allows the connection if the traffic meets the rule conditions and is authenticated using one of the methods specified in the connection security rules. Security options are shown in Figure 7-8.

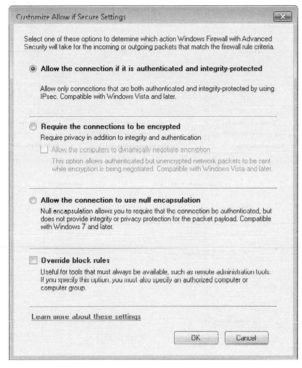

FIGURE 7-8 Security option settings

The default setting requires that the connection be authenticated and integrity protected, but not encrypted. Use the Require The Connection To Be Encrypted option if you want firewall rules to enforce data encryption as well as authentication and integrity protection. The override block rules option allows you to specify a computer account or computer group that can bypass existing block rules.

Rule Scope

A rule scope allows you to specify whether a rule applies to specific source and destination addresses. If you want to create a rule that allows a particular type of traffic but want to limit that traffic to a particular set of network addresses, you need to modify the rule's scope. You can specify a scope when creating a custom rule, but not a standard program or port rule. For these rule types, you can specify the scope by editing the rule's properties after it has been created, as shown in Figure 7-9. You can specify Internet Protocol (IP) addresses or IP address ranges, or use one of the predefined sets of computers that include the Default Gateway, Windows Internet Naming Service (WINS) servers, Dynamic Host Configuration Protocol (DHCP) servers, Domain Name System (DNS) servers, and Local Subnet. You can specify both IPv4 and IPv6 addresses and ranges when configuring a rule's scope.

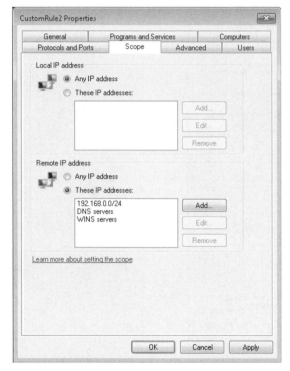

FIGURE 7-9 Configuring rule scope

To modify a rule's scope, perform the following actions:

1. Right-click the rule in the WFAS console and then choose Properties. This opens the Properties dialog box for the rule. Click the Scope tab.

2. If you want to limit the local IP address that the rule applies to (for example, when more than one address is assigned to a network adapter or there are multiple network adapters on your computer), select the These IP Addresses option below Local IP Address. Click Add and specify which address or addresses the rule applies to.

3. If you want to limit the remote IP address that the rule applies to (for example, when you want the rule to only apply to inbound traffic from a specific subnet), select the These IP Addresses option under Remote IP Addresses and click Add to specify the individual IP addresses, network address, or IP address range.

You can use the Advanced options of a rule's properties to specify which network interfaces the rule applies to. This is similar to limiting the local IP addresses that the rule applies to, except it is done by selecting a particular device, not the address attached to that device. On the Advanced tab, you can also configure how a rule responds to traffic that has passed through an edge device such as a Network Address Translation (NAT) router. The options are:

- **Block edge traversal** When selected, the target of the rule is blocked from receiving unsolicited traffic from the Internet through a NAT device.

- **Allow edge traversal** When selected, the target of the rule will process unsolicited traffic directly from the Internet through a NAT device.

- **Defer to user** When selected, the user receives a message informing them of incoming traffic from a NAT device. If the user has sufficient privileges, they can block or allow communication manually.

- **Defer to application** When selected, application settings determine whether incoming traffic from a NAT device is accepted or rejected.

Connection Security Rules

Connection security rules are a special type of rule that deal with authenticated and encrypted traffic. You can use connection security rules to manage how communication occurs between different hosts on the network. You use the New Connection Security Rule Wizard, shown in Figure 7-10, to create connection security rules. Connections can be authenticated using the Kerberos V5 protocol requiring a domain computer and user account or a domain computer account. If you select advanced properties, connections can be authenticated using NTLMv2, computer certificates from a particular certificate authority (CA) or using a pre-shared key.

The different connection security rules work in the following ways:

- **Isolation** Isolation rules allow you to limit communication to hosts that are able to authenticate using specific credentials. For example, you can use an isolation rule to stop computers communicating with any hosts that are not members of an AD DS domain. You can configure an isolation rule to request authentication for inbound and outbound communication, require authentication for inbound communication and request it for outbound communication, or require authentication for all communication.

- **Authentication exemption** These rules allow you to configure exemptions to isolation rules. You can configure authentication exemptions to allow a computer to connect to infrastructure servers, such as DHCP servers and DNS servers, without having to authenticate.

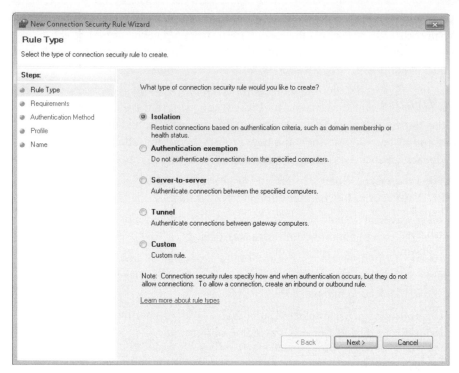

FIGURE 7-10 New connection security rule

- **Server-to-server** These rules allow you to protect connections between specific computers. They differ from isolation rules in that instead of applying to all connections, they apply to connections between hosts at specific addresses.

- **Tunnel** These rules are similar to server-to-server rules, except that they apply to connections through tunnels to remote sites, such as site-to-site links.

> **NOTE CONNECTION SECURITY RULES AND IPSec POLICIES**
>
> The relationship between connection security rules and IPSec policies is similar to the relationship between AppLocker and Software Restriction Policies. Both sets of rules do similar things, but the ones that you use depend on the operating systems used by the client computers in your organization. All editions of Windows 7 and Windows Vista support connection security rules, but Windows XP does not.

Importing and Exporting Firewall Configuration

Most organizations that use clients running Windows 7 apply firewall rules through Group Policy. In the event that you need to support a number of stand-alone clients running Windows 7, you can replicate complex firewall configurations using the WFAS Import Policy and Export Policy options. Importing and exporting policy also allows you to save the current firewall configuration state before you make changes to it. Exported policy files use the .wfw extension. Exported policies use a binary format, not Extensible Markup Language (XML) format like many other Windows 7 configuration files. You can also export and import firewall policies in the same .wfw format using the *netsh advfirewall export* or *netsh advfirewall import* commands.

Managing WFAS with Netsh

You can use the Netsh.exe command-line utility from an elevated command prompt to manage WFAS rules. The advantage of this is that you can combine it with Windows Remote Shell (WinRS), which you will learn about in the next lesson, to manage WFAS rules on other computers running Windows 7 on your network. You can also use Netsh.exe to script the creation of firewall rules on stand-alone computers that are not members of an AD DS domain and hence are not subject to domain-applied Group Policy.

To use Netsh.exe to create WFAS firewall rules, you need to be in the *advfirewall firewall* context. The following are some examples of using WFAS to create firewall rules:

- To create a rule named WebServerRule that applies in the domain profile and allows inbound traffic on TCP port 80, issue the command **netsh advfirewall firewall add rule name="WebServerRule" profile=domain protocol=TCP dir=in localport=80 action=allow.**

- To create a rule named AllowCalc that allows inbound traffic to the Calc.exe application in all network profiles, issue the command **netsh advfirewall firewall add rule name="Calc" dir=in program="c:\windows\system32\calc.exe".**

- To create a rule named BlockFTP that blocks outbound traffic from the Ftp. exe application, issue the command **netsh advfirewall firewall add rule name="BlockFTP" dir=out program="c:\windows\system32\ftp.exe" action=block.**

EXAM TIP

Know when you need to use WFAS to create a rule and when you can use Windows Firewall.

PRACTICE Configuring Windows Firewall

In this practice, you use Windows Firewall and WFAS to configure two different firewall rules. By interacting with the interface, you learn more about the types of rules that you can configure with each tool.

EXERCISE 1 Configuring Firewall Rules with Windows Firewall

In this exercise, you configure a rule that allows incoming traffic to the Internet Backgammon application. To complete this exercise, perform the following steps:

1. Log on to Canberra with the Kim_Akers user account.

2. Click Start, Control Panel, and System And Security.

3. Under Windows Firewall, click Allow A Program Through Windows Firewall.

4. In the Allow Programs To Communicate Through Windows Firewall dialog box, shown in Figure 7-11, click Change Settings.

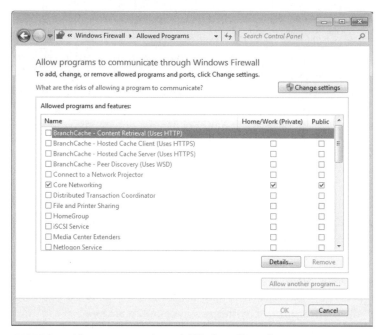

FIGURE 7-11 Allow programs through Windows Firewall

5. Click Allow Another Program. This opens the Add A Program dialog box. Click Browse and navigate to the Program Files\Microsoft Games\Multiplayer\Backgammon folder. Select Bckgzm.exe and click Open.

6. Click Network Location Types and verify that the settings match those shown in Figure 7-12. Click OK and then click Add.

FIGURE 7-12 Choose Network Location Types

7. Verify that a rule for Internet Backgammon now appears in the list of Allowed Programs And Features for the Home/Work (Private) profile, but not the Public profile and then click OK.

EXERCISE 2   Configuring WFAS Rules

In this exercise, you configure a WFAS rule for a hypothetical Internet Relay Chat (IRC) server hosted on a client running Windows 7. You configure the rule to accept only authenticated connections from hosts on a specific subnet.

1. If you have not already done so, log on to the computer named Canberra with the Kim_Akers user account.
2. Click Start. In the Search Programs And Files text box, type **Windows Firewall with Advanced Security,** and click Windows Firewall with Advanced Security. This opens the Windows Firewall With Advanced Security console.
3. Select the Inbound Rules node. In the Actions pane, click New Rule.
4. On the Rule Type page, select Port and then click Next.
5. On the Protocols And Ports page, type **6667** in the Specific Local Ports box, as shown in Figure 7-13, and then click Next.

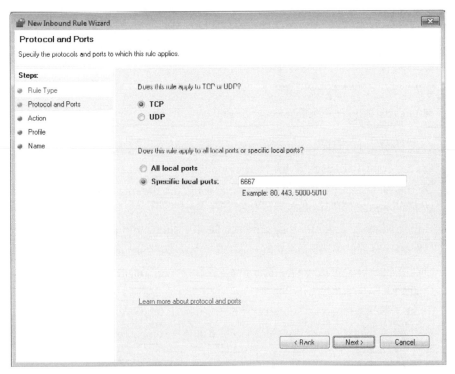

FIGURE 7-13 Specify TCP port 6667

6. On the Action page, select Allow The Connection If It Is Secure and then click Customize.

7. On the Customize Allow If Secure Settings dialog box, select require The Connections To Be Encrypted option and then select the Allow The Computers To Dynamically Negotiate Encryption check box, as shown in Figure 7-14, and click OK.

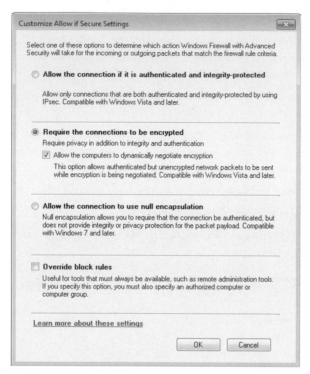

FIGURE 7-14 Customize secure connection settings

8. Click Next. On the Users page of the New Inbound Rule Wizard, click Next.
9. On the Computers page of the New Inbound Rule Wizard, click Next.
10. On the When Does This Rule Apply page, configure the rule to apply only in the Domain and Private profiles, and then click Next.
11. On the Name page, enter the name **IRC Server Rule** and then click Finish.
12. In the list of Inbound Rules, right-click the IRC Server Rule and then choose Properties.
13. Click the Scope tab. In the Remote IP Address section, select These IP Addresses and then click Add.
14. In the This IP Address Or Subnet text box, enter **10.0.10.0/24** and then click OK.
15. Verify that the IRC Server Rule Properties dialog box matches Figure 7-15, and then click OK.

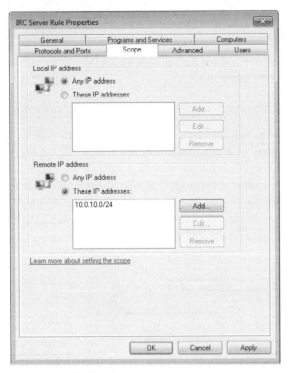

FIGURE 7-15 Configuring rule scope

Lesson Summary

- Windows Firewall and WFAS work together on a client running Windows 7.
- Windows Firewall allows for the creation of basic rules that apply to programs and Windows 7 features. You cannot configure rule scope or authentication settings for Windows Firewall rules.
- Network profiles allow different sets of firewall rules to apply depending on the properties of the network connection. The three network profiles are Domain, Public, and Home Or Work (Private).
- Windows Firewall rules can apply selectively to network profiles. Different network profiles can apply to different network interfaces at the same time.
- WFAS allows you to configure inbound and outbound firewall rules for ports, programs, and services.
- WFAS allows you to configure rule scope and authentication.

Lesson Review

You can use the following questions to test your knowledge of the information in Lesson 1, "Managing Windows Firewall." The questions are also available on the companion DVD if you prefer to review them in electronic form.

> **NOTE ANSWERS**
>
> Answers to these questions and explanations of why each answer choice is correct or incorrect are located in the "Answers" section at the end of the book.

1. You are responsible for managing student laptops that have Windows 7 installed at a small community college. You want to prevent students from uploading files using FTP to FTP sites on the Internet but allow them to send outbound e-mail using the Simple Mail Transfer Protocol (SMTP). Which of the following rules would you configure to accomplish that goal?

   A. Inbound rules

   B. Outbound rules

   C. Isolation rules

   D. Authentication exemption rules

2. You want to create a firewall rule that allows inbound communications on port 80 when your laptop computer with Windows 7 installed is connected to your office network, but blocks inbound communication on TCP port 80 when you are connected to your home network. Which of the following tools could you use to create this rule? (Choose all that apply.)

   A. Windows Firewall

   B. WFAS

   C. Netsh

   D. Netstat

3. What does the command *netsh advfirewall firewall add rule name="CustomRule" profile=domain protocol=TCP dir=in localport=80 action=allow* do when executed from an elevated command prompt?

   A. Creates an inbound rule that applies only in the Domain profile that blocks traffic on port 80

   B. Creates an outbound rule that applies only in the Domain profile that blocks traffic on port 80

   C. Creates an inbound rule that applies only in the Domain profile that allows traffic on port 80

   D. Creates an outbound rule that applies only in the Domain profile that allows traffic on port 80

4. You are configuring firewall rules on a client running Windows 7. You want to allow incoming traffic to the application named Application.exe, but only if it is authenticated. Which of the following steps should you perform to accomplish this goal?

   A. Use Windows Firewall to create a rule

   B. Use WFAS to create a rule

   C. Use the Credential Manager to create a rule

   D. Use the Authorization Manager to create a rule

5. You want Windows 7 to send you a message when the firewall blocks a new program when you are connected to your organization's domain network. Windows 7 should not send you a message when the firewall blocks a new program when you are connected to a public network. Which of the following settings should you configure? (Choose all that apply; each answer forms part of a complete solution.)

   A. In the Home Or Work (Private) Network Location Settings area, select Turn On Windows Firewall and enable Notify Me When Windows Firewall Blocks A New Program.

   B. In the Home Or Work (Private) Network Location Settings area, select Turn On Windows Firewall and disable Notify Me When Windows Firewall Blocks A New Program.

   C. In the Public Network Location Settings area, select Turn On Windows Firewall and enable Notify Me When Windows Firewall Blocks A New Program.

   D. In the Public Network Location Settings area, select Turn On Windows Firewall and disable Notify Me When Windows Firewall Blocks A New Program.

Lesson 2: Windows 7 Remote Management

Remote management allows a user in one location to perform management tasks on a computer in another location. Through remote management, you can perform almost every task remotely that you can perform when you are sitting directly in front of the computer. In this lesson, you learn about the remote management technologies that can be used with Windows 7 including Remote Desktop, Remote Assistance, Windows PowerShell, and Windows Remote Shell (WinRS).

After this lesson, you will be able to:

- Use Windows PowerShell for remote management.
- Use WinRS for remote management.
- Configure Remote Assistance.
- Configure Remote Desktop.

Estimated lesson time: 40 minutes

Remote Desktop

Remote Desktop allows you to log on remotely to a computer running Windows 7 and to interact with that computer it in the same manner as you would if you were sitting in front of it. Remote Desktop allows you to print using printers connected to the remote computer, or print to a local printer from an application running on the remote computer. Remote Desktop functions well as a management tool because it allows employees responsible for managing, maintaining, and configuring client operating systems to perform many of those tasks remotely.

> *NOTE* **REMOTE MANAGEMENT TERMINOLOGY**
>
> For the purposes of clarity, when discussing remote management throughout this lesson, the management computer is the computer that the user is logged on to directly. The remote computer is the computer to which the user is making a remote desktop connection. All remote management technologies require that there be network connectivity between the management computer and the remote computer.

You can perform a logon using Remote Desktop if no one is currently logged on to the remote computer, though the remote computer does need to be switched on. If Wake On LAN is configured for the physical network interface, it is possible for the computer to wake from sleep or hibernate mode when an incoming remote desktop session is detected, though configuring Windows 7 to support this functionality is beyond the scope of the 70-680 exam. If a user locks the screen on their client running Windows 7, it is possible for that user to connect to that client remotely and resume the session over Remote Desktop. It is also possible for the user to disconnect from that session and resume it when they log back on directly.

If another user is logged on when an incoming Remote Desktop session is initiated, she will receive a message indicating that another user wants to log on remotely, as shown in Figure 7-16. The logged-on user has the ability to deny the remote user access, even when the remote user has administrative privileges and the logged-on user does not. If a user is logged on remotely and another user attempts a local logon, the remote user will be prompted in the same way. A currently logged-on user, whether that logon is remote or local, is able to deny another user's logon request. If a user is disconnected, her session remains in memory and she can reconnect at any time, similar to the way a user's session remains in memory when you use the Switch User option from the Shutdown menu.

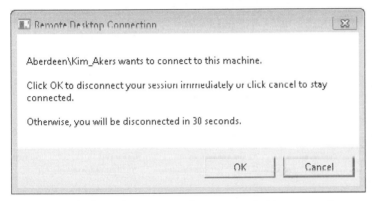

FIGURE 7-16 The logged-on user can deny remote desktop connection.

You can make Remote Desktop connections through NAT devices to hosts on the Internet. A technology available in Windows Server 2008 called Terminal Services Gateway allows users to make Remote Desktop connections from hosts that have Internet connectivity to hosts on an internal protected network. It is possible to make Remote Desktop connections over modem and VPN links. Remote Desktop connections can use both the IPv4 and IPv6 protocol and it is possible to make a Remote Desktop connection when a computer connects to the network using DirectAccess.

Configuring Remote Desktop

You can make remote desktop connections only to computers running the Professional, Enterprise, and Ultimate editions of Windows 7. Other editions of Windows 7 do not support incoming Remote Desktop connections, but all editions include the Remote Desktop client software. Remote Desktop is not enabled by default on computers running Windows 7. You can enable it on the Remote tab of the System Properties dialog box, which is shown in Figure 7-17. When you enable Remote Desktop you need to choose whether to allow connections from computers running any version of Remote Desktop or to restrict connections to computers running Remote Desktop with Network Level Authentication. Only clients running Windows Vista and Windows 7 support Network Level Authentication by default. It is possible to configure computers running Windows XP with SP3 to support Network Level Authentication, but this feature is not enabled by default. If you need to connect to a client running Windows 7 from a client running Windows XP client that does not have SP3 applied, it is necessary to configure the option that allows connections from computers running any version of Remote Desktop.

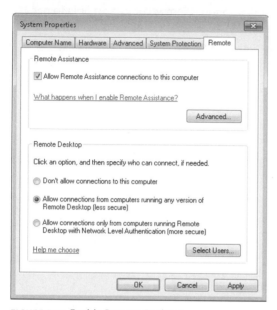

FIGURE 7-17 Enable Remote Desktop

When you enable Remote Desktop, Windows Firewall automatically updates rules to allow Remote Desktop connections to be made to the computer. If you reset Windows Firewall to its default settings, you need to re-enable the Remote Desktop firewall rules manually. You can also re-enable these rules by disabling and then re-enabling Remote Desktop.

If you want to allow a standard user to connect remotely using Remote Desktop, you must add her account to the local Remote Desktop Users group. Only members of the Administrators and Remote Desktop Users local groups are able to make connections to a client running Windows 7 using Remote Desktop. When you click the Select Users button on the Remote tab of the System Properties dialog box, it opens the Remote Desktop Users dialog box, as shown in Figure 7-18. Any user you add using this dialog box is added automatically to the Remote Desktop Users group and this list displays all current members of that group, no matter what method was used to add the user accounts.

You will configure Remote Desktop in the practice at the end of this lesson.

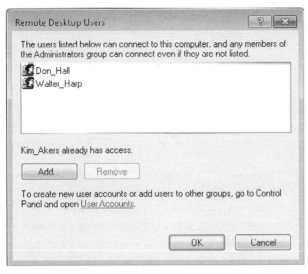

FIGURE 7-18 Remote Desktop Users

Remote Assistance

Both Remote Assistance and Remote Desktop allow the user at the management computer to see the desktop and applications that are present on the remote computer. The difference between Windows Remote Assistance and Remote Desktop is that a user is logged on to the remote computer and initiates the remote assistance session, whereas a Remote Desktop session is initiated on the management computer. Remote Assistance is a support tool used by help-desk staff to allow them to view the screen of the person to whom they are providing assistance. Remote Assistance reduces the need for nontechnical users to accurately describe the problem that they are having with their computers because support personnel can see the desktop directly. Unlike the version of Remote Assistance that shipped with Windows XP, the version of Remote Assistance that is included with Windows 7 does not include a voice client. If you are going to talk to the person whom you are helping using Remote Assistance, you are going to have to use another method, such as the telephone.

Remote Assistance can be used only with the permission of the person that is logged on to the remote computer. Remote Assistance invitations can be used for only a limited time, and once the Remote Assistance application is closed, it is not possible to connect to the remote computer through a Remote Assistance session. The person logged on to the remote computer can terminate the Remote Assistance session at any time. The default connection setting for Remote Assistance has the person providing assistance only able to view, but not interact, with the desktop on the remote computer. The person providing assistance can request control, as shown in Figure 7-19, which allows him to interact directly. This is useful if the person providing assistance needs to respond to a User Account Control prompt. The person receiving the assistance can return the session to view only by clicking the Stop Sharing button on the Windows Remote Assistance control. They can also block the person helping them from viewing their desktop temporarily by pausing the Remote Assistance session.

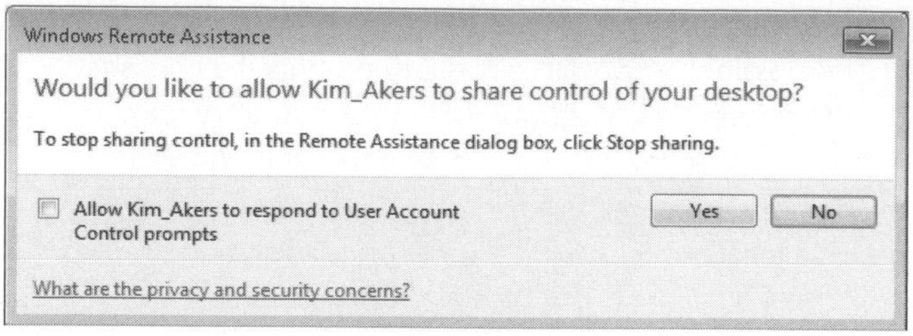

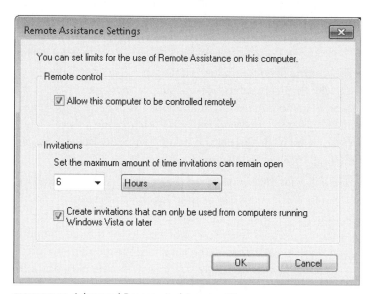

FIGURE 7-19 Permission to share control

Like Remote Desktop, Remote Assistance connections can occur only when there is connectivity between the management computer and the remote computer. This means that you cannot resolve a network connectivity problem using Remote Assistance because that connectivity problem blocks a Remote Assistance connection. The Windows Remote Assistance rule is enabled in Windows Firewall when Windows Remote Assistance is enabled on a computer.

You enable Windows Remote Assistance on the Remote Tab of the System Properties dialog box. Windows Remote Assistance is enabled by default on computers running Windows 7. The advanced Remote Assistance settings, which can be accessed by clicking the Advanced button on the Remote tab of the System Properties dialog box, allow you to configure a maximum time that an invitation can remain open and to limit Remote Assistance so that connections can only be made from computers that are running Windows Vista or later. This dialog box is shown in Figure 7-20.

FIGURE 7-20 Advanced Remote Assistance settings

When you start Windows Remote Assistance, you are presented with the option of configuring an invitation or responding to an invitation, as shown in Figure 7-21. When a user requesting assistance selects the Invite Someone You Trust To Help You option, she is able to choose among three options: saving the invitation as a file, using e-mail to send the invitation, or using Easy Connect. It is possible to use the e-mail option only if a compatible e-mail program is installed on the client running Windows 7. It is important to remember that, unlike previous versions of Windows, Windows 7 does not ship with a built-in e-mail application so you cannot assume that one is automatically present. You can use the Easy Connect connection method only on a local network if the Peer Name Resolution Protocol is present on a local server running Windows Server 2008 or if you want to use Easy Connect to solicit assistance over the Internet (if your router supports this protocol). Easy Connect allows you to send an assistance request without having to forward an invitation.

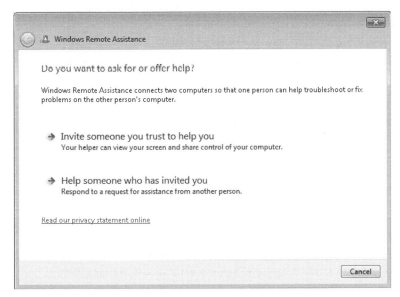

FIGURE 7-21 Asking for or offering remote assistance

Not only must the person providing remote assistance receive an invitation, but she also needs to provide a password that can be given to her only by the person requesting assistance, as shown in Figure 7-22. For security reasons, this password should be provided using a different method to the one used to transmit the invitation file. If the user requesting remote assistance closes the Windows Remote Assistance dialog box, it is not possible for the remote user to make a connection, even if the invitation period has not expired. Once this dialog box is closed, Windows Remote Assistance needs to be restarted and a new remote assistance invitation issued because the previous one is no longer valid.

FIGURE 7-22 Waiting for a connection

When the remotely connecting user makes the connection with the password forwarded to them, the person requesting assistance is given a warning that the remotely connecting user will be able to see whatever is on the desktop, as shown in Figure 7-23. Once the connection is accepted, the Windows Remote Assistance session starts. The session can be terminated by either party at any time.

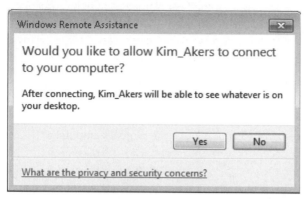

FIGURE 7-23 The allow assistance connection

✔ **Quick Check**

1. What setting do you need to configure to allow Remote Desktop connections from computers running Windows XP Professional SP2.

2. What protocol must be present on local computers running Windows Server 2008 if you are going to forward Windows Remote Assistance invitations using Easy Connect in a LAN environment?

Quick Check Answers

1. You must configure Remote Desktop to allow connections from computers running any version of Remote Desktop, rather than only allowing connections from computers running Remote Desktop with Network Level Authentication.

2. The Peer Name Resolution Protocol feature must be installed on Windows Server 2008 for clients running Windows 7 on a LAN to be able to use Easy Connect.

Windows Remote Management Service

The Windows Remote Management service allows you to execute commands on a remote computer, either from the command prompt using WinRS or from Windows PowerShell. Before you can use WinRS or Windows PowerShell for remote management tasks, it is necessary to configure the target computer using the WinRM command. To configure the target computer, you must run the command *WinRM quickconfig* from an elevated command prompt. Executing *WinRM quickconfig* does the following:

- Starts the WinRM service
- Configures the WinRM service startup type to delayed automatic start
- Configures the LocalAccountTokenFilterPolicy to grant administrative rights remotely to local users
- Configures the WinRM listener on http://* to accept WS-Man requests
- Configures the WinRM firewall exception

If you are attempting to manage a computer remotely that is not a member of the same AD DS domain as the management computer, you may need to configure the management computer to trust the remote computer. This is necessary only when you do not use Hypertext Protocol Secure (HTTPS) or Kerberos to authenticate the remote computer's identity. You need to configure this trust because of the bidirectional nature of remote management traffic and the fact that authentication credentials will be forwarded to the remote computer. You can configure this trust using the following command:

```
winrm set winrm/config/client @{TrustedHosts="remote computer name or IP address"}
```

It is also possible to configure Windows Remote Management through Group Policy. The relevant policies are located in the Computer Configuration\Administrative Templates\ Windows Components\Windows Remote Management node and are split between WinRM Client and WinRM Service policies. These policies relate to authentication settings and TrustedHosts.

Windows Remote Shell for Remote Management

You can use WinRS to execute command-line utilities or scripts on a remote computer. To use WinRS, open a command prompt and prefix the command that you want to run on the remote computer with the *WinRS –r:RemoteComputerName* command. For example, to execute the *Ipconfig* command on a computer named Aberdeen, issue the command:

```
WinRS –r:Aberdeen ipconfig
```

If the computer is on the local network, you can use its NetBIOS name. If the computer is on a remote network, you may need to specify its fully qualified domain name (FQDN). It is also possible to specify credentials to be used on the remote computer. For example, to run the command *net accounts,* which displays information about a computer's password policy on a computer named Aberdeen.contoso.internal using the Kim_Akers user account, issue the command

```
WinRS –r:http://aberdeen.contoso.internal –u:Kim_Akers net accounts
```

If you do not specify a password using the *–p:password* option, you are prompted to enter a password after you execute the command. You can configure WinRS options through Group Policy in the Computer Configuration\Administrative Templates\Windows Components\Windows Remote Shell node. The policies are shown in Figure 7-24 and can be used to configure settings such as idle timeouts, maximum concurrent remote shells, and whether remote shell access is allowed. You will configure and use Windows Remote Shell in a practice exercise at the end of this lesson.

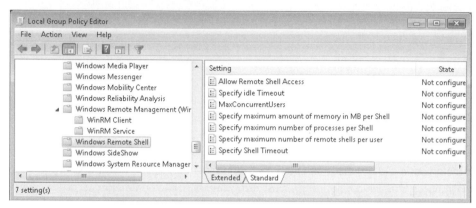

FIGURE 7-24 WinRS policies

Windows PowerShell Remote Management

Windows PowerShell V2 supports remote management of computers. Windows PowerShell V2 is the version of Windows PowerShell that is included with Windows 7. If you want to use a computer running an earlier version of Windows to manage Windows 7 using Windows PowerShell, it is necessary to update to Windows PowerShell V2 or later. You can only use Windows PowerShell to manage a computer remotely if you have configured the Windows Remote Management service as outlined earlier in this lesson. The syntax of remote Windows PowerShell commands is straightforward:

```
Icm hostname {powershell-command}
```

You will use Windows PowerShell remotely in one of the practice exercises at the end of this lesson.

> **MORE INFO   REMOTE WINDOWS POWERSHELL**
>
> To learn more about using Windows PowerShell to manage other computers remotely, consult the following post on the Windows PowerShell Blog: *http://blogs.msdn.com/ powershell/archive/2008/05/10/remoting-with-powershell-quickstart.aspx.*

> **EXAM TIP**
>
> Remember what command you need to execute on a computer if you want to configure the Remote Management Service to allow remote management through Windows PowerShell or WinRS.

Windows 7 Remote Management Options

In this practice, you explore two different remote management technologies that you can use to configure and maintain computers running Windows 7. These technologies are complementary, and there will be situations where you choose to employ one over another. For example, you might use a remote Windows PowerShell session to gather information about a computer while a user is still logged on, or you might use a Remote Desktop session to update a device driver.

EXERCISE 1   Using Remote Desktop for Remote Management

In this exercise, you configure a client running Windows 7 so that it is possible to make a connection to that client using Remote Desktop. You then connect to that client using Remote Desktop to verify the configuration is correct.

1.   Ensure that computer Canberra is turned on.

2.   Turn on computer Aberdeen and log on to it using the Kim_Akers user account.

3.   Open an elevated command prompt. Verify that network connectivity exists between computer Canberra and computer Aberdeen by issuing the command *ping Canberra*, as shown in Figure 7-25. If you are unable to obtain connectivity, enter the following commands from an elevated command prompt on both hosts:

■   netsh advfirewall firewall add rule name="ICMPv4" protocol=icmpv4:any,any dir=in action=allow

■   netsh advfirewall firewall add rule name="ICMPv6" protocol=icmpv6:any,any dir=in action=allow

FIGURE 7-25 Verifying connectivity

4.   Open the Control Panel and click Add Or Remove User Accounts. Click Create A New Account. Enter the user account name Cassie_Hicks as a Standard user and click Create Account.

5. On the Choose The Account You Would Like To Change page, click Cassie_Hicks.

6. On the Make Changes To Cassie_Hicks's Account page, click Create A Password. Enter the password **P@ssw0rd** twice and then, in the Hint box, type the page number of this page. Click Create Password. Close the Change An Account dialog box.

7. Click Start, right-click Computer, and then choose Properties. In the Control Panel Home pane, click Remote Settings.

8. On the Remote tab of the System Properties dialog box, select Allow Connections Only From Computers Running Remote Desktop With Network Level Authentication (More Secure), as shown in Figure 7-26, and then click Select Users.

FIGURE 7-26 Remote Desktop Properties

9. In the Remote Desktop Users dialog box, click Add. In the Select Users dialog box, enter the name **Cassie_Hicks** and then click OK. Click OK twice to close both the Remote Desktop Users dialog box and the System Properties dialog box.

10. Log off of Aberdeen while keeping the computer turned on. Log on to computer Canberra using the Kim_Akers user account.

11. Click Start. In the Search Programs And Files text box, type **Remote Desktop Connection**. Click the Remote Desktop Connection item.

12. In the Remote Desktop Connection dialog box, click Options. In the Computer text area, type **Aberdeen** and in the User Name area, type **Cassie_Hicks,** as shown in Figure 7-27. Click Connect.

13. In the Windows Security, Enter Your Credentials dialog box, enter the password **P@ssw0rd** for the Cassie_Hicks user account and click OK.

FIGURE 7-27 Remote Desktop Client

14. When presented with the warning that the identity of the remote computer cannot be verified, shown in Figure 7-28, click Yes.

FIGURE 7-28 Remote ID verification

15. When the connection has been established, click the Start menu and type **PowerShell** into the Search Programs And Files text box. Click the Windows PowerShell item.

16. At the PowerShell prompt, type the command **$env:ComputerName;$env:UserName** and press Enter. Verify that the command returns the values Aberdeen and Cassie Hicks. Close the PowerShell window and log off of computer Aberdeen.

EXERCISE 2   Using Windows PowerShell and WinRS for Remote Management

In this exercise, you configure a client running Windows 7 so that it can be managed remotely using Windows PowerShell and WinRS. You execute commands remotely to verify that this configuration is correct.

1. Log on to computer Aberdeen with the Kim_Akers computer account.

2. Open an elevated command prompt and issue the command **WinRM Quickconfig.** When prompted, press the Y key and press Enter twice, as shown in Figure 7-29.

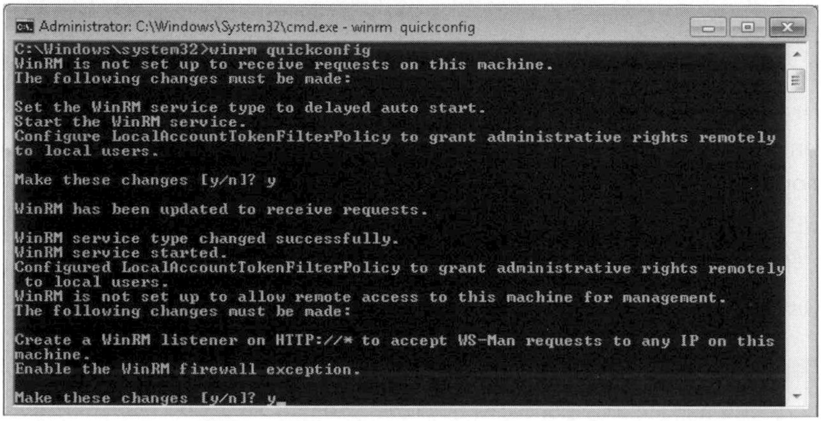

FIGURE 7-29 WinRM Quickconfig

3. Close the Command Prompt window and log off of computer Aberdeen while keeping computer Aberdeen turned on.

4. Log on to computer Canberra using the Kim_Akers user account.

5. Open an elevated command prompt.

6. Enter the command **winrm quickconfig.** Press Enter. Press the Y key and then press Enter when prompted.

7. Enter the command **winrm set winrm/config/client @{TrustedHosts="Aberdeen"}** and press Enter.

8. Enter the command **whoami.** Verify that the result is Canberra\Kim_Akers.

9. Execute the command **winrs –r:Aberdeen whoami.** Verify that the result is Aberdeen\Kim_Akers.

10. Enter the command **ipconfig.** Note the IP address information.

11. Enter the command **winrs –r:Aberdeen ipconfig.** Note the different IP address information.

12. Enter the command **PowerShell** and press Enter. This starts Windows PowerShell.

13. Enter the command **Get-Process | Sort-Object –Property CPU –Descending | Select –First 10** and press Enter. This displays a list of the top 10 processes by CPU usage on Canberra.

14. Enter the command **icm Aberdeen { Get-Process | Sort-Object –Property CPU –Descending | Select –First 10 }** and press Enter. This displays a list of the top 10 processes by CPU usage on Aberdeen.

15. Close Windows PowerShell and the command prompt, and then shut down the operating system and turn off the computer.

Lesson Summary

- Remote Desktop allows you to make a connection to a remote computer and view its desktop as though you were logged on directly.

- When Remote Desktop with Network Level Authentication is enabled, only clients running Windows Vista and Windows 7 can connect. It is possible to connect using a client running Windows XP with SP3, but it requires special configuration and is not supported by default.

- Standard users must be members of the Remote Desktop Users group before they can connect to a client running Windows 7 using Remote Desktop.

- You need to run the command *WinRM Quickconfig* from an elevated command prompt on a client that you want to manage remotely using either WinRS or Windows PowerShell. WinRM Quickconfig configures the Windows Remote Management service and appropriate firewall rules and enables the WinRM listener.

- You can use the *winrs –r:hostname* command to run a command line command remotely on the host named *hostname*.

- Only Windows PowerShell V2 and later support remote Windows PowerShell. Windows PowerShell V2 is the default version of Windows PowerShell included with Windows 7.

- You can use the *icm hostname* command to run PowerShell Command on computer *hostname* remotely.

Lesson Review

You can use the following questions to test your knowledge of the information in Lesson 2, "Windows 7 Remote Management." The questions are also available on the companion DVD if you prefer to review them in electronic form.

> **NOTE ANSWERS**
>
> Answers to these questions and explanations of why each answer choice is correct or incorrect are located in the "Answers" section at the end of the book.

1. You need to manage a computer running Windows 7 from a computer running Windows XP with SP2 when no user is logged on to the computer running Windows 7.

You want connections to be as secure as possible. Which of the following settings on the Remote tab of the System Properties dialog box should you configure?

A. Remote Assistance: Enable The Allow Remote Assistance Connections To This Computer Option

B. Remote Desktop: Don't Allow Connections To This Computer

C. Remote Desktop: Allow Connections From Computers Running Any Version Of Remote Desktop

D. Remote Desktop: Allow Connections Only From Computers Running Remote Desktop With Network Level Authentication

2. You want to user Windows PowerShell on a client running Windows 7 named Alpha to manage a client running Windows 7 named Beta. Which of the following steps do you need to take to do this?

A. Run the command *WinRM Quickconfig* from an elevated command prompt on client Alpha.

B. Run the command *WinRM Quickconfig* from an elevated command prompt on client Beta.

C. Create a WFAS rule for TCP port 80 on client Alpha.

D. Create a WFAS rule for TCP port 80 on client Beta.

3. You are logged on to a client running Windows 7 named Canberra. You want to determine the media access control (MAC) address of a client running Windows 7 named Aberdeen, which is located on another subnet. Both computers are members of the same domain and your domain user account is a member of the local administrator group on both computers. The command *WinRM Quickconfig* has been executed on all clients running Windows 7 in your organization. Which of the following commands should you execute to accomplish your goal?

A. `nslookup Aberdeen`

B. `winrs -r:Aberdeen ipconfig /all`

C. `winrs -r:Canberra ipconfig /all`

D. `arp -a`

4. Which of the following Windows PowerShell commands can you issue on a client running Windows 7 named Canberra to get a list of processes, including CPU and memory usage, on a client running Windows 7 named Aberdeen?

A. `icm Canberra {Get-Process}`

B. `icm Aberdeen {Get-Process}`

C. `winrs -r:Aberdeen Get-Process`

D. `winrs -r:Canberra Get-Process`

5. Which of the following reasons might explain why a helper is unable to connect to a Remote Assistance session when two stand-alone clients running Windows 7 are located on the same LAN?

   A. The WinRM service is disabled on Aberdeen.

   B. Client Aberdeen is configured to accept only Remote Desktop sessions that use Network Level Authentication.

   C. The helper is not a member of the Remote Desktop Users local group on Aberdeen.

   D. The Remote Assistance panel has been closed on client Aberdeen.

Chapter Review

To further practice and reinforce the skills you learned in this chapter, you can perform the following tasks:

- Review the chapter summary.
- Review the list of key terms introduced in this chapter.
- Complete the case scenarios. These scenarios set up real-world situations involving the topics of this chapter and ask you to create a solution.
- Complete the suggested practices.
- Take a practice test.

Chapter Summary

- Windows Firewall can only be configured for applications and features.
- WFAS can be configured for applications, features, services, and ports. It is possible to configure authentication and scope option for WFAS rules.
- Remote Assistance allows a user to forward an invitation to a helper that enables that helper to view the user's screen concurrently. There are several safeguards in place to stop the helper from overriding the user and taking control of the user's computer.
- Remote Desktop allows a user to connect to an existing session that the user has created on a remote client running Windows 7 or to initiate a new session.
- The Windows Remote Management service allows command-line utilities and Windows PowerShell scripts to be run remotely against clients running Windows 7.

Key Terms

Do you know what these key terms mean? You can check your answers by looking up the terms in the glossary at the end of the book.

- **connection security rule**
- **inbound rule**
- **outbound rule**
- **Windows Remote Shell**

Case Scenarios

In the following case scenarios, you apply what you've learned about subjects of this chapter. You can find answers to these questions in the "Answers" section at the end of this book.

Case Scenario 1: University Client Firewalls

You work as a desktop support technician at a local university. All client computers at the university have Windows 7 Enterprise installed. You have several support tickets that you need to resolve. The first ticket involves an academic who wants to run a personal Web site off his laptop computer when he is presenting at conferences and is connected to an ad hoc network. Attendees at his presentations should be able to connect to download information from the site, but people from elsewhere should not be able to connect. The second ticket involves students in the undergraduate laboratory running a stand-alone file sharing application off USB flash drives. You know the port that this application uses, but the name of the application appears to vary. The third ticket involves a postgraduate computer laboratory that has 25 stand-alone clients running Windows 7. You want to ensure that each of these computers has the same WFAS configuration.

With this information in mind, answer the following questions:

1. What steps would you take to resolve the first ticket?

2. What steps would you take to resolve the second ticket?

3. What steps would you take to resolve the third ticket?

Case Scenario 2: Antarctic Desktop Support

Your organization is responsible for supporting a small scientific research facility in Antarctica. The person responsible for IT support at the facility has come down with a serious illness and has been confined to the base medical facility for the next week. In her place, you are providing client operating system support to 30 scientists stationed at the facility. Your office in Tasmania is connected to the base by a high-speed Internet link. All clients running Windows 7 have Remote Desktop enabled.

With these facts in mind, answer the following questions:

1. One of the scientists needs an application installed on their client running Windows 7 that you cannot deploy through Group Policy. You have the ability to elevate your privileges on the computer, but this scientist does not. How can you resolve this situation?

2. Another staff member at the Tasmanian office needs to connect to a client running Windows 7 at the Antarctic base to verify some scientific results but is unable to do so. You check and find that you are able to establish a Remote Desktop connection. What steps can you take to resolve this problem?

3. You need to be able to run Windows PowerShell scripts remotely against the clients running Windows 7. What steps do you need to take before you can do this?

Suggested Practices

To help you master the exam objectives presented in this chapter, complete the following tasks.

Configure Windows Firewall

- **Practice 1**   Configure a WFAS incoming rule for port 1138 for the UDP protocol for IP addresses between 10.10.10.1 and 10.10.10.255.

- **Practice 2**   Configure a WFAS incoming rule for the program Calc.exe in the C:\Windows\System32 folder.

Configure Remote Management

- **Practice 1**   Create and execute a WinRS command that provides a list of all local groups on a remote client running Windows 7.

- **Practice 2**   Create a Windows PowerShell script that lists the free space left on the volumes on a remote computer.

Take a Practice Test

The practice tests on this book's companion DVD offer many options. For example, you can test yourself on just one exam objective, or you can test yourself on all the 70-680 certification exam content. You can set up the test so that it closely simulates the experience of taking a certification exam, or you can set it up in study mode so that you can look at the correct answers and explanations after you answer each question.

> **MORE INFO   PRACTICE TESTS**
>
> For details about all the practice test options available, see the section entitled "How to Use the Practice Tests," in the Introduction to this book.

CHAPTER 8

BranchCache and Resource Sharing

People in the workplace rarely create documents that only they access. This is because organizational data is generally useful only when it is shared among people in the organization. People generally spend countless hours creating and formatting documents in Microsoft Office Word because they expect other people to read those documents. They write documents to explain ideas or to transmit data to other people because, generally, it is not necessary to write a document to explain something to *yourself*. The first part of this chapter looks at the methods you can use to share data stored on computers running Windows 7. This includes the simplified technique of sharing data through HomeGroups and the more complex technique of configuring shared folders. The second part of this chapter looks at how you can restrict the sharing of data, ensuring that only the people who should to be able to view that data are actually able to view it. You can do this by applying file and folder permissions restricting who can access the data and by using encryption to ensure that data is encoded so that only specific people can decode it. The final part of this chapter looks at how you can speed up data access for people that are located in small branch offices in larger organizations through a new Windows 7 feature named BranchCache.

Exam objectives in this chapter:
- Configure shared resources.
- Configure file and folder access.
- Configure BranchCache.

Lessons in this chapter:

Before You Begin

To complete the exercises in the practices in this chapter, you need to have done the following:

- Installed Windows 7 on a stand-alone client PC named Canberra, as described in Chapter 1, "Install, Migrate, or Upgrade to Windows 7."

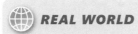

REAL WORLD

Orin Thomas

Although file and folder sharing at the client rather than the server level can be quite useful for small businesses that do not have the resources to deploy a dedicated file server, I've found that if people are not paying attention, shared folders on client computers can cause a lot of problems. Perhaps this is because people think about shared folders on a server and shared folders on a client computer quite differently. When you have a file server, people are very aware that files saved in that location will be visible to other people in the organization. When you deploy file servers, it is relatively simple to set up file shares on the basis of group membership, and people remember that a file that should be visible only to managers gets put in the Managers shared folder. Sure, you can do this with client computers, but it generally takes more effort to configure different shares with specific permissions on each client computer. It takes even more effort to get the people that actually use these computers to remember how permissions actually work.

A colleague of mine had to deal with a meltdown that occurred at one client he worked for because a manager had saved performance reviews to a local folder that was visible to everyone on the network. Although there had been a specific shared folder set up that did limit document access to the administrative assistant and the company director, the manager hadn't paid attention when this was explained to him. He worked off the assumption that no one else would see the reviews because he told only his administrative assistant and the company's director that the documents were present in the shared folder.

Shared printers can cause similar problems. In many small businesses, the people who run the company get the best hardware. The person that ends up with the most fully featured printer gets it because she is the person who owns the company and signs the purchase orders. The printer ends up shared so that the people who might use features such as automatic double-sided printing and collation can actually do so. The downside to this is that these people have to keep going across to the senior staff member's work space to retrieve their printing. At one organization I know, several people had to be given keys to the boss's office so they could access their printing when he was away on business. Rather than move the printer to a more public location, the boss ended up authorizing the purchase of another printer.

Lesson 1: Sharing Resources

Most home networks and very small businesses do not need a dedicated file and print server. There are usually only a few computers, and the number of files that people need to share is minimal. When you do not have access to a dedicated file and print server, you can use the resource sharing options included in Windows 7 to share files, folders, and printers. Windows 7 includes a new feature named HomeGroups, which simplifies the process of sharing files and printers on small networks where Active Directory Domain Services (AD DS) is not present.

After this lesson, you will be able to:

- Configure HomeGroup settings.
- Configure sharing settings using Network And Sharing Center.
- Share folders.
- Manage printer permissions.

Estimated lesson time: 40 minutes

Network And Sharing Center

You can use the Network And Sharing Center, displayed in Figure 8-1, to configure HomeGroup and advanced sharing options. You can use Network And Sharing Center to determine which networks the computer is currently joined to and the network designation assigned to those networks. You can use this tool to reset the designation assigned to an existing network. For example, you can change a Work network to a Home network by clicking the Work Network item under the network name and then clicking the Home Network option in the Set Network Location dialog box. You will learn more about the HomeGroup sharing options later in this lesson.

You can access the Advanced Sharing Settings dialog box by clicking the Change Advanced Sharing Settings item in Network And Sharing Center. You can use this dialog box, shown in Figure 8-2, to configure the sharing options for each different network profile. Because network profiles apply on a per-network interface basis, this means that different sharing options apply on a per-interface basis when a client running Windows 7 connects to multiple networks; for example, when you connect to a home network using a wireless network adapter and to an organizational network using DirectAccess.

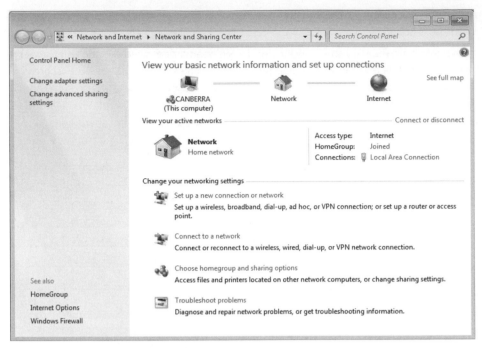

FIGURE 8-1 Network And Sharing Center

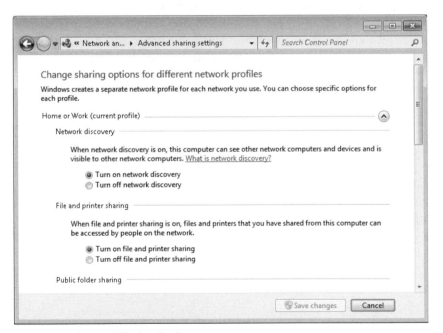

FIGURE 8-2 Advanced Sharing Settings

The sharing options that you can enable, disable, or configure using Advanced Sharing Settings are as follows:

- **Network Discovery** Network Discovery allows the client running Windows 7 to locate other computers and devices on the network. It also makes the client visible to other computers on the network. Disabling Network Discovery does not turn off other forms of sharing.

- **File And Printer Sharing** This setting enables files and printers to be shared with other clients on the network.

- **Public Folder Sharing** Enabling this setting allows network users read and write access to a public folder location. If you disable this folder, users can read and write data only to shared folders to which they have appropriate permissions.

- **Media Streaming** When you enable this setting, users on the network are able to access pictures, music, and videos hosted on the client running Windows 7. The client is also able to locate pictures, music, and videos hosted on other clients running Windows 7 on the network.

- **File Sharing Connections** This option allows you to choose between protecting file-sharing connections using 128-bit encryption or 40- or 56-bit encryption. You would choose the 40- or 56-bit encryption option for devices that do not support 128-bit encryption.

- **Password Protected Sharing** Enabling this option means that only users who have accounts configured locally on the client running Windows 7 are able to access shared resources. To allow users that do not have local accounts access to shared resources, you must disable this option.

- **HomeGroup Connections** This option decides how authentication works for connections to HomeGroup resources. If all computers in the HomeGroup have the same user name and passwords configured, you can set this option to allow Windows to manage HomeGroup connections. If different user accounts and passwords are present, you should configure the option to use user accounts and passwords to connect to other computers. This option is available only in the Home/Work network profile.

HomeGroups

HomeGroups are a simple method through which you can share resources on a home network. You can use HomeGroups only on networks that you have designated as Home networks. You cannot create a HomeGroup on a domain network, but you can join an existing HomeGroup, as shown in Figure 8-3, if one is detected. For example, you could join an existing HomeGroup when you are using your client running Windows 7 on your home network, but where you also have a connection to your organization's domain network through DirectAccess.

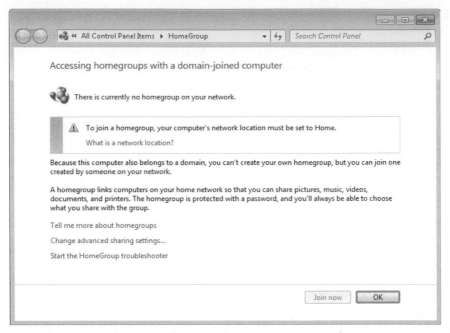

FIGURE 8-3 No HomeGroup on domain network

HomeGroups are visible as a separate node in Windows Explorer. Windows 7 displays HomeGroups by user name and computer name. This is because each user on a client running Windows 7 will share different resources with the network depending on their individual sharing settings. Figure 8-4 shows the Don_Hall (CANBERRA) and Kim_Akers (CANBERRA) HomeGroups. The Kim_Akers (CANBERRA) HomeGroup includes a custom library named Scientific Data. You will create and share this custom library in the practice at the end of this lesson.

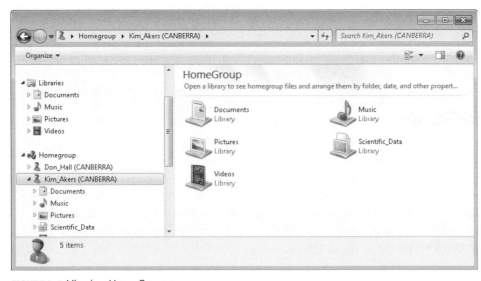

FIGURE 8-4 Viewing HomeGroups

Although only users with Administrative privileges are able to enable the HomeGroup, each standard user can choose which of their libraries to share with the HomeGroup. For example, Kim_Akers can choose to share her Documents, Music, Pictures, and Videos libraries, whereas Don_Hall may choose to share only his Documents library. Users do not need to be logged on for their HomeGroups to be available to other users on the network. Each user's HomeGroup share is available so long as the computer that hosts it is turned on and connected to the home network.

If a HomeGroup is present on the network, the details are displayed when you open the HomeGroup item in the Network And Sharing Center.

To join a HomeGroup if one already exists on your network, perform the following steps:

1. Open the HomeGroup item from the Network And Sharing Center.

2. If a HomeGroup is detected on another computer, the details of this HomeGroup are displayed. Contact the person who configured the HomeGroup and then click Join Now.

3. On the Join A HomeGroup page, shown in Figure 8-5, select which items you want to share with the other computers that are members of the HomeGroup, and click Next.

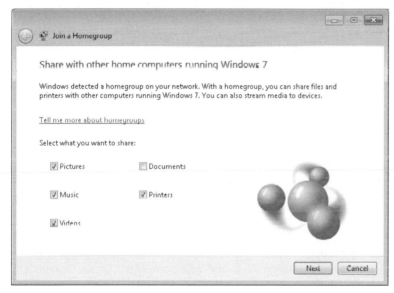

FIGURE 8-5 Share items with HomeGroup

4. Enter the HomeGroup password that you have acquired from the person who created the HomeGroup. Once the password has been accepted, you have joined the HomeGroup.

To leave the HomeGroup, open the HomeGroup item in the Network And Sharing Center and then click Leave.

Shared Folders

Shared folders allow you to share data stored on your computer with other users on your network. You can share individual folders by right-clicking the folder you wish to share, choosing Properties, and then clicking the Share tab of the folder's properties, as shown in Figure 8-6. This page provides two different sharing options: Share and Advanced Sharing. You can use shared folders when you cannot use HomeGroups, such as when you want to share resources on a Work network.

FIGURE 8-6 Sharing tab of folder properties

Clicking Share brings up the File Sharing dialog box, shown in Figure 8-7. You can use this dialog box to set share permissions for local user accounts, the Everyone group, or the HomeGroup. When you connect a client running Windows 7 to a domain, you can also specify domain user accounts and groups. You cannot use this dialog box to specify local groups. The user account that you use to share the folder with is assigned the Owner permission automatically. It is also possible to assign the Read/Write permissions, which allows users to add files, delete files, and modify files in the shared folder, and the Read permission, which allows users to access files in the shared folder but not modify or delete them.

Clicking Advanced Sharing brings up the Advanced Sharing dialog box, shown in Figure 8-8. This dialog box allows you to limit the number of users who are able to access the share. Use this when you need to restrict the number of people that are connected to a share for performance reasons. Clicking Permissions allows you to configure permissions for local groups, local users, domain groups, or domain users.

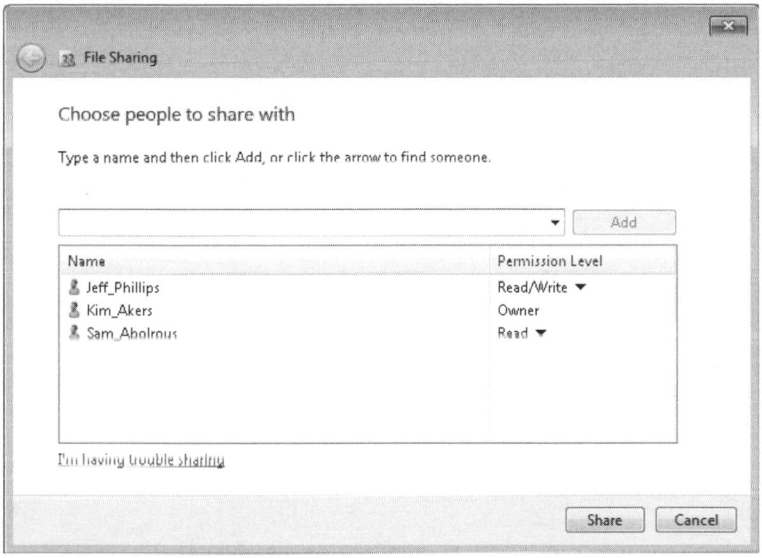

FIGURE 8-7 Basic file sharing

FIGURE 8-8 Advanced Sharing

As you can see in Figure 8-9, these permissions have different names from those that are available from the basic File Sharing dialog box but allow you to do the same things. The Read permission allows a user or group to access a file or folder but does not allow modification or deletion. The Change permission includes the read permission but also allows you to add files, delete files, and modify files in the shared folder. This permission is equivalent to the Read/Write permission in the basic File Sharing dialog box. The Full Control permission includes all the rights conferred by the Change and Read permissions. It also allows the user assigned that permission to modify the permissions of other users. Full Control is equivalent to the basic sharing Owner permission, though unlike basic sharing, where there can only be one user assigned the Owner permission, you can assign the Full Control permission to users and groups.

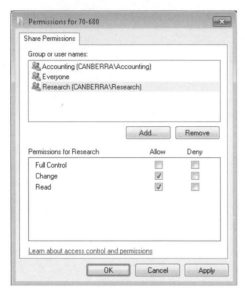

FIGURE 8-9 Advanced permissions

Clicking Caching on the Advanced Sharing dialog box allows you to access the Offline Settings dialog box, as shown in Figure 8-10. Offline settings determine whether programs and files hosted on the shared folder are available when the user, or the computer hosting them, is not available to the network. You will learn more about offline settings in Chapter 11, "BitLocker and Mobility Options."

FIGURE 8-10 Shared folder offline settings

You can manage all shared folders on a client running Windows 7 centrally using the Shared Folders node of the Computer Management console. The Shares node, shown in Figure 8-11, displays all shared folders on the computer. The Sessions node provides details on which remote users currently are connected to shared folders, where they are connecting from and how long they have been connected. The Open Files node displays the folders and files that remote users are accessing. You can edit the properties of an existing share by right-clicking it within this console and selecting properties. You can create a shared folder by right-clicking the Shares node and then clicking New Share. This starts the Create A Shared Folder Wizard. You use this wizard to create a shared folder in a practice exercise at the end of this lesson.

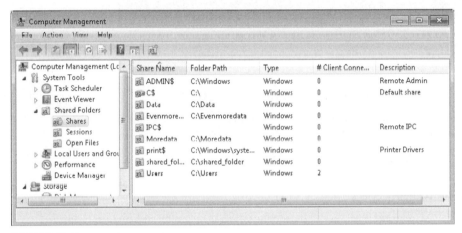

FIGURE 8-11 Viewing shares

The *Net Share* command allows for management of shared folders from the command line. You can script this command to automate the creation of shared folders on clients running Windows 7. To create a shared folder, use the command:

```
net share sharename=drive:path
```

To assign permissions to the shared folder, use the command:

```
net share sharename /grant:user Read/Change/Full
```

You can also use the *Net Share* command to configure caching options as well as limit the number of users that can connect to the shared folder. You can view the properties of a shared folder by running the command

```
net share sharename
```

as shown in Figure 8-12. You can view the properties of all shared folders, including which directories are associated with particular folders, by using the *Net Share* command without any options.

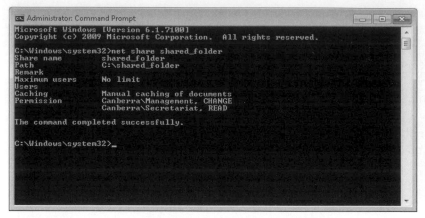

FIGURE 8-12 Shared folder properties

 **Quick Check**

- Which tool can you use to determine which files and folders that users are accessing remotely on a client running Windows 7 configured with shared folders?

Quick Check Answer

- You can use the Shared Folders\Open Files node to determine which files and folders are being accessed remotely on a client running Windows 7.

Libraries

A *library* is a virtualized collection of folders. This means that a library is not a folder that you can locate on the hard disk that contain subfolders but is a collection of links to existing folders. If you navigate to the Libraries folder from the command prompt, you will see that it contains files with the extension *library-ms,* as shown in Figure 8-13. These files are the collection of folder links and each one of them is a separate library.

Libraries allow you to collect folders that exist in many different locations locally and on the network into a single location when viewed from within Windows Explorer. For example, you can configure the Documents library so that it includes document folders located on other computers in the HomeGroup as well as folders located on the computer's hard disk drive. Libraries do not have to be limited to a certain type of file, though it is usually better to restrict them to a specific type of content as a means of simplifying navigation.

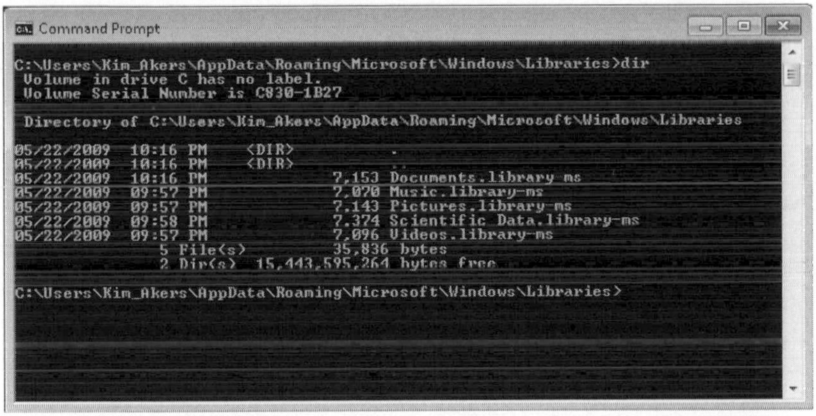

FIGURE 8-13 Libraries from the command line

You can add folders to an existing library by editing that library's properties and clicking Include A Folder, as shown in Figure 8-14. You can use the same Properties page to remove existing folders from a library. You can create a new library by navigating to the Libraries folder and clicking New Library. You will create a new library in the practice exercise at the end of this lesson.

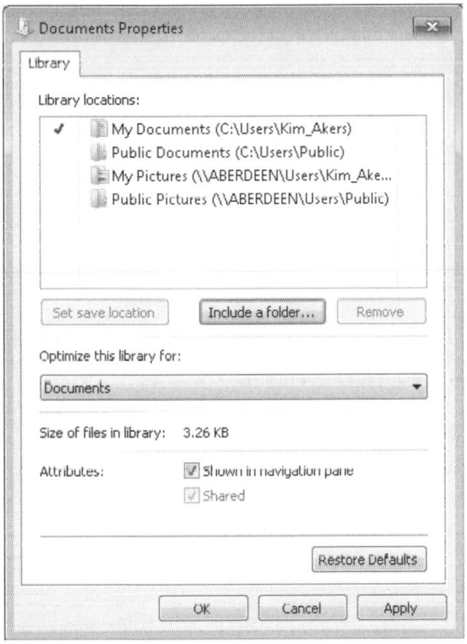

FIGURE 8-14 Library locations

Sharing Printers

Shared printers allow users on the network to send documents to a printer that is connected to a computer running Windows 7. To share a printer, enable printer sharing in HomeGroup or in Advanced Sharing Settings and then locate the printer within Devices And Printers. Right-click the printer that you wish to share, click Printer Properties, click the Sharing tab, and then enable Share This Printer, as shown in Figure 8-15. If you are going to be sharing a printer with computers running previous versions of Microsoft Windows, you can add the drivers for the printer using Additional Drivers. When you add additional drivers, other computers on the network that do not have the printer drivers installed are able to download them from the computer that is sharing the printer.

FIGURE 8-15 Printer sharing options

When you share a printer, the Everyone group is assigned the Print permission by default, as shown in Figure 8-16. This means that all members of the HomeGroup or any user that is a member of the domain in a domain environment can send print jobs to the printer. If several people use the printer, you may wish to assign one of the other available permissions to allow better printer management. The available permissions are:

- **Print** This permission allows a user to print to the printer and rearrange the documents that they have submitted to the printer.

- **Manage This Printer** Users assigned the Manage This Printer permission can pause and restart the printer, change spooler settings, adjust printer permissions, change printer properties, and share a printer.

- **Manage Documents** This permission allows users or groups to pause, resume, restart, cancel, or reorder the documents submitted by users that are in the current print queue.

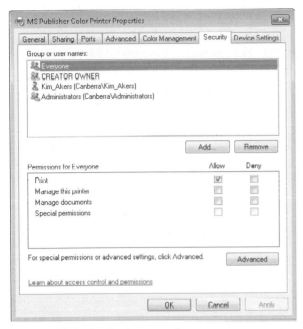

FIGURE 8-16 Printer sharing properties

MORE INFO **MANAGE PRINTER PERMISSIONS**

To learn more about managing printer permissions, consult the following page on TechNet: *http://technet.microsoft.com/en-us/library/cc773372(WS.10).aspx.*

EXAM TIP

Remember what permissions to assign a group to allow them to manage their own documents, but not to manage other documents submitted to a shared printer.

PRACTICE **Sharing Resources**

Rather than deploying a dedicated file server, many small businesses use shared folders hosted off workstations as a method of sharing documents. In this practice, you configure Windows 7 to share data using the built-in HomeGroup functionality as well as sharing through the creation of dedicated shared folders.

EXERCISE 1 Configuring Libraries and HomeGroup Settings

In this exercise, you create a new library and then share it. You also modify the HomeGroup password from the one created during setup to one that is easier for other users of the HomeGroup to remember.

1. Log on to computer Canberra using the Kim_Akers user account.

2. Using Windows Explorer, create the C:\Data, C:\Moredata, and the C:\Evenmoredata folders.

3. Click Start. In the Search Programs And Files text box, type **Libraries**. On the Start menu, click Libraries. This opens the Libraries virtual folder, as shown in Figure 8-17.

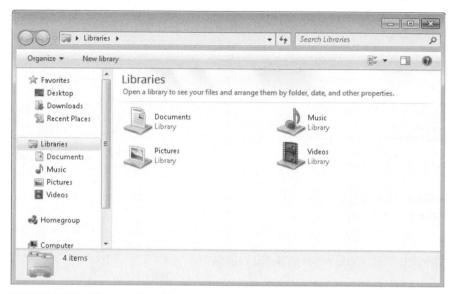

FIGURE 8-17 The Libraries virtual folder

4. Click the New Library item. This creates a new library. Name the library **Scientific_Data**.

5. Right-click the Scientific_Data folder and then choose Properties. This opens the Scientific_Data Properties dialog box. Click Include A Folder, navigate to and select the C:\Data folder, and click Include Folder. Repeat this step for the C:\Moredata and C:\Evenmoredata folders.

6. Verify that the Scientific_Data Properties dialog box matches Figure 8-18, and then click OK.

7. Right-click the Scientific_Data library, choose Share With, and then click HomeGroup (Read).

8. If you are presented with the File Sharing dialog box, shown in Figure 8-19, click Yes, Share The Items.

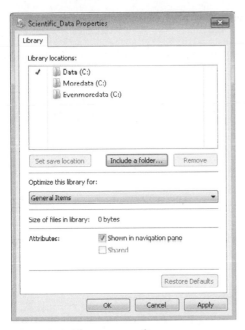

FIGURE 8-18 Library properties

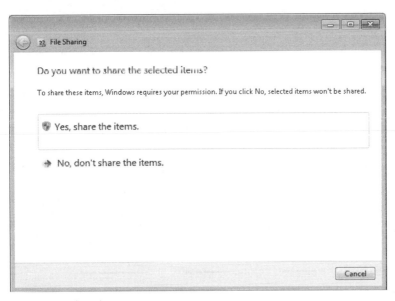

FIGURE 8-19 Share items

9. Click Start. In the Search Programs And Files text box, type **HomeGroup.** In the Start menu, click the HomeGroup item. This opens the HomeGroup control panel.

10. Click the Change The Password item. On the Change Your HomeGroup Password dialog box, click Change The Password.

11. On the Type A New Password For Your HomeGroup page, enter the password **P@ssw0rd** and then click Next.

12. Verify that your HomeGroup password settings match those shown in Figure 8-20, and then click Finish.

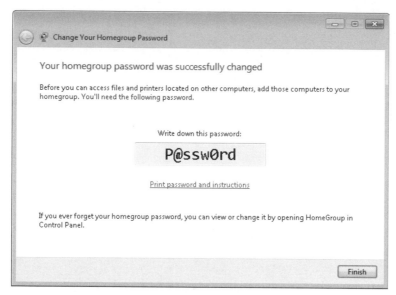

FIGURE 8-20 HomeGroup password changed

EXERCISE 2   Advanced Folder Sharing

In this exercise, you share a folder using the Create A Shared Folder Wizard. You would use this method to share a folder when you connect your computer to a Domain network. When you connect your computer to a domain network, you cannot use the HomeGroup functionality of Windows 7, though it is possible to share libraries directly.

1. If necessary, log on to the Canberra computer using the Kim_Akers user account.

2. Open an elevated command prompt and issue the following commands:

```
Net localgroup Management /add
Net localgroup Secretariat /add
Mkdir c:\shared_folder
```

3. Type **exit** to close the elevated command prompt.

4. Click Start. In the Search Programs And Files text box, type **Computer Management.** In the Start menu, click Computer Management. This opens the Computer Management console.

5. Expand the System Tools\Shared Folders node. Right-click the Shares node and then choose New Share. This starts the Create A Shared Folder Wizard. Click Next.

6. In the Folder Path: text box, type **c:\shared_folder**, as shown in Figure 8-21, and then click Next.

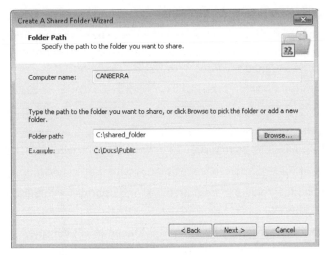

FIGURE 8-21 Specifying a shared folder path

7. In the Name, Description, And Settings page, accept the default settings, and then click Next.

8. On the Shared Folder Permissions page, select Customize Permissions and then click Custom.

9. On the Share Permissions tab, select the Everyone group and then click Remove. Click Add. In the Select Users Or Groups dialog box, type **Management; Secretariat** and then click OK.

10. Configure the Secretariat group with the Read (Allow) permission. Configure the Management group with the Change (Allow) permission, as shown in Figure 8-22. Click OK.

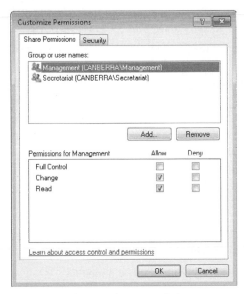

FIGURE 8-22 Custom share permissions

11. Click Finish twice to close the Create A Shared Folder Wizard.

12. From an elevated command prompt, issue the command **net share shared_folder** to verify that the Management group is assigned the Change permission and the Secretariat group has been assigned the Read permission.

Lesson Summary

- HomeGroups can be used on networks that have the Home network location designation. They make it easier to share resources in environments without AD DS.

- Libraries are collections of folders. You can share libraries with the HomeGroup.

- Shared folders allow individual folders to be shared. Sharing options for folders are more detailed than for Libraries.

- You can manage shared folders through the Computer Management console, Windows Explorer, and the *Net Share* command. The Computer Management console allows for the centralized administration of shared folders.

- The Read printer permission allows users to control their own documents. The Manage Documents permission allows users to manage all documents submitted to the printer. The Manage Printers printer permission allows users to control printer settings and configure printer permissions.

Lesson Review

You can use the following questions to test your knowledge of the information in Lesson 1, "Sharing Resources." The questions are also available on the companion DVD if you prefer to review them in electronic form.

> **NOTE** **ANSWERS**
>
> Answers to these questions and explanations of why each answer choice is correct or incorrect are located in the "Answers" section at the end of the book.

1. You are responsible for maintaining a computer running Windows 7 Enterprise that is used in a university laboratory and is hooked up to four different scientific instruments. Each of these instruments outputs its data to a directory named Data. Each instrument's data directory is located on a different volume on the computer's hard disk drive. You want to share this data with other computers in the laboratory through the common HomeGroup. Which of the following should you do? (Choose all that apply; each answer forms part of a complete solution.)

   A. Share each Data folder.

   B. Create a library named Sci_Data.

   C. Add each instrument's separate Data folder to the Sci_Data library.

   D. Share the Sci_Data library using the HomeGroup control panel.

2. You do consulting work for a small business. This small business has a single color laser printer. This printer is shared off the administrative assistant's client running Windows 7. The administrative assistant is not a member of the local Administrators group. You want to allow the administrative assistant to reorder jobs in the print queue and delete them if necessary. The administrative assistant should be able to do this to any documents in the queue. The administrative assistant should not be able to reconfigure printer permissions. Which of the following should you do to accomplish this goal?

   A. Assign the administrative assistant the Print permission.

   B. Assign the administrative assistant the Manage This Printer permission.

   C. Assign the administrative assistant the Manage Documents permission.

   D. Add the administrative assistant's account to the Power Users group.

3. Which of the following tools can you use to determine which shared folders a client running Windows 7 hosts and the local folders that are associated with those shares? (Choose all that apply.)

   A. The *Net Share* command

   B. The Computer Management console

   C. Libraries

   D. Network And Sharing Center

4. You have created a local group on a client running Windows 7 named Accounting. Which of the following share permissions should you assign to the accounting group to ensure that users are able to add, modify, and delete files located in the Accounting shared folder without giving members of the group the ability to modify shared folder permissions?

   A. Read

   B. Modify

   C. Full Control

   D. Owner

5. Which of the following Advanced Sharing Settings options should you configure to ensure that shared resources on a client running Windows 7 are visible to all other computers in the HomeGroup?

   A. Public Folder Sharing

   B. File Sharing Connections

   C. Password Protected Sharing

   D. Network Discovery

Lesson 2: Folder and File Access

In many Windows 7 deployments, multiple people have to use the same computer. When multiple people use the same computer and store their files locally, it becomes necessary to ensure that some form of security exists so that one user is able to look at another user's files only if he has the appropriate permissions. Windows 7 allows you to do this through file and folder permissions, as well as encryption through Encrypting File System (EFS).

After this lesson, you will be able to:
- Configure file and folder permissions.
- Resolve effective permissions issues.
- Encrypt files and folders.

Estimated lesson time: 40 minutes

File and Folder Permissions

You can apply NTFS file and folder permissions to individual user accounts or groups. NTFS file and folder permissions determine access rights to files and folders. These access rights apply whether the user logs on directly to the client running Windows 7 or is accessing the client running Windows 7 over the network. You can set file and folder permissions only to files and folders hosted on NTFS volumes. It is not possible to set file and folder permissions to files and folders hosted on FAT or FAT32 volumes.

There are six standard permissions that can be assigned to a file or a folder. These permissions include the following:

- **Full Control**   When applied to folders, allows the reading, writing, changing, and deletion of files and subfolders. When applied to a file, permits reading, writing, changing, and deletion of the file. Allows modification of permissions on files and folders.

- **Modify**   When applied to folders, allows the reading, writing, changing, and deletion of files and subfolders. When applied to a file, permits reading, writing, changing, and deletion of the file. Does not allow the modification of permissions on files and folders.

- **Read & Execute**   When applied to folders, allows the content of the folder to be accessed and executed. When applied to a file, allows the file to be accessed and executed.

- **List Folder Contents**   Can be applied only to folders, allows the contents of the folder to be viewed.

- **Read**   When applied to folders, allows content to be accessed. When applied to a file, allows the contents to be accessed. Differs from Read & Execute in that it does not allow files to be executed.

- **Write**   When applied to folders, allows adding of files and subfolders. When applied to a file, allows a user to modify, but not delete, a file.

You can assign these permissions to a user or group by viewing a folder's properties and clicking the Security tab. You can configure permissions with the Allow or Deny setting, or provide no setting. Deny permissions always override Allow permissions. If a user is not explicitly assigned an Allow permission, she cannot perform that function.

Figure 8-23 shows that the user Kim Akers has the Read & Execute (Allow), List Folder Contents (Allow), and Read (Allow) permissions for the Temp folder. Other permissions, such as Modify, have been assigned no setting. Unless the Modify (Allow) permission is assigned through membership in another group, Kim Akers is unable to modify files in the Temp folder.

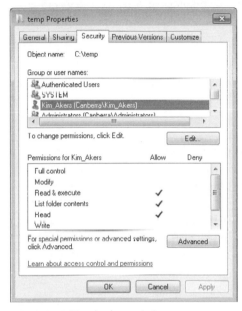

FIGURE 8-23 Standard permissions

When you set the Allow permissions for some permission types, other Allow permissions are included automatically. For example, if you set the Read & Execute (Allow) permission, Windows automatically sets the List Folder Contents (Allow) and Read (Allow) permissions. Similarly, a Deny permission for one permission type can also apply to other permission types. The permissions that also apply when you assign a particular type of permission are included in Table 8-1.

TABLE 8-1 Included Permissions

PERMISSION	INCLUDED
Full Control	Full Control, Modify, Read & Execute, List Folder Contents, Read, Write
Modify	Modify, Read & Execute, List Folder Contents, Read, Write
Read & Execute	Read & Execute, List Folder Contents, Read
List Folder Contents	List Folder Contents
Read	Read
Write	Write

Special Permissions

The six NTFS permissions are actually collections of special permissions. This is why other permissions are included automatically when you assign permissions such as Modify and Read & Execute. The collection of special permissions that are assigned when you assign the Read & Execute permission include all the special permissions that make up the List Folder Contents and Read permissions. The six NTFS permissions are adequate for the majority of situations. If you encounter an unusual situation where you want more granular permissions, you can modify the special permissions. This is done by clicking the Advanced button on the Security tab of a file or folder's properties, clicking Change Permissions, and then clicking Edit. The Permissions Entry dialog box is shown in Figure 8-24.

FIGURE 8-24 Special permissions

The special permissions that make up each of the six NTFS permissions is shown in Table 8-2. The List Folder Contents special permission applies only to folders and does not apply to individual files. Special permissions are included here for the sake of completeness and are unlikely to be addressed directly by the 70-680 exam.

TABLE 8-2 Special Permissions and NTFS Permissions

SPECIAL PERMISSION	FULL CONTROL	MODIFY	READ & EXECUTE	LIST FOLDER CONTENTS	READ	WRITE
Traverse Folder/ Execute File	X	X	X	X		
List Folder/Read Data	X	X	X	X	X	
Read Attributes	X	X	X	X	X	
Read Extended Attributes	X	X	X	X	X	
Create Files/Write Data	X	X				X
Create Folders/ Append Data	X	X				X
Write Attributes	X	X				X
Write Extended Attributes	X	X				X
Delete Subfolders and Files	X					
Delete	X	X				
Read Permissions	X	X	X	X	X	X
Change Permissions	X					
Take Ownership	X					

Inheriting Permissions

Newly created files and folders inherit the permissions that are assigned to the folder in which they are created. For example, if you have a folder named Alpha that has the Modify (Allow) permission assigned to the Development group, any files or folders that you create in folder Alpha also have the Modify (Allow) permission assigned to the Development group by default.

It is possible to override a file or folder's inherited permissions by editing the permissions, clicking Advanced, clicking Change Permissions, and then clearing the Include Inheritable Permissions From This Object's Parent option, as shown in Figure 8-25. When you clear the Include Inheritable Permissions From This Object's Parent option, you have the option of copying the existing permissions so that they apply to the object or removing all inherited permissions. When you edit the Advanced Security settings for a folder, you have the option of replacing the permissions of all existing child objects.

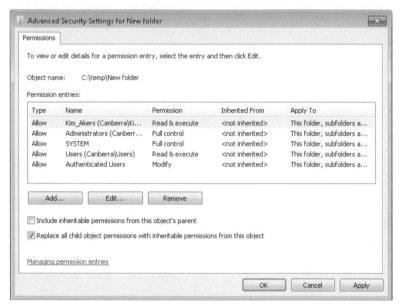

FIGURE 8-25 Permissions inheritance settings

Configuring Permissions with Icacls

Icacls is a command-line utility that you can use to configure and view the NTFS permissions of files and folders on a computer running Windows 7. To use Icacls to view the permissions assigned to a specific file or folder, use the command *Icacls File_or_Folder*. You can use the syntax *Icacls file_or_folder /grant user_or_group:permission*. You can use the */deny* option to set Deny rather than Allow. The NTFS permissions you can assign are:

- F (Full Control)
- M (Modify)
- RX (Read and Execute)
- R (Read)
- W (Write)

For example, to assign the Kim_Akers user account the Modify NTFS permission on the C:\Accounting folder, issue the command

```
Icacls.exe c:\accounting /grant Kim_Akers:(OI)M
```

To assign the Kim_Akers user account the Read & Execute (Deny) permission to the C:\Research folder, issue the command

```
Icacls.exe c:\research /deny Kim_Akers:(OI)RX
```

Icacls can be used to save permissions assigned to files and folders and to restore them. To save all NTFS permissions C:\Test directory and all its subdirectories to a file named Permissions, issue the command

```
Icacls c:\test\* /save permissions /t
```

You can restore permissions using the */restore* option. You can use the ability to save and restore permissions when copying files and folders to different volumes. You will use Icacls to assign permissions in the practice at the end of this lesson.

> **MORE INFO** Icacls
>
> To learn more about Icacls syntax and options, including how to assign special permissions, consult the following TechNet document: *http://technet.microsoft.com/en-us/library/ cc753525(WS.10).aspx.*

Determining Effective Permissions

When a user is a member of multiple groups and those groups are all assigned different permissions to the same folder, it can be difficult to determine the user's effective permission. Permissions are cumulative, and Deny permissions override Allow permissions. This can become very complicated when different groups have multiple Allow permissions. If you do not take a user's group memberships into account, you may miss something important when attempting to figure out the actual permissions that apply to them.

You can use the Effective Permissions tool to calculate a user or group's effective permissions on a file or folder. The Effective Permissions tool analyzes a user's permissions as well as the permissions of all the groups to which the user's account belongs to determine what special permissions the user has to the object in question. To access the Effective Permissions tool, click the Advanced button located on the Security tab of the target file or folder's properties and select the Effective Permissions tab. Click Select, as shown in Figure 8-26, to choose the group or user for which you wish to determine effective permissions. You will determine the effective permissions of a user in the practice exercise at the end of this lesson.

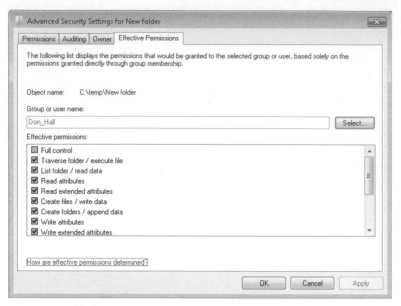

FIGURE 8-26 Effective permissions tool

Copying and Moving Files

Permissions work differently depending on whether you copy a file, move it to a different location on the same volume, or move the file to a different volume. The same inheritance rules that apply to copying or moving files also apply to copying or moving folders.

When you copy a file from one folder to another, the file inherits the permissions of the destination folder. This rule applies whether you are copying between folders on the same volume or folders on different volumes. For example, if you have assigned members of the Research group the Write (Deny) permission on folder Alpha and have assigned the same group the Modify (Allow) permission on folder Beta, members of the Research group have the Modify (Allow) permission on any file copied from folder Alpha to folder Beta. The rules that apply to copying files apply to copying folders. When you copy a folder from one parent folder to another, the folder and all that folder's contents inherit the permissions assigned to the destination folder.

Moving files from one folder to another works differently, depending on whether you are moving from one folder to another on the same volume, or from a folder on one volume to a folder on another. When you move a file between folders on the same volume, the file retains its original permissions. For example, if you have assigned members of the Research group the Write (Deny) permission on folder Alpha and have assigned the same group the Modify (Allow) permission on folder Beta and you move a file from folder Alpha to folder Beta, the file retains its original Write (Deny) permission for the Research group. The same applies if you move a folder. The folder and its contents retain their original permissions when moved to a new location on the same volume.

When you move a file from a folder on one volume to a folder on another volume, the file behaves the same way that it does when you copy it and inherits the permissions of the destination folder. The same applies to a folder. If you move a folder from one volume to another, that folder and all its contents inherit the permissions assigned to the destination folder.

Robocopy.exe is a command-line utility that is included with Windows 7 that allows you to copy files while retaining their existing NTFS permissions. You can also use Robocopy.exe to move files from one volume to another while allowing them to retain their permissions. You should consider Robocopy.exe to be an exception to the normal rules of copying and moving files. In an exam situation, you should assume that the normal rules apply unless the question mentions Robocopy.exe. To use Robocopy.exe to move all files and folders from the folder name C:\Example\ to the folder D:\Destination, use the command

```
Robocopy.exe c:\example d:\destination /copyall /e
```

> **NOTE MOVING TO FAT VOLUMES**
>
> If you move a file or folder to a volume formatted with the FAT or FAT32 file system, all NTFS permissions are lost.

Combined Share and NTFS Permissions

When a user accesses a file hosted on a shared folder, both the share permissions, which you learned about in Lesson 1, and the NTFS permissions apply. The most restrictive permission of the share and the NTFS permissions apply. For example, if a group is assigned the Read permission at the Share level and the Modify permission through file and folder permissions, the user has only Read access to files and folders when connecting to the shared folder over the network. Similarly, if a user has Full Control access at the share level and Read access assigned to the folder through NTFS permissions, the user has only Read access and is unable to modify or delete files and folders hosted on the share.

Configuring Auditing

Auditing allows you to monitor which users and groups access specific files and folders. You most likely do not want to monitor who accesses every document in your organization; you are most likely to use auditing only on sensitive documents. For example, you would use auditing to track who accessed the spreadsheet containing employee salaries, but you would not use auditing to track who accessed the break room cleanup roster. Auditing can tell you who opened a document, who modified a document, and who tried to open a document and failed. You can audit the use of any of the special permissions listed in Table 8-2. You can perform auditing only on volumes that are formatted using the NTFS file system.

The audit policies in Windows 7 allow a greater degree of granularity in tracking audit events compared to the audit policies in previous versions of Windows. For example, in Windows XP, you could audit nine broad event categories: in Windows 7, there are 53 different event categories. This allows you to be more specific about the types of events you audit. To configure auditing to track which users access specific files and folders on clients running Windows 7, do the following:

1. Open the Local Group Policy Editor and navigate to the Computer Configuration\ Windows Settings\Security Settings\Local Policies\Security Options node and set the Audit: Force Audit Policy Subcategory Settings (Windows Vista Or Later) To Override Audit Policy Category Settings policy to Enabled.

2. In the Local Group Policy Editor, navigate to the Computer Configuration\Windows Settings\Security Settings\System Audit Policies – Local Group Policy Object\Object Access node and set the Audit File System policy, as shown in Figure 8-27.

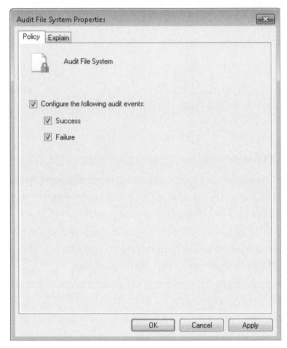

FIGURE 8-27 Configuring audit policies

3. Edit the properties of the file or folder that you wish to audit. On the Security tab, click Advanced, then click the Auditing tab, and then click Continue to elevate privileges.

4. Click Add and add the groups for which you want to audit access. If you want to audit the access of all users, select the Everyone group. Once you have selected the security group, you must select which of the special privileges you want to Audit. Figure 8-28 shows an auditing configuration to track successful file reads, writes, and deletes.

5. Auditing events will now be written to the Security log, which can be accessed using Event Viewer.

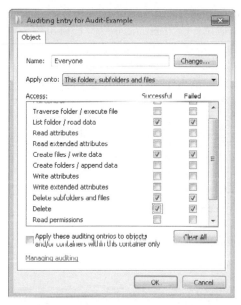

FIGURE 8-28 Auditing entries

MORE INFO **ADVANCED AUDIT POLICY**

To learn more about the advanced auditing options that are available in Windows 7, consult the following TechNet Step-by-Step guide: *http://technet.microsoft.com/en-us/library/dd408940(WS.10).aspx*

 **Quick Check**

- If you move a folder to a new location on the same volume, do the folder and its contents retain their original NTFS permissions?

Quick Check Answer

- Yes. When files or folders are moved to a new location on the same volume, they retain all their original NTFS permissions.

Encrypting File System

Encrypting File System (EFS), a technology available in the Professional, Enterprise, and Ultimate editions of Windows 7, allows for the encryption of individual files and folders. EFS differs from BitLocker To Go because BitLocker enables the encryption of full volumes and does not work directly at the file and folder level. For example, you can use BitLocker to encrypt a universal serial bus (USB) flash drive after you connect it to a client running

Windows 7, and all the files and folders hosted on that drive will be encrypted because the volume hosting them is encrypted. However, assuming that permissions are not configured restrictively, any files stored on that flash drive can be read by any user of that client running Windows 7 as the volume is encrypted to the client running Windows 7 and not any particular user of that client. EFS allows you to encrypt the files and folders stored on that USB flash drive to specific user accounts on the client running Windows 7. EFS encryption works so that even if a user has read access to a file, they cannot actually open the file unless they have the appropriate encryption certificate. You will learn more about BitLocker in Chapter 11.

EFS uses a process known as *public key encryption.* In public key encryption, a user has two keys: a public key, also known as a *certificate,* and a private key. The public key is kept in the computer's store and accessible to everyone. Users can use the public key to encrypt data. The private key is kept in the user's private certificate store and can only be used by the user. The private key decrypts data which has been encrypted using the public key. The first time a user encrypts a file on a computer running Windows 7, the computer creates an EFS certificate and private key.

> **MORE INFO** **HOW EFS WORKS**
>
> EFS certificates only indirectly encrypt files. During the file encryption process, the EFS certificate encrypts another key called the File Encryption Key (FEK). Each file has a unique FEK and the FEK is used to encrypt the target file or folder. Rather than encrypt the whole file multiple times when it needs to be encrypted to multiple keys, the file is encrypted once to the FEK and the FEK is encrypted multiple times, once to each EFS key. Any user that needs to access the encrypted file decrypts the FEK using their private key and then the FEK decrypts the file for access. To learn more about how EFS works, consult the following link on TechNet: *http://technet.microsoft.com/en-us/library/cc962103.aspx.*

You can use EFS only to encrypt files that are stored on volumes formatted with the NTFS file system. Because most USB flash drives come with volumes formatted using FAT32, this means that you need to format them with the NTFS file system prior to being able to use them to store EFS encrypted files and folders. When you encrypt a file or a folder, Windows Explorer displays it with green text rather than the standard black text.

When you encrypt a folder, Windows encrypts all files that you copy to that folder, and all new files that you create in that folder. EFS is not compatible with the file and folder compression feature of Windows 7. When you encrypt a file stored in a compressed folder, the file is decompressed prior to encryption and remains uncompressed while in its encrypted state. If you copy an encrypted file to a compressed folder, the file remains compressed. If you move a compressed file to an encrypted folder, the file decompresses and encrypts. If you copy an EFS encrypted file or folder to a FAT32 volume, Windows 7 automatically decrypts the file when it is written to the destination volume.

You can use EFS to encrypt individual files to multiple users. When you do this, only users that the file is encrypted to are able to read the file contents. Even if other users have the appropriate NTFS permissions to open the file, they are unable to access the file's contents because they are encrypted. You are able to encrypt a file to another user only if that user has an EFS certificate in the computer's store. If you want to encrypt a file to another user and are unable to locate their certificate, you need to get her to log on to the computer and encrypt a file. Once she does this, her EFS certificate is published to the computer store and you are able to use it to encrypt files to their account.

Although EFS allows you to encrypt individual files to multiple user accounts, it does not allow you to encrypt folders to multiple user accounts. It is also not possible to encrypt files to a group, only to multiple, but separate, individual users.

> *NOTE* **EFS IN DOMAIN ENVIRONMENTS**
>
> Active Directory Certificate Services allows the centralized management of EFS certificates in a domain environment. Because the 70-680 exam is primarily concerned with the client running Windows 7, so you will not need to be familiar with integrating EFS with AD DS.

EFS Recovery

Recovery Agents are certificates that allow the restoration of EFS encrypted files. When a recovery agent has been specified using local policies, all EFS encrypted files can be recovered using the recovery agent private key. You should specify a recovery agent before you allow users to encrypt files on a client running Windows 7. You can recover all files that users encrypt after the creation of a recovery agent using the recovery agent's private key. You are not able to decrypt files that were encrypted before a recovery agent certificate was specified.

You create an EFS recovery agent by performing the following steps:

1. Log on to the client running Windows 7 using the first account created, which is the default administrator account.

2. Open a command prompt and issue the command

   Cipher.exe /r:recoveryagent

3. This creates two files: Recoveryagent.cer and Recoveryagent.pfx. Cipher.exe prompts you to specify a password when creating Recoveryagent.pfx.

4. Open the Local Group Policy Editor and navigate to the \Computer Configuration\ Windows Settings\Security Settings\Public Key Policies\Encrypting File System node. Right-click this node and then click Add Data Recovery Agent. Specify the location of Recoveryagent.cer to specify this certificate as the recovery agent.

5. To recover files, use the certificates console to import Recoveryagent.pfx. This is the recovery agent's private key. Keep it safe because it can be used to open any encrypted file on the client running Windows 7.

You can import the recovery agent to another computer running Windows 7 if you want to recover files encrypted on the first computer. You can also recover files on another computer running Windows 7 if you have exported the EFS keys from the original computer and imported them on the new computer. You can use the Certificates console to import and export EFS keys. You can also use Cipher.exe to back up EFS keys.

EFS and HomeGroups

Sharing EFS-encrypted files in HomeGroup environments can be complicated because it requires that each computer in the HomeGroup has the same EFS certificates. In domain environments, it is possible to handle EFS certificates centrally through AD DS and Active Directory Certificate Services. No such central facility exists in HomeGroup environments. Even if users have the same local account names and passwords on each computer in the HomeGroup, each computer generates a unique EFS certificate pair.

If you want to share files encrypted using EFS amongst computers in a HomeGroup, get each user in the HomeGroup to encrypt a file on one computer and then get him to export their EFS keys to a removable USB flash drive using either the Certificates console or the Cipher.exe command. The keys should then be imported on the other computers running Windows 7 in the HomeGroup.

PRACTICE   **Encryption and Permissions**

Although the EFS feature is included with several previous versions of Windows, not every user knows how to encrypt a file. Even experienced administrators have trouble remembering when NTFS permissions applied to files remain and when they are inherited in file move and copy scenarios. In this practice, you learn how to encrypt files and demonstrate to yourself how NTFS permissions are influenced during copy and move procedures.

EXERCISE 1   Encrypting a Single File to Multiple Users

In this exercise, you create a text document and then encrypt it to two different user accounts. Because it is possible to encrypt a document to a user account only if that user account has an existing EFS certificate, the exercise requires you to encrypt a document using two different user accounts before you can encrypt a single document to both users.

1. Log on to computer Canberra with the Kim_Akers user account.

2. Open the Control Panel and then click Add Or Remove User Accounts.

3. On the Manage Accounts page, click Create A New Account. Enter the account name Jeff_Phillips, select Standard User, and then click Create Account.

4. On the Manage Accounts page, click the Jeff_Phillips account and then click Create A Password. Enter the password **P@ssw0rd** twice, and enter the page number of this page in the book as the password hint. Click Create Password. Close the Control Panel.

5. Right-click the Desktop, click New, and then click Folder. Name the folder **Encryption_ Test** and open it.

6. Right-click within the folder, click New, and then click Text Document. Name the document **Encrypt.txt.** Open the text document and enter the text **Configuring Windows 7.** Close the text document and save it.

7. Right-click Encrypt.txt and then choose Properties. On the General tab of the Encrypt. txt Properties dialog box, click Advanced. In the Advanced Attributes dialog box, select the Encrypt Contents To Secure Data check box, as shown in Figure 8-29. Click OK and then click Apply.

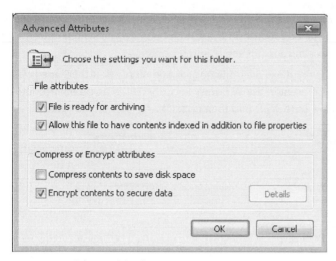

FIGURE 8-29 Advanced Attributes

8. In the Encryption Warning dialog box, select the Encrypt The File Only check box and then click OK. The file is now encrypted.

9. On the General tab of the Encrypt.txt Properties dialog box, click Advanced. In the Advanced Attributes dialog box, click Details. In the User Access To Encrypt.txt dialog box, click Add.

10. In the Windows Security dialog box, shown in Figure 8-30, verify that the only certificate present is the one belonging to Kim_Akers. Click OK.

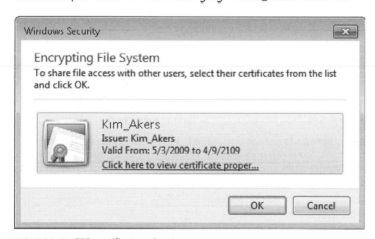

FIGURE 8-30 EFS certificate selection

11. On the Start menu, click the arrow next to Shut Down and then choose Switch User.

12. Log on using the Jeff_Phillips user account.

13. Using the Jeff_Phillips user account, perform steps 5 through 8 and then click OK to close the text file's Properties dialog box.

14. Log off as Jeff_Phillips and resume the Kim_Akers session. The User Access To Encrypt. txt dialog box should still be present on the screen because you switched to the other account and left the existing session active in memory.

15. In the User Access To Encrypt.exe dialog box, click Add. Verify that there are two encryption certificates present in the Windows Security dialog box. Click the Jeff_Phillips certificate, as shown in Figure 8-31, and then click OK.

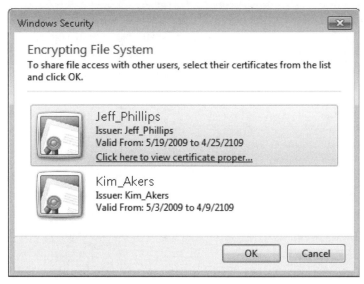

FIGURE 8-31 Additional EFS certificate available

16. Click OK three times to close the Properties dialog box.

EXERCISE 2   Exploring File and Folder Permissions

In this exercise, you explore how file and folder permissions vary when you copy and move files between two folders. You use the Icacls and Effective Permissions tools during this exercise.

1. If you have not done so already, log on to Canberra using the Kim_Akers user account.

2. Open an elevated command prompt and issue the following commands:

```
net localgroup Research /add
net localgroup Accounting /add
net localgroup Research Jeff_Phillips /Add
net localgroup Accounting Jeff_Phillips /Add
mkdir c:\source
mkdir c:\destination
icacls c:\source /grant Research:(OI)(CI)M
icacls c:\destination /grant Accounting:(OI)(CI)RX
icacls c:\destination /deny Jeff_Phillips:(OI)(CI)W
```

3. Open the C:\Source directory in Windows Explorer. Right-click within the folder and create two new text files named Alpha and Beta.

4. Right-click Alpha and then choose Properties. Click the Security tab and then click the Research group. Verify that the permissions are assigned as shown in Figure 8-32. Perform the same actions on Beta.txt to verify that permissions are set identically.

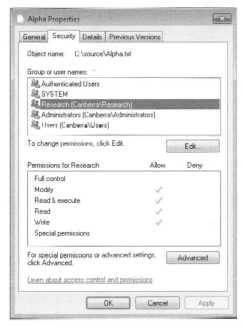

FIGURE 8-32 Permissions for Research group on Alpha.txt

5. From the command prompt, issue the following commands:

```
copy c:\source\alpha.txt c:\destination
move c:\source\beta.txt c:\destination
```

6. View the properties of the file C:\Destination\Alpha.txt and compare it to the properties of C:\Destination\Beta.txt. Note that the permissions assigned to Beta.txt are the same as those prior to the move, but that the permissions of Alpha.txt have changed when the file is copied, specifically the Research and Accounting group permissions and the permissions for user Jeff_Phillips, as shown in Figure 8-33.

7. Edit the properties of file Alpha, click the Security tab, and then click Jeff_Phillips. Note that the Jeff_Phillips account is assigned only the Write (Deny) permission.

8. Click Advanced. In the Advanced Security Settings dialog box, click the Effective Permissions tab.

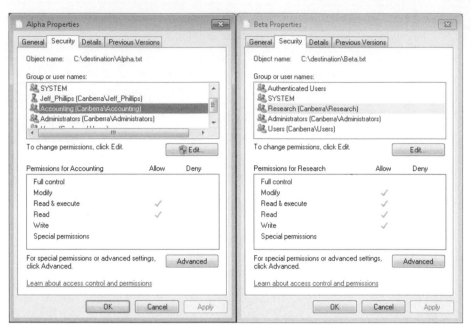

FIGURE 8-33 Permissions comparison

9. Click Select. This opens the Select User Or Group dialog box. Enter the name Jeff_ Phillips and then click OK. Review the effective permissions of the Jeff_Phillips user account, as shown in Figure 8-34. The permissions differ from those assigned to the user account because of permissions assigned through group membership.

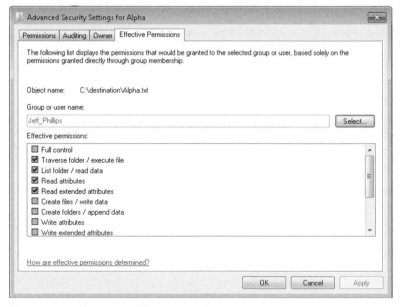

FIGURE 8-34 Determining effective permissions

Lesson Summary

- The Icacls.exe utility can be used to manage NTFS permissions from the command line. You can use this utility to back up and restore current permissions settings.

- There are six basic NTFS permissions: Read, Write, List Folder Contents, Read & Execute, Modify, and Full Control. A Deny permission always overrides an Allow permission.

- You can use the Effective Permissions tool to calculate a user's effective permissions to a file or folder when she is a member of multiple groups that are assigned permission to the same resource.

- The most restrictive permission applies when attempting to determine the result of Share and NTFS permissions.

- Auditing allows you to record which files and folders have been accessed.

- When a file is copied, it inherits the permissions of the folder it is copied to. When a file is moved within the same volume, it retains the same permissions. When a file is moved to another volume, it inherits the permissions of the folder it is copied to.

- When you encrypt a file, it generates an EFS certificate and private key. You can encrypt a file to another user's account only if that user has an existing EFS certificate.

Lesson Review

You can use the following questions to test your knowledge of the information in Lesson 2, "Folder and File Access." The questions are also available on the companion DVD if you prefer to review them in electronic form.

> **NOTE ANSWERS**
>
> Answers to these questions and explanations of why each answer choice is correct or incorrect are located in the "Answers" section at the end of the book.

1. You are logged on to a computer running Windows 7 Enterprise that you share with Jeff Phillips. You want to store some files on an NTFS-formatted USB flash drive that both you and Jeff can access. You want to encrypt these files but do not want to use BitLocker To Go. You are able to encrypt the files, but when you try to add Jeff, you do not see his certificate listed. Which of the following should you do to allow you to use EFS to encrypt files to both your and Jeff's accounts?

   A. Get Jeff to change his password.

   B. Get Jeff to encrypt a file on the computer.

   C. Give Jeff write permission to the files.

   D. Let Jeff take ownership of the files.

2. Which of the following permissions are also set when you apply the Read & Execute (Deny) NTFS permission? (Choose all that apply.)

   A. List Folder Contents (Deny)

   B. Read (Deny)

   C. Modify (Deny)

   D. Write (Deny)

3. Jeff_Phillips's user account is a member of four separate security groups that are each assigned different permissions to a folder on a client running Windows 7. Which of the following tools can you use to determine Jeff's permissions to a file hosted in that folder?

   A. Robocopy

   B. Icacls

   C. Cipher

   D. The Effective Permissions tool

4. The contents of the directory C:\Source are encrypted using EFS. The directory D:\Destination is compressed. Volumes C and D are both NTFS volumes. Which of the following happens when you use Windows Explorer to move a file named Example.txt from C:\Source to D:\Destination? (Choose all that apply; each answer forms part of a complete solution.)

   A. Example.txt remains encrypted

   B. Example.txt becomes compressed

   C. Example.txt retains its original NTFS permissions

   D. Example.txt inherits the NTFS permissions of the D:\destination folder

5. You want to have a record of which user accounts are used to access documents in a sensitive folder on a computer running Windows 7 Enterprise. Which of the following should you do to accomplish this goal?

   A. Configure EFS

   B. Configure auditing

   C. Configure NTFS permissions

   D. Configure BranchCache

Lesson 3: Managing BranchCache

BranchCache is a technology that is new to Windows 7 and Windows Server 2008 R2 that speeds up branch office access to files and Web sites hosted on servers across WAN links. BranchCache works by caching content hosted on remote severs in a cache on the local area network (LAN). Rather than retrieving content across the slower WAN link, clients check the locally hosted cache to see if a copy of the data they are requesting is present. If it is present, and certain conditions are met, the client uses the cached copy. If the requested data is not preset, the data is retrieved across the WAN link, stored in the local cache, and then accessed by the client. The advantage of BranchCache is that it stops the same file being transmitted multiple times across the WAN link and speeds up local access.

> **After this lesson, you will be able to:**
>
> - Use Group Policy to configure BranchCache settings.
> - Use *Netsh* to configure BranchCache settings.
> - Understand the difference between BranchCache distributed cache mode and hosted mode.
>
> **Estimated lesson time: 40 minutes**

BranchCache Concepts

BranchCache is a feature that speeds up branch office access to files hosted on remote networks by using a local cache. Depending on which BranchCache mode is used, that cache is either hosted on a server running Windows Server 2008 R2 or in a distributed manner among clients running Windows 7 on the branch office network. The BranchCache feature is available only on computers running Windows 7 Enterprise and Ultimate editions. BranchCache can cache only data hosted on Windows Server 2008 R2 file and Web servers. You cannot use BranchCache to speed up access to data hosted on servers running Windows Server 2008, Windows Server 2003, or Windows Server 2003 R2.

BranchCache becomes active when the round-trip latency to a compatible server exceeds 80 milliseconds. Several checks occur when a client running Windows 7 uses BranchCache:

- The client checks if the server hosting the requested data supports BranchCache.
- The client checks if the round-trip latency exceeds the threshold value.
- The client checks the cache on the branch office LAN to determine whether the requested data is already cached.
  - If the data is cached already, a check is made to see if the data is up to date and whether the client has permission to access it.
  - If the data is not already cached, the data is retrieved from the server and placed in the cache on the branch office LAN.

Cache modes determine how the branch office cache functions. BranchCache can operate in one of two modes: Hosted Cache mode or Distributed Cache mode. You will learn about these modes during the rest of this lesson.

Hosted Cache Mode

Hosted Cache mode uses a centralized local cache that hosted on a branch office server running Windows Server 2008 R2. You can enable the hosted cache server functionality on a server running Windows Server 2008 R2 that you use for other functions without a significant impact on performance. This is because if you found that files hosted at another location across the WAN were being accessed so frequently that there was a performance impact, you would use a solution like Distributed File System (DFS) to replicate them to the branch office instead of using BranchCache. The advantage of Hosted Cache mode over Distributed Cache mode is that the cache is centralized and always available. Parts of the distributed cache become unavailable when the clients hosting them shut down. You will learn more about Distributed Cache mode later in this lesson.

Hosted Cache mode requires a computer running Windows Server 2008 R2 be present and configured properly in each branch office. You must configure each BranchCache client with the address of the BranchCache host server running Windows Server 2008 R2.

When setting up the Hosted Cache mode server, it is necessary to do the following:

- Install the BranchCache feature.

- Install an Secure Sockets Layer (SSL) certificate where the subject name is set to the fully qualified domain name (FQDN) of the hosted cache server. This involves importing the SSL certificate into the Local Computer's certificate store, making note of the certificate thumbprint, and then binding the certificate using the command *netsh http add sslcert ipport=0.0.0.0:443 certhash=<thumbprint> APPID={d673f5ee-a714-454d-8de2-492e4c1bd8f8}*

- Ensure that all clients that trust the certificate authority that issued the SSL certificate installed on the hosted cache server.

Hosted Cache mode is not appropriate for organizations that do not have their own Active Directory Certificate Services infrastructure or do not have the resources to deploy a dedicated server running Windows Server 2008 R2 to each branch office.

MORE INFO **CONFIGURING HOSTED CACHE SERVERS**

To learn more about configuring a Windows Server 2008 R2 server as a hosted cache server, including how to change the default ports used, consult the following document on TechNet: *http://technet.microsoft.com/en-us/library/dd637793(WS.10).aspx.*

Distributed Cache Mode

Distributed Cache mode uses peer caching to host the branch office cache among clients running Windows 7 on the branch office network. This means that each Distributed Cache mode client hosts part of the cache, but no single client hosts all the cache. When a client running Windows 7 retrieves content over the WAN, it places that content into its own cache. If another BranchCache client running Windows 7 attempts to access the same content, it is able to access that content directly from the first client rather than having to retrieve it over the WAN link. When it accesses the file from its peer, it also copies that file into its own cache.

The advantage of distributed cache mode is that you can deploy it without having to deploy a server running Windows Server 2008 R2 locally in each branch office. The drawback of Distributed Cache mode is that the contents of the cache available on the branch office LAN depend on which clients are currently online. If a client needs a file that is held in the cache of a computer that is shut down, the client needs to retrieve the file from the host server across the WAN.

 Quick Check

- Which BranchCache mode should you use if there are no servers running Windows Server 2008 R2 at your branch office?

Quick Check Answer

- You should use Distributed Cache mode. Hosted Cache mode requires a server running Windows Server 2008 R2 on the LAN.

Configuring BranchCache Clients Running Windows 7

Configuring Windows 7 as a BranchCache client involves enabling BranchCache, selecting either Hosted Cache mode or Distributed Cache mode, and then configuring the client firewall to allow BranchCache traffic. You can configure BranchCache either using Group Policy or by using the *Netsh* command-line utility. The firewall rules that you configure depend on whether you are using Hosted Cache or Distributed Cache mode. You can use predefined firewall rules or manually create them based on protocol and port. The required firewall rules are as follows:

- The BranchCache – Content Retrieval (Uses HTTP) predefined rule. If this rule is not available, create rules that allow inbound and outbound traffic on TCP port 80. This rule is required for both Hosted Cache and Distributed Cache mode. You can create this rule using Windows Firewall With Advanced Security, as shown in Figure 8-35.

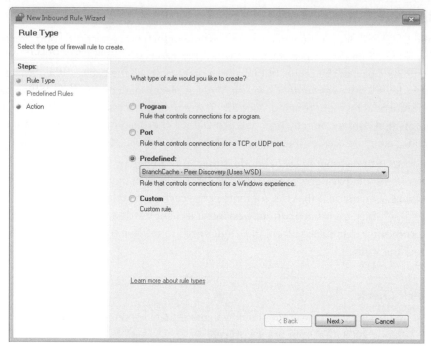

FIGURE 8-35 Predefined BranchCache firewall rule

- The BranchCache – Peer-Discovery (Uses WSD) predefined rule. If this rule is not available, create rules that allow inbound and outbound traffic on UDP port 3702. This rule is only required when using Distributed Cache mode.

- The BranchCache – Hosted Cache Client (HTTPS-Out) predefined rule. It this rule is not available, configure a rule that allows outbound traffic on TCP port 443. This rule is required only when using Hosted Cache mode.

You need to configure the firewall rules only when you configure BranchCache using Group Policy. When you configure BranchCache using *Netsh,* the appropriate firewall rules are set up automatically, as shown in Figure 8-36.

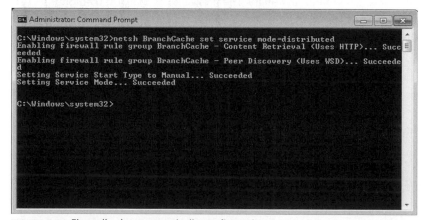

FIGURE 8-36 Firewall rules automatically configured

Configuring BranchCache Using Group Policy

BranchCache can be configured using *Netsh* or through Group Policy. You are more likely to use Group Policy when you want to apply the same settings to a large number of computers. To configure BranchCache on clients running Windows 7 using Group Policy, open the Local Group Policy Editor and navigate to the Computer Configuration\Administrative Templates\ Network\BranchCache node. As Figure 8-37 shows, there are five BranchCache-related policies.

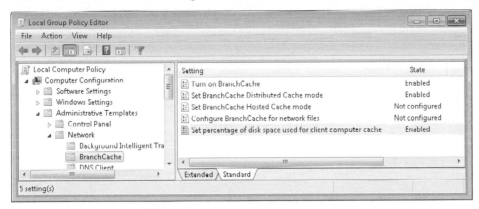

FIGURE 8-37 BranchCache policies

These policies have the following functions:

- **Turn On BranchCache**   This policy enables BranchCache and configures the BranchCache service to start manually. Windows starts the service when you make an attempt to access data on a compatible remote server that exceeds the round-trip latency threshold.

- **Set BranchCache Distributed Cache Mode**   This policy sets the client to use Distributed Cache mode. For this policy to work, you must also have enabled the Turn On BranchCache policy.

- **Set BranchCache Hosted Cache Mode**   This policy sets the client to use Hosted Cache mode. When configuring this policy, as shown in Figure 8-38, it is necessary to specify the location of the host cache server by FQDN. The SSL certificate installed on the server must match the FQDN and the client must trust the issuing certificate authority. For this policy to work, you must also enable the Turn On BranchCache policy.

- **Configure BranchCache For Network Files**   This policy allows you to specify the round-trip latency value that triggers the use of BranchCache. If you do not configure this policy, the default value is 80 milliseconds. You only need to configure this policy if the default value of 80 milliseconds is inappropriate for your organization's network environment.

- **Set Percentage Of Disk Space Used For Client Computer Cache**   This policy allows you to set a custom amount of total disk space the computer uses to store BranchCache files. Other clients on the branch office network are able to access this content if the Distributed Cache mode is used. If you do not enable this policy, the cache size defaults to 5% of the total disk space of the client computer.

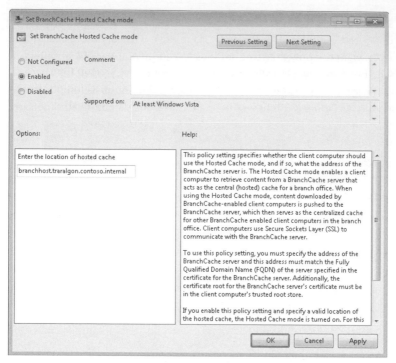

FIGURE 8-38 BranchCache Hosted Cache Mode policy

Configuring BranchCache Using *Netsh*

You can use *Netsh* in the BranchCache context to configure and diagnose problems with BranchCache. There are several options that you can configure using *Netsh,* such as the local caching option, that are not available when you configure BranchCache using Group Policy. Another advantage of using *Netsh* to configure BranchCache is that it automatically enables the relevant firewall rules for each caching mode. When you use Group Policy to enable BranchCache, you must also configure appropriate firewall rules. You learned about these firewall rules earlier in this lesson.

You must run all *Netsh* BranchCache configuration commands, except for the *show status* command, from an elevated command prompt. You can use the following commands to configure BranchCache:

- **Netsh BranchCache reset** This command resets the current BranchCache configuration, disabling and stopping the service, resetting the registry defaults, deleting any cache files, and setting the service start type to Manual. This command also disables any configured BranchCache firewall rules.

- **Netsh BranchCache show status** This command displays the current service mode, including whether that service mode is configured using Group Policy, and displays the current status of the BranchCache service.

- **Netsh BranchCache set service mode=distributed** This command sets the client to use the Distributed Cache mode, starts the BranchCache service, and changes the startup type to Manual. It also enables the BranchCache - Content Retrieval (Uses HTTP) and BranchCache – Peer Discovery (Use WSD) firewall rules.

- **Netsh BranchCache set service mode=local** This command sets the client to use the local cache mode, starts the BranchCache service, and changes the startup type to Manual. It does not enable any firewall rules. When you set the local caching mode, the client stores files retrieved over the WAN in a local cache but does not share the contents of that cache with any other clients on the branch office network. It is only possible to set this mode using *Netsh*.

- **Netsh BranchCache set service mode=hostedclient location=hostedserver** This command sets the client to use the Hosted Cache mode, specifies the location of the hosted cache server, starts the BranchCache service, and changes its startup type to Manual. It also enables the BranchCache - Content Retrieval (Uses HTTP) and BranchCache – Hosted Cache Client (Uses HTTPS) firewall rules.

- **Netsh BranchCache set cachesize** This policy allows you to set the size of the local cache. You can do this as a percentage of hard disk space or by specifying a number of bytes.

- **Netsh BranchCache set localcache** This policy allows you to set the location of the local cache.

Configuration settings applied using Group Policy override settings applied using *Netsh*.

Verifying the State of the BranchCache Service

You can verify the state of the BranchCache service, which must be operational for BranchCache to function, using the Services console. You can open this console by typing **services.msc** into the Search Programs And Files box on the Start menu. To view the properties of the service, double-click the BranchCache service. Verify that the service is started and the startup type is set to Manual, as shown in Figure 8-39.

FIGURE 8-39 BranchCache service status

Configuring File and Web Servers Running Windows Server 2008 R2

BranchCache works only when retrieving data hosted on Web and file servers running Windows Server 2008 R2. To configure a server to support BranchCache, perform the following steps:

1. Install the BranchCache feature on the server running Windows Server 2008 R2 using the Add Features Wizard, as shown in Figure 8-40. The Web server role of Windows Server 2008 R2 automatically uses BranchCache after you install the BranchCache feature.

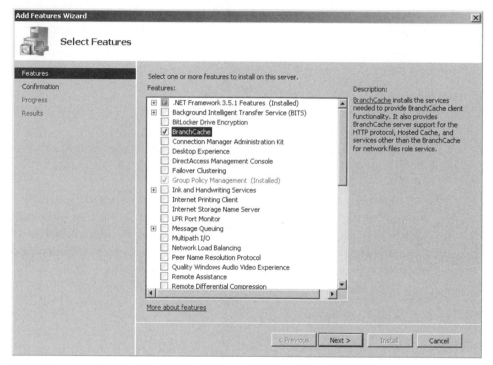

FIGURE 8-40 Installing the BranchCache feature on Windows Server 2008 R2

2. When adding the File Server Role, ensure that you add the BranchCache For Network Files Role service, as shown in Figure 8-41.

3. Edit the Computer Configuration\Administrative Templates\Network\Lanman Server\ Hash Publication for BranchCache policy. Enable the policy and select one of the following options:

   - Allow Hash Publication Only For Shared Folders On Which BranchCache Is Enabled
   - Allow Hash Publication For All Shared Folders

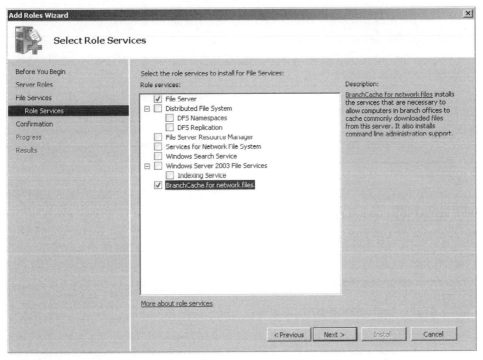

FIGURE 8-41 Installing BranchCache for Network Files

4. If you choose to enable BranchCache only on selected shared folders, use the Share And Storage Management console on the file server running Windows Server 2008 R2 to edit the properties of the share that you want to use with BranchCache, and then click Advanced. In the Advanced dialog box, enable BranchCache, as shown in Figure 8-42.

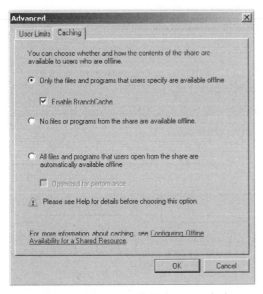

FIGURE 8-42 Enabling BranchCache on each share

EXAM TIP

Remember the syntax of the *netsh branchcache set service* command and that it configures the BranchCache service and firewall rules automatically.

PRACTICE   **BranchCache Configuration**

BranchCache can use the Distributed Cache mode to share a cache of remote files and Web server data among clients running Windows 7 on a branch office network. Distributed Cache mode can be configured using Group Policy or by using the *Netsh* command-line utility.

EXERCISE   **Configuring BranchCache**

In this exercise, you use the *Netsh* command-line utility to configure the BranchCache client settings of a computer running Windows 7. To complete this practice, perform the following steps:

1. Log on to computer Canberra using the Kim_Akers user account.

2. Open an elevated command prompt.

3. Issue the following command:

    `Netsh BranchCache show status`

4. Verify that the service mode is set to disabled and the current status of the service is stopped.

5. Issue the following command:

    `Netsh BranchCache set service mode=distributed`

6. Verify that the status message indicates that two firewall rules have been enabled and the service startup type has been set to Manual.

7. Issue the following command:

    `Netsh BranchCache show status`

8. Verify that the service mode is set to Distributed Caching and the current status of the service is running.

9. Issue the following command:

    `Netsh BranchCache set cachesize size=25 percent=True`

10. Issue the following command:

   `Netsh BranchCache show localcache`

11. Verify that the maximum cache size is set to 25% of hard disk.

12. Issue the following command:

   `Netsh BranchCache reset`

Lesson Summary

- BranchCache is a technology that allows files hosted on remote file servers running Windows Server 2008 R2 to be cached on a branch office network.
- Only Windows 7 Enterprise and Ultimate editions support BranchCache.
- Distributed Cache mode shares the cache among clients running Windows 7.
- Hosted Cache mode requires that a specially configured server running Windows Server 2008 R2 be present on the branch office network.
- When you enable Distributed Cache mode or Hosted Cache mode using *Netsh*, the BranchCache service and firewall rules are configured automatically.

Lesson Review

You can use the following questions to test your knowledge of the information in Lesson 3, "Managing BranchCache." The questions are also available on the companion DVD if you prefer to review them in electronic form.

> **NOTE ANSWERS**
>
> Answers to these questions and explanations of why each answer choice is correct or incorrect are located in the "Answers" section at the end of the book.

1. You want to use BranchCache's hosted cache mode in your organization's branch offices. You have enabled BranchCache on your organization's head office servers. Which of the following steps must you take to accomplish this goal? (Choose all that apply; each answer forms part of a complete solution.)

   A. Deploy at least one server running Windows Server 2008 R2 to each branch office.

   B. Upgrade all branch office client computers to Windows 7 Enterprise.

   C. Upgrade all branch office client computers to Windows 7 Professional.

   D. Deploy at least one Windows Server 2008 Read-Only Domain Controller (RODC) to each branch office.

2. Which of the following tools can you use to configure a group of clients running Windows 7 to use BranchCache in peer caching mode? (Choose all that apply.)

   A. *Net share*

   B. *Netsh*

   C. *Ipconfig*

   D. Local Group Policy Editor

3. You have two computers running Windows 7 Ultimate at one of your organization's branch office locations. All servers in this branch office use Windows Server 2003 R2. You want to configure one of these computers to cache content that it retrieves from a file server running Windows Server 2008 R2 located on the head office network. This file server has the name *fs-alpha.contoso.internal*. The data hosted on this file server is sensitive. The computer you are configuring should not provide cached content to the other computer running Windows 7 Ultimate on the network. Which of the following commands would you use to configure this computer?

   A. `netsh branchcache set service disabled`

   B. `netsh branchcache set service mode=distributed`

   C. `netsh branchcache set service mode=local`

   D. `netsh branchcache set service mode=hostedclient location=fs-alpha.contoso
      .internal`

4. You want to configure clients running Windows 7 Enterprise in a branch office to use BranchCache in Hosted Cache mode. A server running Windows Server 2008 R2 named branch-1.contoso.internal functions as the host on the LAN. Which of the following commands, issued from an elevated command prompt, should you use to configure the clients running Windows 7?

   A. `netsh branchcache set service mode=distributed`

   B. `netsh branchcache set service mode=local`

   C. `netsh branchcache set service mode=hostedserver
      clientauthentication=domain`

   D. `netsh branchcache set service mode=hostedclient location=branch-1.contoso
      .internal`

5. You want to configure clients running Windows 7 Enterprise in a branch office to use BranchCache only if the round-trip network latency when attempting to access files hosted over the WAN exceeds 120 ms. Which of the following policies should you configure to accomplish your goal?

   A. Configure BranchCache For Network Files

   B. Set Percentage Of Disk Space Used For Client Computer Cache

   C. Set BranchCache Distributed Cache Mode

   D. Set BranchCache Hosted Cache Mode

Chapter Review

To further practice and reinforce the skills you learned in this chapter, you can perform the following tasks:

- Review the chapter summary.
- Review the list of key terms introduced in this chapter.
- Complete the case scenarios. These scenarios set up real-world situations involving the topics of this chapter and ask you to create a solution.
- Complete the suggested practices.
- Take a practice test.

Chapter Summary

- HomeGroups allow for the sharing of resources on home networks.
- You can manage shared folders centrally using the Computer Management console.
- Libraries are virtual collections of folders that host similar content.
- NTFS permissions determine which files a user or group can access on a computer.
- Print permissions determine what rights a user has to manage a printer or documents.
- BranchCache is a technology that speeds up branch office access to files in remote locations through the caching of previously accessed files on the branch office network.

Key Terms

Do you know what these key terms mean? You can check your answers by looking up the terms in the glossary at the end of the book.

- **BranchCache**
- **Encrypting File System (EFS)**
- **HomeGroup**
- **library**

Case Scenarios

In the following case scenarios, you apply what you've learned about subjects covered in this chapter. You can find answers to these questions in the "Answers" section at the end of this book.

Case Scenario 1: Permissions and Encryption

A computer running Windows 7 Enterprise named Waverley has two NTFS-formatted volumes, volume C and volume D. The folder C:\Share is shared and has 15 subfolders and hundreds of files. Many of these folders have unique NTFS permissions. You want to move this folder so that it is hosted on volume D because volume C is running out of space. One of the users of computer Waverley will be changing to computer Warrandyte. This user has copied a large number of EFS-encrypted files onto a NTFS-formatted USB flash device.

With these facts in mind, answer the following questions:

1. What steps can you take so that the user is able to read the encrypted files on the USB flash device on computer Warrandyte?

2. What steps can you take to ensure that it is possible to recover all files that are encrypted in future?

3. What steps can you take to move the shared folder to volume D?

Case Scenario 2: Configuring Contoso Branch Offices

You are trying to make the use of WAN bandwidth between Contoso's head office in Melbourne and branch offices in Wangaratta and Traralgon more efficient. All client computers at Contoso have Windows 7 Enterprise installed. Users turn their computers on and off during the day. If possible, you want to store any BranchCache data so that it is always available. There is a Windows Server 2008 R2 RODC at the Traralgon site named rodc.traralgon.contoso.internal, and there is a Windows Server 2008 RODC named rodc.wangaratta.contoso.internal at the Wangaratta site. You do not plan on upgrading any server operating systems in the near future.

With these facts in mind, answer the following questions:

1. Which BranchCache mode should you use at the Wangaratta branch office?

2. Which BranchCache mode should you use at the Traralgon branch office?

3. What steps do you need to take to prepare server rodc.traralgon.contoso.internal to support BranchCache?

Suggested Practices

To help you master the exam objectives presented in this chapter, complete the following tasks.

Configure Shared Resources

Perform this practice when logged on to computer Canberra with the Kim_Akers user account.

- Configure a shared printer. Create a local group named PrinterManagers and assign the Manage Printers permission to this group.

Configure File and Folder Access

Perform both of these practices when logged on to computer Canberra with the Kim_Akers user account.

- **Practice 1**   Use Gpedit.msc and Cipher.exe to configure and assign an EFS recovery agent certificate.
- **Practice 2**   Create a file named Gamma.txt. Use Icacls.exe to assign the Modify (Deny) permission to the file. Use Robocopy.exe to copy Gamma.txt to a new folder while retaining its original permissions.

Configure BranchCache

Perform this practice when logged on to computer Canberra with the Kim_Akers user account.

- Configure computer Canberra using the *Netsh* command to use local caching only.

Take a Practice Test

The practice tests on this book's companion DVD offer many options. For example, you can test yourself on just one exam objective, or you can test yourself on all the 70-680 certification exam content. You can set up the test so that it closely simulates the experience of taking a certification exam, or you can set it up in study mode so that you can look at the correct answers and explanations after you answer each question.

> **MORE INFO**   **PRACTICE TESTS**
>
> For details about all the practice test options available, see the section entitled "How to Use the Practice Tests," in the Introduction to this book.

CHAPTER 9

Authentication and Account Control

U ser Account Control (UAC) is a tool for administrators that alerts you to the fact that what you are trying to do requires administrator privileges. You should not be surprised to encounter a UAC prompt when modifying firewall rules. You would be justifiably wary if you encounter a UAC prompt when trying to open a picture of a cat eating a cheeseburger sent to you by your aunt. One of these tasks should require administrator privileges and one of them should not. UAC can protect your computer from malware because it allows you to notice when a program or document that should not require administrative privileges requests them. UAC rarely affects normal users because, by definition, normal users should not be doing anything that requires administrator privileges. In the first part of this chapter, you learn how to configure UAC for your environment so that it warns you when necessary but keeps out of your way the rest of the time.

Passwords are the primary method through which you secure a computer running Windows 7. The strength of a password is directly proportional to the strength of the security it provides. If passwords are not secure enough for your environment, you can configure Windows 7 to require a smart card before it allows users to log on. Privileges allow users to perform tasks. You can assign privileges, such as allowing a user to back up a computer in its entirety by adding them to the appropriate group or by configuring the appropriate Group Policy. In the second part of this chapter, you learn how to configure password policies, resolve authentication problems, assign privileges, and back up and restore saved credentials.

Exam objectives in this chapter:
- Configure User Account Control (UAC).
- Configure authentication and authorization.

Lessons in this chapter:

Before You Begin

To complete the exercises in the practices in this chapter, you need to have done the following:

- Installed Windows 7 on a stand-alone client PC named Canberra, as described in Chapter 1, "Install, Migrate, or Upgrade to Windows 7."

 **REAL WORLD**

Orin Thomas

The UAC prompt doesn't appear capriciously. UAC lets you know if software is doing something suspicious. If you are messing around with the guts of your operating system, you should expect a couple of UAC prompts. This is because you are making substantive changes to the operating system, and you need administrator privileges to do that. However, if you are doing something normal with your computer, such as playing a game or running a word processor (something that shouldn't require administrative privileges), and you are prompted by UAC, your first thought shouldn't be "Oh, not that annoying prompt again!" You should be thinking, "Now what on Earth made it do that?" Normal programs do not require administrative privileges to run. This is the key thing to understand about UAC. If UAC does interrupt when you are doing something that isn't related to your computer configuration, you should get suspicious. UAC is a red flag, a warning you should pay attention to. UAC is the computer's way of asking you, "Are you sure you want to let this program have administrative rights?" The answer to this question is important. To take control of your computer, malware needs to elevate its privileges so that it can run with administrative rights. Malware authors have a whole bag of tricks that they use to try to get you to run their programs. Sometimes malware try to get you to execute it by piggybacking on another program that you run on a regular basis. You run the program, thinking it is something else and then bang, pwnd! UAC cannot stop you from running the malware, but it warns you when the program tries to do something that requires admin privileges. If you do get prompted when you are doing something that you should be able to do without administrator rights, UAC lets you proceed if you so choose. Of course, if your computer does end up infected with malware, you won't be able to say that you weren't warned.

Lesson 1: Managing User Account Control

User Account Control (UAC) is a tool that you will likely use only if your user account is a member of the local administrators group. This is because UAC is disabled by default for standard users, which means that standard users do not, by default, encounter a UAC prompt. UAC settings can be tailored to better meet the needs of your organization. In this lesson, you learn how to configure UAC so that it does not have to run on the Secure Desktop, how to require administrators to enter their credentials rather than just clicking OK, and to configure UAC so that administrators assisting standard users can access elevated privileges.

> **After this lesson, you will be able to:**
> - Configure local security policies related to UAC.
> - Configure behavior of the User Account Control elevation prompt.
> - Configure the behavior of Secure Desktop.
>
> **Estimated lesson time: 40 minutes**

User Account Control (UAC)

UAC is a security feature of Windows 7 that informs you when the action that you want to undertake requires an elevation of privileges. If you logged on with a user account that was a member of the local administrators group in previous versions of Microsoft Windows, such as Windows XP, you automatically had administrator-level access at all times. This, by itself, was not a problem because recommended good practice was that people logged on with accounts that were members of the local administrator group only when they needed to do something related to administration. The problem with this is that people tended to use their administrator account as their normal user account. It was convenient for them because they did not have to log off and log on again each time they wanted to do something related to systems administration. Unfortunately, this behavior presented a security problem because any program run by a user logged on with an administrative account runs with the rights and privileges of that user. UAC resolves this problem by allowing a user that is a member of the local Administrators group to run as a standard user most of the time and to briefly elevate their privileges so that they are running as administrators when they attempt to carry out specific administration-related tasks.

To understand UAC, you need to understand the following concepts:

- **Privilege elevation** All users of clients running Windows 7 run with the rights of a standard user. When a user attempts an act that requires administrative privileges, such as creating a new user account, her rights need to be raised from those of a standard user to those of an administrative user. This increase in rights is termed *privilege elevation*. UAC is a gateway to privilege elevation. It allows users who are members of the local Administrators group to access administrative rights, but ensures that the person accessing the Administrative rights is aware that they are doing so.

This privilege elevation occurs only for a specific task. Another task executed at the same time that also requires privilege elevation generates its own UAC prompt.

- **Admin Approval mode** Admin Approval mode is where an administrator must give explicit approval for elevation to occur by responding to the UAC prompt. The UAC prompt might require either clicking yes, called *prompting for consent,* or entering a user name and password, which is called *prompting for credentials.*

- **Secure Desktop** *Secure Desktop* ensures that malware is unable to alter the display of the UAC prompt as a method of tricking you into allowing administrative access. When you configure UAC to use the Secure Desktop, the desktop is unavailable when a UAC prompt is triggered. You must respond to the UAC prompt before you can interact with the computer. The dimmed screen is actually a screen shot of the current desktop, which is why if you have video running in the background and a UAC prompt uses Secure Desktop, the video appears to freeze. If you do not respond to a UAC prompt on a Secure Desktop after 150 seconds, Windows automatically denies the request for privilege elevation, and the computer returns to the standard desktop.

UAC Settings

You can determine how intrusive UAC is by configuring the User Account Control Settings dialog box, shown in Figure 9-1. You can access this dialog box from the User Accounts control panel by clicking the Change User Account Control Settings item. The dialog box consists of a slider that allows you to adjust UAC notifications between Always Notify and Never Notify.

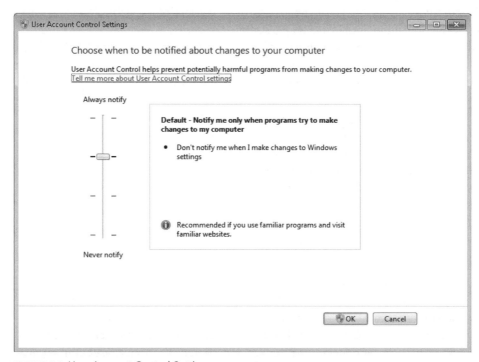

FIGURE 9-1 User Account Control Settings

If you make an adjustment using this slider, you are prompted by UAC informing you that the program named UserAccountControlSettings is trying to make a change to your computer. You can see this dialog box in Figure 9-2. This dialog box is a security measure that ensures that malware is unable to modify your UAC settings without you being aware of it. If you see this message and you have not modified UAC yourself, it is likely that malware is attempting to compromise the integrity of your computer.

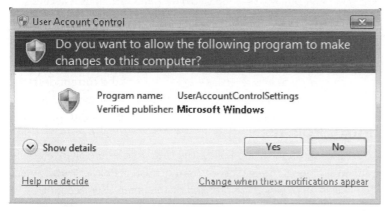

FIGURE 9-2 UAC settings change warning

The settings that you can configure using the slider do the following:

- **Always Notify**   This is the most secure setting. You are prompted before programs make changes to your computer or Windows settings that require administrator permissions. During notification, your desktop appears dimmed. This is because Secure Desktop has become active. You must respond to the UAC prompt before it is possible to do anything else with the computer. If you do not respond to the UAC prompt after 150 seconds, Windows automatically denies the request for privilege elevation, and the computer returns to the standard desktop.

- **Notify Me Only When Programs Try To Make Changes To My Computer**   When this option is set, you are prompted before programs make changes to your computer or Windows settings that require administrator permissions. Notification occurs on the Secure Desktop. If you do not respond to the UAC prompt after 150 seconds, Windows automatically denies the request for privilege elevation.

- **Notify Me Only When Programs Try To Make Changes To My Computer (Do Not Dim My Desktop)**   With this option, you are prompted before programs make changes that require administrator permissions. You are not prompted if you try to make changes to Windows settings that require administrator permissions using programs that are included with Windows. You are prompted if a program that is not included with Windows attempts to modify Windows settings.

- **Never Notify**   When logged on as an administrator, you are not notified before programs make changes to your computer or to Windows settings. If you are logged on as a standard user, any changes that require administrative privileges are automatically denied.

User Account Control Policies

You primarily manage UAC settings through Group Policy. The UAC policies are all located in the Computer Configuration\Windows Settings\Security Settings\Local Policies\Security Options node. There are 10 policies, all of which are prefixed by the name User Account Control, as shown in Figure 9-3.

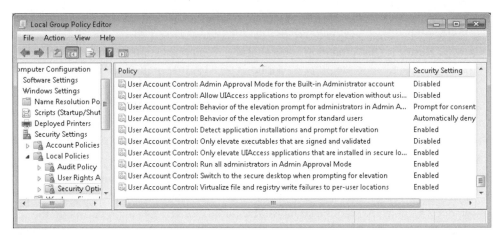

FIGURE 9-3 User Account Control policies

In the next few sections, you learn more about these policies and how they influence the operation of User Account Control.

UAC: Admin Approval Mode For The Built-In Administrator Account

UAC: The Admin Approval Mode For The Built-In Administrator Account policy controls how Administrator Approval mode works for the built-in Administrator account. The built-in Administrator account is disabled by default, so this policy is relevant only if you have enabled the built-in Administrator account using the Accounts: Administrator Account Status policy, which is also located in the Security Options node. The default setting of this policy is Disabled. If you enable the built-in Administrator account, privilege elevation occurs automatically without a UAC prompt. If you enable the policy and the built-in Administrator account, the built-in account receives UAC prompts when attempting tasks that require privilege elevation.

UAC: Behavior Of The Elevation Prompt For Administrators In Admin Approval Mode

UAC: The Behavior Of The Elevation Prompt For Administrators In Admin Approval Mode policy functions in a similar way to the User Account Control Settings dialog box that was covered earlier in this lesson. It allows you to configure how intrusive UAC is for users that log on to a client running Windows 7 with administrative privileges. Unlike the UAC Settings dialog box, which has four settings, the UAC: Behavior Of The Elevation Prompt For Administrators In Admin Approval Mode policy, shown in Figure 9-4, has six settings.

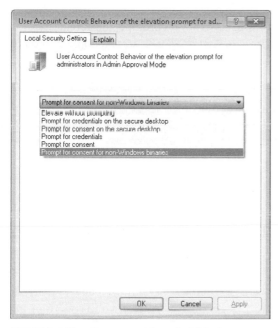

FIGURE 9-4 Elevation prompt for administrators

These settings work as follows:

- **Elevate Without Prompting** This is the least secure setting and is the equivalent of disabling UAC. Requests for elevation are approved automatically.

- **Prompt For Credentials On The Secure Desktop** UAC always prompts the administrator for a password, as shown in Figure 9-5, on the Secure Desktop.

FIGURE 9-5 Prompt for credentials

■ **Prompt For Consent On The Secure Desktop**   UAC always prompts the administrator
for consent on the Secure Desktop, as shown in Figure 9-6. This setting does not require
the user to enter a password.

FIGURE 9-6 Consent prompt

■ **Prompt For Credentials**   The user must enter a password. The Secure Desktop is used
only if the UAC: Switch To The Secure Desktop When Prompting For Elevation policy is
enabled (that policy's default setting).

■ **Prompt For Consent**   This policy prompts for consent. The Secure Desktop is used
only if the UAC: Switch To The Secure Desktop When Prompting For Elevation policy is
enabled (that policy's default setting).

■ **Prompt For Consent For Non-Windows Binaries**   This is the policy's default setting.
UAC prompts only when an application that is not a part of the Windows operating
system requests elevation. Applications that are a part of the Windows operating
system and that request elevation do not trigger a UAC prompt.

UAC: Behavior Of The Elevation Prompt For Standard Users

The UAC: Behavior Of The Elevation Prompt For Standard Users policy, shown in Figure 9-7, determines whether and how Windows prompts a user who does not have administrative privileges for privilege elevation. The default option automatically denies elevation requests. Windows does not provide the user with any direct indication that this denial has occurred, though they can infer it by the fact that they are unable to do whatever they were trying to do that prompted the attempt at elevation in the first place. The other options are to prompt for credentials on the Secure Desktop or to prompt for credentials. Credentials are required because another user account, one that has administrative privileges, is necessary to approve any elevation request.

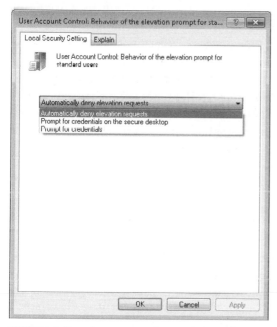

FIGURE 9-7 Elevation requests for standard users

UAC: Detect Application Installations And Prompt For Elevation

The UAC: Detect Application Installations And Prompt For Elevation policy determines whether an application installer is able to request an elevation of privilege. The default setting is enabled, allowing the installation of software once consent or appropriate credentials have been provided. This policy is often disabled in enterprise environments where software is distributed through Group Policy and the direct use of application installers is not necessary.

UAC: Only Elevate Executables That Are Signed And Validated

When you enable the UAC: Only Elevate Executables That Are Signed And Validated policy, UAC provides an elevation prompt only for executable files that have digital signatures from a trusted certificate authority (CA). If an application has no digital signature, or has a signature from a CA that is not trusted, UAC does not allow elevation. This policy is disabled by default and should be used only in environments where all applications that require elevation are digitally signed.

UAC: Run All Administrators In Admin Approval Mode

The UAC: Run All Administrators In Admin Approval Mode policy dictates whether Windows provides UAC for users with administrative privileges when they perform a task that requires elevation. The default setting of the policy is Enabled. When this policy is disabled, users with administrative privileges are elevated automatically when they perform a task that requires elevation. Disabling this policy disables UAC for all users with administrative rights.

UAC: Switch To The Secure Desktop When Prompting For Elevation

The UAC: Switch To The Secure Desktop When Prompting For Elevation policy determines whether the UAC prompt is displayed on the Secure Desktop when a user is prompted for elevation. Secure Desktop dims the screen and requires that a user respond to the UAC prompt before being able to continue using the computer. This functions as a security measure, ensuring that malware is unable to disguise the appearance of a UAC prompt as a way of tricking an administrator into providing consent. This policy is enabled by default. If this policy is disabled and the UAC: Behavior Of The Elevation Prompt For Administrators In Admin Approval Mode policy is set to either the Prompt For Consent or Prompt For Credentials setting on the Secure Desktop, Secure Desktop is still used.

UAC: Virtualize File And Registry Write Failures To Per-User Locations

Many older applications attempt to write data to the Program Files, Windows, or Windows\ System32 folder, or the HKLM\Software\ registry area. Windows 7 does not allow applications to write data to these secure locations. To support these applications, Windows 7 allows applications to believe that they have successfully written data to these locations, when in reality, Windows 7 has redirected this data to virtualized per-user locations. When the UAC: Virtualize File And Registry Write Failures To Per-User Locations policy is disabled, Windows blocks applications from writing data to protected locations. This policy is enabled by default.

UAC: Allow UIAccess Applications To Prompt For Elevation Without Using Secure Desktop

User Interface Accessibility (UIAccess) programs are a special type of program that can interact with Windows and applications on behalf of a user. Examples include on-screen keyboard and Windows Remote Assistance. The UAC: Allow UIAccess Applications To Prompt For Elevation Without Using Secure Desktop policy determines whether UIAccess applications, which are identified as such by the properties of the application, are able to issue a UAC prompt without using Secure Desktop. The default setting for this policy is Disabled.

You should enable this policy when it is necessary for remote assistance helpers to respond to UAC prompts that occur during a remote assistance session. During normal operation, if a UAC prompt is triggered during a remote assistance session, the remote computer displays the UAC prompt on the Secure Desktop. Unfortunately for the helper, the Secure Desktop is not available to them when they are connected over a remote assistance session. The only way that a helper can respond to these UAC prompts is if Secure Desktop is not invoked when using UIAccess applications. This policy is only necessary if UAC prompts are configured for standard users. If this policy is not enabled, elevation is not possible for standard users so the helper will not get an opportunity to provide credentials.

UAC: Only Elevate UIAccess Applications That Are Installed In Secure Locations

The UAC: Only Elevate UIAccess Applications That Are Installed In Secure Locations policy applies only to applications that request execution with the UIAccess integrity level. The default setting for this policy is Enabled, which means that only applications that are installed in the Windows\System32 folder and the Program Files\ folder and its subdirectories are able to request execution with this special integrity level. Disabling this policy allows programs that are installed in any location to request execution with the UIAccess integrity level. Programs requesting execution with UIAccess integrity level must have a digital signature issued by a trusted CA independent of this policy setting.

Secpol and Local Security Policy

The Local Security Policy console (also known as Secpol.msc), shown in Figure 9-8, is available in the Administrative Tools section of the Control Panel. The console displays a subset of the policies available in the Local Group Policy editor. You can use the Local Security Policy console to edit what appears in the Computer Configuration\Windows Settings\Security Settings node of the Local Group Policy editor. The advantage of the Local Security Policy console over the Local Group Policy Console is that the Local Security Policy console is focused specifically on security settings. Every task that you can accomplish with the Local Security Policy console, you can also complete using the Local Group Policy Editor.

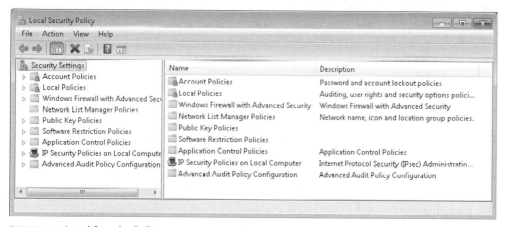

FIGURE 9-8 Local Security Policy

You can use both the Local Group Policy Editor and the Local Security Policy console to import and export security-related Group Policy settings. You can use this import and export functionality to apply the same security settings to stand-alone computers that are not part of a domain environment. Exported security files are written in Security Template .inf format. As well as using Local Group Policy Editor and the Local Security Policy console to import policies that are stored in .inf format, you can apply them using the Secedit.exe command-line utility. You use the Local Group Policy Editor in the practice which follows.

EXAM TIP

Understand the difference between prompt for consent and prompt for credentials.

PRACTICE **Configuring User Account Control**

UAC can be configured to better meet the needs of the administrators and users in your environment. In this practice, you configure different UAC options and evaluate them to get a better idea of what configuration options are available.

EXERCISE 1 **Configuring UAC Settings**

In this exercise, you configure UAC settings and take note at how different settings influence the function of UAC.

1. Log on to computer Canberra using the Kim_Akers user account.

2. Click Start. In the In the Search Programs And Files text box, type **User Accounts.** Click the User Accounts item on the Start menu.

3. Click the Manage Another Account item. Note that you are not prompted by UAC to start the Manage Accounts control panel. Click Go To The Main User Accounts Page.

4. Click the Change User Account Control settings item. Note that you are not prompted by UAC when clicking this item.

5. On the Choose When To Be Notified About Changes To Your Computer page, move the slider to Always Notify. Click OK.

6. At the User Account Control prompt, click Yes.

7. Click the Manage Another Account item. Note that this time, you are prompted by UAC and that the screen is dimmed, indicating that the Secure Desktop feature is active. Click No to cancel the UAC prompt.

8. Click the Change User Account Control settings item. Note that you are now prompted by UAC with the Secure Desktop when you click this item. Click Yes.

9. On the Choose When To Be Notified About Changes To Your Computer page, return the slider to the Default – Notify Me Only When Programs Try To Make Changes To My Computer setting. Click OK. Click Yes when prompted by the UAC prompt.

10. Close the User Accounts control panel.

EXERCISE 2   Configuring and Exporting UAC Policies

In this exercise, you configure User Account Control policies using the Local Security Policy editor.

1. If you have not done so already, log on to computer Canberra using the Kim_Akers user account.

2. Using Windows Explorer, create the C:\Export folder.

3. In the In the Search Programs And Files text box, type **Edit Group Policy.** Click the Edit Group Policy item.

4. Ensure that the Computer Configuration\Windows Settings\Security Settings node is selected. Open the Action menu and then choose Export Policy.

5. Save the exported policy as C:\Export\Base_policy.inf

6. Within Security Settings, select the Local Policies\Security Options node. Double-click the User Account Control: Behavior Of The Elevation Prompt For Administrators In Admin Approval Mode policy.

7. Select the Prompt For Credentials On The Secure Desktop setting, as shown in Figure 9-9, and then click OK.

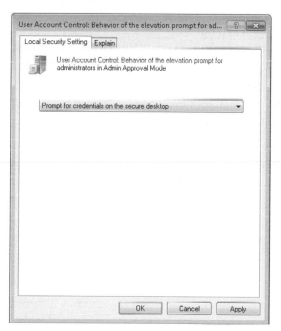

FIGURE 9-9 Prompt For Credentials On The Secure Desktop

8. Click Start. In the In the Search Programs And Files text box, type **gpupdate /force** and press Enter.

9. Click Start. In the In the Search Programs And Files text box, type **User Accounts**. Click the User Accounts item on the Start menu.

10. Click the Change User Account Control Settings item. Note that you are required to enter your user name and password on the Secure Desktop, as shown in Figure 9-10. Enter your password and then click Yes.

FIGURE 9-10 Entering credentials

11. Notice that the User Account Control Settings slider has been set to the most secure option rather than the default setting that you set it to in the previous exercise. Click Cancel to dismiss the dialog box.

12. Ensure that the Computer Configuration\Windows Settings\Security Settings node is selected. Open the Action menu and then click Import Policy. Import the C:\Export\Base_policy.inf policy. If you receive an error, click OK.

13. In the In the Search Programs And Files text box, type **gpupdate /force**.

14. In the User Accounts control panel, click the Change User Account Control Settings item. Note that the User Account Control Settings opens and that you do not have to enter credentials. You should also note that the slider has been returned to the default position.

15. Close all open windows and log off.

Lesson Summary

- You can use the Local Security Policy console or the Local Group Policy Editor to edit security-related group policies.
- When UAC is configured to use Secure Desktop, an administrator must respond directly to the prompt before being able to continue using the computer.
- UAC can be configured to prompt for consent or prompt for credentials. Prompting for consent requires that the administrator simply assents to the elevation. Prompting for credentials requires the administrator to his password to allow elevation.

- By default, Windows 7 does not prompt standard users. You can configure UAC to prompt standard users for credentials. They must then provide the credentials of a user that is a member of the local administrators group.

Lesson Review

You can use the following questions to test your knowledge of the information in Lesson 1, "Managing User Account Control." The questions are also available on the companion CD if you prefer to review them in electronic form.

> **NOTE ANSWERS**
>
> Answers to these questions and explanations of why each answer choice is correct or incorrect are located in the "Answers" section at the end of the book.

1. Which policy setting should you configure to ensure that the Windows 7 built-in Administrator account must respond to a UAC prompt before elevating privileges?

    A. UAC: Behavior Of The Elevation Prompt For Administrators In Admin Approval Mode: Elevate Without Prompting

    B. UAC: Admin Approval Mode For The Built-In Administrator Account: Enabled

    C. UAC: Admin Approval Mode For The Built-In Administrator Account: Disabled

    D. UAC: Behavior Of The Elevation Prompt For Administrators In Admin Approval Mode: Prompt For Consent For Non-Windows Binaries

2. Which of the following policy settings should you configure to ensure that users that are not members of the local Administrators group on a client running Windows 7 are prompted for credentials when they perform an action that requires the elevation of privileges?

    A. User Account Control: Behavior Of The Elevation Prompt For Standard Users: Automatically Deny Elevation Requests

    B. User Account Control: Behavior Of The Elevation Prompt For Standard Users: Prompt For Credentials

    C. User Account Control: Behavior Of The Elevation Prompt For Administrators In Admin Approval Mode: Prompt For Credentials

    D. User Account Control: Behavior Of The Elevation Prompt For Administrators In Admin Approval Mode: Prompt For Consent

3. You are responsible for managing a student lab that has 30 stand-alone clients running Windows 7. These clients are not members of a domain, though are members of the same HomeGroup. You have configured a set of UAC policies on a reference computer.

You want to apply these policies to each of the 30 client computers in the lab. Which of the following tools could you use to do this? (Choose all that apply.)

A. Local Group Policy Editor console

B. Computer Management console

C. User Account Control settings

D. Local Security Policy

4. You are in the process of phasing out older applications at your organization. You want to ensure that older applications that attempt to write data to protected locations such as the \Windows\System32 folder fail and are not redirected by Windows into writing data elsewhere. Which of the following policies should you configure to accomplish this goal?

A. UAC: Only Elevate Uiaccess Applications That Are Installed In Secure Locations

B. UAC: Only Elevate Executables That Are Signed And Validated

C. UAC: Behavior Of The Elevation Prompt For Standard Users

D. UAC: Virtualize File And Registry Write Failures To Per-User Locations

5. You want users that are members of the local Administrators group to be prompted for credentials when performing a task that requires elevation, but you do not want them to have to respond to this prompt on the Secure Desktop. You have configured the User Account Control: Behavior Of The Elevation Prompt For Administrators In Admin Approval mode to Prompt for Credentials. Users that are members of the local administrators group are being forced onto the Secure Desktop during the UAC process. Which of the following policy settings should you configure to resolve this problem?

A. UAC: Admin Approval Mode For The Built-in Administrator Account

B. UAC: Behavior Of The Elevation Prompt For Administrators In Admin Approval Mode

C. UAC: Switch To The Secure Desktop When Prompting For Elevation

D. UAC: Behavior Of The Elevation Prompt For Standard Users

Lesson 2: Windows 7 Authentication and Authorization

When a user forgets his password, he is unable to log on to his computer. If he cannot log on to his computer, he cannot do his job. In this lesson, you learn about the methods Windows 7 provides through which you can deal with a forgotten password, from the preventative creation of a password reset disk to having a member of the Administrators local group log on and reset the password. Passwords are not the only way that you can authenticate to a client running Windows 7. Windows 7 supports multifactor authentication, primarily by including drivers that support the Personal Identity Verification (PIV) smart card standard and policies that can require a smart card to log on. In this lesson, you also learn about a new feature named Credential Manager. Credential Manager allows you to back up, restore, and manage saved credentials, such as those for Web sites and terminal services servers. You also learn about assigning user rights and configuring password policies.

> **After this lesson, you will be able to:**
> - Back up and restore credentials with Credential Manager.
> - Administer certificates with Certificate Manager.
> - Use runas to run commands with alternate credentials.
> - Configure account and smart card policies.
> - Resolve authentication issues.
>
> **Estimated lesson time: 40 minutes**

Credential Manager

Credential Manager stores logon user name and passwords for network resources, including file servers, Web sites, and terminal services servers. Credential Manager stores user name and password data in the Windows Vault. You can back up the Windows Vault and restore it on other computers running Windows 7 as a method of transferring saved credentials from one computer to another. Although Credential Manager can be used to back up some forms of digital certificates, it cannot be used to back up and restore the self-signed Encrypting File System (EFS) certificates that Windows 7 generates automatically when you encrypt a file. For this reason, you must back up EFS certificates using other tools. You will learn about backing up EFS certificates later in this lesson.

As Figure 9-11 shows, it is possible to add credentials to the Windows Vault by selecting Remember My Credentials in the Windows Security dialog box. Whenever you choose to remember your credentials, using Windows Internet Explorer, Windows Explorer, or Remote Desktop Connection, Credential Manager transfers them to the Windows Vault.

FIGURE 9-11 Remember My Credentials

You can also preemptively add credentials to Windows Vault for resources prior to actually accessing them. To add credentials to the Windows Vault, perform the following steps:

1. Open Credential Manager by typing **Credential Manager** into the Search Programs And Files text box and then clicking Credential Manager on the Start menu.

2. Click the Add a Windows Credential item.

3. In the Add a Windows Credential dialog box, shown in Figure 9-12, enter the Internet or network address, user name, and password of the credential that you want stored in the Windows Vault.

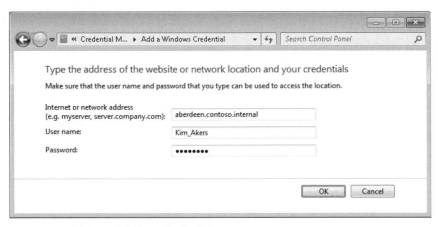

FIGURE 9-12 Adding a Windows Credential

To modify an existing password or to remove an existing credential, click the credential within Credential Manager and then click either the Edit item or the Remove From Vault item, respectively. You can see these items in Figure 9-13. Clicking Edit allows you to modify the user name and password stored in the vault. You would use the edit functionality to update an existing stored password. It is important to note that the existing password is not displayed but is shown as a series of dots. You cannot use Credential Manager to determine what an existing stored password is—only that the password itself is stored.

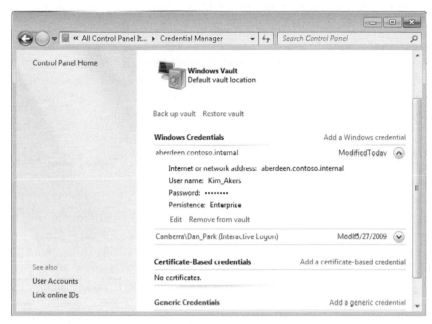

FIGURE 9-13 Editing and removing credentials

You can use the Back Up Vault and Restore Vault items, shown in Figure 9-13, to back up and restore credential data, or to transfer credential data between computers. This can be especially useful if a user has a significant number of credentials stored on their computer running Windows 7 and does not want to have to re-enter all of them when they move to a new computer. The backup process involves pressing the Ctrl, Alt, and Del keys at the same time to enter the backup password to protect the credentials on the Secure Desktop. You must also press Ctrl, Alt, and Del keys to enter the password on the Secure Desktop that you assigned to the backup when restoring the Windows Vault. You will back up and restore the Windows Vault in the practice at the end of this lesson.

Using Runas to Run Programs as Another User

The Runas command-line utility enables you to run programs using the credentials of another user. To run the application named Application.exe with an option, enclose the application and the option within quotation marks. To run the program *application.exe /option* as user Kim_Akers on computer Canberra, issue the command:

```
Runas /user:Canberra\Kim_Akers "application.exe /option"
```

When you enter this command, you have to enter the password of the target account. Once you have done this, the application runs using the target user's security context. The default setting loads the target user's profile. You can also use the *profile* option to force the target user's profile to be loaded. When the target user's profile is loaded, you can access files encrypted to the target user's account because the EFS certificates are stored with the user profile data. Use the *noprofile* option to stop the profile being loaded.

The *savecred* option allows you to save the credentials of the target user account. You have to enter the password the first time you use the *savecred* option. To access stored credentials with future Runas commands, use the *savecred* option and specify the account name. Saved credentials are stored within the Windows Vault and can be managed using Credential Manager. To use runas with the *savecred* option, use the command:

```
Runas /savecred /user:computername\user name "application.exe /option"
```

You cannot use the Runas command to execute an application that requires elevation if the target user account is configured to prompt for consent or prompt for credentials. You can use the Runas command to execute an application that requires elevation if the target user account is the built-in administrator account. The built-in administrator account is disabled by default, but it can be enabled through Group Policy. To run the Local Group Policy Editor console from a standard user account when the built-in administrator account has been enabled using Group Policy, use the command:

```
runas /user:administrator "mmc gpedit.msc"
```

You can use the *savecred* option to save the local Administrator account credentials so that they can be used automatically in the future. You should be careful when doing this because of the security risk that it poses.

Configuring User Rights

You can configure user rights through the Computer Configuration\Windows Settings\ Security Settings\Local Policies\User Rights Assignment node of Group Policy. This node contains 44 policies, most of which relate to operating system functions that are unlikely to be tested on the 70-680 exam. Most administrators configure user rights by adding users to specific local groups rather than by modifying specific user rights group policies. For example, you can allow a user to back up files and directories by assigning them to the Backup Operators group rather than by modifying the Back Up Files and Directories policy. The same applies to using Remote Desktop. You can add a user account to the Remote Desktop Users group, or you can modify the Allow Log On Through Remote Desktop Services policy. It is usually easier to add members to the appropriate local groups because it is easier to keep track of which users have been assigned specific rights by examining group membership than it is to examine Group Policy settings. The Windows 7 built-in groups that you can add users to as a method of assigning them rights are as follows:

- **Administrators** Members of this group have unrestricted access to the client running Windows 7.

- **Backup Operators** Members of this group are able to override file and folder access restrictions for the purpose of backing up data.

- **Cryptographic Operators** Members of this group are able to perform cryptographic operations. This policy is used only when Windows 7 is deployed in a special configuration called common criteria mode. In this mode administrators are able to read and write all settings except those related to the cryptography of IPsec policy.

- **Distributed COM Users** Members of this group are able to manipulate Distributed COM objects on this computer.

- **Event Log Readers** Members of this group can read data stored in the event logs.

- **Network Configuration Operators** Members of this group can change Transmission Control Protocol/Internet Protocol (TCP/IP) address settings.

- **Performance Log Users** These users can schedule the logging of performance counters, enable trace providers, and collect event traces.

- **Performance Monitor Users** These users can access performance counter data locally and remotely.

- **Power Users** This group is included for backward compatibility.

- **Remote Desktop Users** Members of this group are able to log on remotely through remote desktop.

- **Replicator** This group is used to support file replication in domain environment.

MORE INFO **DEFAULT LOCAL GROUPS**

You can learn more about the default local groups by navigating to the following Microsoft TechNet Web site: *http://technet.microsoft.com/en-us/library/cc771990.aspx*. You should be aware that some of the groups on this list are relevant only to domain environments.

 **Quick Check**

- How can you delete credentials that you stored when using Runas with the */savecred* option?

Quick Check Answer

- You can delete the credentials using Credential Manager.

Smart Cards

Smart cards store digital certificates that you can use for authentication. Smart cards are more secure than authenticating using user names and passwords. This is because it is possible for someone else to learn and use a person's user name and password without that person being aware of it, but it is very difficult for someone else to possess a smart card without the owner of the smart card becoming aware of the fact that she no longer has it. If a smart card is missing, an administrator can revoke the certificate stored on the smart card. This makes the missing smart card useless.

Windows 7 supports the PIV standard that was issued by the National Institute of Standards and Technology (NIST). Support for this standard allows Windows 7 to obtain drivers for smart cards from Windows Update or a PIV-compliant mini-driver that is included with Windows 7. The advantage of this is that you can use smart cards directly with Windows 7 without requiring specific vendor software.

Smart cards allow you to implement multifactor authentication on clients running Windows 7. *Multifactor authentication* requires a user to authenticate using two or more separate methods. The user might have to provide a user name/password and smart card, or a user name/password and biometric ID, such as a fingerprint. The most common form of multifactor authentication used with clients running Windows 7 in enterprise environments is smart card and password authentication. Biometric authentication is more likely to be used on portable stand-alone clients running Windows 7 and cannot be integrated into Active Directory Domain Services (AD DS) without third-party products.

> **MORE INFO** **BIOMETRICS IN WINDOWS 7**
>
> Although Biometric authentication is unlikely to be tested on the 70-680 exam, you can learn more about support for Biometrics at the following Microsoft TechNet Web page: *http://technet.microsoft.com/en-us/library/dd367857.aspx.*

Windows 7 has the following policies related to smart cards. These policies are located in the Computer Configuration\Windows Settings\Security Settings\Local Policies\Security Options node and are as follows:

- **Interactive Logon: Require Smart Card**   When this policy is enabled, users are able to log onto the computer only using a smart card. When the policy is disabled, which is the default setting, users can log on using any method.

- **Interactive Logon: Smart Card Removal Behavior**   This policy allows you to determine how the computer reacts when a user removes his smart card. The default setting is for no action to be taken if a smart card is removed. The other options that are available are:

  - **Lock Workstation**   When you implement this setting, Windows 7 locks the screen if the user removes the smart card. The user can only unlock the screen by reinserting the smart card.

  - **Force Logoff**   When you implement this setting, the user is forcibly logged off.

  - **Disconnect If A Remote Desktop Services Session**   This policy applies to what is known as Terminal Services sessions hosted on Windows Server 2008. Terminal Services is renamed Remote Desktop Services in Windows Server 2008 R2. This policy forces a disconnection from the Remote Desktop Services session when the user removes his smart card.

MORE INFO **SMART CARDS IN WINDOWS 7**

To learn more about using smart cards with Windows 7, consult the following Microsoft TechNet Web page: *http://technet.microsoft.com/en-us/library/dd367851.aspx*.

Account Policies

Password and account lockout policies, which can be found under the Computer Configuration\Windows Settings\Security Settings node of Group Policy, allow you to configure how passwords work on clients running Windows 7. You can use these policies to configure settings such as the length of time a user can use the same password before needing to change it, whether accounts are locked out after a number of invalid passwords are entered, and whether passwords must meet a set of complexity requirements.

You can configure the following password policies:

- **Enforce Password History** Use this policy to ensure that people do not use a small set of passwords that they rotate through each time they are asked to update their password. When you configure the Enforce Password History, Windows 7 remembers a certain number of prior passwords and does not allow users to set their new password to one they have used previously. When configuring this policy, you specify how many passwords Windows remembers.

- **Maximum Password Age** The maximum number of days that a person can keep the same password. Once this limit expires, users must change their password. If a user account has the Password Never Expires setting enabled (not recommended), it is not subject to this policy.

- **Minimum Password Age** Use this policy to require that a new password be kept for a minimum number of days before the user is allowed to change it. This stops users from rapidly changing passwords so that they can go through their existing password history and end up keeping the same password they had before they were asked to change it the first time.

- **Minimum Password Length** Use this policy to ensure that passwords have a minimum number of characters.

- **Password Must Meet Complexity Requirements** Use this policy to require passwords to include three of the following: uppercase letters, lowercase letters, numbers, and symbols. When you enforce this policy, passwords also cannot contain part of the user's first name, last name, or user name.

- **Store Passwords Using Reversible Encryption** Use this policy only if you are using older applications that use older authentication technologies. This policy makes password storage less secure.

You can configure the following account lockout policies:

- **Account Lockout Duration** Use this policy to configure the length of time an account is locked out before a user can attempt to log in again.

- **Account Lockout Threshold**   Use this policy to configure the number of times a user can enter an incorrect password before Windows locks out the account.
- **Reset Account Lockout Counter After**   Use this policy to specify the period in which Windows records invalid logon attempts. For example, if you set this period to 30 minutes and the Account Lockout Threshold policy is set to 3, three invalid logon attempts in 30 minutes triggers a lockout whereas three invalid logon attempts in 31 minutes will not. A valid logon automatically resets the account lockout counter.

Resolving Authentication Issues

The most common authentication issue that users face is that they have forgotten their password. There are two methods that you can use to deal with this problem: password reset disks and resetting user account passwords. Password reset disks, which can include universal serial bus (USB) storage devices, have the advantage that they allow a user to recover a forgotten password without losing encrypted data. The downside of password reset disks is that you must create one prior to the password being lost. Another disadvantage is that they can be used by anyone to recover that specific account's password, so they must be kept in a secure location because anyone who has access to the disk can gain access to the user's computer.

You can create a password reset disk, which can store password reset data on a floppy disk or a USB flash disk, by using the Create A Password Reset Disk item in the User Accounts Control Panel. Clicking the Create A Password Reset Disk item starts the Forgotten Password Wizard. When you use the wizard, you check which removable storage device you will store the data on and then enter the current user account password, as shown in Figure 9-14. You can activate the Password Reset Wizard once an incorrect password is entered on the Windows 7 logon screen. When using this wizard, the user specifies the password reset disk's location (either floppy disk or USB device) and then enters the new password. The user still has access to all her encrypted data.

FIGURE 9-14 Creating a password reset disk

If a user has forgotten her password and there is no password reset disk available, it will be necessary to change the password. This can be done through the Users node of the computer management console or by using the Manage Accounts option within the User Accounts control panel. Only members of the local Administrators group can change another user's password. When you change a user's password, the user loses all access to EFS-encrypted files, personal certificates, and stored passwords that are stored with the Windows Vault in Credential Manager, as displayed in Figure 9-15. If the user has backed up these passwords and certificates, it is possible to recover some items by restoring the Windows Vault. If the user has backed up her EFS key, she can access her encrypted files by restoring that key. You will learn about backing up and restoring EFS keys later in this lesson. It is also possible for an administrator to recover EFS-encrypted files if there is an existing EFS recovery agent configured for the computer. You learned about creating EFS recovery agents in Chapter 8, "BranchCache and Resource Sharing."

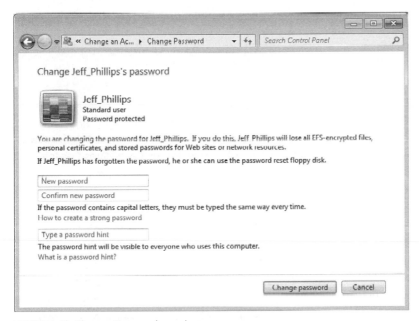

FIGURE 9-15 Change Password warning

If you have configured account lockout policies, a user may have his account locked out if he enters an incorrect password the number of times specified in the policy. You can unlock the account by editing the account properties using the Computer Management Console and removing the check next to the Account Is Locked Out setting, as shown in Figure 9-16. Only members of the local Administrators group can unlock accounts. Unlocking an account does not reset the account password and has no impact on stored credentials or EFS certificates. A user that has an unlocked account still needs to remember his password before he is able to log on to the computer running Windows 7.

FIGURE 9-16 Account lockout

Managing Certificates

Although you cannot use Credential Manager to back up EFS certificates, Windows 7 includes three other tools that you can use to perform this task. These are the Certificates Console (Certmgr.msc), the Manage File Encryption Certificates tool, and the Cipher.exe command-line tool. Each of these tools can be used to back up or export an existing EFS certificate to a password-protected PFX file. This PFX file can then be imported on other computers, or back to the original computer if necessary, either by using these tools, or double-clicking the PFX file using Windows Explorer.

Most users will use the Manage Your File Encryption Certificates tool, shown in Figure 9-17, to back up their EFS certificates because it is easier to use than other tools. This tool comprises a wizard that can be used either to back up your certificates or to configure EFS to use a smart card. The tool is accessed by typing **Manage File Encryption Certificates** into the Search Programs And Files text box. Using the wizard, you select the certificate that you want to back up, the location where the backup will be stored, and the password used to protect the backup.

The Certificates console, shown in Figure 9-18, can also be used to back up EFS certificates. This console can be opened by typing **certmgr.msc** into the Search Programs And Files text box. Certificates can be exported to password-protected PFX files by right-clicking the certificate that you want to export and then clicking Export. This console is less likely to be used by normal users because it is less intuitive than the Manage Your File Encryption Certificates tool. You have to remember that your EFS certificate is stored under the Personal\Certificates node, something that might not be obvious to a non-technical user.

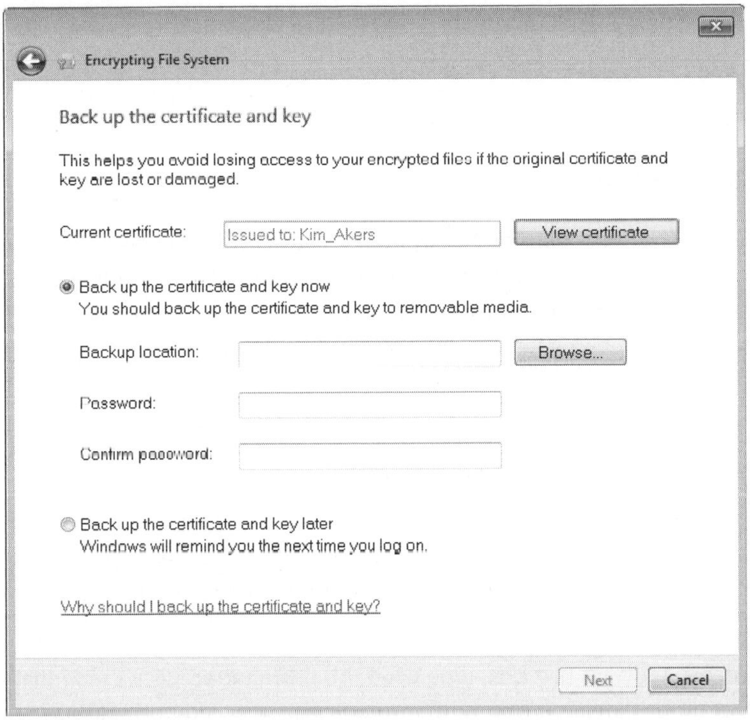

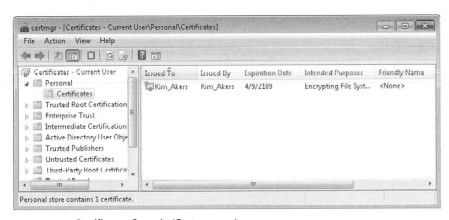

FIGURE 9-17 Backup EFS certificate

FIGURE 9-18 Certificates Console (Certmgr.msc)

EFS keys can also be backed up from the command line using the Cipher.exe command-line utility. When you back up your key, you are provided with a warning on the desktop that this is about to take place and are asked to provide a password to protect the exported key. The command to back up an EFS certificate is:

```
Cipher.exe /x filename.pfx
```

PRACTICE **Managing Credentials**

The Windows Vault allows you to store login and password information. This is very useful if you need to access resources outside a domain network and you have trouble remembering all of the unique passwords and login names that you have to use for each different research. In this practice, you explore the Windows Vault and the Runas utility. You get an understanding of each utility's function and how you might use them when deploying Windows 7 in your own network environment.

EXERCISE 1 **Exploring Runas Credentials and Credential Manager**

In this exercise, you use the Runas command to run several applications using another user's credentials. You save those credentials to the Windows Vault, verify that they have been saved, and then remove them. To complete this exercise, perform the following steps:

1. Log on to computer Canberra with the Kim_Akers user account.

2. In the Search Programs And Files text box, type **Credential Manager.** Click Credential Manager. Verify that no credentials are currently stored under any categories. Close Credential Manager.

3. Open an elevated command prompt and issue the following command:

   ```
   Net user Dan_Park P@ssw0rd /ADD
   ```

4. Close the elevated command prompt. Open a normal command prompt and issue the following command, which opens Notepad:

   ```
   Runas /savecred /user:Canberra\Dan_Park notepad
   ```

5. Enter the password **P@ssw0rd** when prompted. Close Notepad. Enter the following command at the command prompt:

   ```
   Runas /user:Canberra\Dan_Park write
   ```

6. Note that you needed to enter the password to run WordPad. Close WordPad. Enter the following command from the command prompt to open Microsoft Paint:

   ```
   Runas /savecred /user:Canberra\Dan_Park mspaint
   ```

7. Note that you did not need to enter a password because the saved credentials were used. Close Paint.

8. In the Search Programs And Files text box, type **Credential Manager.** Click Credential Manager. Click the Canberra\Dan_Park item under Windows Credentials, as shown in Figure 9-19.

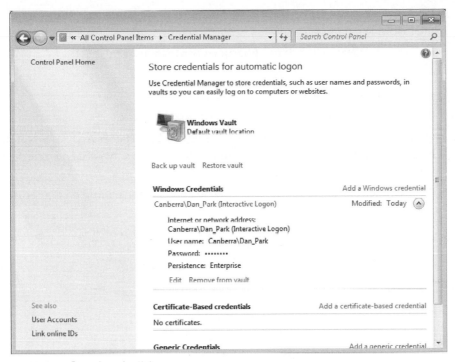

FIGURE 9-19 Stored credentials

9. Click Remove From Vault to remove the Dan_Park credentials. Click Yes when prompted by the Delete Windows Credential dialog box. From the command prompt, again issue the following command:

```
Runas /savecred /user:Canberra\Dan_Park mspaint
```

10. Note that this time you must enter credentials because they are no longer stored in the Windows Vault (though by running this command, you have again added them).

EXERCISE 2   Adding a Credential and Backing Up and Restoring Windows Vault

In this exercise, you add a credential to the one that was added to the Windows Vault at the end of the previous exercise. You then add yet another credential. From there, you back up the Windows Vault, delete the existing credentials, and then restore them by restoring the Windows Vault. To complete this exercise, perform the following steps:

1. If you have not done so already, log on to computer Canberra with the Kim_Akers user account. Use Windows Explorer to create the directory C:\Vault.

2. In the In the Search Programs And Files text box, type **Credential Manager.** Click Credential Manager.

3. Verify that the Canberra\Dan_Park (Interactive Logon) credential is present in Credential Manager. You re-created this credential in step 9 of Exercise 1.

4. Click Add a Windows Credential. In the Add A Windows Credential dialog box, enter the following credentials:
   - Internet Or Network Address: **Aberdeen.contoso.internal**
   - User name: **Sam_Abolrous**
   - Password: **P@ssword**

5. Click OK to close the Add A Windows Credential dialog box.

6. Click the Back Up Vault item. This opens the Stored User Names And Passwords dialog box. In the Back Up To text box, click Browse. Navigate to C:\Vault\, enter the name **Winvault,** and click Save. Click Next.

7. Press Ctrl, Alt, and Delete at the same time to continue the backup on the Secure Desktop, as shown in Figure 9-20.

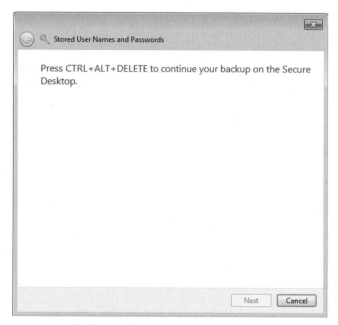

FIGURE 9-20 Backup on Secure Desktop

8. Enter the backup password **P@ssw0rd** twice and then click Next. Click Finish.

9. Use the Credential Manager to remove the Aberdeen.contoso.internal and Canberra\Dan_Park (Interactive Logon) credentials.

10. Click the Restore Vault item.

11. Click Browse to browse to C:\Vault\Winvault.crd and then click Next.

12. Press Ctrl, Alt, and Delete at the same time to continue restoring logon credentials on the Secure Desktop.

13. Enter the password **P@ssw0rd** on the Stored User Names And Password dialog box, as shown in Figure 9-21, and then click Next.

FIGURE 9-21 Restoring password

14. Click Finish when you are informed that your logon credentials have been restored.

15. Close and reopen Credential Manager to verify that the deleted logon credentials have been recovered.

Lesson Summary

- Credential Manager allows you to manage passwords for Web sites, terminal services and remote desktop sessions, stand-alone network resources, and smart card certificates. You can use Credential Manager to back up and restore these credentials.

- The Runas utility allows you to run programs using alternate credentials. You can use the */savecred* option to store the password associated with these alternate credentials.

- You can use Certmgr.msc, Cipher.exe, or the Manage File Encryption Certificates tool to back up EFS certificates.

- Users can create a password reset disk to assist them if they forget their password. Password reset disks must be created before the password is forgotten.

- Members of the local administrators group can reset the passwords of users that have forgotten them.

- Group policies can be configured to enforce multifactor authentication by requiring users to log on with smart cards.

- You can assign rights to users by adding them to the appropriate built-in local group or by assigning them rights through Group Policy.

Lesson Review

You can use the following questions to test your knowledge of the information in Lesson 2, "Windows Authentication and Authorization." The questions are also available on the companion CD if you prefer to review them in electronic form.

> **NOTE   ANSWERS**
>
> Answers to these questions and explanations of why each answer choice is correct or incorrect are located in the "Answers" section at the end of the book.

1. You have used Runas with the */savecred* option to save the credentials of an administrator account on a client running Windows 7. You have finished performing the tasks that you needed to and now want to remove those credentials from the computer. Which of the following tools could you use to do this?

   A. Runas

   B. Credential Manager

   C. The Certificates console

   D. UAC settings

2. You want to ensure that users are forcibly logged off from their computers running Windows 7 if they remove their smart cards. Which of the following policies and settings should you configure to accomplish this goal? (Choose all that apply; each answer forms part of a complete solution.)

   A. Interactive Logon: Smart Card Removal Behavior Properties: No Action

   B. Interactive Logon: Smart Card Removal Behavior Properties: Lock Workstation

   C. Interactive Logon: Smart Card Removal Behavior Properties: Force Logoff

   D. Interactive Logon: Require Smart Card: Enabled

3. A user has forgotten the password to the stand-alone desktop computer running Windows 7 that she uses at your organization. The user does not have a reset disk. You have an account on this computer that is a member of the local Administrators group. Which of the following steps can you take to resolve this user's authentication problem?

   A. Unlock her account

   B. Reset her password

   C. Create a password reset disk for her account

   D. Create a password reset disk for your account

4. You want to ensure that users of stand-alone clients running Windows 7 in your organization change their passwords every three weeks. Which of the following policies should you configure on each computer to accomplish this goal?

   A. Enforce Password History

   B. Minimum Password Length

   C. Minimum Password Age

   D. Maximum Password Age

5. Which of the following tools can users use to back up EFS certificates created when they encrypt a file on a stand-alone computer running Windows 7? (Choose all that apply.)

   A. Credential Manager

   B. The Manage File Encryption Certificates tool

   C. The Certificate Manager console

   D. Cipher.exe

Chapter Review

To further practice and reinforce the skills you learned in this chapter, you can perform the following tasks:

- Review the chapter summary.
- Review the list of key terms introduced in this chapter.
- Complete the case scenarios. These scenarios set up real-world situations involving the topics of this chapter and ask you to create a solution.
- Complete the suggested practices.
- Take a practice test.

Chapter Summary

- UAC can be configured to either prompt for credentials or prompt for consent. When prompting for credentials, you must enter your user account password.
- When Secure Desktop is implemented, users must respond to a UAC prompt before being able to continue working with their computer.
- UAC is configured through Group Policy.
- Credential Manager stores credentials entered into Internet Explorer, Remote Desktop Connection, and through Windows Explorer when connecting to remote servers. You can back up and restore these credentials.
- Password policies determine how often passwords need to be changed, whether users are locked out for entering successive incorrect passwords, and how complex passwords may be.
- Forgotten passwords can be recovered using the Password Recovery Tool. An administrator can reset a forgotten password, but credential data and encrypted files may be lost.
- You can back up EFS certificates using Certmgr.msc, Cipher.exe, or the Manage File Encryption Certificates tool.
- You can enforce multifactor authentication on a client running Windows 7 by configuring smart card policies.

Key Terms

Do you know what these key terms mean? You can check your answers by looking up the terms in the glossary at the end of the book.

- **multifactor authentication**
- **privilege elevation**
- **Secure Desktop**

Case Scenarios

In the following case scenarios, you apply what you've learned about subjects covered in this chapter. You can find answers to these questions in the "Answers" section at the end of this book.

Case Scenario 1: User Account Control at Coho Vineyard

You are developing UAC policies for the deployment of clients running Windows 7 at Coho Vineyard. Administrators often have to help out standard users using remote assistance. At times, it is necessary for administrators to perform actions that require elevation. Administrators should have to provide their authentication credentials when performing an act that triggers an elevation prompt. The administrators should be able to continue using other parts of the operating system and should not have to respond to the elevation prompt immediately. All approved applications at Coho Vineyard have been digitally signed by the application publisher.

With these facts in mind, answer the following questions:

1. Which policies do you need to configure to support the elevation requirements for administrators?

2. Which policies do you need to configure to support elevation during remote assistance?

3. Which policy do you need to configure to ensure that only approved applications can initiate elevation?

Case Scenario 2: Resolving Password Problems at Wingtip Toys

Wingtip Toys has 20 people that have stand-alone computers running Windows 7. One of the users recently had a problem where he forgot his password. You were able to reset this user's password, but the user lost access to several important encrypted documents as well as all his stored Web site credentials. You are in the process of developing a policy to ensure that this type of data loss does not happen again. You also want to ensure that users do not keep the same passwords because several appear to have been using the same password for the last few months without changing it, even though your company policy states that passwords should be changed every month.

With these facts in mind, answer the following questions:

1. What steps can you take to ensure that users do not lose access to encrypted documents or credentials if their password is reset?

2. What steps can you take to ensure that users are able to recover their own forgotten passwords?

3. What steps can you take to ensure that users regularly change their passwords and do not use the same small number of passwords?

Suggested Practices

To help you master the exam objectives presented in this chapter, complete the following tasks.

Configure User Account Control (UAC)

You should perform the first practice and then test it using one of the standard user accounts that you have created in previous exercises. The second practice requires two computers to test.

- **Practice 1** Configure UAC policies using the Local Security Policy console so that standard users are prompted for credentials when performing an activity that requires elevated privileges, such as attempting to run an elevated command prompt.

- **Practice 2** Configure UAC policies using the Local Security Policy console so that a user in the helper role is able to respond to a UAC prompt by entering their credentials when connected remotely using Remote Assistance. Use the computer named Aberdeen, which you configured in Chapter 6, "Network Settings," as the computer from which the Remote Assistance invitation is sent.

Configure Authentication and Authorization

You should perform both of these practices. The first exercise requires you to have access to a floppy disk or a USB storage device.

- **Practice 1** Create a password reset disk for a user account other than the Kim_Akers user account. Use the password reset disk to log on to an account.

- **Practice 2** Use Manage File Encryption Certificates tool to back up an EFS certificate.

Take a Practice Test

The practice tests on this book's companion CD offer many options. For example, you can test yourself on just one exam objective, or you can test yourself on all the 70-680 certification exam content. You can set up the test so that it closely simulates the experience of taking a certification exam, or you can set it up in study mode so that you can look at the correct answers and explanations after you answer each question.

> **MORE INFO** **PRACTICE TESTS**
>
> For details about all the practice test options available, see the section entitled "How to Use the Practice Tests," in the Introduction to this book.

CHAPTER 10

DirectAccess and VPN Connections

Virtual private networks (VPNs) allow you to access a workplace network remotely, whether you are just down the road from the office at a local coffee shop or in an airport lounge on the other side of the world. If the infrastructure in your office is set up correctly, all you need to use a VPN is to have access to the Internet. Once you have a successful Internet connection, you can access all resources on the corporate network.

In this chapter, you learn about new virtual private networking technologies included with Windows 7 as well as others with which you may already be familiar. One of these new technologies allows your computer running Windows 7 to reconnect automatically to an existing VPN session if something disrupts your connection, or when you switch one Internet service provider (ISP) to another. DirectAccess, another new feature, is a different kind of VPN solution that provides an always-on connection to a corporate network that becomes active as soon as the client running Windows 7 detects a connection to the Internet. In reading this chapter, you also learn about how to deal with clients that require remediation before they are able to access networks that use Network Access Protection (NAP) and how to configure Remote Desktop to access internal network servers without having to configure a VPN connection.

Exam objectives in this chapter:
- Configure DirectAccess.
- Configure remote connections.

Lessons in this chapter:

Before You Begin

To complete the exercises in the practices in this chapter, you need to have done the following:

- Installed Windows 7 on a stand-alone client PC named Canberra, as described in Chapter 1, "Install, Migrate, or Upgrade to Windows 7."
- To perform the exercises in Lesson 2, you should ensure that the Canberra client running Windows 7 has an active Internet connection.

REAL WORLD

Orin Thomas

The biggest drawback to being able to work anywhere is being able to work anywhere. I've found myself plugged into work in a lot of strange places, from a transit lounge in Bangkok when I was waiting for a flight to Copenhagen, to the balcony of a hotel suite on an island in the Great Barrier Reef. I always tell myself that I will just spend a few more moments catching up with my workload. Hamsters in running wheels probably say the same thing to themselves as well. Whereas in the past it was relatively easy to get away, modems that work in range of a cellular tower to give you Internet access and VPN connections that use that Internet access as a bridge to the office mean that the office is wherever you are. The office no longer ends at the front door—it extends itself to anywhere there is Internet connectivity. Some of the technologies that you learn about in this chapter further blur that distinction between home and work. When we talk about these technologies, we sell them with the promise that they allow corporate network access for people traveling on company business. Although that is the sales pitch, in reality you will find that many people use these remote access technologies at home after work hours to connect to the office to get just a little more work done. In the last decade, the line between the workplace and the home has become difficult to draw. The functionality provided by some of the technologies that you learn about in this chapter make drawing that line even more challenging.

Lesson 1: Managing DirectAccess

DirectAccess is a new technology in Windows 7 that eventually may replace traditional VPN solutions such as Point-to-Point Tunneling Protocol (PPTP), Layer 2 Tunneling Protocol/Internet Protocol Security (L2TP/IPsec), and Secure Socket Tunneling Protocol (SSTP). DirectAccess is an automatic connectivity solution that allows clients running Windows 7 to connect seamlessly to the corporate intranet the moment they establish a connection to the global Internet. The change from traditional solutions to DirectAccess will not occur overnight. Organizations have to make substantive changes to their network infrastructure, adopt new server and client technologies, and commit fully to IPv6. In this lesson, you learn about the benefits of DirectAccess, the technologies that support it, and what you need to do to implement it in your organization.

After this lesson, you will be able to:

- Use Netsh to configure DirectAccess clients.
- Configure DirectAccess authentication.
- Describe DirectAccess infrastructure requirements.

Estimated lesson time: 30 minutes

Understanding DirectAccess

DirectAccess is an always-on, IPv6, IPsec VPN connection. If a properly configured computer is able to connect to the Internet, DirectAccess automatically connects that computer to a properly configured corporate network. DirectAccess differs from the VPN solutions that you will learn about in Lesson 2, "Remote Connections," in the following ways:

- The connection process is automatic and does not require user intervention or logon. The DirectAccess connection process starts from the moment the computer connects to an active network. From the user's perspective, the computer always has access to the corporate intranet, whether she is sitting at her desk or when she has just connected to a Wi-Fi hot spot at a beachside cafe. Traditionally, users must initiate VPN connections to the corporate intranet manually.

- DirectAccess is bidirectional, with servers on the intranet being able to interact with the client running Windows 7 in the same way that they would if the client was connected to the local area network (LAN). In many traditional VPN solutions, the client can access the intranet but servers on the intranet cannot initiate communication with the client.

- DirectAccess provides administrators with greater flexibility in controlling which intranet resources are available to remote users and computers. Administrators can integrate DirectAccess with NAP to ensure that remote clients remain up to date with virus definitions and software updates. Administrators can also apply connection security policies to isolate servers and hosts.

The DirectAccess Process

The DirectAccess process is automatic. It requires no intervention on the part of the person
who is logging on to the computer running Windows 7. A portable computer that is taken
home and connected to a home Internet network can still receive software and Group Policy
updates from servers on the corporate network even if the user has not logged on. Clients
running Windows 7 use the following process to establish a DirectAccess connection:

1. The client running Windows 7 configured with DirectAccess connects a network.
   In most cases this occurs prior to user logon when the client running Windows 7 first
   connects to the network.

2. During the network identification phase, whenever a computer running Windows 7
   detects that it is connecting to a new network or resuming a connection to an existing
   network, the client attempts to connect to a specially configured intranet Web site.
   An administrator specifies this Web site address when configuring DirectAccess on the
   DirectAccess server, and you will learn how to do this later in the lesson. If the client
   can contact the Web site, Windows 7 concludes that it has connected to the corporate
   network and no further action is necessary.

3. If the client running Windows 7 is unable to contact the specially configured intranet
   Web site, the client attempts to determine whether a native IPv6 network is present.
   If a native IPv6 network is present and the client has been assigned a public IPv6
   address, DirectAccess makes a direct connection to the DirectAccess server across the
   Internet.

4. If a native IPv6 network is not present, Windows 7 attempts to establish an IPv6 over
   IPv4 tunnel using first the 6to4 and then Teredo transition technologies. You learned
   about Teredo and 6to4 in Chapter 6, "Network Settings."

5. If the client running Windows 7 cannot establish a Teredo or 6to4 connection due
   to an intervening firewall or proxy server, the client running Windows 7 attempts to
   connect using Internet Protocol–Hypertext Protocol Secure (IP-HTTPS). IP-HTTPS
   encapsulates IPv6 traffic over a HTTPS connection. IP-HTTPS is likely to work because
   few firewalls that allow connections to the Internet block traffic on TCP port 443.

6. The DirectAccess IPsec session is established when the client running Windows 7 and
   the DirectAccess server authenticate with each other using computer certificates.
   DirectAccess supports only certificate-based authentication.

7. The DirectAccess server checks the appropriate Active Directory Domain Services (AD DS) group to verify that the computer and user have authorization to connect using DirectAccess.

8. The DirectAccess client now has access to appropriately configured resources on the corporate network.

Table 10-1 summarizes DirectAccess client configurations and the corresponding method of communicating using IPv6 with the DirectAccess server. When you configure the DirectAccess server, you configure it to support all these different connection methods. You do this because you cannot be certain of what conditions exist on the remote network from which the DirectAccess client is attempting to connect. IP-HTTPS is tried last because it provides a poorer performance compared to the other connection methods.

TABLE 10-1 DirectAccess Connection Methods

CLIENT NETWORK CONNECTION	DIRECTACCESS CONNECTION METHOD
Public IPv6 address	Public IPv6 address
Public IPv4 address	6to4
Private (NAT) IPv4 address	Teredo
Client unable to connect to network due to firewall, but is connected to the Internet	IP-HTTPS

DirectAccess Client Configuration

Only domain-joined clients running Windows 7 Enterprise and Ultimate editions support DirectAccess. You cannot use DirectAccess with other editions of Windows 7 or earlier versions of Microsoft Windows, such as Windows Vista or Windows XP. When configuring a client for DirectAccess, you must add the client's domain computer account to a special security group. You specify this security group when running the DirectAccess wizard on the DirectAccess server. You will learn how to configure this special group later in this lesson.

Clients receive their DirectAccess configuration through Group Policy. This differs from traditional VPN configuration where connections are configured manually or distributed through the connection manager administration kit. Once you have added the computer's client account to the designated security group, you need to install a computer certificate on the client for the purpose of DirectAccess authentication. An organization needs to deploy Active Directory Certificate Services so that clients can automatically enroll with the appropriate certificates.

DirectAccess Manual Configuration

As mentioned earlier, DirectAccess clients get their configuration through Group Policy. This Group Policy is filtered so that it only applies to computers that are members of specific DirectAccess security groups. The policies that apply through this filtering are located in the Computer Configuration\Administrative Templates\TCPIP Settings\IPv6 Transition Technologies node. You can see this collection of policies in Figure 10-1.

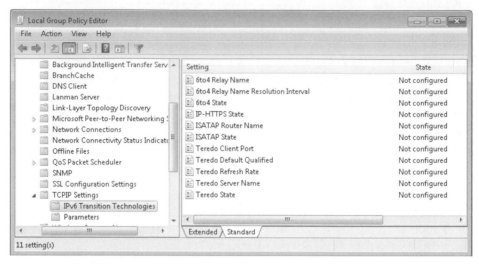

FIGURE 10-1 DirectAccess group policies

As computers must be domain-joined and be specifically added to security groups configured to support DirectAccess, there is little scope for local administrators to have to modify local policies on individual client running Windows 7 computers. When you configure DirectAccess on the DirectAccess server, it creates a GPO at the domain level and filters it for a specific security group. This GPO applies the following policies:

- **6to4 Relay Name**   This policy sets the 6to4 relay name and is configured to use one of the public IPv4 addresses applied to the DirectAccess server.

- **IP-HTTPS State**   This policy sets the Uniform Resource Locator (URL) of the IP-HTTPS server, which will be the FQDN of one of the public IPv4 addresses applied to the DirectAccess server. The default policy state uses IP-HTTPS as a connection of last resort. It is possible to set this policy to always use IP-HTTPS even if other connectivity options, such as 6to4 or Teredo, are available.

- **Teredo Default Qualified**   This policy determines whether Teredo will be used. It is set to enabled for DirectAccess clients.

- **Teredo Server Name**   This policy sets the address of the Teredo server. This address will be one of the public IPv4 address assigned to the DirectAccess server.

The final policy that is configured when you set up the DirectAccess server is the name resolution policy. The DirectAccess name resolution policy is located in the Computer Configuration\Policies\Windows Settings\Name Resolution Policy and is shown in Figure 10-2.

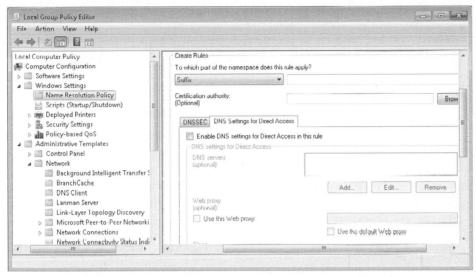

FIGURE 10-2 DirectAccess name resolution

Although it is possible to configure DirectAccess-related settings using the *Netsh* command-line utility, it is important to remember that Group Policy settings override settings manually configured using Netsh. The commands that you can use to configure DirectAccess settings are as follows:

```
Netsh interface ipv6 set teredo enterpriseclient IPv4_address
Netsh interface 6to4 set relay IPv4_address
Netsh interface httpstunnel add interface client https://fqdn/IPHTTPS
```

The first command configures Teredo. The IPv4 address that you assign using this command should be one of the public IPv4 addresses of the DirectAccess server. The second command configures 6to4 and again uses one of the public IPv4 addresses of the DirectAccess server. The final command configures IP-HTTPS. You should use the FQDN that maps to one of the public IPv4 addresses, as well as the installed SSL certificate, on the DirectAccess server.

> **MORE INFO** **CONFIGURING DIRECTACCESS CLIENTS MANUALLY**
>
> For more information on manually configuring DirectAccess clients, consult the following Microsoft TechNet document: *http://technet.microsoft.com/en-us/library/dd637798.aspx*.

Troubleshooting DirectAccess

You can determine if a client has made a successful DirectAccess connection by clicking on the Network Connection icon. When the status message displays "Internet and Corporate Access," as shown in Figure 10-3, the computer running Windows 7 has connected successfully to DirectAccess. If the status message shows "Local and Internet Access," there is no connection to the DirectAccess server.

Currently connected to:

Network
Internet and Corporate access

Open Network and Sharing Center

FIGURE 10-3 The Internet and Corporate Access message

As you learned earlier, DirectAccess clients use digital certificates to authenticate with the DirectAccess server. If a computer does not have a valid computer certificate issued by a certificate authority (CA) that the DirectAccess server is configured to trust for the purpose of DirectAccess authentication, it cannot connect successfully. DirectAccess clients and the DirectAccess server almost always receive their certificates from an Active Directory Certificate Services Certificate Authority that is integrated into the domain. This ensures that both client and server trust each other's certificates. To verify that a computer certificate is present and valid on a client running Windows 7, perform the following actions:

1. Open a blank Microsoft Management Console by typing **mmc** into the In The Search Programs And Files text box.

2. Add the Certificates snap-in for the local Computer account.

3. Navigate to the Certificates (Local Computer)\Personal\Certificates node and verify that the computer has enrolled a certificate for the intended purposes of Client Authentication and Server Authentication, as shown in Figure 10-4.

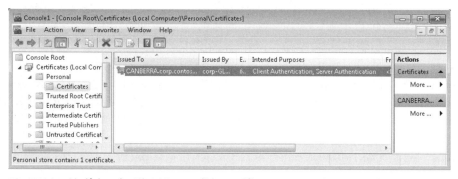

FIGURE 10-4 Verifying the DirectAccess client certificate

You can verify the current DirectAccess configuration using several command-line utilities. To verify the DirectAccess client's settings for 6to4, issue the command

```
Netsh interface 6to4 show relay
```

When the client is assigned DirectAccess configuration through Group Policy, this command displays one of the public IPv4 addresses assigned to the Direct Access server as the relay address. If the relay setting is set to Default, the DirectAccess Group Policy has not been applied properly. Similarly, when DirectAccess configuration is applied through Group Policy, you should see one of the two public addresses assigned to the DirectAccess server when you verify the Teredo configuration. You can verify the Teredo configuration by issuing the command

```
Netsh interface ipv6 show teredo
```

You can also get information about the IP-HTTPS configuration by issuing the command

```
Netsh interface httpstunnel show interfaces
```

> **MORE INFO   TROUBLESHOOTING DIRECTACCESS**
>
> For more information on troubleshooting DirectAccess, consult the following Microsoft TechNet document: *http://technet.microsoft.com/en-us/library/dd637786.aspx*.

 **Quick Check**

- Which IPv6 transition technology does DirectAccess use if you are in a remote location and your computer has been assigned a public IPv4 address, but not a public IPv6 address?

Quick Check Answer

- DirectAccess uses the 6to4 IPv6 transition technology if the client is assigned a public IPv4 address but not a public IPv6 address.

Configuring the DirectAccess server

You configure DirectAccess primarily by configuring the DirectAccess server. When you configure the DirectAccess server, you also end up configuring the necessary Group Policy Objects (GPOs) that support DirectAccess. Prior to installing DirectAccess, you should ensure that the DirectAccess server meets the following requirements:

- The computer needs to have Windows Server 2008 R2 installed and be a member of a domain.
- This server must have two network adapters.
- One of these network adapters needs to a direct connection to the Internet. You must assign this adapter two consecutive public IPv4 addresses.
- The second network adapter needs a direct connection to the corporate intranet.
- The computer needs digital certificates to support server authentication. This includes having a computer certificate that matches the fully qualified domain name (FQDN) that is assigned to the IP addresses on the DirectAccess server's external network interface.

You should also create at least one global security group in AD DS that you use with DirectAccess. You can give this group any name that you like, though it is easier to keep track of it if you give it a DirectAccess-related name. It is possible to create and specify multiple DirectAccess-related security groups if necessary. You create multiple groups when you need to differentiate access to segments of the corporate intranet.

To install DirectAccess on a server running Windows Server 2008 R2, add the DirectAccess Management Console feature using the Add Features Wizard, as shown in Figure 10-5. Installing the DirectAccess Management Console allows you to configure and manage DirectAccess features. Installing the DirectAccess Management console also requires that you add the Group Policy Management feature. The Group Policy Management feature is necessary because the DirectAccess setup wizard creates DirectAccess-related GPOs that configure DirectAccess clients. You need to run the DirectAccess setup wizard with a user account that has permissions to create and apply GPOs in the domain.

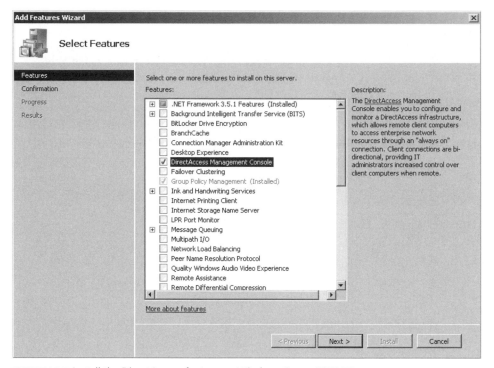

FIGURE 10-5 Install the DirectAccess feature on Windows Server 2008 R2

After you install the DirectAccess Management console, you can configure the DirectAccess server. To do this, perform the following steps:

1. Open the DirectAccess Management console from the Administrative Tools menu on the computer running Windows Server 2008 R2. This opens the DirectAccess Management console, shown in Figure 10-6.

FIGURE 10-6 DirectAccess console

2. Select the Setup node. In the details pane, in the Remote Clients area, click Configure. This opens the DirectAccess Client Setup dialog box. Click Add and then specify the name of the security groups to which you add computer accounts when you want to grant access to DirectAccess to specific clients running Windows 7. Those groups can have any names. The one in Figure 10-7 is called DA_Clients.

FIGURE 10-7 DirectAccess client groups

3. Use the DirectAccess Server Setup item to specify which interface is connected to the Internet and which interface is connected to the internal network. Performing this step will enable IPv6 transition technologies on the DirectAccess server, as shown in Figure 10-8. You use this item to specify the CA that client certificates must ultimately come from, either directly or through a subordinate CA. You also must specify the server certificate used to secure IP-HTTPS traffic.

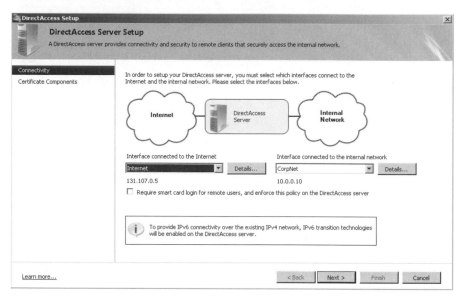

FIGURE 10-8 DirectAccess Server Setup

4. On the Infrastructure Server Setup page, you specify the location of the internal Web site (known as the Network Location Server) that DirectAccess clients attempt to contact to determine whether they are connected to the corporate intranet or a remote location. You must ensure that you secure this Web site with a Web server certificate, as shown in Figure 10-9. You also use this dialog box to specify which DNS servers and domain controllers the DirectAccess clients are able to contact for authentication purposes.

5. The final step involves specifying which resources on the corporate intranet are accessible to DirectAccess clients. The default setting is to allow access to all resources. In more secure environments, it is possible to use isolation policies to limit the contact to the membership of specific security groups. For example, you might create a security group and add the computer accounts of some file servers and mail servers, but not others.

6. When you click Finish, DirectAccess interfaces with a domain controller and creates two new GPOs in the domain. The first of these is targeted at the security groups that contain the computer accounts of DirectAccess clients. The second GPO is targeted at the DirectAccess server itself. You can see these GPOs in Figure 10-10.

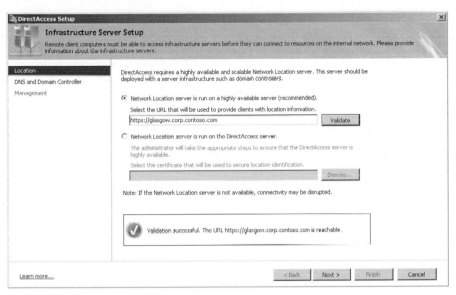

FIGURE 10-9 Specifying the network location server

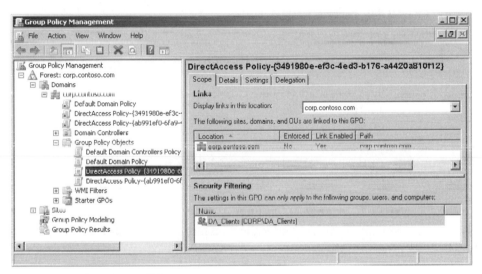

FIGURE 10-10 Direct Access GPOs

DirectAccess relies upon several other components in a Windows Server 2008 R2 network infrastructure. The domain in which you install the DirectAccess server must also have the following:

- At least one domain controller running Windows Server 2008 R2 and DNS server on the internal network.

- A server running Windows Server 2008 with Active Directory certificates installed, either as an enterprise root CA or an enterprise subordinate CA.

To make internal network resources available to remote DirectAccess clients, you need to do one of the following:

- Ensure that all internal resources that will be accessed by DirectAccess support IPv6.
- Deploy ISATAP on the intranet. ISATAP allows intranet servers and applications to be reached by tunneling IPv6 traffic over an IPv4 intranet.
- Deploy an NAT-PT device. NAT-PT devices allow hosts that only support IPv4 addresses to be accessible to DirectAccess clients using IPv6.

All application servers that DirectAccess clients access need to allow ICMPv6 traffic in Windows Firewall with Advanced Security (WFAS). You can accomplish this by enabling the following firewall rules using Group Policy.

- Echo Request – ICMPv6-in
- Echo Request – ICMPv6-out

The following ports on an organization's external firewall must be open to support DirectAccess:

- **UDP port 3544**   Enables Teredo traffic.
- **IPv4 protocol 41**   Enables 6to4 traffic.
- **TCP port 443**   Allows IP-HTTPS traffic.
- **ICMPv6 and IPv4 Protocol 50**   Required when remote clients have IPv6 addresses.

EXAM TIP

Remember which conditions necessitate the use of Teredo, 6to4, and IP-HTTPS on DirectAccess clients.

PRACTICE   **Configure DirectAccess with Netsh**

DirectAccess requires a Windows Server 2008 R2 network infrastructure, so it is not possible to simulate DirectAccess on a client running Windows 7 without also having access to several servers running Windows Server 2008 R2. In this practice, you simulate manually configuring different IPv6 DirectAccess components using Netsh.

EXERCISE 1   **Netsh DirectAccess Configuration**

In this exercise, you simulate setting DirectAccess policies using the *Netsh* command-line utility. In reality, DirectAccess configuration comes through Group Policy, though there may be circumstances, such as when a client has been out of the office for some time and when the DirectAccess server address has changed, where you need to perform this type of manual configuration.

1. Log on to computer Canberra using the Kim_Akers user account and open an elevated command prompt.

2. Enter each of the following commands and press Enter:

```
Netsh interface ipv6 set teredo enterpriseclient 131.107.0.5
Netsh interface 6to4 set relay 131.107.0.5
```

3. Now enter the following diagnostic commands and press Enter after each one to verify that the correct configuration was set. The configuration should match the IP address 131.107.0.5:

```
Netsh interface 6to4 show relay
Netsh interface ipv6 show teredo
```

Lesson Summary

- DirectAccess allows a client running Windows 7 Enterprise or Ultimate edition to connect automatically to a corporate intranet when an active Internet connection is established without requiring user intervention.

- If a client running Windows 7 has a public IPv6 address, a direct IPv6 connection is made. If the client has a public IPv4 address, a connection is made using the 6to4 transition technology. If the client has a private IPv4 address, a connection is made using the Teredo transition technology. If the client has a private IPv4 address and is behind a firewall that restricts most forms of network traffic, a connection using IP-HTTPS is made.

- DirectAccess clients require computer certificates from a CA that is trusted by the DirectAccess server. The DirectAccess server requires a certificate from a CA trusted by the DirectAccess client.

- DirectAccess clients must be members of an AD DS domain. DirectAccess clients must be members of a special domain security group which has been configured during the setup of the DirectAccess server.

- A DirectAccess server must run Windows Server 2008 R2. A domain controller running Windows Server 2008 R2 and a DNS server must also be present on the internal network to support DirectAccess.

Lesson Review

You can use the following questions to test your knowledge of the information in Lesson 1, "Managing DirectAccess." The questions are also available on the companion DVD if you prefer to review them in electronic form.

> **NOTE ANSWERS**
>
> Answers to these questions and explanations of why each answer choice is correct or incorrect are located in the "Answers" section at the end of the book.

1. A client running Windows 7 is connecting to a hotel network. Clients on the hotel network are assigned IP addresses in the 10.0.10.0 /24 range. The hotel firewall blocks all traffic except that on ports 25, 80, and 443. Which DirectAccess connectivity method does the client use to make the connection?

   A. Teredo

   B. 6to4

   C. Globally routable IPv6 address

   D. IP-HTTPS

2. You have 10 stand-alone laptop computers running Windows 7 Professional. You want to configure these computers so that they can use DirectAccess to access the internal network when users connect to remote networks. Your internal network has a Windows Server 2008 R2 functional level domain. Which of the following steps must you take before you can accomplish this goal? (Choose all that apply.)

   A. Upgrade the computers to Windows 7 Ultimate.

   B. Join the computers to the domain.

   C. Configure AppLocker policies.

   D. Configure BranchCache policies.

3. Which of the following computers can you configure as a DirectAccess server?

   A. A server running Windows Server 2008 R2 with two network adapters that has been assigned two consecutive public IPv4 addresses

   B. A server running Windows Server 2008 R2 with one network adapter that has been assigned two consecutive public IPv4 addresses

   C. A server running Windows Server 2008 R2 with two network adapters that has been assigned one public IPv4 address

   D. A server running Windows Server 2008 R2 with one network adapter that has been assigned one public IPv4 address

4. Kim Akers, who uses the Kim_Akers user account, has been using a computer running Windows 7 Enterprise named laptop-122 with DirectAccess to access the internal corporate network when working remotely. Laptop-122 is a member of the Direct_Access domain security group. Laptop-122 has developed a fault and Kim has been given Laptop-123, which also runs Windows 7 Enterprise and is joined to the Contoso.internal domain. When Kim is working remotely, she is unable to connect to the internal network. Which of the following steps should you take to resolve this problem?

   A. Add the computer account for Laptop-123 to the Direct_Access group in the domain.

   B. Add the computer account for Laptop-123 to the Direct_Access group on Laptop-123.

   C. Add the Kim_Akers user account to the Direct_Access group in the domain.

   D. Add the Kim_Akers user account to the Direct_Access local group on Laptop-123.

5. Your client running Windows 7 is connected to a hotel network, has an address on the 192.168.10.0 /24 network, and is located behind a Network Address Translation (NAT) device. The network blocks all outbound traffic except that on ports 80 and 443. You want the address of the DirectAccess IP-HTTPS server to be set correctly. Which of the following commands could you use?

   A. *ipconfig*

   B. *netsh interface 6to4 show relay*

   C. *netsh interface ipv6 show teredo*

   D. *netsh interface httpstunnel show interfaces*

Lesson 2: Remote Connections

Although not every edition of Windows 7 supports DirectAccess, every edition of Windows 7 supports VPN using the PPTP, L2TP/IPsec, SSTP, and IKEv2 protocols. Traditional VPN technology is important because, except for IKEv2, these technologies are compatible with existing remote access infrastructures and do not require an organization to upgrade any servers to Windows Server 2008 R2. PPTP and L2TP/IPsec VPNS are also compatible with third-party remote access solutions. This is important if your organization does not rely upon a Windows Server remote access infrastructure. In this lesson, you learn about how to deal with clients that have been restricted to NAP quarantine and how to configure the Remote Desktop Client to access Remote Desktop Services servers on protected internal network without having to configure a VPN connection.

> **After this lesson, you will be able to:**
> - Establishing VPN connections.
> - Configuring VPN authentication.
> - Setting up VPN Reconnect.
> - Manage VPN security auditing.
> - Configure NAP quarantine remediation.
>
> **Estimated lesson time: 40 minutes**

Virtual Private Networks

VPNs allow people to make connections to remote networks over the Internet. VPN users can access resources on the LAN such as e-mail, shared folders, printers, databases, and calendars when they are using their computers in an out-of-office location. All they need to access a VPN is to have an active Internet connection and for the relevant VPN infrastructure to be set up on the corporate network to which they are connecting. Configuring VPNs means that resources on protected corporate networks can be made available to authorized users on the Internet through the VPN without making those resources directly available to users on the Internet. VPNs are like tunnels that allow specific authorized users from the Internet access to a configured list of internal network resources. Users without administrative privileges are able to create remote access connections. It is possible to limit user rights to create or modify remote access connections by configuring policies in the User Configuration\Administrative Templates\Network\Network Connections node of Group Policy.

When you create a VPN connection, you need to specify the address of the VPN server that you are connecting to and your authentication credentials. You can create a new VPN connection in the Network And Sharing Center by clicking Set Up A New Connection Or Network and then Connect to a Workplace. When you create a new VPN connection,

Windows 7 sets the VPN type to Automatic. You can configure a connection to use a specific VPN protocol, but if you do this, Windows 7 does not try to use other VPN protocols If the protocol you select is not available. You will create a VPN connection and then edit its properties to use a specific VPN protocol in the practice at the end of this lesson.

When a VPN connection type is set to Automatic, Windows 7 attempts to make a connection using the most secure protocol. Clients running Windows 7 can use four different VPN protocols, which differ in the types of encryption and data protection they offer. The most secure protocols support:

- **Data confidentiality**   The protocol encrypts your data so that third parties cannot read it as it crosses public networks.
- **Data integrity**   You will know if a third party tampers with your data in transit.
- **Replay protection**   Ensures that the same data cannot be sent more than once. In a replay attack, an attacker captures and then resends data.
- **Data origin authentication**   The sender and receiver can be sure of the origin of transmitted and received data.

The VPN protocols supported by Windows 7, listed from least to most secure, are:

- **PPTP**   PPTP VPNs are the least secure form of VPN. Because PPTP VPNs do not require access to a public key infrastructure (PKI), they are also the most commonly deployed type of VPN. PPTP connections can use the MS-CHAP, MS-CHAPv2, EAP, and PEAP authentication protocols. PPTP connections use MPPE to encrypt PPTP data. PPTP connections provide data confidentiality but do not provide data integrity or data origin authentication. Some older NAT devices do not support PPTP. Windows 7 uses PPTP to support incoming VPN connections. You will learn about configuring Windows 7 to support incoming VPN connections later in this lesson.
- **L2TP/IPsec**   L2TP/IPsec VPN connections are more secure than PPTP. L2TP/IPsec provides per-packet data origin authentication, data integrity, replay protection, and data confidentiality. L2TP/IPsec uses digital certificates, so it requires access to a certificate services infrastructure. Most third-party VPN solutions support L2TP/IPsec. L2TP/IPsec cannot be used behind NAT unless the client and server support IPsec NAT Traversal (NAT-T). Windows 7, Windows Server 2003, and Windows Server 2008 support NAT-T. You can configure L2TP to use either certificate-based authentication or a pre-shared key by configuring the advanced properties, as shown in Figure 10-11.
- **SSTP**   SSTP VPN tunnels use port 443, meaning that SSTP VPN traffic can pass across almost all firewalls that allow Internet access, something that is not true of the PPTP, L2TP/IPsec, and IKEv2 VPN protocols. SSTP works by encapsulating PPP traffic over the SSL channel of the HTTPS protocol. SSTP supports data origin authentication, data integrity, replay protection, and data confidentiality. You cannot use SSTP through a Web proxy that requires authentication.

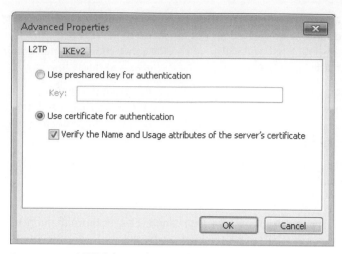

FIGURE 10-11 L2TP Advanced Properties

- **IKEv2** IKEv2 is a VPN protocol new to Windows 7 and is not present in previous versions of Windows. IKEv2 supports IPv6 and the new VPN Reconnect feature. IKEv2 supports Extensible Application Protocol (EAP) and computer certificates for client-side authentication. This includes Microsoft Protected EAP (PEAP), Microsoft Secured Password (EAP-MSCHAP v2), and Microsoft Smart Card or Other Certificate, as shown in Figure 10-12. IKEv2 does not support POP, CHAP, or MS-CHAPv2 (without EAP) as authentication protocols. IKEv2 supports data origin authentication, data integrity, replay protection, and data confidentiality. IKEv2 uses UDP port 500. When you configure a new Windows 7 VPN connection with the default settings, Windows 7 attempts to make an IKEv2 connection first.

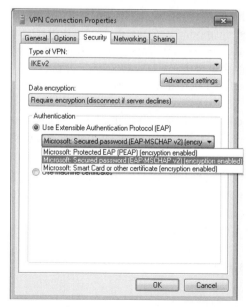

FIGURE 10-12 Authentication protocols supported by IKEv2

VPN Authentication Protocols

Windows 7 supports different authentication protocols for both dial-up and VPN connections. There are two broad categories of authentication protocol: password-based authentication protocols and certificate-based authentication protocols. Certificate-based authentication protocols require the deployment of a PKI solution such as Active Directory Certificate Services. When you use a certificate-based authentication protocol, it is necessary to deploy certificates tied to user accounts, computer accounts, or both types of account. The properties of these protocols are as follows:

- **PAP (Password Authentication Protocol)**   This protocol uses unencrypted passwords for authentication. This protocol is not enabled by default for Windows 7 VPN connections and is not supported by remote access servers running Windows Server 2008. You would enable this protocol only to connect to an older third-party VPN server that does not support other more secure protocols.

- **CHAP (Challenge Authentication Protocol)**   This is a password-based authentication protocol. Although remote access servers running Windows Server 2008 do not support this protocol, it is enabled by default for Windows 7 VPN connections and it allows you to connect to third-party VPN servers that do not support other more secure protocols.

- **MS-CHAPv2 (Microsoft Challenge Handshake Authentication Protocol version 2)**   MS-CHAPv2 is a password-based authentication protocol. You can configure a VPN connection that uses this protocol to use the credentials of the currently logged on user for authentication.

- **PEAP/PEAP-TLS (Protected Extensible Authentication Protocol with Transport Layer Security)**   This is a certificate-based authentication protocol where users authenticate using certificates. Requires the installation of a computer certificate on the VPN server.

- **EAP-MS-CHAPv2/PEAP-MS-CHAPv2**   The most secure password-based authentication protocols available to VPN clients running Windows 7; requires the installation of a computer certificate on the VPN server. Does not require a client certificate.

- **Smart Card or Other Certificate**   Use this protocol when users are authenticating VPN connections using a smart card or a certificate installed on this computer. The properties for this authentication protocol are shown in Figure 10-13.

You can configure which VPN authentication protocols are supported for a connection by editing a VPN connection's properties in the Network Connections control panel, as shown in Figure 10-14. Windows first tries to use the most secure authentication protocol that is enabled and then falls back to less secure protocols if they are available.

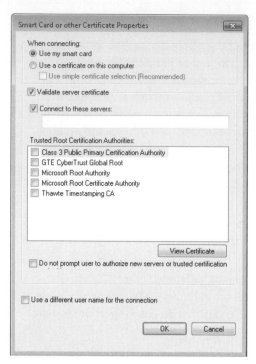

FIGURE 10-13 Smart Card or other Certificate options

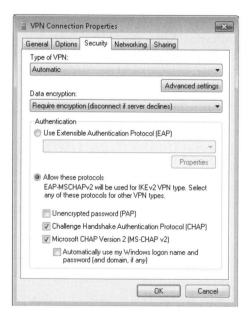

FIGURE 10-14 VPN Authentication protocols

VPN Reconnect

VPN Reconnect is a feature new to Windows 7. When you connect to a VPN server using the PPTP, L2TP/IPsec, or SSTP protocol and you suffer some sort of network disruption, you can lose your VPN connection and need to restart it. If you were transferring a file, downloading e-mail, or sending a print job, you need to start over from the beginning. VPN Reconnect allows clients running Windows 7 to reconnect automatically to a disrupted VPN session even if the disruption has lasted for 8 hours. VPN Reconnect also works if connecting to a new Internet access point causes the disruption. For example, a user might be using a VPN connection to his corporate network while connected to a wireless network at an airport coffee shop. As the time of his flight's departure approaches, he moves from the coffee shop to the airport lounge, which has its own Wi-Fi network. With VPN Reconnect, the user's VPN connection is reestablished automatically when he achieves Internet connectivity with the new network. With a traditional VPN solution, this user would have to reconnect manually once he connected to the new wireless network in the airport lounge, and any existing operations occurring across the VPN would be lost. Unlike DirectAccess, which only some editions of Windows 7 support, all editions of Windows 7 support VPN Reconnect.

VPN Reconnect uses the IKEv2 tunneling protocol with the MOBIKE extension. The MOBIKE extension allows VPN clients to change their Internet addresses without having to renegotiate authentication with the VPN server. Only VPN servers running Windows Server 2008 R2 support IKEv2. You cannot use IKEv2 if your organization has a routing and remote access server running Windows Server 2003, Windows Server 2003 R2, or Windows Server 2008.

You can configure VPN Reconnect with a maximum timeout of 8 hours, as shown in Figure 10-15. After the period specified in the Network Outage Time setting has expired, it is necessary for the user to reconnect manually. You will create and configure an IKEv2-based VPN connection in the practice exercise at the end of this lesson.

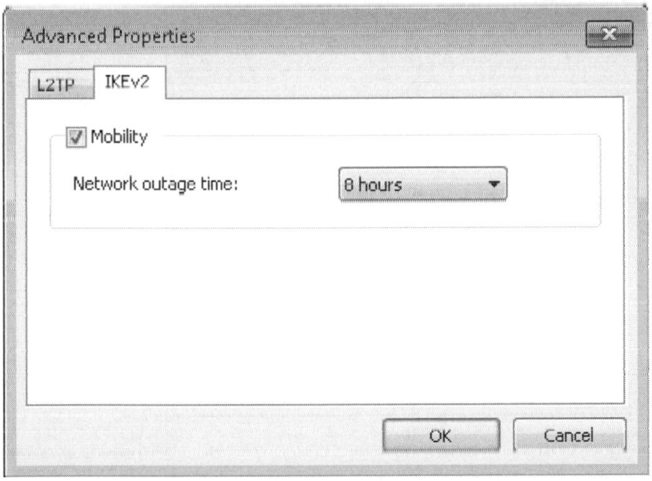

FIGURE 10-15 IKEv2 Advanced Properties

NAP Remediation

NAP is a technology in Windows Server 2008 that restricts network access based on an assessment of a client computer's health. A compliant client that meets the health benchmark is able to access the network. If the computer does not meet the health benchmark, it is noncompliant. NAP blocks noncompliant clients from accessing the network. NAP can be used for clients on the LAN, but also can be used for VPN, RD Gateway, and DirectAccess clients. Administrators can configure NAP to restrict network access based on the following criteria:

- Does a client have antivirus software installed and up to date?
- Does a client have anti-spyware software installed and up to date?
- Does a client have Windows Firewall enabled?
- Are automatic update enabled?
- Have all software updates been installed on the client computer?

Administrators specify these criteria through Security Health Validators (SHVs). Administrators configure SHVs to specify the components of the system health benchmark. Figure 10-16 shows the Windows 7 SHV that is included with Windows Server 2008 R2.

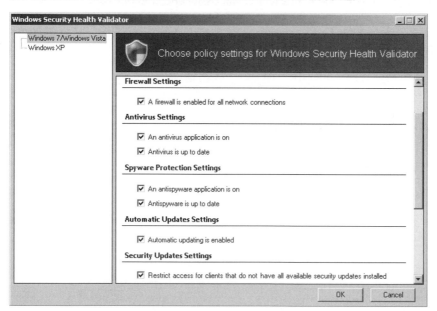

FIGURE 10-16 Windows Security Health Validator

Administrators can configure NAP to perform a process of remediation on client computers that do not meet the specified health benchmarks. When NAP applies to VPN connections, this often means providing access to a remediation network. A remediation network is a special network that hosts the services that would allow the client to come back into compliance. Noncompliant clients can communicate with hosts on the remediation network but not other hosts on the internal corporate network. A remediation network could include a Windows Server Update Services (WSUS) server so that the client can get the most recent software updates and an antivirus update server so that the client can reach a compliant state and be granted access to the network.

It is possible for a client running Windows 7 to perform some steps automatically towards remediation when the Security Center service is enabled. This service interacts with the Windows 7 Action Center. If this service is enabled and the appropriate NAP policies are configured within the remote access infrastructure, clients might automatically bring themselves into compliance by switching on items like the Windows Firewall, running Windows Update, and initiating the process of updating antivirus and anti-spyware software.

In environments without remediation networks, it is necessary for users to bring the computer into compliance manually before they will be able to establish a successful remote access connection. If your organization uses NAP with its remote access infrastructure, you should ensure that users know what steps they need to take to get their clients running Windows 7 compliant so they will be able to access the internal network.

> **MORE INFO** **NAP**
>
> To find out more about NAP, consult the Network Access Protection TechCenter at the following address: *http://technet.microsoft.com/en-us/network/bb545879.aspx.*

Remote Desktop and Application Publishing

Windows Server 2008 R2 Remote Desktop Services, known as Terminal Services on Windows Server 2008 and Windows Server 2003, allows people to connect using the Remote Desktop Connection client to a server on which they can run applications. You learned about making Remote Desktop connections to clients running Windows 7 in Chapter 7, "Firewall and Remote Management."

RD (Remote Desktop) Gateway, formerly known as Terminal Services Gateway, allows users on the Internet to make Remote Desktop connections to servers on internal networks without the user having to initiate a VPN connection. Connections can only be made to specially configured Remote Desktop hosts on the internal network. Users are unable to access all resources on network, as is the case with a traditional VPN or DirectAccess.

> **MORE INFO** **RD GATEWAY**
>
> To learn more about RD Gateway, consult the following Microsoft TechNet article: *http://technet.microsoft.com/en-us/library/dd560672.aspx.*

To connect using an RD Gateway server, navigate to the Advanced tab of the Remote Desktop Connection Properties dialog box and click Settings under Connect From Anywhere. This opens the RD Gateway Server Settings dialog box. This dialog box allows you to specify RD Gateway settings, including whether or not you want the RD Gateway to be detected automatically, whether to use a specific RD Gateway server, as shown in Figure 10-17, or you can specify Do Not Use an RD Gateway Server, which is the default setting.

FIGURE 10-17 RD Gateway server settings

You can also apply RD Gateway configuration through Group Policy rather than configuring it manually. The relevant policies are located in the User Configuration\Administrative Templates\ Windows Components\Remote Desktop Services\RD Gateway node, as shown in Figure 10-18.

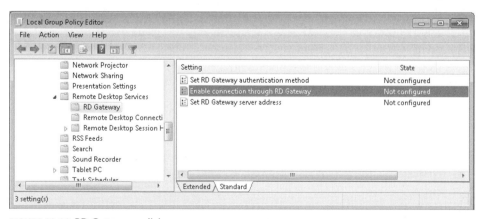

FIGURE 10-18 RD Gateway policies

These policies work as follows:

- **Set RD Gateway authentication method** When the policy is set to Not Configured or Disabled, the authentication method specified by the user is used. When enabled, the administrator can choose to allow the user to change the setting, or the administrator can select among the following options:
  - Ask for credentials, use NTLM protocol
  - Ask for credentials, use Basic protocol
  - Use the locally logged on credentials
  - Use a smart card

- **Enable Connection through RD Gateway** When this policy is enabled, Remote Desktop Client automatically tries to connect through the configured RD Gateway if it is unable to connect automatically to the target Remote Desktop Services server. This policy can be enforced only if the Set RD Gateway server address policy is configured. A policy option allows users to override this setting.

- **Set RD Gateway server address** When the policy is set to Not Configured or Disabled, clients automatically detect whether RD Gateway is required. If required, the RD Gateway specified by the user is used. When this policy is set to Enabled, the address of the RD Gateway server specified in the policy is used. The address of the RD Gateway server must match the name of the SSL certificate installed on the RD Gateway server.

RemoteApp allows applications that reside on Remote Desktop Services servers to have their display output shown in Remote Desktop clients. This differs from a standard Remote Desktop Connection window where the user sees the entire remote desktop in a window. For example, if you publish the Microsoft Office Excel 2007 application through Remote Desktop Services RemoteApp and the user runs it, the user sees an Excel 2007 application window just as she would if the application were running locally. Remote Desktop Services RemoteApp applications appear in the Start menu just like other locally installed applications. The difference with RemoteApp is that the application runs on the Remote Desktop Services server, with only the application display appearing on the client.

You can use RemoteApp applications over the Internet if the RemoteApp program shortcuts or publications include the address of an RD Gateway server. You configure the RD Gateway server address prior to publishing applications by using the RemoteApp Deployment Settings dialog box, shown in Figure 10-19. This dialog box is available through the RemoteApp manager on a computer running Windows Server 2008 R2. If you publish a RemoteApp application through Group Policy or by distributing a remote desktop shortcut (.rdp) file prior to configuring an RD Gateway, you have to republish the application and redistribute the file.

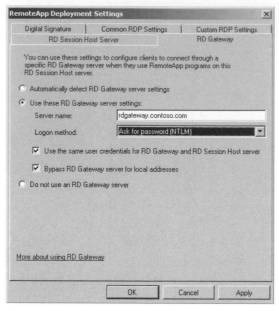

FIGURE 10-19 RD Gateway settings for RemoteApp

> **MORE INFO** **REMOTEAPP**
>
> To learn more about Remote Desktop Services RemoteApp, consult the following Microsoft TechNet Web page: *http://technet.microsoft.com/en-us/library/cc755055.aspx.*

Dialup Connections

A large number of people still access the Internet using dial-up connections to their ISPs. Windows 7 supports dial-up connections to ISPs so long as a compatible modem is available. Modems can include land-line and cellular devices, and they can be included as a part of their portable computer's hardware or as universal serial bus (USB) attachments.

To set up a dial-up connection, perform the following steps:

1. In Network And Sharing Center click Set Up A New Connection Or Network. On the Choose A Connection Option page, shown in Figure 10-20, select Set Up A Dial-Up Connection and then click Next.

2. In the Create A Dial-up Connection dialog box, shown in Figure 10-21, enter the phone number of the ISP, the ISP user name and password, a connection name, and whether you want other users of the computer to be able to use this connection.

3. If you need to configure dialing rules, such as country code, carrier code, a specific number to access an outside line, or switch between pulse and tone dialing, you can click the Dialing Rules item to specify these settings.

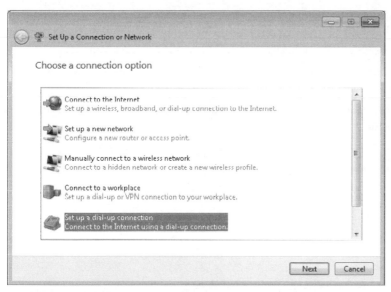

FIGURE 10-20 Set Up Dial-up Connection

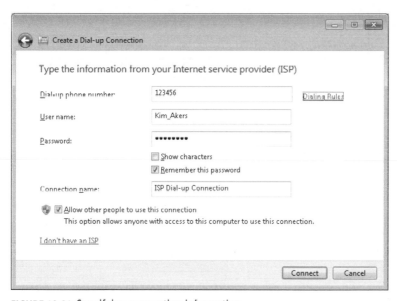

FIGURE 10-21 Specifying connection information

Configuring Windows 7 to Accept Incoming Connections

You can configure Windows 7 to accept incoming VPN and dial-up connections. When you configure Windows 7 to accept incoming VPN and dial-up connections, the client running Windows 7 is able to function as a VPN and dial-up server. Windows 7 supports incoming

VPNs that use the PPTP protocol and allows only one incoming connection at a time. To configure Windows 7 to support incoming connections, perform the following steps:

1. Open the Network Connections page, which is accessible through the Network And Sharing Center. Press Alt to bring up the menu bar. Click File and then click New Incoming Connection.

2. Select which users can access the computer remotely using VPN or dial-up, as shown in Figure 10-22, and then click Next.

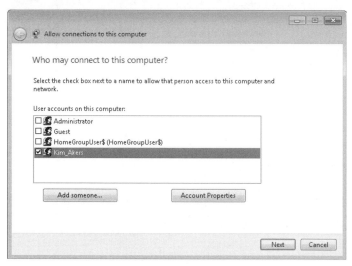

FIGURE 10-22 Selecting remote users

3. On the How Will People Connect? page, shown in Figure 10-23, select the types of connections that you wish to support. Your options include Through The Internet and Through A Dial-Up Modem.

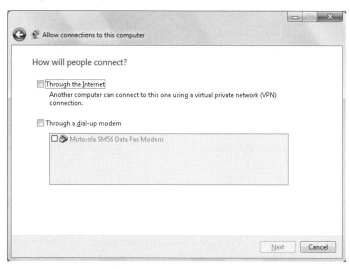

FIGURE 10-23 Configuring the incoming connection type

4. On the Networking Software Allows This Computer To Accept Connections From Other Kinds Of Computers page, select which networking components will be enabled for the incoming connections. The default settings have IPv4 and File And Printer Sharing enabled. IPv6 is disabled by default.

5. By clicking the Properties for each network component type, you can decide whether a remote user can have access to the LAN that the computer running Windows 7 is connected to. As Figure 10-24 shows, you can also specify how the client gets its address, either through Dynamic Host Configuration Protocol (DHCP), through an IP address pool, or by allowing the incoming client to specify its own IP address.

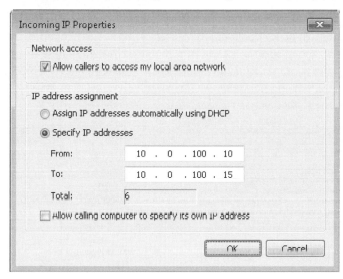

FIGURE 10-24 Incoming IP address properties

6. Click Allow to allow the connections. The Network Connections control panel contains a new item called Incoming Connections, as shown in Figure 10-25. You can modify the properties of incoming connections and specify which users you will permit to initiate incoming connections by right-clicking the Incoming Connections item and selecting Properties.

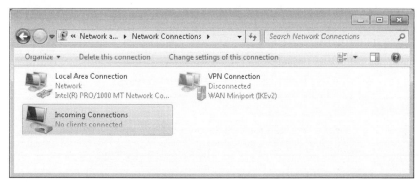

FIGURE 10-25 Incoming connection configured

Auditing Remote Connections

If you configure Windows 7 to support incoming VPN or dial-up connections, you may want to audit those connections. Auditing incoming connections provides you with a record of which users have connected to the client running Windows 7 remotely. If you are using basic auditing, you should enable the Computer Configuration\Windows Settings\Security Settings\Local Policies\Audit Policy\Audit Logon Events policy. This policy records all attempts to log on and off the computer to which the policy applies.

If you enable the Computer Configuration\Windows Settings\Security Settings\Local Policies\Security Options\Audit: Force Audit Policy Subcategory Settings policy, you can use the more detailed auditing policies that are available in the Computer Configuration\Windows Settings\Security Settings\Advanced Audit Policy Configuration\System Audit Policies\Logon\Logoff node. This node contains the Audit Logon and Audit Logoff policies. Auditing these specific policies reduces the amount of account logon and logoff activity that is audited when compared to the more general account auditing setting mentioned earlier. You can view audited account logon and logoff events in the Security log in Event Viewer, as shown in Figure 10-26.

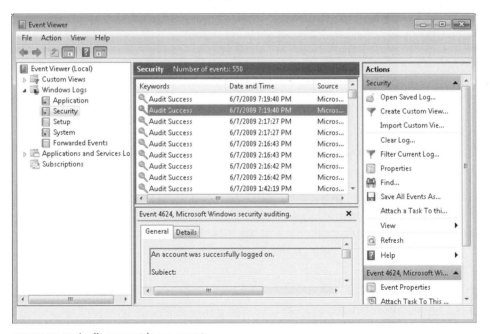

FIGURE 10-26 Audit account logon event

EXAM TIP
Remember what protocol is required for VPN Reconnect.

Configure Remote Connections

When you are configuring VPN connections, you always need to know three things: the address of the VPN server, the user name you connect with, and the password associated with that account. Windows 7 tries all VPN protocols, starting with IKEv2 and working through SSTP, L2TP/IPsec, and finally PPTP, so it is not necessary to specify which protocol a VPN connection uses, though you can do this later by editing the VPN connection's properties. The following practice relates to the configuration of VPN connections.

EXERCISE 1   Configure a VPN Connection

In this exercise, you configure a VPN connection. Perform the following steps:

1. Log on to computer Canberra with the Kim_Akers user account.

2. Right-click the Network Status icon and then choose Open Network And Sharing Center. This opens the Network And Sharing Center.

3. Click Set Up A New Connection Or Network. In the Set Up A Connection Or Network wizard, shown in Figure 10-27, click Connect To A Workplace and then click Next.

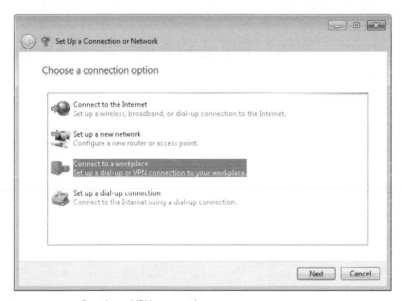

FIGURE 10-27 Creating a VPN connection

4. On the How Do You Want To Connect? page, click Use My Internet Connection (VPN).

5. On the Type The Internet Address To Connect To page, enter the name **remote-access .contoso.com.** Select the Allow Other People To Use This Connection check box and the Don't Connect Now; Just Set It Up So I Can Connect Later check box, as shown in Figure 10-28. Click Next.

FIGURE 10-28 VPN connection address

6. On the Type Your User Name And Password page, enter the user name and password that will be used to authenticate with the Routing and Remote Access server. You can also enter the user account's domain, as shown in Figure 10-29. Click Create and then click Close.

FIGURE 10-29 VPN credentials

EXERCISE 2 Modify VPN Connection Properties

In this exercise, you modify the properties of the VPN connection that you configured to the Contoso VPN server earlier. Perform the following steps:

1. If you have not already done so, log on to computer Canberra with the Kim_Akers user account.

2. Right-click the Network Status icon and then click Open Network And Sharing Center. This opens the Network And Sharing Center.

3. In the Network And Sharing Center control panel, click Change Adapter Settings.

4. In the Network Connections control panel, right-click VPN Connection and then choose Properties. This brings up the VPN Connection Properties dialog box.

5. Click the Security tab. Using the Type Of VPN drop-down menu, select IKEv2, as shown in Figure 10-30. Note that the Authentication options change when you select this VPN type.

FIGURE 10-30 VPN connection security

6. Click Advanced Settings. On the Advanced Properties page, change the Network Outage Time to 8 hours and then click OK.

7. Close the VPN Connection Properties dialog box.

Lesson Summary

- Clients running Windows 7 support the PPTP, L2TP/IPsec, SSTP, and IKEv2 VPN protocols.

- The IKEv2 VPN protocol is required if you want to use the VPN Reconnect feature. VPN Reconnect also requires a VPN server running Windows Server 2008 R2.

- The SSTP protocol allows users to access VPNs from behind most firewalls because it uses the same port as HTTPS traffic.

- RD Gateways allow Remote Desktop Connection access to Remote Desktop hosts on an organization's internal network without requiring that the external client use a VPN connection. RD Gateway also allows RemoteApp applications to be published to clients on the Internet.

- EAP-MS-CHAPv2 is the strongest password-based authentication protocol, and it is the only password-based authentication protocol that can be used with IKEv2.

- You can create a VPN or dial-up connection using the Create New Connection Wizard, which is available from the Network And Sharing Center.

- Windows 7 can function as a dial-up and VPN server if you configure incoming connections.

- NAP can be used to block remote access connections made by clients running Windows 7 that do not meet designated health benchmarks. These clients can be redirected to remediation networks that contain resources that allow them to become compliant.

Lesson Review

You can use the following questions to test your knowledge of the information in Lesson 2, "Remote Connections." The questions are also available on the companion DVD if you prefer to review them in electronic form.

> **NOTE ANSWERS**
>
> Answers to these questions and explanations of why each answer choice is correct or incorrect are located in the "Answers" section at the end of the book.

1. Which of the following VPN types support the VPN Reconnect feature of Windows 7?

    A. PPTP

    B. L2TP/IPsec

    C. SSTP

    D. IKEv2

2. You work as a consultant for a small business that has a Windows Server 2008 network infrastructure. Each person that works at this business has a laptop computer running Windows 7 Professional. Several of the employees regularly stay at small motels around the country, and some have complained that they are unable to establish VPN connections to the office even though they are able to browse the Web using the motel Internet connection. Which of the following VPN protocols should you configure to resolve this problem?

    A. SSTP

    B. IKEv2

C. PPTP

D. L2TP/IPsec

3. Your organization's Routing and Remote Access server has Windows Server 2003 R2 installed. Which of the following protocols can you use to connect to the VPN server?

   A. SSTP

   B. IKEv2

   C. PPTP

   D. L2TP/IPsec

4. Which of the following authentication protocols can you use to connect to an IKEv2 VPN? (Choose all that apply.)

   A. PEAP

   B. EAP-MSCHAP v2

   C. Microsoft Smart Card or Other Certificate

   D. CHAP

5. You have connected to a free Wi-Fi access point at the local library with your computer running Windows 7 Professional. You want to connect to the server remote-desktop. contoso.internal so that you can run some special line-of-business applications. Your organization has a remote desktop gateway server at the address rdgateway.contoso. com. There are currently no VPN connections configured on your computer. How can you connect to remote-desktop.contoso.internal?

   A. Configure a DirectAccess connection and then connect to remote-desktop .contoso.internal using Remote Desktop Connection.

   B. Configure Remote Desktop Connection to use the Remote Desktop Gateway at remote-desktop.contoso.internal and then connect to rdgateway.contoso.com.

   C. Configure Remote Desktop Connection to use the Remote Desktop Gateway at rdgateway.contoso.com and then connect to remote-desktop.contoso.internal.

   D. Configure a DirectAccess connection and then connect to rdgateway.contoso.com using Remote Desktop Connection.

Chapter Review

To further practice and reinforce the skills you learned in this chapter, you can perform the following tasks:

- Review the chapter summary.
- Review the list of key terms introduced in this chapter.
- Complete the case scenarios. These scenarios set up real-world situations involving the topics of this chapter and ask you to create a solution.
- Complete the suggested practices.
- Take a practice test.

Chapter Summary

- DirectAccess allows clients to connect to an internal corporate network whenever they have an active Internet connection.
- DirectAccess requires clients running Windows 7 Enterprise or Ultimate, as well as a DirectAccess server running Windows Server 2008 R2.
- DirectAccess can use native IPv6 connections or the Teredo, 6to4, and IP-HTTPS IPv6 to IPv4 transition technologies.
- Windows 7 supports PPTP, L2TP/IPsec, SSTP, and IKEv2 VPNs. IKEv2 VPNs support the VPN Reconnect feature.
- RD Gateway servers allow Remote Desktop Clients to connect to internal Remote Desktop Services servers without the need for a VPN or DirectAccess connection.

Key Terms

Do you know what these key terms mean? You can check your answers by looking up the terms in the glossary at the end of the book.

- **DirectAccess**
- **RemoteApp**

Case Scenarios

In the following case scenarios, you apply what you've learned about subjects of this chapter. You can find answers to these questions in the "Answers" section at the end of this book.

Case Scenario 1: Wingtip Toys DirectAccess

Wingtip Toys currently has 40 laptop computers running Windows Vista Business. Wingtip Toys wants to deploy DirectAccess because many of the users of these computers would prefer an automatic connection to the company network when they are in remote locations, rather than relying on a manual VPN connection. Wingtip Toys wants to replace their existing server running Windows Server 2003 R2 x64 Routing and Remote Access with a DirectAccess server. This server has two network cards and is assigned two consecutive public IPv4 addresses on the Internet interface. This server is a member of the Wingtiptoys.internal domain. The server has already been assigned the appropriate computer certificates.

With these facts in mind, answer the following questions:

1. What steps should Wingtip Toys take to create the DirectAccess server?
2. What type of group should you create to support DirectAccess?
3. What steps should you take to prepare client computers to use DirectAccess?

Case Scenario 2: Remote Access at Tailspin Toys

Tailspin Toys is deploying Windows 7 Professional to 300 laptop computers. You want to ensure that future VPN users will be able to stay connected to their VPN sessions if they switch from using a public Wi-Fi connection to using the cellular modem cards provided to them by the company. Users should be able to authenticate with their user names and passwords. Your existing VPN infrastructure uses NAP. The current Routing and Remote Access server is running the Windows Server 2008 x64 operating system. This system blocks VPN access to clients running Windows Vista Professional that do not have the most recent software updates or antivirus definitions installed. Presently, NAP blocks noncompliant clients from accessing the network. These clients cannot access the VPN until they connect to the corporate network directly and are able to download antivirus and software updates. You want to upgrade your quarantine network so that noncompliant clients can undergo remediation while connected remotely. Tailspin Toys has an Active Directory Certificate Services deployment.

With these facts in mind, answer the following questions:

1. What steps do you need to take to support VPN Reconnect at Tailspin Toys?
2. What additions should you make to the quarantine network so that clients can become compliant?
3. Which authentication protocol should you use for Tailspin Toys?

Suggested Practices

To help you master the exam objectives presented in this chapter, complete the following tasks.

Configure DirectAccess

If you have access to two servers or virtual machines running Windows Server 2008 R2, perform the following practices:

- **Practice 1** Configure the first server running Windows Server 2008 R2 as a domain controller, a DNS server, and an Active Directory Certificate Services server.

- **Practice 2** Configure the second server running Windows Server 2008 R2 as a DirectAccess server. To do so, review the requirements for a DirectAccess server listed in Lesson 1.

Configure Remote Connections

If you have access to two servers or virtual machines running Windows Server 2008 R2, perform the following practices:

- **Practice 1** Configure the first server running Windows Server 2008 R2 as a domain controller and install Remote Desktop services. Configure the second server running Windows Server 2008 R2 as an RD Gateway server. Connect using a client running Windows 7 to Remote Desktop services on the domain controller using the RD Gateway server.

- **Practice 2** Configure the first server running Windows Server 2008 R2 as a domain controller and install Remote Desktop services. Configure the second server running Windows Server 2008 R2 as a Routing and Remote Access server. Connect to the Routing and Remote Access server using a client running Windows 7 that is configured to use only an IKEv2 VPN connection.

Take a Practice Test

The practice tests on this book's companion DVD offer many options. For example, you can test yourself on just one exam objective, or you can test yourself on all the 70-680 certification exam content. You can set up the test so that it closely simulates the experience of taking a certification exam, or you can set it up in study mode so that you can look at the correct answers and explanations after you answer each question.

> **MORE INFO**   **PRACTICE TESTS**
>
> For details about all the practice test options available, see the section entitled "How to Use the Practice Tests," in the Introduction to this book.

CHAPTER 11

BitLocker and Mobility Options

Portable computers bring unique challenges to IT departments that these workers do not face with more traditional desktop computer deployments. One of these challenges is ensuring that a person using a portable computer is able to use the computer for a maximum amount of time when she is not able to connect to a power outlet. Another challenge is ensuring that a user is able to access important files even when she is unable to connect to the network. A third challenge is ensuring that no one outside the organization is able to recover confidential data on a misplaced or stolen portable computer. In this chapter, you learn about several technologies that assist you in addressing these challenges.

BitLocker and BitLocker To Go provide full volume data encryption that protects data if the computer or storage device hosting it is stolen or lost. The Offline Files feature enables you to access data hosted on shared folders when a computer cannot connect to the shared folder host server's network. Windows 7 power plans allow you to balance system performance with battery life, allowing you to increase performance when energy consumption is less important and to switch over to preserving battery charge when you need to use a portable computer away from a power supply for an extended amount of time.

Exam objectives in this chapter:
- Configure BitLocker and BitLocker To Go.
- Configure mobility options.

Lessons in this chapter:

Before You Begin

To complete the exercises in the practices in this chapter, you need to have done the following:

- Installed the Windows 7 operating system on a stand-alone client PC named Canberra, as described in Chapter 1, "Install, Migrate, or Upgrade to Windows 7."

- Make sure you have access to a small removable USB storage device. This device should not host any data.

- Note that a Trusted Platform Module (TPM) chip is not required for the practice exercise at the end of this lesson.

 REAL WORLD

Orin Thomas

Once, when I was working on a Self-Paced Training Kit, I received a chapter back from editing a few minutes before I was about to board a plane. Unfortunately, the plane I was about to board was going to take me from Melbourne, Australia, to Copenhagen, Denmark, with a stopoff for two hours in Bangkok, Thailand. This is one of those journeys that is within spitting distance of going literally halfway around the world. As I find it almost impossible to sleep on airplanes, I knew that I'd be unable to work after more than 24 hours in transit. Dealing with it now was better than dealing with it in a jet-lagged state on the other side of the world. Besides, I had never been to Copenhagen, and I didn't want to spend my first day there after I'd recovered from jet lag tapping away on my laptop in my hotel room. Given that you can buy a small car for the price of a first-class ticket from Melbourne to Copenhagen, I was in economy class without any way to power my laptop computer. Going through a chapter after editing can take some time, more time than usually afforded by my laptop computer's battery. My laptop wasn't a "newfangled, lasts for 8 hours on one battery" laptop, but one that would do three hours on a good day if I didn't push it hard. Unfortunately, I needed more than three hours to finish what I needed to do. This is where creating a custom power plan came in. I turned everything down. The screen gave off almost no light, the processor was restricted to a few percent of its maximum speed, and every non-critical device was switched off. The computer was sluggish, but it provided me with enough power that I was able to use it through the entire flight from Melbourne to Bangkok. This gave me enough time to complete my work on the chapter. When I arrived at Bangkok, I still had enough power to connect the laptop to the Internet through my mobile phone and send the revised chapter back to my editor. When I got to Copenhagen, I could concentrate fully on taking in a city I had never visited before. One day, when I get a new laptop that has a bit more battery life, I reckon I could configure a power plan that might get me all the way through a flight from Melbourne to Copenhagen. Until then, Melbourne to Bangkok will have to do!

Lesson 1: Managing BitLocker

Several studies have found that the staff at a medium-sized business loses an average of two laptop computers each year. These studies have determined that the cost of a lost laptop computer to an organization can exceed 20 times the value of the laptop computer itself, adding up to tens of thousands of dollars. The biggest cost involved with a lost laptop computer is determining what data was stored on the computer and the impact of that data finding its way into the hands of a competing organization. Often, it can be difficult to ascertain exactly what data may have been stored on a misplaced computer. When you assume a worst-case scenario, that cost can rise very high. Universal serial bus (USB) flash devices present a similar problem. People often use them to transfer important data from home to the workplace. Because these devices are small, they are easy to misplace. When one of these devices is lost, there is a chance, however small, that some sensitive data may find its way into the hands of a competing organization.

Research that has measured the cost of lost equipment has also found that the cost to an organization of losing a laptop computer was significantly lower for organizations that could be sure that a full disk encryption solution such as BitLocker protected all data on their portable computers. This was because in these cases, organizations could be sure that a competing organization was unable to recover any important data that might be stored on a misplaced computer or device. This significantly reduced the cost to the organization of the loss because it did not have to determine what might be stored on the lost equipment because that data was effectively irretrievable. In this lesson, you learn how to configure the BitLocker and BitLocker To Go features in Windows 7 so that if someone in your organization loses a laptop computer or USB flash device, you can be certain that the person who finds it is unable to recover any data stored on the device.

After this lesson, you will be able to:

- Configure BitLocker and BitLocker To Go Policies.
- Manage Trusted Platform Module PINs.
- Configure Startup Key storage.
- Configure Data Recovery Agent support.

Estimated lesson time: 40 minutes

BitLocker

BitLocker is a full volume encryption and system protection feature that is available on computers running the Enterprise and Ultimate editions of Windows 7. The function of BitLocker is to protect computers running Windows 7 from offline attacks. Offline attacks include booting using an alternative operating system in an attempt to recover data stored on the hard disk and removing the computer's hard disk and connecting it to another computer in an attempt to access the data it contains.

BitLocker provides full encryption of a computer's volumes. Without the BitLocker encryption key, the data stored on the volume is inaccessible. BitLocker stores the encryption key for the volume in a separate safe location, and it releases this key, making the data on the volume accessible, only after it is able to verify the integrity of the boot environment.

BitLocker provides the following benefits:

- It prevents an attacker from recovering data from a stolen computer unless that person also steals the passwords that provide access to the computer. Without the appropriate authentication, the hard disk remains encrypted and inaccessible.

- It simplifies the process of hard disk drive disposal. Rather than having to wipe a computer's hard disk, you can be sure that without the accompanying BitLocker key, any data on the disposed hard disk is irrecoverable. Many organizations have suffered security breaches because people have been able to recover data on hard disk drives after the hard disk has theoretically been disposed of.

- It protects the integrity of the boot environment against unauthorized modification by checking the boot environment each time you turn on the computer. If BitLocker detects any modifications to the boot environment, it forces the computer into BitLocker recovery mode.

Although BitLocker does provide some forms of protection, BitLocker does not protect data hosted on the computer once the computer is fully active. If there are multiple users of a computer and BitLocker is enabled, BitLocker cannot stop them from reading each other's files if file and folder permissions are not properly set. BitLocker encrypts the hard disk, but that encryption does not protect data from attack locally or over the network once the computer is operating normally. To protect data from access on a powered-up computer, configure NTFS permissions and use Encrypting File System (EFS). You learned about these technologies in Chapter 8, "BranchCache and Resource Sharing."

> **MORE INFO**   **BitLocker EXECUTIVE OVERVIEW**
>
> For a more detailed summary of the functionality of BitLocker in Windows 7, consult the following executive overview document hosted on Microsoft TechNet: *http://technet.microsoft .com/en-us/library/dd548341(WS.10).aspx.*

BitLocker Modes

You can configure BitLocker to function in a particular mode. The mode that you choose depends on whether you have a Trusted Platform Module (TPM) on your computer and the level of security that you want to enforce. The modes involve selecting a combination of TPM, personal identification number (PIN), and startup key. A startup key is a special cryptographically generated file that is stored on a separate USB device. The available BitLocker modes are as follows:

- **TPM-only mode** In TPM-only mode, the user is unaware that BitLocker is functioning and does not have to provide any passwords, PINs, or startup keys to start the computer. The user becomes aware of BitLocker only if there is a modification to the boot environment, or if she removes her hard disk drive and tries to use it on another computer. TPM-only mode is the least secure implementation of BitLocker because it does not require additional authentication.

- **TPM with startup key** This mode requires that a USB device hosting a preconfigured startup key be available to the computer before the computer can boot into Microsoft Windows. If the device hosting the startup key is not available at boot time, the computer enters recovery mode. This mode also provides boot environment protection through the TPM.

- **TPM with PIN** When you configure this mode, the user must enter a PIN before the computer boots. You can configure Group Policy so that it is possible to enter a password containing numbers, letters, and symbols rather than a simple PIN. If you do not enter the correct PIN or password at boot time, the computer enters recovery mode. This mode also provides boot environment protection through the TPM.

- **TPM with PIN and startup key** This is the most secure option. You can configure this option through Group Policy. When you enable this option, a user must enter a startup PIN and have the device hosting the startup key connected before the computer will boot into Windows. This option is appropriate for high-security environments. This mode also provides boot environment protection through the TPM.

- **BitLocker without a TPM** This mode provides hard disk encryption but does not provide boot environment protection. This mode is used on computers without TPM chips. You can configure BitLocker to work on a computer that does not have a TPM chip by configuring the Computer Configuration\Administrative Templates\Windows Components\BitLocker Drive Encryption\Operating System Drives\Require Additional Authentication At Startup policy. This policy is shown in Figure 11-1. When you configure BitLocker to work without a TPM chip, you need to boot with a startup key on a USB storage device.

Managing the TPM Chip

Most implementations of BitLocker store the encryption key in a special chip on the computer's hardware known as the TPM chip. The TPM Management console, shown in Figure 11-2, allows administrators to manage the TPM. Using this console, you can store TPM recovery information in Active Directory Domain Services (AD DS) clear the TPM, reset the TPM lockout, and enable or disable the TPM. You can access the TPM Management console from the BitLocker Drive Encryption control panel by clicking the TPM Administration icon.

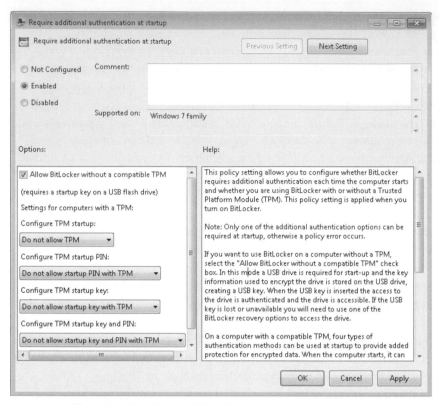

FIGURE 11-1 Allow BitLocker without a TPM chip

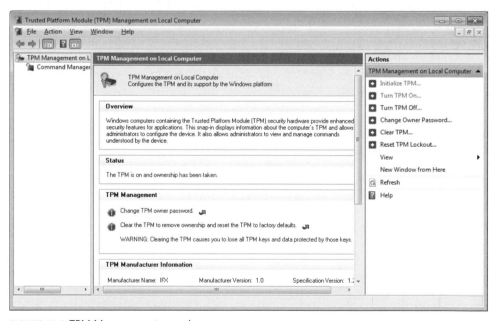

FIGURE 11-2 TPM Management console

Configuring a BitLocker DRA

Data Recovery Agents (DRAs) are special user accounts that you can use to recover encrypted data. You can configure a DRA to recover BitLocker-protected drives if the recovery password or keys are lost. The advantage of a DRA is that you can use it organization-wide, meaning that you can recover all BitLocker-encrypted volumes using a single account rather than having to recover a specific volume's recovery password or key.

The first step you must take in configuring BitLocker to support DRAs is to add the account of a DRA to the Computer Configuration\Windows Settings\Security Settings\Public Key Policies\BitLocker Drive Encryption node, as shown in Figure 11-3. A DRA account is a user account enrolled with a special type of digital certificate. In organizational environments, this digital certificate is almost always issued by an AD DS certificate authority (CA).

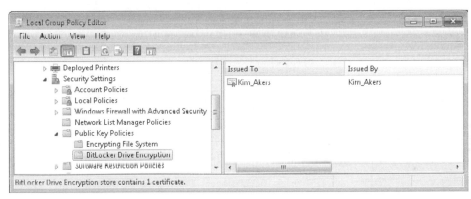

FIGURE 11-3 Assigning the recovery key

After you have configured the DRA, It is also necessary to configure the Computer Configuration\Administrative Templates\Windows Components\BitLocker Drive Encryption\Prove The Unique Identifiers For Your Organization policy to support DRA recovery. BitLocker works with DRAs only when an identification field is present on a volume and the value matches that configured for the computer. Figure 11-4 shows this policy configured with the identification field set to ContosoBitLockerSelfHost. You also use this policy when denying write access to removable devices not protected by BitLocker. You will learn more about denying write access to removable devices later in this lesson.

After you have configured the DRA and the Identifiers, you need to configure the following policies to allow specific volume types to utilize the DRA:

- Choose How BitLocker-Protected Operating System Drives Can Be Recovered
- Choose How BitLocker-Protected Fixed Drives Can Be Recovered
- Choose How BitLocker-Protected Removable Drives Can Be Recovered

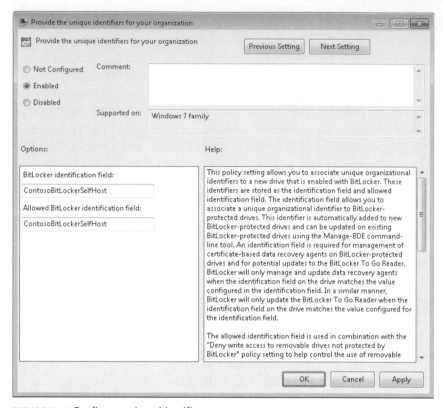

FIGURE 11-4 Configure unique identifiers

Each of these policies is similar in that you configure it to allow the DRA. You can also configure a recovery password and a recovery key for each volume type, as shown in Figure 11-5. You can use any of the items you specify in these policies for recovery. These policies also allow you to force the backup of recovery passwords and keys to AD DS. It is even possible to block the implementation of BitLocker unless backup to AD DS is successful. You should not enable the option of backing up data to AD DS when clients running Windows 7 are not members of an AD DS domain.

In some cases, you may have already enabled BitLocker on a volume prior to preparing a DRA. You can update a volume to support a DRA by using the *manage-bde –SetIdentifier* command on the encrypted volume from an elevated command prompt. You can verify the identifier setting by using the *manage-bde –status* command and checking the Identification Field setting in the resulting output. To verify that the DRA is configured properly, issue the *manage-bde –protectors –get* command. This lists the certificate thumbprint assigned to the DRA. To recover data from a volume protected by a DRA, connect the volume to a working computer that has the DRA private key installed and use the *manage-bde.exe –unlock <drive> -Certificate –ct <certificate thumbprint>* command from an elevated command prompt. You will use some of these commands in the practice at the end of this lesson.

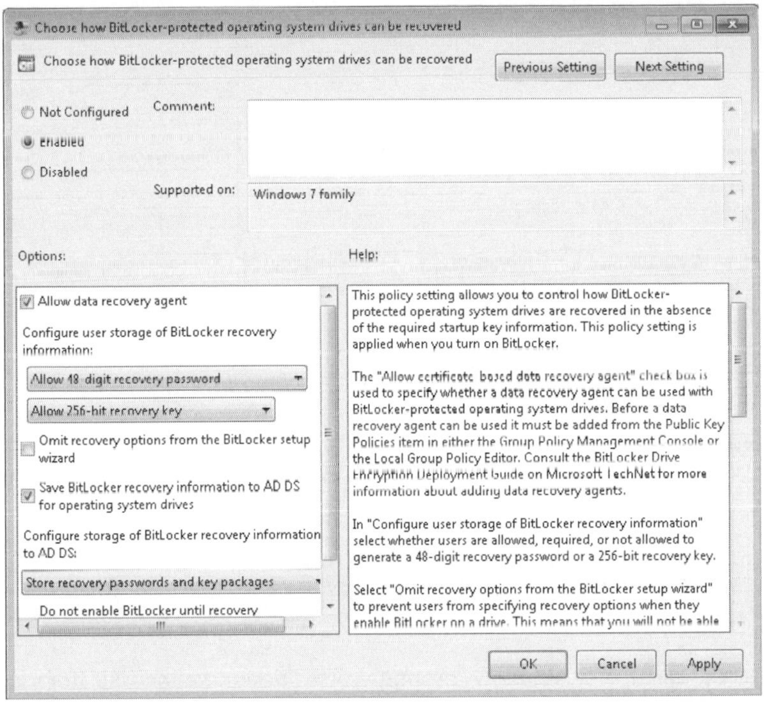

FIGURE 11-5 Recovery policies

> **MORE INFO** **CONFIGURING A BitLocker DRA**
>
> To learn more about configuring a BitLocker DRA, consult the following Microsoft TechNet article: *http://technet.microsoft.com/en-us/library/dd875560(WS.10).aspx.*

Enabling BitLocker

To enable BitLocker on a computer, open the BitLocker Drive Encryption control panel and then click Turn On BitLocker. A user must be a member of the local Administrators group to enable BitLocker on a computer running Windows 7. When you click Turn On BitLocker, a check is performed to see if your computer has the appropriate TPM hardware, or has the appropriate Group Policy if that hardware is not present, to support BitLocker. If the TPM hardware is not present and Group Policy is not configured appropriately, an error message is displayed informing you that the computer does not support BitLocker and you are unable to implement BitLocker.

The next step in configuring BitLocker is to configure which authentication choice to use with BitLocker. You learned about the different BitLocker modes—TPM-only, TPM with startup key, TPM with PIN, and TPM with startup key and PIN—earlier in this lesson. If you are using BitLocker without a TPM, you only have the option of requiring a Startup key, as shown in Figure 11-6. You can configure the option to require TPM with startup key and PIN only through Group Policy.

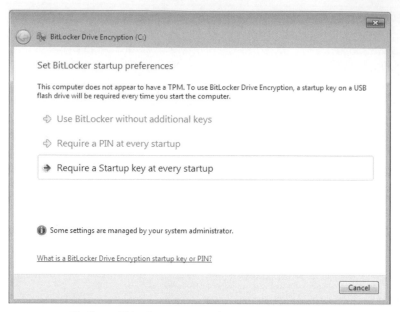

FIGURE 11-6 Configure BitLocker startup options

If you choose to require a startup key, Windows prompts you to designate the USB storage device that hosts the startup key. Windows then writes the startup key to the designated device. The next step in the BitLocker process involves storing the recovery key, as shown in Figure 11-7. The recovery key is different from the startup key or PIN. You should store the recovery key in a different location to the startup key. That way, if you lose your startup key, you have not also lost the recovery key.

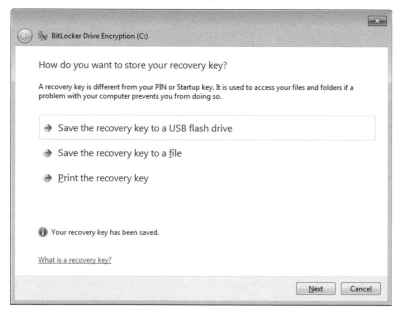

FIGURE 11-7 Save the recovery key

The last step before you enable BitLocker on a computer is running the System Check, as shown in Figure 11-8. This check verifies that BitLocker can work with your computer and that there is not a problem with the configured startup key or TPM chip. Although this check takes time, you should run it because all data on the computer may be lost if there is a problem with one of the BitLocker features. For example, if you are using BitLocker without a TPM, this check allows you to discover whether the USB device that you have stored the startup key on is accessible to the computer prior to booting into Windows. Even though the startup key may be present on the device, if the BIOS does not support accessing the USB device at the appropriate time, BitLocker locks out the computer. If that is the case, you cannot use BitLocker on this computer. It is much better to discover this type of problem prior to activating BitLocker than having to go through the BitLocker recovery process.

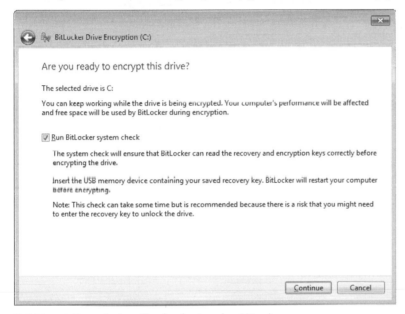

FIGURE 11-8 Run a System Check prior to using BitLocker

The system check test involves a reboot. After the test completes successfully, BitLocker begins the encryption process. The encryption process occurs in the background. A user with administrative privileges can pause and resume the encryption process if necessary. BitLocker is not fully active until the encryption process is completed.

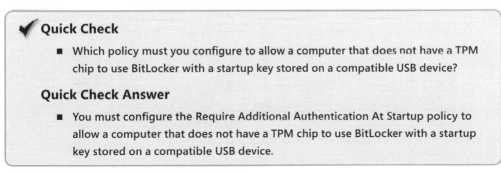

✔ **Quick Check**

- Which policy must you configure to allow a computer that does not have a TPM chip to use BitLocker with a startup key stored on a compatible USB device?

Quick Check Answer

- You must configure the Require Additional Authentication At Startup policy to allow a computer that does not have a TPM chip to use BitLocker with a startup key stored on a compatible USB device.

BitLocker To Go

BitLocker To Go is a feature that is available in the Enterprise and Ultimate editions of Windows 7. Computers running these editions of Windows 7 can configure a USB device to support BitLocker To Go. Other editions of Windows 7 can read and write data off BitLocker To Go devices, but they cannot configure a device to use BitLocker To Go. BitLocker To Go allows for removable storage devices to be encrypted using BitLocker. BitLocker To Go differs from BitLocker in previous versions of Windows because it allows you to use BitLocker-encrypted removable storage devices on other computers if you have the appropriate password. Although BitLocker in Windows Vista SP1 and later did allow you to encrypt BitLocker removable storage devices, the process of using a BitLocker-encrypted device on another computer was complicated and involved performing BitLocker recovery.

BitLocker To Go does not require that the computer have a TPM chip or that Group Policy be configured to allow some other form of authentication such as a startup key. If you configure appropriate policies, devices protected by BitLocker To Go can be used in read-only mode with computers running Windows XP and Windows Vista.

BitLocker To Go Policies

The Removable Data Drives node of the BitLocker Drive Encryption policy node contains six policies that allow you to manage BitLocker To Go, as shown in Figure 11-9.

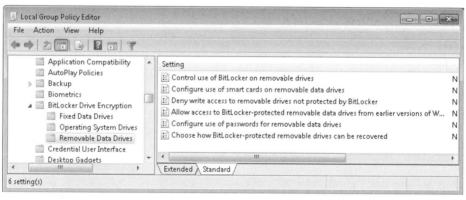

FIGURE 11-9 Removable drive policies

- **Control Use of BitLocker On Removable Drives**   This policy includes two settings that can be enabled. The first setting allows users to apply BitLocker protection to removable drives. The second allows users to suspend and decrypt BitLocker protection on removable drives. If this policy is disabled, users are unable to use BitLocker To Go.

- **Configure Use Of Smart Cards On Removable Data Drives**   This policy allows you to enable and/or require use of smart cards to authenticate user access to a removable drive. When this policy is disabled, users cannot use smart cards to authenticate access to removable drives protected with BitLocker.

- **Deny Write Access To Removable Drives Not Protected By BitLocker** Configuring this policy allows you to stop users from writing data to removable devices that are not BitLocker-protected. Within this policy, you can enable the Do Not Allow Write Access To Drives Configured In Another Organization setting, which allows you to limit the writing of data to removable devices configured with a specific BitLocker identification string. This string is configured using the Provide The Unique Identifiers For Your Organization Policy that you learned about earlier in this lesson and which was shown earlier in Figure 11-4. When this policy is enabled, users can still read data from removable devices that are not protected by BitLocker or have another organization's identifier. If this policy is disabled, users can write data to removable devices whether or not they have been configured with BitLocker.

- **Allow Access To BitLocker-Protected Removable Data Drives From Earlier Versions of Windows** Use this policy to allow or restrict BitLocker-protected removable devices formatted with the FAT file system from being accessed on previous versions of Windows. This policy does not apply to NTFS-formatted removable devices. You can configure this policy to allow the installation of BitLocker To Go Reader, a program that allows previous versions of Windows read access to BitLocker-protected removable devices. BitLocker To Go Reader must be present on a computer running a previous version of Windows for that computer to be able to read BitLocker-protected removable devices. When this policy is disabled, FAT-formatted BitLocker-protected removable devices cannot be unlocked on computers running previous versions of Windows.

- **Configure Use Of Passwords For Removable Data Drives** This policy determines whether a password is required to unlock a removable data drive protected by BitLocker, as shown in Figure 11-10. The policy allows password complexity requirements to be enforced. If this policy is disabled, users are not allowed to use passwords with removable devices.

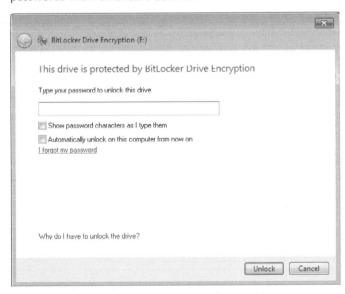

FIGURE 11-10 Password to access encrypted removable storage

- **Choose How BitLocker-Protected Removable Drives Can Be Recovered** This policy allows you to specify the methods that can be used to recover BitLocker-protected removable devices. You can configure removable drives to use the DRA specified in the Computer Configuration\Windows Settings\Security Settings\Public Key Policies\ BitLocker Drive Encryption node. You can also configure a recovery password and a recovery key. Using this policy, you can specify whether BitLocker recovery information is stored within AD DS.

Once a removable device supports BitLocker To Go, it is possible to manage it either by right-clicking it within Windows Explorer or by clicking Manage BitLocker within the BitLocker Drive Encryption control panel. This opens the dialog box shown in Figure 11-11. This dialog box allows you to change the password assigned to the device, configure the device so that you can unlock it with a smart card, save the recovery key, remove the password from the device, or configure the computer to automatically unlock the device whenever it is connected.

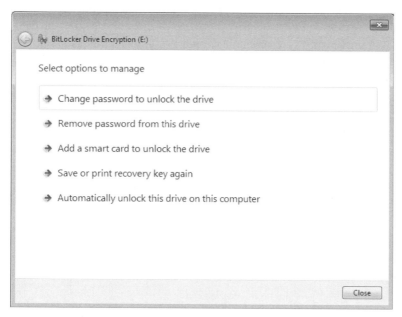

FIGURE 11-11 Change BitLocker To Go options

BitLocker Recovery

Encrypted volumes are locked when the encryption key is not available. When the operating system volume is locked, you can boot only to recovery mode. In recovery mode, you can enter the BitLocker password or you can attach the USB device that has the recovery key stored and restart the computer. Once you enter the recovery password or key, you can boot your computer normally. The following events trigger recovery mode:

- The boot environment changes. This could include one of the boot files being modified.
- TPM is disabled or cleared.

- An attempt is made to boot without the TPM, PIN, or USB key being provided.
- You attach a BitLocker-encrypted operating system volume to another computer.

If you need to perform a task that would normally trigger recovery mode, such as modifying the boot files, it is possible to disable BitLocker temporarily. You should temporarily disable BitLocker when upgrading the computer's BIOS or making any modification to the startup environment, such as configuring Windows 7 to dual-boot with a virtual hard disk (VHD) installation of the operating system. Once you have finished the configuration changes, you can re-enable BitLocker. The changes that you made when BitLocker was disabled do not trigger recovery mode.

Manage-bde.exe

Manage-bde.exe is the BitLocker command-line utility. You must use Manage-bde.exe from an elevated command prompt. Manage-bde.exe allows you to unlock locked BitLocker volumes and allows you to modify BitLocker PINs, passwords, and keys. Table 11-1 lists common Manage-bde.exe parameters. You will use Manage-bde.exe in the practice exercise at the end of the lesson.

TABLE 11-1 Common Manage-bde.exe Parameters

PARAMETER	FUNCTION
-status	Displays BitLocker status
-on	Encrypts a volume and turns BitLocker on
-off	Decrypts a volume and turns BitLocker off
-pause/-resume	Pauses or resumes encryption or decryption
-lock	Prevents access to BitLocker-protected data
-unlock	Allows access to BitLocker-encrypted data
-SetIdentifier	Configures the identifier for a volume
-changepin	Modifies the PIN for a volume
-changepassword	Modifies a volume's password
-changekey	Modifies a volume's startup key

EXAM TIP

Remember which policy to configure to allow computers without TPM chips to use BitLocker.

PRACTICE **Configuring BitLocker To Go**

In this practice, you configure Group Policies so that users are able to write data only to specially prepared removable storage devices that support BitLocker To Go. Implementing similar policies in a real-world environment ensures that data stored on a removable storage device is safe from third-party access if the owner of the removable storage device loses it in a public place.

EXERCISE 1   Configuring BitLocker To Go Policies

In this exercise, you configure BitLocker To Go–related Group Policy settings.

1. Log on to computer Canberra using the Kim_Akers user account.

2. Ensure that the USB storage device that you will encrypt using BitLocker To Go is attached to the computer.

3. Use the Disk Management console to format the USB storage device with the FAT32 file system.

4. Disconnect the USB storage device from the computer

5. In the Search Programs And Files text box, type **gpedit.msc.** This opens the local Group Policy Editor.

6. Navigate to the Computer Configuration\Administrative Templates\Windows Components\BitLocker Drive Encryption node.

7. Edit the Provide The Unique Identifiers For Your Organization policy. Enable the policy and set the BitLocker Identification Field and the Allowed BitLocker Identification Field to ContosoBitLocker, as shown in Figure 11-12, and then click OK.

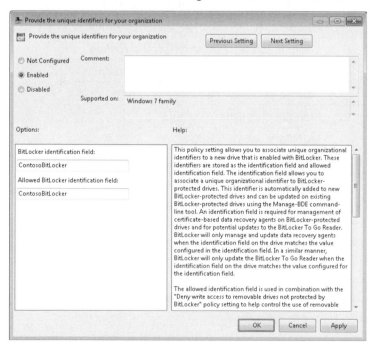

FIGURE 11-12 Configure identifiers

8. Open the Removable Data Drives node and then set the Deny Write Access To Removable Drives Not Protected By BitLocker policy to Enabled. Then select the Do Not Allow Write Access To Devices Configured In Another Organization check box. Click OK.

9. Enable the Allow Access To BitLocker-Protected Removable Data Drives From Earlier Versions Of Windows policy.

10. Set the Configure Use Of Passwords For Removable Data Drives policy to Enabled. Select the Require Password For Removable Data Drive check box, set the Configure Password Complexity For Removable Data Drives to Allow Password Complexity, as shown in Figure 11-13, and then click OK.

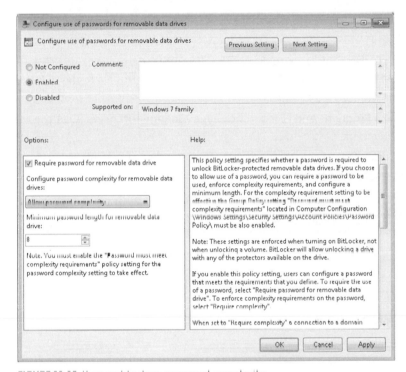

FIGURE 11-13 Removable drive password complexity

11. Close the Local Group Policy Editor and then reboot the computer.

EXERCISE 2   Testing the Application of BitLocker To Go Policies

In this exercise, you encrypt a removable storage device and verify that it is possible to write data to the device only when the device has been configured with BitLocker.

1. After computer Canberra has rebooted at the end of Exercise 1, log on with the Kim_Akers user account.

2. After you have logged on, connect the USB storage device that you prepared in Exercise 1. Verify that the message displayed in Figure 11-14 appears.

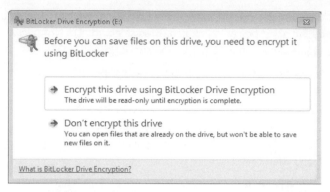

FIGURE 11-14 Removable device warning

3. Click Don't Encrypt This Drive to dismiss this dialog box. Create a file on the desktop named Test.txt. Using Windows Explorer, attempt to copy this file to the USB storage device. This prompts a message informing you that the disk is write-protected.

4. In the Search Programs And Files text box, type **Manage BitLocker.** Click the Manage BitLocker item.

5. In the BitLocker Drive Encryption control panel, click the Turn On BitLocker item next to the removable USB drive, as shown in Figure 11-15.

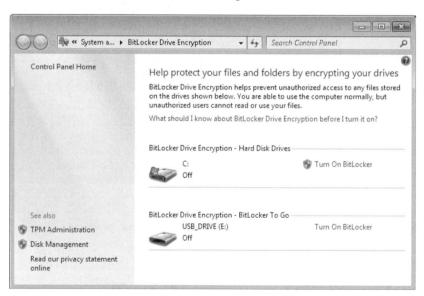

FIGURE 11-15 The BitLocker control panel

6. On the Choose How You Want To Unlock The Drive page, enter the password **P@ssw0rd** twice and then click Next.

7. On the How Do You Want To Store Your Recovery Key? page, click Save The Recovery Key To A File and save the recovery key on the desktop. Click Next.

8. On the Are You Ready To Encrypt This Drive? page, click Start Encrypting. Windows starts encrypting the drive.

9. When the removable drive has stopped encrypting, open an elevated command prompt and issue the command **manage-bde –status e:** (where e: is the volume identifier of the USB storage device). Verify that the Identification Field setting matches ContosoBitLocker, as shown in Figure 11-16.

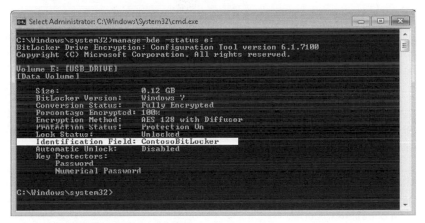

FIGURE 11-16 Check BitLocker status

10. Use Windows Explorer to copy the file Test.txt from the desktop to the USB storage device, and verify that you are now able to write data to the device.

11. Disconnect and then reconnect the storage device. Verify that you need to enter a password to access the storage device.

Lesson Summary

- BitLocker offers full volume encryption and system protection for computers running the Enterprise and Ultimate editions of Windows 7.

- TPM chips are required for BitLocker boot integrity protection. TPM PINs can be backed up to AD DS.

- BitLocker can use five different modes: TPM-only, TPM with PIN, TPM with startup key, TPM with PIN and startup key, and startup key without TPM. The startup key without TPM mode can be enabled only by configuring Require Additional Authentication At Startup Group Policy.

- DRAs can be configured for the recovery of BitLocker-encrypted volumes.

- BitLocker To Go provides BitLocker encryption to removable storage devices. Computers running the Enterprise and Ultimate editions of Windows 7 can configure removable devices. Computers running other editions of Windows 7 cannot configure removable devices, but they can read and write data to BitLocker To Go–protected devices.

- BitLocker To Go–protected removable storage devices can be protected with passwords.

- BitLocker To Go storage devices can be accessed from computers running Windows Vista and Windows XP through a utility named BitLocker To Go Reader if Group Policy is configured to allow this.

Lesson Review

You can use the following questions to test your knowledge of the information in Lesson 1, "Managing BitLocker." The questions are also available on the companion DVD if you prefer to review them in electronic form.

NOTE ANSWERS

Answers to these questions and explanations of why each answer choice is correct or incorrect are located in the "Answers" section at the end of the book.

1. Which of the following policies must you configure when setting up a DRA to recover the operating system volume for BitLocker? (Choose all that apply; each answer forms part of a complete solution.)

    A. Computer Configuration\Administrative Templates\Windows Components\Provide The Unique Identifiers For Your Organization

    B. Computer Configuration\Administrative Templates\Windows Components\Choose Default Folder For Recovery Password

    C. Computer Configuration\Administrative Templates\Windows Components\Choose How Users Can Recover BitLocker-Protected Drives

    D. Computer Configuration\Windows Settings\Security Settings\Public Key Policies\ BitLocker Drive Encryption

    E. Computer Configuration\Administrative Templates\Windows Components\ BitLocker Drive Encryption\Operating System Drives\Choose How BitLocker-Protected Operating System Drives Can Be Recovered

2. You want to block users from writing data to removable drives if those drives are not BitLocker-protected. Users should not be able to write data to drives configured with BitLocker by organizations other than your own. Which of the following policies must you configure to accomplish this goal? (Choose all that apply; each answer forms part of a complete solution.)

    A. Control Use Of BitLocker On Removable Drives

    B. Store BitLocker Recovery Information In Active Directory Domain Services

    C. Deny Write Access To Removable Drives Not Protected By BitLocker

    D. Provide The Unique Identifiers For Your Organization

3. Which of the following policies should you configure to allow a computer without a TPM chip that is running Windows 7 Enterprise to utilize BitLocker to protect its hard disk drive?

    A. Require Additional Authentication At Startup

    B. Allow Enhanced PINs for Startup

    C. Configure TPM Platform Validation Profile

    D. Configure Minimum PIN Length For Startup

4. Which of the following BitLocker policies should you configure to ensure that BitLocker To Go Reader is available on all FAT-formatted removable devices protected with BitLocker?

    A. Configure Use Of Passwords For Removable Data Drives

    B. Allow Access To BitLocker Protected Removable Data Drives From Earlier Versions Of Windows

    C. Choose How BitLocker-Protected Removable Drives Can Be Recovered

    D. Control Use Of BitLocker On Removable Drives

5. Which of the following tools can you use to determine the identification string assigned to a BitLocker-protected volume?

    A. Manage-bde.exe

    B. Cipher.exe

    C. Bcdedit.exe

    D. Sigverif.exe

Lesson 2: Windows 7 Mobility

Correctly configuring the power settings of computers, especially when there are many computers in use across an organization, can lead to substantial reductions in an organization's energy requirements. Refinements in the way that Windows 7 uses energy mean that an organization upgrading computer hardware from Windows XP to Windows 7 brings noticeable efficiencies in energy usage. This can provide two important benefits for an organization: reducing the organization's impact on the environment and reducing the amount of money spent on electricity.

Offline Files is a feature relevant to portable computers that allows content that is stored on shared folders to be cached temporarily on mobile computers so that it can still be accessed and worked on when the mobile computer is no longer connected to the office environment. When the computer reconnects to the environment that hosts the shared folder, the offline content is synced, updating the content on servers and clients as necessary.

> **After this lesson, you will be able to:**
> - Manage Offline Files.
> - Manage Windows 7 power settings.
> - Configure Windows 7 power policies.
>
> **Estimated lesson time: 40 minutes**

Offline Files

The Offline Files feature of Windows 7 allows a client to locally cache files hosted in shared folders so that they are accessible when the computer is unable to connect directly to the network resource. The Offline Files feature is available to users of the Professional, Enterprise, and Ultimate editions of Windows 7. You can use the Offline Files feature to ensure access when a client computer is out of the office or when a temporary disruption, such as a wide area network (WAN) link failing between a branch office and a head office, blocks access to specially configured shared folders.

When a user makes a file available for offline access, Windows 7 stores a copy of that file within a local cache. When the file server that hosts the file is no longer available, such as when a user disconnects from the network, the user can continue to work with the file stored within the local cache. When the file server that hosts the file becomes available, Windows 7 synchronizes the copy of the file in the cache with the copy of the file hosted on the shared folder. A user can make a file available offline by right-clicking the file and then clicking the Always Available Offline option, as shown in Figure 11-17. When the offline file cache becomes full, the files in the cache that are least used are dropped to make room for newer ones. Windows 7 does not remove manually cached files unless a user specifically deletes them.

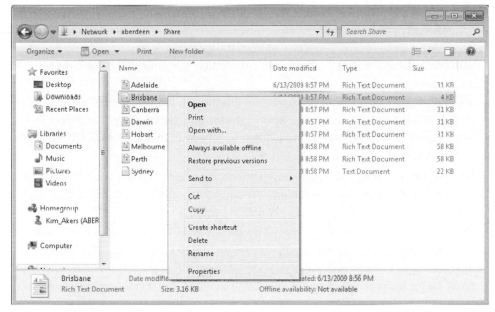

FIGURE 11-17 Make a file available offline

Files available offline are shown as Always Available in Windows Explorer. Figure 11-18 shows a file available offline named Brisbane. If a user modifies a file that she has made available offline, that file synchronizes with the shared folder when the user again connects to the network and the modified file replaces the one on the shared folder. If the file on the shared folder is changed and the file in the local cache remains unchanged, the synchronization process overwrites the file in the local cache. If both the file on the shared folder and the file in the local cache have been modified, it is necessary to use Sync Center to resolve the conflict. You will learn more about using Sync Center to resolve conflicts with Offline Files later in this lesson.

FIGURE 11-18 Brisbane file is Always Available

The Offline Files feature in Windows 7 has the four following modes of operation:

- **Online mode**   Changes made to files are applied to the file share and then to the local cache. Read requests are satisfied from the local cache. Synchronization occurs automatically and a user can initiate synchronization manually. This is the default mode of operation.

- **Auto offline mode**   When a network error is detected, Windows 7 transitions to auto offline mode. File operations occur against the local cache. Windows 7 attempts to reconnect automatically every two minutes. If reconnection is successful, Offline Files automatically transitions to online mode.

- **Manual offline mode**   The transition to offline mode is forced when user selects the Work Offline item in Windows Explorer. A computer must be returned to online mode manually by clicking Work Online in Windows Explorer.

- **Slow-link mode**   This mode is enabled by default in Windows 7 and triggered when the link speed falls below the default value of 64,000 bits per second. This value can be configured through policy. In this mode, file operations are performed against the local cache. Users can synchronize manually, but automatic synchronization does not occur. Computer transitions to online mode when link speed exceeds configured value.

Some functionalities, like the Previous Versions of Files feature that allows you to retrieve the previous version of a file from a shadow copy on the server, are not available in auto offline or offline mode.

Offline File Policies

You configure Offline Files through Offline Files policies, located in the Computer Configuration\Administrative Templates\Network\Offline Files node of a Group Policy Object. There are 28 policies, some of which are shown in Figure 11-19.

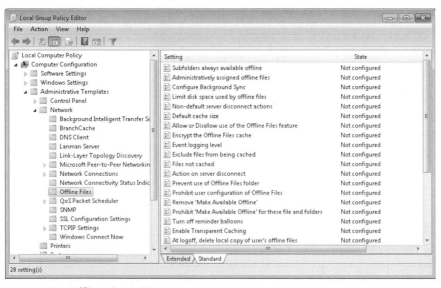

FIGURE 11-19 Offline Files policies

Several important policies available in this node include:

- **Administratively Assigned Offline Files**   Lists all network files and folders that are always available for offline use without requiring user interaction.

- **Configure Background Sync**   This policy applies in slow-link mode and determines how often background synchronization occurs.

- **Non-Default Server Disconnect Actions**   Determines whether the computer automatically goes into offline mode when computer detects that it is disconnected from offline file servers.

- **Encrypt The Offline Files Cache**   Ensures that the offline files cache is encrypted.

- **Configure Slow Link Mode**   Enabled by default on Windows 7, allows the computer to use slow-link mode.

- **Configure Slow Link Speed**   The bandwidth value in bits per second where a network is considered slow.

Transparent Caching

When you enable *transparent caching,* Windows 7 keeps a cached copy of all files that a user opens from shared folders on the local volume. The first time a user opens the file, the file is stored in the local cache. When the user opens the file again, Windows 7 checks the file to ensure that the cached copy is up to date and if it is, opens that instead. If the copy is not up to date, the client opens the copy hosted on the shared folder, also placing it in the local cache. Using a locally cached copy speeds up access to files stored on file servers on remote networks from the client. When a user changes a file, the client writes the changes to the copy of the file stored on the shared folder. When the shared folder is unavailable, the transparently cached copy is also unavailable. Transparent caching does not attempt to keep the local copy synced with the copy of the file on the remote file server as the Offline Files feature does. Transparent caching works on all files in a shared folder, not just those that you have configured to be available offline.

Transparent caching is appropriate for WAN scenarios and has several similarities to the BranchCache feature that you learned about in Chapter 8. Some significant differences are that clients on the local area network do not share the cache and that file servers hosting the shared folders do not need to be running Windows Server 2008 R2 to support transparent caching. It is also possible to use transparent caching on clients running Windows 7 Professional and on clients that are not members of an AD DS domain, something that is not possible with BranchCache. Windows 7 triggers transparent caching when the round-trip latency value exceeds the amount specified in the Enable Transparent Caching policy, shown in Figure 11-20.

> **MORE INFO**   **TRANSPARENT CACHING**
>
> To learn more about the transparent caching features of Windows 7, consult the following Microsoft TechNet Web page: *http://technet.microsoft.com/en-us/library/dd637828.aspx.*

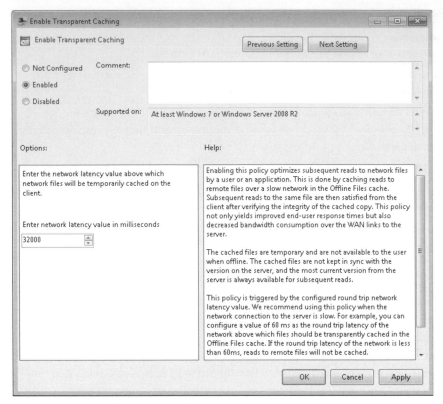

FIGURE 11-20 Enable Transparent Caching

Offline File Exclusions

Administrators can configure Offline File policies to exclude specific file types from being available offline. You can do this by configuring the Exclude Files From Being Cached Policy, as shown in Figure 11-21. File types are specified in the policy through their file name extension. For example, to block all Windows Bitmap files, use the extension designation *.bmp. When you configure this policy, users are unable to create files of this type in folders configured to be available offline.

Using Sync Center

You can use Sync Center to synchronize files, manage offline files, and resolve synchronization conflicts manually. Sync Center is located within the Control Panel or by typing **Sync Center** into the Search Programs and Files text box on the Start menu. Clicking Manage Offline Files opens the Offline Files dialog box, shown in Figure 11-22. This dialog box is also available using the Offline Files control panel. Using this dialog box, you can disable offline files, view offline files, configure disk usage for offline files, configure encryption for offline files, and configure how often Windows 7 should check for slow network conditions.

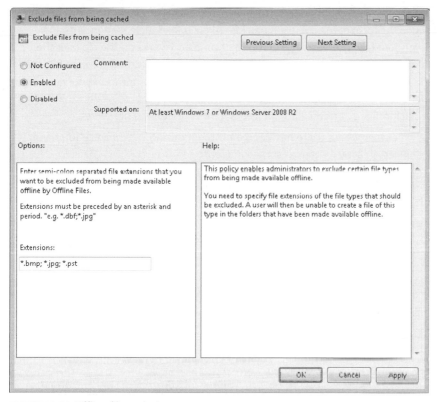

FIGURE 11-21 Offline file exclusions

FIGURE 11-22 The Offline Files dialog box

A sync conflict occurs when changes occur to a file made available offline both on the file server and within the local cache. For example, Kim Akers makes a file named Brisbane. doc available offline. Kim takes her portable computer home and works on the file over the weekend. Sam Abolrous goes into the office on the weekend and works on the copy of Brisbane. doc stored on the file server. When Kim reconnects her portable computer to the network, Sync Center notifies her that there is a sync conflict. Kim can then use this tool to resolve the conflict between the file she modified at home and the file Sam modified on the file server.

You can see a list of files where there has been a problem during synchronization if you click View Sync Conflicts in Sync Center, as shown in Figure 11-23.

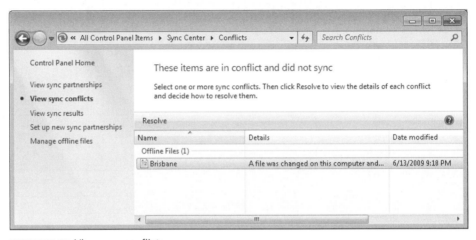

FIGURE 11-23 View sync conflicts

When you click Resolve within the View Sync Conflicts area, you can choose among three actions:

- **Keep the local version**   The version of the file that is stored on the local computer will be kept. This version overwrites the changed version of the file on the file share.
- **Keep the server version**   The version of the file that is stored on the file share is kept, and the changes made to the local version are lost.
- **Keep both versions**   The version on the local computer is renamed and then saved to the file share. The version of the file on the file share keeps the original name.

Figure 11-24 shows these options as applied to the earlier example of Kim Akers and the modified offline file.

Configuring Shared Folders for Offline Files

Users can make files available offline only if the shared folder that hosts these files supports offline files. You can configure a shared folder on a computer running Windows 7 to support offline files by performing the following steps:

FIGURE 11-24 Resolve the conflict

1. Edit the properties of the folder that you want to configure to support offline files.

2. On the Sharing tab, click Advanced Sharing.

3. In the Advanced Sharing dialog box, click Caching. This brings up the Offline Settings dialog box, shown in Figure 11-25. Use this dialog box to choose between allowing only the files that a user specifies to be available offline, all files to be available offline, or no files to be available offline.

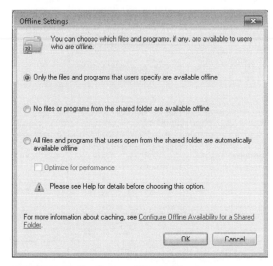

FIGURE 11-25 Configure offline settings

Windows 7 Power Configuration

Power plans are collections of settings that specify how a computer running Windows 7 uses energy. A new computer running Windows 7 comes with three power plans named High Performance, Balanced, and Power Saver. Many original equipment manufacturers (OEMs) also supply their own custom Windows 7 power plans that they may precisely optimize for a specific hardware configuration. In general, the High Performance power plan allows hardware to run at its maximum speed but uses more energy, and the Power Saver plan configures hardware devices in such a way that they use less energy with a corresponding reduction in performance. When a portable computer is running on battery power, it runs for a shorter amount of time before the battery drains completely when configured to use the High Performance power plan compared to when the same computer is set to use the Power Saver power plan. You can use the Power Options control panel, shown in Figure 11-26, to select a power plan for a client running Windows 7. The default power plan for a newly installed client running Windows 7 is Balanced.

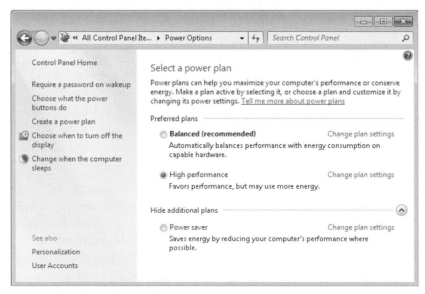

FIGURE 11-26 Select a power plan

Windows 7 allows you to configure basic and advanced settings for each plan. The settings that you can configure depend on your computer's hardware configuration. The Edit Plan Settings dialog box, shown in Figure 11-27, allows you to configure a plan's basic settings. Some computers do not support the Dim The Display or Adjust Plan Brightness settings. When you configure the basic settings of a plan, you configure different values for when the computer is plugged in or when the computer is running on internal battery power. On desktop computers that do not use an internal battery, it is possible to configure only the Plugged In settings.

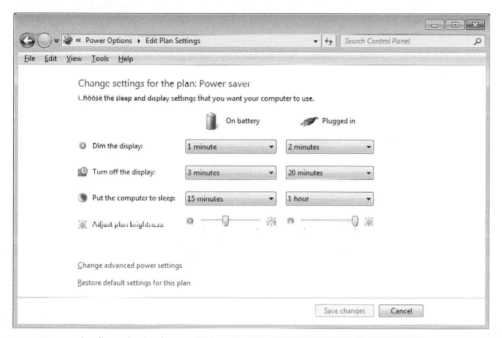

FIGURE 11-27 Configure basic plan settings

A user who has an account that is not a member of the local Administrators group is able to modify what the power and sleep buttons do. If they are able to elevate privileges, they can also specify whether a password is required when the computer wakes from the sleep state. You can configure these options by clicking Choose What The Power Buttons Do, which opens the Power Options System Settings dialog box, shown in Figure 11-28. The options that you can configure are Sleep, Hibernate, Shut Down, and Do Nothing.

Windows 7 supports the following sleep, shutdown, and hibernation modes:

- **Sleep**   When Windows 7 is in the Sleep state, the processor and the majority of system devices are in a turned-off state. The computer's RAM remains in a turned-on state so that it can maintain the user's open applications and documents. Devices that are configured to wake the computer from sleep, such as USB mice, keyboards, and network cards, remain in a turned-on state. If the computer is not woken after a configurable amount of time, the computer transitions to the Hibernate state. You can wake a computer from sleep by using the keyboard or mouse.

FIGURE 11-28 Configure power buttons

- **Hybrid Sleep** Hybrid Sleep is a power-saving feature that is used with desktop computers that do not have a battery-based power backup. If a desktop computer is in Sleep mode and suffers an interruption to its power supply, data loss may occur. The contents of the computer's RAM are stored both in the RAM in a low-power state and as a special file on the hard disk. When the Hybrid Sleep option is enabled, computers put to sleep use Hybrid Sleep rather than ordinary Sleep mode.

- **Hibernate** When Windows 7 is in the Hibernate state, all devices are turned off and the contents of the computer's RAM are stored in a special file on the operating system volume. All devices are in a turned-off state. You can turn on a computer that is hibernating only by using the power buttons.

- **Shutdown** In the Shutdown state, the contents of RAM are not preserved. All devices are in a turned-off state.

> **MORE INFO** **Windows 7 POWER MANAGEMENT**
>
> For more information about the new power management features available in Windows 7, including Wake On LAN, consult the following Microsoft TechNet article: *http://technet .microsoft.com/en-us/library/dd744300(WS.10).aspx.*

Advanced Power Plan Settings

To configure the advanced power plan settings, click the Change Advanced Power Settings item in the Edit Plan Settings dialog box. Unlike the basic plan settings, which a user who is not a member of the local administrators group can modify, only a user with elevated privileges can modify advanced power plan settings. The advanced plan settings are shown in Figure 11-29.

FIGURE 11-29 Advanced power settings

Using the Advanced Settings dialog box in Power Options, you can configure the following settings for both the On Battery and Plugged In states:

- **Require A Password On Wakeup**   Specifies whether a password is required after the computer resumes from hibernation or sleep.

- **Turn Off Hard Disk**   Specifies the period of inactivity after which to turn off the hard disk drive.

- **Desktop Background Settings**   Specifies whether animated desktop backgrounds, such as the slideshow background, are available when the computer is on battery or plugged in.

  - **Wireless Adapter Settings**   Configure the power performance of the wireless adapter. Possible settings are Maximum Performance, Low Power Saving, Medium Power Saving, and Maximum Power Saving. Different settings influence the performance of the adapter, reducing the adapter's maximum range and speed.

- **Sleep** This setting allows you to configure the Sleep and Hibernation periods for a computer. You learned about the difference between Sleep, Hybrid Sleep, and Hibernate earlier in this lesson. The options are the following:

  - **Sleep After** Specifies the period of inactivity after which the computer is put into sleep mode

  - **Allow Hybrid Sleep** Specifies whether the computer can use Hybrid Sleep

  - **Hibernate After** Specifies the period of sleep after which the computer goes into hibernation

  - **Allow Wake Timers** Specifies whether timed events should be allowed to wake the computer from sleep

- **USB Settings** Specifies whether selective suspend is enabled for USB.

- **Power Buttons And Lid** Specifies what happens to the computer when you close a laptop computer's lid, when you press the power button, and when you press the sleep button. Options include Do Nothing, Sleep, Hibernate, and Shut Down.

- **PCI Express** Specifies whether Windows 7 can utilize the PCI Express Link State Power Management feature with idle devices. This can be configured to Moderate Power Savings, Maximum Power Savings, or Off.

- **Processor Power Management** Specifies a minimum processor state and a maximum processor state in terms of percentage. It is also possible to specify whether the system cooling policy is active.

- **Display** Specifies the period after which to dim the display and the period after which to turn off the display. It is also possible to specify the display brightness during normal use and the display brightness when set to the dim setting.

- **Multimedia Settings** This section contains the following policies:

  - **When Sharing Media** Configure the computer's response when a remote computer is accessing media over the network. Options include allowing the computer to sleep, prevent idling to sleep, and allowing the computer to enter Away mode.

  - **Video Playback Settings** Options include optimizing video quality, balanced and optimize power savings.

- **Battery** Specifies the Reserve, Low, and Critical battery levels as a percentage. It is also possible to specify what action that the computer should take when the battery reaches the Low and Critical levels. Actions include Do Nothing, Sleep, Hibernate, and Shut Down.

If the three power plans may not meet your specific needs, it is possible to create a custom power plan. To create a custom plan, click Create A Power Plan in the Power Options control panel. You can delete a custom power plan so long as the plan that you want to delete is not currently active. You cannot delete any of the default power plans. You will create a custom power plan in the practice exercise at the end of this lesson.

Power-Related Group Policies

Group Policy settings related to Power Management are located in the Computer Configuration\ Administrative Templates\System\Power Management node. This node contains five nodes, as shown in Figure 11-30.

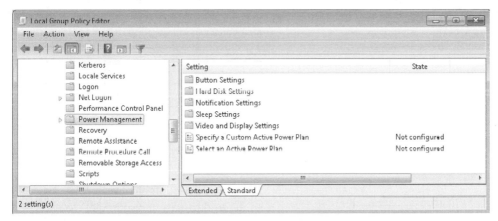

FIGURE 11-30 Power-related Group Policies

You can configure all the settings that you learned about in the section entitled "Advanced Power Plan Settings," earlier in this chapter, through these policies. There are several additional settings, located in the Sleep Settings node, that you can configure only through Group Policy. These settings are as follows:

- Allow Applications To Prevent Automatic Sleep
- Allow Automatic Sleep With Open Network Files
- Turn On The Ability For Applications To Prevent Sleep Transition

Each of these policies relates to whether applications or open network files can prevent a computer from entering the Sleep state automatically. When these policies are disabled, only direct user input is taken into account when determining whether the computer should enter the Sleep state. These policies have no impact when a user puts the computer into the Sleep state manually.

Command-line Power Configuration

Powercfg.exe is a command-line utility that you can use from an administrative command prompt to manage Windows 7 power settings. It is possible to use Powercfg.exe to configure a number of Windows 7 power-related settings that you cannot configure through Group Policy or the Advanced Plan Settings dialog box. You can use Powercfg.exe to configure specific devices so that they are able to wake the computer from the Sleep state. You can also use Powercfg.exe to migrate power policies from one computer running Windows 7 to another by using the import and export functionality. Table 11-2 contains a list of some of the Powercfg.exe options and the tasks that they can be used to accomplish.

TABLE 11-2 Powercfg.exe Options

COMMAND OPTION	FUNCTION
-list	Lists all the current power schemes.
-query <scheme_guid>	Displays the contents of the specified power scheme.
-change	Use this to change a specific setting in the current power scheme.
-hibernate	Use this to enable or disable the Hibernate feature.
-devicequery <option>	Lists devices that can wake the computer, as follows: ■ **Wake_From_Any** Lists all devices that support waking the computer from any Sleep state. ■ **Wake_Armed** Lists all devices currently configured to wake the computer from any Sleep state.
-deviceenablewake <devicename>	Enables the device to wake the computer from Sleep state.
-devicedisablewake <devicename>	Disables the device from waking the computer from Sleep state.
-import / -export	Allows you to migrate a power policy by import and exporting power plans.
-lastwake	Provides information on what event last triggered the computer to wake from sleep.
-requests	List application and driver power requests that may prevent a computer from entering Sleep mode.
-requestsoverride	Allows you to override a particular application or driver power request to stop it from blocking the computer from entering Sleep mode.
-energy	Check the computer for common energy-efficiency and battery life problems. Provides report in Hypertext Markup Language (HTML) format.

MORE INFO **Powercfg.exe**

For more information on Powercfg.exe, consult the following Microsoft TechNet document: *http://technet.microsoft.com/en-us/library/cc748940.aspx.*

PRACTICE Managing Power Plans

Custom power plans allow you to configure power management settings that best suit the individual needs of your organization. In this practice, you explore the process of creating a custom power plan and then simulate migrating that plan to other computers running Windows 7.

EXERCISE 1 Creating a Custom Power Plan

In this exercise, you create a custom power plan based on the Power Saver power plan and configure advanced plan settings.

1. Log onto computer Canberra using the Kim_Akers user account.

2. In the Search Programs And Files text box, type **Power Options.** Click the Power Options item to open the Power Options control panel.

3. Select the Power Saver plan and then click Create A Power Plan.

4. On the Create A Power Plan page, select the Power Saver plan and then enter the custom name **Extreme Power Saver,** as shown in Figure 11-31, and click Next.

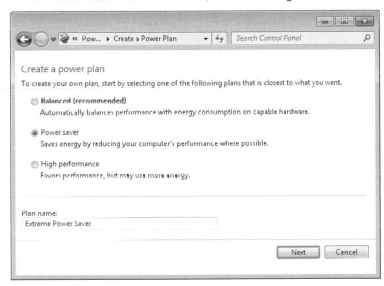

FIGURE 11-31 New custom power plan

5. On the Change Settings For the Plan: Extreme Power Saver page, click Create. In the Power Options control panel, click Change Plan Settings. On the Edit Plan Settings dialog box, click Change Advanced Power Settings.

6. In the Power Options Advanced Settings dialog box, shown in Figure 11-32, click Change Settings That Are Currently Unavailable.

FIGURE 11-32 Power Options Advanced Settings dialog box

7. Change the Require A Password On Wake Up setting to No.

8. Expand the Power Buttons And Lid node. Set the Sleep Button action to Hibernate.

9. Expand the Processor Power Management node. Set the Maximum Processor State to 80%. Click OK. Close the Edit Plan Settings dialog box.

EXERCISE 2 Migrating a Power Plan

In this exercise, you use the Powercfg.exe command-line utility to export the plan that you created in Exercise 1. You then delete the plan you created and import it as a substitute for importing the plan on another computer.

1. At an elevated command prompt, type **powercfg.exe –list.** This should provide output similar to that shown in Figure 11-33, though the power scheme globally unique identifiers (GUIDs) will be different. Take a note of the GUID assigned to the Extreme Power Saver plan. You may want to use the command prompt ability to mark and copy data to copy the GUID to memory because you will need this identifier in step 4.

2. Create the directory C:\Export if it does not already exist. Change into this directory.

3. Issue the command **powercfg.exe –energy.** When the command finishes executing, issue the command *start energy-report.html*. This opens Windows Internet Explorer with the report, as shown in Figure 11-34. Review the report and then close the Internet Explorer window.

FIGURE 11-33 List of plans and GUIDs

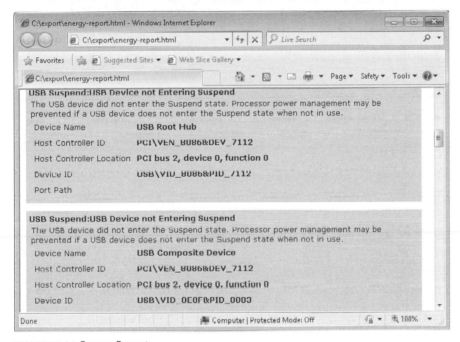

FIGURE 11-34 Energy Report

4. Issue the command **powercfg.exe –export extreme.pow {GUID},** where {GUID} is the GUID of the Extreme Power Saver plan.

5. Issue the command **powercfg.exe –setactive SCHEME_BALANCED.**

6. Verify that the Balanced power scheme is set by issuing the command **powercfg.exe –list.** Make a note of the GUID assigned to the Extreme Power Saver plan.

7. Enter the **command powercfg.exe –delete {GUID},** where {GUID} is the GUID of the Extreme Power Saver plan.

8. Verify that the Extreme Power Saver plan has been deleted by issuing the command **powercfg.exe –list**. You should see only three power schemes, as shown in Figure 11-35.

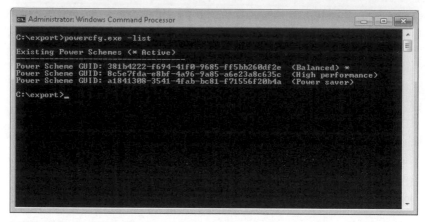

FIGURE 11-35 Verifying deletion of the power plan

9. Issue the command **powercfg.exe –import c:\export\extreme.pow**.

10. Verify that the power scheme has been imported successfully by issuing the command **powercfg.exe –list**. You should see that the Extreme Power Saver plan is now available.

Lesson Summary

- Offline Files is a feature of Windows 7 Professional, Enterprise, and Ultimate editions that allows a user to manipulate a file that is hosted on a shared folder when he is not connected to the network that hosts the shared folder.

- Offline Files creates a cached copy of the file on the local computer that is synchronized automatically with the file server whenever connectivity to the file server is established.

- Sync Center can be used to perform a manual synchronization of offline files. Sync Center can also be used to resolve synchronization conflicts that occur when an offline file and a shared file are modified during the same period.

- Transparent caching provides automatic caching of files on shared folders that are on remote networks. Transparently cached files are available only to the local computer and are not synchronized as offline files are.

- Power Plans control how a computer running Windows 7 uses energy. Normal users can select a power plan to meet their needs without having to elevate privileges.

- The default Windows 7 Power Plan is Balanced. Other plans that ship with Windows 7 include Power Saver and High Performance.

- Powercfg.exe can be used to import and export power policies, allowing you to migrate them between computers.

Lesson Review

You can use the following questions to test your knowledge of the information in Lesson 2, "Windows 7 Mobility." The questions are also available on the companion DVD if you prefer to review them in electronic form.

1. Which of the following commands can you use to generate a list of devices on a computer running Windows 7 that are currently configured to wake the computer from any sleep state?

   A. powercfg.exe –devicequery all_devices

   B. powerctg.exe –hibernate on

   C. powercfg.exe –devicequery wake_armed

   D. powercfg.exe –list

2. Sam Abolrous has a user account on a client running Windows 7. This user account is not a member of the local Administrators group. Which of the following power settings tasks can Sam perform? (Choose all that apply.)

   A. Choose a different power plan

   B. Create a new power plan

   C. Change what the power buttons do

   D. Change the Require A Password On Wakeup setting

3. Which of the following tools can you use to migrate a custom power plan from one computer running Windows 7 to another?

   A. The Power Options control panel

   B. Gpedit.msc

   C. Powercfg.exe

   D. Bcdedit.exe

4. Kim Akers has set the file Brisbane.doc (which is hosted on an office file server) to be available offline using her portable computer running Windows 7. Kim goes home for the weekend and works on Brisbane.doc. Same Abolrous comes into the office on the weekend and works on the copy of Brisbane.doc stored on the office file server. Which of the following tools can Kim use to resolve the conflict that occurs when she connects her computer to the office network?

   A. Credential Manager

   B. The Sync Center control panel

    C. HomeGroup

    D. Network And Sharing Center

5. Which of the following policies should you enable to ensure that clients running Windows 7 are able to cache files on shared folders if the round-trip latency to the remote file server exceeds a specific value in milliseconds without having to specify that a file is available offline?

    A. Configure Slow Link Speed

    B. Configure Slow Link Mode

    C. Exclude Files From Being Cached

    D. Transparent caching

Chapter Review

To further practice and reinforce the skills you learned in this chapter, you can perform the following tasks:

- Review the chapter summary.
- Review the list of key terms introduced in this chapter.
- Complete the case scenarios. These scenarios set up real-world situations involving the topics of this chapter and ask you to create a solution.
- Complete the suggested practices.
- Take a practice test.

Chapter Summary

- BitLocker protects computers against offline attacks by providing full hard disk encryption as well as protection for the boot environment.
- BitLocker To Go provides full volume encryption for USB removable storage devices. These storage devices can be accessed on other computers if the appropriate password is used.
- Offline Files allows files hosted on specially configured shared folders to be used when a computer is not connected to the network.
- Sync Center can be used to resolve conflicts between Offline Files and those stored on shared folders.
- Transparent caching is an automatic caching technology that speeds up access to files located on file shares on distant networks.
- Power plans allow users to balance computer performance against energy consumption. Power plans can be migrated using a command-line utility.

Key Terms

Do you know what these key terms mean? You can check your answers by looking up the terms in the glossary at the end of the book.

- **Data Recovery Agent (DRA)**
- **Transparent Caching**
- **Offline Files**

Case Scenarios

In the following case scenarios, you apply what you've learned about subjects covered in this chapter. You can find answers to these questions in the "Answers" section at the end of this book.

Case Scenario 1: Accessing Offline Files at Contoso

Contoso's Australian division has its head office located in Melbourne and branch offices in Wagga Wagga, Maroochydore, and Wangaratta. The file server in Melbourne, named fs1.melbourne.au.contoso.com, has Windows Server 2008 installed. Several users at the Melbourne office have configured files hosted on shared folders to be available offline. Sometimes other users edit these files when the users who made them available offline are out of the office. Several clients in the branch offices need to retrieve files from the Melbourne file server, but they experience delays due to WAN congestion. Branch office clients run Windows 7 Professional and are not members of the Contoso domain. You have configured a branch office client with a custom power plan. You want to use this power plan with other clients running Windows 7 at the branch office sites.

With these facts in mind, answer the following questions:

1. What tool should you use to configure other branch office clients with the custom power plan?

2. How can you speed up access to files stored on fs1.melbourne.au.contoso.com for clients in Wagga Wagga, Wangaratta, and Maroochydore?

3. What tool should you advise head office users to use to resolve offline file synchronization conflicts?

Case Scenario 2: Using BitLocker at Tailspin Toys

Tailspin Toys has recently deployed a large number of computers running Windows 7 Enterprise. The company has distributed 32-GB USB flash drives for use with these computers. After a senior manager left her flash drive in an airport lounge, you have been asked to review security policies with respect to these devices. It is important that unauthorized third parties are unable to recover data if one of these devices is lost. Users should be unable to store data on these devices unless that data is encrypted by Tailspin Toys. Users should be able to access the data stored on these devices on their home computers. Home computers run either Windows XP or Windows Vista.

With these facts in mind, answer the following questions:

1. What can you do to allow people to use their USB storage devices at home on their computers running Windows XP and Windows Vista?

2. What can you do to ensure that users are able to write information only to BitLocker-protected removable devices from Tailspin Toys?

3. What can you do to ensure that it is possible to recover removable volumes when people have forgotten their password or lost their key?

Suggested Practices

To help you master the exam objectives presented in this chapter, complete the following tasks.

Configure BitLocker and BitLocker To Go

This practice requires a computer that has a compatible TPM chip. If you do not have a computer that has a compatible TPM chip, or you are using a virtual machine, do not perform this practice.

- **Practice 1** Configure a computer with a TPM chip to use BitLocker to protect all attached volumes. The volume encryption process takes some time.

- **Practice 2** Remove BitLocker from the computer configured in Practice 1. The BitLocker removal process takes some time.

Configure Mobility Options

This practice requires that you have both computer Canberra and computer Aberdeen available and able to connect to each other. You configured computer Aberdeen for the practice exercises in several previous chapters. In this practice, you explore offline files functionality and resolve an offline files conflict.

- **Practice 1** Configure a shared folder on computer Aberdeen. Create some temporary files in the folder using WordPad. Connect to this shared folder over the network from computer Canberra. When logged on to computer Canberra, make one of the files that you created on computer Aberdeen available offline.

- **Practice 2** After you have made the file that you created on computer Aberdeen available offline on computer Canberra, shut down computer Aberdeen. Make modifications to this file on computer Canberra and then shut down computer Canberra. Start computer Aberdeen and modify the same file that you made offline on computer Canberra. Start computer Canberra. Use the Sync Center to resolve the conflict between the offline file modified on computer Canberra and the shared file modified on computer Aberdeen.

Take a Practice Test

The practice tests on this book's companion DVD offer many options. For example, you can test yourself on just one exam objective, or you can test yourself on all the 70-680 certification exam content. You can set up the test so that it closely simulates the experience of taking a certification exam, or you can set it up in study mode so that you can look at the correct answers and explanations after you answer each question.

> **MORE INFO**   **PRACTICE TESTS**
>
> For details about all the practice test options available, see the section entitled "How to Use the Practice Tests," in the Introduction to this book.

CHAPTER 12

Windows Update and Windows Internet Explorer

K eeping computers secure is one of an IT professional's most important responsibilities. This task has become increasingly difficult as attackers become more sophisticated. Malware authors respond rapidly to the publication of new updates, reverse engineering them to learn more about the vulnerabilities that the updates address. What this means in practical terms is the longer you take to apply a released update, the more time you give to attackers to exploit the vulnerabilities that are fixed by the update. In the first part of this chapter, you learn which methods and technologies that you can use to keep clients running Windows 7 up to date so that you can ensure the safety and security of the users in your organization.

Windows Internet Explorer 8 is the browser most commonly used with Windows 7. Browsing the Internet and intranet is becoming as much a critical activity in business as using a word processor or managing a spreadsheet. In the second part of this chapter, you learn how to configure two new privacy technologies that are included with Internet Explorer 8: InPrivate Browsing and InPrivate Filtering. You learn how to extend the functionality of Internet Explorer by configuring and managing accelerators and add-ons. You also learn about how you can configure Internet Explorer to be more secure, through customizing privacy options and configuring zone settings.

Exam objectives in this chapter:

- Configure updates to Windows 7.
- Configure Internet Explorer.

Lessons in this chapter:

Before You Begin

To complete the exercises in the practice in this chapter, you need to have done the following:

- Install Windows 7 on a stand-alone client PC named Canberra, as described in Chapter 1, "Install, Migrate, or Upgrade to Windows 7."

- Ensure that computer Canberra has an active connection to the Internet.

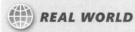

REAL WORLD

Orin Thomas

Many security incidents would not have occurred if administrators and users had kept their computers up to date with software updates, antivirus definitions, and service packs. This is because a significant number of attacks against computers exploit problems that the vendor has previously patched with a released update. Many famous viruses and worms attacked security vulnerabilities that Microsoft had already fixed. For example, Code Red, Nimda, and Sasser were successful because a large number of people did not keep their computers current with software updates. If almost every administrator diligently applied updates, we would never have heard of these viruses because they would have been unable to infect computers. Applying updates in a timely manner is important because security researchers have estimated that exploit code becomes available for the vulnerability that a new update addresses within a week of the update's release. One of the most important aspects of your career as an IT professional who supports client computers is to ensure that the clients you are responsible for managing stay current with software updates. This immunizes computers that you manage from malware infections. You also do not want to be in a position to have to explain to your manager why you did not manage to find the time to install the update that would have protected your organization's computers from the attack when the next big virus or worm hits.

Lesson 1: Updating Windows 7

Your responsibility for managing a computer does not end once the operating system and applications are installed, appropriate settings configured, and the user logs on for the first time. As an IT Pro responsible for managing clients running Windows 7, it is likely that you will spend more time ensuring that software updates and service packs are applied in a timely manner than you will ever spend on deploying the operating system to new computers. In this lesson, you learn about what steps you can take to automate the deployment of software updates. You learn about the functionality of the Windows Update client built into Windows 7, and you learn about centralized update deployment solutions like Windows Server Update Services (WSUS).

> **After this lesson, you will be able to:**
> - Manage updates to Windows 7.
> - Configure update-related group policies.
> - Configure and update sources.
>
> **Estimated lesson time: 40 minutes**

Configuring Windows Update

The Windows Update control panel is the primary tool you use to manage software updates on clients running Windows 7. Through this control panel, a user with Administrator privileges is able to check for updates, change update settings, review installed updates, and review hidden updates. A user who is unable to elevate privileges is able to use this control panel to check for and install updates. Windows Update relies upon the Windows Update service. This service is enabled by default on all clients running Microsoft Windows.

When installing Windows 7, the installation routine asks you to set the Windows Update defaults. The options are to use recommended settings, install important updates only, or have Windows 7 ask about update settings again later. If you choose the default settings, Windows Update attempts to detect and install updates classified as Important and Recommended every day at 3:00 A.M. If the computer is not switched on at 3:00 A.M., the computer performs a check for updates and installs them the next time it is turned on.

Administrators and standard users can manually check for updates by clicking the Check For Updates item in the control panel. The computer needs to be able to contact the update source to be able to check for updates. The update source can be the Microsoft Update servers on the Internet or a local update server. You will learn more about configuring Windows Update to use a local update server later in this lesson. After you check for updates, the Windows Update control panel lists all available updates that can be installed, as shown in Figure 12-1. When you manually check for updates as opposed to waiting until the scheduled update time, Windows Update checks only for updates. Manually checking for updates does not automatically download and install updates. You can also manually check for updates from the command line by issuing the following command:

```
Wuauclt.exe /detectnow
```

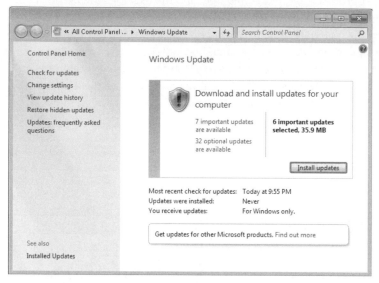

FIGURE 12-1 Windows Update control panel

Updates can have one of the three following classifications:

- **Important Updates** Important updates often address critical security issues. In some cases, updates with the important classification address security issues where an exploit is already available to attackers on the Internet.

- **Recommended Updates** Recommended updates often address functionality issues. The Recommended update shown in Figure 12-2 addresses a problem that Internet Explorer had with unresponsive Web sites.

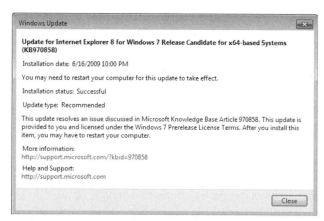

FIGURE 12-2 Properties of a Recommended Update

- **Optional Updates** Optional updates provide items such as driver updates and language packs. Figure 12-3 shows the Russian Language Pack, which is an optional update for Windows 7.

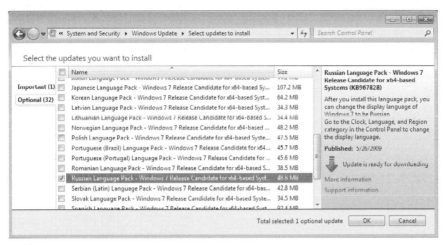

FIGURE 12-3 Optional language pack update

How Windows Update deals with this update depends on how you have configured update settings. You can manually configure how Windows Update deals with updates by clicking the Change Settings item. This opens the Change Settings dialog box, shown in Figure 12-4. Through this dialog box, you can configure how Windows 7 deals with important updates, the frequency at which updates are checked, whether recommended updates are treated in the same fashion as important updates, and whether users without administrative privileges are able to install updates on the computer. Only users with administrative privileges are able to change Windows Update settings. The options that you can configure with this dialog box are as follows:

- **Install Updates Automatically (Recommended)** Windows Update installs updates automatically at the time specified. This is the default setting for Windows Update.

- **Download Updates But Let Me Choose Whether To Install Them** Updates are downloaded to the computer, and the user is notified that the updates are available for installation.

- **Check For Updates But Let Me Choose Whether To Download And Install Them** The user is notified that updates are available for download and install.

- **Never Check For Updates (Not Recommended)** Windows Update does not check for updates, but updates can still be checked for and installed manually.

- **Give Me Recommended Updates The Same Way I Receive Important Updates** This means that Recommended Updates are treated in the same manner as Important Updates. Optional updates still need to be installed manually.

- **Allow All Users To Install Updates On This Computer** This option is enabled by default. If you disable this option, only user accounts that are members of the local Administrators group can install updates.

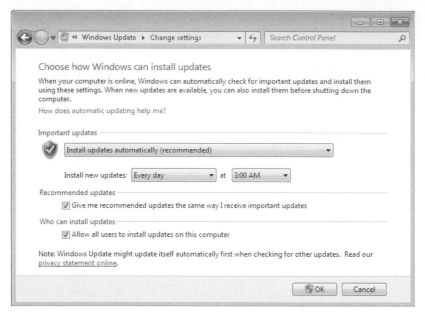

FIGURE 12-4 Changing how Windows can install updates

The View Update History control panel, shown in Figure 12-5, allows you to view a list of all updates that have been successfully or unsuccessfully installed on a computer, as well as the date they were installed and their importance classification. Clicking on an update within the View Update History control panel allows you to find out more information about the update. This information provides a summary of the update and also provides a link to a Knowledge Base article that also provides detailed information about the update. Knowledge Base articles also provide information about any potential problems that an update might cause. If you install an update on a client running Windows 7 and start experiencing problems, you should consult the Knowledge Base article related to the update to determine if these problems have been documented and if there are any workarounds to deal with the issues related to the update. Knowing the Knowledge Base ID of an update is also important if you want to delete the update. The Knowledge Base ID is a six-digit number, often preceded by the letters KB, such as KB123456.

When reviewing updates that are available for installation, you can also right-click an update and select Hide Update. Choosing to hide an update effectively declines the update. This means that the update does not install and that Windows Update does not present that particular update for installation through Windows Update in the future. Only users with Administrative privileges are able to hide updates. Declining an update does not mean that the update cannot be installed at a later stage. Through the Restore Hidden Updates item in the Windows Update control panel, you are able to restore updates that were hidden in the past. Restoring a hidden update means that the update will be available the next time an update check occurs. The Restore Hidden Updates control panel is shown in Figure 12-6.

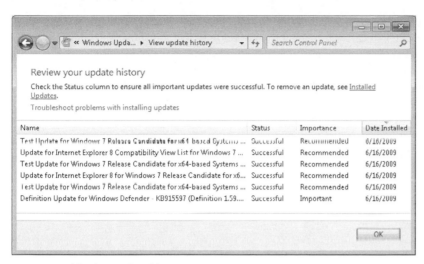

FIGURE 12-5 Viewing update history

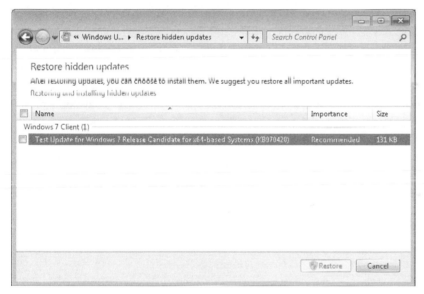

FIGURE 12-6 Restoring hidden updates

It is possible to uninstall an update that has already been installed. A user who is a member of the local Administrators group can uninstall an update. This is done through the Programs and Features control panel. You can also access this panel by clicking the Installed Updates item in the Windows Update control panel. Unlike the View Update History dialog box, you are presented only with the Knowledge Base identifier of the update. This means that you must know the Knowledge Base identifier of an update to uninstall it. As you learned earlier, you can determine the Knowledge Base identifier of a particular update by using the View Update

History control panel and double-clicking the update. This displays an update information dialog box from which you can determine the Knowledge Base ID, as shown in Figure 12-7.

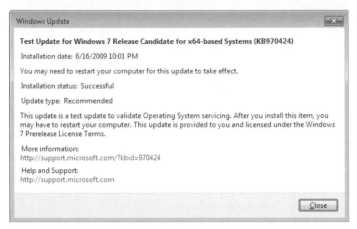

FIGURE 12-7 Update information

When you uninstall an update, it does not appear in the list of hidden updates, but it does become available again if you check for new updates. It is important to remember to hide any update after you uninstall it. For example, you might install an update only to find that it causes a conflict with some custom software deployed in your organization. You choose to uninstall the update to restore the functionality of the custom software. You can then use the Hide Update function to hide the update until the software vendor is able to develop a fix that makes the custom software compatible with the update. This will ensure that other users who have the ability to install updates do not inadvertently install the update until the custom software fix is available. Figure 12-8 shows the Installed Updates control panel, from which you can uninstall an update.

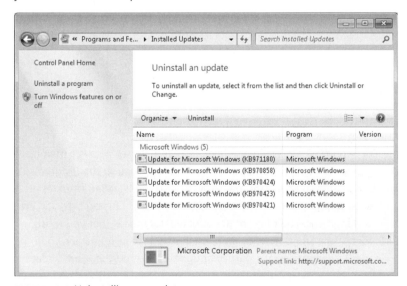

FIGURE 12-8 Uninstalling an update

Updates for Other Microsoft Products

The default Windows Update settings retrieve updates only for the Windows operating system and included applications. You can upgrade Windows Update so that updates for all Microsoft software, including Microsoft Office, can be detected and installed through Windows Update. To do this, click the Find Out More item next to Get Updates For Other Microsoft Products. This opens a Web page that hosts an update allowing you to extend the functionality of Windows Update. Installing this update adds a section to the Change Settings control panel, shown in Figure 12-9, that allows Windows Update to provide update for other Microsoft products. It is also possible for Windows Update to deliver updates that are available from an alternate update source like WSUS. You will learn about WSUS later in this chapter.

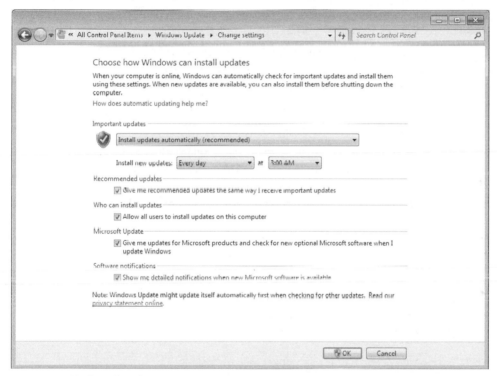

FIGURE 12-9 Updates for other Microsoft products

Configuring Windows Update to Use a Proxy Server

Occasionally, on networks that have specific firewall and proxy configurations, Windows Update clients are unable to contact the Microsoft Update servers on the Internet. There are several ways to deal with this problem. The first is to deploy a WSUS server on the local area network (LAN) and have the clients download updates from the WSUS server. When setting up the WSUS server, you can configure it to use the proxy. Alternatively, it is possible to configure a client running Windows 7 manually so that Windows Update can communicate with the Microsoft Update servers through the proxy. Although you can configure Internet Explorer to use a proxy through Internet Options, Windows Update cannot use these settings directly. You can configure clients running Windows 7 to determine proxy settings in two ways:

- **Use Web Proxy Auto Detect (WPAD)**   This feature allows computer services to locate an available proxy by querying a Dynamic Host Configuration Protocol (DHCP) option or checking a Domain Name System (DNS) record.

- **Use the Netsh.exe command-line tool**   Although Windows Update does not use the Internet Options settings directly, you can use the Netsh.exe command-line tool to import the proxy settings configured for Internet Explorer. To accomplish this goal, use the following command from an elevated command prompt:

```
netsh winhttp import proxy source=ie
```

MORE INFO   **WEB PROXY AUTO DETECT**

For more information on configuring Web Proxy Auto Detect on DNS and DHCP servers, consult the following document on Microsoft TechNet: *http://technet.microsoft.com/en-us/ library/cc713344.aspx*.

Installing Windows 7 Update Files Manually

In some cases, such as when you are dealing with stand-alone computers that are not connected to a network, it is necessary to install update files directly. You can download Windows 7 update files directly from Microsoft's Web site. You can find these updates related to each update's security bulletin. Update files have the .msu extension. If you want to script the installation of a number of MSU files, you can use the Wusa.exe utility. When chaining the installation of updates, you should use the */norestart* parameter after each update except the last one that you want to install. For example, you might have a script that installs three updates with the commands:

```
Wusa.exe d:\windows6.1-kb123456-x64.msu /quiet /norestart
Wusa.exe d:\windows6.1-kb123457-x64.msu /quiet /norestart
Wusa.exe d:\windows6.1-kb123458-x64.msu /quiet
```

MORE INFO   **WINDOWS UPDATE STAND-ALONE INSTALLER**

For more information about the Windows Update Stand-alone installer (Wusa.exe), consult the following article: *http://support.microsoft.com/kb/934307*.

 Quick Check

- Which Windows Update–related tasks can a user with standard privileges complete?

Quick Check Answer

- A user with standard privileges is able to install updates. A user with standard privileges is unable to hide or uninstall updates. A user with standard privileges cannot change update settings.

Action Center

Action Center, shown in Figure 12-10, provides a central reporting area for problems related to security and maintenance. Action Center notifications appear in taskbar balloons that remind users that they should address certain issues related to their computer. Action Center can provide security and maintenance warning messages on the following subjects:

- Windows Update
- Internet security settings
- Network firewall
- Spyware and related protection
- User Account Control (UAC)
- Virus Protection
- Windows Backup
- Windows Troubleshooting

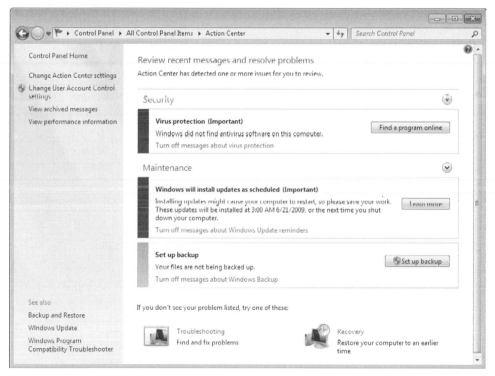

FIGURE 12-10 Action Center

Action Center relies upon the Security Center service being active. If this service is not active, the Action Center does not function. Other networking services, such as Network Access Protection (NAP), which is used to keep computers that do not have updates installed from connecting to either local corporate networks or virtual private networks (VPNs) also rely on the Security Center service being active. A user with administrative privileges can configure Action Center to customize which message types are displayed, as shown in Figure 12-11. You can reach this dialog box by clicking the Change Action Center settings item in the Action Center Control panel. You will learn more about Action Center in Chapter 13, "Monitoring and Performance."

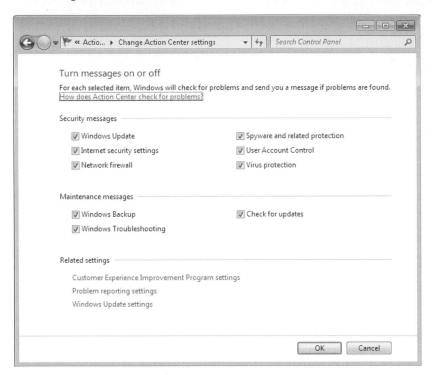

FIGURE 12-11 Action Center settings

Understanding Windows Server Update Services

Windows Update retrieves updates from the Microsoft Update servers on the Internet. Although this configuration works well for small deployments, when there are more than 10 computers running Windows 7 in a single location, you can make significant bandwidth savings by deploying a centralized software update solution like Windows Server Update Services (WSUS), System Center Essentials, or System Center Configuration Manager (SCCM) 2007. These products function as a local Microsoft Update server. Rather than each client downloading the same update over an organization's Internet connection, the local update server can download an update once to the LAN, and then each client can retrieve the update off the local update server. Because System Center Essentials and SCCM software update deployments build off WSUS, this lesson concentrates primarily on WSUS. Clients running Windows 7 require that the WSUS server be running WSUS 3.0 with Service Pack 1 or later.

MORE INFO **SCCM 2007**

To learn more about SCCM 2007, navigate to the following Web site: *http://www.microsoft*
.com/systemcenter/configurationmanager/en/us/default.aspx.

WSUS allows administrators to deploy updates according to a schedule that best meets
the needs of the organization. A drawback of relying on Microsoft Update is that updates are
released according to Microsoft's schedule, which does not give an organization time to test
that an update is fully compatible with their client computers if Windows Update has been
configured to install any detected updates. When an organization uses WSUS, it can test an
update on a small group of computers before deploying it to all computers in the organization.
Figure 12-12 shows the WSUS server console on a computer running Windows Server 2008.

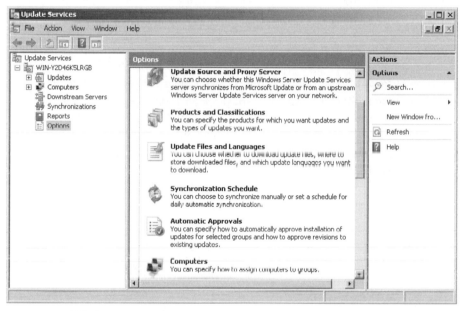

FIGURE 12-12 WSUS server console

In many WSUS deployments, an administrator takes control of updates centrally. This means
that the decision as to which updates to install and when to install them occurs centrally rather
than on each client computer. Administrators can enforce these decisions through update
policies. You will learn about configuring update policies later in this lesson.

WSUS allows administrators to organize client computers into groups. Groups allow for the
staggered deployment of updates. This means that you can deploy updates on some computers
but not on others. You create groups on the WSUS server. After the groups are created on
the WSUS server, you can configure a client to join a group by configuring the Enable Client
Side Targeting policy, which you will learn about later in this lesson, or by manually assigning
computers to groups using the WSUS console, as shown in Figure 12-13.

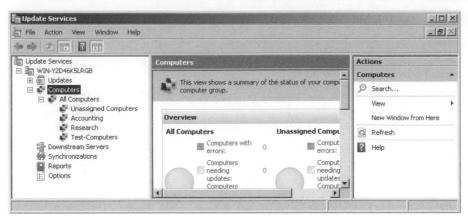

FIGURE 12-13 WSUS computer groups

WSUS also allows administrators centrally to roll back the installation of an update across all computers in the organization. For example, if an update causes a problem in an organization that relies only on Microsoft Update, administrators have to uninstall and then hide the update on each computer in the organization manually. If an update causes a problem in an organization that uses WSUS, the update administrator can roll back the update from WSUS, which removes that update from all client computers in the organization. It is not necessary to hide a rolled back update because the WSUS server makes approved updates available only to Windows Update clients.

> **MORE INFO** **WSUS**
>
> To learn more about WSUS, consult the Windows Server Update Services TechCenter at the following Microsoft TechNet address: *http://technet.microsoft.com/en-us/wsus/default.aspx*.

Windows Update Policies

Although you can configure some settings, such as when the computer will check for updates and how the computer will deal with updates using the Windows Update Control Panel, you configure most Windows Update settings by configuring Group Policy. The Computer Configuration\Administrative Templates\Windows Components\Windows Update Group Policy node contains 16 policies, as shown in Figure 12-14.

You can configure Windows Update using these policies as follows:

- **Do Not Display "Install Updates And Shut Down" Option In Shut Down Windows Dialog Box**   This policy allows you to configure whether the Shut Down menu displays the Install Updates And Shut Down option. The default setting has this option available.

- **Do Not Adjust Default Option To "Install Updates And Shut Down" in Shut Down Windows Dialog Box**   When this policy setting is enabled, the user's last shutdown choice is the default shutdown option. When this policy setting is disabled or is not

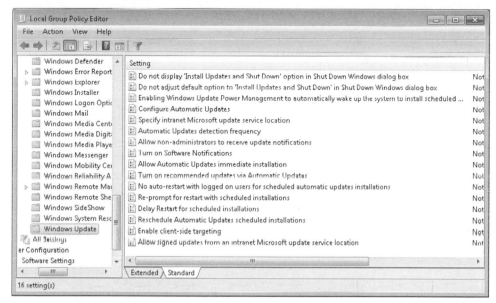

FIGURE 12-14 Windows Update policies

configured, Install Updates and Shut Down is the default option if updates are available for installation. This policy is deprecated when the Do Not Display "Install Updates And Shut Down" Option In Shut Down Windows Dialog Box policy is enabled.

- **Enabling Windows Update Power Management To Automatically Wake The System To Install Scheduled Updates** This policy allows Windows Update to wake a hibernating computer to install updates. Updates does not install if the computer is hibernating on battery power.

- **Configure Automatic Updates** This policy, shown in Figure 12-15, allows you to configure update detection, download, and installation settings. Several of these settings are similar to the ones that you can configure through the Windows Update control panel. You can configure the following settings using this policy:

  - **Notify For Download And Notify For Install** Windows Update does not download updates. Windows Update notifies the user that updates are available for download and installation.

  - **Auto Download And Notify For Install** Windows Update downloads updates and notifies the user that updates are available for installation.

  - **Auto Download And Schedule The Install** Windows Update downloads and installs updates without user intervention.

  - **Allow Local Admin To Choose Setting** This setting configured using Windows Update control panel is used for update download and notification.

  - **Install Day and Install Time** Use these settings to configure the day and time that Windows Update will install updates.

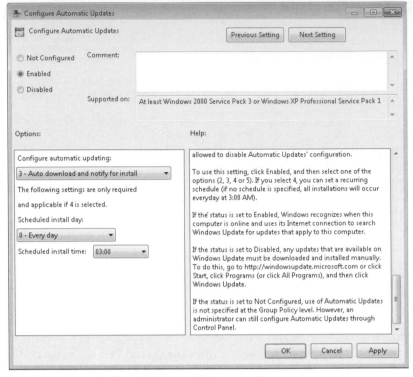

FIGURE 12-15 Configuring the Automatic Updates policy

- **Specify Intranet Microsoft Update Service Location** This policy, shown in Figure 12-16, allows you to specify the location of an internal update server, such as one running WSUS. This policy is the only way that you can configure Windows Update to use an alternate update server. Using this policy, you can specify the update server and the statistics server. In most cases, these are the same servers. The updates server is where the updates are downloaded from, and the statistics server is the server where clients report update installation information.

- **Automatic Updates Detection Frequency** Configure this policy to specify how often Windows Update checks the local intranet update server for updates. This policy does not work if you configure a client to retrieve updates from the Windows Update servers.

- **Allow Non-Administrators To Receive Update Notifications** This policy specifies whether users who are not members of the local Administrators group are able to install updates.

- **Turn On Software Notification** When you enable this policy, Windows Update presents users with information about optional updates.

- **Allow Automatic Updates Immediate Installation** When you enable this policy, updates that do not require a restart install automatically. Updates that do require a restart are not installed until the conditions set in the Configure Automatic Updates policy are met.

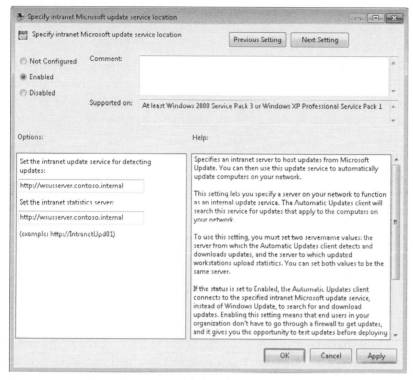

FIGURE 12-16 Specifying intranet update location

- **Turn On Recommended Updates Via Automatic Updates** Use this policy to configure Windows Update to install recommended updates as well as important updates.

- **No Auto-Restart With Logged On Users For Scheduled Automatic Updates Installation** When you enable this policy, Windows Update waits until the currently logged on user logs off if Windows Update installs updates that requiring a restart. If you disable or do not configure this policy and the Configure Automatic Updates policy is set to install updates at a specific time, Windows Update gives the logged-on user a 5-minute warning prior to restarting to complete the installation.

- **Re-prompt For Restart With Scheduled Installations** Use this policy to set the amount of time that a user can postpone a scheduled restart when the Configure Automatic Updates policy is set to install updates at a specific time.

- **Delay Restart For Scheduled Installations** Through this policy, you can specify the amount of time that Windows waits before automatically restarting after a scheduled installation. This policy applies only if the Configure Automatic Updates policy is set to install updates at a specific time.

- **Reschedule Automatic Updates Scheduled Installations** You can use this policy to configure a computer that has missed a scheduled update to perform the update a specific number of minutes after startup. For example, use this policy to ensure that a computer that was switched off at the scheduled update time installs updates 1 minute after starting up. Disabling this policy means that updates install at the next scheduled time.

- **Enable Client-Side Targeting**   This policy allows you to place computers into different software update groups. Different software update groups allow the software update administrator to target the deployment of updates, allowing updates to be deployed to specific groups of computers in the organization rather than all computers in the organization.

- **Allow Signed Updates From An intranet Microsoft Update Service Location**   This policy allows updates from third-party vendors to be distributed from the Automatic Updates location so long as those updates are digitally signed by a trusted publisher.

Microsoft Baseline Security Analyzer

The Microsoft Baseline Security Analyzer (MBSA) tool allows you to scan client computers to determine if they have all currently available software updates installed. This tool allows administrators in environments that do not use a central update solution like WSUS to locate client computers that are not up to date with security updates. If you do not use a utility like the MBSA tool, you need to access Windows Update on each computer to determine whether a particular computer has all updates installed. The MBSA tool is important in the latter stages of an operating system's life cycle. This is because more updates are available for an operating system the longer that operating system is available, and it becomes increasingly time consuming to determine if a particular update is missing.

As Figure 12-17 shows, the MBSA tool can check a computer for updates based on Microsoft Update, or can scan a computer based on updates that were approved on a WSUS server. You can also use the MBSA tool to determine if there are problems with a computer's security configuration, such as whether common administrative vulnerabilities are present and weak passwords are set. You can use the MBSA tool to scan servers as well as clients, so it is possible to check for other vulnerabilities, such as those that are present in Internet Information Server (IIS) and Microsoft SQL Server. To scan a computer, you need to have administrator access on the local computer and administrator access on any remote computer that you are scanning. This requirement ensures that you cannot use the MBSA tool as an attack tool to scan other people's computers to determine which vulnerabilities they may possess. You cannot use version 2.1 and earlier of the MBSA tool to scan computers running Windows 7.

> *MORE INFO*   **MBSA**
>
> To get more information about the MBSA, consult the following Microsoft TechNet Web page: *http://technet.microsoft.com/en-au/security/cc184923.aspx*.

 EXAM TIP
Remember the function of the Specify Intranet Microsoft Update Service Location policy.

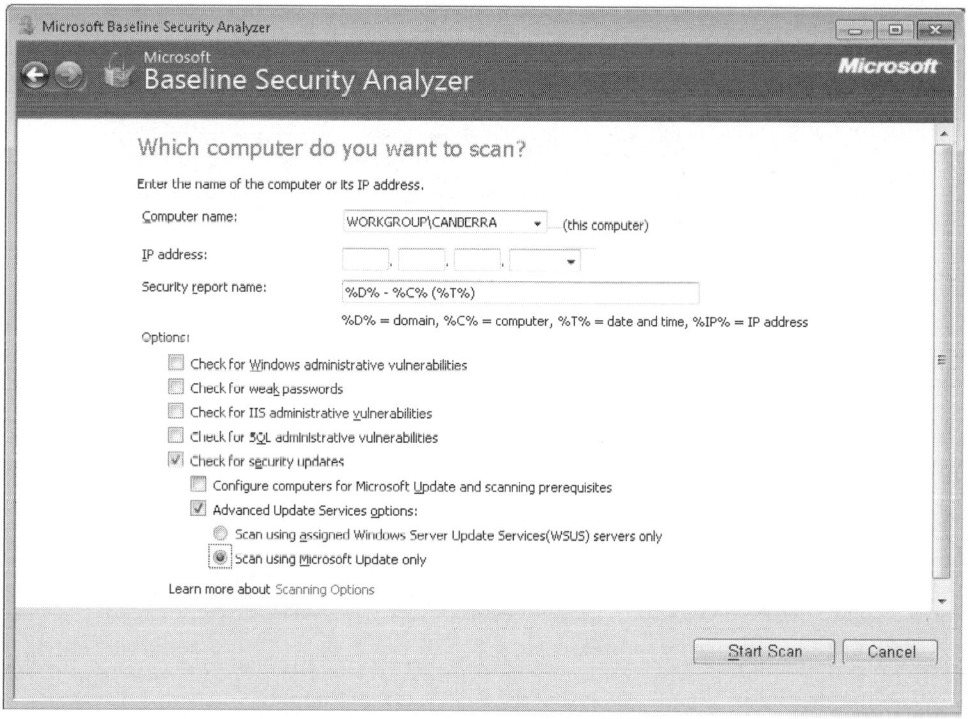

FIGURE 12-17 Microsoft Baseline Security Analyzer

Configuring Windows Update

In this practice, you configure Windows Update using both the Windows Update control panel and the Local Group Policy Editor.

EXERCISE 1 Configure Windows Update Using the Control Panel

In this exercise, you configure Windows Update so that it can obtain updates not only for the operating system and the default applications that ship with Windows, but so that it can obtain updates for other Microsoft applications such as Office. To complete this practice, you must connect computer Canberra to the Internet and perform the following steps:

1. Log on to computer Canberra using the Kim_Akers user account.

2. In the Search Programs And Files text box, type **Windows Update** and then press Enter.

3. On the Windows Update control panel, click the Find Out More item next to Get Updates For Other Microsoft Products. This opens a Web browser window, as shown in Figure 12-18.

4. Select the I Agree To The Terms Of Use For Microsoft Updates check box and then click Install. When presented with the User Account Control dialog box, click Yes.

5. Close the Web browser windows. In the Windows Update control panel, click the Change Settings item.

6. Verify that the Give Me Updates For Microsoft Products And Check For New Optional Microsoft Software When I Update Windows item is present and enabled.

FIGURE 12-18 Getting more updates

7. Use the drop-down menu to set the installation update time to Friday at 5.00 P.M. Verify that settings match those shown in Figure 12-19 and then click OK. Close the Windows Update control panel.

FIGURE 12-19 Verifying practice exercise settings

EXERCISE 2 Configuring Windows Update Through Group Policy

You can configure several Windows Update settings using the Local Group Policy Editor that you cannot configure using the Windows Update control panel. In this exercise, you configure a computer to wake if it is in hibernation when the assigned automatic update period occurs, you allow updates to install automatically if they do not require a restart, and you ensure that an automatic restart does not occur if a user is currently logged on to the computer. To complete this exercise, perform the following steps:

1. If you have not done so already, log on to computer Canberra with the Kim_Akers user account.

2. In the Search Programs And Files text box, type **gpedit.msc** and then press Enter. The Local Group Policy Editor opens.

3. Navigate to the Computer Configuration\Administrative Templates\Windows Components\Windows Update node.

4. Enable the Enabling Windows Update Power Management To Automatically Wake Up The System To Install Scheduled Updates policy.

5. Enable the Allow Automatic Updates Immediate Installation policy.

6. Enable the No Auto-Restart With Logged On Users For Scheduled Automatic Updates Installations policy.

7. Close the Local Group Policy Editor, type **gpupdate /force** into the In the Search Programs And Files text box, and press Enter.

Lesson Summary

- Windows Update allows software updates to be downloaded automatically to clients running Windows 7 from the Microsoft Update servers or a local update source, such as a WSUS server.

- You can configure Windows Update to automatically download and install updates, download and notify the logged-on user that updates are available for installation, or notify the logged-on user that updates are available for download and installation.

- Users with standard privileges are able to install and check for updates using Windows Update. Only users with administrative privileges are able to change Windows Update settings or change the update source from Microsoft Update to a local WSUS server.

- Users with administrative privileges are able to hide updates. A hidden update is not installed on the computer. A hidden update can be unhidden and installed at a later stage. Users with administrative privileges are able to uninstall previously installed updates. An uninstalled update becomes available for installation again unless hidden by an administrator.

Lesson Review

You can use the following questions to test your knowledge of the information in Lesson 1, "Updating Windows 7." The questions are also available on the companion DVD if you prefer to review them in electronic form.

> **NOTE ANSWERS**
>
> Answers to these questions and explanations of why each answer choice is correct or incorrect are located in the "Answers" section at the end of the book.

1. When Windows 7 is configured according to its default settings, which of the following tasks can a standard user perform with respect to Windows Update?

   A. Uninstall updates

   B. Install updates

   C. Change when updates are installed

   D. Change update download and installation behavior

   E. Hide updates

2. You have just discovered that an update rated as Important and published through Windows Update last week causes a conflict with a custom software package that is critical to your organization's business process when installed on clients running Windows 7. This conflict stops the custom software package from running. You have talked to the custom software package's vendor and you have been assured that it will have a fix ready within two months. All clients running Windows 7 are configured with the default Windows Update settings. What steps should you take to allow the custom software package to run while also ensuring that normal users do not install the update at any time before the fix from the vendor becomes available but do not miss out on other important updates published through Windows Update? (Choose all that apply; each answer forms part of a complete solution.)

   A. Change update settings

   B. Uninstall the update

   C. Hide the update

   D. Install the update

3. Even though you have configured scheduled updates to occur during the lunch hour, you have found that a significant percentage of the computers are not turned on at this time. You want to ensure that any updates scheduled for installation install soon after these computers start up again. Which of the following policies should you configure to accomplish this goal?

   A. Re-Prompt For Restart With Scheduled Installations

   B. Delay Restart For Scheduled Installations

C. Reschedule Automatic Updates Scheduled Installations

D. No Auto-Restart With Logged On Users For Scheduled Automatic Updates Installation

4. Which of the following policies should you configure if you want a client running Windows 7 to use a WSUS server located at updates.contoso.internal as a source of updates rather than the Microsoft Update servers?

A. Turn Off Software Notification

B. Automatic Updates Detection Frequency

C. Configure Automatic Updates

D. Specify Intranet Microsoft Update Service Location

5. You manage 30 separate clients running Windows 7 in an organization that does not use a WSUS server. All clients are members of a Windows Server 2008 Active Directory Domain Services (AD DS) domain. Which of the following tools can you use to determine if a particular software update is missing from these computers?

A. Microsoft Update

B. WSUS

C. Group Policy Management Console

D. MBSA

Lesson 2: Configuring Internet Explorer

Although alternatives are freely available, Internet Explorer is the browser most commonly used with Windows. A large number of settings make Internet Explorer highly configurable, but at the same time, it is a little daunting to manage for the uninitiated administrator. In this lesson, you learn the specifics of configuring Internet Explorer to render pages in Compatibility View; configuring Internet Explorer security; and configuring add-ons to enhance the browser's functionality, manage certificates, and manage InPrivate mode browsing.

> **After this lesson, you will be able to:**
> - Configure Internet Explorer Compatibility View.
> - Configure Internet Explorer security settings.
> - Configure Internet Explorer providers.
> - Manage Internet Explorer add-ons.
> - Control InPrivate mode.
> - Manage certificates for secure Web sites.
>
> **Estimated lesson time: 40 minutes**

Internet Explorer Compatibility View

Internet Explorer Compatibility View allows sites designed for previous versions of Internet Explorer to display correctly for users of Internet Explorer 8. You can enable Compatibility View for a page by clicking the broken page icon at the end of the address bar. You can configure Compatibility View settings through the Compatibility View Settings dialog box. You can access this dialog box by clicking Compatibility View Settings on the Tools menu of Internet Explorer.

Through this dialog box, you can configure Internet Explorer to use Compatibility View automatically for a list of Web sites distributed through Windows Update. This list includes high-profile Web sites that function better in Compatibility View, as well as other Web sites that have submitted their details to Microsoft. By default, Internet Explorer displays all intranet sites in Compatibility View. Intranet sites are determined based on the Local Intranet zone. You will learn about zones later in this lesson. You can disable Compatibility View for intranet sites using the Compatibility View Settings dialog box. You can also use this dialog box to configure Internet Explorer to display specific Web sites with Compatibility View. Figure 12-20 shows Internet Explorer configured to display the Web site Contoso.com in Compatibility View. You can also force Internet Explorer to display all Web sites in Compatibility View by checking the Display All Websites In Compatibility View option.

FIGURE 12-20 Compatibility View settings

Group Policies related to Compatibility View are located in the Administrative Templates\ Windows Components\Internet Explorer\Compatibility View node. You can find this node in both the Computer Configuration and the User Configuration sections of Group Policy. These policies have the following functions:

- **Turn On Internet Explorer 7 Standards Mode**   If you enable this policy, Internet Explorer will display all Web sites in Compatibility View.
- **Turn Off Compatibility View**   Use this policy to disable Compatibility View.
- **Turn Off Compatibility View Button**   The policy allows you to disable the Compatibility View button.
- **Include Updated Web Site Lists From Microsoft**   This policy configures Compatibility View to use an updated list of sites published by Microsoft through Windows Update.
- **Use Policy List Of Internet Explorer 7 Sites**   This policy lists the sites for which Internet Explorer uses Compatibility View. Users can add sites using Compatibility View Settings but cannot remove the default list of sites.

Configuring Security Settings

Internet Explorer allows you to configure different levels of security for different types of Web sites by segmenting Web sites into security zones. The security settings that Internet Explorer uses for a Web site depend on the corresponding security zone. The different security zones are as follows:

- **Local Intranet**   Sites in the Local Intranet zone are computers on your organizational intranet. Internet Explorer can be configured to detect intranet sites automatically. It is also possible to add Web sites to this zone by clicking the Advanced button on the

Local Intranet sites dialog box, as shown in Figure 12-21. The default security level of this zone is Medium-Low. Protected Mode is not enabled by default for sites in this zone.

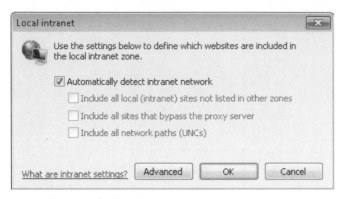

FIGURE 12-21 Local Intranet

- **Trusted Sites** Sites in the Trusted Sites zone often require elevated privileges. Only select Web sites should be added to this zone because Internet Explorer uses fewer security precautions with sites that are placed in this zone. The default security level for this zone is Medium. Protected Mode is not enabled by default for sites in this zone. Sites are added through the Trusted Sites dialog box. The default setting requires all sites in the Trusted Sites zone to be secured with a Secure Sockets Layer (SSL) certificate.

- **Restricted Sites** Sites in this zone are potentially malicious. You should only add sites to this zone if it is necessary to visit dangerous Web sites. The default security level for this zone is High. Internet Explorer Protected Mode is enabled by default for sites in this zone.

- **Internet** This zone hosts all Web sites that are not contained in the Local Internet, Trusted Sites, or Restricted Sites zone. Sites in this zone are blocked from viewing private data from other Web sites. Sites in this zone are unable to make changes to Windows 7. The default security level of this zone is Medium-High. Protected Mode is enabled by default for sites in this zone.

You can use the slider, shown in Figure 12-22, to adjust the security level assigned to a zone. You can also configure whether a zone uses Protected Mode and Configure Custom Zone settings. Protected Mode is a technology that forces Internet Explorer to run as a low-integrity process. The security architecture of Windows 7 means that processes that are assigned lower integrities are unable to interact directly with objects that are assigned higher integrities. This means that any malware that might compromise the browser is blocked from causing damage to Windows 7 because it is unable to cause problems as a low-integrity process. The design of Windows 7 allows the processes that run in each tab to be separate from each other. This means that a tab that has a Web site in Protected Mode can run alongside a tab that has a site that is not running in Protected Mode. Sites that you do not trust, such as those on the Internet or within the Restricted Sites zone, are run in Protected Mode.

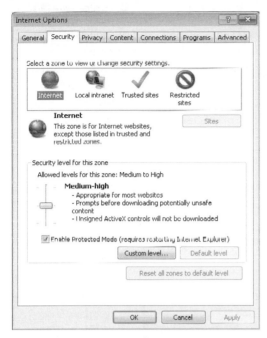

FIGURE 12-22 Security tab of Internet options

The three default security levels are Medium, Medium-High, and High. Each level is more restrictive, with High being the most restrictive. You can use the Custom Level button to configure a custom level of security for a zone, as shown in Figure 12-23. Items that can be configured include ActiveX control behavior, scripting, and user authentication settings. Unless your organization has unusual security requirements, the default security levels are usually sufficient.

FIGURE 12-23 Custom security-level settings

You can configure advanced security options on the Advanced tab of Internet Options, as shown in Figure 12-24. Using this dialog box, you can configure settings such as whether Internet Explorer performs certificate revocation checks, whether the SmartScreen Filter is enabled by default, which versions of SSL and Transport Layer Security (TLS) are supported, whether Windows Authentication is supported, and whether Internet Explorer should provide a warning if there is a mismatch between the SSL certificate and the Web site address. You will learn about configuring SSL certificate options and SmartScreen Filter later in this lesson.

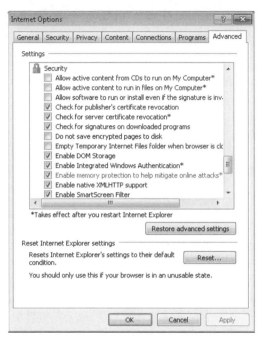

FIGURE 12-24 Advanced Internet options

> **MORE INFO** **INTERNET EXPLORER ENHANCED SECURITY CONFIGURATION**
>
> To learn more about running Internet Explorer with enhanced security settings, consult the following Microsoft TechNet Web page: *http://technet.microsoft.com/en-us/library/dd883248.aspx.*

SmartScreen Filter

SmartScreen Filter is an Internet Explorer feature that blocks browsing to Web sites that are known to host malware or be related to phishing. *Phishing* is where criminals configure a Web site to look similar to one that a user regularly visits, such as a bank Web site, in an attempt to lure the user into providing authentication credentials. SmartScreen Filter works to protect users in the following ways:

- **Analyzes Web pages that you visit for suspicious characteristics**   If a Web page is determined to have suspicious characteristics, SmartScreen Filter displays a message advising you to proceed with caution.

- **Checks the sites that you visit against a list of regularly updated known phishing and malware sites**   When you navigate to a site on this list, SmartScreen Filter blocks you with a warning about the site's problematic content.

- **Checks files that you download from Web sites against known malware**   SmartScreen Filter presents you with a warning notifying you that the download has been blocked for your safety.

You can check a Web site manually if you are suspicious about it by selecting SmartScreen Filter from the Safety menu and then clicking Check This Website. When you do this, the SmartScreen Filter dialog box, shown in Figure 12-25, is displayed. You can use the Report Unsafe Website button to report a Web site that you believe hosts malware or may be related by phishing. The Web site is then checked by Microsoft and added to the list of dangerous Web sites as appropriate.

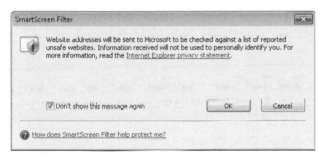

FIGURE 12-25 SmartScreen Filter

Managing InPrivate Mode

InPrivate Mode consists of two technologies: InPrivate Filtering and InPrivate Browsing. Both *InPrivate Filtering* and *InPrivate Browsing* are privacy technologies that restrict the amount of information available about a user's browsing session. InPrivate Browsing restricts what data is recorded by the browser, and InPrivate Filtering is used to restrict what information about a browsing session can be tracked by external third parties.

Users can open an InPrivate Browsing window by clicking the InPrivate Browsing option in the safety menu. When Internet Explorer is functioning in InPrivate Mode, the InPrivate indicator is displayed in the address bar, as shown in Figure 12-26. The InPrivate indicator reminds users that Internet Explorer is not storing their browsing data. You should remind users that although browsing activity is not recorded locally, organizations are still able to monitor browsing activities using other methods such as examining proxy logs.

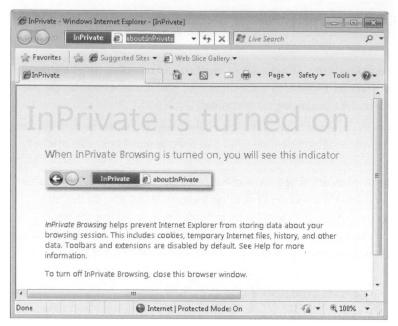

FIGURE 12-26 InPrivate Browsing

Web browsing data is stored while the InPrivate session is active. For example, users could log in to their Webmail account and have the necessary cookies stored temporarily as part of the InPrivate session. They would also be able to navigate back through sites they have visited during the session. The advantage of InPrivate mode is that all this data is deleted automatically when the browser window is closed. Although it is possible to delete a certain amount of browsing history using the Delete Browsing History item in the Safety menu, as one of the exercises at the end of this lesson demonstrates, not all browsing data is deleted when you use this tool.

Many Web pages present content from other Web sites on their pages. For example, advertisements are rarely provided by the Web site you are visiting; rather, they are supplied by a third-party company. When you visit a Web site that is configured in this manner, some data about your visit is transmitted back to the advertising company. When you browse to several sites that use the same advertising company, the advertising company is able to tie together data about your visits to the different Web sites to which they provide advertising. For example, suppose that a single company provides advertising content for separate sites A, B, and C. If you visit sites A, B, and C, tracking data sent back to the company reveals information about your Web browsing habits. This methodology is not limited to advertising and applies to any content served to multiple Web sites by third parties. If you enable InPrivate filtering, Internet Explorer blocks third parties from tracking your browsing sessions across multiple separate Web sites in this manner. You must enable InPrivate Filtering manually each time you start a new browsing session.

You can use the InPrivate Filtering Settings dialog box, shown in Figure 12-27, to configure InPrivate Filtering. You can block content, allow the user to choose content to block or allow, or turn InPrivate Filtering off automatically. The InPrivate Filtering Settings dialog box also displays a list of content providers that provide content across multiple sites. You can also import and export InPrivate Filtering rules using the Manage Add-Ons control panel.

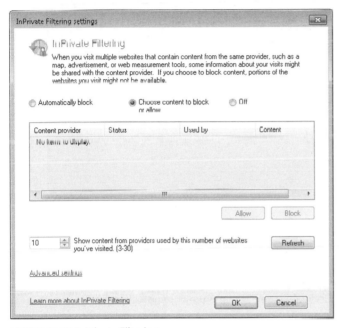

FIGURE 12-27 InPrivate Filtering

You can manage InPrivate mode centrally through the InPrivate policies. These policies are available in the Administrative Templates\Windows Components\Internet Explorer node of both the Computer Configuration and User Configuration areas. A list of these policies is shown in Figure 12-28. These policies have the following functions:

- **Turn Off InPrivate Filtering** When this policy is enabled, users cannot use InPrivate Filtering.

- **Turn Off InPrivate Browsing** When this policy is enabled, users cannot use InPrivate Browsing.

- **Do Not Collect InPrivate Filtering Data** This policy disables the collection of data used by the InPrivate Filtering Automatic Mode.

- **Disable Toolbars and Extensions When InPrivate Browsing Starts** When this policy is enabled, additional toolbars and extensions are disabled when an InPrivate Browsing session starts.

- **InPrivate Filtering Threshold** The value specified in this policy sets the number of different Web sites that a user browses to that a third-party item can be referenced from before it is blocked. Allowable values range from 3 to 30.

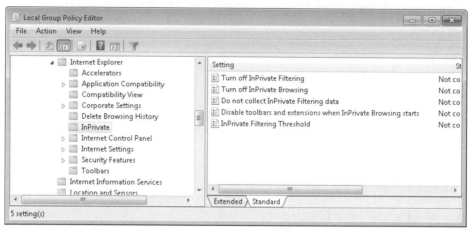

FIGURE 12-28 InPrivate Browsing policies

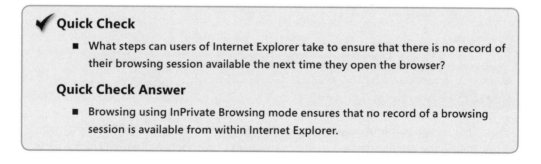

Quick Check

- What steps can users of Internet Explorer take to ensure that there is no record of their browsing session available the next time they open the browser?

Quick Check Answer

- Browsing using InPrivate Browsing mode ensures that no record of a browsing session is available from within Internet Explorer.

Add-Ons and Search Providers

Add-ons extend the functionality of Internet Explorer. Add-ons are usually downloaded and installed separately rather than being included with Internet Explorer. You manage add-ons through the Manage Add-Ons dialog box, shown in Figure 12-29. Internet Explorer add-ons fall into the following categories:

- **Toolbars and Extensions** This area lists browser toolbars and extensions. Toolbars are additions to browsers that add extra functionality to the browser interface. Extensions allow the browser to perform additional functions, such as playing media or opening some types of document file within the browser that the browser does not support natively.

- **Search Providers** These allow users to search the Internet automatically using the Internet Explorer search window. A new window or tab is opened to display the results of the search query on the search engine provider's home page.

- **Accelerators** Accelerators allow users to perform actions after selecting text. Internet Explorer ships with several default accelerators, though users can add more accelerators by clicking the Find More Accelerators item. The default accelerator categories are:
  - **Blog** This category of accelerator allows you to post selected information directly to a specially configured blog.
  - **E-mail** This category of accelerator allows you to send the selected information in an e-mail. Using the accelerator opens the e-mail program associated with the accelerator and paste the selected text into a new e-mail message.
  - **Map** This category of accelerator allows you to perform a search of an online mapping service based on text selected in the browser. You will use a mapping accelerator in the practice at the end of this lesson.
  - **Translate** This category of accelerator allows you to translate selected text into another language using an online translation engine.
- **InPrivate Filtering** Through the InPrivate Filtering area, you can configure InPrivate Filtering items. You can import and export InPrivate Filtering rules using this tool.

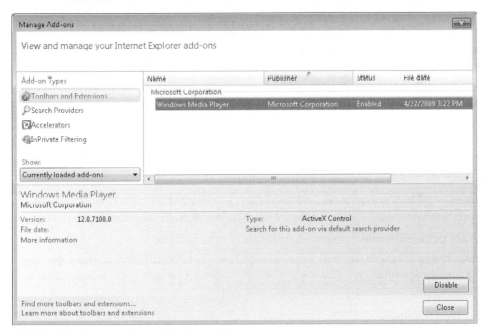

FIGURE 12-29 Managing Internet Explorer add-ons

Add-ons are usually installed either by navigating to a Web page that hosts the add-on installer or by downloading and installing the software in the traditional manner. When you choose to install an accelerator from a Web site, Internet Explorer queries you to make sure that you intend to add the accelerator, as shown in Figure 12-30. You should ensure that you install add-ons only from Web sites that you trust.

FIGURE 12-30 Adding an accelerator

You can use the Manage Add-Ons dialog box to disable or remove add-ons. You might choose to disable an add-on if you were experiencing problems with Internet Explorer and you were trying to determine if the add-on was responsible for those problems. Once you had ascertained that a specific add-on was causing the problems, you can then use the Manage Add-Ons dialog box to remove that add-on. Windows 7 allows standard users to add, remove, and disable add-ons by default.

Accelerator policies are located under the Windows Components\Internet Explorer node of both the Computer Configuration and User Configuration settings. The following Accelerator-related group policies are available:

- **Deploy Non-Default Accelerators** Allows additional accelerators to be deployed. Users are unable to remove these accelerators.

- **Deploy Default Accelerators** Allows default accelerators to be specified. Users can add additional accelerators, but cannot modify the defaults specified by the policy.

- **Turn Off Accelerators** Allows all accelerators to be disabled.

- **Use Policy Accelerators** This policy restricts the use of accelerators to those that are distributed through Group Policy.

Pop-Up Blocker

The Pop-Up Blocker blocks pop-up and pop-under windows from appearing automatically when you browse to a page using Internet Explorer. You can configure Pop-Up Blocker settings by clicking the Pop-Up Blocker Settings item under Pop-Up Blocker on the Tools menu in Internet Explorer. The Pop-Up Blocker Settings dialog box allows you to configure the blocking level, exceptions, whether a sound plays when a pop-up is blocked, and whether the information bar triggers when a pop-up is blocked. The default blocking setting of

Medium blocks most automatic pop-up windows. The Low setting allows pop-ups only from secure sites, and the High setting blocks all pop-ups.

Exceptions are sites where the Pop-Up Blocker does not block pop-ups. Figure 12-31 shows exceptions for the sites *http://www.contoso.com* and *http://www.tailspintoys.com*. Allowing pop-up information to display in the information bar allows users to view a pop-up window if necessary. Unless you configure the High setting, Internet Explorer does not block pop-ups from sites that are in the Local Intranet or Trusted Sites security zone. The default Windows 7 settings allow users without administrative privileges to modify the Pop-Up Blocker settings through the Pop-Up Blocker Settings control panel.

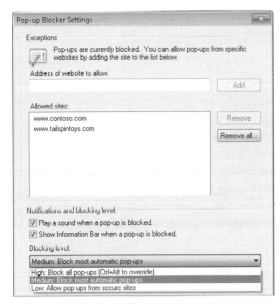

FIGURE 12-31 Pop-Up Blocker settings

Configuring SSL Certificates

SSL certificates provide two useful functions for users of Web browsers. SSL certificates allow users to verify the identity of the Web site to which they are connecting and ensure that communication between the browser and the Web site is secured through encryption.

When a user browses to a site that is protected by an SSL certificate, a gold lock icon is displayed in the address bar to indicate that the connection is secure. Users are able to click this gold lock icon to view information about the Web site, as shown in Figure 12-32. Clicking the View Certificates item on the Website Identification pop-up allows you to view details of the certificate. These details include which certificate authority (CA) issued the certificate, when the certificate issue date, when the certificate expires, and the identity of the root CA that is at the top of the certification path. Clicking the Should I Trust This Site? item provides general advice on whether you should trust the Web site.

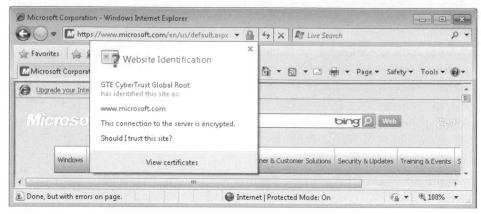

FIGURE 12-32 Web site identification information

Internet Explorer provides a warning when you navigate to a secure Web site where there is a problem with the SSL certificate. For example, in Figure 12-33, the name that is on the certificate used on the Web site *https://www.contoso.com* is not *www.contoso.com*. Internet Explorer blocks navigation to this Web site automatically. A user needs to click the Continue To This Website (Not Recommended) item to navigate to the Web site. This problem can arise if a Web site has recently changed its name and is still using the certificate related to its old name. Alternatively, it could be that the domain has been hijacked or some other problem has occurred with the site that would affect security. You should advise users to be cautious if they encounter this error, and they should definitely not provide sensitive information to a Web site where the SSL certificate and the Web site name do not match. This is because you are unable to verify the Web site's identity without a proper certificate. Even if a site is legitimate, you should be cautious about providing sensitive information over the Internet to any organization that is unable to keep its SSL certificate up to date.

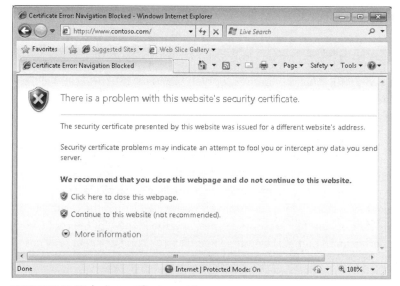

FIGURE 12-33 Web site certificate problem

Internet Explorer blocks navigation to a Web site if the application detects the following types of certificate errors:

- **Web site address does not match address in certificate**   This error occurs when a Web site is using a digital certificate issued to a different Web address. It often happens when an organization hosts multiple Web sites off the same server.

- **Web site certificate has been revoked**   This error indicates that the security certificate was obtained or used fraudulently by the Web site. The organization responsible for issuing the certificate has revoked the certificate, indicating that the Web site should no longer be trusted.

- **Web site certificate is out of date**   This error occurs when the current date is either before or after the certificate validity period. For example, you would receive this error for a certificate that is configured to be valid from 2100 to 2150, and you would receive this error for a different certificate that was valid from 1996 to 2000. Web sites must renew certificates with certificate authorities on a regular basis.

- **Web site certificate is not from a trusted source**   This error indicates that the Web site certificate that has been issued from a CA that is not trusted by Internet Explorer. This error occurs often with Web servers on intranet sites. If you encounter this error on an Internet site, you should not trust the Web site because many phishing sites use fake identity certificates to attempt to trick users into believing they are legitimate. You will learn more about configuring Internet Explorer to trust legitimate sources later in this lesson.

- **Problem found with security certificate**   This error occurs when Internet Explorer detects a problem with a Web site certificate that does not fall into the above categories. This error can occur if someone has tampered with the certificate, or the certificate has become corrupted. You should not trust Web sites where Internet Explorer finds a problem with the security certificate.

When dealing with secure sites on non-public networks, such as a corporate intranet, you may encounter Web site certificates issued by a CA that Internet Explorer does not trust. This often occurs because organizations set up their own internal Public Key Infrastructure (PKI) to distribute certificates to internal hosts and do not need a publicly validated SSL certificate to identify an internal server. In most organizations that set up their own PKIs, clients automatically trust the issuing CAs because it is possible to publish their certificates through AD DS. You can configure Internet Explorer to trust a CA by navigating to the CA's Web site to obtain and install its certificate.

You can view the current list of certificates on the Content page of the Internet Options dialog box, as shown in Figure 12-34. You can clear currently cached SSL certificates by clicking Clear SSL State. You can view current certificates by clicking Certificates and you can view trusted CAs by clicking Publishers. You can use the Certificates or the Publishers button to import or export certificates. For example, if you had received an e-mail with the CA certificate of an organization's internal CA, you could configure Internet Explorer to trust that CA by importing its certificate through this dialog box.

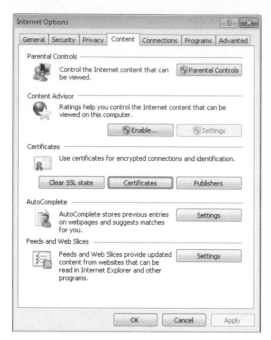

FIGURE 12-34 Managing certificates

PRACTICE **InPrivate mode and Add-Ons**

In this practice, you examine how InPrivate Browsing works and also manage Internet Explorer add-ons. InPrivate Browsing is a feature that many people who use shared computers are interested in because they want to keep the details of their Web browsing activities hidden from other people who may use the computer. Computer Canberra must be able to connect to the Internet to complete both of the exercises in this practice.

EXERCISE 1 Exploring InPrivate Mode

In this exercise, you explore the InPrivate Mode in Internet Explorer 8. InPrivate Mode reduces the amount of data stored about a browsing session. In this exercise, you browse normally, browse in InPrivate Mode, and then compare the difference. To complete this exercise, perform the following steps.

1. Log on to computer Canberra using the Kim_Akers user account.

2. Open Internet Explorer from the Taskbar. If you are presented with the Welcome To Internet Explorer 8 Wizard, click Ask Me Later.

3. Ensure that only one tab is open. In the address bar, type the address **http://www.bing.com** and then press Enter.

4. In the search engine text box, type **70-680 site:microsoft.com** and then click the search button. This should produce a result similar to that shown in Figure 12-35.

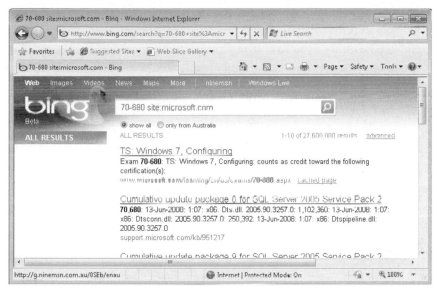

FIGURE 12-35 Searching for 70-680

5. Click the TS: Windows 7, Configuring link. This takes you to the Web page for the 70-680 TS: Windows 7, Configuring exam. On the right side of the page, under Related Services, click E-Reference Libraries. This opens the E-Reference Libraries page.

6. From the Safety menu, click Delete Browsing History. In the Delete Browsing History dialog box, ensure that all items are selected, as shown in Figure 12-36, and then click Delete.

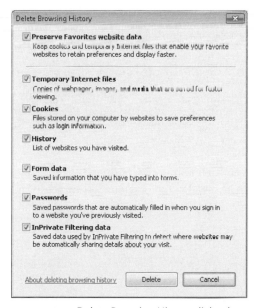

FIGURE 12-36 Delete Browsing History dialog box

7. Once the browsing history is deleted, close Internet Explorer.

8. Open Internet Explorer again. From the Tools menu, click Reopen Last Browsing Session. This opens the last page that you visited in the previous session, even though you deleted the browsing history.

9. Click the drop-down arrow next to the address bar and verify that all pages that you browsed to in the previous session, including the contents of the Bing.com search results, are stored within the reopened browser session, as shown in Figure 12-37.

FIGURE 12-37 Last session data still available

10. Close Internet Explorer.

11. Open Internet Explorer again. From the Safety menu, click InPrivate Browsing. This opens the InPrivate Browsing window.

12. In the InPrivate Browsing window address bar, enter the address **http://www.bing.com** and then press Enter.

13. In the search text box, type **Windows 7 site:microsoft.com** and then press Enter.

14. In the search results, click the Welcome to Windows 7 link that corresponds to the Uniform Resource Locator (URL) *http://www.microsoft.com/windows/windows-7/default.aspx*. This opens the Windows 7 home page.

15. Close all open Internet Explorer windows.

16. Open Internet Explorer again. From the Tools menu, click Reopen Last Browsing Session. Verify that none of the pages involved in the previous session searching for Windows 7 information are present, either in the browsing history or within the previous session.

17. Close Internet Explorer.

EXERCISE 2   Manage Internet Explorer Add-Ons

In this exercise, you configure and manage add-ons for Internet Explorer. To complete this exercise, perform the following steps:

1. If you have not done so already, log on to computer Canberra with the Kim_Akers user account.

2. Open Internet Explorer. In the Tools menu, click Manage Add-ons. This opens the Manage Add-Ons dialog box.

3. Select the Search Providers option and then click the Find More Search Providers item. This causes Internet Explorer to navigate to a Web page that hosts an add-on gallery. In the Add-on Gallery, select a search provider and then click Add To Internet Explorer. In the Add Search Provider dialog box, shown in Figure 12-38, click Add.

FIGURE 12-38 Adding a search provider

4. Close and then open the Manage Add-ons dialog box. Verify that the search provider that you installed is now available. Select the Accelerators option and then click Find More Accelerators. Internet Explorer again navigates to the Web page that hosts an add-on gallery. This time it presents a list of accelerators. Click the Mapping category. Locate a mapping accelerator, as shown in Figure 12-39, and then click Add To Internet Explorer.

5. On the Do You Want To Add This Accelerator? page, click Add. Close and reopen the Manage Add-ons dialog box and verify that the maps accelerator that you chose has been added.

6. Click on the newly installed maps accelerator and then click Set As Default. Click Close to close the Manage Add-ons dialog box.

7. In Internet Explorer, navigate to the following URL: *http://www.microsoft.com/ presspass/inside_ms.mspx*.

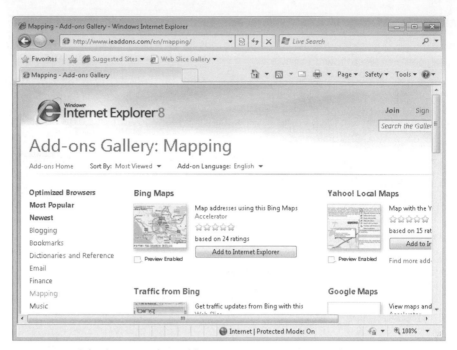

FIGURE 12-39 Selecting a search provider

8. Select the text that says

   One Microsoft Way

   Redmond, WA 98052-7329

   USA

9. Click the accelerator icon and then click the map accelerator that you selected. Internet Explorer now navigates to a page that shows a map of the Microsoft campus.

10. From the Tools menu, click Manage Add-ons. Click Accelerators and then click the maps accelerator that you installed. Click on Disable to disable this accelerator. Click Close to close the Manage Add-Ons dialog box.

11. Close Internet Explorer.

Lesson Summary

- Compatibility View allows pages that do not render correctly in Internet Explorer 8, but which render correctly in Internet Explorer 7, to be displayed properly in Internet Explorer 8. You can configure Compatibility View manually, use a list of Web sites provided by Microsoft and updated through Windows Update, or manually configure a list of sites that Internet Explorer should use Compatibility View with.

- Security settings are configured primarily by assigning sites to zones. Sites that require elevated privileges should be assigned to the Trusted Sites zone. Sites that are on the intranet are automatically assigned to the Local Intranet zone, though this may require manual configuration in some circumstances. All other sites are assigned to the Internet zone. The Restricted Sites zone is used only for Web sites that may present security risks but must be visited.

- Add-ons enhance the functionality of Internet Explorer. Users with standard permissions can add, remove, and disable add-ons unless configured Group Policy dictates otherwise. Accelerators allow users to select text on a Web page and then automatically perform another function, such as translating the text or forwarding it to their blog. Providers allow additional search providers to be added to the search window.

- InPrivate Browsing stops Internet Explorer from storing information about a browsing session. InPrivate Filtering stops third-party Web sites from gaining data when browsing across multiple sites.

- Internet Explorer provides warnings if a Web site's address does not match the SSL certificate that it presents to the client, if the certificate has expired, if the certificate has been revoked, or if the certificate has become corrupt.

Lesson Review

You can use the following questions to test your knowledge of the information in Lesson 2, "Configuring Internet Explorer." The questions are also available on the companion DVD if you prefer to review them in electronic form.

> **NOTE ANSWERS**
>
> Answers to these questions and explanations of why each answer choice is correct or incorrect are located in the "Answers" section at the end of the book.

1. You are spending several weeks working as a contractor at Contoso. You attempt to connect using Internet Explorer to the timesheet Web application hosted at *https://timesheet.contoso.internal*. You receive a message that the Web site certificate has not been issued by a trusted source. Which of the following steps can you take to resolve this problem?

   A. Configure the security level of the Intranet Zone.

   B. Turn off the Pop-up Blocker.

   C. Start InPrivate Browsing and revisit the Web site.

   D. Visit the Contoso.internal CA using Internet Explorer and install the CA certificate.

2. Developers at your organization have come up with a custom blogging tool and accelerator that allows blogs to be posted directly to the corporate intranet. You want users to be able to highlight interesting text that they find on Web pages and blog it directly to the intranet server. You want to ensure that users do not accidentally blog using the default Blog With Windows Live accelerator. Which of the following steps

should you take on each computer to accomplish this goal? (Choose all that apply; each answer forms part of a complete solution.)

    A. Disable the Blog With Windows Live accelerator.

    B. Install the custom blog accelerator.

    C. Set the Blog With Windows Live accelerator as the default Blog accelerator for Internet Explorer.

    D. Disable the custom blog accelerator.

3. You want to ensure that Internet Explorer does not display any pop-up windows except those from the site *http://www.wingtiptoys.com*. Which of the following Pop-Up Blocker settings should you configure on the Pop-Up Blocker Settings dialog box? (Choose all that apply; each answer forms part of a complete solution.)

    A. Configure *http://www.wingtiptoys.com* as an exception.

    B. Set the blocking level to Medium.

    C. Set the blocking level to High.

    D. Set the blocking level to Low.

4. Your organization has recently acquired several subsidiaries. Each subsidiary has their own separate Internet site and these sites have unique fully qualified domain names (FQDNs). All clients use Windows 7 Enterprise with the default settings. Several subsidiary intranet Web sites do not display properly in Internet Explorer on Windows 7, but they display without problems in Internet Explorer on clients running Windows XP and Windows Vista. All clients running Windows 7 are members of the same AD DS domain. Which of the following configuration changes should you make to Group Policy to resolve this problem?

    A. Enable the Turn Off InPrivate Browsing policy.

    B. Enable the Turn Off InPrivate Filtering policy.

    C. Enable the Turn Off Compatibility View policy.

    D. Configure the Use Policy List Of Internet Explorer 7 Sites policy.

5. You want to ensure that third-party Web sites that provide content to a variety of sites that you visit are not able to track you across those sites during a browsing session. Which of the following actions should you take, after starting Internet Explorer, to ensure that this does not occur?

    A. Start an InPrivate Browsing session

    B. Enable InPrivate Filtering

    C. Disable Pop-up Blocker

    D. Disable SmartScreen Filter

Chapter Review

To further practice and reinforce the skills you learned in this chapter, you can perform the following tasks:

- Review the chapter summary.
- Review the list of key terms introduced in this chapter.
- Complete the case scenarios. These scenarios set up real-world situations involving the topics of this chapter and ask you to create a solution.
- Complete the suggested practices.
- Take a practice test.

Chapter Summary

- Windows Update is a feature built into Windows 7 that manages how software updates are downloaded and installed.
- Windows Update can retrieve updates from the Microsoft Update servers on the Internet or from a local update source, such as a WSUS server.
- Some Windows Update servers can be configured through the Windows Update control panel, but most settings are configured through Group Policy.
- InPrivate Browsing mode stops Internet Explorer from recording a browsing session.
- Internet Explorer add-ons extend the functionality of Internet Explorer.
- Internet Zones allow Web sites to be classified according to how trustworthy they are.

Key Terms

Do you know what these key terms mean? You can check your answers by looking up the terms in the glossary at the end of the book.

- **InPrivate Browsing**
- **InPrivate Filtering**

Case Scenarios

In the following case scenarios, you apply what you've learned about subjects of this chapter. You can find answers to these questions in the "Answers" section at the end of this book.

Case Scenario 1: Windows Update at Contoso

Contoso has three Australian offices. The head office is in the city of Canberra. There are branch offices in the cities of Adelaide and Brisbane. All client computers at Contoso have Windows 7 Enterprise installed, are configured so that you can log on to them remotely using Remote Desktop Connection, and have power features that support waking from hibernation. You have just installed the WSUS role in the Canberra office. You want computers in the Canberra office to use the WSUS server for updates, but you want to have computers in the Adelaide and Brisbane offices retrieve updates from Microsoft Update. Another issue that you must deal with relates to a custom software application installed on computers in the Adelaide and Brisbane offices. You have just heard from the software vendor that a recent update, which is associated with KB123456, has caused the custom software application to behave erratically.

With these facts in mind, answer the following questions:

1. Which policy should you configure for the computers in the Canberra office to ensure that they use the local WSUS server rather than the Microsoft Update servers on the Internet?

2. Which policy should you configure to ensure that computers wake for the installation of software updates?

3. How should you remove update KB123456 from the computers at the Brisbane and Adelaide offices and how can you ensure that it will not be installed until a fix for the custom software application is available?

Case Scenario 2: Internet Explorer at Wingtip Toys

You have recently overseen the deployment of 100 computers running Windows 7 Enterprise at WingTip Toys. WingTip Toys and its subsidiary, Tailspin Toys, sell high-performance, remote-controlled aircraft. As part of the Windows 7 deployment, you need to deal with the following post-migration issues:

- Some members of the research department have concerns that their Web browsing sessions across a variety of Web sites are being tracked by third-party competitor organizations. Although this is something that they have been aware of for some time, several have read that Windows 7 includes special technologies to deal with this problem.

- After several incidents where company information was posted on external blogs accidentally, you want to minimize the use of accelerators with Internet Explorer 8.

- The company has two external Web sites: *http://www.tailspintoys.com* and *http://www.wingtiptoys.com*. These Web sites do not render well in Internet Explorer 8, though they appear normal in Internet Explorer 7 running on clients running Windows XP and Windows Vista. The company has plans to update the sites, but no firm timetable has been set.

With this information in mind, answer the following questions:

1. What steps can you take to ensure that users are not able to use any accelerators with Internet Explorer?

2. What steps can members of the research department take to ensure that their browsing sessions are not tracked across multiple Web sites?

3. How can you ensure that the sites *http://www.tailspintoys.com* and *http://www.wingtiptoys.com* are always rendered in Compatibility View by clients at WingTip Toys?

Suggested Practices

To help you master the exam objectives presented in this chapter, complete the following tasks.

Configure Updates to Windows 7

You can complete these practices only if you are connected to the Internet.

-   **Practice 1**   Run Windows Update, check for available updates, and then install available updates marked Important or Recommended. Reboot the computer if necessary.

-   **Practice 2**   Once available updates have installed and no more updates are available, uninstall one of the updates. Use the Windows Update control panel to again check for updates and verify that the update that you uninstalled is now available for installation. Use the Windows Update control panel to hide this update. Use Windows Update to again check for updates and verify that no Important or Recommended updates are available. Unhide the update. Use Windows Update again to check for available updates. Install the unhidden update.

Configure Internet Explorer

You can complete practices only if you are connected to the Internet.

-   **Practice 1**   Add accelerators to Internet Explorer for the Blog, E-mail, and Translate categories.

-   **Practice 2**   Navigate to the Security tab of Internet Options. Using the Custom Level button, view the individual settings that apply to each zone. Note which zones allow the user to download signed and unsigned ActiveX controls.

Take a Practice Test

The practice tests on this book's companion DVD offer many options. For example, you can test yourself on just one exam objective, or you can test yourself on all the 70-680 certification exam content. You can set up the test so that it closely simulates the experience of taking a certification exam, or you can set it up in study mode so that you can look at the correct answers and explanations after you answer each question.

> **MORE INFO   PRACTICE TESTS**
>
> For details about all the practice test options available, see the section entitled "How to Use the Practice Tests," in the Introduction to this book.

CHAPTER 13

Monitoring and Performance

This chapter looks at monitoring resources and performance on a computer running Windows 7. It considers the various tools that tell you what resources are available on a computer and report problems encountered in using a resource. The chapter discusses performance monitoring, establishing baselines and logs, and determining where bottlenecks might occur before they happen. It looks at checking the potential of the computer to perform resource-intensive tasks and how to capture both local events and events on other computers.

Sometimes services, processes, and applications encounter problems and the chapter considers how you can deal with them. Sometimes the tools provided by the operating system are not exactly what you require, and the chapter looks at how you can create standard scripts to address any problems you encounter without requiring a high level of programming expertise.

You need to manage and configure services, configure page files and memory cache, configure services, manage processes, configure your desktop, and, if necessary, change your boot environment. The chapter discusses all these requirements.

Exam objectives in this chapter:

- Monitor systems.
- Configure performance settings.

Lessons in this chapter:

Before You Begin

To complete the exercises in the practices in this chapter, you need to have done the following:

- Installed the Windows 7 operating system on a stand-alone client PC, as described in Chapter 1, "Install, Migrate, or Upgrade to Windows 7." You need Internet access to complete the exercises.

- Optionally installed Windows 7 on a second PC, as described in Chapter 6, "Network Settings." A second computer is not required for the practice exercises but will enable you to complete the suggested practices at the end of this chapter.

- If you have two physical computers that are not otherwise on the same network, you need to connect their Ethernet ports with a crossover cable or by using an Ethernet switch.

- You need a universal serial bus (USB) flash memory device with at least 200 MB usable free space, or a second internal or external hard disk.

- The computer you use for the practice exercises (Canberra) needs to have an optical drive that can write to DVD-ROM.

 REAL WORLD

Ian McLean

You can usually justify a server upgrade to management, even though many managers don't know what a server is.

There aren't many servers. With virtualization, they are fewer than ever before. They are mysterious black boxes that do incomprehensible things. If the network administrator says the servers need an upgrade, the expense probably isn't huge in the general scheme of things.

Senior managers may not typically be technically aware (when you find one that is, it can be scary) but they are emphatically not fools, especially where money is concerned. You can justify extra cash to upgrade half a dozen servers. When it comes to upgrading 500 workstations, it's a different ball game.

So gathering performance statistics about your workstations is just as important as gathering them about your servers. You can have the fastest servers on the market, but if your client computers aren't up to the job, you have a poorly performing network. Even the thinnest of thin clients have bottlenecks, especially when it comes to network resource.

You will need to upgrade your hardware, if not right now, then in a year or two. Start preparing your case. Ensure that you have defined sensible baselines. Keep track of the small but cumulative performance drops as your equipment ages and user expectations increase. Start preparing a good case right now for the upgrades you need in the future. Don't wait for tomorrow, or else tomorrow somebody else might be doing your job.

Lesson 1: Monitoring Systems

As an IT professional with at least one year's experience, you will have come across some of, if not all, the tools and utilities described in this lesson. Windows 7 offers tools to measure performance, set baselines, identify bottlenecks, display resources, measure system stability and reliability, and so on.

It is sometimes not easy to select the right tool for the job. Often you can use several tools to obtain the same information or carry out the same configuration, but one of them does it more efficiently than the others. It is relatively straightforward to use one or more tools to gather information about a computer system. Interpreting that information may be more difficult. This lesson attempts to split the various tools into different functional groups and describe how the tools in each group complement each other.

> **After this lesson, you will be able to:**
>
> - Use performance tools to view real-time performance data, collect data in Data Collector Sets (DCSs), and generate reports that identify actual or potential resource bottlenecks.
> - Examine failures and potential problems related to software installations and other significant system changes.
> - Gather event subscriptions from source computers and store them on a destination computer
> - Access the Windows Experience Index and choose computer software based on that index.
>
> **Estimated lesson time: 50 minutes**

Performance Monitoring and Reporting

Monitoring performance data and comparing it to established baselines is crucial to determining the health of your client computers, as is examining events in the event logs. Many events are informational, but you should not ignore them because of that. Your skill and experience as an administrator must determine what you should address and what you can safely ignore. You should never ignore warning and error events that indicate real and immediate problems.

As an IT professional, you probably have experience with Windows performance tools such as Performance Monitor and the Reports tool. You might not be familiar with DCSs that use performance counters to generate performance logs and can, in turn, be read by Performance Monitor and the Reports tool. DCSs provide a replacement for Performance Logs and Alerts in earlier operating systems.

Your aim is to monitor and improve performance, identify potential bottlenecks, and upgrade the appropriate resources. You especially want to identify sources of critical performance problems that could make a computer unacceptably slow or completely unusable.

Performance Monitor

In Windows 7, you can open Performance Monitor by accessing Control Panel, specifying All Control Panel Items, selecting Performance Information And Tools, clicking Advanced Tools in the Performance Information And Tools window, and clicking Open Performance Monitor. However it is easier to type **perfmon** in the Start menu search box (or at a command prompt). The Performance dialog box lets you access Performance Monitor, DCSs, and the Reports tool. Select Performance Monitor on the tree pane.

You can add counters by clicking the green + button on the Performance Monitor toolbar, expanding the object (such as Memory), selecting the counter, and clicking Add. You can specify whether you want to display a single instance of a counter or a total of all instances. For example, if a computer has more than one CPU, you could select a counter that monitors the usage of a single CPU or a counter that monitors total CPU usage. Figure 13-1 shows Performance Monitor displaying real-time data.

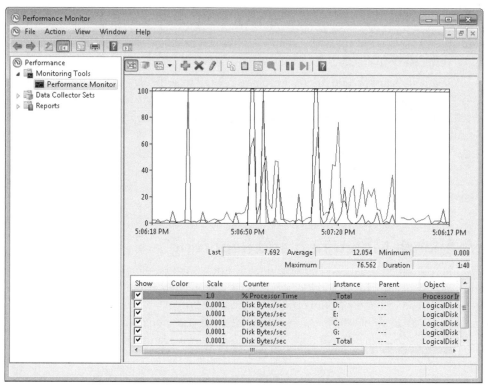

FIGURE 13-1 Performance Monitor displaying real-time data

Each line on the graph appears in a different color. To make it easier to view a specific graph, select its counter and press Ctrl+H. The selected counter appears bold and in black on the graph. To change the appearance and refresh rate of the chart, right-click Performance Monitor and then select Properties. The five tabs of the Performance Monitor Properties dialog box provide access to different configuration options, as follows:

- **General** In the Graph Elements group, you can adjust the Sample Every box to change how frequently the graph updates. You can also specify whether the Legend, Value Bar, and Toolbar are displayed and whether the Report and Histogram views show Default, Maximum, Minimum, Average, or Current values. Figure 13-2 shows the General tab.

FIGURE 13-2 The General tab of Performance Monitor Properties

- **Source** On this tab, you can choose whether to display current activity in real time or show log files that you have saved using a DCS

- **Data** On this tab, in the Counters list, select the counter that you want to configure and adjust Color, Width, and Style.

- **Graph** By default, Performance Monitor begins overwriting graphed counter values on the left portion of the chart after the specified duration is reached. If you want to record counter values over a long period of time, you likely want to see the chart scroll from right to left. To do this, select the Scroll style. You can also select one of the following chart types by clicking the Change Graph Type button on the toolbar or by pressing Ctrl+G.

  - **Line** This is the default setting and shows values as lines on the chart.

  - **Histogram** This shows a bar graph with the current, maximum, minimum, or average counter values displayed. If you have a large number of counters, a histogram is easier to read than a line chart.

  - **Report** This lists the current, maximum, minimum, or average counter values in a text report.

- **Appearance** If you keep multiple Performance Monitor windows open simultaneously, you can use this tab to change the color of the background or other elements.

Data Collector Sets

Data collector sets (DCSs) gather system information, including configuration settings and performance data, and store it in a data file. You can use Performance Monitor to examine the data file and analyze detailed performance data, or you can generate a report that summarizes this information.

Windows 7 includes the following built-in DCSs:

- **System Performance**   You can use this DCS when troubleshooting a slow computer or intermittent performance problems. It logs processor, disk, memory, and network performance (Internet Protocol versions 4 and 6) counters and kernel trace data.

- **System Diagnostics**   You can use this DCS when troubleshooting reliability problems such as problematic hardware, driver failures, or STOP errors. It logs all the information included in the System Performance DCS, plus detailed system information. Figure 13-3 shows some of the counters included in the System Diagnostics data set.

To use a DCS, right-click it and then select Start. The System Performance DCS has a default overall duration of 10 minutes. The System Diagnostics DCS collector set has a default overall duration of 1 minute. To stop a DCS manually, right-click it and then click Stop.

After running a DCS, you can view a summary of the data that it has gathered in the *Performance Monitor\Reports* node. To view the most recent report for a DCS, right-click the DCS and then click *Latest Report*. You can then view the report by accessing it in the *Reports* node, as shown in Figure 13-4.

You can also add performance counter alerts to DCSs. This enables you to monitor and detect an alert, which you can then use to start a batch file, send you an e-mail, or call you on a pager. For example, if you configured an alert to trigger when free space on a logical volume falls below 30 percent, you could add this to a DCS and use it to trigger a batch file that archives the data on the volume.

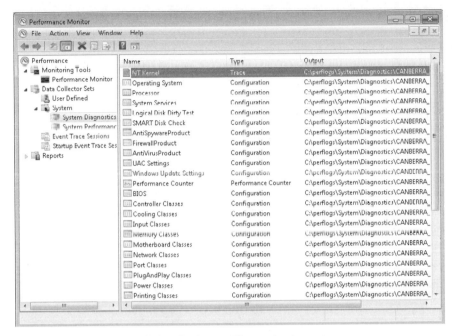

FIGURE 13-3 Counters included in the System Diagnostics data set

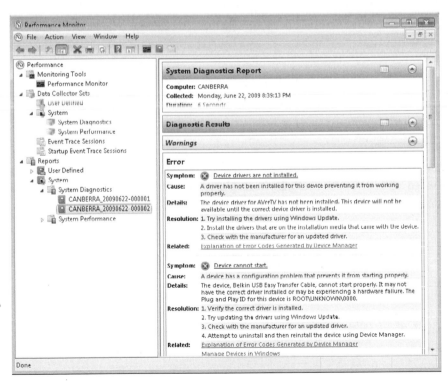

FIGURE 13-4 Accessing a report for the System Diagnostics data set

Data logging uses a large amount of system resources, and performance log files can become very large. To minimize the performance impact of performance data logging, log the minimum amount of information you require. For example, use System Performance instead of System Diagnostics whenever possible because System Performance includes fewer counters.

Creating a Data Collector Set

If you have a performance problem or want to analyze and possibly improve the performance of a client computer, you can use DCSs to gather performance data and compare it against your baselines. The following high-level procedure creates a custom DCS:

1. In the Performance Monitor console (not the Performance Monitor tool that you can access from the console), expand Data Collector Sets, right-click User Defined, select New, and then select Data Collector Set. This starts the Create New Data Collector Set Wizard.

2. On the Create New Data Collector Set page, specify a name for the set. Ensure that Create From A Template (Recommended) is selected. Click Next.

3. On the Which Template Would You Like To Use? page, choose from one of the standard templates (Basic, System Diagnostics, or System Performance). Click Next.

4. On the Where Would You Like The Data To Be Saved? page, click Next to accept the default location for the data.

5. On the Create The Data Collector Set page, leave Run As set to the default to create and run the DCS using the logged-on user's credentials. Alternatively, click Change and specify alternative administrative credentials.

6. Select one of the following three options, and then click Finish:

   - Open Properties For This Data Collector Set
   - Start This Data Collector Set Now
   - Save And Close

Custom DCSs are located under the User Defined node within Data Collector Sets. You can schedule when a DCS runs and configure its stop conditions. You can also start a DCS manually by right-clicking it and selecting Start.

> **MORE INFO**   **CREATING DCSS**
>
> For more information about the various methods of creating DCSs, see *http://technet.microsoft.com/en-us/library/cc749337.aspx*.

Customizing Data Collector Sets

A custom DCS logs only the performance data defined in the template that you choose. To add your own data sources to a DCS, you must update it after you create it.

To add a performance data source (such as a performance counter) to a DCS, right-click the DCS, select New, and then select Data Collector. The Create New Data Collector Wizard opens. On the What Type Of Data Collector Would You Like To Create? page, specify the data collector name, select the type, and then click Next. You can choose from the following types of data collectors:

- **Performance Counter Data Collector** This type of data collector enables you to collect performance statistics over long periods of time for later analysis. You can use it to set baselines and analyze trends.

- **Event Trace Data Collector** This type of data collector enables you to collect information about system events and activities.

- **Configuration Data Collector** This type of data collector stores information about registry keys, Windows Management Instrumentation (WMI) management paths, and the system state.

- **Performance Counter Alert** This type of data collector (sometimes termed an *Alert data connector*) enables you to configure an alert that is generated when a particular performance counter exceeds or drops below a specific threshold value.

You can add as many data collectors to a DCS as you need. To edit a data collector, select it in the Data Collector Sets\User Defined node. In the Details pane, right-click the data collector and click Properties.

> **MORE INFO** **DCS PROPERTIES**
>
> For more information about configuring DCS properties, see *http://technet.microsoft.com/ en-us/library/cc749267.aspx.*

If a DCS includes performance counters, you can view the counter values in Performance Monitor by right-clicking the report, clicking View, and then clicking Performance Monitor. Performance Monitor then displays the data logged by the DCS rather than real-time data.

Creating Data Collectors from the Command Prompt

You can create data collectors from an elevated command prompt by using the *Logman* utility. For example, you can use the following commands to create the various types of data collector listed in the previous section:

- **Logman create counter** This command creates a Performance Counter data collector. For example, the *logman create counter my_perf_log -c "\Processor(_Total)\% Processor Time"* command creates a counter called *my_perf_log* that records values for the *% Processor Time* counter in the *Processor(_Total)* counter instance.

- **Logman create trace** This command creates an Event Trace data collector. For example, the *logman create trace my_trace_log -o c:\trace_log_file* command creates an event trace data collector called *my_trace_log* and outputs the results to the *C:\trace_log_file* location.

- **Logman create config**   This command creates a Configuration data collector. For example, the *logman create config my_cfg_log –reg HKEY_LOCAL_MACHINE\ SOFTWARE\Microsoft\Windows\CurrentVersion* command creates a configuration data collector called *my_cfg_log* using the *HKEY_LOCAL_MACHINE\SOFTWARE\ Microsoft\Windows\CurrentVersion* registry key.
- **Logman create alert**   This command creates an Alert data collector. For example, the *logman create alert my_alert -th "\Processor(_Total)\% Processor Time>90"* command creates an alert called *my_alert* that fires when the *% Processor Time* performance counter in the *Processor(_Total)* counter instance exceeds a value of *90*.

You can also use the *Logman* utility to query data collector output; for example, the *logman query "my_perf_log"* command lists the data collectors contained in the *my_perf_log* DCS. You can start and stop DCSs, for example, by using the commands *logman start my_perf_log* and *logman stop my_perf_log*. You can delete a DCS, for example, by using the command *logman delete my_perf_log*, and you can use *logman update* to update a performance counter, a trace counter, an alert, or a configuration. *Logman* enables you to export the information in DCSs to and import information from an XML file.

> ***MORE INFO*** **LOGMAN**
>
> For more information about the *Logman* utility, see *http://technet.microsoft.com/en-us/ library/cc753820.aspx*.

Generating a System Diagnostics Report

When you create and use a DCS, you generate a report that is placed in User Defined Reports in the Reports tool in the Performance Tools console. However, the Reports tool also contains a system diagnostic report, sometimes known as a *computer health check* (although the term *health check* is more commonly used on server rather than client computers).

A system diagnostics report gives you details about the status of hardware resources, system response times, and processes on the local computer, along with system information and configuration data. You would generate a system diagnostics report if you were looking for ways to maximize performance and streamline system operation. You need to be a member of the local Administrators group or equivalent to generate a system diagnostics report.

If you use the Performance Tools console to look at the system diagnostics report, you see a copy of that report the last time it was compiled. To generate and display a system diagnostic report that is completely up to date, enter the following into the Search box on the Start menu:

```
perfmon /report
```

If you prefer, you can instead enter **perfmon.exe /report** in an elevated command prompt. Whatever method you choose, the command generates a diagnostics report (this typically takes 60 seconds) and displays it in the Resource and Performance Monitor, as shown in Figure 13-5. You can scroll down the report and expand any of its sections.

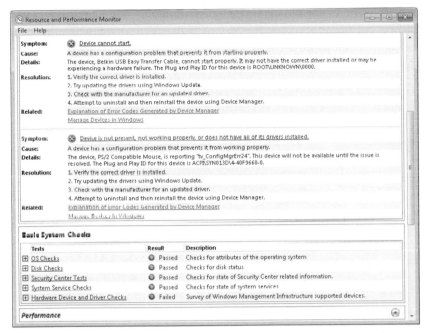

FIGURE 13-5 System diagnostics report in the Resource and Performance Monitor

For example, expanding the failed basic system check called Hardware Device And Driver Checks in the Resource and Performance Monitor results in the screen shown in Figure 13-6, which indicates there are problems with three of the Plug and Play (PnP) devices.

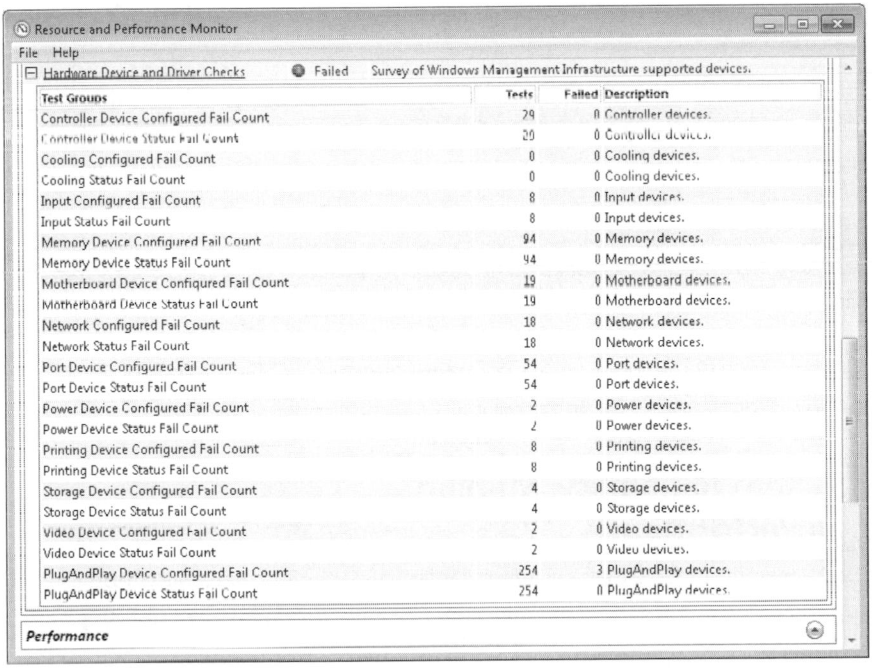

Test Groups	Tests	Failed	Description
Controller Device Configured Fail Count	29	0	Controller devices.
Controller Device Status Fail Count	29	0	Controller devices.
Cooling Configured Fail Count	0	0	Cooling devices.
Cooling Status Fail Count	0	0	Cooling devices.
Input Configured Fail Count	8	0	Input devices.
Input Status Fail Count	8	0	Input devices.
Memory Device Configured Fail Count	94	0	Memory devices.
Memory Device Status Fail Count	44	0	Memory devices.
Motherboard Device Configured Fail Count	19	0	Motherboard devices.
Motherboard Device Status Fail Count	19	0	Motherboard devices.
Network Configured Fail Count	18	0	Network devices.
Network Status Fail Count	18	0	Network devices.
Port Device Configured Fail Count	54	0	Port devices.
Port Device Status Fail Count	54	0	Port devices.
Power Device Configured Fail Count	2	0	Power devices.
Power Device Status Fail Count	2	0	Power devices.
Printing Device Configured Fail Count	8	0	Printing devices.
Printing Device Status Fail Count	8	0	Printing devices.
Storage Device Configured Fail Count	4	0	Storage devices.
Storage Device Status Fail Count	4	0	Storage devices.
Video Device Configured Fail Count	2	0	Video devices.
Video Device Status Fail Count	2	0	Video devices.
PlugAndPlay Device Configured Fail Count	254	3	PlugAndPlay devices.
PlugAndPlay Device Status Fail Count	254	0	PlugAndPlay devices.

FIGURE 13-6 Displaying the basic system check for Hardware Device And Driver Checks

You can expand Performance, Software Configuration, Hardware Configuration, CPU, Network, Disk, Memory, and Report Statistics. For example, expanding Software Configuration lets you access more information, as shown in Figure 13-7, although no faults or warnings are displayed in this screen shot. If a fault was detected, you can explore further by expanding any of the nodes marked with a + symbol.

FIGURE 13-7 Expanding Software Configuration in Resource and Performance Monitor

Expanding Report Statistics lets you access computer information, files, and processed events and discover Payload GUIDs, as shown in Figure 13-8.

Tracking System Reliability, Stability, and Overall Performance

Windows 7 offers several tools to assess system reliability and stability. Reliability Monitor keeps a record of software changes and updates and lets you correlate system changes with

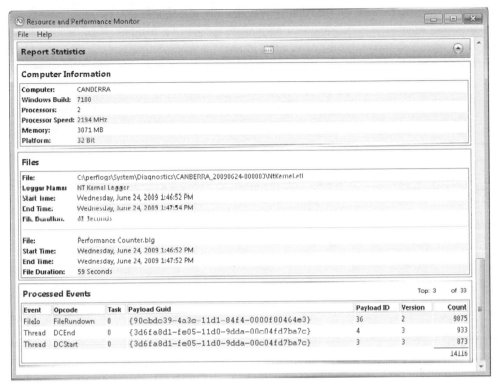

FIGURE 13-8 Expanding Report Statistics in Resource and Performance Monitor

crashes and reboots; the Action Center monitors your computer and reports problems with security, maintenance, and related services; and the Windows Experience Index measures the capability of your computer's hardware and software configuration and expresses this as a base score.

Reliability Monitor

Reliability Monitor tracks a computer's stability. Computers that have no reboots or failures are considered stable and can (eventually) achieve the maximum system stability index of 10. The more reboots and failures that occur on a computer, the lower the system stability becomes. The minimum index value is zero. The system stability index is not an exact measure of reliability because, sometimes, installing a new service pack or update requires a reboot, which initially lowers the index value but ultimately makes a system more reliable than it was before. However, Reliability Monitor provides valuable information about what system changes were made before a problem occurred. The easiest way to open Reliability Monitor is to type **perfmon /rel** in the Start menu Search box and click View Reliability History

You can use Reliability Monitor to diagnose intermittent problems. For example, if you install an application that causes the operating system to fail intermittently, it is difficult to correlate the failures with the application installation. Figure 13-9 shows how Reliability

Monitor can be used to indicate that Windows and application failures and a video hardware error occurred on the Canberra computer on June 22 following an update of a video driver on June 21. If you obtained this result on a test network, you might consider obtaining more information before updating the driver on your production network.

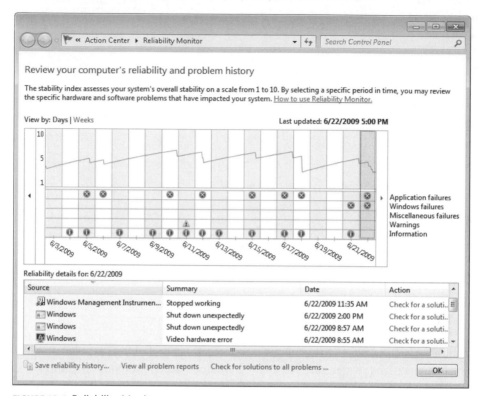

FIGURE 13-9 Reliability Monitor

The Stability Index

The stability index is based on data collected over the lifetime of a system. Each day in the stability chart is associated with a graph point showing its stability index rating. The stability index is a weighted measurement calculated from the number of failures seen over a rolling historical period. The index value is calculated over the preceding 28 days, although the results for considerably more days can be displayed.

Recent failures are weighted more heavily than past failures so that improvement over time is reflected in an ascending stability index when a reliability issue has been resolved. Days when the computer is turned off or is in a sleep or hibernate state are not included when calculating the stability index.

If there is not enough data to calculate a steady stability index, the line on the graph is dotted. For example, until Reliability Monitor has 28 days of data, the stability index is displayed as a dotted line, indicating that it has not yet established a valid baseline. When enough data has been recorded to generate a steady stability index, the line is solid. If there are any significant changes to the system time, an information icon appears on the graph for each day on which the system time was adjusted.

Reliability Monitor maintains up to a year of history for stability and reliability events. The Stability Chart displays a rolling graph organized by date.

 Quick Check

- What would a stability index of 10 indicate?

Quick Check Answer

- The maximum value of the stability index is 10. This value indicates that the computer has been stable over the previous 28 days with no failures or reboots. It also indicates that no software updates and service packs that require a reboot have been applied during that time.

The Stability Chart

The Stability Chart in Reliability Monitor displays a graph of the stability index on a day-to-day basis. Rows in the lower half of the chart track reliability events that either contribute to the stability measurement for the system or provide related information about software installation and removal. When one or more reliability events of each type are detected, an icon appears in the column for that date.

For software installs and uninstalls an information icon indicates a successful event and a warning icon indicates a failure. For all other reliability event types, an error icon indicates a failure. If more than 30 days of data are available, you can use the left and right arrow keys on the keyboard to find dates outside the visible range.

Using the Action Center

The Action Center, available under System And Security in Control Panel, monitors your computer and reports problems with security, maintenance, and related settings that help indicate your computer's overall performance. It notifies users if there is a problem with the network firewall, antivirus, anti-spyware, or Windows Update on their computers running Windows 7. When the status of a monitored item changes (for example, your antivirus software becomes out of date), Action Center notifies you with a message in the notification area on the taskbar. The status of the item in Action Center changes color to reflect the severity of the message, and Action Center recommends an action. The Action Center is shown in Figure 13-10.

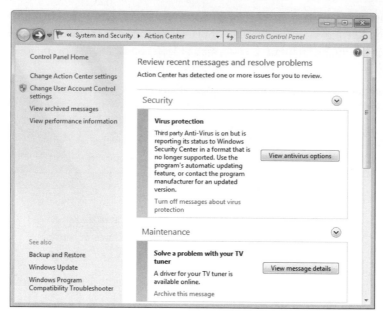

FIGURE 13-10 The Action Center

Changing Action Center Settings

If you prefer to keep track of an item yourself and you do not want to see notifications about its status, you can turn off notifications for the item in the Change Action Center Settings dialog box, shown in Figure 13-11.

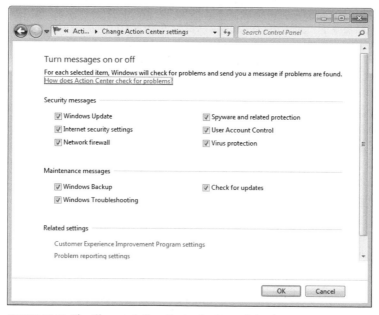

FIGURE 13-11 The Change Action Center Settings dialog box

When you clear the check box for an item on the Change Action Center Settings dialog box, you no longer receive any messages and do not see the item's status in Action Center. Microsoft recommends checking the status of all items listed because that can help warn you about security issues.

The Windows Experience Index

From Action Center, you can archive messages and view the messages you have archived. You can click a link to change User Account Control (UAC) settings, as described in Chapter 9, "Authentication and Account Control." However, the link in the Action Center that best measures the computer's current performance level is to the Windows Experience Index in the Performance Information And Tools dialog box, as shown in Figure 13-12.

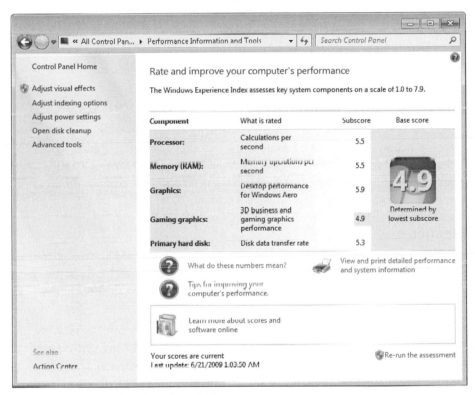

FIGURE 13-12 The Windows Experience Index

The Windows Experience Index measures the capability of your computer's hardware and software configuration and expresses this as a base score. A higher base score generally means that your computer will perform better and faster especially when performing resource-intensive tasks.

Each hardware feature receives an individual subscore and the base score is determined by the lowest subscore. The base score is not an average of the combined subscores. However, the subscores can give you a view of how the features that are most important to you will perform and can help you decide which features to upgrade. Remember that if you are not interested in gaming and very high-quality three-dimensional graphics, you might purchase a computer that has very adequate processor, memory, and hard disk resources but has a lower-cost graphics hardware device. Such a computer is adequate for your purposes but does not have a high base score.

While bearing this in mind, you can use the base score as at least a rough guide when you are selecting software to run on your computer. For example, if your computer has a base score of 3.3, then you would be wise to purchase only software packages that require a base score of 3 or lower. Interactive games applications are a good example of the type of software package that require a high Windows Experience Index.

The scores range from 1.0 to 7.9. The Windows Experience Index is designed to accommodate advances in computer technology. As hardware speed and performance improve, higher score ranges will be enabled. The standards for each level of the index generally stay the same. However, in some cases, new tests might be developed that can result in lower scores. If you have replaced or upgraded hardware on your computer, you need to recalculate the Windows Experience Index.

Using System Tools to Investigate Processes and Services

As an IT professional, you probably have used Task Manager and accessed Resource Manager from that tool, although you may not be aware of the Resource Manager enhancements that Windows 7 provides. Process Explorer is a downloadable advanced system tool that offers many of the features of Task Manager and Resource Manager and you can use this tool to investigate resource usage, handles, and dynamic-link library (DLL) files.

Task Manager

If an application stops responding, Windows 7 tries to find the problem and fix it automatically. Alternatively, if the system seems to have crashed completely and Windows 7 has not resolved the problem, you can end the application by opening Task Manager and accessing the Applications tab.

The Performance tab in Task Manager provides details about how a computer is using system resources—for example, RAM and CPU. As shown in Figure 13-13, the Performance tab has four graphs. The first two show the percentage of CPU resource that the system is using, both at the moment and for the past few minutes. A high percentage usage over a significant period indicates that programs or processes require a lot of CPU resources. This can affect computer performance. If the percentage appears frozen at or near 100 percent, a program might not be responding. If the CPU Usage History graph is split, the computer either has multiple CPUs, a single dual-core CPU, or both.

If processor usage is consistently high—say 80 percent or higher for a significant period— you should consider installing a second processor or replacing the current processor even if the Windows Experience Index subscore does not identify the processor as a resource bottleneck. However, before you do so, it is worth capturing processor usage data by using Performance Monitor rather than relying on snapshots obtained by using Task Manager.

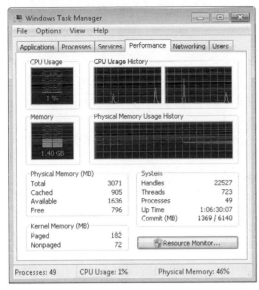

FIGURE 13-13 The Performance tab in Task Manager

The next two graphs display how much RAM is being used, both at the moment and for the past few minutes. The percentage of memory being used is listed at the bottom of the Task Manager window. If memory use appears to be consistently high or slows your computer's performance noticeably, try reducing the number of programs that are open at one time (or encourage users you support to close any applications they are not currently using). If the problem persists, you might need to install more RAM or implement ReadyBoost.

Three tables below the graphs list various details about memory and resource usage. In the Physical Memory (MB) table, *Total* is the amount of RAM installed on your computer, *Cached* refers to the amount of physical memory used recently for system resources, and *Free* is the amount of memory that is currently unused and available.

In the Kernel Memory (MB) table, *Total* is the amount of memory being used by the core part of Windows, called the kernel; *Paged* refers to the amount of virtual memory the kernel is using; *Nonpaged* is the amount of RAM memory used by the kernel.

The System table has five fields: Handles, Threads, Processes, Up Time, and Page File Handles are pointers that refer to system elements. They include (but are not limited to) files, registry keys, events, or directories. Lesson 2, "Configuring Performance Settings," discusses page file configuration.

If you need more information about how memory and CPU resources are being used, click Resource Monitor. This displays the Resource Monitor, which is discussed later in this lesson. You require elevated privileges to access Resource Monitor.

You can determine how much memory an individual process uses by selecting the Task Manager Processes tab. As shown in Figure 13-14, the Memory (Private Working Set) column is selected by default. A private working set indicates the amount of memory a process is using that other processes cannot share. This information can be useful in identifying a "leaky" application—an application which, if left open, uses more and more memory resource and does not release memory resource that it is no longer using.

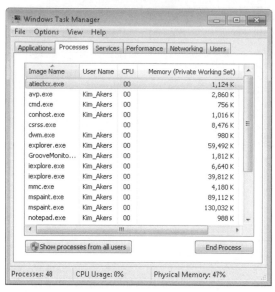

FIGURE 13-14 The Processes tab in Task Manager

You can click View, click Select Columns, and then select a memory value to view other memory usage details on the Processes tab. You can use the Task Manager Processes tab to end a process, to end a process tree (which stops the process and all processes on which it depends), and to set process priority. To change the priority of a process, right-click the process and click Set Priority. You can choose Realtime, High, Above Normal, Normal, Below Normal, or Low.

The Task Manager Services tab shows which services are running and which are stopped. You can stop or start a service or go to a process that depends on that service. If you want more details about or more control over the services available on a computer, you can click Services to access the Services administrative tool. You require elevated privileges to use the Services tool.

The Task Manager Networking tab lets you view network usage. The Users tab tells you what users are connected to the computer and lets you disconnect a user. The Applications tab shows you the running applications and (as previously stated) enables you to close a crashed application.

 **Quick Check**

- You want to change the priority of a process on a computer. How do you do this?

Quick Check Answer

- Open Task Manager. In the Processes tab, right-click the process and click Set Priority. You can choose Realtime, High, Above Normal, Normal, Below Normal, or Low.

EXAM TIP

In Windows 7, you right-click a process and click Set Priority to observe or configure its priority level. In Windows Vista, you click Select Priority. Examiners often test this sort of change to determine whether candidates have properly studied the new operating system or whether they are relying on their experience with the previous one.

Resource Monitor

Windows 7 offers an enhanced version of the Resource Monitor tool. Windows 7 Resource Monitor allows you to view information about hardware and software resource use in real time. You can filter the results according to the processes or services that you want to monitor. You can also use Resource Monitor to start, stop, suspend, and resume processes and services, and to troubleshoot unresponsive applications. You can start Resource Monitor from the Processes tab of Task Manager or by entering **resmon** in the Search box on the Start menu.

Resource Monitor always starts in the same location and with the same display options as the previous session. You can save your display state at any time and then open the configuration file to use the saved settings. However, filtering selections are not saved as part of the configuration settings.

Resource Monitor includes five tabs: Overview, CPU, Memory, Disk, and Network. The Overview tab, shown in Figure 13-15, displays basic system resource usage information. The other tabs display information about each specific resource. If you have filtered results on one tab, only resources used by the selected processes or services are displayed on the other tabs. Filtered results are denoted by an orange bar below the title bar of each table.

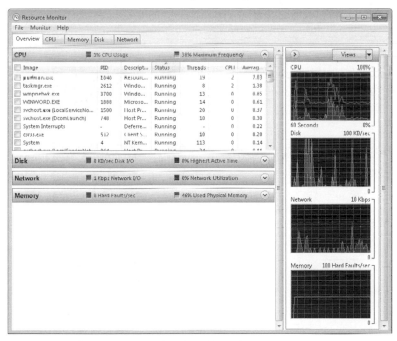

FIGURE 13-15 The Resource Monitor Overview tab

Each tab in Resource Monitor includes multiple tables that provide detailed information about the resource featured on that tab. The first table displayed is always the key table, and it contains a complete list of processes using the resource included on that tab. For example, the key table on the Overview tab contains a complete list of processes running on the system.

You can filter the detailed data in tables other than the key table by one or more processes or services. To filter, select the check box in the key table next to each process or service that you want to highlight. To stop filtering for a single process or service, clear its check box. To stop filtering altogether, clear the check box next to Image in the key table. If you have filtered results, the resources used by the selected processes or services are shown in the graphs as an orange line.

You can change the size of the graphs by clicking Views and selecting a different graph size. You can hide the chart pane by clicking the arrow at the top of the pane. To view definitions of data displayed in the tables, move the mouse pointer over the column title about which you want more information.

For example, to identify the network address that a process is connected to, click the Network tab and then click the title bar of TCP Connections to expand the table. Locate the process whose network connection you want to identify. You can then determine the Remote Address and Remote Port columns to see which network address and port the process is connected to. Figure 13-16 shows the System process is currently connected to IPv4 addresses 192.168.123.138 and 192.168.123.176, both on port 445.

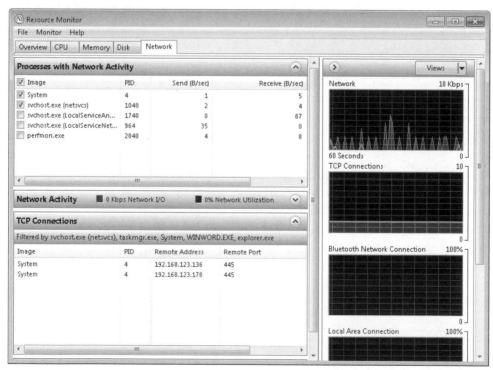

FIGURE 13-16 Identifying network addresses that a process is connected to

On the Memory tab, shown in Figure 13-17, you can review the memory available to programs. Available memory is the combined total of standby memory and free memory. Free memory includes zero page memory.

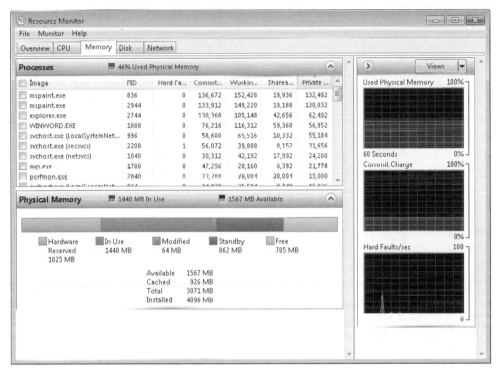

FIGURE 13-17 The Resource Monitor Memory tab

Resource Monitor displays real-time information about all the processes running on your system. If you want to view only the data related to selected processes, you can filter the detailed results by selecting the check boxes next to the names of the processes you want to monitor in any of the tabs. Selected processes are moved to the top of the Image column. After you have selected at least one process for filtering, the Associated Handles and Associated Modules tables on the CPU tab contain data related to your selection. Tables that contain only filtered results include an orange information bar below the title bar of the table.

Resource Monitor allows you to end or suspend processes and start, stop, or restart services. You should use Resource Monitor to end a process only if you are unable to close the program by normal means. If an open program is associated with the process, it closes immediately and you lose any unsaved data. If you end a system process, this might result in system instability and data loss.

To end a process, right-click the executable name of the process that you want to end in the Image column of the key table of any Resource Monitor tab and click End Process. To end all processes dependent on the selected process, click End Process Tree. To resume a process, right-click the executable name of the program that you want to resume, and then click Resume Process.

To stop, start, or restart a service using Resource Monitor access the CPU tab and click the title bar of Services to expand the table. In Name, right-click the service that you want to change, and then click Stop Service, Start Service, or Restart Service.

Applications that are not responding might be waiting for other processes to finish, or for system resources to become available. Resource Monitor allows you to view a process wait chain, and to end processes that are preventing a program from working properly.

A process that is not responding appears as a red entry in the CPU table of the Overview tab and in the Processes table of the CPU tab. To view the process wait chain, right-click the executable name of the process you want to analyze in the Image column on the key table of any Resource Monitor tab and click Analyze Wait Chain.

If the process is running normally and is not waiting for any other processes, no wait chain information is displayed. If, on the other hand, the process is waiting for another process, a tree organized by dependency on other processes is displayed. If a wait chain tree is displayed, you can end one or more of the processes in the tree by selecting the check boxes next to the process names and clicking End Process.

Handles (as stated previously in this section) are pointers that refer to system elements. They include (but are not limited to) files, registry keys, events, or directories. Modules are helper files or programs. They include (but are not limited to) DLL files.

To use Resource Monitor to view all handles and modules associated with a process, in the Image column of the CPU tab, select the check box next to the name of the process for which you want to see associated handles and modules. Selected processes move to the top of the column. Click the title bars of the Associated Handles and Associated Modules tables to expand them. An orange bar below the title bar of each table shows the processes you have selected. Review the results in the detail tables.

If you need to identify the processes that use a handle, click the Search Handles box in the title bar of the Associated Handles table. Type the name of the handle you want to search for, and then click Search. For example, searching for *c:\windows* returns all handles with *c:\windows* as part of the handle name. The search string is not case sensitive, and wildcards are not supported.

Process Explorer

Process Explorer is not part of Windows 7, but you can download it at *http://technet.microsoft .com/en-us/sysinternals/bb896653.aspx*, expand the archive into a folder (such as *C:\ProcessExplorer*), and start it by entering **c:\processexplorer\procexp.exe** in the Search box on the Start menu. Process Explorer tells you which program has a particular file or directory open and displays information about which handles and DLLs processes have opened or loaded. You can use either Process Explorer or Resource Monitor to determine which applications are responsible for activity on your hard disk, including which files and folders are being accessed.

When it opens, Process Explorer displays a list of the currently active processes, as shown in Figure 13-18. You can toggle the lower pane on and off and select to view handles or DLLs.

In Handle mode, you can see the handles that the process selected in the top window has opened. The Process Explorer search capability discovers which processes have particular handles opened or DLLs loaded.

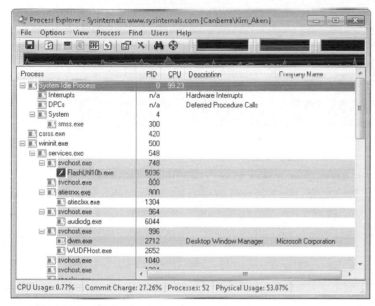

FIGURE 13-18 Process Explorer opening page

MORE INFO   **ADVANCED SYSTEM TOOLS AND COMMAND-LINE UTILITIES**

For more information about advanced system tools for Windows, including their corresponding command-line utilities, see *http://technet.microsoft.com/en-us/sysinternals/default.aspx*.

Process Explorer includes a toolbar and mini-graphs for CPU, memory, and I/O history. The mini-graphs show history of system activity, and resting the mouse over a point on a graph displays the associated time and the process information. For example, the tooltip for the mini-CPU graph shows the process that was the largest consumer of CPU. Clicking on any of the mini-graphs opens the System Information screen, as shown in Figure 13-19. Difference highlighting helps you see what items change between refreshes. Items—including processes, DLLs, and handles—that exit or are closed show in red and new items show in green.

System Information graphs display the CPU usage history of the system, committed virtual memory usage, and I/O throughput history. Red in the CPU usage graph indicates CPU usage in kernel mode, whereas green is the sum of kernel-mode and user-mode execution. When Committed Virtual Memory reaches the system Commit Limit, applications and the system become unstable. The Commit Limit is the sum of most of the physical memory and the sizes of any paging files. In the I/O graph, the blue line indicates total I/O traffic, which is the sum of all process I/O reads and writes between refreshes, and the pink line shows write traffic.

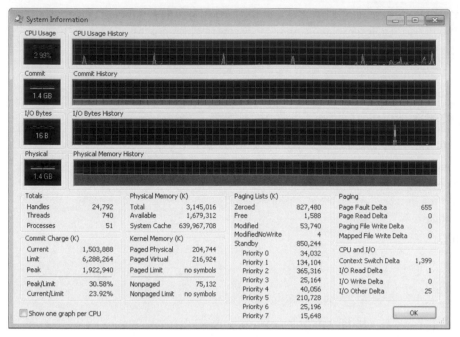

FIGURE 13-19 Process Explorer System Information screen

You can reorder columns in Process Explorer by dragging them to their new position. To select which columns of data you want visible in each of the views and the status bar, click Select Columns on the View menu or right-click a column header and click Select Columns. You can save a column configuration and its associated settings by clicking Save Column Set on the View menu.

On the Options menu, you can choose to have Process Explorer open instead of Task Manager whenever Task Manager is started, or you can ensure that the Processor Explorer window is always on top and always visible. You can specify that only one instance of Process Explorer is open at any one time.

> **NOTE** **THE VIEWING ADVANCED DETAILS IN SYSTEM INFORMATION OPTION**
>
> The View Advanced Details In System Information option, available when you click Advanced Tools in The Performance Information And Tools dialog box, provides detailed information about system configuration. It does not, however, directly address performance issues. The dialog box in which this information is presented is called System Information. Take care to distinguish between this dialog box, which is provided in Windows 7, and the System Information feature of Process Explorer, which is a downloadable tool.

Logging and Forwarding Events and Event Subscriptions

As an experienced IT professional, you almost certainly have used Event Viewer and event logs, and this section discusses these tools only briefly before going on to event forwarding and event subscriptions, with which you might be less familiar.

Details about event subscriptions can be found in the Subscriptions tab of the event log Properties dialog box. The General tab of this dialog box gives details such as current log size, maximum log size, and the action to take when maximum log size is reached. The easiest way to start Event Viewer is to enter **eventvwr** in the Start menu Search box.

Event Viewer displays event logs, which are files that record significant events on a computer—for example, when a user logs on or when a program encounters an error. You will find the details in event logs helpful when troubleshooting problems. The events recorded fall into the following categories:

- Critical
- Error
- Warning
- Information

The security log contains two more event categories, Audit Success and Audit Failure, that are used for auditing purposes.

Event Viewer tracks information in several different logs. Windows logs include the following:

- **Application** Stores program events. Events are classified as error, warning, or information, depending on the severity of the event. The critical error classification is not used in the Application log.
- **Security** Stores security-related audit events that can be successful or failed. For example, the security log will record an audit success if a user trying to log on to the computer was successful.
- **System** Stores system events that are logged by Windows 7 and system services. System events are classified as critical, error, warning, or information.
- **Forwarded Events** Stores events that are forwarded by other computers.

Custom Views

You can create custom views by clicking Create Custom View on the Event Viewer Action menu, specifying the source logs or events and filtering by level, time logged, event ID, task category, keywords, user, or computer. You are unlikely to specify all these criteria, but this facility enables you to refine your search to where you think a problem might be occurring rather than searching through a very large number of events. Figure 13-20 shows a custom view specification.

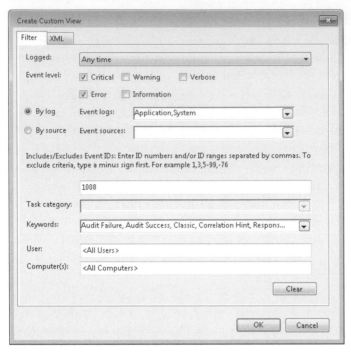

FIGURE 13-20 Specifying a custom view

A filter is not persistent. If you set up a filter to view specific information in an event log, you need to configure the same filter again the next time you want to see the same information. Custom views are persistent, which means you can access them whenever you open Event Viewer. You can save a filter as a custom view so it becomes persistent and you do not need to configure it for each use. The Action menu also allows you to import custom views from another source and to connect to another computer. You need to have an administrator-level account on that computer.

Applications and Services Logs

Event Viewer provides a number of Applications and Services logs. These include logs for programs that run on the computer and detailed logs that store information about specific Windows services. For example, these logs can include the following:

- Hardware Events
- Internet Explorer
- Key Management Service
- Media Center
- A large number of Microsoft Windows logs
- Microsoft Office Diagnosis
- Microsoft Office Sessions
- Windows PowerShell

Attaching Tasks to Events

Sometimes you want to be notified by e-mail if a particular event occurs, or you might want a specified program to start, such as one that activates a pager. Typically, you might want an event in the Security log—such as a failed logon, or a successful logon by a user who should not be able to log on to a particular computer—to trigger this action. To implement this functionality, you attach a task to the event so that you receive a notification.

To do this, open Event Viewer and navigate to the log that contains the event about which you want to be notified. Typically, this would be the Security log in Windows logs, but you can implement this in other Windows logs or in Applications and Services logs if you want to. You click the event and click Action, click the event and go to the Actions pane, or right-click the event. You then select Attach Task To This Event.

This opens the Create A Basic Task Wizard. You name and describe the task and then click Next. The next screen summarizes the event, and you can check that you have chosen the correct event before clicking Next. The next screen gives you the option of starting a program, sending an e-mail, or specifying a message. When you make your choice and click Next, you configure the task. For example, if you want to send an e-mail, you would specify source address, destination address, subject, task, attachment (if required), and Simple Mail Transfer Protocol (SMTP) server. You click Next and then click Finish.

Using Network Diagnostics with Event Viewer

When you run Windows Network Diagnostics, as described in Chapter 6, any problem found, along with solution or solutions, is displayed in the Network Diagnostics dialog box. If, however, more detailed information about the problem and potential solutions is available, Windows 7 saves this in one or more event logs. You can use the information in the event logs to analyze connectivity problems or help interpret the conclusions.

You can filter for network diagnostics and Transmission Control Protocol/Internet Protocol (TCP/IP) events by specifying (for example) Tcpip and Tcpiv6 event sources and capturing events from these sources in a custom view.

If Network Diagnostics identifies a problem with a wireless network, it saves information in the event logs as either helper class events or informational events. Helper class events provide a summary of the diagnostics results and repeat information displayed in the Network Diagnostics dialog box. They can also provide additional information for troubleshooting, such as details about the connection that was diagnosed, diagnostics results, and the capabilities of the wireless network and the adapter being diagnosed.

Informational events can include information about the connection that was diagnosed, the wireless network settings on the computer and the network, visible networks and routers or access points in range at the time of diagnosis, the computer's preferred wireless network list, connection history, and connection statistics—for example, packet statistics and roaming history. They also summarize connection attempts, list their status, and tell you what phases of the connection failed or did not start.

Event Forwarding and Event Subscriptions

Event forwarding enables you to transfer events that match specific criteria to an administrative (or collector) computer. This enables you to manage events centrally. A single *event log* on the collector computer holds important events from computers anywhere in your organization. You do not need to connect to the local event logs on individual computers.

Event forwarding uses Hypertext Transfer Protocol (HTTP) or, if you need to provide an additional encryption and authentication layer for greater security, Hypertext Transfer Protocol Secure (HTTPS) to send events from a source computer to a collector computer. Because event forwarding uses the same protocols that you use to browse Web sites, it works through most firewalls and proxy servers. Event forwarding traffic is encrypted whether it uses HTTP or HTTPS.

To use event forwarding, you must configure both the source and collector computers. On both computers, start the Windows Remote Management (WinRM) and the Windows Event Collector services. On the source computer, configure a Windows Firewall exception for the HTTP protocol. You might also need to create a Windows Firewall exception on the collector computer, depending on the delivery optimization technique you choose.

You can configure collector-initiated or source-initiated subscriptions. In collector-initiated subscriptions, the collector computer retrieves events from the computer that generated the event. You would use a collector-initiated subscription when you have a limited number of source computers and these are already identified. In this type of subscription, you configure each computer manually.

Subscriptions

In a source-initiated subscription (sometimes termed a *source computer–initiated subscription*), the computer on which an event is generated (the source computer) sends the event to the collector computer. You would use a source-initiated subscription when you have a large number of source computers and you configure these computers through Group Policy.

In a source-initiated subscription, you can add additional source computers after the subscription is established and you do not need to know immediately which computers in your network are to be source computers. In collector-initiated subscriptions, the collector computer retrieves events from one or more source computers. Collector-initiated subscriptions are typically used in small networks. In source-initiated subscriptions, the source computers forward events to the collector computer. Enterprise networks use source-initiated subscriptions.

A collector computer needs to run Windows Server 2008 R2, Windows Server 2008, Windows 7, Windows Vista, or Windows Server 2003 R2. A source computer needs to run Windows XP with SP2, Windows Server 2003 with SP1 or SP2, Windows Server 2003 R2, Windows Vista, Windows 7, Windows Server 2008, or Windows Server 2008 R2.

In a collector-initiated subscription, you first manually configure one or more source computers and the collector computer. When the source computers and the collector computer are configured, you can create an *event subscription* to determine what events should be transferred.

Configuring a Collector-Initiated Subscription

To configure a computer running Windows 7 so that a collector computer can retrieve events from it, open an elevated command prompt and use the *Winrm* (Windows Remote Management) command-line tool to configure the WinRM service by entering the following command:

```
winrm quickconfig
```

You can abbreviate this to *winrm qc.* Windows displays a message similar to that shown in Figure 13-21. The changes that must be made depend on how the operating system is configured. You enter **Y** to make these changes. Note that if any of your network connector types is set to public, you must set it to private for this command to work.

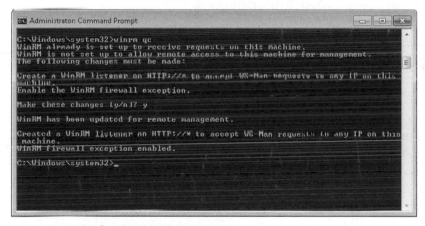

FIGURE 13-21 Configuring the WinRM service

Next, add the computer account of the collector computer to the local Event Log Readers group or the local Administrators group on the source computer. You can do this by using the Local Users And Groups MMC snap-in or by entering a net command in an elevated command prompt.

You can add the collector computer account to the local Administrators group or the Event Log Readers group on the source computer. If you do not require the collector computer to retrieve events in Security Event logs, it is considered best practice to use the Event Log Readers group. However, if you do need to transfer Security Event log information, you must use the local Administrators group.

By default, the Local Users And Groups MMC snap-in does not permit you to add computer accounts. You must click the Object Types button in the Select Users, Computers, Or Groups dialog box and select the Computers check box. You can then add computer accounts.

To configure a computer running Windows 7 to collect events, open an elevated command prompt and enter the following command to configure the Windows Event Collector service:

```
wecutil qc
```

When you have configured the source and collector computers, you next configure the event subscription by specifying what events the collector computer needs to retrieve and the event sources (specifically the source computers) from which it must retrieve them.

EXAM TIP

Distinguish between *Winrm* and *Wecutil*. *Winrm* is used to configure WinRM and is typically used on the source computer. *Wecutil* is used to configure the Windows Event Collector service and is typically used on the collector computer.

Configuring a Source-Initiated Subscription

Source-initiated subscriptions are typically used in enterprise networks in which you can use Group Policy to configure a number of source computers. To configure a source-initiated subscription, you configure the collector computer manually and then use Group Policy to configure the source computers. When the collector computer and source computers are configured, you can create an event subscription to determine which events are forwarded.

Source-initiated subscriptions (sometimes termed *source computer–initiated subscriptions*) enable you to configure a subscription on a collector computer without defining the event source computers. You can then set up multiple remote event source computers by using Group Policy to forward events to the event collector computer. By contrast, in the collector-initiated subscription model, you must define all the event sources in the event subscription.

To configure the collector computer in a source-initiated subscription, you need to use command-line commands entered in an elevated command prompt. If the collector and source computers are in the same domain, you must create an event subscription Extensible Markup Language (XML) file (called, for example, Subscription.xml) on the collector computer, open an elevated command prompt on that computer, and configure WinRM by entering the following command:

```
winrm qc -q
```

Configure the Event Collector service on the same computer by entering the following command:

```
wecutil qc -q
```

Create a source-initiated subscription on the collector computer by entering the following command:

```
wecutil cs configuration.xml
```

To configure a source computer to use a source-initiated subscription, you first configure WinRM on that computer by entering the following command:

```
winrm qc -q
```

You then use Group Policy to add the address of the event collector computer to the SubscriptionManager setting. From an elevated command prompt, start Group Policy by entering the following command:

```
%SYSTEMROOT%\System32\gpedit.msc
```

In Local Group Policy Editor, under Computer Configuration, expand Administrative Templates, expand Windows Components, and select Event Forwarding. Note that you do not have this option if you have already configured your computer as a collector computer.

Right-click the SubscriptionManager setting and select Properties. Enable the SubscriptionManager setting and then click Show. Add at least one setting that specifies the event collector computer. The SubscriptionManager Properties window contains an Explain tab that describes the syntax for the setting.

After the SubscriptionManager setting has been added, run the following command to ensure that the policy is applied:

```
gpupdate /force
```

Creating an Event Subscription

To receive events transferred from a source computer to a collector computer, you must create one or more event subscriptions. Before setting up a subscription, configure both the collector and source computers as previously described. To create a subscription on a collector computer, perform the following procedure:

1. In Event Viewer, right-click Subscriptions and select Create Subscription.

2. If prompted, click Yes to configure the Windows Event Collector Service to start automatically.

3. In the Subscription Properties dialog box shown in Figure 13-22, type a name for the subscription. You can also type a description if you want.

4. Select and configure the type of subscription you want to create—Collector Initiated or Source Computer Initiated. Specify Computers or Computer Groups.

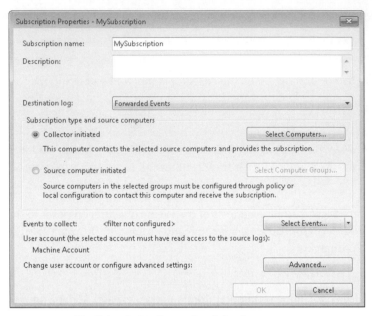

FIGURE 13-22 The Subscription Properties dialog box

5. Click the Select Events button in the Subscription Properties dialog box to open the Query Filter dialog box. Use this dialog box to define the criteria that forwarded events must match. Then click OK.

6. If you want, you can click the Advanced button in the Subscription Properties dialog box to open the Advanced Subscription Settings dialog box. You can configure three types of subscriptions: Normal, Minimize Bandwidth, and Minimize Latency.

> **NOTE SPECIFYING THE ACCOUNT THE SUBSCRIPTION USES**
>
> Use the Advanced Subscription Settings dialog box to configure the account the subscription uses. Whether you use the default Machine Account setting or specify a user, you must ensure that the account is a member of the source computer's Event Log Readers group (or, if you are collecting Security Event log information, the local Administrators group).

7. Click OK in the Subscription Properties dialog box to create the subscription.

PRACTICE Using Performance Monitor to Generate a Snapshot of Disk Performance Data

In this practice, you take a snapshot of performance data on your Canberra computer. You then view this data in graph, histogram, and report format. You will probably obtain different results from the Canberra computer in your practice network. Before you carry out this practice, connect a second storage device, such as a second hard disk or USB flash memory, to your computer.

EXERCISE 1   Add and Monitor Disk Counters

In this exercise, you add counters that enable you to monitor the performance of your system (C:) hard disk volume. If you have additional volumes on a single hard disk or additional hard disks on your system, you can extend the exercise to monitor them as well.

> **NOTE   DISKPERF**
>
> Both logical and physical disk performance counters are enabled on demand by default on Windows 7. The *Diskperf* command still exists, and you can use it to enable or disable disk counters forcibly for older applications that use *ioctl_disk_performance* to retrieve raw counters.

> **MORE INFO   THE *IOCTL_DISK_PERFORMANCE* FILE**
>
> For more information about *Ioctl_disk_performance,* see *http://msdn.microsoft.com/en-us/library/ms804569.aspx.* Note, however, that this is an older feature and is unlikely to be tested in the 70-680 examination.

A bottleneck affecting disk usage and speed has a significant impact on a computer's overall performance. To add counters that monitor disk performance, perform the following procedure:

1. Log on to the Canberra computer using the Kim_Akers account.
2. Open Performance Monitor.
3. In Performance Monitor, click the Add button (the green + symbol).
4. In the Add Counters dialog box, ensure that Local Computer is selected in the Select Counters From Computer drop-down list.
5. Select the Show Description check box.
6. Select any counters currently listed in the Added Counters pane and click Remove.
7. In the Counter Selection pane, expand LogicalDisk and select % Free Space. In the Instances Of Dialog Box pane, select C:, as shown in Figure 13-23. The LogicalDisk\% Free Space counter measures the percentage of free space on the selected logical disk drive. If this falls below 15 percent, you risk running out of free space for the operating system to store critical files.
8. Click Add to add this counter.
9. In the Counter Selection pane, expand PhysicalDisk and select % Idle Time. In the Instances Of Dialog Box pane, select C:, as shown in Figure 13-24. This counter measures the percentage of time the disk was idle during the sample interval. If this value falls below 20 percent, the disk system is said to be saturated, and you should consider installing a faster disk system.
10. Click Add to add this counter.

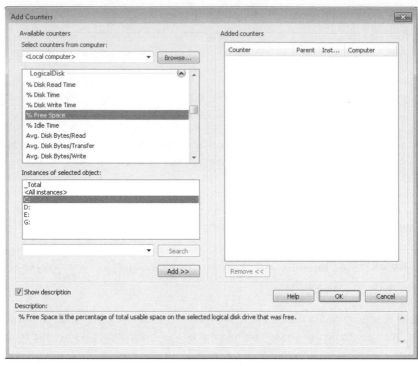

FIGURE 13-23 Selecting the Logical Disk\% Free Space Counter for the C: drive

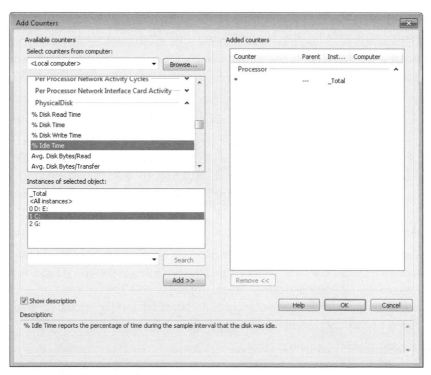

FIGURE 13-24 Selecting the Physical Disk\% Idle Time Counter for the C: drive

11. Use the same technique to add the C: instance of the PhysicalDisk\Avg. Disk Sec/Read counter. This counter measures the average time in seconds to read data from the disk. If the value is larger than 25 milliseconds (ms), the disk system is experiencing latency (delay) when reading from the disk. In this case, consider installing a faster disk system.

12. Use the same technique to add the C: instance of the PhysicalDisk\Avg. Disk Sec/Write counter. This counter measures the average time in seconds to write data to the disk. If the value is larger than 25 ms, the disk system is experiencing latency (delay) when writing to the disk. In this case, consider installing a faster disk system.

> **MORE INFO** **PHYSICALDISK\% DISK TIME COUNTER**
>
> Because the value in the PhysicalDisk\% Disk Time counter can exceed 100 percent, many administrators prefer to use PhysicalDisk\% Idle Time, PhysicalDisk\Avg. Disk Sec/Read, and PhysicalDisk\Avg. Disk Sec/Write counters to obtain a more accurate indication of hard disk usage. For more information about the PhysicalDisk\% Disk Time counter, see *http://support.microsoft.com/kb/310067*.

13. Use the same technique to add the C: instance of the PhysicalDisk\Avg. Disk Queue Length counter. This counter indicates how many I/O operations are waiting for the hard drive to become available. If the value of this counter is larger than twice the number of spindles in a disk array the physical disk itself might be the bottleneck.

14. Use the same technique to add the Memory\Cache Bytes counter. This counter indicates the amount of memory being used for the file system cache. There might be a disk bottleneck if this value is greater than 300 MB.

15. Check that the Add Counters dialog box shows the same counters and instances as Figure 13-25. Click OK.

> **NOTE** **COUNTER INCLUDED BY DEFAULT**
>
> The Processor\%Processor Time counter is included by default and you do not need to add it. It does not appear in the list in Figure 13-25, but you can see it in the line graph, histogram, and report views shown in Exercise 2.

16. Do not close Performance Monitor. Go directly to Exercise 2.

EXERCISE 2   Set Performance Monitor Properties and Monitor Disk Performance

In this exercise, you set the sample interval and duration, read data from, and write data to the disk volume you are monitoring. You view the results in line, histogram, and report formats. Perform this exercise immediately after Exercise 1.

1. In the Performance Monitor Action pane, click More Actions and then click Properties.

2. On the General tab of the Performance Monitor Properties dialog box, in the Graph Elements section, change the Sample Every value to 5 and the Duration value to 300. Click OK.

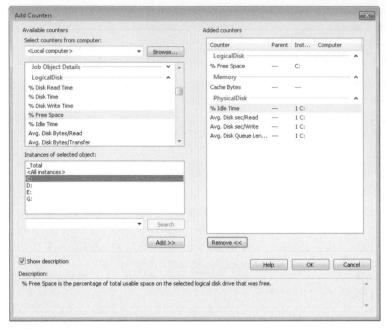

FIGURE 13-25 Counters and instances added

3. Copy a file or folder (about 100 MB in size) from your C: drive to your attached storage device.

4. Copy a file or folder (about 100 MB in size) from your attached storage device to your C: drive.

5. View the line graph in Performance Monitor, as shown in Figure 13-26. This might not easily provide the information you are looking for.

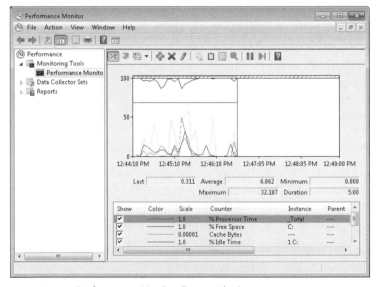

FIGURE 13-26 Performance Monitor line graph view

6. In the Change Graph drop-down list, select Histogram Bar. View the histogram in Performance Monitor, as shown in Figure 13-27.

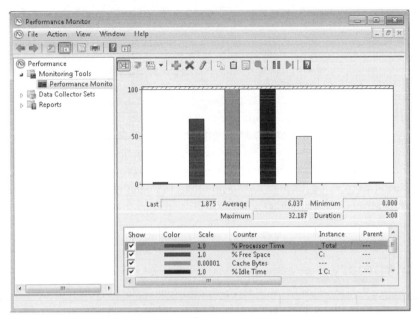

FIGURE 13-27 Performance Monitor histogram view

7. In the Change Graph drop-down list, select Report. View the Report in Performance Monitor, as shown in Figure 13-28.

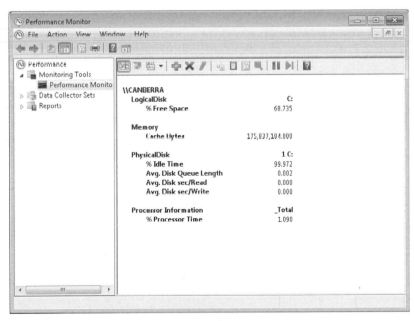

FIGURE 13-28 Performance Monitor report view

8. Analyze the counter values in light of the information given about each counter in Exercise 1. The results shown in the screen shots indicate that adequate free space remains on the C: volume and no problem occurred when copying a fairly large file or folder. Cache memory usage was significant, but this is normal and acceptable in this operation. The results you obtain are likely to be different.

> **NOTE FILE CACHING**
>
> To obtain meaningful results, Exercise 2 asked you to obtain line, histogram, and report views for the same copying operations. Had you been asked to repeat the copy operations to obtain the histogram and report views, the results would have been different. This is because Windows 7 would have cached the file or folder after the first copy and the subsequent results would have reflected only the impact of writing the file to disk and retrieving it from RAM. Using the tools is relatively straightforward; interpreting the results sometimes is not.

Lesson Summary

- You can use Performance Monitor to view performance data in real time or performance counter values captured in DCSs. A system diagnostics report gives you details about the status of hardware resources, system response times, and processes on the local computer, along with system information and configuration data.

- Reliability Monitor tracks a computer's stability. It can also tell you when events that could affect stability (such as the installation of a software application) occurred and whether any restarts were required after these events. Action Center monitors your computer and reports problems with security, maintenance, and related settings. The Windows Experience Index indicates the suitability of your current computer hardware for running resource-intensive applications.

- Task Manager gives you a snapshot of resource usage and lets you manage applications, service, and protocols. Resource Monitor allows you to view information about hardware and software resource use in real time. Process Explorer performs the same functions as Task Manager but gives you additional controls and more detailed system information.

- Event Viewer lets you access and filter event logs and create custom views. You can attach tasks to events and configure event forwarding and event subscriptions so that a central computer can store events generated on one or more source computers.

Lesson Review

You can use the following questions to test your knowledge of the information in Lesson 1, "Monitoring Systems." The questions are also available on the companion DVD if you prefer to review them in electronic form.

1. You have upgraded the hardware on a computer so that it can run an application that requires a large amount of processor resource. You use the Windows Experience Index tool to generate a new base score. The subscores for each feature are as follows:

    - Processor   5.1
    - Physical Memory (RAM)   3.3
    - Graphics   3.6
    - Gaming Graphics   2.3
    - Primary Hard Disk   5.3

    Based on these figures, what is the Windows Experience Index base score?

    A. 2.3

    B. 3.9

    C. 5.1

    D. 4.4

2. A client running Windows 7 is experiencing intermittent performance problems. You suspect the problems might be caused by an application that you recently installed but you have forgotten exactly when you did this. Which tool or feature would you use to determine when the application was installed?

    A. Reliability Monitor

    B. Action Center

    C. DCSs

    D. Performance Monitor

3. Which of the following types of information are stored in Reliability Monitor? (Choose all that apply; each correct answer presents part of a complete solution.)

    A. An application failed and needs to be restarted.

    B. A Windows error occurred and the system was rebooted.

    C. An application was uninstalled.

    D. A service was stopped.

    E. A device driver failed.

4. You are configuring a client running Windows 7 named Canberra to retrieve events from a computer running Windows 7 named Aberdeen. Both computers are on the same workgroup. Which of the following commands would you run on the collector computer to configure the Event Collector service?

    A. `wecutil qc`

    B. `winrm qc`

C. `winrm qc -q`

   D. `%SYSTEMROOT%\System32\gpedit.msc`

5. You want to use Performance Monitor to display performance data captured in a DCS. You open the tool and access the Performance Monitor Properties dialog box. On which tab can you choose whether to display current activity in real time or log files that you have saved using a DCS?

   A. General

   B. Source

   C. Data

   D. Graph

   E. Appearance

Lesson 2: Configuring Performance Settings

This lesson looks at configurations that can affect the performance of your computer and the tools that Windows 7 provides to display and reconfigure performance settings and resolve performance issues. If you do not like the tools provided, you can use Windows Management Instrumentation (WMI) scripts to write your own.

Many factors affect performance, such as the appearance of your screen or your browser window, the services and processes that are running on your computer, and the priorities and processor affinity that you assign to various processes. Performance is affected by your cache and page file settings, by the services and applications that start automatically or run even when not required, and by what processes are running and the amount of resources each consumes.

> **After this lesson you will be able to:**
> - Use a variety of Windows tools to inspect and configure settings that affect Windows 7 performance.
> - Write WMI scripts that return system information and use the WMI tools.
> - Troubleshoot performance issues.
>
> **Estimated lesson time: 45 minutes**

Obtaining System Information Using WMI

WMI lets you access system management information and is designed to work across networks. It provides a consistent model of the managed environment and a WMI class for each manageable resource. A WMI class is a description of the properties of a managed resource and the actions that WMI can perform to manage that resource. A managed resource is any object (computer hardware, computer software, service, or user account) that can be managed by using WMI.

To use WMI, you write scripts that use the WMI scripting library. This library lets you work with WMI classes that correspond to managed resources. You can use this approach to manage resources such as disk drives, event logs, and installed software.

You can use Windows Script Host (WSH), Microsoft Visual Basic Scripting Edition (VBScript), Microsoft JScript, or scripting languages such as ActivePerl to write WMI scripts that automate the management of aspects of your network. Typically, Windows Imaging (WIM) files have .vbs extensions.

You can write scripts to manage event logs, file systems, printers, processes, registry settings, scheduled tasks, security, services, shared folders, and so on. You can create WMI-based scripts to manage network services, such as the Domain Name System (DNS), and to manage client-side network settings, such as whether a computer is configured with static

Internet Protocol version 4 (IPv4) address settings or whether it obtains these settings from a Dynamic Host Configuration Protocol (DHCP) server. WMI scripts can monitor and respond to entries in an event log, modifications to the file system or the registry, and other real-time operating system changes.

A WMI script works with WMI classes, which are representations of physical features or services on a computer. Each class can contain one or more objects or instances and the objects have attributes. You can display the value of each attribute or pass this on to another routine for analysis.

Typically, you type WIM scripts using a text editor such as Microsoft Notepad and save them as *.vbs* files in a directory (for example, *C:\WIM_Scripts*) that you have created for this purpose. Be wary of using word processing software such as Microsoft Office Word for this process. Word processing software often uses different styles of quotation marks for different fonts (to cite one example), and this can cause syntax errors. You can run WIM scripts from an elevated command prompt by using the *Cscript* utility, and you can create batch files that run scripts at scheduled intervals or when triggered by an event.

For example, the following WIM script accesses instances of the *Win32_Battery* class (there is only one) and prints out the value of the *EstimatedChargeRemaining* attribute. The code looks more complex than it actually is. You can substitute other WIM classes and find the values of their attributes by substituting the class and the attributes in this routine.

```
strComputer = "."
Set objSWbemServices = GetObject("winmgmts:\\" & strComputer)
Set colSWbemObjectSet = objSWbemServices.InstancesOf("Win32_Battery")
For Each objSWbemObject In colSWbemObjectSet
Wscript.Echo "Remaining Charge: " & objSWbemObject.EstimatedChargeRemaining & "
percent."
Next
```

Figure 13-29 shows the output from this script file, saved as Battery.vbs in the C:\WMI_Scripts folder. Note that if you run this script on a desktop computer, it should complete without error, but it does not give an output.

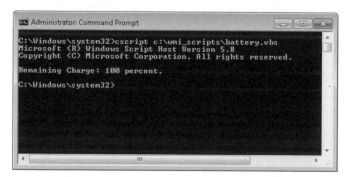

FIGURE 13-29 Estimated battery charge remaining read by a WMI script

You can substitute other WIM classes and find the values of their attributes by substituting the class and the attributes in the previous script. For example, *FreePhysicalMemory* is an attribute of objects in the *Win32_OperatingSystem* class (typically, there would be only one object in this class). The following WMI script outputs the free physical memory on a computer in kilobytes:

```
strComputer = "."
Set objSWbemServices = GetObject("winmgmts:\\" & strComputer)
Set colSWbemObjectSet - objSWbemServices.InstancesOf ("Win32_OperatingSystem")
For Each objSWbemObject In colSWbemObjectSet
Wscript.Echo "Free physical memory: " & objSWbemObject.FreePhysicalMemory & " KB."
Next
```

Figure 13-30 shows the output from this script file, saved as Memory.vbs in the C:\WMI_Scripts folder.

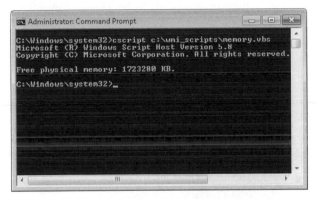

FIGURE 13-30 Free physical memory read by a WMI script

> **MORE INFO** **LIST OF WMI CLASSES**
>
> You can obtain a list of WMI classes and their attributes at *http://msdn.microsoft.com/ en-us/library/aa394554(VS.85).aspx*. For a complete WMI reference, see *http://msdn.microsoft .com/en-us/library/aa394572(VS.85).aspx*.

> **WARNING** **WMI CLASSES**
>
> If you use a WMI class, ensure that Windows 7 supports it. For example, the class *Win32_LogicalMemoryConfiguration* is deprecated and not supported. If you specify this class and run your script on a computer running Windows 7, this generates a 0x80041010 error.

You can write scripts that manage WMI classes that contain a number of objects. For example, the *Win32_Services* class contains all the services that run on a computer. The following script lists all these services:

```
strComputer = "."
Set objSWbemServices = GetObject("winmgmts:\\" & strComputer)
Set colSWbemObjectSet = objSWbemServices.InstancesOf ("Win32_Service")
For Each objSWbemObject In colSWbemObjectSet
Wscript.Echo "Display Name: " & objSWbemObject.DisplayName & vbCrLf
Next
```

You can expand the previous script to determine the state (started or stopped) and the start mode for each service as follows:

```
strComputer = "."
Set objSWbemServices = GetObject("winmgmts:\\" & strComputer)
Set colSWbemObjectSet = objSWbemServices.InstancesOf ("Win32_Service")
For Each objSWbemObject In colSWbemObjectSet
Wscript.Echo "Display Name: " & objSWbemObject.DisplayName & vbCrLf
& " State: " & objSWbemObject.State & vbCrLf
& " Start Mode: " & objSWbemObject.StartMode
Next
```

Figure 13-31 shows some of the output from the preceding script.

FIGURE 13-31 Determining the state and start mode of each service

You use WMI to administer managed resources. These include the computer system, Active Directory Domain Services (AD DS), disks, peripheral devices, event logs, files, folders, file systems, networking features, operating system subsystems, performance counters, printers, processes, registry settings, security, services, shared folders, users and groups, Windows Installer, device drivers, Simple Network Management Protocol (SNMP) management information base (MIB) data, and so on.

When you write scripts that interact with WMI-managed resources, the term *instance* is used to refer to the managed resource in the script. For example, the following script returns the drive letter for each logical disk drive on your computer:

```
strComputer = "."
Set objSWbemServices = GetObject("winmgmts:\\" & strComputer)
Set colSWbemObjectSet = objSWbemServices.InstancesOf ("Win32_LogicalDisk")
For Each objSWbemObject In colSWbemObjectSet
Wscript.Echo objSWbemObject.DeviceID
Next
```

You can prompt for input in a WMI script and store this in a variable. For example, the following (partial) script prompts the user for a password and stores it in the string variable *strPassword*, which could, for example, be used with the *Connect.Server* function to connect to a server on the network:

```
strComputer = "."
Wscript.StdOut.Write "Please enter the administrator password: "
strPassword = Wscript.StdIn.ReadLine
```

The next script is a more complete routine that you can adapt for your own purposes. It uses the *inputbox* function to prompt for a computer name and then uses the *MsgBox* function to display information about that computer's printers, processes, and processor. The code is not significantly more complex than the previous examples — you are simply displaying the values of object attributes—but using the built-in functions gives the script a professional feel:

```
computer = inputbox ("What computer do you want to check? (Press Enter if this
computer)","Computer")
set WMI = GetObject("WinMgmts://" & computer)
If computer="" then computer = "this computer"

List = ""
Set objs = WMI.InstancesOf("Win32_Printer")
For each obj in objs
        List = List & obj.Caption & ", "
Next
List=Left(List, Len(List)-2)
MsgBox List,64,"Printers on " & computer

List = ""
Set objs = WMI.InstancesOf("Win32_Process")
For each obj in objs
List = List & obj.Description & ", "
Next
List=Left(List, Len(List)-2)
MsgBox List,64,"Processes on " & computer
```

```
List = ""
set objs = WMI.InstancesOf("Win32_Processor")
For each obj in objs
        List = List & obj.Description & ", "
Next
List=Left(List, Len(List)-2)
MsgBox List,64,"Processor on " & computer
```

Note that if you specify the Aberdeen computer when you run this script on Canberra, you need to ensure the \\Canberra\Kim_Akers account has administrator rights on Aberdeen. Only a local administrator can run a WMI script on a computer, although if you have the appropriate rights, running WMI scripts on remote computers is straightforward. The script is possibly more relevant to an enterprise environment where Domain and Enterprise Admins have rights on every machine. Also, ensure that the firewalls are not blocking the information. Figure 13-32 shows the list of processes on Canberra displayed in a message box.

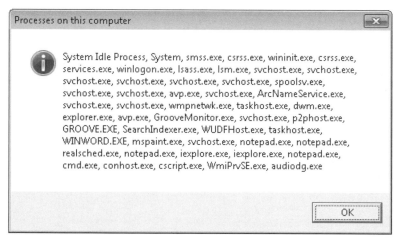

FIGURE 13-32 Processes on this computer (Canberra)

WMI consists of three primary features: the Common Information Model Object Manager (CIMOM), also known as the WMI service; the Common Information Model (CIM) repository, also known as the WMI repository; and WMI providers. Together, these features provide an infrastructure through which configuration and management data is defined, exposed, accessed, and retrieved.

WMI Providers

WMI providers, such as Win32 and the built-in Event Log provider, act as intermediaries between the CIMOM and a managed resource. Providers request information from and send instructions to WMI-managed resources on behalf of applications and scripts. Providers expose the managed resource to the WMI infrastructure using a standards-based access model, communicate with their respective managed resources by using the native application programming interfaces (APIs) of the managed resource, and communicate with the CIMOM by using WMI programming interfaces. Windows 7 introduces additional providers for Windows PowerShell and virtualization.

To create an application that manages Windows subsystems, you typically use the Win32 APIs. Without WMI, you would need to call these APIs yourself. Unfortunately, Win32 APIs cannot be called from a script, and you would need to use a programming language such as C++ or Microsoft Visual Basic. Writing C++ or Virtual Basic code is typically much more difficult than writing a script.

When you use WMI providers, you do not have to worry about calling the Win32 APIs because WMI does that for you. Also, you do not have to worry about differences between various APIs because you use a standard set of WMI commands and WMI translates those commands into commands that the APIs understand.

WMI providers are generally implemented as DLLs in the SystemRoot\System32\Wbem directory. The built-in providers, also known as *standard providers*, supply data and management functions from well-known operating system sources, such as the Win32 subsystem, event logs, performance counters, and the registry.

The CIMOM

The CIMOM handles the interaction between consumers and providers. It acts as the WMI information broker and all WMI requests and data flow through the CIMOM. When you write a WMI script, the script is directed to the CIMOM. However, the CIMOM does not directly handle your request. For example, suppose that you request a list of all the services installed on a computer. The CIMOM does not actually retrieve the list of services for you. Instead, it locates the appropriate WMI provider and asks the provider to retrieve the list. When the list has been retrieved, the CIMOM returns the information to you.

The WMI Service

The WMI service (Winmgmt.exe) implements the CIMOM on Windows 7. You can start and stop it from an elevated command prompt like any other service (for example, *net stop winmgmt*). Be aware, however, that if you stop the WMI service, this also stops the Security Center and IP Helper services. If the WMI service is stopped and you run a script or an application that requires WMI, the service automatically restarts.

The CIM Repository

Management applications, administrative tools, and scripts make requests to the CIMOM to retrieve data, subscribe to events, or to perform some other management-related task. The CIMOM retrieves the provider and class information necessary to service consumer requests from the CIM repository. The CIMOM uses the information obtained from the CIM repository to hand off consumer requests to the appropriate WMI provider.

The CIM repository holds the schema, also called the *object repository* or *class store,* which defines all data exposed by WMI. The schema is similar to the AD DS schema and is built on the concept of classes. A class is a blueprint of a WMI-manageable resource. However, unlike

AD DS classes, CIM classes typically represent dynamic resources. Instances of resources are not stored in the CIM repository but are dynamically retrieved by a provider based on a consumer request. This means that the term *repository* is somewhat misleading. Although the CIM is a repository and is capable of storing static data, its primary role is storing the blueprints for managed resources.

The operational state for most WMI-managed resources changes frequently (for example, all the events in all event logs on a computer) and is read on demand to ensure that the most up-to-date information is retrieved. This can sometimes cause queries to run slowly if a lot of information needs to be retrieved, but this is preferable to using the computer resource that would be required to maintain an up-to-date repository of frequently changing data.

CIM Classes

CIM classes are organized hierarchically and child classes inherit from parent classes. The Distributed Management Task Force (DMTF) maintains the set of core and common base classes from which system and application software developers derive and create system-specific or application-specific extension classes. Classes are grouped into namespaces, logical groups representing a specific area of management. CIM classes include both properties and methods. Properties describe the configuration and state of a WMI-managed resource; methods are executable functions that perform actions on the WMI-managed resource associated with the corresponding class.

> **MORE INFO** **DMTF**
>
> For more information about the Distributed Management Task Force, visit the DMTF home page at *http://www.dmtf.org/home/*.

WMI Consumers

A WMI consumer can be a script, an enterprise management application, a Web-based application, or some other administrative tool that accesses and controls management information available through the WMI infrastructure. For example, the script listed earlier that discovered and listed the logical disk drives on your computer is a WMI consumer. An application can be both a WMI provider and a WMI consumer (for example, Microsoft Application Center and Microsoft Operations Manager).

WMI Scripting Library

The WMI scripting library provides the set of automation objects through which scripting languages such as VBScript access the WMI infrastructure. The WMI scripting library is implemented in a single automation feature named Wbemdisp.dll that is stored in the SystemRoot\System32\Wbem directory. The Automation objects in the WMI scripting library provide a consistent and uniform scripting model for WMI-managed resources.

Variable Naming Convention

WMI scripts typically follow a consistent convention when naming variables. Each variable is named according to the automation object name in the WMI scripting library and is prefaced with *obj* (to indicate an object reference) or *col* (to indicate a collection object reference). For example, a variable that references an object called *SWbemServices* is named *objSWbemServices*; a variable that references an object called *SWbemObject* is named *objSWbemObject*; and a variable that references an object called *SWbemObjectSet* is named *colSWbemObjectSet*.

This convention is not mandatory, but it helps you understand the type of WMI object that you are working with in a WMI script. Following a consistent naming convention makes your code easier to read and to maintain, especially if you are not the person doing the maintenance.

The WMI Administrative Tools

You can download the WMI Administrative Tools at *http://www.microsoft.com/downloads/ details.aspx?FamilyID=6430f853-1120-48db-8cc5-f2abdc3ed314&DisplayLang=en,* although it is probably easier to go to *http://www.microsoft.com/downloads* and search for "WMI Administrative Tools."

The WMI Administrative Tools include the following:

- **WMI Common Information Model (CIM) Studio** Enables you to view and edit classes, properties, qualifiers, and instances in a CIM repository; run selected methods; and generate and compile Managed Object Format (MOF) files.

- **WMI Object Browser** Enables you to view objects, edit property values and qualifiers, and run methods.

- **WMI Event Registration Tool** Enables you to configure permanent event consumers, and to create or view instances of event consumers, filters, bindings, and timer system classes.

- **WMI Event Viewer** Displays events for all instances of registered consumers.

WMI CIM Studio

WMI CIM Studio is designed primarily for use by developers, particularly those who are writing providers. It assists developers to create WMI classes in the CIM repository. WMI CIM Studio uses a Web interface to display information and relies on a collection of ActiveX features installed on the system when it runs for the first time. The tool enables developers to:

- Connect to a chosen system and browse the CIM repository in any namespace available
- Search for classes by their name, by their descriptions, or by property names
- Review the properties, methods, and associations related to a given class
- See the instances available for a given class of the examined system
- Perform queries in the WMI Query Language (WQL)
- Generate an MOF file based on selected classes
- Compile an MOF file to load it in the CIM repository

WMI CIM Studio also provides wizards for generating and compiling MOF files and for generating framework provider code. When you start WMI CIM Studio from the WMI Tools menu, you first need to click the Information bar and permit ActiveX tools to run. You then select a namespace in the Connect To Namespace dialog box or use the default namespace *Root\CIMV2*. Figure 13-33 shows the WMI CIM Studio tool.

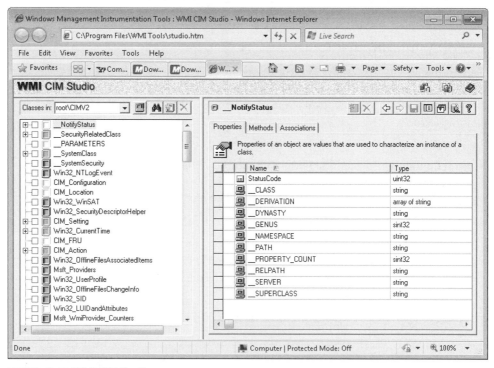

FIGURE 13-33 WMI CIM Studio

WMI CIM Studio contains a Class Explorer and a Class Viewer. When you select classes in the Class Explorer, their details appear in the Class Viewer. WMI CIM Studio wizards generate and compile MOF files.

You can use WMI CIM Studio to view the class inheritance tree for any namespace in your system or on a network by specifying the namespace path in the Classes In box, by clicking the Classes In arrow and selecting the namespace in the history list, or by browsing to a namespace.

You can search for a specific class in the namespace by clicking Search For Class in Class Explorer. In the Search For Class dialog box, select one or more check boxes under Search Options to select the type of search to perform: by class name, class description, or property name. Enter the full or partial text value to use for this search, and click Go. The results of the search appear in the Search Results pane. Click the class to view and then click OK. This displays the chosen class in Class Explorer.

You can display the properties of a class by selecting the class in Class Explorer and then clicking the Properties tab in Class Viewer. Symbols (for example, a key represents a key property) let you identify the following information about a class:

- Key properties
- System properties
- Inherited properties
- Writable properties
- The values contained in property arrays

WMI CIM Studio lets you display instances of an existing class by accessing a table of all instances of the class and viewing the associations of an instance. You can also define and display custom views of instances. You can add and delete class definitions in Class Explorer, and you can modify class definitions by adding, editing, or deleting properties, qualifiers, and methods. You can add and delete instances of a class.

You can execute regular methods on instances in WMI CIM Studio if the instances are implemented and not disabled. Click the class in Class Viewer and click Instances. Right-click the instance you want to work with and select Go To Object. Click the Methods tab in Class Viewer, right-click the method, and select Execute Method. The Parameters column shows the parameters defined for the method and their default values. Before executing the method, you can configure the parameters by editing their values.

The WQL Query Builder lets you write, save, and execute WQL queries. To use this feature, click the WQL Query symbol in Class Viewer. The MOF Generator Wizard in Class Explorer enables you to generate an MOF file for class definitions and instances from an existing repository. Typically, you run this wizard when you have created a new class or when you want to export existing repository information to another computer. You can compile the MOF file into a repository—importing any class definitions or instances from the MOF file into the current repository—by using the MOF Compiler Wizard. This wizard checks the syntax of an MOF file and creates binary MOF files.

WMI Object Browser

Unlike WMI CIM Studio, the WMI Object Browser is designed for use by system managers. This tool enables you to display the object tree for a CIM repository, view object details, edit object information, and run selected methods. You start WMI Object Browser from the WMI Tools menu and you need to click the Information bar and enable ActiveX controls. You can select a namespace or accept the default.

WMI Object Browser contains an Object Explorer and an Object Viewer. When you select objects in the Object Explorer, their details appear in the Object Viewer. Figure 13-34 shows the WMI Object Browser.

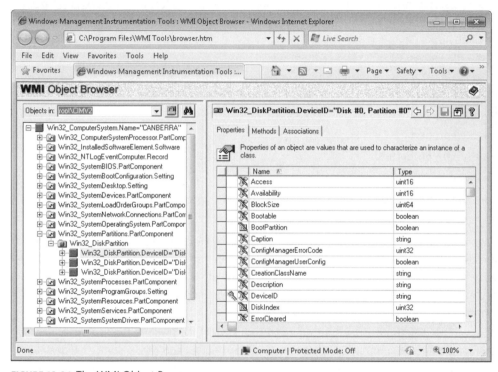

FIGURE 13-34 The WMI Object Browser

The left pane of the WMI Object Browser contains the Object Explorer, which shows the object tree for the current namespace (by default, the *Root\CIMV2* namespace on the local computer). You can select a different local namespace or a namespace on a remote computer. The Object Explorer shows a hierarchy of the instances that are found in the selected namespace and any instance in the namespace can be selected as the root of the tree.

The tree shows regular objects and grouping nodes. Grouping nodes are not objects themselves but instead are used to organize objects. The symbols next to the names indicate the type of object or node. Resting the mouse over an object in the tree displays the object's path, which identifies the object in the namespace.

The right pane of WMI Object Browser shows the Object Viewer. You can select the Properties, Methods, or Associations tab for an object. Figure 13-35 displays the Associations tab. The Object Viewer displays the title of the current view above the tabs. For a single object, the title is the object path of the instance currently displayed. For a multiple-object table, the title describes the group of objects currently displayed.

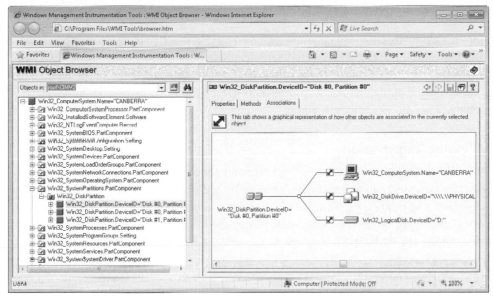

FIGURE 13-35 WMI Object Browser Associations tab

WMI Object Browser enables you to do the following:

- Display the object tree contained in a specified CIM repository
- Reroot the object tree.
- Display properties, methods, and associations for a selected object.
- Display instances of grouped objects.
- Display property and object qualifiers.
- Execute methods on a selected object.
- Edit property values and object and property qualifiers.

You can view the object tree for any namespace in your system or on a network by entering the namespace path in the Objects In box or selecting it in the history list. You can also browse for a namespace or right-click the object whose namespace you want to display and click Go To Namespace. The root of the namespace can be changed temporarily in a session or permanently through the schema.

When you select a grouping node in the Object Explorer, the Object Viewer displays an instance table showing all objects in the namespace that belong to the selected group and the common properties of those objects. You can also display the details for any individual instance from the instance table by right-clicking the instance and clicking Go To Object. This displays the object's Properties tab. From the Properties tab, you can double-click a property to display property qualifiers. When the Properties tab is selected, you can right-click anywhere in the Object Viewer grid and select Object Qualifiers. Selecting the Properties tab also enables you to edit the Value field of properties that are not read-only. To return to the instance table, reselect the grouping node.

From the Methods tab in the Object Viewer, you can right-click a method and select Execute Method. The Method Parameters window displays the parameters used when executing the selected method. The Parameters column shows the parameters defined for this method and their default values. You can configure parameters by editing the values in this table before you execute the method.

WMI Event Registration

The WMI Event Registration tool is designed primarily for developers. It provides a graphical interface for what you can also accomplish programmatically. You need to install Windows Management and create a repository of classes on the target computer before you can use the WMI Event Registration Tool. You can do this by compiling an MOF file in the system directory where the WMI Core is installed. To compile the MOF file, type the following at the command-line prompt:

```
mofcomp <filename>.mof
```

However, by default, the WMI Event Registration tool uses the Eviewer.mof file found in the WMI Tools directory. This file is compiled automatically when Windows Management first starts, so the WMI Event Viewer consumer is registered as a permanent event consumer by default and you can open the WMI Event Registration tool and investigate its features.

> **MORE INFO**   **COMPILING MOF FILES**
>
> You can find out more about compiling MOF files by downloading the Windows 7 Platform software development kit (SDK) and accessing the "Mofcomp" topic in the Windows Management Instrumentation (WMI) section. However, this topic is beyond the scope of this book and the 70-680 examination.

You start the WMI Event Registration Tool from the WMI Tools menu and need to allow blocked ActiveX content on the Information bar and specify a root, as with the other tools. From the drop-down menu near the top-left of the WMI Event Registration Tool, you can select Filters, Consumers, or Timers. Double-clicking an item in the left pane opens the View Class Properties dialog box, as shown in Figure 13-36. This lets you access the Properties, Methods, and Associations tabs.

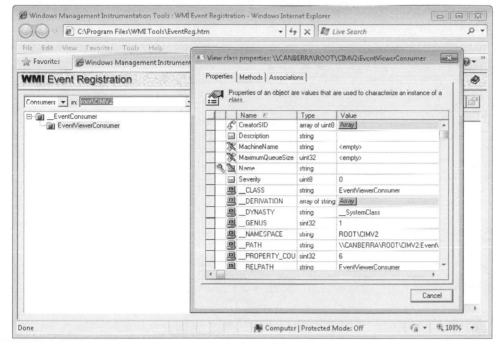

FIGURE 13-36 The WMI Event Registration tool

The WMI Event Registration Tool enables you to create, display, and modify the event consumers, filters, and timers for a given namespace and any bindings between filters and consumers. You can use the tool to do the following:

- View properties of the defined consumer, filter, and timer system classes and instances
- Add or delete event consumer instances
- Add or delete event filter instances
- Add or delete event timer instances
- Edit instance properties
- Register consumers for events by binding consumer and filters

WMI Event Viewer

WMI Event Viewer is a permanent event consumer that lets you sort and view the details of events generated in WMI by Windows Management or by event providers. Event objects are forwarded to any consumers registered for these types of events. You can register WMI Event Viewer for any event filters and view incoming events that match the filters.

You can open WMI Event Viewer from the WMI Tools menu. However, as a permanent event consumer, it is started automatically by WMI whenever an event occurs that needs to be forwarded to it. To register WMI Event Viewer for different types of events, you use the

WMI Event Registration Tool. This tool can be started either independently from the WMI Tools menu or from WMI Event Viewer tool by clicking the Register For Events control, as shown in Figure 13-37.

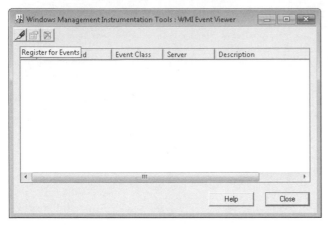

FIGURE 13-37 The Register For Events control in WMI Event Viewer

WMI Event Viewer enables you to carry out the following tasks:

- View Windows Management–generated events and event information, such as the event's date and time, class, point of origin, and description
- View event instance properties
- Start the WMI Event Registration Tool
- Clear the display

The Eviewer.mof file, installed in the WMI Tools directory along with WMI Event Viewer, contains the classes and instances required to declare and register the WMI Event Viewer Consumer Provider with the WMI event subsystem. This MOF file is compiled automatically when the Windows Management Service is first started, so that the WMI Event Viewer consumer is registered as a permanent event consumer by default.

All permanent event consumers, including WMI Event Viewer, require specific distributed component object model (DCOM) permissions to start automatically on a remote computer for a registered event. To set the DCOM launch permissions for WMI Event Viewer so you can monitor events on a remote computer, carry out the following procedure:

1. Run the Dcomcnfg.exe program from an elevated command prompt on the remote computer.

2. On the Applications tab of the Distributed COM Configuration Properties dialog box, select WMI Event Viewer, as shown in Figure 13-38, and click Properties.

3. On the Security tab of the WMI Event Viewer Properties dialog box, select Customize and click Edit.

4. Click Add.

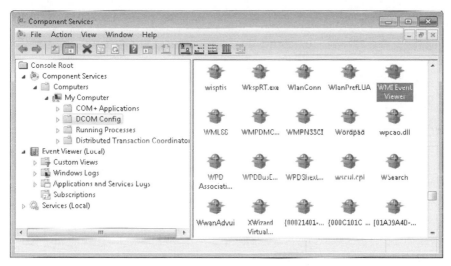

FIGURE 13-38 Selecting WMI Event Viewer in Component Services

5. In the Add Users And Groups dialog box, type **Everyone.**

6. Click Add. Ensure that all permissions check boxes are selected and then click OK. Note that WMI Event Viewer enables users and event consumers to access event information. It is not a configuration tool. Therefore, there are no security implications to setting these permissions.

Using the System Configuration Tool

You open System Configuration (MSConfig) by entering **msconfig** in the Start menu Search box, the Run box, or the command prompt. The principal purpose of this tool is to troubleshoot the Windows startup process. MSConfig modifies which programs run at startup, edits configuration files, and enables you to control Windows services and access Windows Performance and Troubleshooting tools.

You can use the System Configuration tool to configure Windows 7 to perform a diagnostic startup that loads a minimum set of drivers, programs, and services. Figure 13-39 shows the General tab of the System Configuration tool, on which you can specify Normal Setup or Diagnostic Setup. You can also customize a Selective Setup and control whether to load System Services and Startup Items. You can select the System Services and Startup Items to load and start on the Services and Startup tabs, respectively, in the System Configuration tool.

It is a good idea to look carefully at the list of programs on the Startup tab. Some software packages—for example, software that detects viruses and other malware—should run at startup and continue to run unless you have a reason to disable them. Other software packages, particularly third-party software, install themselves so that they run at startup whether they need to or not. The more unnecessary programs you have running, the slower your computer goes.

FIGURE 13-39 The General tab of System Configuration

Services are more difficult to manage than packages because of service dependencies. You might see that a service you have never heard of before runs at startup and decide to change its startup type, only to find that half a dozen essential services all depend on the one that is no longer running. The System Configuration tool lets you experiment with a computer on your test network before making changes to production computers.

> **NOTE DISABLING SERVICES WITH MSCONFIG**
>
> Although you can use MSConfig to disable services, this does not change the current state of the service. For example, you can use MSConfig to disable the running Diagnostic Policy service, but the service remains running until you reboot the computer.

The Boot tab of the System Configuration tool lets you specify the source of your boot files and, if desired, make that source the default. For example, in the Boot tab shown in Figure 13-40, the computer is dual-boot, with operating systems on both the C: and D: volumes. It can also boot into Windows 7 Ultimate from a virtual hard drive (VHD). On the Boot tab, you can specify the timeout, which is how long the boot system waits for instructions before booting from its default source.

You can specify Safe Boot and the type of Safe Boot to use (Minimal, Alternate Shell, Active Directory Repair, or Network). You can specify a No-Graphical User Interface (GUI) boot, or, if you are having problems with a video driver, specify a boot that uses the Base Video (lowest-resolution and color-depth) driver. You can require a Boot Log and Operating System (OS) Information. You can use reconfigured boot settings only once or make then permanent.

Clicking Advanced on the Boot tab lets you specify a Debug Port and Baud Rate for remote debugging and the Number Of Processors and Maximum Memory available to the boot process.

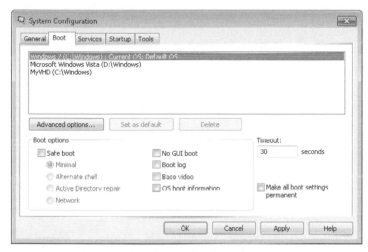

FIGURE 13-40 The Boot tab of System Configuration

On the Startup tab, you can disable automatic startup for an application by clearing the check box beside the item. You can disable automatic startup for all items by clicking Disable All. This does not prevent the software from running—it merely stops it from starting automatically when the computer boots. The Services tab works in much the same way, in that you can disable or enable automatic startup of a single service or of all services. You can also determine what third-party services are running by selecting the Hide All Microsoft Services check box.

The Tools tab performs a very useful function. Not only are all the available tools listed, but you can enable any tool from this tab. This is often easier than trying to remember or deduce the tool's place in the Control Panel hierarchy, whether the tool is a Microsoft Management Console (MMC) snap-in, or what file you need to access from the command prompt to start the tool. The tab also lists the file and file path for the application that runs each tool.

EXAM TIP

You can use either Task Manager or System Configuration to start and stop services on a computer running Windows 7 without rebooting the computer.

Using the Services Console

The Services console, an MMC snap-in, lists the same services as does the Services tab of the System Configuration tool, but it provides more information about each service and more service management options. For example, the Services console tells you the service startup type (not just whether or not it is running) and the logon details.

You can access the Services console by entering **services.msc** in the Search box on the Start menu, in the Run box, or in a command-prompt window. You can also access the tool from the Tools tab of the System Configuration tool.

When you right-click a service in the Services console, you can start it, stop it, restart it, pause it, and resume it. You can access the Properties dialog box for the service and select the General, Log On, Recovery, and Dependencies tabs.

The General tab lets you specify the startup type. This can be Automatic, Automatic (Delayed Start) Manual, or Disabled. You should consider the following when specifying the startup type:

- If a service is configured as Automatic, it starts at boot time. Some services also automatically stop when no longer required. However, if you find that you do not need a service, configure its start type as Manual or Disabled.

- If a service is configured as Automatic (Delayed Start), it starts just after boot time. Configuring this setting can result in a faster boot, but if you need the service to be up and running when you boot, configure it as Automatic. If, on the other hand, you do not need a service, configure its start type as Manual or Disabled.

- Manual mode allows Windows 7 to start a service when needed. In practice, some services do not start up when required in Manual mode. If you find that you need a service, configure it as Automatic.

- If you configure a service as Disabled, it does not start even if needed. Unless you have a very good reason for disabling a service, configure its startup type as Manual instead.

The General tab, shown in Figure 13-41, also tells you whether a service is currently started, lets you start or stop it (as appropriate), and specifies the start parameters.

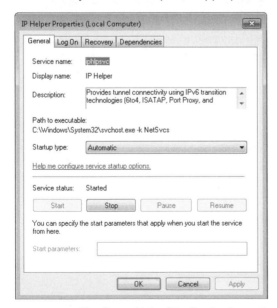

FIGURE 13-41 The General tab of the Service Properties dialog box

The Logon tab typically specifies that the service logs on with a Local System account. You can specify another account if you need to do so, typically a local Administrator account on the computer on which the service is running.

The Recovery tab specifies the actions that you take if a service fails. You can specify actions for the first failure, the second failure, and subsequent failures.

If you click Run A Program, you need to type the full path for the program that you want to run. Programs or scripts that you specify should not require user input. If you click Restart The Computer, you need to specify how long the computer waits before restarting. You can also create a message to send automatically to remote users before the computer restarts.

If you select Enable Actions For Stops With Errors, you can trigger the recovery actions when service stops with an error.

The Dependencies tab lists the services, system drivers, and load order groups that a service depends on. If a service is not running when you expect it to be, you might have disabled another service that it depends on.

Configuring Performance Options

The Performance Options tool is a Windows 7 Performance And Analysis tool that you can access by clicking Advanced Tools on the Performance Information And Tools dialog box and then clicking Adjust The Appearance And Performance Of Windows.

The Visual Effects tab of this tool is shown in Figure 13-42. You can let Windows decide what is best for your computer, adjust for best appearance, adjust for best performance, or select Custom and specify the appearance settings for your computer manually. If you select Custom, you can choose which visual effects to turn off, one by one. There are 18 visual effects that you can control, such as whether shadows are displayed under screen icons or under the mouse pointer.

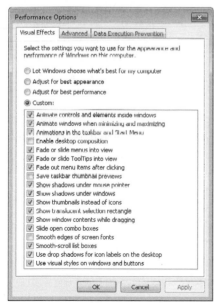

FIGURE 13-42 The Visual Effects tab of the Performance Options tool

On the Advanced tab, you can adjust for the best performance of programs or background services. If your computer is running applications (as a typical workstation does), you would specify Adjust For Best Performance Of Programs. On a server that is functioning as a Web server (for example), you would specify Adjust For Best Performance Of Background Services.

On the same tab, you can adjust page file settings. A page file is an area of disk space that can be used as paged virtual memory when running memory-intensive operations (such as print spooling) or if the system RAM is not adequate to cope with the demands of applications that are running. You can allow Windows 7 to manage memory paging (the default), as shown in Figure 13-43, or you can manually specify virtual memory allocation. If RAM is a serious bottleneck on your computer or you are running some extremely memory-intensive applications, you might want to specify memory-paging settings manually. Otherwise, you should accept the defaults.

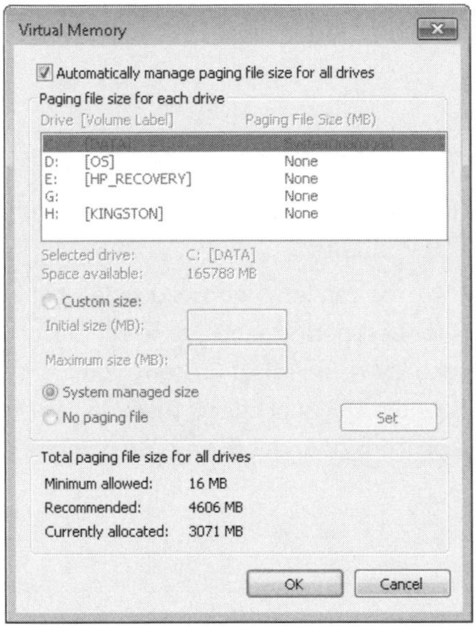

FIGURE 13-43 Virtual memory default settings

Data Execution Prevention (DEP) helps prevent damage to your computer from viruses and other security threats. Malware attacks your operating system by attempting to execute code from the sections of a computer's memory reserved for Windows 7 and other authorized programs. DEP helps to protect your computer by monitoring programs and ensuring that they use computer memory safely. If DEP detects a program on your computer that attempts to use memory incorrectly, it closes the program and notifies you.

The Data Execution Prevention tab on the Performance Options tool lets you choose whether to turn on DEP for essential Windows programs and services only (the default) or to turn on DEP for all programs and services except those that you specify. For example, in a test environment where application developers are testing applications that could inadvertently cause security problems on the computer, you would choose to enforce DEP for all programs and services and possibly specify only those in which you have complete confidence as exceptions.

Configuring Hard Disk Write Caching

Write caching uses high-speed volatile RAM to collect write commands sent to data storage devices and cache them until the slower storage media (either physical disks or flash memory) can deal with them. You can manage write caching on the Policies tab of the device's Properties dialog box that you access from Device Manager.

For USB flash memory devices (for example), you can specify the Quick Removal option, as shown in Figure 13-44. This option is typically the best choice for devices that you are likely to remove from the system frequently, such as USB flash drives, memory cards, or other externally attached storage devices.

FIGURE 13-44 The Quick Removal option for removable storage

When you select the Quick Removal option, Windows 7 manages commands sent to the device using write-through caching. In write-through caching, the device operates on write commands as if there were no cache. The cache may still provide a small performance benefit, but the emphasis is on treating the data as safely as possible. The main benefit is that you can remove the storage device from the system quickly without risking data loss. For example, if a flash drive were to be accidentally pulled out of its port, the data being written to it is much less likely to be lost if the Quick Removal option is specified.

You should select the Better Performance option for devices that you intend to remove from the system infrequently. If you choose this option and the device is disconnected from the system before all the data is written to it (for example, if you remove a USB flash drive), you could lose data.

If you select Enable Write Caching On This Device (the default) on a hard disk, this improves system performance but a power outage or system failure might result in data loss. By default, Windows 7 employs cache flushing and periodically instructs the storage device to transfer all data waiting in the cache to the storage media. If you select Turn Off Windows Write Cache Flushing On The Device, these periodic data transfer commands are inhibited. Not all hard disk devices support this feature. Figure 13-45 shows the Policies tab for a hard disk.

FIGURE 13-45 The Policies tab for a hard disk

If high data transfer performance is your main objective, you should select the Better Performance option for removable storage and select Enable Write Caching On The Device for hard disks. These are the defaults if the system hardware and storage device support these features. However, if your system or power source has known issues with sustaining power, you should not use these settings. In general, it is best to use the Safe Removal applet before you remove any external storage device from your system.

Troubleshooting Performance Problems with Event Viewer

As an IT professional, you sometimes are required to to view details of software and hardware problems affecting Windows performance to troubleshoot these problems. You can view event logs in Event Viewer, as described in Lesson 1 of this chapter, and filter by event type. The events you are looking for are mostly found in the Operational container under Diagnostic-Performance, which you access by expanding Microsoft and then Windows in the Event Viewer tree pane.

However, there is a more straightforward method of accessing this information. Click the Performance Information And Tools item of Control Panel. Click Advanced Tools in this dialog box, and then click View Performance Details In Event Log. This opens Event Viewer and displays the events in the Operational container, as shown in Figure 13-46. Examining a critical error shows that, for example, the Canberra computer had a problem during the boot process.

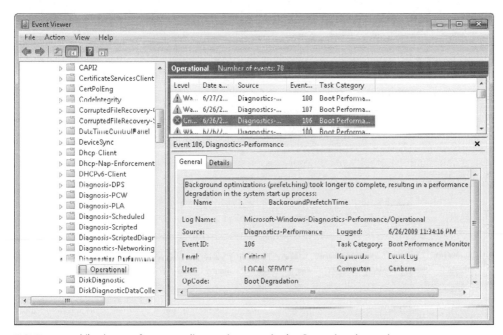

FIGURE 13-46 Viewing performance diagnostic events in the Operational container

---

NOTE **DEVICE DRIVERS**

If a device is not working properly, then this has an effect on performance that is often catastrophic. You need to ensure that (in general) the latest device drivers are installed for all your devices. The exception is when a new device driver does not work as well as its predecessor, in which case you need to roll back to the old device driver. Chapter 4, "Managing Devices and Disks," discusses this topic in detail.

NOTE **POWER PLANS**

Power plans and configuring power settings are mentioned in the examination objectives covered in this chapter. However, Chapter 11, "BitLocker and Mobility Options," discusses these topics in depth, and there is no point duplicating that material here.

Using Task Manager to Configure Processes

Lesson 1 described how you use Task Manager to close failed applications and manage services. You can also use the tool to configure the processes that implement services. If a process is particularly significant and should be allocated more resources, you can set a higher priority for that process. If a process is using too many resources, or if the speed at which a process works is unimportant, you can assign it a lower priority and hence free resources for other processes.

If your computer has more than one processor, you can configure the affinity of your processes to use a particular processor. By default, processes that install on a multiprocessor computer are set to use whatever processor is available. If an additional processor is added retrospectively to a computer, however, processes might require configuration so they can use that processor. For example, if Task Manager or Performance Monitor counters show that one processor on a dual-processor computer is heavily used and the other is not, you should change the affinity so resource-intensive processes use both processors. You also have the option of changing the affinity of some processes so that they use only the second processor.

To determine what process or processes are used by a service, right-click the service in the Services tab of Task Manager and click Go To Process. This selects the Processes tab and highlights the relevant process. To change the priority of a process, right-click the process and click Set Priority. As shown in Figure 13-47, you can choose one of six priority levels. Do not select Realtime, though—this could seriously affect the operation of other processes on your computer.

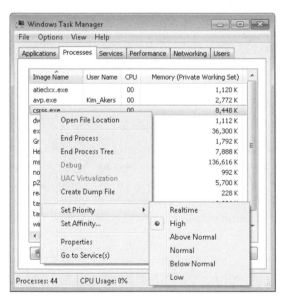

FIGURE 13-47 Setting process priority in Task Manager

To determine the affinity of a process and change it if necessary, right-click the process and click Set Affinity. You cannot change the affinity of certain system processes, and you cannot change affinity if the computer has only one processor. Otherwise, the Processor Affinity dialog box appears, as shown in Figure 13-48, and you can configure process affinity.

FIGURE 13-48 The Processor Affinity dialog box

Configuring Networking Performance

Networking performance on an enterprise network depends upon a large number of factors, such as the type of Ethernet or wireless connections used, the speed of switches and routers, the number of devices on a network, and so on. However, in a small network, users tend to define networking performance by the speed of connection to other computers on the network (if they are transferring files) and the performance of their Internet connections.

Configuring Internet Options can have a significant effect on networking performance and on computer performance in general. As an IT professional, you are aware that temporary Internet files can take up a considerable amount of disk space and should be deleted on a regular basis. You know that users with excessively large mailboxes can experience lengthy logon times, especially when they are downloading their profiles from a central server in the enterprise environment. These however, are matters that involve user training rather than configuration.

The Internet Options dialog box offers configuration options that can affect networking performance. You can access this dialog box from Network And Internet on Control Panel or from your browser. On the General tab, you can delete temporary Internet files and other downloaded information such as Web form information. However, in the context of networking performance settings, the most significant tab in the dialog box is the Advanced tab, shown in Figure 13-49.

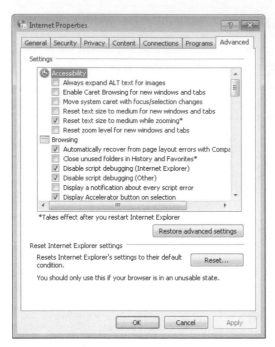

FIGURE 13-49 The Internet Options Advanced tab

The Advanced tab enables you to configure Accessibility, Browsing, International, Multimedia, Printing, and Security settings. Some of these have little or no impact on performance, whereas others can affect performance considerably. Typically, for example, Accessibility features would not be considered a performance issue, but if large font or caret browsing is set for a user that does not need them, then the perceived performance for that user is reduced.

The Browsing settings can impinge on performance. For example, if you do not disable script debugging and display notifications about script errors, the user's browsing experience slows down. These settings are useful if you are debugging a new Web site that runs scripts but are inappropriate for the standard user. Even the simplest setting, such as choosing to always underline links, can slow browsing on a slow or heavily used site.

If you are accessing sites that provide multimedia files for either streaming or downloading you can choose (for example) whether to play sounds and animations, automatically resize images, or use smart image dithering. In general effects that enhance the user's multimedia experience often also slow down site access and browsing.

The more secure a site is, the slower it tends to be because of additional security checks. Typically, this is something you and your users need to accept. You should not reduce security merely to shorten access times. Nevertheless, it is probably not necessary to warn users whenever they browse from an HTTPS secure site to an insecure HTTP site.

Windows Performance Analysis Tools

The Windows Performance Toolkit (WPT) contains performance analysis tools that are new to the Windows SDK for Windows 7, Windows Server 2008, and Microsoft .NET Framework 3.5. WPT can be used by a range of IT Professionals including system administrators, network administrators, and application developers. The tools are designed for measuring and analyzing system and application performance on Windows Vista, Windows Server 2008, Windows Server 2008 R2, and Windows 7.

Windows performance analysis tools analyze a wide range of performance problems including application start times, boot issues, deferred procedure calls (DPCs), interrupt service requests (ISRs), system responsiveness issues, application resource usage, and interrupt storms.

These tools ship with the Microsoft Windows SDK for Windows Server 2008 and .NET Framework 3.5, which you can download at *http://www.microsoft.com/downloads/details .aspx?FamilyId=F26B1AA4-741A-433A-9BE5-FA919850BDBF&displaylang=en* (although it is probably easier to go to the Microsoft Download Center at *http://www.microsoft.com/ downloads* and search for it). This SDK provides documentation, samples, header files, libraries, and tools to develop applications for Windows XP; Windows Server 2003; Windows Vista; Windows Server 2008; Windows Server 2008 R2; Windows 7; and .NET Framework versions 2.0, 3.0, and 3.5. You download and install the SDK in the practice later in this lesson.

The WPT is released as an MSI installer (one per architecture) and contains the Performance Analyzer tool suite, consisting of the following tools:

- **The Trace Capture, Processing, and Command-Line Analysis tool (Xperf.exe)** This tool captures traces, processes them for use on a computer, and supports command-line (action-based) trace analysis.

- **The Visual Trace Analysis tool (Xperfview.exe)** This tool presents trace content in the form of interactive graphs and summary tables.

- **The On/Off Transition Trace Capture tool (Xbootmgr.exe)** This tool automates on/off state transitions and captures traces during these transitions.

The Trace Capture, Processing, and Command-Line Analysis Tool

Xperf.exe is a command-line tool that provides the following features:

- Event Tracing for Windows (ETW) trace control
- ETW trace merging and enhancements by including other events
- Executable image and symbol identification
- Trace dump capabilities
- Support for post-processing

This tool manages the end-to-end operations that are needed to generate a trace file for analysis. You use Xperf.exe in the practice later in this lesson.

Xperf.exe enables events in the operating system by using groups and flags. These flags enable and disable events from providers in various parts of the operating system. For example, flags can direct the kernel, services, and applications to one or more trace files by using log sessions with custom configurations. You can then merge all traces into a single aggregate trace file that is referred to as a merged trace file.

When Xperf generates this file, it collects additional information from the operating system and adds it to the aggregate trace. You can process the merged trace file on any supported operating system without reference to the system that generated the trace. You can then use Performance Analyzer (Xperfview.exe) to analyze the merged file, you can post-process the merged file into a text file, or you can use actions to do other types of processing. Actions produce summarized outputs that are specific to an area of interest, such as boot, shutdown, suspend, and resume operations, or to a type of system event, such as sampled profile, context switches, DPCs and ISRs, disk I/O, registry accesses, file accesses, or system configuration.

The Visual Trace Analysis Tool

The Visual Trace Analysis tool, or Performance Analyzer, is used to view the information from a single trace file generated by Xperf.exe. You can use the following command to start Performance Analyzer:

```
xperf file.etl
```

Xperf.exe forwards the file name to Performance Analyzer, which then opens and displays the data in the file. You can also run Performance Analyzer directly by entering **xperfview** in the Search box on the Start menu, the Run command box, or the command prompt. A Performance Analyzer trace is displayed in the practice later in this lesson.

The On/Off Transition Trace Capture Tool

Xbootmgr.exe collects information during the on/off transition phases of Windows 7. You can capture data during any of the following phases:

- Boot
- Shutdown
- Sleep and resume
- Hibernate and resume

After issuing a trace command, the test computer resets within 5 seconds.

The On/Off Transition Trace Capture tool can automate a reboot cycle during which the computer running Windows 7 is shut down and rebooted multiple times. You can analyze the captured data by using the Xperf.exe and Xperfview.exe tools.

Downloading and Using the Windows Performance Analysis Tools

In this practice, you download and install the Microsoft Windows SDK for Windows Server 2008 and .NET Framework 3.5, then install the WPT and use the Xperf.exe tool to generate a trace.

EXERCISE 1   Downloading and Installing the SDK

In this exercise, you download and install the SDK. The exercise gives a direct link to the SDK download file, but you might find it easier to browse to this link. Perform the following steps:

1. Log on to the Canberra computer with the Kim_Akers account.

2. Insert a blank recordable DVD-ROM into your optical drive. Close the Autoplay box.

3. Open your browser and access *http://www.microsoft.com/downloads/details .aspx?FamilyId=F26B1AA4-741A-433A-9BE5-FA919850BDBF&displaylang=en*.

4. Click Download.

5. In the File Download box, click Open. The download takes some time.

6. If prompted, click Allow to close the Internet Explorer Security dialog box.

7. In the Windows Disc Image Burner, select Verify The Disc After Burning, and then click Burn.

8. When you have burned and verified the DVD-ROM, it ejects automatically. Close the Windows Disc Image Burner. Insert the DVD-ROM into the optical drive.

9. In the Autoplay box, click Run Setup.exe.

10. If prompted, click Yes to clear the User Account Control (UAC) dialog box.

11. The Windows SDK Setup Wizard opens. Click Next.

12. Read the License terms, select I Agree, and then click Next.

13. Click Next to accept the Folder defaults.

14. Click Next to accept the Installation Options defaults.

15. Click Next to start the Installation.

16. Click Finish when installation completes. Read the SDK release notes.

EXERCISE 2   Installing the Windows Performance Toolkit

In this exercise, you install the 32-bit version of the Windows Performance Toolkit. If your computer is running a 64-bit operating system, choose Xperf_64.msi instead of Xperf_86.msi. You need to have installed the SDK in Exercise 1 before you attempt this exercise.

1. If necessary, log on to the Canberra computer with the Kim_Akers account.

2. Open My Computer and navigate to C:\Program Files\Microsoft SDKs\Windows\ v6.1\Bin.

3. Double-click the Xperf_86.msi file. The Microsoft Windows Performance Toolkit Setup Wizard starts. Click Next.

4. Accept the License Agreement. Click Next.

5. Click Typical and then click Install.

6. If prompted, click Yes to clear the UAC dialog box.

7. Click Finish when setup completes.

EXERCISE 3   Using Xperf.exe to Generate Traces

In this exercise, you use the Trace Capture, Processing, and Command-Line Analysis Tool (Xperf.exe) to generate a kernel trace and a user trace. You combine the traces and process the results into a text file. You need to have completed Exercises 1 and 2 before you attempt this exercise.

1. If necessary, log on to the Canberra computer with the Kim_Akers account.

2. Open an elevated command prompt.

3. Start the kernel trace. The kernel session does not need a specified name because its name is unique. The groups Base and Network are enabled on the kernel provider. The trace is collected in a file called *Kernel.etl*. To accomplish this, enter the following command:

   ```
   xperf -on Base+Network -f kernel.etl
   ```

4. Start a user trace named UserTrace and enable the provider's Microsoft-Windows-Firewall to it. This trace is collected in a file called User.etl. To accomplish this task, enter the following command:

   ```
   xperf -start UserTrace -on Microsoft-Windows-Firewall -f user.etl
   ```

5. Stop the UserTrace session so the user-mode provider no longer produces events to this session. To accomplish this, enter the following command:

   ```
   xperf -stop UserTrace
   ```

6. Stop the kernel session. To accomplish this, enter the following command:

   ```
   xperf -stop
   ```

7. Merge the user and kernel traces into a single trace called Single.etl. To accomplish this, enter the following command:

   ```
   xperf -merge user.etl kernel.etl single.etl
   ```

8. Process the binary trace file Single.etl into a text file called C:\Mytrace.txt. To accomplish this, enter the following command:

   ```
   xperf -i single.etl -o c:\mytrace.txt -a dumper
   ```

Figure 13-50 shows the Xperf commands used in this procedure. Note that there was a problem loading a DLL associated with the On/Off Transition Trace Capture Tool, but this tool was not used so the procedure completed satisfactorily. Figure 13-51 shows a portion of the text file that was created. Figure 13-52 shows the combined trace (Single.eti) displayed in the Performance Analyzer.

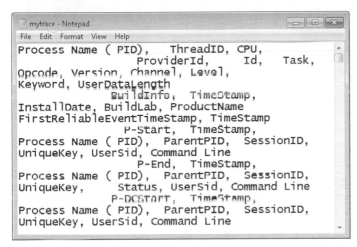

FIGURE 13-50 Xperf commands used to capture and merge traces

```
Process Name ( PID),     ThreadID, CPU,
                        ProviderId,    Id,    Task,
Opcode, Version, Channel, Level,
Keyword, UserDataLength
                BuildInfo,  TimeStamp,
InstallDate, BuildLab, ProductName
FirstReliableEventTimeStamp, TimeStamp
                P-Start,  TimeStamp,
Process Name ( PID),  ParentPID,  SessionID,
UniqueKey, UserSid, Command Line
                P-End,  TimeStamp,
Process Name ( PID),  ParentPID,  SessionID,
UniqueKey,     Status, UserSid, Command Line
                P-DCStart,  TimeStamp,
Process Name ( PID),  ParentPID,  SessionID,
UniqueKey, UserSid, Command Line
```

FIGURE 13-51 Trace information captured in a text file

Lesson Summary

- You can write WMI scripts to customize the system information you retrieve from a computer and generate your own performance-measuring tools.

- The System Configuration Tool modifies which programs run at startup, edits configuration files, and enables you to control Windows services and access Windows Performance and Troubleshooting tools. The Services console lets you manage and configure services and gives you more options than either the Services tab of Task Manager or the Services tab of the System Configuration tool.

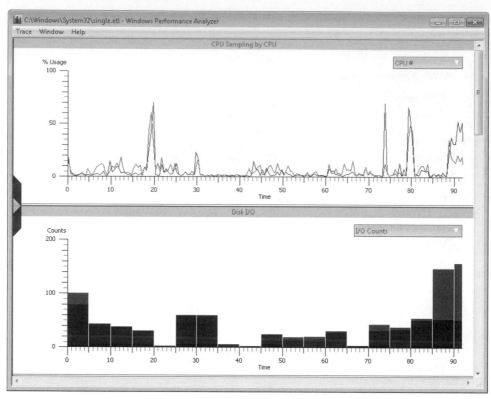

FIGURE 13-52 Captured trace displayed in Performance Analyzer

- The Performance Options tool lets you configure visual effects and specify whether the system is adjusted for best performance of applications or background services. It lets you configure page file (virtual memory) settings and DEP.

- The Windows Performance Analysis tools, downloaded as part of the Windows Server 2008 SDK, analyze a wide range of performance problems including application start times, boot issues, DPCs, ISRs, system responsiveness issues, application resource usage, and interrupt storms.

Lesson Review

You can use the following questions to test your knowledge of the information in Lesson 2, "Configuring Performance Settings." The questions are also available on the companion DVD if you prefer to review them in electronic form.

> **NOTE ANSWERS**
>
> Answers to these questions and explanations of why each answer choice is correct or incorrect are located in the "Answers" section at the end of the book.

1. What WIM tool do you use to view Windows Management–generated events and event information, such as the event's date and time, class, point of origin, and description?

   A. WMI CIM Studio

   B. WMI Object Browser

   C. WMI Event Registration Tool

   D. WMI Event Viewer

2. Which Windows Performance Analysis tool captures user and kernel traces and can merge them to form a combined trace?

   A. Performance Analyzer

   B. On/Off Transition Trace Capture

   C. Trace Capture, Processing, and Command-Line Analysis

   D. Visual Trace Analysis

3. Which tool provided by Windows 7 helps you determine which applications are responsible for activity on your hard disk, including which files and folders are being accessed?

   A. Process Explorer

   B. Resource Monitor

   C. Task Manager

   D. Windows Experience Index

4. A number of processor-intensive applications have been performing slowly on your computer. As a result, you add a second processor. This does not solve your problem, however, and you examine processor usage with Task Manager and Performance Monitor. You deduce that several key processes are using only the original processor. How do you ensure that these processes use whatever processor is available?

   A. Configure Process Affinity on the Processes tab of Task Manager.

   B. Configure Process Priority on the Processes tab of Task Manager.

   C. Select Adjust For Best Performance Of Programs on the Advanced tab of the Performance Options tool.

   D. Reconfigure Virtual Memory settings on the Advanced tab of the Performance Options tool.

5. Your computer is configured to dual-boot between Windows Vista Professional and Windows 7 Enterprise. Currently, it boots into Windows Vista by default. You want to specify Windows 7 as the startup default operating system and configure how Windows 7 reacts in the event of a system failure. You boot the computer into Windows 7. What tool do you use to accomplish your goal?

   A. The Services console

   B. Performance Options

   C. Task Manager

   D. System Configuration

Chapter Review

To further practice and reinforce the skills you learned in this chapter, you can perform the following tasks:

- Review the chapter summary.
- Review the list of key terms introduced in this chapter.
- Complete the case scenarios. These scenarios set up real-world situations involving the topics of this chapter and ask you to create a solution.
- Complete the suggested practices.
- Take a practice test.

Chapter Summary

- Windows 7 tools such as Performance Monitor, Reliability Monitor, the Action Center, and the Windows Reliability Index let you gauge whether your computer is performing as it should, whether it needs more resources to do what you want it to do, and where performance bottlenecks are occurring.
- Tools such as Task Manager give you a snapshot of how your computer is currently performing, whereas event logs can store historical events in addition to warning you when problems occur, and DCSs can hold both current and historical counter values so you can compare a computer's performance with how it was performing at a specified past time.
- Tools specific to measuring and troubleshooting computer performance include WMI scripts, the System Configuration tool, the Services console, the Performance Options tool, and the Windows Performance Analysis tools.

Key Terms

Do you know what these key terms mean? You can check your answers by looking up the terms in the glossary at the end of the book.

- **Data Collector Set (DCS)**
- **event forwarding**
- **event log**
- **event subscription**
- **performance counter**

Case Scenarios

In the following case scenarios, you will apply what you've learned about network settings. You can find answers to these questions in the "Answers" section at the end of this book.

Case Scenario 1: Using Data Collector Sets and Event Forwarding

James Seymour is an IT professional administering the production network at Tailspin Toys. Recently, users have been experiencing intermittent performance problems when accessing a file server running Windows Server 2008 R2 from their computers running Windows 7. James checks resource usage on the file server by using Task Manager but sees no indication of excessive processor, memory, disk, or network resource usage. He needs to monitor these resources over a period of time rather than look at a real-time snapshot, and to monitor resources both when the performance problems are occurring and when they are not. From his computer running Windows 7, James opens Performance Monitor and connects to the file server.

With these facts in mind, answer the following questions:

1. How does James generate performance logs that help him analyze disk, network, processor, and memory resource usage on the server, both when problems are occurring and when performance is normal?

2. James knows roughly when problems started to occur. How can he check what applications were installed or upgraded at that time?

3. Recently, a number of your users have had problems downloading files and e-mail because the space on their local disks had reached a critical limit. James needs to create a proactive method of identifying low disk space problems on computers running Windows 7 on the Tailspin Toys network so he can ask his desktop support technicians to free disk space on client computers before critical limits are reached. How does he monitor client computers for low disk space events?

Case Scenario 2: Troubleshooting Performance Issues on a Client Computer

James is troubleshooting performance issues on a client running Windows 7 at Wingtip Toys. This is normally a desktop support job, but the computer belongs to the CEO, so James needs to do the job himself and come up with some quick solutions.

With these facts in mind, answer the following questions:

1. James runs Task Manager and finds that one of the two processors on the computer is heavily used whereas the second is hardly used at all. He checks the records and finds that one of his team had installed the second processor retrospectively because the

CEO had heard that another processor would improve performance on her computer. How does James ensure the processor resource is properly used?

2. James needs to quickly scan events in the event logs that are specifically related to performance. He knows he can create filters and custom views, but this would take time, and he needs answers now. How does James quickly access the appropriate events?

3. The CEO has a habit of pulling her USB flash memory device out of her computer without using the Safe Removal applet, especially when she is in a hurry. She has previously lost data on the USB device, but when a CEO loses data, it is (of course) the fault of technical support, not the CEO. How should James minimize the risk of data loss on the USB device?

Suggested Practices

To help you master the exam objectives presented in this chapter, complete the following tasks.

Use the Performance Monitoring Tools

- **Practice 1** Look at the standard DCSs available and experiment with creating your own. DCSs provide a powerful method of managing current and historical performance on your computer, and the only way to become comfortable with them is to use them.

- **Practice 2** It is part of any IT professional's job not only to carry out the tasks required to keep computer and network equipment performing efficiently, but also to report on these tasks to colleagues and to management. You will be judged on the clarity and relevance of your reports, and they will be a factor in your budget allocation. Learn to generate good reports.

Manage Event Logging

- This topic often seems complex at first, but it becomes clearer when you have practiced configuring subscriptions and forwarding events. You can do this initially with only two computers on your test network. Become proficient before you need to do it on a production network.

Write WMI Scripts

- Sample WMI scripts can be found on the Internet and in textbooks in your organization's library. The easiest way to learn scripting (or any other type of programming) is to understand and adapt other people's scripts before you try to write your own from scratch.

Take a Practice Test

The practice tests on this book's companion DVD offer many options. For example, you can test yourself on just one exam objective, or you can test yourself on all the 70-680 certification exam content. You can set up the test so that it closely simulates the experience of taking a certification exam, or you can set it up in study mode so that you can look at the correct answers and explanations after you answer each question.

> **MORE INFO** **PRACTICE TESTS**
>
> For details about all the practice test options available, see the section entitled "How to Use the Practice Tests," in the Introduction to this book.

CHAPTER 14

Recovery and Backup

M odern computer hardware is reliable, and it is unusual that a computer system crashes completely and needs a complete restoration. Typically crashes are hardware-related, and you can replace a hardware component and even an entire motherboard while keeping system and user files on your hard disk intact. Nevertheless files, folders, and even entire volumes can be lost, sometimes through user error, through disk failure, or because a virus forces you to wipe the hard disk.

Recovery and backup, therefore, remain core components of an IT professional's job. Well-documented procedures on production networks are typically in place if a server recovery is required and servers are often grouped in failover configurations. If user data is not held and backed up centrally, then regular backups of essential files on client computers need to be scheduled. These should happen without user intervention, preferably late at night when the backup does not impinge on the user experience.

In this chapter, you learn how to back up both files and folders and system images, and to schedule backups so they occur automatically at a specified time. You learn how to quickly restore a vital file that a user has lost or overwritten. You learn how to create and restore the system image of an entire system volume.

Exam objectives in this chapter:

- Configure backup.
- Configure system recovery options.
- Configure file recovery options.

Lessons in this chapter:

Before You Begin

To complete the exercises in the practices in this chapter, you need to have done the following:

- Installed the Windows 7 operating system on a stand-alone client PC, as described in Chapter 1, "Install, Migrate, or Upgrade to Windows 7."
- Added a second hard disk to your computer. This can be an internal hard disk or an external universal serial bus (USB) disk formatted with the NTFS file system. You need at least 20 GB of free space on this disk.

 REAL WORLD

Ian McLean

Many people use the terms *backup* and *copy* interchangeably. When I finish working on this chapter tonight, I'll copy it to a USB flash drive that I'll store in a separate location from my computer, so that if the computer crashes or is stolen, I haven't lost my work. On a weekly basis, all my user files are backed up automatically to an external hard disk that I can plug into another computer if necessary. In both cases, I'm protecting my data. So, what's the difference?

When a file is backed up, its archive attribute is set. If the file is not altered, it will not be backed up again during a scheduled backup. If there's more than one user using a computer, a backup backs up all the users' files. A standard user can copy only his or her own files.

File copying can't save registry settings or other system settings. File copying can't create a complete image of a computer or a system volume. Backups are compressed and take up less disk space than copies. Compression during backup and decompression during restore happen automatically and are invisible to the user. You cannot use the Restore Files Wizard to restore files you have copied.

Copies aren't marked as previous versions. You can't restore them using the Restore Previous Versions feature. You can copy files from any medium to any medium. You can't back up files that are stored on FAT media. You can back up files only to a hard disk (internal, external, or network drive), optical media, a virtual hard disk (VHD), or another computer.

Finally, you can copy files that you have encrypted. You can't back up encrypted files. However, there lies the rub when it comes to copying. Should you, as an IT professional, encourage the users you support to copy their files? You instinctively support the notion that users should be aware of the need to protect their data (at least I do), but the press just loves stories of lost USB flash drives containing confidential information. (It's quite easy to lose optical disks, too, but it seems to be flash memory that excites the journalists.) Either ensure that all users encrypt their files or stop them making copies.

Either way, you won't be popular.

Lesson 1: Backup

In this lesson, you use the Backup And Restore console to schedule a file and folder backup and to create a system repair disk. You learn how to set a schedule for file and folder backup and specify what files and folders you want to back up. You can also use the Backup And Restore console to create an image of a complete volume. However, if you want to schedule System Image backups, you need to use a batch file containing command-line commands, and you will learn how to create a System Image backup from an elevated command prompt.

A *System Image* is a copy of all the files and folders on the system disk (and other specified hard disks) on a computer. You can use a System Image backup to restore the computer to exactly what its configuration was when the System Image backup was created.

After this lesson you will be able to:

- Use the Backup And Restore console to schedule a file and folder backup and to perform a System Image backup.
- Create a system repair disk.
- Understand the backup file structure and backup sets.
- Create a System Image backup from an elevated command prompt.

Estimated lesson time: 35 minutes

Scheduling Backups with the Backup And Restore Console

Windows 7 Backup uses shadow copies to take a snapshot of your files, allowing the backup to completely back up files even if they are open. Backups are configured and scheduled by using the Backup And Restore console under System And Security in Control Panel. The first time you use the Backup And Restore console—when no scheduled backups are configured on your computer—it looks similar to Figure 14-1.

In this case, one of your first tasks should be to configure regular backups by clicking Set Up Backup. You are prompted for a backup destination, as shown in Figure 14-2.

You can select the following types of backup destination:

- **A second internal hard drive**   Hard drives are secure (especially when formatted using the NTFS system), relatively inexpensive, and typically always available. You can install the drive in another computer if you want to restore backed up data to that computer. However, installing a second hard drive in a computer and switching an internal hard drive to another computer is by no means as straightforward as inserting or unplugging an external device. If your computer has two internal hard drives and you have chosen to implement a dual-boot system with an operating system on both of these drives, you cannot use either of the hard drives as a backup destination for the other.

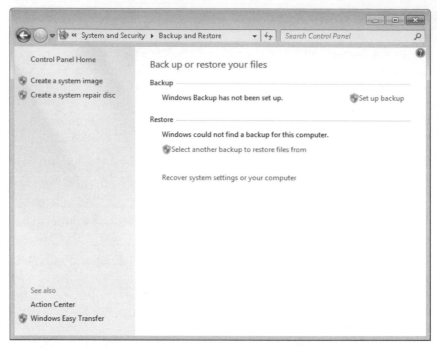

FIGURE 14-1 The Backup And Restore console when no backups are configured

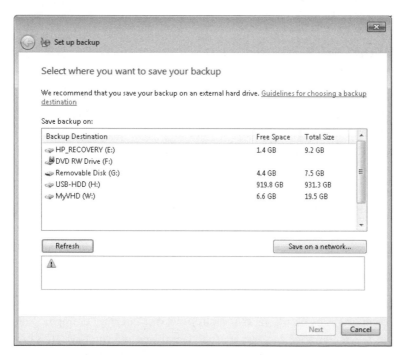

FIGURE 14-2 Selecting a backup destination

- **An external hard drive**   External hard drives are more expensive to purchase than internal hard drives, although you need to balance this against the cost of fitting the internal drive. They can be removed and stored in a secure location. However, they are typically slower than internal hard drives and tend to be less reliable, mainly because they are by default formatted using FAT rather than NTFS. You cannot use an external hard drive for a System Image backup unless you convert its filing system to NTFS. Because it is easily removable, it is more likely that an external hard drive will be missing when a scheduled backup is required.

- **DVD-ROM**   Optical disks are inexpensive and can be archived in a secure location. You can back up to both CD-ROMs and DVD-ROMs, but in practice, a typical backup would need a large number of CD-ROMs. You probably need a number of DVD-ROMs. You cannot save scheduled System Image backups on DVD-ROMs. DVD-ROMs can become corrupted over time, but the timeframe for this is a number of years.

- **USB flash drives**   Flash drive memory is considerably less expensive and flash drive devices support much more memory than they did three or even two years ago. Nevertheless, they typically support a lot less memory than hard drives and quickly fill up if you needed to keep copies of older backups. You cannot save System Image backups to flash memory. A flash drive must be able to hold more than 1 GB if you want to save a backup on it. Flash drives can be stored offsite and are small and easy to carry. They are also easy to lose.

- **Network location**   If your computer is short of disk space, you can back it up to a network location on another computer or network storage. Note that this is not the same as the situation in a production environment, where users' Documents libraries are stored on a file server and an administrator backs up the file server. You can save your backups on a network location only on computers running Windows 7 Professional, Windows 7 Ultimate, and Windows 7 Enterprise, and you need to provide credentials so that Windows Backup can access the network.

- **A VHD**   In Windows 7, you can specify a VHD as a backup location. However, the VHD file should not be on the physical disk that you are backing up, or else you could lose your backup if the disk fails. You can also carry out a System Image backup of an entire volume to a VHD disk image file. On Windows 7 Ultimate and Enterprise editions, you can use the Bcdedit tool to make a VHD bootable so you can boot the computer from a backed-up system image.

When you have selected your backup medium, click Next and then either let Microsoft Windows choose the files and folders to be backed up or select them manually. If you let Windows choose what is backed up, your backup includes data files that are saved locally in libraries, on the desktop, and in default Windows folders for all users with accounts on the computer. Default Windows folders include AppData, Contacts, Desktop, Downloads, Favorites, Links, Saved Games, and Searches. If the drive you are saving your backup on is formatted using the NTFS file system and has enough disk space, a System Image of your programs, your operating system, and all drivers and registry settings is also included in the backup. However, regular System Image backup cannot be scheduled through the Backup And Restore console.

If you choose to select which files you want to be backed up, you can choose local files and folders except for Program files (applications), files stored on hard disks that are formatted using the FAT file system, files in the Recycle Bin, and temporary files on drives smaller than 1 GB. You can also specify whether your backup includes a System Image of your drive or drives that contain an operating system (assuming that your backup destination supports this).

You can optionally select the Additional Data item. This backs up items such as Favorites, Saved Games, Searches, Desktop data, and Links. You also have the option of backing up the Documents library. If you want to ensure a particular directory is backed up, specify it directly; or if you let Windows choose the folders to back up, add the directory to the Documents library. When you let Windows choose, it always backs up the Documents library.

EXAM TIP

Remember that libraries are virtual folders. You can add folders to libraries. You cannot move folders to libraries.

When you choose (or let Windows choose) what you want to back up, you are prompted to review your backup settings. By default, backups occur every Sunday at 7:00 P.M. If this is not convenient, you can click Change Schedule. When you are happy with the settings, you click Save Settings And Run Backup. The backup runs immediately (and again at the next time scheduled). Figure 14-3 shows the Backup And Restore console as it appears after you have configured a scheduled backup.

The Backup And Restore console supports two kinds of backup:

- **System Image** The System Image backup backs up an entire volume to a .vhd disk image file (which has been compacted to remove empty space). This type of backup enables you to quickly restore a computer and all running applications. However, if you want to boot from this image, as you can in Windows Enterprise and Ultimate editions, you need to ensure that the image is kept up to date. Otherwise, you boot with an image that is unsafe because updates that address known vulnerabilities are not installed. Chapter 2, "Configuring System Images," addresses this issue.

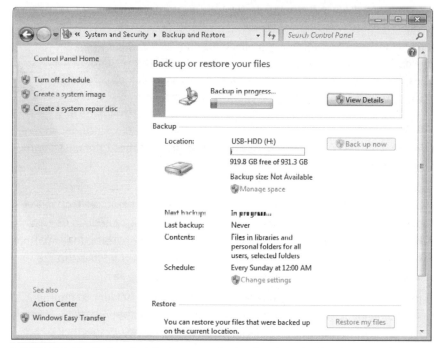

FIGURE 14-3 The Backup And Restore console showing that a backup has started

- **Files and folders** You can store files and documents to compressed (.zip) files. File backups are incremental by default. Also, file backups do not back up system files, program files, Encrypting File System (EFS)–encrypted files, temporary files, files in the Recycle Bin, or user profile settings. File backups can back up to either local media or a shared folder on the network.

NOTE **MOUNTING A SYSTEM IMAGE IN MICROSOFT WINDOWS VIRTUAL PC**

You can also mount a system image created by System Image backup in Windows Virtual PC, which is included when you install Windows XP Mode.

MORE INFO **VIRTUAL PC AND WINDOWS XP MODE**

For more information about Virtual PC and Windows XP Mode, access *http://www.microsoft .com/windows/virtual-pc/* and follow the links.

EXAM TIP

Remember that the Backup And Restore utility in Windows 7 writes System Image backups in VHD format. In Windows 7 Enterprise and Ultimate editions, you can mount a backup in the Disk Management console by using the Diskpart utility and then use the Bcdedit utility to make the VHD bootable. The Backup And Restore utility does not store System Image backups in any other file format, such as ISO, WIM, or BAK.

Backup And Restore in Windows 7 supports backing up data files to CD-ROM, DVD-ROM, hard disk (including VHD files), or a network location. You can use Backup And Restore to write a System Image backup to an internal hard disk drive, an external hard disk drive (if formatted with the NTFS file system) and a network location. You cannot use Backup And Restore to write a System Image backup to a USB flash drive, a writable DVD, or a tape drive.

Bear in mind that you can save your backups on a network location only on computers running Windows 7 Professional, Windows 7 Ultimate, and Windows 7 Enterprise. Remember also that tape drives are not supported by the Backup And Restore utility.

> *NOTE* **BitLocker**
> You cannot select a backup destination that has BitLocker enabled.

File and Folder Backups

The Backup And Restore console graphical user interface (GUI) manually initiates backup and restore sessions and schedules automatic backups. You need to schedule client computers that store important data for automatic backup. After you first configure automatic file backup using the Backup And Restore console, Windows 7 regularly backs up your files. The first time a backup is performed, a full backup is done, including all important user documents. Subsequent backups are incremental, backing up only changed files. Older backups are discarded if the disk begins to run out of space.

For example, if you configure a nightly scheduled backup and change a file every day, a copy of that file is stored in each day's Backup Files folder. By storing multiple versions of a single file, Windows 7 gives users the opportunity to choose from several older copies of a file when using the Previous Versions tool (described in Lesson 3, "Recovering Files and Folders"). When you restore files, you need only restore from a single backup because Windows 7 automatically locates the most recent version of each file. Windows 7 uses shadow copy (described in Lesson 3) to back up the last saved version of a file. Therefore, if a file is open during the backup, that file will be backed up. However, any changes the user made since last saving the file are not backed up.

You need administrator credentials to configure scheduled backups or to manually initiate a backup. However, restoring files does not require administrator privileges unless a user attempts to restore another user's file.

If you perform a file backup to a shared network folder, the credentials used to run the backup must have Full Control share and NTFS permissions for the destination folder (known as Co-owner permissions in the Windows 7 Setup Wizard). To reduce security risks, you should set up a user account that is used only by the backup application and configure share and NTFS permissions to grant access only to the backup user. The backup account requires administrative privileges to the computer being backed up, but it needs permissions only to the share and folder on the target computer.

File and Folder Backup Structure

When a user chooses to perform a backup to an external hard disk, Windows 7 automatically creates a folder in the root of the hard disk using the computer name. Within that folder, backups are saved in the format: *Backup Set* <year-month-day> <time>. For example, if your computer name is Canberra, your backup location is H:, and you backed up on July 4, 2009, at 16:36:39, your backup is located in *H:\Computer\Backup Set 2009-07-04 163639,* as shown in Figure 14-4.

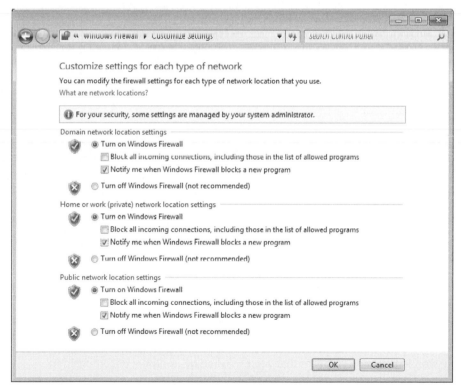

FIGURE 14-4 Backup set

The folder structure is created when you first perform a backup. However, the name of the Backup Set folder is never updated, so the date indicated by the folder name is older than the dates of the files contained within the folder. A new Backup Set folder is created only when you perform a full backup.

Within each Backup Set folder, Backup creates a series of folders that are named using the date on which the incremental backup was performed. Additionally, Backup creates a Catalogs folder within the root Backup Set folder. Figure 14-5 shows the backup folder structure for the Canberra computer. The File And Folder backup is stored in the Canberra folder. A System Image backup was not performed in this instance because this is implemented later in this lesson using commands entered in an elevated command prompt. However, if a System Image backup had been implemented, it would be stored in the WIndowsImageBackup folder on the H: drive. File permissions on all folders and files are restricted to administrators, who have full control, and to the user who configured the backup, who has read-only permissions by default.

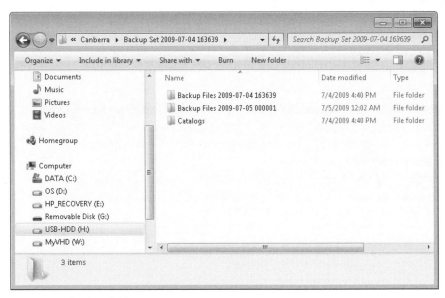

FIGURE 14-5 Backup folder structure

Within each of the backup folders is a series of compressed (.zip) files named Backup files *xxx*.zip, where *xxx* is an incremental number to make each file name unique. For example, a backup folder might contain the following files:

- Backup files 1.zip
- Backup files 2.zip
- Backup files 3.zip

These are standard compressed files that you can open by using the decompression capabilities in Windows 7 or by using third-party tools. Because Windows 7 can search compressed files, you can find a backup of a specific file by searching the backup folders and then extracting that file from the compressed folder without needing to access the Backup And Restore console directly. You can restore files backed up in Windows 7 even if your computer is booted into a different operating system.

The Catalogs folder contains a file named GlobalCatalog.wbcat. This contains an index of the individual files that have been backed up and the compressed file in which the backup is contained. Windows 7 uses this information to quickly locate a file for restoration. The Catalogs folder also contains a list of file permissions for each backed-up file. Therefore, permissions are intact if you restore files using the Backup And Restore tool. However, if you restore a file from the compressed folder directly, the file inherits the permissions of the parent folder into which it is restored rather than keeping the file permissions of the original file.

Implementing System Image Backups

System Image backups make a block by block backup of your system volume to a .vhd file, which is stored on local storage such as a second hard disk. You can store a .vhd file on a second hard disk even when that disk holds another operating system. Subsequent backups to the same media automatically perform an incremental backup. Only the portions of the hard disk that have changed are copied to the existing System Image backup. Only a single version of the System Image backup is stored.

The Backup And Restore console does not provide a graphical tool for scheduling System Image backups. You need to create a System Image backup manually from the Backup And Restore console whenever you have made significant changes to a computer's configuration. Take care that if you restore a System Image backup and boot from it, or if you make the VHD bootable for failover protection, your computer could be vulnerable unless the System Image includes security updates.

Although you cannot use Backup And Restore to schedule System Image backups, you can use the Wbadmin command-line utility to perform this function. For example, to initiate a System Image backup of the C: drive to the H: drive, you run the following command from an elevated command prompt:

```
wbadmin start backup –backuptarget:h: -include:c: -quiet
```

A portion of the output of this command is shown in Figure 14-6. Note that the H: drive needs to be formatted with the NTFS file system if it is to be used for a System Image backup. Note also that if the volume being backed up (in this case the C: drive) contains a VHD and if that VHD is mounted, the files on that VHD are not backed up. The first time you initiate a System Image backup, it backs up every block on the system volume. Each subsequent time, it updates the previous backup.

As with any command-line routine, you can put this command into a batch file and schedule it by using Windows Task Scheduler. You need to configure the task to run with administrative privileges. You do this by specifying an administrative user account and selecting the Run With Highest Privileges check box on the General tab of the task's Properties dialog box.

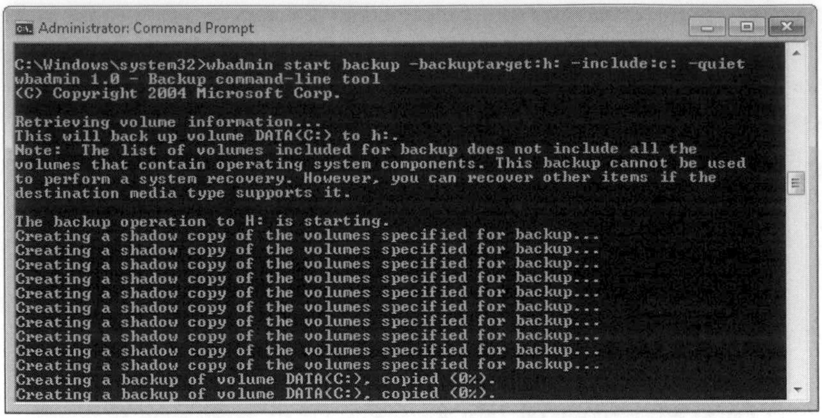

FIGURE 14-6 Performing a System Image backup using the Wbadmin utility

> **MORE INFO   Wbadmin**
>
> For more information about the Wbadmin utility, see *http://technet.microsoft.com/en-us/library/cc754015.aspx*.

System Image Backup Structure

When you create a System Image backup, Windows 7 creates a WindowsImageBackup folder in the root of the backup media. Within this folder, it creates a folder with the current computer's name. It then creates a Catalog folder containing the GlobalCatalog and BackupGlobalCatalog files, and a Backup *<year>-<month>-<date> <time>* folder containing the disk image file.

To back up an entire volume, System Image creates a VHD disk image file. VHD files were discussed in detail in Chapter 2.

System Image backups also create the following files:

- A MediaId file in the *<ComputerName>* folder to identify the disk image
- GlobalCatalog and BackupGlobalCatalog files in the Catalog folder to track the backup image versions
- Extensible Markup Language (XML) files in the Backup folder that contain configuration settings for the backup file

> **NOTE   COMPLETE PC BACKUP**
>
> A System Image backup is sometimes termed a *complete PC backup* because it backs up all the files in one or more volumes. However, be aware that a System Image backup can be used to back up only one volume in a computer that holds several. If you are using System Image backup to back up all volumes on your computer, your destination is typically a network share.

Quick Check

- You want to schedule System Image Backup to run every two weeks. How would you do this?

Quick Check Answer

- You would create a batch file that uses the Wbadmin utility to perform a System Image backup. You would use Task Scheduler in the Computer Management console to schedule this task to run on a specified day at a specified time every two weeks.

PRACTICE Configuring a File and Folder Backup

In this practice, you reconfigure your backup to include important files on your computer. You should adjust the procedure to back up your own files on your Canberra computer. You also create a system repair disk.

EXERCISE 1 Reconfiguring a Backup

In this exercise, you specify files and folders on files on your Canberra computer that you want to back up on a regular basis. You also redefine the backup schedule. The exercise assumes you have already configured a file and folder backup on Canberra specifying the default settings.

1. Log on to the Canberra computer with the Klm_Akers account.
2. Open Control Panel, click System And Security, and click Backup And Restore.
3. In the Backup And Restore window, click Change Settings.

NOTE THE CHANGE SETTINGS OPTION

The Change Settings option is not available unless you have configured a backup schedule and performed a backup. As discussed earlier in this lesson, you are prompted to do this the first time you open the Backup And Restore console.

4. Select a destination volume, for example a second internal hard disk drive or a USB external hard disk drive.
5. Click Next. On the Set Up Backup page, select Let Me Choose. Click Next.
6. Choose the files you want to back up. Your choice will probably be different from that shown in Figure 14-7. Do not select the Include A System Image Of *whatever system volumes Windows selects* check box.
7. Click Next.
8. On the Review Your Backup Settings page, click Change Schedule.

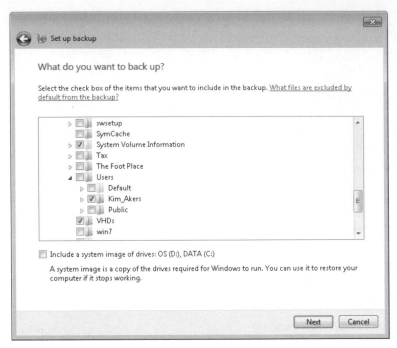

FIGURE 14-7 Choosing the files that you want to back up

9. Select a backup schedule of 12:00 A.M. (Midnight) and Daily, as shown in Figure 14-8.

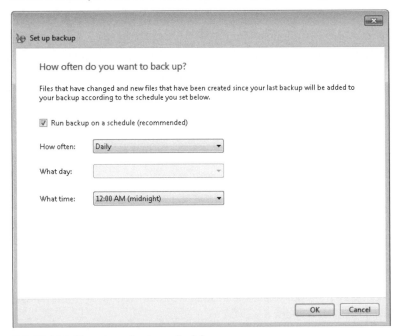

FIGURE 14-8 Choosing a backup schedule

10. Click OK. Review your backup settings. If they are OK, click Save Settings And Exit.

EXERCISE 2 Creating a System Repair Disk

In this exercise, you create a system repair disk for the Canberra computer.

1. Log on to the Canberra computer with the Kim_Akers account.

2. Open Control Panel, click System And Security, and click Backup And Restore.

3. In the Backup And Restore dialog box, click Create A System Repair Disk.

4. Insert a blank writable DVD-ROM disk in the Canberra computer.

5. Click Create Disk.

6. The Creating A System Repair Disk dialog box appears, as shown in Figure 14-9. Click Close.

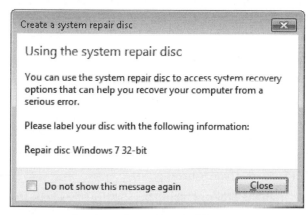

FIGURE 14-9 Creating a System Repair disk

Lesson Summary

- You can use the Backup And Restore console to schedule a file and folder backup and to start such a backup immediately.

- You can use the Backup And Restore console to start a System Image backup but not to schedule such a backup. You can, however, start a System Image backup from the command line and schedule a batch file with Task Scheduler to perform such a backup regularly.

- Whenever a file and folder backup occurs, it creates a backup set.

Lesson Review

You can use the following questions to test your knowledge of the information in Lesson 1, "Backup." The questions are also available on the companion DVD if you prefer to review them in electronic form.

> **NOTE ANSWERS**
>
> Answers to these questions and explanations of why each answer choice is correct or incorrect are located in the "Answers" section at the end of the book.

1. Clients running Windows 7 Enterprise on your employer's production network are all configured to perform a file and folder backup to a second internal hard disk every Sunday at 7:00 P.M. Company policy dictates the same setting for each computer. This is to let Windows decide what is backed up. A user has created a folder on her computer called C:\Contracts. She wants to ensure that the folder and its contents are backed up. What do you ask her to do?

   A. Ask her to open the Backup And Restore console and click Change Settings. Have her select Let Me Choose on the What Do You Want To Back Up? page, and then specify the C:\Contracts folder.

   B. Ask her to open the Backup And Restore console and click Change Settings. Ask her to configure her backup destination to be a network share on the company file server.

   C. Ask her to add the C:\Contracts folder to her Documents library.

   D. Ask her to open the Backup And Restore console and click Backup Now.

2. A user on your company network creates a new file and works on it during the day. He saves the file but decides he no longer needs it and deletes it just before the office closes. Overnight, a file and folder backup takes place. The next morning, the user decides he needs the file after all. He calls you for help. What action can you take?

   A. Restore the file from the previous night's backup.

   B. Restore the Recycle Bin from the previous night's backup. The file will be in the restored Recycle Bin.

   C. Restore the file from an older backup.

   D. Ask the user to open his Recycle Bin.

3. Kim Akers has an administrator account on a computer running Windows 7 Enterprise. Don Hall has a standard account on the same computer. Both users have Microsoft Office Word and Microsoft Office Excel files saved in their Documents library. Don stores Microsoft Office PowerPoint presentations in a subfolder of his Documents library named Presentations. He also stores digital photographs in his Pictures library. Don has created a folder called Secret in his Documents library and has encrypted the folder and its contents. He stores confidential files in that folder. When Don last logged on, he deleted some personal files but did not empty his Recycle Bin. Kim is logged on to the computer. She has plugged in a USB flash memory device that holds personal files but has not yet copied any of these files to the computer. She has never formatted the flash memory device. The computer is configured to let Windows decide what files and folders to back up. Kim opens the Backup And Restore console but does not change any settings. She clicks Backup Now. Which files are backed up? (Choose all that apply.)

   A. The Word and Excel files in Don's Documents library

   B. The Word and Excel files in Kim's Documents library

C. The PowerPoint files in Don's Presentation folder

D. The digital photographs in Don's Pictures library

E. The files in Don's Secret folder

F. The files in Don's Recycle Bin

G. The files on Kim's USB flash memory device

4. You have recently installed Windows 7 Ultimate on a laptop computer, installed applications such as Office, and downloaded and installed all outstanding updates. The computer has two internal hard disks, both formatted with the NTFS file system. You also have an external USB hard disk that you have plugged into the laptop. You used the *convert fs/ntfs* command to convert the external hard drive to the NTFS file system. You have an 8-GB USB flash memory device and the laptop contains a DVD-ROM writer. In your workplace, you can plug in to the corporate network and connect to a network share on a file server running Windows Server 2008 R2. On what devices can you create a full System Image backup of the laptop's system volume? (Choose all that apply.)

A. The second internal hard disk

B. The external hard disk

C. The USB flash drive

D. Multiple DVD-ROMs

E. The network share

5. You want to centralize backups by backing up all client computers in your company's production network to a network share on a file server running Windows Server 2008 R2. All your client computers run Windows 7, but because your company has grown through a series of mergers, some run Windows 7 Professional, some run Windows 7 Enterprise, and some run Windows 7 Ultimate. Which computers can you back up to a network share?

A. Only the computers running Windows 7 Ultimate

B. Only the computers running Windows 7 Enterprise

C. Only the computers running either Windows 7 Ultimate or Windows 7 Enterprise

D. All your company's client computers

Lesson 2: System Recovery

This lesson discusses how to restore corrupt or misconfigured system settings to a previous working system configuration. It looks at system protection, restore points, system recovery, and restoring a System Image.

The chapter considers boot options, advanced recovery methods, and how you recover from the situation when a system change prevents your computer from booting normally.

After this lesson you will be able to:

- Create a restore point manually.
- Perform a system restore to a selected restore point.
- Restore from a System Image backup.
- Boot from the Windows 7 installation DVD-ROM and run a system repair.
- Use the Advanced Boot Options.
- Configure System Protection.

Estimated lesson time: 30 minutes

Performing a System Restore

Windows 7 creates system restore points on a regular schedule and prior to events such as the installation of applications and drivers. A *restore point* contains information about registry settings and other system information. Windows 7 generates restore points automatically before implementing significant system changes. You can manually create restore points and restore a computer system to a selected restore point.

If you install an application or driver that causes your computer to become unstable, you should first attempt to uninstall the application or roll back the driver. If this does not solve the problem, you can restore system files and settings by performing a system restore to restore the computer to its last system restore point. A *system restore* returns a computer system to a selected restore point. System restores do not alter user files. Note that a system restore is not the same as a System Image restore, which is discussed later in this lesson.

The most straightforward way of starting a system restore is to enter **system restore** in the Start menu Search box and click the appropriate link. In Control Panel, you can also access All Control Panel Items, click Recovery, and click Open System Restore. In addition, you can start a system restore from the System Protection tab of the System Properties dialog box. You do this in the Practice Session later in this lesson. If you boot the from the installation media, you can select Repair Your Computer and then select Use The System Restore option. You need elevated privileges to run system restore. The System Restore Wizard is shown in Figure 14-10.

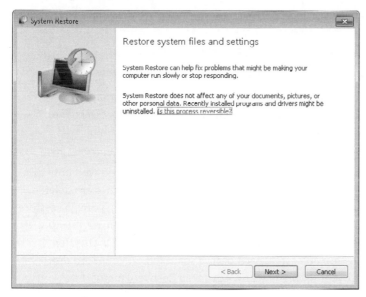

FIGURE 14-10 The System Restore Wizard

When you perform a system restore following a normal boot or following a boot that uses the Last Known Good Configuration (Advanced) option, a restore point is created that enables you to undo the changes if they do not fix your problem. However, if you perform a system restore when the computer is in Safe Mode or by using the System Recovery options, you cannot undo the restore operation. In this case, if your problem is not resolved, you can run another system restore and choose a different restore point.

A system restore restores Windows system files, programs, and registry settings. It can also make changes to scripts, batch files, and other types of executable files created by any user on your computer. System restores do not affect personal files, and they cannot help you restore a deleted file. However, this means that if you have added or altered any user documents since the last restore point was created, you will not lose your changes if you run a system restore. If you need to restore personal files, you can do this from a file and folder backup. If you need previous versions of personal files, you can use the Restore From A Previous Version feature described in Lesson 3.

The System Restore Wizard automatically recommends the most recent restore point created before a significant change, such as software installation. You can also choose from a list of restore points. Microsoft advises using restore points created just before the date and time you started noticing problems. The descriptions of automatically created restore points correspond with the name of an event, such as an update installing through Windows Update. System restores return your computer to the state that it was in before your chosen restore point.

Windows 7 reserves disk space for system restores and restore points are saved until this disk space is filled up. At this point, as new restore points are created, old ones are deleted. If you turn off system protection (the feature that creates restore points) on a disk, all restore points are deleted from that disk. When you turn system protection back on, new restore points are created. For a system restore to be effective, you need to ensure that system protection is enabled and you have at least 300 MB of free space left on your hard disk. If a system restore does not fix your problem, try an Advanced Recovery method.

> **NOTE SMALL HARD DISKS**
>
> If your hard disk is smaller than 300 MB, you need 50 MB of free space for a system restore to work. However, hard disks of this size are very uncommon.

System Protection

System protection regularly creates and saves information about your computer's system files and settings. It also saves previous versions of files that you have modified. It saves these files in restore points, which are created just before significant system events, such as the installation of a program or device driver. Restore points are also created automatically every seven days if no other restore points were created in the previous seven days. You can create restore points manually at any time.

System protection is automatically on for the drive that holds the operating system and can be enabled only for drives that are formatted using the NTFS file system. It enables you to use system restore and to restore files to previous versions. You will configure system protection, create a restore point, and perform a system restore in the practice later in this lesson.

Advanced Recovery Methods

The advanced methods available by clicking Advanced Recovery Methods in the Recovery window under All Control Panel Items in Control Panel can return Windows to a usable state if it is badly damaged. The Advanced Recovery Methods dialog box is shown in Figure 14-11.

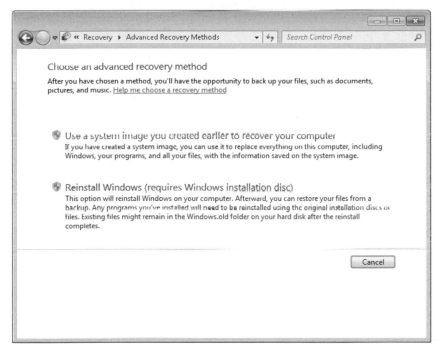

FIGURE 14-11 The Advanced Recovery Methods dialog box

The first method uses a System Image backup, which was described in Lesson 1. The second method reinstalls Windows, either from a recovery image provided by your computer manufacturer or from the original Windows installation files. Both methods can result in loss of data. Before beginning either method, you are prompted to back up your personal files to an external location, such as a USB hard disk. The procedure for restoring from a System Image backup is described in the next section. Note that restoring from a System Image backup is not the same as performing a system restore.

Restoring from a System Image Backup

A System Image restore rewrites the entire contents of a system volume. Therefore, you restore from a System Image backup by booting from the Windows 7 Installation DVD-ROM and loading System Recovery tools or by pressing F8 during the boot process. Restoring from a System Image backup enables you to quickly get a computer running after you replace a failed hard disk, or if the operating system installation has been corrupted (for example, by malware that cannot be removed except 0 by wiping the disk). It is sometimes known as *complete recovery* or *complete PC Restore*.

This procedure assumes that the System Recovery Options (otherwise known as the Windows Recovery Environment, or Windows RE) files are present on the DVD-ROM. If not, you can boot from the installation DVD-ROM and press F8 during the boot to access the Advanced Boot Options, as described in the next section of this lesson.

To restore a System Image backup, perform the following steps:

1. Ensure the backup medium is connected to your computer.

2. Insert the Windows 7 DVD-ROM. Ensure that the computer BIOS is configured to boot from the DVD-ROM.

3. Restart your computer. When prompted to boot from DVD-ROM, press any key.

4. Windows 7 Setup loads. When prompted, select your regional preferences and then click Next.

5. Click Repair Your Computer.

6. In the System Recovery Options dialog box, click Restore Your Computer Using A System Image. If the backup was saved to a DVD-ROM, insert the DVD-ROM now. Click Next. The Windows System Image Restore Wizard starts.

7. On the Select A System Image Backup page, the most recent backup is automatically selected. If this is the backup you want to restore, click Next. Otherwise, click Select A System Image, click Next, and then select the desired backup.

8. On the Choose Additional Restore Options page, select the Format And Repartition Disks check box if you want to reformat the disk and overwrite all data, or if the disk is not formatted. If you do not want to overwrite all the data on your current disk, do not select this check box. Click Next.

9. Click Finish. When prompted, click Yes to confirm.

Windows System Image Restore reads the data from the backup and overwrites existing files. Typically, the restore will take from 30 through 60 seconds per gigabyte. You can restore to a different-sized hard disk, provided that the hard disk is large enough to store the backup. After the restore is complete, the computer restarts using the restored system volume.

Advanced Boot Options and System Recovery Options

On a computer running Windows 7, you can access the Advanced Boot Options by restarting the computer and holding the F8 key down while it reboots. You can do this when you boot from the installation DVD-ROM or when you boot from hard disk. This gives you a method of accessing repair tools, such as a system restore, when inappropriate changes to the system result in the computer being unable to boot from its system volume. You can then access one of the following options:

- **Safe Mode**   This loads a minimal set of drivers.
- **Safe Mode With Networking**   This loads the least number of drivers that will enable basic operation plus network connectivity.
- **Safe Mode With Command Prompt**   This loads a minimal set of drivers and starts Windows 7 with a command-line interface.
- **Enable Boot Logging**   This logs details about the boot process. Specifically, it creates a file named Ntbtlog.txt, which lists all drivers that load during startup, including the last file to load before a failure occurs.

- **Enable Low Resolution Video**   This loads only the most basic default screen drivers. You use this option if you have loaded a new video driver and now can no longer read the screen.
- **Last Known Good Configuration (Advanced)**   This boots the computer into the last configuration that is known to have worked.
- **Directory Services Restore Mode**   This is not relevant to a client computer.
- **Debugging Mode**   This enables kernel debugging and System Image restore.
- **Disable Automatic Restart On System Failure**   This lets you read the information on the blue STOP screen, which otherwise disappears as the computer reboots.
- **Disable Driver Signal Enforcement**   This allows you to load unsigned drivers.
- **Start Windows Normally**   This attempts to start Windows 7 normally. If you booted from the installation DVD-ROM, selecting this option starts Setup and Windows 7 installation begins.

The Last Known Good Configuration is discussed later in this lesson. Debugging Mode starts the kernel debugger. When you select this option, Windows Preinstallation Environment (Windows PE) loads and System Recovery Options (otherwise known as Windows RE) starts.

System Recovery Options

When you select Debugging Mode in Advanced Boot Options, the System Recovery Options dialog box asks you to select a Keyboard Input Method (typically a U.S. keyboard) and then gives you the choice of two options:

- Use Recovery Tools That Can Help Fix Problems Starting Windows
- Restore Your Computer Using A System Image You Created Earlier

The second option starts a System Image restore, as discussed earlier in this lesson. This is the Windows 7 equivalent of the Complete PC Restore implemented in previous operating systems (and is often given that name in Help files and Microsoft TechNet documentation).

If you select the first option, you are asked to select an operating system to repair (assuming that more than one is available). When you click Next, the dialog box that appears is similar to the Windows Recovery Environment options selection found in previous operating systems. You have the following choices:

- **Startup Repair**   Automatically fixes problems that prevent Windows from starting. If Windows 7 had boot problems during a previous restart, a normal boot (without accessing the Advanced Boot dialog box) gives you the option of selecting Startup Repair. Figure 14-12 shows the dialog box you are presented with in this situation.
- **System Restore**   Gives you another method of starting a system restore to a previous restore point, as discussed earlier in this lesson. Because you can access this menu when you boot from a DVD-ROM, this lets you repair your system when recent changes to system settings prevent your computer from booting normally.

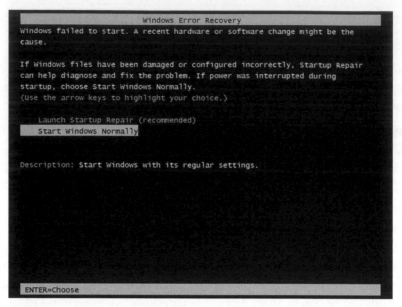

FIGURE 14-12 The Startup Repair option

- **System Image Recovery** Enables you to implement a System Image restore. You would choose this option if your hard disk failed or needed to be wiped. If system changes are causing problems, you would choose the System Restore option.

- **Windows Memory Diagnostic** Analyzes the computer memory (RAM) for hardware problems.

- **Command Prompt** Gives access to the file system, volumes, and files through a command-line interface.

> **NOTE** **USING RECOVERY TOOLS**
>
> If Windows RE is included in your installation DVD-ROM, you can boot from the Windows 7 installation media, select Repair Your Computer, and then select the option to use recovery tools to access the System Recovery Options. However, you can use the method described previously (pressing F8) whether the Windows RE files are present on your DVD-ROM or not and whether you boot from your installation DVD-ROM or from hard disk.

 Quick Check

- You use the Enable Boot Logging option in Advanced Boot Options. What file does this create and what information is stored in this file?

Quick Check Answer

- Enable Boot Logging creates a file named Ntbtlog.txt, which lists all drivers that load during startup, including the last file to load before a failure occurs.

The Last Known Good Configuration (Advanced)

The Last Known Good Configuration (Advanced) feature in Advanced Boot Options is a recovery option that you use to start your computer with the most recent settings that worked. Last Known Good Configuration (Advanced) restores registry information and driver settings that were in effect the last time the computer started successfully.

You should use the Last Known Good Configuration (Advanced) feature when you cannot start Windows 7 after you make a change to your computer, or when you suspect that a change that you just made is causing a problem—for example, if you cannot start Windows after you install a new video driver. When you start your computer by using the Last Known Good Configuration (Advanced) feature, Windows 7 uses the configuration stored in the following registry key:

HKEY_LOCAL_MACHINE\System\CurrentControlSet

Figure 14-13 shows the Control key within the CurrentControlSet registry key. When your computer restarts and you log on, your current configuration in ControlSet001 is copied to CurrentControlSet and becomes the Last Known Good Configuration. Take care, therefore, if you see messages about error events being written to Event Viewer while your logon screen is active. If you log on at this point, you cannot return to the previous Last Known Good Configuration, although you can perform a system restore to previous restore points.

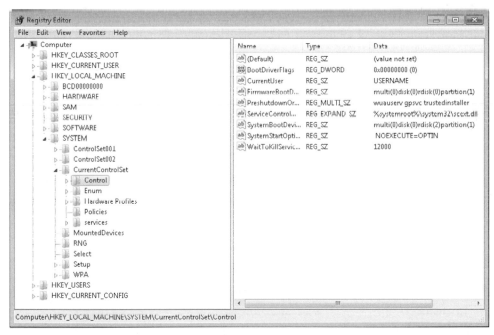

FIGURE 14-13 The CurrentControlSet registry key

Windows 7 Boot Options

Windows 7 implements a boot loader, a boot configuration and storage system called Boot Configuration Data (BCD), and a boot option editing tool called Bcdedit. In Chapter 2, you saw how you can use the Bcdedit tool to make VHDs bootable on computers running Windows 7 Enterprise and Ultimate editions.

Windows 7 includes the following boot loader features:

- Windows boot manager (Bootmgr.exe)
- Windows operating system loader (Winload.exe)
- Windows resume loader (Winresume.exe)

When a computer with multiple boot entries includes at least one entry for Windows 7, Windows Boot Manager starts the system and interacts with the user. It displays the boot menu, loads the selected system-specific boot loader, and passes the boot parameters to the boot loader.

Boot Configuration Data

On Windows 7, boot options and BCD are stored in the BCD store. BCD provides a common interface for all computers running Windows 7 and enables administrators to assign rights for managing boot options. BCD is available at run time and during all phases of setup, including resuming after hibernation.

You can use the Bcdedit utility to manage BCD remotely and manage BCD when the system boots from media other than the media on which the BCD store resides. This feature is important for debugging and troubleshooting, especially when a BCD store must be restored while running Startup Repair from DVD-ROM, from USB-based storage media, or remotely. For example the following command forces the use of the Video Graphics Array (VGA; low resolution) display driver on reboot:

```
bcdedit /set vga on
```

The following command enables kernel debugging for the current operating system boot entry:

```
bcdedit /debug on
```

The following command disables kernel debugging for an operating system boot entry specified by its global unique identifier (GUID):

```
bcdedit /debug <GUID> off
```

You can use the Bcdedit utility to do the following:

- Create a BCD store
- Rebuild BCD
- Add entries to a existing BCD store
- Modify existing entries in a BCD store

- Delete entries from a BCD store
- Export entries to a BCD store
- Import entries from a BCD store
- List currently active settings
- Query entries of a particular type
- Apply a global change to all entries
- Change the default time-out value

MORE INFO   **BCD BOOT OPTIONS**

For more information about BCD boot options, see *http://msdn.microsoft.com/en-us/library/aa906217.aspx*.

You can use the Bcdedit utility to edit boot options in Windows 7. You must be a member of the local Administrators group to use Bcdedit. You can also use the Windows Management Instrumentation (WMI) interface to programmatically change the boot options. Chapter 13, "Monitoring and Performance," discussed WMI in detail.

MORE INFO   **THE BCD WMI INTERFACE**

For more information about the BCD WMI interface and the Windows Software Development Kit (SDK), see *http://msdn.microsoft.com/en-us/library/aa362692.aspx*.

Rolling Back Drivers

Sometimes you can encounter problems because a recently installed driver for a hardware device is incompatible with other drivers or with the hardware in your computer. The classic situation is when you update a video driver and find that when you restart your computer, you cannot see your screen.

In this case, you need to return your computer to its state before you updated the driver. If you have not logged on since the driver was updated, you can boot using Last Known Good Configuration (Advanced) in Advanced Boot Options. If you cannot use Last Known Good Configuration (Advanced) you would next consider performing a system restore.

Typically, you would boot into Advanced Boot Options by using the F8 key and selecting Debugging Mode or boot from DVD-ROM and select Repair Your Computer. In either case, you would access the System Restore option and restore your system settings to the system restore point that was created before you installed the problem driver. It is a good idea to create a system repair point before you make any significant changes to a computer, such as installing a new driver.

However, it is not always convenient to use Last Known Good Configuration (Advanced) or a system restore. The driver could have been installed through Windows Update with other important and recommended updates that you do not want to roll back. In this case, you need to boot the computer either into Safe Mode or Enable Low Resolution Video (if your problem is a video driver) and roll back the driver. Managing drivers and using Device Manager were discussed in detail in Chapter 4, "Managing Devices and Disks."

On the Drivers tab of the device's Properties dialog box, shown in Figure 14-14, you can choose to uninstall or disable the driver. If the device was a monitor, this would result in the default low-resolution driver being used, but in other types of devices, it would probably result in the device not working at all.

FIGURE 14-14 Drivers tab of a device Properties box

Your choice, therefore, should be to roll back the driver. This rolls back to the previous driver that was used (and worked satisfactorily) before the new device driver was installed. One of the main functions of Safe Mode and the Enable Low Resolution Video option is to allow you to make changes to device drivers when these are causing problems. Note that the Roll Back option is enabled only if a driver for a device has been installed that overwrote a previous driver.

| PRACTICE | Configuring System Protection, Creating a Restore Point, and Performing a System Restore |

In this practice, you configure system protection on a hard disk on which it is not configured by default. You then manually create a restore point. You make a system change (uninstall a driver) and then perform a system restore to the restore point you created. Finally, you check that the system change has been reversed.

EXERCISE 1 Configure System Protection

In this exercise, you configure system protection on a hard disk that does not hold a system partition and therefore does not have system protection on by default. You can choose any hard disk you want, but you will likely use the second internal hard disk if one exists on your computer. If you are saving your backups on an external hard disk, you can choose to do this provided that this disk is formatted with the NTFS filing system, although in practice you are unlikely to enable system protection on a device used only to store backups. System protection configuration is discussed in more detail in Lesson 3. Perform the following procedure:

1. If necessary, log on to the Canberra computer with the Kim_Akers account.

2. In Control Panel, click System And Security. In the System And Security window, click System.

3. In the System window, click System Protection. This accesses the System Protection tab of the System Properties dialog box, as shown in Figure 14-15.

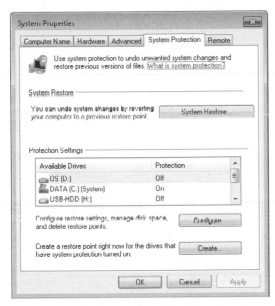

FIGURE 14-15 The System Protection tab of the System Properties dialog box

4. Select the drive on which you want to configure system protection and then click Configure.

5. In the System Protection dialog box for the selected drive, select Restore System Settings And Previous Versions Of Files. Configure the Maximum Usage setting (the maximum disk capacity that you want to use to store restore points) by using the slider control, as shown in Figure 14-16.

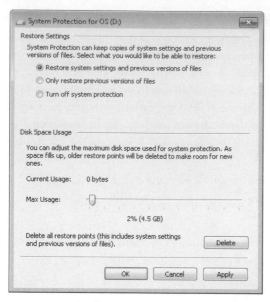

FIGURE 14-16 Configuring system protection for a selected disk drive

6. Click OK.

7. On the System Protection tab of the System Properties dialog box, ensure that system protection for the disk drive you selected is set to On. Click OK.

EXERCISE 2 Create a Restore Point Manually

In this exercise, you manually create a restore point named Trial Restore Point.

1. If necessary, log on to the Canberra computer with the Kim_Akers account and access the System Protection tab of the System Properties dialog box, as described in Exercise 1.

2. Click Create.

3. In the Create A Restore Point dialog box, type **Trial Restore Point.** Click Create. Windows 7 creates a restore point. This can take some time.

4. Click Close.

EXERCISE 3 Perform a System Restore

In this exercise, you make a system change. You then perform a system restore to the Trial Restore Point and check the system change is reversed.

1. If necessary, log on to the Canberra computer with the Kim_Akers account.

2. On the Start menu, right-click Computer and choose Manage.

3. In the left pane of the Computer Management console, select Device Manager.

4. Choose a device that you are not using right now. Right-click the device and choose Properties.

5. Click Driver to access the Driver tab, as shown in Figure 14-17.

FIGURE 14-17 The Driver tab for the chosen device

6. Click Uninstall. Click OK to confirm that you want to uninstall the driver.

7. Access the System Protection tab of the System Properties dialog box, as described in Exercise 1.

8. Click System Restore.

9. On the Restore System Files And Settings page of the System Restore Wizard, click Next.

10. In the Restore Your Computer To The State It Was In Before The Selected Event dialog box, ensure that Trial Restore Point is selected, as shown in Figure 14-18. Click Next.

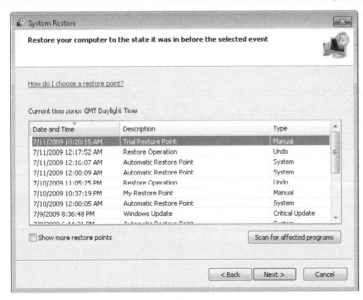

FIGURE 14-18 Selecting a restore point

11.   Click Finish. Click Yes to confirm that you want to continue. Windows 7 performs a system restore and the Canberra computer reboots.

12.   Log on to the Canberra computer with the Kim_Akers account.

13.   Click Close to close the System Restore Completed Successfully box.

14.   Access the Driver tab of the device you chose earlier, as described in steps 2 through 5 in this exercise.

15.   Check that the device driver is no longer uninstalled (that is, the Uninstall button is enabled).

Lesson Summary

- If system protection is configured on a disk drive, restore points are created automatically when you make significant system changes. You can also manually create a restore point.

- You can restore your system settings to a selected restore point.

- You can restore your entire computer from a System Image backup to how it was when the backup was taken.

- You can boot from the Windows 7 installation DVD-ROM and run a System Repair, or you can access the Advanced Boot Options by pressing the F8 key during a reboot. Both techniques access tools that let you investigate boot and system problems.

Lesson Review

You can use the following questions to test your knowledge of the information in Lesson 2, "System Recovery." The questions are also available on the companion DVD if you prefer to review them in electronic form.

1.   You are testing unsigned device drivers on a computer on an isolated test network. You install a display driver and find that the computer boots to a blank screen. You restart the computer and press F8. What Advanced Boot Options could you choose to help remedy the situation? (Choose all that apply.)

   A.   Safe Mode

   B.   Enable Boot Logging

C. Enable Low Resolution Video

D. Last Known Good Configuration (Advanced)

E. Disable Driver Signal Enforcement

2. You are deciding on which storage devices you want to configure system protection. System protection is enabled by default on your C: drive, which holds your system files. No other storage device on your computer has system protection enabled. On which of the following storage devices can you enable system protection? (Choose all that apply.)

    A. Your second internal hard disk, formatted with NTFS

    B. An external USB hard disk formatted with FAT

    C. A USB flash drive

    D. Your optical drive

    E. A mounted VHD created on your second internal hard disk

3. You are investigating instability and boot problems on a computer running Windows 7 Enterprise. You boot using the Last Known Good Configuration (Advanced) option and perform a system restore. This does not solve your problems, and you want to undo the system restore. Can you do this, and what is the reason for your answer?

    A. No. You can undo a system restore only if you initiate it from the System Recovery tools.

    B. No. You can undo a system restore only if you carry it out after booting normally.

    C. Yes. You can always undo a system restore, no matter how you booted the computer or how you initiated the restore.

    D. Yes. You can undo a system restore that you perform after either booting normally or booting using Last Known Good Configuration (Advanced).

4. You are troubleshooting instability problems on a computer running Windows 7 Ultimate and suspect that they might be related to hardware faults in RAM. You access the System Recovery options. Which option is most likely to help you diagnose the problem?

    A. Windows Memory Diagnostic

    B. Startup Repair

    C. System Restore

    D. System Image Recovery

5. What command-line utility can you use in Windows 7 to edit boot options?

    A. Bootmgr.exe

    B. Winload.exe

    C. Bcdedit.exe

    D. Winresume.exe

Lesson 3: Recovering Files and Folders

This lesson looks at previous versions of files and folders created as shadow copies by the Volume Shadow Copy Service (VSS) when a restore point is created or held in backup sets created by a file and folder backup. It discusses how you can restore previous versions of files even when these files have been renamed or deleted.

The lesson looks at file and folder recovery and the Recover Files Wizard and describes how you use this wizard to restore user profile information. System Protection was introduced in Lesson 2, and this lesson considers System Protection settings in more detail.

After this lesson you will be able to:

- Recover a previous version of a file or folder.
- Recover a file and folder from backup.
- Restore a renamed or deleted file.
- Restore a user profile.

Estimated lesson time: 35 minutes

Restoring Damaged or Deleted Files by Using Previous Versions

Previous versions are either backups of files and folders that you create by using the Backup And Restore console and restore by accessing the same tool and using the Restore Files Wizard, or they are shadow copies. *Shadow copies* are copies of files and folders that Windows 7 automatically saves when it creates a restore point. You can decide whether to restore from backup or restore from a shadow copy. The file you restore from backup will be the version of the file that was current when the backup was taken. You may have a shadow copy that is more recent than the backed-up file, or you may want to restore an older version.

You can use previous versions of files to restore damaged files or files that you, or users you support, accidentally modify or delete. You can access previous versions, save them to a different location, or restore a previous version of a damaged file to its original location.

Restoring Files and Folders

Windows 7 makes restoring files and folders from backup straightforward. You can restore a file or folder to its original location or to a different location. Typically, you restore a file to its original location if it is corrupted or has been accidentally overwritten, but sometimes you want to restore to a different location to test that your backup and restore procedures are working correctly without the risk of overwriting your current files and folders. This is known as a *dummy restore*.

To restore a file or folder from backup, click Restore My Files in the Backup And Restore console. By default, files and folders are restored from the latest backup. If you want to use an earlier backup, click Choose A Different Date, select the date and time from the list you are presented with, and click OK.

On the first page of the Restore Files Wizard, you have the option of clicking Search and specifying all or part of a file or folder name, clicking Browse For Files and selecting a file, or clicking Browse For Folders and selecting a folder. You select a file or folder and click Add File or Add Folder as appropriate. Figure 14-19 shows a Word file called Backup and Restore selected for restoration.

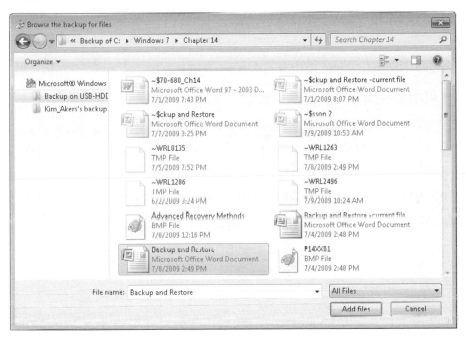

FIGURE 14-19 Selecting a file to restore

When you have selected the files or folders that you want to restore, click Next on the Restore Files Wizard. You then have the option of restoring to the original location or specifying a different location to perform a dummy restore. You can either type in the dummy restore location or browse to it. Your dummy restore location can be on an internal or external hard disk, a USB flash memory device, an optical drive, a VHD, or (in Windows 7 Ultimate, Enterprise, and Professional editions only) a network share.

When you have specified where you want to restore your files or folders (or accepted the default), click Restore. If a file or folder with the same name already exists at that location, you are given the options of Copy And Replace; Don't Copy; and Copy, But Keep Both Files (as with any normal file-copying operation). If you want, you can select the Do This For All Conflicts check box. You then select the action that you want Windows 7 to take. If you want, you can review the stored files. Finally, click Finish.

Shadow Copies

Shadow copies are automatically saved as part of a restore point. If system protection is enabled, Windows 7 automatically creates shadow copies of files that have been modified since the last restore point was created. By default, new restore points are created every seven days or whenever a significant system change (such as a driver or application installation) occurs.

You can access previous versions of a file or folder by right-clicking the file or folder in Windows Explorer and clicking Restore Previous Versions. As shown in Figure 14-20, you then see a list of available previous versions of the file or folder. The list includes both backed-up files and shadow copies if both types are available.

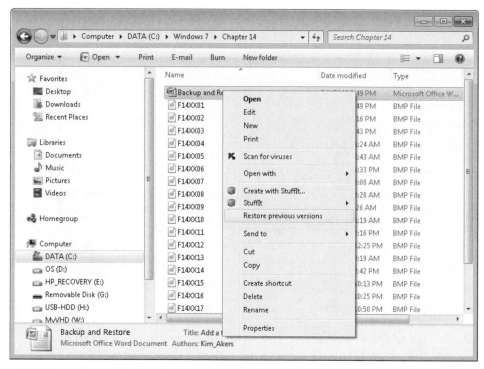

FIGURE 14-20 Selecting Restore Previous Versions

If you want to restore a previous version of a file or folder, right-click the file or folder and click Restore Previous Versions. Select the item that you want to restore and then click Restore, as shown in Figure 14-21. You need to take care to select the previous version that you want to restore because that file or folder will replace the current version on the computer and the replacement cannot be undone. If the Restore option is unavailable, you cannot restore a previous version of the file or folder (possibly because the file structure has been changed). You might, however, be able to open the previous version or save it to a different location.

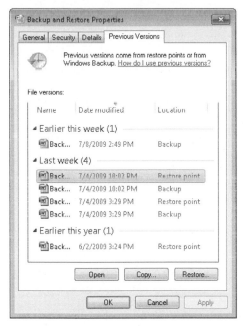

FIGURE 14-21 Selecting a previous version to restore

You can use the Previous Versions tab of the Backup And Restore Properties dialog box to recover previous versions of files directly from restore points on your hard disk or from a backup. If you need to restore a backup copy, you carry out the same procedure. In this case, when you click Restore, Windows 7 opens the Restore Files Wizard.

If you cannot find shadow copies of some files, system protection might not be turned on for that hard disk or the file might be an offline file. Offline files are copies of files that are stored on shared network folders. Shadow copies are not available for offline files. Shadow copies are unavailable for files and folders that are required for Windows 7 to work. For example, there is no shadow copy of the system folder (the folder that the operating system is installed in) or its contents.

Recovering Renamed and Deleted Files

You can restore a renamed file or folder from a shadow copy, but you need to know the location that the file or folder was saved to. You do this in the practice in this lesson.

You cannot directly recover a deleted file that has been removed from the Recycle Bin. However, you can recover a previous version of the folder that the file was in. Take care, because recovering the folder overwrites other files in the folder with their previous versions. The procedure to recover an accidentally deleted file that has been removed from the Recycle Bin is as follows:

1. Identify the folder that contained the deleted file.
2. Create a new folder and copy the contents of the folder you identified into the new folder.

3. Replace the folder you identified with its most recent previous version.

4. Copy the contents of the new folder back into the previous version folder. Permit any old versions of files to be overwritten by the newer versions in the new folder. The file that was deleted will be in the previous version folder but will not be affected by the copy operation because that file will not be in the new folder.

5. Finally, you can delete the new folder.

Recovering Several Previous Versions of the Same File

If you recover a previous version of a file or folder (either created when a restore point was created or from backup) to its original location, it overwrites the existing file or folder. If you then restore another previous version of the same file or folder to its original location, it in turn overwrites the version you created earlier.

Sometimes you want to recover and retain several versions of the same file for historical reasons or in the course of an audit or an investigation. In this case, you would use the Copy function on the Previous Version tab of the Backup And Restore Properties dialog box shown previously in Figure 14-21.

For example, suppose that you want to restore several previous versions of a file going back the last four weeks. Your first step should be to create a new folder to hold these files. You right-click the current file, click Restore Previous Versions, select the previous version that you want to recover, and click Copy to copy it to the new folder (not to the folder that holds the current version). You then rename the file you have recovered, typically by appending a month and day (such as Backup_and_restore_7_12.docx). You do this for all the files in which you are interested, renaming each in turn. The renaming is necessary because all the previous versions of the same file have the same name by default, and you do not want any file to be overwritten.

The Volume Shadow Copy Service

VSS manages and implements shadow copies, which are used for backup and to create previous versions when a restore point is generated, and manages volume snapshots. When you initiate a file and folder backup from the Backup And Restore console, the VSS creates a snapshot of the volume that contains the files and folders to be backed up, and the snapshots are backed up rather than the files themselves. This speeds up the backup process and enables you to back up files on disk even when the file is open and you are working on it. Note that the backup process does not back up the changes you have made to an open file since the last time you saved it. The shadow copy creates volumes that match the original volumes at the shadow copy point of time.

VSS is installed on computers running Windows 7. As shown in Figure 14-22, its startup type is Manual. The service starts as needed. If the service does not start when required, shadow copies are unavailable for backup and Windows Backup does not succeed. Nor can you create restore points and previous versions. In this case, check the service and ensure that it has not been disabled.

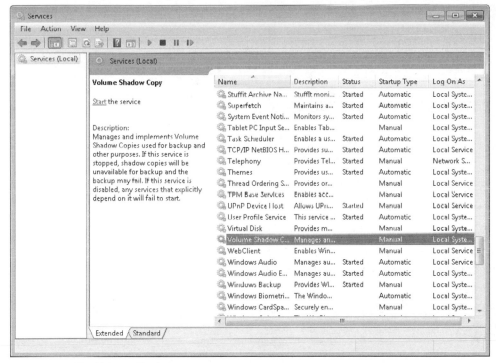

FIGURE 14-22 The Volume Shadow Copy Service

Restoring User Profiles

When you perform a file and folder backup, by default you back up all the files (the Documents library, Pictures library, Favorites folder, and so on) associated with each of the users on the computer. Information specific to a particular user is known as the *user profile*. In a small network, user profiles are stored locally. In a domain-based enterprise network, you can store user profiles on a server and download them to a client computer whenever a user logs on. The second type of profile, known as a *roaming profile,* enables a user to log on at any client computer in a domain; see that it is configured with his or her personal settings; and access his or her libraries, Internet favorites, contacts, and so on. As shown in Figure 14-23, user profiles can take up a lot of storage space.

If you need to reverse recent changes to a user profile, you can restore the latest backup of the user's profile by running the Restore Files Wizard from the Backup And Restore console. Typically, if you are restoring a user profile, you restore folders. Restoring individual files is a lengthy process.

If you click Restore My Files in the Backup And Restore console and then click Browse For Folders in the Restore Files Wizard, you find a folder specific to each user on the computer in the left pane of the Browse The Backup For Folders Or Drives dialog box. If you select one of these folders, you obtain a list of folders similar to that shown in Figure 14-24. These folders contain all the files and settings specific to the specified user.

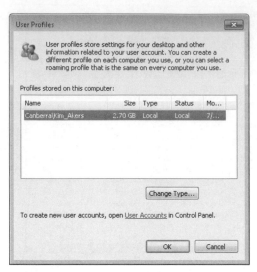

FIGURE 14-23 A user profile taking up 2.7 GB storage space

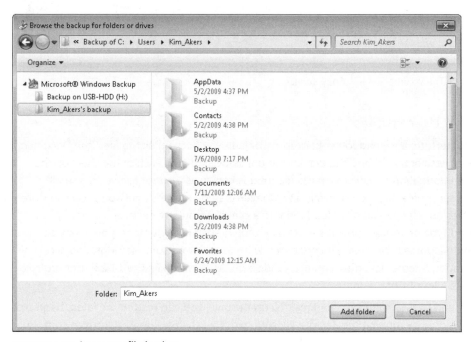

FIGURE 14-24 A user profile backup

You can select each of the folders that you want to restore in turn and click Add Folder. You need to return to the Browse The Backup For Folders Or Drives page for each folder you want to restore. When you have finished specifying folders, your Restore Files Wizard page should look similar to Figure 14-25.

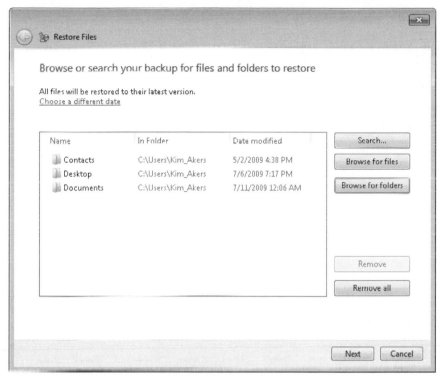

FIGURE 14-25 Specifying the user profile folders to restore

> **NOTE** **SPECIFYING FILES**
>
> If you want to specify a file in addition to (or instead of) the folders you are restoring, click Browse For Files rather than Browse For Folders. You can specify both files and folders in a restore.

You then click Next and proceed as you would with a normal file and folder restore. If you are restoring corrupted user profile information, you would typically restore to the original location.

Configuring System Protection and Disk Usage

You accessed the System Protection tab of the System Properties dialog box in a practice exercise in Lesson 2, when you were creating a restore point. In the exercise, you clicked Configure and enabled system protection for a disk drive. A drive needs to have system protection enabled if it is to be included in a restore point, which means that system protection is also required for previous copies to be generated on that drive. You will not find previous copies of files and folders on drives that do not have system protection enabled.

It is appropriate at this point to examine the System Protection dialog box more closely. This dialog box for the C: drive is shown in Figure 14-26. This figure is similar to (but not the same as) Figure 14-16 in Lesson 2.

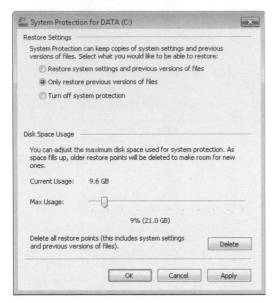

FIGURE 14-26 System protection settings

The Restore Settings section of the System Protection dialog box presents you with the following options:

- **Restore System Settings And Previous Versions Of Files**   You typically use this setting on disk drives that hold a system volume, for which this is the default setting. It enables the creation of restore points that hold system information to be used during a system restore. If user files are held on the same drive, previous versions of the files are generated when a restore point is created. Typically, Disk Space Usage is set to a relatively low value (for example, 10 percent) because the disk drive is mainly used to hold system files that are seldom updated.

- **Only Restore Previous Versions Of Files**   You typically use this setting on disk drives that you use for file storage and that do not contain system files, such as a second internal hard disk. If you create a restore point that includes a drive with this level of system protection, previous versions of the files are generated. Typically, you would allocate a high percentage of Disk Space Usage (for example, 40 percent) for system protection so a large number of previous versions can be held.

- **Turn Off System Protection**   You typically use this setting on disk drives that are backup destinations. You do not need to create previous versions of backup files because backup file sets already perform this function. Typically, you would configure this setting on an external USB disk used as a backup medium.

Configuring Disk Space Usage is a matter of individual judgment, although the general guidelines are that it should be set to a low volume for system disks and a high value for data disks. When the disk space allocated to system protection is used up, the oldest previous versions are overwritten. If you are in an environment where users want to access versions of files that are several months old, you might need to allocate a lot of disk space for that purpose. If users seldom need to access previous versions that are more than a week old, you can allocate a lower percentage.

Similarly, you need to think carefully about which of the Restore Settings options you choose. Although you typically select Restore System Settings And Previous Versions Of Files for a drive that holds system files, you might have a computer with a single hard disk and your priority might be to store as many previous versions of files and folders as possible. In this case, you could decide to select Only Restore Previous Versions Of Files and accept the fact that a system restore might not solve the problem of a misconfigured system setting or roll back a problem driver.

PRACTICE   **Recovering a File You Have Renamed**

In this practice, you recover the previous version of a file you have renamed.

EXERCISE   Recovering a Renamed File

In this exercise, you select a file that has a number of previous versions and rename it. You then discover that you need to recover an older version of the file. You recover the previous version with its original file name. You do not need to elevate privileges to complete this exercise. However, the procedure, as written, asks you to log in by using an administrator-level account. Unless you have sophisticated users, recovering a renamed file would typically be an administrative function.

The procedure asks you to find a file (such as a Word document or an Excel spreadsheet) that has a number of previous versions. Hopefully, several such files exist on your computer. If not, you need to create a file, perform a file and folder backup, edit the file, and create a restore point. The procedures for performing backups and manually creating a restore point are described earlier in this chapter. The figures in the exercise show a file called *Lesson 2.docx* being used for this purpose. You can choose a suitable file on your Canberra computer. To recover a previous copy of a renamed file, perform the following steps:

1. If necessary, log on to the Canberra computer using the Kim_Akers account

2. Open Windows Explorer by double-clicking Computer on the Start menu.

3. Navigate to a folder in which you store personal files.

4. Open the folder and right-click a file that you amend regularly. Select Restore Previous Versions.

5. Check that previous copies of the file exist, as shown in Figure 14-27.

FIGURE 14-27 Previous versions of a selected file

6. Close the file Properties dialog box.

7. Right-click the file and rename it.

8. Right-click the renamed file. As shown in Figure 14-28, the Restore Previous Versions option is no longer available.

9. To restore a previous version of the file, right-click the folder in which it is saved in the left-hand Windows Explorer pane, as shown in Figure 14-29, and choose Restore Previous Versions.

FIGURE 14-28 No previous versions of the renamed file

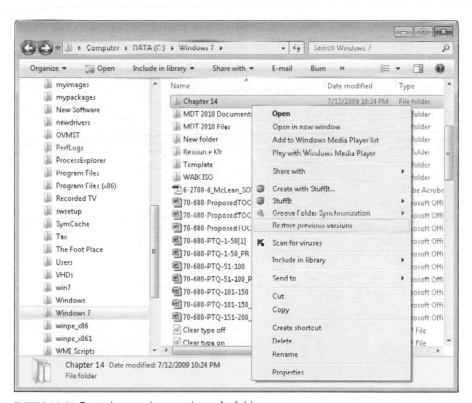

FIGURE 14-29 Restoring previous versions of a folder

10. Select a previous version of the folder that is likely to contain the file you want to restore, as shown in Figure 14-30, and then click Open.

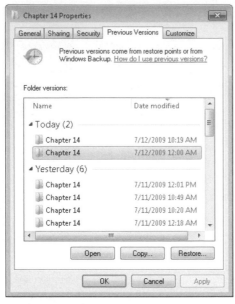

FIGURE 14-30 Selecting the previous version of a folder that contains the file you want to restore

11. As shown in Figure 14-31, the previous version of the file that you want to restore should be in the previous version of the folder. Right-click the file and copy it.

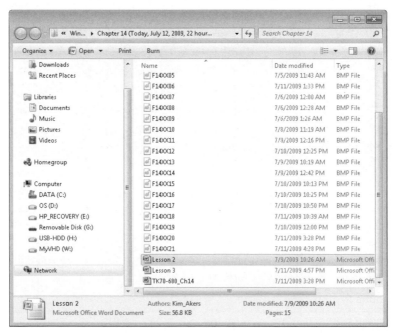

FIGURE 14-31 The previous version of the file you renamed in the recovered folder

12. Close the previous version of the folder. Paste the file to wherever you want to store it. It is a good idea to open it and make sure it is the version that you want.

Lesson Summary

- You can recover a previous version of a file or folder from shadow copies created when a restore point was created or from backup sets.
- You can restore a renamed or deleted file by restoring a previous version of the folder in which the original file was saved.
- You can restore user settings and user-related data such as desktop settings, contacts, and favorites by restoring a user profile.
- You can configure system protection on internal and external hard drives and VHDs formatted using the NTFS file system. Previous versions of files and folders are created when you create a restore point on a drive where system protection is configured.

Lesson Review

You can use the following questions to test your knowledge of the information in Lesson 3, "Recovering Files and Folders." The questions are also available on the companion DVD if you prefer to review them in electronic form.

NOTE ANSWERS

Answers to these questions and explanations of why each answer choice is correct or incorrect are located in the "Answers" section at the end of the book.

1. A user telephones your help desk. She has just accidentally deleted a file she was working on earlier that day. You have configured her computer to carry out backups every evening, and you installed a new graphics driver two days ago. How should you advise the user to retrieve her file?

   A. Open the Backup And Restore console and restore the file from backup.

   B. Use the Restore Previous Versions feature to restore the file.

   C. Open her Recycle Bin, right-click the file, and choose Restore.

   D. Perform a system restore.

2. An employee who works from home telephones your help desk. A virus attack has deleted his computer's single internal hard disk. He carried out a System Image backup on his computer three months ago and automatically backs up his personal files every night. He uses an external USB hard drive formatted with the NTFS file system to hold his backups. All his personal files are in his Documents library. What do you advise? (Choose all that apply; the answers form a complete solution.)

   A. Carry out a System Image restore.

   B. Carry out a system restore.

C. Use Restore Previous Versions to restore his Documents library from a shadow copy.

D. Use Restore My Files in the Backup And Restore console to restore his Documents library folder.

3. Your computer running Windows 7 Enterprise has two internal hard disks. System protection is configured by default on the C: drive, which holds the operating system and installed applications. The D: drive is a 500-GB hard disk formatted with the NTFS filing system, and you use it to store your personal files. You want to store previous versions going back several months and therefore intend to reserve 200 GB of this disk for system protection. You are not using either of your internal disks for backup; instead, you store your backups on a 1-TB external USB hard disk. How do you configure system protection on your D: drive? (Choose all that apply; each answer forms part of the complete solution.)

A. Select Restore System Settings And Previous Versions Of Files

B. Select Only Restore Previous Versions Of Files

C. Set the Max Usage slider control to 40 percent

D. Set the Max Usage slider control to 4 percent

4. Your company's chief accountant consults you with a question about a financial spreadsheet. She needs to recover the version of this particular spreadsheet that existed six months ago because it is needed for a financial audit. Using Restore Previous Versions, you find that the oldest version stored is dated three months ago. How can you recover the required file?

A. Edit the System Protection properties for the volume that hosts the file. Use the Max Usage slider to increase the maximum proportion of the hard disk capacity used for system protection to 70 percent.

B. Perform a system restore. Select a system restore point that was created six months ago.

C. Edit the System Protection properties for the volume that hosts the file. Select the Only Restore Previous Versions Of Files setting.

D. Use the Backup And Restore console to recover the file from a backup set generated six months ago.

5. A user telephones your help desk. Her Favorites list is corrupt and she is having problems accessing the Web sites she visits regularly. All the computers in your organization are backed up every night with a file and folder backup that uses default settings. A restore point was created on all the company's client computers 24 hours ago because a new device driver was installed. You performed a System Image backup on all the computers in your organization three weeks ago. The user is not

computer-literate and you need to fix the problem for her. What is the most efficient way to do so?

A. Perform a system restore.

B. Perform a System Image restore.

C. Use the Restore Files Wizard to restore the Favorites folder in the user's backed-up profile.

D. Access the History tab under Favorites on the user's browser. Browse to recently visited sites and add them to Favorites.

Chapter Summary

- You can use the Backup And Restore console to start and to schedule a file and folder backup and to start (but not schedule) a System Image backup. You can perform a System Image backup from an elevated command prompt. You can restore your entire computer from a System Image backup to the way it was when the backup was taken. You can restore files, folders, and user profile information from file and folder backup sets.

- Restore points are created automatically when you make significant system changes. You can also manually create a restore point and you can restore your system settings to a selected restore point. You configure system protection on a disk drive to enable restore point creation and specify the proportion of disk capacity that system protection uses.

- Advanced Boot Options and System Repair let you address problems when a computer does not boot normally.

- You can recover a previous version of a file or folder from shadow copies created when a restore point was created or from backup sets. You can restore a renamed or deleted file with its original file name.

Chapter Review

To further practice and reinforce the skills you learned in this chapter, you can perform the following tasks:

- Review the chapter summary.
- Review the list of key terms introduced in this chapter.
- Complete the case scenarios. These scenarios set up real-world situations involving the topics of this chapter and ask you to create a solution.
- Complete the suggested practices.
- Take a practice test.

Key Terms

Do you know what these key terms mean? You can check your answers by looking up the terms in the glossary at the end of the book.

- **dummy restore**
- **restore point**
- **shadow copy**
- **System Image**
- **system restore**

Case Scenarios

In the following case scenarios, you apply what you've learned about recovery and backup. You can find answers to these questions in the "Answers" section at the end of this book.

Case Scenario 1: Supporting Backup And Restore

James Seymour is an IT professional working for a large computer retailer that provides help-desk advice to home users. The retailer mostly sells computers that run Windows 7.

Answer the following questions:

1. A user has accidently deleted all the data in a file and then saved the file to hard disk and closed the application. He has not scheduled automatic file and folder backups. He has been working with the file for over a week. During that week, he has installed a number of application packages. What does James tell him?

2. A user has configured automatic file and folder backup to take place at midnight every night. She has accepted the default of letting Windows decide what files and folders to back up. A file that her son is working on for a school project has been corrupted. She is concerned that because she did not specify her son's Documents library, he cannot restore the file from backup. What does James tell her?

3. A user recently installed third-party software that is causing problems on his computer. He also has problems uninstalling the software. He understands that he can use a system restore to restore the computer to its last restore point, but he is afraid he might lose some important files that he has created recently. What does James tell him?

4. A user's computer has a single hard disk that contains two partitions. She has tried to create a System Image backup on the partition that does not hold her operating system, but the Create A System Image Wizard does not give her that option. She wants to know how she can create such a backup. What does James tell her?

Case Scenario 2: Addressing System and Configuration Issues

James Seymour provides technical support for Lucerne Publishing, a small publishing company that has only one office. Lucerne's network does not use Active Directory Domain Services (AD DS) and is configured as a workgroup. All computers on the network run Windows 7 Professional. James has an administrator account on all Lucerne's computers. All other employees have standard accounts except for the boss, Don Hall, who has an Administrator account on his own computer but not on any others. Unfortunately, Don is not as knowledgeable about computers as he thinks he is.

With this information in mind, answer the following questions:

1. Don boots his computer and accesses the Advanced Boot Options. He selects Disable Driver Signal Enforcement, which lets him install and try out unsigned display drivers

he has downloaded from various Internet sites. However, when he installs the first of these drivers, the computer reboots and the monitor screen is completely blank. Don asks James how he can quickly get his computer working again. What advice does James give?

2. Don thinks he knows a better way of solving the previous problem. He will boot from the installation media and perform a System Image restore. Fortunately, he speaks to James first. James knows that the last System Image backup performed on Don's computer happened three months ago. What does he advise?

3. The computers at Lucerne Publishing have two internal hard disks. The first holds the operating system and applications, and the second holds user data. Backups are done to a network share on a server on the network. Don inspects the system protection settings that James has configured on the second hard disk. He understands that a higher Disk Usage setting results in more previous versions being stored. He suggests a setting of 90 percent rather than the 40 percent James has configured. What does James tell him?

Suggested Practices

To help you master the exam objectives presented in this chapter, complete the following tasks.

Perform Backups

- **Practice 1** Create a batch file that performs a System Image backup. Use Task Scheduler to schedule this backup for every two weeks.

- **Practice 2 (optional)** If you have a second computer running Windows 7 Ultimate on your test network (such as the Aberdeen computer), create a network share on that computer and perform a file and folder backup on the Canberra computer that uses that network share.

Configure System Recovery

- **Practice 1** You can boot from the installation DVD-ROM and perform a system recovery in one of two ways—either by pressing the F8 key on boot to access the Advanced Boot Options or by selecting Repair My Computer. You need to be familiar with running a system restore when a computer cannot boot normally.

- **Practice 2** Access the More Information link given in Lesson 2 to learn more about the Bcdedit utility and the command syntax. Practice using this utility.

- **Practice 3 (optional)** If you created a bootable VHD in Chapter 2, restore a recent System Image backup to that VHD and boot from that system image.

Recover Files and Folders

- **Practice 1** Delete one of your files (preferably one that you no longer need) and remove it from the Recycle Bin. Recover the file and ensure that other files in the same folder are the most recent versions.

- **Practice 2** Delete all your Internet favorites (it is a good idea to copy your Favorites folder somewhere safe first). Restore your Favorites folder from your user profile backup.

Take a Practice Test

The practice tests on this book's companion DVD offer many options. For example, you can test yourself on just one exam objective, or you can test yourself on all the 70-680 certification exam content. You can set up the test so that it closely simulates the experience of taking a certification exam, or you can set it up in study mode so that you can look at the correct answers and explanations after you answer each question.

> **MORE INFO** **PRACTICE TESTS**
>
> For details about all the practice test options available, see the section entitled "How to Use the Practice Tests," in the Introduction to this book.

Answers

Chapter 1: Lesson Review Answers

Lesson 1

1. Correct Answer: C

   A. **Incorrect:** LoadState.exe is part of the User State Migration Tool (USMT) utility and cannot be used to prepare a USB storage device as a Windows 7 installation source.

   B. **Incorrect:** ScanState.exe is part of USMT and cannot be used to prepare a USB storage device as a Windows 7 installation source.

   C. **Correct:** You can use the Diskpart utility to prepare a USB storage device so you can boot from it to install Windows 7.

   D. **Incorrect:** Bcdedit is used to modify boot configuration, but It cannot be used to prepare a USB storage device so that it is possible to boot from it to install Windows 7.

2. Correct Answer: D

   A. **Incorrect:** You need to install the operating systems in the order that they were released by Microsoft. Later operating systems are designed to detect existing installations of earlier operating systems, but earlier operating systems cannot detect the installation of later operating systems.

   B. **Incorrect:** You need to install the operating systems in the order in which they were released. Later operating systems are designed to detect existing installations of earlier operating systems, but earlier operating systems cannot detect the installation of later operating systems.

   C. **Incorrect:** You need to install the operating systems in the order in which they were released. Later operating systems are designed to detect existing installations of earlier operating systems, but earlier operating systems cannot detect the installation of later operating systems.

   D. **Correct:** You need to install Windows XP first, Windows Vista, and then Windows 7 because that is the order that Microsoft released them. This allows you to boot among the three operating systems.

3. **Correct Answers: B and D**

   A. **Incorrect:** An x86 version of Windows 7 can utilize a maximum of 4 GB of RAM.

   B. **Correct:** An x64 versions of Windows 7 can utilize more than 4 GB of RAM.

   C. **Incorrect:** An x86 version of Windows 7 can utilize a maximum of 4 GB of RAM.

   D. **Correct:** An x64 versions of Windows 7 can utilize more than 4 GB of RAM.

4. **Correct Answer: B**

   A. **Incorrect:** A computer does not require a DVD-ROM drive for a network-based installation from WDS.

   B. **Correct:** To deploy over the network using WDS requires the computer either a PXE-compliant network adapter or be booted from a WDS discover image.

   C. **Incorrect:** A computer does not require a USB 2.0 slot for a network-based installation from WDS.

   D. **Incorrect:** A computer does not require a HDMI port for a network-based installation from WDS.

5. **Correct Answer: B**

   A. **Incorrect:** Two volumes are the minimum number required to support dual-booting between Windows XP and Windows 7.

   B. **Correct:** Two volumes are the minimum number required to support dual-booting between Windows XP and Windows 7. The Windows 7 installation routine creates an extra 200-MB system volume on one of these volumes when you install Windows 7, but two volumes is the minimum number required on a Windows XP computer prior to attempting to install Windows 7 for dual-boot configuration.

   C. **Incorrect:** Two volumes are the minimum number required to support dual-booting between Windows XP and Windows 7.

   D. **Incorrect:** Two volumes are the minimum number required to support dual-booting between Windows XP and Windows 7.

Lesson 2

1. **Correct Answer: B**

   A. **Incorrect:** You cannot upgrade Windows Vista Enterprise to Windows 7 Home Professional. Windows Vista Enterprise (x86) only can be upgraded to Windows 7 Enterprise (x86) or Ultimate (x86).

   B. **Correct:** Windows Vista Enterprise (x86) only can be upgraded to Windows 7 Enterprise (x86) or Ultimate (x86).

   C. **Incorrect:** You cannot upgrade an x86 version of Windows Vista to an x64 version of Windows 7.

   D. **Incorrect:** You cannot upgrade an x86 version of Windows Vista to an x64 version of Windows 7.

2. **Correct Answers: A, B, and D**

   A. **Correct:** It is not possible to perform a direct upgrade from Windows XP to Windows 7, so a migration is necessary.

   B. **Correct:** It is not possible to perform a direct upgrade between an x86 version of Vista and an x64 version of Windows 7.

   C. **Incorrect:** You can perform a direct upgrade from Windows Vista Enterprise (x64) to Windows 7 Enterprise (x64).

   D. **Correct:** It is not possible to upgrade from an (x64) version of Windows Vista to an (x86) version of Windows 7.

3. **Correct Answer: D**

   A. **Incorrect:** Sysprep cannot be used to upgrade between editions of Windows 7.

   B. **Incorrect:** You cannot use Windows PE to upgrade between editions of Windows 7.

   C. **Incorrect:** WDS requires a server with WDS installed. The question specifies that there are no other computers on the home network.

   D. **Correct:** A user can utilize Windows Anytime Upgrade with a home Internet connection to upgrade from Windows 7 Home Premium to Windows 7 Ultimate.

4. **Correct Answer: A**

   A. **Correct:** The Windows 7 Upgrade Advisor can examine the configuration of a computer running Windows Vista to determine if any of the applications installed on that computer are known to have compatibility problems with Windows 7.

   B. **Incorrect:** Sysprep is used to prepare a computer for imaging. It cannot report whether particular applications have compatibility problems with Windows 7.

   C. **Incorrect:** The USMT is used to migrate user profile data from one computer to another. It cannot report whether particular applications have compatibility problems with Windows 7.

   D. **Incorrect:** Windows PE is a minimal operating system that is used for maintenance tasks. It cannot report whether particular applications have compatibility problems with Windows 7.

5. **Correct Answers: A and C**

   A. **Correct:** You can upgrade Windows 7 Home Premium (x86) to Windows 7 Professional (x86).

   B. **Incorrect:** You cannot upgrade an x86 version of Windows 7 to an x64 version of Windows 7.

   C. **Correct:** You can upgrade from Windows 7 Home Premium (x86) to Windows 7 Ultimate (x86).

   D. **Incorrect:** You cannot upgrade an x86 version of Windows 7 to an x64 version of Windows 7.

Lesson 3

1. **Correct Answers: B, C, and D**

   A. **Incorrect:** Windows 2000 does not support offline migration using the USMT.

   B. **Correct:** Windows XP Professional supports offline migration using the USMT.

   C. **Correct:** Windows Vista supports offline migration using the USMT.

   D. **Correct:** Windows 7 support offline migration using the USMT.

2. **Correct Answers: B and C**

   A. **Incorrect:** File Settings and Transfer Wizard is a Windows XP utility; it cannot be used to migrate data to Windows 7.

   B. **Correct:** USMT can be used to transfer user encryption certificates from a computer running Windows XP Professional to a computer running Windows 7 Professional.

   C. **Correct:** Windows Easy Transfer can be used to transfer user encryption certificates from a computer running Windows XP Professional to a computer running Windows 7 Professional.

   D. **Incorrect:** Robocopy.exe cannot be used to transfer user encryption certificates from a computer running Windows XP Professional to a computer running Windows 7 Professional.

3. **Correct Answer: B**

   A. **Incorrect:** MigDocs.xml contains rules about locating user documents.

   B. **Correct:** MigUser.xml contains rules about migrating user profiles and user data.

   C. **Incorrect:** MigApp.xml contains rules about the migration of application settings.

   D. **Incorrect:** Config.xml contains information about what features to exclude from a migration.

4. **Correct Answer: C**

   A. **Incorrect:** Windows Anytime Upgrade is a tool used to upgrade from one edition of Windows 7 to another. It does not contain USMT 4.0

   B. **Incorrect:** Windows Upgrade Advisor is a tool that advises you whether hardware and software used with a computer running Windows Vista is compatible with Windows 7.

   C. **Correct:** The WAIK contains USMT 4.0.

   D. **Incorrect:** The Microsoft Application Compatibility Toolkit does not include USMT 4.0.

5. **Correct Answer: C**

   A. **Incorrect:** Uncompressed migration stores use the most hard disk space as it creates a copy of the data being migrated in a separate directory structure.

   B. **Incorrect:** Compressed migration stores create a compressed copy of the data being migrated in a separate directory structure.

   C. **Correct:** Hard-link migration stores create a set of hard links to all data that will be migrated in a separate location but do not actually duplicate that data on the volume.

Chapter 1: Case Scenario Answers

Case Scenario 1: Installing Windows 7 at Contoso

1. You could use WDS or a USB storage device as an installation source for deploying Windows 7. Because you do not have access to Windows PE, you cannot use a network share.

2. You could use a USB storage device as an installation source for deploying Windows 7. Because you do not have access to Windows PE, you cannot use a network share. You would not use WDS when you need to deploy operating systems to only five computers at each location.

3. Windows 7 Enterprise supports BitLocker hard disk drive encryption and is available to volume license customers. Although Windows 7 Ultimate also supports BitLocker hard disk drive encryption, it uses a retail license rather than a volume one.

Case Scenario 2: Migrating User Data at Fabrikam

1. Side-by-side migrations are appropriate because you are moving users in the branch offices from old computers to new computers. Wipe-and-load migrations are appropriate only when the same computer hardware is being used.

2. You should perform a wipe-and-load because the users in the head office will be using the same hardware and should not be able to boot into the x86 version of Windows 7 Enterprise after the upgrade is complete.

3. Use Windows Easy Transfer with the network method.

Chapter 2: Lesson Review Answers

Lesson 1

1. **Correct Answer: D**
   A. **Incorrect:** To capture a Windows 7 WIM image, you need to boot to Windows PE 3.0 (Windows PE).
   B. **Incorrect:** To capture a Windows 7 WIM image, you need to boot to Windows PE 3.0 (Windows PE). Also, the Windows SIM tool opens Windows images, creates answer files, and manages distribution shares and configuration sets. It does not create WIM images.
   C. **Incorrect:** To capture a Windows 7 WIM image, you need to boot to Windows PE 3.0 (Windows PE). Also, the DISM tool applies updates, drivers, and language packs to a Windows image. It does not create WIM images.
   D. **Correct:** To capture a Windows 7 WIM image, you boot to Windows PE 3.0 (Windows PE) and use the ImageX tool.

E. **Incorrect:** The Windows SIM tool opens Windows images, creates answer files, and manages distribution shares and configuration sets. It does not create WIM images.

F. **Incorrect:** The DISM tool applies updates, drivers, and language packs to a Windows image. It does not create WIM images.

2. **Correct Answers: A and E**

   A. **Correct:** The Windows SIM tool in Windows AIK automates the creation of an unattend answer file. In the Windows SIM Answer File pane, under Settings, you can select the appropriate setting and enter the required value in the right column.

   B. **Incorrect:** DISM applies updates, drivers, and language packs to a Windows image. You cannot use it to create an answer file.

   C. **Incorrect:** The Deployment Workbench tool lets you access MDT 2010 documentation, gives you a checklist of tasks you need to perform before you can deploy an operating system, enables you to create and configure a task sequence, and lets you view deployment points and create a deployment share. However, you cannot use it to create an answer file.

   D. **Incorrect:** Sysprep.exe prepares a computer for image deployment. You can use an answer file to automate the Sysprep process, but you cannot use Sysprep.exe to create an answer file.

   E. **Correct:** Although Windows SIM automates the process, some experienced administrators prefer to generate an unattend answer file directly by using a text editor such as Microsoft Notepad.

3. **Correct Answers: A, C, F, G, and H**

   A. **Correct:** You need the ImageX tool and Windows PE tools to create a system image on the reference computer. You also need the Oscdimg tool to generate an ISO file and create bootable Windows PE media. Therefore, you need to install the Windows AIK.

   B. **Incorrect:** It is not essential that you use an answer file to configure the reference computer, although this is the method Microsoft recommends. If you prefer, you can configure the computer manually.

   C. **Correct:** You need to install an operating system on your reference computer so you can image it.

   D. **Incorrect:** The question does not stipulate how the image is distributed and MDT is one of several possible methods. If you do use MDT and deploy the image on a large number of destination computers, you will probably install it on a server.

   E. **Incorrect:** The question does not stipulate how the image is distributed, and WDS is one of several possible methods. The question also does not state whether the destination computers are PXE-compatible.

   F. **Correct:** You need to boot the reference computer into Windows PE to image it.

G. **Correct:** Your goal is to create an image of the reference computer. You use the ImageX tool to do this.

H. **Correct:** You are distributing the image to several computers. You therefore need to prepare the reference computer for imaging by using *sysprep /generalize* and *sysprep /oobe*.

4. Correct Answer: C

A. **Incorrect:** *Sysprep /audit* restarts the computer into audit mode. This lets you add additional drivers or applications to Windows 7 and to test an installation before it is sent to a user. It does not remove unique system information from the installation.

B. **Incorrect:** *Sysprep /oobe* restarts the computer in Windows Welcome mode. This enables end users to customize their Windows 7 operating system, create user accounts, and name the computer. It does not remove unique system information from the installation.

C. **Correct:** *Sysprep /generalize* removes all unique system information from the Windows 7 installation. The SID is reset, system restore points are cleared and event logs are deleted.

D. **Incorrect:** *Sysprep /unattend*, followed by the name of an answer file, applies settings in that answer file to Windows 7 during unattended installation. It does not remove unique system information from the installation.

5. Correct Answer: A

A. **Correct:** The *oobeSystem* Windows Setup configuration pass applies settings to Windows 7 before Windows Welcome starts.

B. **Incorrect:** The *auditSystem* Windows Setup configuration pass processes unattended Setup settings while Windows 7 is running in system context before a user logs on to the computer in Audit mode. It does not apply settings to Windows 7 before Windows Welcome starts.

C. **Incorrect:** The *specialize* Windows Setup configuration pass creates and applies system-specific information such as network settings, international settings, and domain information. It does not apply settings to Windows 7 before Windows Welcome starts.

D. **Incorrect:** The *offlineServicing* Windows Setup configuration pass applies updates to a Windows image. It also applies packages, including software fixes, language packs, and other security updates. During this pass, you can add drivers to a Windows 7 image before that image is installed. It does not apply settings to Windows 7 before Windows Welcome starts.

Lesson 2

1. Correct Answer: B

A. **Incorrect:** A VHD is created as a file with a .vhd extension. You need to specify the file name Systemvhd.vhd.

B. **Correct:** This creates the VHD file as specified.

C. Incorrect: The size (or maximum size) of the VHD is specified in megabytes, not gigabytes. Therefore it needs to be 20000, not 20.

D. Incorrect: A VHD is created as a file with a .vhd extension. You need to specify the file name Systemvhd.vhd. Also, the size (or maximum size) of the VHD is specified in megabytes, not gigabytes. Therefore it needs to be 20000, not 20.

2. **Correct Answer: C**

A. Incorrect: This command forces Windows 7 to automatically detect the HAL when creating the boot entry.

B. Incorrect: This deletes a VHD entry from the Boot menu.

C. Correct: This tests if the boot entry has been created successfully.

D. Incorrect: This returns the GUID of the specified VHD.

3. **Correct Answer: D**

A. Incorrect: This command replaces an install image. Typically, you use this command when you have updated an install image and want to overwrite the old image file.

B. Incorrect: This command enables the Auto-Add policy on the WDS server.

C. Incorrect: This command creates a discover image.

D. Correct: This command adds an install image as specified.

4. **Correct Answer: A**

A. Correct: The Offline Virtual Machine Servicing Tool works with the SCVMM. Its main function is to create and implement a scheduled task that brings VHDs and virtual machines online for just long enough for them to obtain updates to their system images, typically from a WSUS server.

B. Incorrect: The SCVMM is a prerequisite for installing and running the Offline Virtual Machine Servicing Tool. However, it is the latter tool that implements scheduled boots from VHDs that are normally offline.

C. Incorrect: The Windows Deployment Services MMC snap-in is a GUI tool that is available when you install the WDS server role. It enables you to create, modify, and export disk images. It cannot implement scheduled boots from VHDs that are normally offline.

D. Incorrect: WDSUTIL is a command-line tool that is available when you install the WDS server role. It enables you to create, modify, and export disk images and to pre-stage client computers. It cannot implement scheduled boots from VHDs that are normally offline.

Chapter 2: Case Scenario Answers

Case Scenario 1: Generating a System Image

1. You should generate a WIM image file. You use the ImageX tool in Windows AIK to do this.

2. You should generate an ISO image file. You use the Oscdimg tool in Windows AIK to do this.

3. You can use the USMT tool in Windows AIK to transfer user data from computers running Windows Vista Ultimate to computers running Windows 7 Ultimate.

Case Scenario 2: Working with VHDs

1. You can boot only the computer running Windows 7 from the operating system captured on its VHD. Only Windows 7 Enterprise and Windows 7 Ultimate can be booted when installed on a VHD.

2. You need to run *sysprep /generalize* to strip hardware-specific information such as the SID from the image generated from the reference computer.

Chapter 3: Lesson Review Answers

Lesson 1

1. **Correct Answers: B and D**

   A. **Incorrect:** The DISM */image* option specifies the folder that contains the mounted 0image, not the source image.

   B. **Correct:** The */recurse* parameter causes all the drivers in the folder C:*drivers* and its subfolders to be added to the mounted image.

   C. **Incorrect:** The DISM */image* option specifies the folder that contains the mounted image, not the source image.

   D. **Correct:** This command would work, although Answer B would be the preferred solution Typically, you would use the */driver* parameter multiple times if the drivers were not in the same file structure (for example, C:\Printerdriver and C:\Scannerdriver).

2. **Correct Answer: A**

   A. **Correct:** The amount of writeable space available on a Windows PE system volume when booted in RAMdisk mode is known as the Windows PE system volume scratch space. You can use the */get-scratchspace* DISM option to obtain a value for this.

   B. **Incorrect:** This command returns the path to the root of the Windows PE image at boot time, known as the target path.

   C. **Incorrect:** This command determines whether the Windows PE profiling tool is enabled or disabled.

   D. **Incorrect:** Profiling (file logging) is disabled by default. This command enables it. However, the command does not return the amount of writeable space available on a Windows PE system volume when booted in RAMdisk mode.

3. **Correct Answer: D**

   A. **Incorrect:** The */set-syslocale* option sets the language for non-Unicode programs (also called the system locale) and the font settings. You can do this only in an offline-mounted image.

   B. **Incorrect:** The */set-userlocale* option configures a per-user setting that determines the default sort order and the default settings for formatting dates, times, currency, and numbers. You can do this only in an offline-mounted image.

C. Incorrect: The */set-inputlocale* option sets the input locale and keyboard layout. You can do this only in an offline-mounted image.

D. Correct: In an online working operating system, you can query international settings but not configure them. The DISM option */get-intl* is the only option that can be used with an online image.

4. **Correct Answer: B**

A. Incorrect: The mounted image is in C:\Mount, not C:\Textfiles\Answer. The answer file is in C:\Textfiles\Answer, not C:\Mount.

B. Correct: This command applies the file Unattend.xml in the folder C:\Textfiles\Answer to an image mounted in the C:\Mount folder.

C. Incorrect: The DISM option that applies an answer file to a mounted image is */apply-unattend*, not */apply*.

D. Incorrect: The DISM option that applies an answer file to a mounted image is */apply-unattend*, not */apply-answer*.

5. **Correct Answer: C**

A. Incorrect: The */get-appinfo* DISM option returns information about Windows Installer (*.msi*) applications. The */get-packageinfo* option returns information about packages implemented as cabinet (.cab) files.

B. Incorrect: The */get-appinfo* DISM option returns information about Windows Installer (.msi) applications. The */get-featureinfo* option returns information about Windows Features.

C. Correct: The */get-appinfo* DISM option returns information about Windows Installer (.msi) applications.

D. Incorrect: The */get-appinfo* DISM option returns information about Windows Installer (.msi) applications. The */get-apppatchinfo* option returns information about application patches (.msp files).

Lesson 2

1. **Correct Answer: B**

A. Incorrect: MDT 2010 can add updates, applications, and language packs to a WIM system image that can then be installed on client computers and VHDs. However, it does not update VHDs directly.

B. Correct: You can use the Offline Virtual Machine Servicing Tool to keep offline VHD files that contain installations of Windows 7 up to date with service packs and software updates.

C. Incorrect: You can use the BCDEdit command-line tool to add a boot entry for a VHD. The tool does not update VHDs.

D. Incorrect: You can use the Offline Virtual Machine Servicing Tool with VMM 2007 and either WSUS 3.0, SCCM 2007, or Configuration Manager 2007 R2. However, Configuration Manager 2007 R2 does not update VHDs directly.

2. **Correct Answer: D**

   A. **Incorrect:** When you boot a reference client computer from a WDS capture image, the Windows Deployment Services Image Capture Wizard enables you to capture a system image from that computer and export it to the WDS server. It does not directly specify the source directory in which the WIM file resides, specify whether setup or Sysprep files are required, or move the file to the distribution share.

   B. **Incorrect:** The SCCM 2007 Task Sequence Editor creates and modifies task sequences. In the New Task Sequence Wizard, you can select Install An Existing Image, Build A Reference Operating System Image, or Create A New Custom Task Sequence. However the wizard creates task sequences. It does not directly specify the source directory in which the WIM file resides, specify whether setup or Sysprep files are required, or move the file to the distribution share.

   C. **Incorrect:** You access the Create Distribution Share Wizard from the MDT 2010 Deployment Workbench console. This wizard lets you create a distribution share that will hold the WIM file, but it does not specify the source directory in which the WIM file resides, specify whether setup or Sysprep files are required, or move the file to the distribution share.

   D. **Correct:** You access the New OS Wizard from the MDT 2010 Deployment Workbench console. This wizard lets you specify the source directory in which the WIM file resides, specify whether setup or Sysprep files are required, and then move the file to the distribution share.

3. **Correct Answer: C**

   A. **Incorrect:** WDS deploys install images across the network. You do not need to install them on removable bootable media.

   B. **Incorrect:** When you boot a target computer from the network, WDS presents you with a boot menu on the target machine that enables you to boot from a boot image. This is delivered over the network and you do not need to install this image from bootable removable media. Note that the choice specifies a standard boot image. Discover and capture images are special types of boot image.

   C. **Correct:** If your target computers are not PXE-compliant, they cannot boot from the network. Therefore, you need to boot them from a discover image on removable, bootable media.

   D. **Incorrect:** If you want to capture the image of a reference computer, you boot it from a capture image. Capture images appear on the boot menu in the same way as standard boot images and you do not need to install them on bootable removable media.

4. **Correct Answers: A, E, and F**

   A. **Correct:** The WDS server role needs to be installed on a server in an AD DS domain.

   B. **Incorrect:** WDS can work with MDT 2010 to implement LTI, but it does not require MDT 2010 to deploy images.

   C. **Incorrect:** SQL Server is required with SCCM 2007 and MDT 2010 to implement ZTI. However, SQL Server is not a WDS requirement.

D. **Incorrect:** SCCM 2007 is required with SQL Server and MDT 2010 to implement ZTI. However, SCCM 2007 is not a WDS requirement.

E. **Correct:** WDS typically deploys to PXE-compliant target client computers that rely on DHCP for their IP configuration.

F. **Correct:** The WDS server role needs to be installed on a server in a network that contains at least one DNS server.

5. **Correct Answer: A**

A. **Correct:** To make the image bootable, you use BCDboot from Windows PE to initialize the BCD store and copy boot environment files to the system partition. On restart, the target computer boots into Windows 7 Ultimate.

B. **Incorrect:** DISM enables you to manage and manipulate a WIM image. It does not make an image bootable when you have installed it on a target computer.

C. **Incorrect:** You use BCDEdit to make media such as VHD and USB flash memory bootable. However, it does not make an image bootable when you have installed it on a target computer.

D. **Incorrect:** You used ImageX to create the WIM image on the source computer and install it on the target computer. However, ImageX cannot make the installed image bootable.

Chapter 3: Case Scenario Answers

Case Scenario 1: Deploying an Image with More Than One Language Pack

1. Don requires the following:
   - A technician computer with the Windows AIK tools installed and enough available space on the hard disk drive to both hold the master image and mount this image.
   - The Windows image (.wim file) that he wants to service.
   - The drivers (.inf files), update packages (.cab or .msu files), and the language packs (.cab files) that he will use to service the image.

2. Don's first task is to copy an instance of the master image to the technician computer. Microsoft does not recommend mounting an image from a network share.

3. Don uses DISM to mount the image. He then uses DISM commands to apply the update, add the new driver, and change the relevant settings. He checks that both language packs are installed on the image and the correct international settings can be configured. If it is likely that he will service the image regularly, he should create a script using the DISM command-line options. Don uses DISM to verify that the appropriate driver and other packages were added (or removed, if necessary) from the image. Finally, he commits and dismounts the image.

Case Scenario 2: Deploying an Image to 100 Client Computers

1. You need to ensure that all critical and recommended updates, particularly security updates, have been installed. Also, if any new hardware devices are to be used with the new computers that are not Plug and Play, you need to install the device drivers on the reference computer. You need to test the installation thoroughly. Finally, you need to use the Sysprep tool to generalize the computer configuration prior to the image capture.

2. You need to create a capture image on the WDS server.

3. You restart the reference computer and press F12 to boot from the network. On the boot menu, select the capture image and follow the procedure to create the computer's system image. You transfer the resulting WIM file to the WDS server. You boot each target computer from the network (if necessary, configuring the BIOS boot order to do so). You choose the standard boot image (not the capture image) from the boot menu and select the install image you created from the reference computer. The image is installed, and Setup continues normally.

Chapter 4: Lesson Review Answers

Lesson 1

1. Correct Answers: A and C
   A. **Correct:** The device must be signed with a valid digital certificate that is recognized by Windows 7 and is in the Trusted Publishers store. Otherwise, administrator privileges are required to install the device.
   B. **Incorrect:** Digital certificates are stored in the Trusted Publisher store, not device drivers.
   C. **Correct:** The device driver must be stored in the device driver store. Otherwise, administrator privileges are required to copy the driver to that store.
   D. **Incorrect:** The device does not need to connect through a USB port. It could, for example, be a PS/2 keyboard.
   E. **Incorrect:** Although Microsoft signs many drivers, a Microsoft signature is not essential. The digital certificate needs to be from a trusted CA. For example, in the domain environment, it could be a self-signed certificate.

2. Correct Answer: B
   A. **Incorrect:** You use this procedure to determine the power requirements of each device, not the bandwidth requirements.
   B. **Correct:** This procedure enables you to view the bandwidth requirements of each device in the Bandwidth-Consuming Devices list on the Advanced tab.
   C. **Incorrect:** The Details tab can give you a great deal of information (for example, the device-type GUID) but does not indicate bandwidth requirements. Also, the devices listed are not necessarily those on the USB hub.
   D. **Incorrect:** IEEE 1394 bus host controllers are not USB devices. Also, the Resources tab does not show bandwidth requirements.

3. **Correct Answers: A and D**

   A. **Correct:** This permits non-administrators to install any device in the device setup class, provided that the device driver is in the driver store.

   B. **Incorrect:** This instructs Windows 7 to search for a device driver in any folder and subfolder on the C: drive. However, administrator privileges are required to copy the driver to the driver store and install it.

   C. **Incorrect:** The Trusted Publisher store holds digital certificates that authenticate driver signatures. It does not hold device drivers.

   D. **Correct:** When a driver is staged, it is placed in the device driver store and non-administrators can install the device, provided they have permission to install devices in the appropriate device setup class.

4. **Correct Answer: B**

   A. **Incorrect:** This prevents automatic installation of drivers downloaded from Windows Update but does not remove the Web site from the search path.

   B. **Correct:** This prevents Windows 7 from searching for device drivers in Windows Update.

   C. **Incorrect:** The DevicePath registry entry does not list the Windows Update Web site specifically.

   D. **Incorrect:** This installs drivers from Windows Update if Windows 7 judges they are the best drivers based on inbuilt criteria. It does not prevent Windows 7 from searching for device drivers in Windows Update.

5. **Correct Answer: A**

   A. **Correct:** This stops the device driver and immediately disables the device.

   B. **Incorrect:** This ensures the device is disabled the next time the computer restarts. You would likely do this if you discovered the device was giving problems. However, it does not stop the device immediately to allow you to investigate.

   C. **Incorrect:** The Disable control is available for PnP devices but not for devices listed under Non-Plug And Play Drivers. You should use the Stop control instead.

   D. **Incorrect:** The Uninstall control is available for PnP devices but not for devices listed under Non-Plug And Play Drivers. In any case, you want to stop the driver, not uninstall it.

Lesson 2

1. **Correct Answer: A**

   A. **Correct:** This Diskpart command converts the selected disk to a GPT disk.

   B. **Incorrect:** This Diskpart command converts the selected disk to an MBR disk.

   C. **Incorrect:** This Diskpart command converts a selected dynamic disk to a static disk.

   D. **Incorrect:** This Diskpart command converts a selected static disk to a dynamic disk.

2. **Correct Answer: C**

   A. **Incorrect:** This is a valid strategy for Windows 7 Enterprise or Ultimate edition, but you cannot make a VHD bootable on a computer running Windows 7 Home Premium.

   B. **Incorrect:** RAID-0 (disk striping) offers no fault tolerance and you cannot store operating system files on a RAID-0 volume.

   C. **Correct:** You can use a RAID-1 volume to mirror the disk that holds your operating system and provide fault tolerance.

   D. **Incorrect:** RAID-0 (disk striping) offers fault tolerance and failover protection. However, you cannot store operating system files on a RAID-5 volume.

3. **Correct Answer: B**

   A. **Incorrect:** Enabling this policy permits remote users to access removable storage devices in remote sessions. It does not deny all access to all types of external storage devices.

   B. **Correct:** Enabling this policy denies all access to all types of external storage devices. It overrides any access rights granted by other policies.

   C. **Incorrect:** Enabling this policy denies read access to USB removable disks, portable media players, and cellular phones. It does not deny all access to all types of external storage devices.

   D. **Incorrect:** Enabling this policy denies write access to USB removable disks, portable media players, and cellular phones. It does not deny all access to all types of external storage devices.

4. **Correct Answer: B**

   A. **Incorrect:** To create the largest possible RAID-0 (striped) volume, you omit the *size* parameter. Specifying a size of zero does not do this.

   B. **Correct:** This command creates the largest possible RAID-0 volume.

   C. **Incorrect:** The *create volume raid* command creates a RAID-5 volume. Also, to specify the largest possible volume you omit the *size* parameter.

   D. **Incorrect:** This command creates the largest possible RAID-5 volume.

5. **Correct Answer: D**

   A. **Incorrect:** If you had used the *mountvol /n* or the *diskpart automount* command on Aberdeen to prevent new volumes from being added to the system, the volume would not be mounted and would not receive a drive letter. However, the question explicitly states that you did not do this.

   B. **Incorrect:** When you move a basic volume to another computer, it receives the next available drive letter on that computer. However, you are moving a dynamic volume.

   C. **Incorrect:** The G: drive letter is neither the next available letter on Aberdeen nor the drive letter to which the volume had been allocated on Canberra. There is no reason for this drive letter to be allocated.

   D. **Correct:** When moved to a new computer, dynamic volumes retain the drive letter they had on the previous computer, in this case H:.

Chapter 4: Case Scenario Answers

Case Scenario 1: Enforcing a Driver Signing Policy

1. The Dxdiag tool diagnoses any problems with the video card and will tell you whether the driver is WHQL approved.

2. The Sigverif tool scans the computer and detects any unsigned drivers.

3. The Msinfo32 tool lists the resources and tells you what driver uses what resources. In particular, you should investigate Conflicts/Sharing under Hardware Resources.

4. Driver Verifier Monitor tests the device driver under configurable stress conditions.

Case Scenario 2: Managing Disks

1. You would create a RAID-1 (mirror) array to hold your operating system and would mirror Drive 0 with 200 GB of the allocated space on Drive 2.

2. You would create a RAID-5 (striping with parity) volume using the unallocated space on Drives 1 and 3 (both 200 GB) and the 200 GB unallocated space that remains on Drive 2. A RAID-5 volume offers fault tolerance and reduced data access times. Although a RAID-0 array would provide a greater usable data storage capacity and a greater improvement in performance, it is not fault-tolerant.

3. Three 200 GB portions of unallocated disk would result in a RAID-5 array with 400 GB of usable storage capacity.

Chapter 5: Lesson Review Answers

Lesson 1

1. **Correct Answer: A**

   A. **Correct:** You should install the Windows XP Mode feature and install the application under Windows XP. Windows XP Mode runs a fully virtualized copy of Windows XP on a computer that has the Windows 7 Professional, Enterprise, or Ultimate operating system installed. Applications that work on Windows XP and that have compatibility problems that cannot be resolved using the ACT function in Windows XP Mode.

   B. **Incorrect:** You should not create a custom compatibility fix because the question already indicates that you have been unsuccessful in configuring a custom compatibility mode, which is a collection of such fixes.

   C. **Incorrect:** A shim is the previous name for a custom compatibility fix. The question text already indicates that you have been unsuccessful in configuring a custom compatibility mode, which is a collection of these fixes.

   D. **Incorrect:** You should not configure the application installer to run in Windows XP Professional SP2 mode because you have already found that you are unable to get the application working using the tools included in the ACT. The ACT provides more compatibility mode options than those built into Windows 7. If an application functions under the built-in Windows 7 compatibility modes, it can work under the ACT modes.

2. **Correct Answer: D**

   A. **Incorrect:** Although the application may function in the Windows 98/Windows Me compatibility mode, you only have evidence that the application functions on the Windows 2000 operating system, so you should use this compatibility mode first and try others only if the Windows 2000 mode is unsuccessful.

   B. **Incorrect:** Although the application may function in the Windows NT 4.0 (Service Pack 5) compatibility mode, you only have evidence that the application functions on the Windows 2000 operating system, so you should use this compatibility mode first and try others only if the Windows 2000 mode is unsuccessful.

   C. **Incorrect:** You should not configure the application to run under Windows XP (Service Pack 2) compatibility mode because you have evidence that the application does not function on computers running Windows XP.

   D. **Correct:** You should configure the application to run under the Windows 2000 compatibility mode because you know that the application functions on computers with Windows 2000 installed.

3. **Correct Answer: B**

   A. **Incorrect:** You cannot use the compatibility troubleshooter to troubleshoot .cab files. You must extract the contents of the .cab file to find the executable file that contains the application installer.

   B. **Correct:** The Program Compatibility troubleshooter works only with executable files.

   C. **Incorrect:** You cannot use the compatibility troubleshooter to troubleshoot .msi installer files. The Program Compatibility troubleshooter only works with executable files that have the .exe extension.

   D. **Incorrect:** You cannot use the compatibility troubleshooter to troubleshoot .zip files. You need to extract the contents of the .zip file to find the executable file that contains the application installer.

4. **Correct Answer: C**

   A. **Incorrect:** You should not configure the application to run in Windows XP (Service Pack 3) compatibility mode because the problem is that the application does not prompt for elevation. The program will still be unable to prompt for elevation when running in this compatibility mode.

   B. **Incorrect:** You should not configure the application to run in 256-color mode. This compatibility option should be used only when the application has display problems.

   C. **Correct:** You should enable the Run This Program As An Administrator compatibility option if the application is not configured to prompt for elevation when administrative privileges are required. This will allow the program to run with administrative privileges once the user responds to a User Account Control prompt.

   D.   **Incorrect:** You should not enable the Disable Desktop Composition compatibility option. You should enable this option when you need the Aero interface disabled when the application executes.

5. **Correct Answer: B**

   A.   **Incorrect:** You can use the IEAK to configure Internet Explorer. You cannot use this toolkit to determine whether an existing Web site displays correctly for users of Internet Explorer 8, which is the default browser of Windows 7.

   B.   **Correct:** The ACT includes the Internet Explorer Compatibility Test Tool. This tool can be used to evaluate whether a Web site is compatible with Internet Explorer 8, which is the default browser of Windows 7.

   C.   **Incorrect:** The Windows AIK includes tools that assist in deploying the Windows operating system. You cannot use this toolkit to determine whether an existing Web site displays correctly for users of Internet Explorer 8, which is the default browser of Windows 7.

   D.   **Incorrect:** The MDT is a solution accelerator that assists in the planning and deployment of operating systems to client computers. You cannot use this toolkit to determine whether an existing Web site displays correctly for users of Internet Explorer 8, which is the default browser of Windows 7.

Lesson 2

1. **Correct Answer: D**

   A.   **Incorrect:** AppLocker cannot be used to block the execution of applications on computers running Windows Vista or Windows 7 Professional.

   B.   **Incorrect:** AppLocker cannot be used to block the execution of applications on computers running Windows Vista or Windows 7 Professional.

   C.   **Incorrect:** AppLocker cannot be used to block the execution of applications on computers running Windows Vista or Windows 7 Professional.

   D.   **Correct:** Because you cannot use AppLocker to block the execution of applications on Windows Vista or Windows 7 Professional, you should use Software Restriction Policies to accomplish the same objective.

2. **Correct Answer: A**

   A.   **Correct:** Publisher rules allow you to block applications based on which software vendor wrote the application.

   B.   **Incorrect:** Path rules do not allow you to block applications based on which software vendor wrote the application, as the question stipulates; they allow you to block an executable file based on its location.

   C.   **Incorrect:** Hash rules do not allow you to block applications based on which software vendor wrote the application, as the question stipulates; they allow you to block a specific executable file based on a hash value generated from that file.

3. Correct Answers: B and C

    A. **Incorrect:** You should not create AppLocker publisher rules. Publisher rules can be used only when the file that is the subject of the rule has been signed digitally by the publisher.

    B. **Correct:** You should create an AppLocker hash rule because it is not possible to create a publisher rule due to the lack of digital signature.

    C. **Correct:** You should configure AppLocker enforcement to audit executable rules. This allows you to ensure that the rules relating to applications function before you enforce them in a production environment.

    D. **Incorrect:** You should not configure AppLocker enforcement to audit Windows Installer rules because you are interested in the functionality of executable rules.

4. Correct Answer: C

    A. **Incorrect:** You should not configure Group Policy to set the Application Management service to start automatically. The Application Management service is used to process installation, removal, and enumeration requests for software deployed through Group Policy. The service that you want to configure to start automatically is the Application Identity service.

    B. **Incorrect:** As the Software Restriction Policies are functioning properly, you do not need to modify the settings of services related to the computers running Windows 7 Professional.

    C. **Correct:** For AppLocker policies to function properly, you need to have the Application Identity service functioning. The default setting on Windows 7 is to have this service disabled. Through Group Policy, you can force this service to start automatically, which allows AppLocker policies to be enforced.

    D. **Incorrect:** Because the Software Restriction Policies are functioning properly, you do not need to modify the settings of services related to the computers running Windows 7 Professional.

5. Correct Answer: A

    A. **Correct:** You need to create a new hash rule for the application. Hash rules need to be updated whenever you apply an update to an application. This is because the update changes the characteristics of the file so that it no longer matches the hash rule generated for it originally.

    B. **Incorrect:** Because the application is not signed digitally, you cannot use a publishing rule to manage it with AppLocker.

    C. **Incorrect:** Because other AppLocker policies are functioning, you can infer that the Application Identity service is active and its status does not need to be modified.

    D. **Incorrect:** The Application Management service is related to software installation, removal, and enumeration through Group Policy. This service does not affect AppLocker policies directly.

Chapter 5: Case Scenario Answers

Case Scenario 1: Configuring Application Compatibility at Fabrikam

1. Edit the properties of application Alpha. Configure the application to run using the Windows XP Service Pack 3 compatibility mode.

2. Edit the properties of the Beta application. On the compatibility tab, enable the Run This Program As An Administrator option. This enables the Run As Administrator option without having to right-click the application each time to enable this functionality.

3. You can use the ACT to configure compatibility options for Application Gamma.

Case Scenario 2: Restricting Applications at Contoso

1. Configure an AppLocker executable rule that uses a file hash of the data collection application. You cannot use a publisher rule because the application is not digitally signed.

2. Configure this rule to apply to the Everyone group. Block the execution of the application, but configure an exception for the Scientists group.

3. The in-house developers would need to sign the application digitally before you can create a publisher rule for it.

Chapter 6: Lesson Review Answers

Lesson 1

1. **Correct Answer: C**

   A. **Incorrect:** The *Ping* command is used to test connectivity. It does not display the IP configuration of a computer's interfaces.

   B. **Incorrect:** The *Tracert* command is used to test connectivity to a device on a remote network and return information about the intermediate hops. It does not display the IP configuration of a computer's interfaces.

   C. **Correct:** The *Ipconfig* command displays the IP configuration of a computer's interfaces.

   D. **Incorrect:** The *Netstat* tool displays protocol statistics. It does not display the IP configuration of a computer's interfaces.

2. **Correct Answers: B, C, and D**

   A. **Incorrect:** This accesses the Local Area Network (LAN Settings) dialog box. You can select automatic configuration, specify an automatic configuration script, or specify a proxy server. The dialog box does not display connection properties.

B. Correct: This procedure accesses the Local Area Connections Properties dialog box.

C. Correct: This is an alternative method of accessing the Local Area Connections Properties dialog box.

D. Correct: Double-clicking the LAN connection opens the Local Area Connection Status dialog box. Clicking Properties accesses the Local Area Connections Properties dialog box.

3. **Correct answer: D**

   A. Incorrect: DNS resolves computer names to IP addresses. You are pinging the computers by their IPv4 addresses, not their computer names, and a DNS service is not required for the commands to succeed.

   B. Incorrect: All computers on the same subnet must have the same subnet mask.

   C. Incorrect: The subnet is isolated and no gateway is required to send traffic to other networks. You do not need to define a gateway to implement connectivity between two computers within the same subnet.

   D. Correct: By default Windows Firewall blocks the Ping command. You need to enable ICMPv4 traffic at both firewalls. At an elevated command prompt on both computers, enter **netsh advfirewall firewall add rule name="ICMPv4"**.

4. **Correct Answer: B**

   A. Incorrect: This sets a /24 subnet mask. The question specifies a /25 subnet mask (255.255.255.128).

   B. Correct: This configures a static IPv4 address 10.0.10.162 on the 10.0.10.128/25 subnet.

   C. Incorrect: This specifies dynamic configuration.

   D. Incorrect: The 10.0.10.128/25 subnet has an IPv4 address range 10.0.10.129 through 10.0.10.254. The IPv4 address 10.0.10.16 is not on this subnet.

5. **Correct Answers: C and D**

   A. Incorrect: The command *netsh interface ipv4 show route* shows route table entries, but it does not display IPv6 routes.

   B. Incorrect: The command *tracert –d* traces the route of an IP packet through an internetwork. It lists the path the packet took and the delays encountered at each hop. The *–d* flag prevents the tool from resolving IPv4 addresses to host names. The command does not display a route table.

   C. Correct: The command *route print* displays both the IPv4 and IPv6 route tables.

   D. Correct: The command *netstat –r* displays the same output as the route print command.

   E. Incorrect: The command *netstat –a* displays all active connections and the TCP and UDP ports on which the computer is listening. It does not display a route table.

Lesson 2

1. **Correct Answer: A**

   A. **Correct:** Typically you would use a site-local address. If every device on the subnet had a global address, you could also use global addresses, but this option is not given in the question.

   B. **Incorrect:** If you use link-local addresses, you need to specify their interface IDs. Also, link-local addresses are not dynamically registered in Windows DDNS. It is therefore much easier to use site-local addresses and typically they are used for this purpose.

   C. **Incorrect:** Only two special addresses exist, :: and ::1. Neither can implement IPv6 connectivity over a private network.

   D. **Incorrect:** An anycast address is configured only on a router and cannot implement IPv6 connectivity over a private network. Also, it is not a unicast address.

2. **Correct Answer: B**

   A. **Incorrect:** The address fec0:0:0:0:fffe::1 is a site-local unicast IPv6 address that identifies a node in a site or intranet. This type of address is the equivalent of an IPv6 private address (for example, 10.0.0.1), and is not globally routable and reachable on the IPv6 Internet.

   B. **Correct:** The address 21cd:53::3ad:3f:af37:8d62 is a global unicast address. This type of address is the IPv6 equivalent of an IPv4 public unicast addresses and is globally routable and reachable on the IPv6 Internet.

   C. **Incorrect:** The address fe80:d1ff:d166:7888:2fd6 is a link-local unicast IPv6 address and is autoconfigured on a local subnet. It is the equivalent of an IPv4 APIPA address (for example, 169.254.10.123), and it is not globally routable or reachable on the IPv6 Internet.

   D. **Incorrect:** The loopback address ::1 identifies a loopback interface and is equivalent to the IPv4 loopback address 127.0.0.1. It is not globally routable or reachable on the IPv6 Internet.

3. **Correct Answer: D**

   A. **Incorrect:** ARP is a broadcast-based protocol used by IPv4 to resolve IPv4 addresses to MAC addresses. It does not manage the interaction of neighboring nodes and resolve IPv6 addresses to MAC addresses.

   B. **Incorrect:** DNS is a service rather than a protocol. It resolves computer names to IP addresses. It does not manage the interaction of neighboring nodes and resolve IPv6 addresses to MAC addresses.

   C. **Incorrect:** DHCPv6 assigns stateful IPv6 configurations. It does not manage the interaction of neighboring nodes and resolve IPv6 addresses to MAC addresses.

   D. **Correct:** ND uses ICMPv6 messages to manage the interaction of neighboring nodes and resolve IPv6 addresses to MAC addresses.

4. **Correct Answer: A**

   A. Correct: This is a Teredo compatibility address. Teredo addresses start with 2001.

   B. Incorrect: This is a 6to4 compatibility address. 6to4 addresses start with 2002.

   C. Incorrect: This is a link-local ISATAP address. Look for 5efe followed by the hexadecimal representation of an IPv4 address, in this case 10.0.2.143.

   D. Incorrect: This is a site-local Ipv6 address. It is not an IPv4-to-IPv6 compatibility address.

5. **Correct Answer: C**

   A. Incorrect: A PTR resource record performs a reverse lookup and resolves an IPv4 or IPv6 address (depending on the reverse lookup zone specified) to a host name.

   B. Incorrect: An A (address) resource record resolves a host name to an IPv4 address.

   C. Correct: An AAAA (quad-A) resource record resolves a host name to an IPv6 address.

   D. Incorrect: A host resource record is another name for an A record. It resolves a host name to an IPv4 address.

Lesson 3

1. **Correct Answer: C**

   A. Incorrect: The user's computer works fine in the office. There is no need to reconfigure the office network.

   B. Incorrect: The order in which the user's computer accesses networks is not the problem. The problem occurs when her computer is within range of two wireless networks and switches between them.

   C. Correct: The likely cause of the reported behavior is that the lounge area of the hotel is within range of (and possibly equidistant between) two wireless networks and keeps switching between them. You can disable this feature or tell the user how to do so. You need to warn the user that if she moves to another part of the hotel, she might need to reconnect to a network.

   D. Incorrect: The user's laptop is working in the office and her hotel room. There is nothing wrong with her wireless adapter.

2. **Correct Answer: A**

   A. Correct: The MAC address is unique to an interface and does not change. MAC ensures that only computers whose wireless interfaces have one of the listed MAC addresses can access a wireless network. Be aware that if a new computer needs to access the network, or if you replace the wireless adapter in a computer, you need to register the new MAC address in the WAP.

   B. Incorrect: Most networks are configured by using DHCP so IPv4 addresses can change. Even in networks where IPv4 addresses are statically configured, it is unlikely that the WAP supports IPv4 address control.

C. **Incorrect:** WEP is an encryption method that ensures that third parties cannot read messages if they intercept them. It does not determine which computers can access a network.

D. **Incorrect:** Like WEP, WPA is an encryption method and does not determine which computers can access a network.

3. **Correct Answers: C, E, and F**

A. **Incorrect:** The Network Diagnostic tool is not a system tool and can't be accessed from the System Tools menu.

B. **Incorrect:** You run the Windows Network Diagnostic tool when you have a problem. It is not a tool that you schedule to run on a regular basis and it is not in the task scheduler library.

C. **Correct:** You can run the Network Diagnostic tool from the Network And Sharing Center.

D. **Incorrect:** You cannot access the Windows Network Diagnostic tool from the Adapter Properties dialog box. This dialog box is used for configuration, not diagnosis.

E. **Correct:** You can run the Windows Network Diagnostic tool when you fail to connect to a Web page.

F. **Correct:** You can run the Windows Network Diagnostic tool for a specific connection by accessing the Network Connections dialog box.

4. **Correct Answer: B**

A. **Incorrect:** Windows Firewall protects Don's computer and is enabled by default. His neighbor is accessing his WAP, not his computer.

B. **Correct:** Don found the WAP setup easy because he accepted all the defaults and did not set up any security. He needs to change his SSID from its default value. He should also configure encryption and set up a passphrase. He should change the access password. He should consider restricting access by MAC address.

C. **Incorrect:** Changing the WAP channel can solve problems related to interference from mobile phones or microwave ovens (for example). It does not affect access to a network.

D. **Incorrect:** ICS enables other computers to obtain their IPv4 configuration from the ICS computer. Unless Don has non-wireless computers connected through a wired interface to his wireless computer, he does not need to set up ICS. Additional wireless computers obtain their configurations directly from the WAP. This has no bearing on whether his neighbor can access his network.

5. **Correct Answer: D**

A. **Incorrect:** This specifies LaserF2 as the default printer whatever floor Sam is on and whatever network he is connected to. This causes problems because Sam cannot connect to LaserF2 when he is on the third floor.

B. **Incorrect:** This specifies LaserF3 as the default printer whatever floor Sam is on and whatever network he is connected to. This causes problems because Sam cannot connect to LaserF3 when he is on the second floor.

C. Incorrect: This specifies LaserF3 as the default printer when Sam is on the second floor and LaserF2 as the default printer when Sam is on the third floor. This causes problems because LaserF3 is on a network that is not accessible from the second floor and LaserF2 is on a network that is not accessible from the third floor.

D. Correct: This specifies LaserF2 as the default printer when Sam is on the second floor and LaserF3 as the default printer when Sam is on the third floor, which is the required scenario.

Chapter 6: Case Scenario Answers

Case Scenario 1: Implementing IPv4 Connectivity

1. Your friend needs to set up ICS on the computer that connects to his modem. He needs to ensure that the other computers on his network obtain their IPv4 configuration automatically. When he has configured ICS on the first computer, he should reboot the other two.

2. He should plug the WAP into his cable modem though its WLAN connection. He then should connect the three wired desktop computers to the Ethernet ports on the WAP and configure the WAP from one of them using its Web interface. He can connect the wireless computer to his network through Network And Sharing Center or by clicking the Wireless icon on the bottom left section of his screen.

Case Scenario 2: Implementing IPv6 Connectivity

1. Site-local IPv6 addresses are the direct equivalent of private IPv4 addresses and are routable between VLANs. However, you could also consider configuring every device on your network with an aggregatable global unicast IPv6 address. NAT and CIDR were introduced to address a lack of IPv4 address space, and this is not a problem in IPv6. You cannot use only link-local IPv6 addresses in this situation because they are not routable.

2. This is a Teredo address associated with a Teredo tunnel. It is used to implement compatibility between IPv6 and IPv4.

Case Scenario 3: Using Laptop Computers Running Windows 7 on Wireless Networks

1. Windows 7 introduces location-aware printing. The employee can use the office printer as her default printer while at Margie's Travel and her inkjet printer as her default printer while at home. The switchover is seamless and automatic provided that both printers are designated as the default printers.

2. Windows 7 introduces the Network Printer Installation Wizard. This is easier to use than the Add Printer Wizard and users can install printers without requiring administrative privileges.

3. The employee is unfortunate because his desk is located where two wireless networks overlap. If it is impractical to move the employee's desk, you can disable automatic switching. This solves the problem, but the employee should be advised that he would need to connect to a network manually if he moves to some other areas in the building.

Chapter 7: Lesson Review Answers

Lesson 1

1. **Correct Answer: B**

   A. **Incorrect:** Inbound rules are used to block traffic from the network to the computer. You want to block a specific type of network traffic from the computer to the network, which necessitates the use of outbound rules.

   B. **Correct:** Outbound rules allow you to block and allow traffic that originates on the computer from traveling out to the network. You should configure an outbound rule to block students from using FTP to upload files to sites on the Internet and an outbound rule to allow students to use SMTP to send e-mail.

   C. **Incorrect:** Isolation rules are used to limit the hosts that a computer can communicate with to those that meet a specific set of authentication criteria. They cannot be used to block an outbound specific protocol.

   D. **Incorrect:** Authentication exemption rules are used in conjunction with Isolation rule to allow connections to be made without requiring that authentication occur. Authentication exemption rules apply to inbound traffic rather than outbound.

2. **Correct Answers: B and C**

   A. **Incorrect:** Windows Firewall does not allow you to create firewall rules for specific network locations on the basis of port address. Windows Firewall does not allow you to create rules that differentiate between the home and work network locations. You can only create rules that differentiate on the basis of home and work or public network locations.

   B. **Correct:** You can use WFAS to create firewall rules on the basis of port address and on the basis of network location.

   C. **Correct:** You can use the *Netsh* command-line utility to create WFAS rules. WFAS rules allow you to create firewall rules on the basis of port address and on the basis of network location.

   D. **Incorrect:** Netstat is a tool used to provide information about network traffic. You cannot use Netstat to create firewall rules.

3. **Correct Answer: C**

   A. **Incorrect:** The rule in the question allows traffic rather than blocks traffic.

   B. **Incorrect:** The rule in the question applies to inbound traffic rather than outbound traffic.

   C. **Correct:** This rule, called CustomRule, applies in the domain profile and allows inbound TCP traffic on port 80. You can create WFAS rules using Netsh in the *advfirewall* context.

   D. **Incorrect:** The rule in the question is an inbound rule rather than an outbound rule.

4. **Correct Answer: B**
    A. **Incorrect:** Although you can create rules based on applications using Windows Firewall, you cannot use this tool to create rules that require that incoming connections be authenticated.
    B. **Correct:** WFAS allows you to create detailed rules that include the ability to allow incoming traffic only if it is authenticated.
    C. **Incorrect:** Credential Manager stores authentication credentials. It cannot be used to create firewall rules that require authentication.
    D. **Incorrect:** Authorization Manager allows you to configure roles for the delegation of administrative privileges. You cannot use Authorization Manager to create firewall rules that require authentication.

5. **Correct Answers: A and D**
    A. **Correct:** You should configure Windows Firewall to notify you when it blocks a program in the Home Or Work (Private) Network Location Settings area. This ensures that you receive a message when a new program is blocked when connected to this network profile.
    B. **Incorrect:** You should not disable the setting related to receiving a message when a new program is blocked in the Home Or Work (Private) Network Location Settings area because this means that you do not receive a message when a program is blocked.
    C. **Incorrect:** You should not enable the setting related to receiving a message when a new program is blocked in the Public Network Location Settings area because this notifies you when a new program is blocked. The question text states that you should not be notified when this occurs.
    D. **Incorrect:** You should disable the setting related to receiving a message when a new program is blocked in the Public Network Location Settings area because this ensures that you are not notified when a program is blocked.

Lesson 2

1. **Correct Answer: C**
    A. **Incorrect:** You should not enable Remote Assistance. Remote Assistance requires that someone is logged on to the computer that you wish to manage remotely.
    B. **Incorrect:** You should not enable the Remote Desktop: Don't Allow Connections To This Computer option because that blocks the ability to make Remote Desktop connections.
    C. **Correct:** You should enable the Remote Desktop: Allow Connections From Computer Running Any Version Of Remote Desktop setting because this allows you to connect to a computer running Windows 7 from a computer running Windows XP with SP2.
    D. **Incorrect:** You should not enable the Remote Desktop: Allow Connections Only From Computers With Network Level Authentication as clients running Windows XP with SP2 are unable to connect to clients running Windows 7 when this option is enabled. Windows XP requires SP3 and special configuration to use Network-Level Authentication.

2. **Correct Answer: B**

   A. **Incorrect:** You need to configure client Beta rather than client Alpha using the *WinRM Quickconfig* command.

   B. **Correct:** You need to run the command *WinRM Quickconfig* on client Beta before you can manage it remotely from client Alpha using Windows PowerShell. This command starts the WinRM service, configures a listener for the ports that send and receive WS-Management protocol messages, and configures firewall exceptions.

   C. **Incorrect:** It is not necessary to create a firewall rule on client Alpha.

   D. **Incorrect:** Although it is necessary to create a firewall rule on client Beta, it is also necessary to configure a listener for WS-Management protocol messages and to start the WinRM service. All these tasks can be accomplished by running the *WinRM quickconfig* command. Only one of these tasks can be accomplished by creating a firewall rule.

3. **Correct Answer: B**

   A. **Incorrect:** The command *nslookup Aberdeen* provides the computer's IP address but does not provide the MAC address.

   B. **Correct:** The command *winrs –r:Aberdeen ipconfig /all* runs the command *ipconfig /all* on Aberdeen but displays the results on the computer that you are logged on to, which in this case is computer Canberra. *Ipconfig /all* displays a computer's MAC address.

   C. **Incorrect:** You should not use the command *winrs –r:Canberra ipconfig /all* because this displays computer Canberra's IP address information, not the IP address information of computer Aberdeen.

   D. **Incorrect:** The command *arp –a* displays information about IP addresses and MAC addresses on the same subnet but does not display MAC address information about computers on remote subnets. To use this command to determine another computer's MAC address, you also have to know that computer's IP address.

4. **Correct Answer: B**

   A. **Incorrect:** The Windows PowerShell command *icm Canberra {Get-Process}* displays process information from computer Canberra, not computer Aberdeen.

   B. **Correct:** The Windows PowerShell command *icm Aberdeen {Get-Process}* opens a remote Windows PowerShell session to computer Aberdeen and runs the *Get-Process* cmdlet, which displays process information, including listing data about CPU and memory usage.

   C. **Incorrect:** You cannot use WinRS to invoke a Windows PowerShell cmdlet. You must use Windows PowerShell with the syntax *icm remotehost {PowerShell Cmdlet}* to use Windows PowerShell remotely.

   D. **Incorrect:** You cannot use WinRS to invoke a Windows PowerShell cmdlet. You must use Windows PowerShell with the syntax *icm remotehost {PowerShell Cmdlet}* to use Windows PowerShell remotely. In this example, WinRS targets computer Canberra rather than computer Aberdeen.

5. **Correct Answer: D**

A. **Incorrect:** The WinRM service is required for remote use of Windows PowerShell and Remote Shell. The WinRM service is not required for Remote Assistance.

B. **Incorrect:** A client does not have to be configured to accept Remote Desktop sessions to use Remote Assistance, so this setting does not explain why the connection cannot be made. Clients running Windows 7 always support Network Level Authentication.

C. **Incorrect:** The helper does not need to log on to the target computer when participating in a Remote Assistance session, so it does not matter what groups her user account is a member of. A Remote Assistance session allows the helper to see the desktop of the currently logged-on user, so everything that is done within that session is done with the currently logged-on user's privileges.

D. **Correct:** If the Remote Assistance panel is closed, it stops any possible Remote Assistance connection.

Chapter 7: Case Scenario Answers

Case Scenario 1: University Client Firewalls

1. Configure a Windows Firewall rule that allows incoming Web traffic on the local subnet. This allows people at the conference to connect to the Web site but does not allow people from other networks to make similar connections.

2. You should configure a port-based outbound rule to block the file sharing program in the undergraduate computer lab. Port-based rules allow you to block specific ports and can be useful when the programs that use those ports have different identities.

3. You could create a set of firewall rules on a reference computer and export them to a USB flash device. You could then import the firewall rules on each of the other stand-alone computers in the postgraduate computer laboratory.

Case Scenario 2: Antarctic Desktop Support

1. As installing the application requires the ability to elevate privileges, you need to connect to the client running Windows 7 using Remote Desktop and log on.

2. Add the user's account to the Remote Desktop Users group on the client running Windows 7 at the Antarctic base. If the user at the Tasmanian office is using a client running Windows XP, ensure that the settings on the client running Windows 7 in Antarctica do not require Network Level Authentication.

3. Before you can run Windows PowerShell scripts remotely against the clients running Windows 7, you need to run the WinRM Quickconfig command from an elevated command prompt on each computer.

Chapter 8: Lesson Review Answers

Lesson 1

1. Correct Answers: B, C, and D

    A. **Incorrect:** You do not need to share each data folder; you can add them to a common library and then share the library using HomeGroups.

    B. **Correct:** You should create a new library named Sci_Data, add each instrument's separate data folder to the library, and then share it using the HomeGroup control panel.

    C. **Correct:** You should create a new library named Sci_Data, add each instrument's separate data folder to the library, and then share it using the HomeGroup control panel.

    D. **Correct:** You should create a new library named Sci_Data, add each instrument's separate data folder to the library, and then share it using the HomeGroup control panel.

2. Correct Answer: C

    A. **Incorrect:** The Print permission allows a user to manage their documents but not the documents of others.

    B. **Incorrect:** Users that you assign the Manage This Printer permission are able to reconfigure printer permissions. They are not able to manage the documents of other users directly, though they can assign themselves the Manage Documents permission and accomplish this task indirectly.

    C. **Correct:** When you assign a person the Manage Documents permission, she is able to reorder any documents in the queue and cancel them.

    D. **Incorrect:** The Power Users group is included for backward compatibility with earlier versions of Windows. Assigning a user to the Power Users group does not confer any printer permissions.

3. Correct Answers: A and B

    A. **Correct:** You can use the *net share* command to view share names and the folders with which those folders are associated.

    B. **Correct:** You can use the Computer Management console to view share names and the folders with which those shares are associated.

    C. **Incorrect:** Libraries allows you to configure libraries. You cannot use Libraries to determine which shared folders a client running Windows 7 hosts because it is possible to host shared folders that are not libraries.

    D. **Incorrect:** You can use Network And Sharing Center to configure sharing options, but you cannot use Network And Sharing Center to determine which shared folders a client running Windows 7 hosts.

4. Correct Answer: B

    A. **Incorrect:** You should not assign the Read permission. If you assign this permission, users are unable to modify or delete files.

B. Correct: You should assign the Modify permission because this allows users to add, modify, and delete files located in the accounting shared folder.

C. Incorrect: You should not assign the Full Control permission because then users have the ability to modify shared folder permissions.

D. Incorrect: You cannot assign the Owner permission to groups. When you use basic sharing, Windows automatically assigns this permission to the user who shares the folder.

5. **Correct Answer: D**

A. Incorrect: Enabling this option does not ensure that shared resources are visible to other computers in the HomeGroup. This option allows HomeGroup readers to read and write files in the public folder.

B. Incorrect: Enabling this option does not ensure that shared resources are visible to other computers in the HomeGroup. This option controls the encryption level of file sharing connections.

C. Incorrect: Password Protected Sharing restricts access to shared resources hosted on the client. Only users with local accounts on the client are able to access shared resources when Password Protected Sharing is enabled. Enabling this option does not ensure that shared resources are visible to other computers in the HomeGroup.

D. Correct: Network Discovery allows the client to find other computers on the network. It also allows other computers on the network to view resources shared by the client.

Lesson 2

1. **Correct Answer: B**

A. Incorrect: Jeff needs an EFS certificate for you to be able to encrypt a file that he can access. Changing a password does not generate an EFS certificate.

B. Correct: If Jeff encrypts a file on the computer, it generates an EFS certificate. You can then use this EFS certificate to encrypt the file to his account.

C. Incorrect: Jeff does not need write access to the file for you to be able to use EFS to encrypt the file to his account. Jeff needs an encryption certificate, which can be generated by having Jeff encrypt a file on the computer.

D. Incorrect: Letting Jeff take ownership of the files does not allow you to use EFS to encrypt the file to his account. Jeff needs an encryption certificate, which can be generated by having Jeff encrypt a file on the computer.

2. **Correct Answers: A and B**

A. Correct: When you apply the Read & Execute (Deny) permission, Windows also automatically applies the List Folder Contents (Deny) and Read (Deny) permissions.

B. Correct: When you apply the Read & Execute (Deny) permission, Windows also automatically applies the List Folder Contents (Deny) and Read (Deny) permissions.

C. **Incorrect:** Windows does not apply the Modify (Deny) permission when you apply the Read & Execute (Deny) permission.

D. **Incorrect:** Windows does not apply the Write (Deny) permission when you apply the Read & Execute (Deny) permission.

3. **Correct Answer: D**

A. **Incorrect:** Robocopy can be used to copy files and their associated NTFS permissions but cannot be used to calculate permissions.

B. **Incorrect:** Icacls can be used to display permissions but cannot be used to calculate the result of cumulative permissions.

C. **Incorrect:** Cipher is used to manage certificates and cannot be used to calculate the result of cumulative permissions.

D. **Correct:** The Effective Permissions tool can be used to calculate the result of cumulative permissions that accrue through multiple group memberships.

4. **Correct Answers: A and D**

A. **Correct:** Encrypted files remain encrypted when copied or moved to compressed folders.

B. **Incorrect:** Encrypted files remain encrypted when copied or moved to compressed folders. Only unencrypted files become compressed when moved to compressed folders.

C. **Incorrect:** Files retain their original NTFS permissions only when they are moved between folders on the same volume. If you move them between volumes, they inherit the permissions of the destination folder. You can use Robocopy to move files and retain their NTFS permissions, but Robocopy was not mentioned in the question text.

D. **Correct:** Files that are moved using Windows Explorer inherit the NTFS permissions assigned to their destination folder.

5. **Correct Answer: B**

A. **Incorrect:** EFS can be used to limit which users can access a document by encrypting it only to certain user accounts, but it cannot be used to track which user accounts have been used to access files.

B. **Correct:** Auditing allows you to track which user accounts are used to access files and folders. You can configure auditing to track successful and failed attempts to use any of the special permissions.

C. **Incorrect:** You cannot use NTFS permissions to record which user accounts are used to access documents; you can only use NTFS permissions to restrict which user accounts are used to access documents.

D. **Incorrect:** BranchCache is used to speed up access to files across the wide area network (WAN); it cannot be used to record which user accounts access documents in a sensitive folder.

Lesson 3

1. **Correct Answers: A and B**

   A. **Correct:** If you are going to use hosted cache mode, it is necessary to deploy at least one server running Windows Server 2008 R2 with the BranchCache feature enabled in each branch office.

   B. **Correct:** Windows 7 Enterprise and Ultimate editions support BranchCache. You must upgrade clients to one of these operating systems if they are going to utilize BranchCache.

   C. **Incorrect:** Windows 7 Professional does not support the BranchCache feature.

   D. **Incorrect:** A Windows Server 2008 RODC is not necessary to support BranchCache.

2. **Correct Answers: B and D**

   A. **Incorrect:** You can use *Net share* to manage shared folders on a client running Windows 7, but you cannot use it to enable and configure BranchCache. You can use it to enable BranchCache on a computer that hosts a shared folder, but BranchCache needs to be enabled and configured before you can do this.

   B. **Correct:** You can use *Netsh* in the BranchCache context and the Local Group Policy Editor to configure BranchCache on a client running Windows 7.

   C. **Incorrect:** *Ipconfig* provides IP address configuration information. You cannot use *Ipconfig* to configure BranchCache on a client running Windows 7.

   D. **Correct:** You can use *Netsh* in the BranchCache context and the Local Group Policy Editor to configure BranchCache on a client running Windows 7.

3. **Correct Answer: C**

   A. **Incorrect:** If you use the command *netsh branchcache set service disabled,* the content accessed over the WAN link is not cached locally.

   B. **Incorrect:** If you use the command *netsh branchcache set service mode=distributed,* it is possible that the content will be shared with the other computer running Windows 7 Ultimate, although in a properly configured environment, file and folder permissions would restrict access.

   C. **Correct:** You should use the command *netsh branchcache set service mode=local,* because this allows the computer running Windows 7 Ultimate to satisfy requests from its local cache without allowing that cache to be accessible to other computers on the network.

   D. **Incorrect:** You should not use the command *netsh branchcache set service mode=hostedclient location=fs-alpha.contoso.internal.* You can use the hostedclient mode only if there is a server running Windows Server 2008 R2 that has BranchCache enabled on your LAN.

4. **Correct Answer: D**

   A. **Incorrect:** The command *netsh branchcache set service mode=distributed* configures Distributed Cache mode rather than Hosted Cache mode. The question specifies that the clients use Hosted Cache mode.

   B. **Incorrect:** The command *netsh branchcache set service mode=local* sets the client to use local caching only. The question specifies that the clients use Hosted Cache mode.

   C. **Incorrect:** The command *netsh branchcache set service mode=hostedserver clientauthentication=domain* is used to configure the host server and cannot be used to configure a Hosted Cache mode client.

   D. **Correct:** To configure a BranchCache client to use a particular server in Hosted Cache mode, issue the command *netsh branchcache set service mode=hostedclient location=servername*. You must specify the name of the local server running Windows Server 2008 R2 that functions as the BranchCache host when configuring Hosted Cache mode.

5. **Correct Answer: A**

   A. **Correct:** The Configure BranchCache For Network Files policy allows you to set the latency value above which network files are cached by client computers in the branch office.

   B. **Incorrect:** The Set Percentage Of Disk Space Used For Client Computer Cache policy configures the cache size, it cannot be used to configure latency settings.

   C. **Incorrect:** Configuring the Set BranchCache Distributed Cache Mode policy sets the client to use Distributed Cache Mode. You cannot configure latency settings using this policy.

   D. **Incorrect:** Configuring the Set BranchCache Hosted Cache Mode policy sets the client to use Hosted Cache Mode. You cannot configure latency settings using this policy.

Chapter 8: Case Scenario Answers

Case Scenario 1: Permissions and Encryption

1. You need to export the user's private key from computer Waverley and import it to computer Warrandyte.

2. Create a recovery agent certificate using Cipher.exe. Use the Local Group Policy Editor to assign this certificate as a recovery agent.

3. You can use Robocopy.exe or Icacls.exe to move the files from one volume to another while retaining their existing permissions. If you just move the files, the permissions will be lost.

Case Scenario 2: Configuring Contoso Branch Offices

1. You should use Distributed Caching mode in the Wangaratta branch office because you are unable to deploy a server running Windows Server 2008 R2 to this location and Windows Server 2008 does not support BranchCache.

2. You should configure the Hosted Cache mode at the Traralgon office because this ensures that a maximum number of files are available in the centralized cache. Hosted Cache allows the cache to remain online, unlike Distributed Cache, which requires that all clients remain online. A server running Windows Server 2008 R2 is present at the Traralgon branch office to support Hosted Cache mode.

3. Install the BranchCache feature on the server and configure shared folders to support BranchCache. Run the command *set service mode=hostedserver clientauthentication=domain* on the server.

Chapter 9: Lesson Review Answers

Lesson 1

1. **Correct Answer: B**

   A. **Incorrect:** You should not configure the policy UAC: Behavior Of The Elevation Prompt For Administrators In Admin Approval Mode: Elevate Without Prompting. This policy relates to all administrator accounts except the built-in administrator account, which must be managed with other policies.

   B. **Correct:** You should configure the UAC: Admin Approval Mode For The Built-In Administrator Account policy to Enabled. This ensures that the built-in administrator account must respond to a UAC prompt when performing a task that requires elevated privileges.

   C. **Incorrect:** You should not configure the UAC: Admin Approval Mode For The Built-In Administrator account policy to Disabled. This policy setting disables the UAC prompt for the built-in administrator account.

   D. **Incorrect:** You should not configure the policy UAC: Behavior Of The Elevation Prompt For Administrators In Admin Approval Mode: Prompt For Consent For Non-Windows Binaries. This policy relates to all administrator accounts except the built-in administrator account, which must be managed with other policies.

2. **Correct Answer: B**

   A. **Incorrect:** You should not configure the User Account Control: Behavior Of The Elevation Prompt For Standard Users: Automatically Deny Elevation Requests policy. When this policy is configured, standard users receive no prompt when they perform a task that requires elevation, and the elevation attempt automatically fails.

   B. **Correct:** You should configure the User Account Control: Behavior Of The Elevation Prompt For Standard Users: Prompt For Credentials policy. This ensures that a standard user is prompted for credentials when an attempt is made at elevation.

   C. **Incorrect:** You should not configure the User Account Control: Behavior Of The Elevation Prompt For Administrators In Admin Approval Mode: Prompt For Credentials because this policy relates to approval for administrator accounts rather than standard user accounts.

D. **Incorrect:** You should not configure the User Account Control: Behavior Of The Elevation Prompt For Administrators In Admin Approval Mode: Prompt For Consent because this policy relates to approval for administrator accounts rather than standard user accounts. This policy also provides a prompt for consent rather than a prompt for credentials.

3. **Correct Answers: A and D**

   A. **Correct:** You can use the Local Group Policy Editor console to import and export security-related policies. You could export the policies from the reference computer and then import them on each of the 30 client computers in the lab.

   B. **Incorrect:** You cannot use the Computer Management console to import or export UAC policies.

   C. **Incorrect:** You cannot use the User Account Control settings control panel item to import and export UAC policies.

   D. **Correct:** You can use the Local Security Policy console to import and export security-related policies. You could export the policies from the reference computer and then import them on each of the 30 client computers in the lab.

4. **Correct Answer: D**

   A. **Incorrect:** The UAC: Only Elevate Uiaccess Applications That Are Installed In Secure Locations policy does not deal with the writing of data to protected locations. This policy deals with a special class of applications that interact with the operating system in an unusual way and restricts their execution based on location within the file system.

   B. **Incorrect:** The UAC: Only Elevate Executables That Are Signed And Validated policy does not deal with the writing of data to protected locations. It is used to restrict privilege elevation requests to applications that are digitally signed.

   C. **Incorrect:** The UAC: Behavior Of The Elevation Prompt For Standard Users policy does not deal with the writing of data to protected locations; instead, it is used to configure Windows to provide UAC prompts for standard users.

   D. **Correct:** The UAC: Virtualize File And Registry Write Failures To Per-User Locations policy determines whether application writes to protected locations are redirected elsewhere. Disabling this policy ensures that an application that attempts to write data to a protected location fails.

5. **Correct Answer: C**

   A. **Incorrect:** You should not configure the UAC: Admin Approval Mode For The Built-In Administrator account. This policy relates to how UAC works for the built-in administrator account. To accomplish your goal, you need to disable the switch to Secure Desktop policy.

   B. **Incorrect:** You should not configure the UAC: Behavior Of The Elevation Prompt For Administrators In Admin Approval Mode policy. This policy is already properly configured. To accomplish your goal, you need to disable the switch to Secure Desktop policy.

   C. **Correct:** You need to disable the UAC: Switch To The Secure Desktop When Prompting For Elevation. If this policy is enabled, UAC prompts always appear on the Secure

Desktop. If this policy is disabled, whether a UAC prompt appears on the Secure Desktop depends on the setting in the UAC: Behavior of the elevation prompt for administrators in Admin Approval Mode policy.

D.   **Incorrect:** You should not configure the UAC: Behavior Of The Elevation Prompt For Standard Users policy. This policy relates to standard users and does nothing to disable Secure Desktop for administrators. To accomplish your goal, you need to disable the switch to Secure Desktop policy.

Lesson 2

1.   Correct Answer: B

A.   **Incorrect:** You cannot remove saved Runas credentials using the Runas command. You must use the Credential Manager.

B.   **Correct:** You can use the Credential Manager to remove credentials saved using the Runas command.

C.   **Incorrect:** You cannot use the Certificates console to remove credentials saved using the Runas command. The Certificates console is used to manage certificates.

D.   **Incorrect:** You cannot use UAC settings to remove credentials saved using the Runas command. The User Account Control settings dialog box is used to change which situations trigger UAC prompts.

2.   Correct Answers: C and D

A.   **Incorrect:** You should not configure the Interactive Logon: Smart Card Removal Behavior Properties: No Action policy because this allows users to remove their smart cards but still remain logged on.

B.   **Incorrect:** You should not configure the Interactive Logon: Smart Card Removal Behavior Properties: Lock Workstation because this locks the workstation rather than forcibly logging off the user that removed the smart card.

C.   **Correct:** You should configure the Interactive Logon: Smart Card Removal Behavior Properties: Force Logoff policy setting because you want users logged off when they remove their smart cards.

D.   **Correct:** You should configure the Interactive Logon: Require Smart Card: Enabled policy because this requires users to log on using a smart card.

3.   Correct Answer: B

A.   **Incorrect:** The question does not state that the account has been locked; it says that the user has forgotten her password. Unlocking an account works only if a user knows her password. It does not reset her password.

B.   **Correct:** You need to reset her password. The user loses access to encrypted files if she has not backed up her EFS key. The user also loses access to any saved credentials stored in Windows Vault.

C. **Incorrect:** You can create a password reset disk for an account only if you know the account password. You cannot create a password reset disk for another user account or for one where the user has forgotten her password.

D. **Incorrect:** You should not create a password reset disk for your own account because this does not help resolve the user's problem.

4. **Correct Answer: D**

A. **Incorrect:** The Enforce Password History policy ensures that a user is unable to use a recently used password when changing his password. It does not ensure that a user must change his password after a certain amount of time.

B. **Incorrect:** The Minimum Password Length policy ensures that a user's password meets a minimum length requirement. It does not ensure that a user must change his password after a certain amount of time.

C. **Incorrect:** The Minimum Password Age policy stops a user changing his password for a minimum amount of time after the most recent password change. It does not ensure that a user changes his password after a certain amount of time.

D. **Correct:** The Maximum Password Age policy ensures that a user must change his password after a certain amount of time has expired. In this case, you would set the policy to 21 days.

5. **Correct Answers: B, C, and D**

A. **Incorrect:** Credential Manager can back up Web site credentials, user names and passwords, and some forms of digital certificates, but it cannot back up self-signed EFS certificates generated by Windows 7 when you first encrypt a file.

B. **Correct:** You can use the Manage File Encryption Certificates tool to back up EFS certificates to a password-protected PFX file.

C. **Correct:** You can use the Certificate Manager console to export an EFS certificate to a password-protected PFX file.

D. **Correct:** Cipher.exe is a command-line tool that you can use to back up an EFS certificate to a password-protected PFX file.

Chapter 9: Case Scenario Answers

Case Scenario 1: User Account Control at Coho Vineyard

1. You need to configure the UAC: Behavior Of The Elevation Prompt For Administrators In Admin Approval Mode policy and set it to Prompt For Credentials. You also need to set the UAC: Switch To The Secure Desktop When Prompting For Elevation policy to Disabled. This ensures that administrators are prompted for credentials but do not have to respond immediately to the prompt.

2. You need to configure the UAC: Behavior Of The Elevation Prompt For Standard Users policy to ensure that standard users are prompted for credentials when they perform an act that requires elevation. You also need to configure the UAC: Allow UIAccess Applications To Prompt For Elevation Without Using Secure Desktop policy. Doing this allows remote user interaction with the UAC prompt when connected through UIAccess applications.

3. You need to configure the UAC: Only Elevate Executables That Are Signed And Validated policy. You can use this policy because all applications that might require elevation at Coho Vineyard have digital signatures.

Case Scenario 2: Resolving Password Problems at Wingtip Toys

1. Ensure that users back up their EFS key. This can be done using Cipher.exe, the Manage File Encryption Certificates tool, or through Certmgr.msc. The users should use Credential Manager to back up their stored Web site passwords.

2. Get each user to create his or her own password reset disk.

3. Configure the Maximum Password Age policy and configure the Enforce Password History policy.

Chapter 10: Lesson Review Answers

Lesson 1

1. Correct Answer: D
   A. **Incorrect:** Teredo is appropriate when a client has a private IPv4 address and when no firewall blocks traffic on UDP port 3544. Because this port is blocked, the client uses IP-HTTPS.
   B. **Incorrect:** To use 6to4, the client must have a public IPv4 address. The question states that the client has been assigned a private IPv4 address.
   C. **Incorrect:** To use a globally routable IPv6 address, the client must be assigned a globally routable IPv6 address.
   D. **Correct:** IP-HTTPS is used when the DirectAccess client is assigned a private IPv4 address on a network that allows Internet access but that has a firewall that restricts most forms of network traffic.

2. Correct Answers: A and B
   A. **Correct:** Only Windows 7 Ultimate and Enterprise editions support the DirectAccess feature.
   B. **Correct:** Only domain-joined clients running Windows 7 are able to use DirectAccess.

C.   **Incorrect:** AppLocker policies control which applications can execute on a client running Windows 7. AppLocker policies do not relate to DirectAccess.

D.   **Incorrect:** BranchCache policies allow clients in branch offices to cache WAN content locally. BranchCache policies do not relate to DirectAccess.

3.   **Correct Answer: A**

A.   **Correct:** The DirectAccess server needs to have two network adapters and needs to be assigned two consecutive public IPv4 addresses.

B.   **Incorrect:** The DirectAccess server needs to have two network adapters. One network adapter must be assigned to the internal network, and the other must be accessible to the Internet.

C.   **Incorrect:** The DirectAccess server needs to be assigned two consecutive public IPv4 addresses.

D.   **Incorrect:** The DirectAccess server needs to have two network adapters. One network adapter must be assigned to the internal network and the other must be accessible to the Internet.

4.   **Correct Answer: A**

A.   **Correct:** DirectAccess configures special GPOs that contain the DirectAccess configuration settings. These GPOs are applied to specific security groups that contain computer accounts. A computer must be a member of these specific security groups for it to be configured to use DirectAccess.

B.   **Incorrect:** DirectAccess configuration occurs through the application of Group Policy based on computer account domain group membership. It does not rely on local group membership.

C.   **Incorrect:** The computer account must be a member of the domain security group, not the user account.

D.   **Incorrect:** The computer account must be a member of the domain security group, not a user account that is a member of a local group.

5.   **Correct Answer: D**

A.   **Incorrect:** The *ipconfig* command displays IP address configuration. It does not display information about DirectAccess IP-HTTPS server configuration.

B.   **Incorrect:** The *netsh interface 6to4 show relay* command displays 6to4 information. 6to4 can be used when a computer is assigned a public address, rather than a private one, and is not behind a NAT device.

C.   **Incorrect:** The *netsh interface ipv6 show teredo* command displays Teredo information. Teredo cannot be used if a hotel network firewall blocks all traffic except that on port 80 and 443.

D.   **Correct:** The *netsh interface httpstunnel show interfaces* command shows information related to the DirectAccess IP-HTTPS configuration.

Lesson 2

1. **Correct Answer: D**

   A. Incorrect: PPTP VPNs do not support the VPN Reconnect feature in Windows 7

   B. Incorrect: L2TP/IPsec VPNs do not support the VPN Reconnect feature in Windows 7.

   C. Incorrect: SSTP VPNs do not support the VPN Reconnect feature in Windows 7.

   D. Correct: The IKEv2 VPN type is the only VPN type that supports the VPN Reconnect feature in Windows 7.

2. **Correct Answer: A**

   A. Correct: SSTP VPN connections work using the same ports as secure Web browsing connections. This allows users who can browse the Web using a motel Internet connection to connect through VPN.

   B. Incorrect: IKEv2 uses UDP port 500, which is likely to be blocked by firewalls that block other forms of traffic except common protocols used by Web browsers.

   C. Incorrect: PPTP uses port 1723, which is likely to be blocked by firewalls that block other forms of traffic except common protocols used by Web browsers.

   D. Incorrect: L2TP/IPsec uses UDP port 1701, which is likely to be blocked by firewalls that block other forms of traffic except common protocols used by Web browsers.

3. **Correct Answers: C and D**

   A. Incorrect: SSTP is supported only on Routing and Remote Access servers running Windows Server 2008 and Windows Server 2008 R2.

   B. Incorrect: IKEv2 is supported only on Routing and Remote Access servers running Windows Server 2008 R2.

   C. Correct: PPTP is supported by Routing and Remote Access servers running Windows Server 2003 R2.

   D. Correct: L2TP/IPsec is supported by Routing and Remote Access servers running Windows Server 2003 R2.

4. **Correct Answers: A, B, and C**

   A. Correct: You can use the PEAP authentication protocol with an IKEv2 VPN.

   B. Correct: You can use the EAP-MSCHAP v2 authentication protocol with an IKEv2 VPN.

   C. Correct: You can use Microsoft Smart Card or Other Certificate to authenticate an IKEv2 VPN.

   D. Incorrect: You cannot use the CHAP protocol with an IKEv2 VPN. IKEv2 VPNs can be authenticated only using EAP or computer certificates.

5. **Correct Answer: C**

   A. Incorrect: DirectAccess is not available on computers running Windows 7 Professional. If DirectAccess were available, this solution would work.

B. Incorrect: You should not configure Remote Desktop Connection to use the Remote Desktop Gateway at remote-desktop.contoso.internal and then connect to rdgateway. contoso.com as the remote desktop gateway is located at rdgateway.contoso.com. In this answer, the positions of the RD gateway server and the remote desktop services server are switched.

C. Correct: You should configure Remote Desktop Connection to use the Remote Desktop Gateway at rdgateway.contoso.com and then connect to remote-desktop.contoso.internal.

D. Incorrect: DirectAccess is not available on computers running Windows 7 Professional. If it were, you would want to connect to remote-desktop.contoso.internal rather than to the Remote Desktop Gateway server.

Chapter 10: Case Scenario Answers

Case Scenario 1: Wingtip Toys DirectAccess

1. Upgrade the server to Windows Server 2008 R2. The rest of the server's configuration supports DirectAccess because it is a member of the domain, has two consecutive public IP addresses assigned to its Internet interface, and has the appropriate computer certificates installed. You can install the DirectAccess feature on this server once it has been upgraded to the newer operating system.

2. You should create a global security group in the Wingtip Toys domain.

3. Upgrade the client computers to Windows 7 Enterprise or Ultimate edition. Add them to the security group that you have configured to support DirectAccess. Install computer certificates.

Case Scenario 2: Remote Access at Tailspin Toys

1. Windows 7 Enterprise supports IKEv2 VPNs, though Windows Server 2003 R2 x64 Routing and Remote Access servers do not. It is necessary to upgrade the Routing and Remote Access server to Windows Server 2008 R2 to support IKEv2 VPNs.

2. Install an antivirus update server and a WSUS server on the quarantine network so that clients can update themselves to become compliant.

3. You should use the EAP-MS-CHAPv2 authentication protocol because this allows password authentication.

Chapter 11: Lesson Review Answers

Lesson 1

1. **Correct Answers: A, D, and E**

   A. Correct: A BitLocker-encrypted volume must be configured with a unique identifier to be used with a DRA. You must configure the Prove The Unique Identifiers For Your Organization policy to assign this identifier.

B. Incorrect: The Choose Default Folder For Recovery Password policy allows the recovery password to be saved in a particular location. A recovery password is different for a DRA, which involves a special certificate that can be used to recover all BitLocker-encrypted volumes in an organization.

C. Incorrect: The Choose How Users Can Recover BitLocker Protected Drivers policy specifies whether recovery occurs via a password or a USB flash drive and key. This is separate from a DRA, which involves a special certificate that can be used to recover all BitLocker-encrypted volumes in an organization.

D. Correct: You need to specify the DRA to be used in the Computer Configuration\ Windows Settings\Security Settings\Public Key Policies\BitLocker Drive Encryption policy to configure BitLocker to support DRAs.

E. Correct: You need to configure the Choose How BitLocker-Protected Operating System Drives Can Be Recovered policy and specify that a DRA can be used to recover protected operating system drives.

2. **Correct Answers: C and D**

A. Incorrect: The Control Use Of BitLocker On Removable Drives policy allows BitLocker to be used on removable drives. You cannot use this policy to restrict usage of removable drives only to those configured with BitLocker.

B. Incorrect: The Store BitLocker Recovery Information In Active Directory Domain Services policy, which applies to clients running Windows Vista rather than Windows 7, allows for BitLocker recovery keys to be stored within AD DS. You cannot use this policy to restrict usage of removable drives only to those configured with BitLocker.

C. Correct: You need to configure the Deny Write Access To Removable Drives Not Protected By BitLocker policy. This policy allows you to deny write access to drives not protected by BitLocker and to specify which BitLocker identifiers are associated with your organization.

D. Correct: The Provide The Unique Identifiers For Your Organization policy allows you to specify which BitLocker identifiers are associated with your organization. If the BitLocker identifier that is used with a removable device does not match one of the identifiers configured in this policy and the Deny Write Access To Removable Drives Not Protected By BitLocker policy is configured appropriately, users are unable to write data to these removable devices.

3. **Correct Answer: A**

A. Correct: By configuring the Require Additional Authentication At Startup policy, it is possible to disable the BitLocker requirement that a computer have a compatible TPM chip.

B. Incorrect: The Allow Enhanced PINs for Startup policy allows you to use an enhanced PIN with startup. Configuring this policy does not allow you to bypass the BitLocker requirement for a TPM chip.

C. Incorrect: The Configure TPM Platform Validation Profile policy configures how the TPM chip secures the BitLocker encryption key. Configuring this policy does not allow you to bypass the BitLocker requirement for a TPM chip.

> **D. Incorrect:** The Configure Minimum PIN Length For Startup policy allows you to configure a minimum PIN length for the startup PIN. Configuring this policy does not allow you to bypass the BitLocker requirement for a TPM chip.

4. **Correct Answer: B**

> **A. Incorrect:** The Configure Use Of Passwords For Removable Data Drives policy allows you to configure password policies for removable data drives. You cannot use this policy to ensure that BitLocker To Go Reader is available on all FAT-formatted removable devices protected with BitLocker.

> **B. Correct:** The Allow Access To BitLocker-Protected Removable Data Drives From Earlier Versions Of Windows policy allows you to ensure that BitLocker To Go Reader is available on all FAT-formatted removable devices protected with BitLocker.

> **C. Incorrect:** The Choose How BitLocker-Protected Removable Drives Can Be Recovered policy allows you to configure removable device recovery options. You cannot use this policy to ensure that BitLocker To Go Reader is available on all FAT-formatted removable devices protected with BitLocker.

> **D. Incorrect:** The Control Use Of BitLocker On Removable Drives policy determines whether you can use BitLocker with removable devices on the computer to which the policy applies. You cannot use this policy to ensure that BitLocker To Go Reader is available on all FAT-formatted removable devices protected with BitLocker.

5. **Correct Answer: A**

> **A. Correct:** You can use the *Manage-bde.exe* command-line utility to determine the identification string assigned to a BitLocker-protected volume.

> **B. Incorrect:** The Cipher.exe utility allows you to manage EFS rather than BitLocker encryption. You cannot use Cipher.exe to determine the identification string associated with a BitLocker-protected volume.

> **C. Incorrect:** The Bcdedit.exe utility allows you to manage boot configuration. You cannot use Bcdedit.exe to determine the identification string associated with a BitLocker-protected volume.

> **D. Incorrect:** The Sigverif.exe utility allows you to verify the digital signatures of files. You cannot use Sigverif.exe to determine the identification string associated with a BitLocker-protected volume.

Lesson 2

1. **Correct Answer: C**

> **A. Incorrect:** The command *powercfg.exe –devicequery all_devices* lists all devices. It does not provide information about which devices are configured to wake the computer from any sleep state.

> **B. Incorrect:** The command *powercfg.exe –hibernate* enables the hibernate option. You cannot use this command to provide a list of devices that are configured to wake the computer from any sleep state.

C. Correct: The command *powercfg.exe –devicequery wake_armed* displays a list of devices on a computer running Windows 7 that are configured to wake the computer from any sleep state.

D. Incorrect: The command *powercfg.exe –list* displays a list of all power schemes in the current user's environment. It does not display a list of devices that are configured to wake the computer from a sleep state.

2. **Correct Answers: A, B, and C**

   A. Correct: A user account that is not a member of the local administrators group can be used to select a different power plan.

   B. Correct: A user account that is not a member of the local administrators group can be used to create a new power plan.

   C. Correct: A user account that is not a member of the local administrators group can be used to change what the power buttons do.

   D. Incorrect: A user account that is not a member of the local administrators group cannot be used to change the Require A Password On Wakeup setting.

3. **Correct Answer: C**

   A. Incorrect: You cannot use the Power Options control panel to migrate a custom power plan from one computer running Windows 7 to another.

   B. Incorrect: Although you can use the Local Group Policy Editor (Gpedit.msc) to edit power plan settings, you cannot use the Local Group Policy Editor to migrate power plan settings. Only security-related settings can be migrated using the Local Group Policy Editor.

   C. Correct: You can use Powercfg.exe to migrate a power plan from one computer running Windows 7 to another.

   D. Incorrect: Bcdedit.exe is used to modify a computer's boot configuration; it cannot be used to modify a power plan.

4. **Correct Answer: B**

   A. Incorrect: Credential Manager is used to manage stored authentication credentials. You cannot use Credential Manager to resolve offline file sync conflicts.

   B. Correct: The Sync Center control panel can be used to resolve offline file sync conflicts.

   C. Incorrect: HomeGroup is used to manage HomeGroup settings. HomeGroup cannot be used to resolve offline file sync conflicts.

   D. Incorrect: Network And Sharing Center cannot be used to resolve offline file sync conflicts. Network And Sharing Center is used to manage network configuration.

5. **Correct Answer: D**

   A. Incorrect: The Configure Slow Link Speed policy allows you to configure a threshold value for transitioning to Slow Link mode. Slow Link mode works with files configured to be available offline. The question states that it is not necessary to specify that a file is available offline.

B. Incorrect: The Configure Slow Link Mode policy allows you to configure the computer to be able to use Slow Link mode, which is the default setting for clients running Windows 7. Slow Link mode works with files configured to be available offline. The question states that it is not necessary to specify that a file is available offline.

   C. Incorrect: The Exclude Files From Being Cached policy is used to block certain file types from being available offline. This policy cannot be used to configure a client running Windows 7 to cache files.

   D. Correct: Transparent caching allows Windows 7 to cache files locally when the round-trip latency to the remote file server exceeds a specific value in milliseconds.

Chapter 11: Case Scenario Answers

Case Scenario 1: Accessing Offline Files at Contoso

1. You need to use Powercfg.exe to export the custom power plan from the reference computer and import the custom power plan on each of the other branch office computers. Group Policy cannot be used with computers that are not members of an AD DS domain.

2. Enable transparent caching. You cannot enable BranchCache because none of the file servers at Contoso have the Windows Server 2008 R2 operating system installed.

3. Sync Center is the tool used to resolve offline file synchronization conflicts.

Case Scenario 2: Using BitLocker at Tailspin Toys

1. You can allow users to use BitLocker To Go–encrypted USB storage devices on computers that are running Windows XP or Windows Vista by configuring the Allow Access To BitLocker-Protected Removable Data Drives From Earlier Versions Of Windows policy.

2. You can restrict removable device usage through Group Policy so that only devices that are protected by BitLocker To Go and which have a specific organizational string configured within BitLocker can be used on clients running Windows 7. You can do this through the Deny Write Access To Removable Drives Not Protected By BitLocker policy and through the Provide The Unique Identifiers For Your Organization policy.

3. You can configure a DRA to be used with removable volumes and configure policies to back up keys and passwords to AD DS.

Chapter 12: Lesson Review Answers

Lesson 1

1. **Correct Answer: B**

   A. Incorrect: Uninstalling installed updates requires elevated privileges and cannot be performed with a standard user account.

B. Correct: The default Windows 7 Windows Update settings allow standard users to install updates.

C. Incorrect: The default Windows 7 Windows Update settings do not allow standard users to change when updates are installed. It is necessary to use elevated privileges to perform these tasks.

D. Incorrect: The default Windows 7 Windows Update settings do not allow standard users to change update download and installation behavior. It is necessary to use elevated privileges to perform these tasks.

E. Incorrect: The default Windows 7 Windows Update settings do not allow standard users to hide updates. It is necessary to use elevated privileges to perform this task.

2. **Correct Answers: B and C**

A. Incorrect: You should not change the update settings. Changing the update settings to stop updates being installed does not ensure that other important updates published through Windows Update are deployed to clients running Windows 7.

B. Correct: You should uninstall the update. This allows the custom software package to run.

C. Correct: You should hide the update after uninstalling the update. If you do not hide the update, the update becomes available for installation. Because standard users are able to install updates by default, this could lead to the problematic update being reinstalled. Once the fix for the custom software application becomes available, you can unhide the update and then reinstall it.

D. Incorrect: You should not install the update. This causes problems with the custom software application.

3. **Correct Answer: C**

A. Incorrect: You should not configure the Re-Prompt For Restart With Scheduled Installations policy because it sets the amount of time that a user can postpone a scheduled restart. It does not ensure that updates scheduled for installation when the computer was switched off are installed the next time the computer is switched on.

B. Incorrect: You should not configure the Delay Restart For Scheduled Installations policy because it determines how long Windows waits before automatically restarting after a scheduled installation. It does not ensure that updates scheduled for installation when the computer was switched off are installed the next time the computer is switched on.

C. Correct: You should configure the Reschedule Automatic Updates Scheduled Installations policy because it allows you to configure a computer that is switched off during the scheduled update period to install updates after it is turned on.

D. Incorrect: You should not configure the No Auto-Restart With Logged On Users For Scheduled Automatic Updates Installation policy because it allows a user to remain logged on when installed updates require a restart. It does not ensure that updates scheduled for installation when the computer was switched off are installed the next time the computer is switched on.

4. **Correct Answer: D**

   A. **Incorrect:** You should not configure the Turn Off Software Notification policy. This policy relates to user notification about available updates. You cannot use it to configure Windows Update to use a WSUS server rather than the Microsoft Update servers.

   B. **Incorrect:** You should not configure the Automatic Updates Detection Frequency policy. This policy determines how often Windows Update checks for updates. You cannot use it to configure Windows Update to use a WSUS server rather than the Microsoft Update servers.

   C. **Incorrect:** You should not configure the Configure Automatic Updates policy. This policy configures which updates should be installed and whether they should be downloaded or installed, or whether the logged-on user should be notified. You cannot use it to configure Windows Update to use a WSUS server rather than the Microsoft Update servers.

   D. **Correct:** You should configure the Specify Intranet Microsoft Update Service Location policy because it allows you to specify a local WSUS server for updates.

5. **Correct Answer: D**

   A. **Incorrect:** Microsoft Update does not provide centralized reports for organizations telling them which clients in the organization are missing specific updates. Microsoft Update serves as the source for updates in organizations that do not use solutions like WSUS, System Center Essentials 2007, and SCCM 2007.

   B. **Incorrect:** Because a WSUS server is not deployed in the organization, you cannot use a WSUS server to determine if updates are missing.

   C. **Incorrect:** You cannot use the Group Policy Management Console to determine whether updates are missing. The Group Policy Management Console is used to manage Group Policy in a domain environment.

   D. **Correct:** You can use the MBSA to scan computers that you have administrative privileges to as a way of determining if they are missing software updates.

Lesson 2

1. **Correct Answer: D**

   A. **Incorrect:** You should not configure the security level of the Intranet Zone. The security level manages how Internet Explorer deals with downloads and cookies. Configuring this setting does not enable Internet Explorer to trust the CA that issued the certificate to *timesheet.contoso.internal*.

   B. **Incorrect:** Turning off the Pop-Up Blocker allows pop-ups, but does not allow Internet Explorer to trust this Web site certificate.

   C. **Incorrect:** Browsing to the Web site using InPrivate Mode does not allow Internet Explorer to trust the certificate issued to the Web site. Using InPrivate Mode stops Internet Explorer from recording browser navigation information.

   D. **Correct:** Because the Web site's certificate has been issued by an internal CA and you do not work for the organization directly, Internet Explorer has not been configured to trust the internal CA. To trust the internal CA, navigate to its Web site and download and install the CA's certificate.

2. **Correct Answers: A and B**

   A. **Correct:** To ensure that users do not accidentally blog using the default Blog With Windows Live accelerator, you should disable it.

   B. **Correct:** To ensure that users are able to use the custom blog accelerator, it is necessary to install the accelerator.

   C. **Incorrect:** You should not set the Blog With Windows Live accelerator as the default Blog accelerator for Internet Explorer. Because you do not want users to use this accelerator accidentally, you should disable it.

   D. **Incorrect:** You should not disable the custom blog accelerator because you want users to use this accelerator to blog to the intranet site.

3. **Correct Answers: A and C**

   A. **Correct:** You should configure the *www.wingtiptoys.com* site as an exception so that pop-up windows on this site are displayed by Internet Explorer.

   B. **Incorrect:** You should not set the blocking level to Medium because this lets pop-ups through from sites other than those that are on the exception list.

   C. **Correct:** You should configure the blocking level to High because this blocks all pop-up windows except those from sites on the exceptions list.

   D. **Incorrect:** You should not set the blocking level to Low because this lets pop-ups through from sites other than those that are on the exception list.

4. **Correct Answer: D**

   A. **Incorrect:** The problem is not related to InPrivate Browsing; the problem is related to Compatibility View as indicated by the statement in the question that the Web sites display without problems on Windows XP and Vista clients running Internet Explorer. Although Windows XP and Vista clients can run Internet Explorer 8, this hint suggests that compatibility is the issue.

   B. **Incorrect:** The problem is not related to InPrivate Filtering; the problem is related to Compatibility View as indicated by the statement in the question that the Web sites display without problems on Windows XP and Vista clients running Internet Explorer. Although Windows XP and Vista clients can run Internet Explorer 8, this hint suggests that compatibility is the issue.

   C. **Incorrect:** The question states that the Web sites display without problems on Windows XP and Vista clients running Internet Explorer. Although Windows XP and Vista clients can run Internet Explorer 8, this hint suggests that compatibility is the issue. Disabling Compatibility View does not resolve the problem.

   D. **Correct:** You should configure the list of intranet sites that do not display properly through the Use Policy List Of Internet Explorer 7 Sites policy. Internet Explorer displays these sites using Compatibility View.

5. **Correct Answer: B**

   A. Incorrect: Starting an InPrivate Browsing session does not stop third-party Web sites from tracking you if they provide content to multiple sites that you visit. InPrivate Browsing sessions still accept cookies and transmit data.

   B. Correct: Enabling InPrivate Filtering allows Internet Explorer to locate and block content from third-party Web sites that appear across multiple separate sites during a browsing session.

   C. Incorrect: Disabling the Pop-Up Blocker does not block third-party Web sites that provide content to a number of sites that you visit from tracking your browsing session across those sites. Disabling the Pop-Up Blocker means that you are presented with pop-up Web pages that normally would be blocked.

   D. Incorrect: You should not disable SmartScreen Filter. SmartScreen Filter protects you from phishing attacks. If you disable SmartScreen Filter, Internet Explorer does not warn you when you visit a Web site that contains malicious software or is suspected of being involved in phishing.

Chapter 12: Case Scenario Answers

Case Scenario 1: Windows Update at Contoso

1. You should configure the Specify Intranet Microsoft Update Service Location policy for the computers in the Canberra office. This policy allows you to specify the local WSUS server address.

2. You should configure the Enabling Windows Update Power Management To Automatically Wake Up The System To Install Scheduled Updates. When this policy is configured on compatible computers, the computer wakes from hibernation at the scheduled update time.

3. Log on to each computer at the Brisbane and Adelaide offices remotely using Remote Desktop. Uninstall the update and then hide the update. This ensures that the update is not installed again automatically.

Case Scenario 2: Internet Explorer at Wingtip Toys

1. You can disable the use of Internet Explorer accelerators through Group Policy. Although it is possible to disable accelerators manually, unless you disable accelerators through Group Policy, it is possible for users to reinstall them, or other accelerators, manually.

2. Instruct them to enable InPrivate Filtering. InPrivate Filtering stops browsing sessions being tracked across multiple sites. InPrivate Browsing does not block browsing sessions being tracked across multiple sites; it blocks browsing history and data being recorded by Internet Explorer.

3. Add them to the list of sites to use with Compatibility View, either through the Compatibility View Settings dialog box or by distributing the list through Group Policy.

Chapter 13: Lesson Review Answers

Lesson 1

1. **Correct Answer: B**

   A. **Incorrect:** On the General tab, you can specify how frequently the graph updates and how much data is displayed in the graph before Performance Monitor begins overwriting the graph on the left portion of the chart. You can also specify whether Legend, Value Bar, and Toolbar are displayed and whether the Report and Histogram views show Default, Maximum, Minimum, Average, or Current values. You cannot choose whether to display current activity in real time or show log files saved using a DCS.

   B. **Correct:** On the Source tab, you can choose whether to display current activity in real time or log files saved using a DCS. If you display a log file, you can use this tab to control the time range that is displayed in the Performance Monitor window.

   C. **Incorrect:** You can use the Data tab to configure the display of specific counters. In the Counters list, you can select the counter that you want to configure and adjust Color, Width, and Style. You can increase or decrease the Scale value. You cannot choose whether to display current activity in real time or log files saved using a DCS.

   D. **Incorrect:** You can use the Graph tab to select the scroll style and the type of graph to display. You cannot choose whether to display current activity in real time or log files saved using a DCS.

   E. **Incorrect:** If you keep multiple Performance Monitor windows open simultaneously you can use the Appearance tab to change the color of the background or other elements. This makes it easier to distinguish between the windows. You cannot choose whether to display current activity in real time or log files saved using a DCS.

2. **Correct Answer: A**

   A. **Correct:** You can use the Wecutil utility to configure the Event Collector service.

   B. **Incorrect:** The *Winrm* command configures WinRM. Typically, you run it on a source computer. You can run it on the collector computer if you are configuring a source-initiated conscription, but this is not relevant to this scenario because Canberra is retrieving events from Aberdeen. In any case, this command does not configure the Event Collector service.

   C. **Incorrect:** The *Winrm* command configures WinRM. Here, you are running it in quiet mode. Whether you use the *-q* switch or not, the command does not configure the Event Collector service.

   D. **Incorrect:** This command starts the Group Policy MMC snap-in. You can use Group Policy to add source computers to a source-initiated conscription, but this is not relevant to this scenario. In any case, the command does not configure the Event Collector service.

3. **Correct Answers: A, B, C, and E**

   A. **Correct:** Application failures are recorded in Reliability Monitor.

   B. **Correct:** Windows errors are recorded in Reliability Monitor.

C. **Correct:** Application installs and uninstalls are recorded in Reliability Monitor.

D. **Incorrect:** A service starting or stopping is typically recorded in the event log, not Reliability Monitor.

E. **Correct:** Device driver failures are recorded in Reliability Monitor.

4. **Correct Answer: A**

A. **Correct:** Reliability Monitor tracks application installations. It enables you to determine whether what applications have been installed and exactly when the installations occurred.

B. **Incorrect:** Action Center can tell you if an application or device driver is not working properly. It cannot tell you when an application was installed.

C. **Incorrect:** DCSs capture current performance and configuration data. They cannot tell you when in the past an application was installed.

D. **Incorrect:** You can use Performance Monitor to view performance counters in real time or analyze performance data in a DCS. However, Performance Monitor does not record when an application was installed.

5. **Correct Answer: A**

A. **Correct:** The lowest subscore determines the base score, even though this computer is not primarily used for three-dimensional graphics and gaming.

B. **Incorrect:** 3.9 is the average of the subscores. However, the lowest subscore determines the base score, not the average.

C. **Incorrect:** 5.1 is a significant score because the computer is used for processor-intensive operations. However, the question asks for the base score, and the lowest subscore determines the base score.

D. **Incorrect:** 5.3 is the highest subscore. The lowest subscore determines the base score, not the highest.

Lesson 2

1. **Correct Answer: D**

A. **Incorrect:** WMI CIM Studio enables you to view and edit classes, properties, qualifiers, and instances in a CIM repository; run selected methods; and generate and compile MOF files. It does not enable to view Windows Management–generated events and event information, such as the event's date and time, class, point of origin, and description.

B. **Incorrect:** WMI Object Browser enables you to view objects, edit property values and qualifiers, and run methods. It does not enable to view Windows Management–generated events and event information, such as the event's date and time, class, point of origin, and description.

C. **Incorrect:** WMI Event Registration Tool enables you to configure permanent event consumers, and to create or view instances of event consumers, filters, bindings, and timer system classes. It does not enable to view Windows Management–generated events and event information, such as the event's date and time, class, point of origin, and description.

D. **Correct:** WMI Event Viewer displays events for all instances of registered consumers. It enables to view Windows Management–generated events and event information, such as the event's date and time, class, point of origin, and description.

2. **Correct Answer: C**

   A. **Incorrect:** The Performance Analyzer tool (Xperfview.exe) can display captured traces. It cannot capture images.

   B. **Incorrect:** The On/Off Transition Trace Capture tool (Xbootmgr.exe) collects information during the on/off transition phases of Windows 7. It does not capture user and kernel traces, and it does not merge traces.

   C. **Correct:** The Trace Capture, Processing, and Command-Line Analysis tool (Xperf.exe) captures user and kernel traces and can merge them to form a combined trace.

   D. **Incorrect:** Visual Trace Analysis is another name for the Performance Analyzer tool (Xperfview.exe). It displays captured images, but it does not capture images.

3. **Correct Answer: B**

   A. **Incorrect:** Process Explorer helps you determine which applications are responsible for activity on your hard disk, including which files and folders are being accessed. However it is a downloadable tool and is not provided by Windows 7.

   B. **Correct:** The Resource Monitor tool, provided as part of Windows 7, helps you determine which applications are responsible for activity on your hard disk, including which files and folders are being accessed.

   C. **Incorrect:** Task Manager tells you what applications, services, and processes are running on your computer. It gives system details, such as the numbers of handles and threads in use, and it provides a snapshot of processor usage. However, it does not help you determine which applications are responsible for activity on your hard disk.

   D. **Incorrect:** The Windows Experience Index measures the ability of your computer to run resource-intensive applications, such as games and business graphics. It does not help you determine which applications are responsible for activity on your hard disk.

4. **Correct Answer: A**

   A. **Correct:** Process affinity determines whether a process uses a specified processor or whether it can use whatever processor is available. From the symptoms described, a number of significant processes are tied to the original processor and need to be configured so they can use the second processor. You configure process affinity in Task Manager.

   B. **Incorrect:** Process priority determines how fast a process works and what access it has to resources compared to other processes. It does not determine which processor or processors that it can use.

C. Incorrect: You can use the Performance Options tool to adjust for best performance of programs or background services. In a client computer you would normally specify the best performance of programs. This does not affect which processor that running processes can use.

D. Incorrect: Virtual memory settings specify the amount of disk space that can be used as paged memory. This does not affect which processor that running processes can use.

5. **Correct Answer: D**

    A. Incorrect: The Services console lists the services available on a computer, provides information about each service, and offers service management options. For example, the Services console tells you the service startup type and the logon details. It does not enable you to specify the startup operating system in a dual-boot configuration or to configure how Windows 7 reacts to a system failure.

    B. Incorrect: The Performance Options tool enables you to configure visual effects, to maximize performance for applications or background services, and to configure DEP settings. It does not enable you to specify the startup operating system in a dual-boot configuration or to configure how Windows 7 reacts to a system failure.

    C. Incorrect: Task Manager gives you a snapshot of resource usage and enables you to stop crashed applications, to stop and start services, and to set process priority and affinity. It does not enable you to specify the startup operating system in a dual-boot configuration or to configure how Windows 7 reacts to a system failure.

    D. Correct: System Configuration (Msconfig) enables you to specify the startup operating system in a dual-boot configuration and configure how Windows 7 reacts to a system failure.

Chapter 13: Case Scenario Answers

Case Scenario 1: Using Data Collector Sets and Event Forwarding

1. James uses DCSs to record a performance baseline when the server is performing normally. He then runs the same DCSs manually when a performance problem occurs. If the performance problems occur at a certain time of day, he can schedule the performance data sets to record data at that time over an extended period. He uses Performance Monitor to analyze the results, compare them with the baseline, and identify the factors that could be causing the problems.

2. James accesses the server through Remote Desktop and runs Reliability Monitor. This shows the applications that were installed or updated on the server at about the time that problems began to occur.

3. James uses event forwarding to transfer low disk space events to a central server. He then monitors the server event log to identify computers with low disk space by attaching a task that informs him that a low-disk-space event has been logged.

Case Scenario 2: Troubleshooting Performance Issues on a Client Computer

1. James needs to set the affinity of processes on the computer, particularly those that use a lot of processor resources. It is probable that these processes are configured to use only the original processor. James is already using Task Manager, which is the tool he needs for configuring process affinity.

2. James clicks the Performance Information And Tools item in Control Panel, clicks Advanced Tools in this dialog box, and then clicks View Performance Details In Event Log. This opens Event Viewer and displays the events in the Operational container under Diagnostic-Performance, which is where he is most likely to find events related to performance issues.

3. On the Policies tab of the USB Device Properties dialog box, James should select the Quick Removal option. Data transfer between the computer and the USB device may be slightly slower, but if the flash drive is accidentally (or deliberately) pulled out of its port, the data being written to it is much less likely to be lost.

Chapter 14: Lesson Review Answers

Lesson 1

1. **Correct Answer: C**
   A. **Incorrect:** This is against company policy, which stipulates that Windows chooses the files and folders to back up. Also, there is no indication in the question that the user is a local administrator or backup operator on her computer, so she probably does not have the permissions required to change backup settings.
   B. **Incorrect:** Changing the backup destination does not affect what files and folders are backed up. Also, the user probably does not have the appropriate permissions for this task.
   C. **Correct:** When Windows chooses what to back up, it always backs up the Documents library.
   D. **Incorrect:** Performing an immediate backup does not affect what files and folders are backed up. Also, the user probably does not have the appropriate permissions to do this.

2. **Correct Answer: D**
   A. **Incorrect:** The file was created on the previous day and was deleted before the overnight backup occurred, so it was not backed up.
   B. **Incorrect:** The Recycle Bin is not backed up during a file and folder backup.
   C. **Incorrect:** The file was created during the previous day and deleted before it could be backed up. If there is a file of the same name in a previous backup, it will not be the same file.
   D. **Correct:** The overnight backup makes no changes to the Recycle Bin. The file was deleted the previous evening, so it is in the Recycle Bin.

3. **Correct Answers: A, B, C, and D**

    A. **Correct:** Don's Word and Excel files in his Documents library are backed up by default. Don does not need to be logged into the computer.

    B. **Correct:** Kim's Word and Excel files in her Documents library are backed up by default.

    C. **Correct:** Don's Presentation folder is in his Documents library and is backed up by default.

    D. **Correct:** Don's Picture library is backed up by default.

    E. **Incorrect:** Encrypted files and folders are not backed up (even if they are in a Documents library).

    F. **Incorrect:** Files in the Recycle Bin are not backed up.

    G. **Incorrect:** By default, a USB flash memory device is formatted with the FAT filing system. Files on such a device are not backed up.

4. **Correct Answers: A, B, and E.**

    A. **Correct:** You can use Backup And Restore to write a System Image backup to an internal hard disk.

    B. **Correct:** You can use Backup And Restore to write a System Image backup to an external hard disk (if formatted with the NTFS file system).

    C. **Incorrect:** You cannot use Backup And Restore to write a System Image backup to an 8-GB USB flash drive, although you can use this media for file and folder backups.

    D. **Incorrect:** You cannot use Backup And Restore to write a System Image backup to an optical drive, although you can use this media for file and folder backups.

    E. **Correct:** You can use Backup And Restore to write a System Image backup to a network share provided the computer is running **Windows 7** Professional, **Windows 7** Ultimate, or **Windows 7** Enterprise.

5. **Correct Answer: D**

    A. **Incorrect:** Computers running Windows 7 Ultimate offer all Windows 7 features. However, they are not the only computers running Windows 7 that can be backed up to a network share.

    B. **Incorrect:** Computers running Windows 7 Enterprise are installed with a bulk license and are intended for use in large numbers in the enterprise environment. However, they are not the only computers running Windows 7 that can be backed up to a network share.

    C. **Incorrect:** Some features, such as booting from a VHD, require either Windows 7 Ultimate or Windows 7 Enterprise. However, the ability to back up to a network share is not one of these features.

    D. **Correct:** You can save backups to a network share on computers running **Windows 7** Professional, **Windows 7** Ultimate, and **Windows 7** Enterprise.

Lesson 2

1. **Correct Answers: A, C, and D**

   A. **Correct:** Safe Mode loads a minimal set of drivers. The computer will boot successfully and you can roll back the unsigned driver.

   B. **Incorrect:** Enable Boot Logging creates a file named Ntbtlog.txt, which lists all drivers that load during startup, including the last file to load before a failure occurs. This does not help in this situation, where you want to boot without loading the problem driver.

   C. **Correct:** Enable Low Resolution Video loads the default, low-resolution display driver. The problem driver does not load, and you can boot the computer and roll back this driver.

   D. **Correct:** You have not logged on since the problem driver was installed. Last Known Good Configuration (Advanced) loads the previously installed driver and is the preferred option in this situation because it involves the least administrative effort.

   E. **Incorrect:** Disable Driver Signal Enforcement lets you install unsigned drivers. Presumably you have already configured the computer to do this. This option does not enable you to roll back the problem driver.

2. **Correct Answers: A and E**

   A. **Correct:** You can enable system protection on internal hard disks, which are typically formatted with NTFS.

   B. **Incorrect:** You can enable system protection on external hard disks, but only if they are formatted with NTFS.

   C. **Incorrect:** You cannot enable system protection on USB flash drives.

   D. **Incorrect:** You cannot enable system protection on optical drives.

   E. **Correct:** System protection can be enabled on mounted VHDs.

3. **Correct Answer: D**

   A. **Incorrect:** You can undo a system restore if you perform it after booting using Last Known Good Configuration (Advanced). You cannot undo a system restore if you initiate it from the System Recovery tools.

   B. **Incorrect:** You can undo a system restore that you perform after either booting normally or booting using Last Known Good Configuration (Advanced).

   C. **Incorrect:** You can undo the system restore in this instance because you performed it after booting using Last Known Good Configuration (Advanced). It is incorrect to say that you can always undo a system restore no matter how you booted the computer or how you initiated the restore.

   D. **Correct:** If you perform a system restore after either booting normally or booting using Last Known Good Configuration (Advanced), this creates a restore point that enables you to undo the system restore.

4. **Correct Answer: A**

   A. **Correct:** Windows Memory Diagnostic analyses the computer memory (RAM) for hardware problems.

   B. **Incorrect:** Startup Repair automatically fixes problems that prevent Windows from starting. It is unlikely to help you diagnose hardware problems associated with RAM.

   C. **Incorrect:** System Restore restores system files and settings to the last restore point. It is used when a system change such as installing an application or a driver causes problems. It cannot help resolve hardware problems.

   D. **Incorrect:** System Image Recovery restores your system configuration from a System Image backup you made previously. You would typically choose this option if your hard disk failed or needed to be wiped. System Image Recovery cannot help resolve hardware problems.

5. **Correct Answer: C**

   A. **Incorrect:** Bootmgr.exe is the Windows Boot Manager. It runs the boot process, but you cannot use it to edit boot options.

   B. **Incorrect:** Winload.exe is the Windows operating system loader. It loads the selected operating system, but you cannot use it to edit boot options.

   C. **Correct:** You use Bcdedit.exe to edit boot options. You can also use the utility to manage BCD remotely and manage BCD when the system boots from media other than the media on which the BCD store resides.

   D. **Incorrect:** Windows 7 uses the Winresume.exe utility to resume from hibernation. You cannot use this utility to edit boot options.

Lesson 3

1. **Correct Answer: C**

   A. **Incorrect:** This action restores the file that existed on the previous evening. The user would lose the changes she made today.

   B. **Incorrect:** Previous versions include the backup version created on the previous evening and shadow copies. Probably the last shadow copy was made two days ago when the installation of a graphics driver generated a restore point. Previous versions would not include the version the user accidentally deleted.

   C. **Correct:** The user deleted the file recently, so it is still in her Recycle Bin. It contains all the information that it contained when it was deleted.

   D. **Incorrect:** A system restore does not restore a deleted user file.

2. **Correct Answers: A and D**

   A. **Correct:** A System Image restore restores the computer to the way it was three months ago.

   B. **Incorrect:** All restore points were deleted when the hard disk was wiped, so a system restore would not help. The user needs to reinstall any software he installed in the last three months, install (or allow Windows Update to install) three months of updates, and ensure that his virus and spyware definitions are up to date, but these options were not given in the question.

C. **Incorrect:** All shadow copies were deleted when the hard disk was wiped. Also, a Documents library is a virtual folder, not a physical folder.

D. **Correct:** A System Image restore ensures that the user has a working computer. However, the contents of his Documents library is three months out of date. He needs to restore his Documents library from backup.

3. Correct Answers: B and C

A. **Incorrect:** The D: drive does not hold system files, so you do not need to store system settings.

B. **Correct:** This creates previous versions of the files and folders on the D: drive whenever a restore point is created.

C. **Correct:** This allocates 200 GB of the 500-GB disk capacity for system protection.

D. **Incorrect:** This allocates only 20 GB of the 500-GB disk capacity for system protection. You want to allocate 200 GB.

4. Correct Answer: D

A. **Incorrect:** System protection settings are not retrospective. The previous versions of this file older than three months have already been deleted, and increasing the disk space that is allocated to system protection does not bring them back.

B. **Incorrect:** System restore does not restore user files.

C. **Incorrect:** System protection settings are not retrospective. This setting prevents system settings for the relevant volume being stored when a restore point is created and therefore leaves more space for previous versions. However, it does not bring back a file that has already been deleted because of lack of disk space.

D. **Correct:** You should use the Backup And Restore console to recover the file. This is the only way you can recover a file that is six months old.

5. Correct Answer: C

A. **Incorrect:** A system restore does not restore a corrupted Favorites folder.

B. **Incorrect:** A System Image restore restores the computer to the way it was three weeks ago. This restores the user's Favorites folder, but it would not include any Web sites added in the last three weeks. All the user's other files will also be three weeks old and would need to be restored from backup or previous versions.

C. **Correct:** This restores the user's Favorites folder to the way it was 24 hours ago. Any Web sites added since can be added again manually.

D. **Incorrect:** The browser history tells you the sites that the user browsed to recently. This is not the same as the contents of the Favorites folder.

Chapter 14: Case Scenario Answers

Case Scenario 1: Supporting Backup and Restore

1. In this situation, shadow copies of the file exist. James advises the user to recover his file by right-clicking it, selecting Restore Previous Versions, and selecting the most recent shadow copy.

2. Automatic scheduled file and folder backups by default back up the Documents libraries for all users with accounts on the computer. The user's son can use the Restore Files Wizard to restore his file from backup.

3. System Restore can restore the computer system to a restore point created before the new software was installed without deleting or modifying the user files currently on the computer. However, it is still a good idea to back up important files before carrying out a system restore (or any other major operation).

4. The user cannot place a System Image on the same disk that holds her operating system. She needs to create the backup on an external hard disk or on one or more DVD-ROM rewritable disks.

Case Scenario 2: Addressing System and Configuration Issues

1. Don has several options, such as booting into Safe Mode, enabling low resolution video from the Advanced Boot Options, or performing a system restore. However, the quickest way of getting his computer working again is to boot using the Last Known Good Configuration (Advanced) option. Because Don has not logged on since the driver was installed, this boots the computer using the previously installed driver.

2. Performing a System Image restore gives Don a working computer, but it used a system image that is three months old. If he did this, Don would need to install user files and his user profile from file and folder backup sets and reinstall any applications he has installed in the last three months. A System Image restore is used as a last resort when a disk drive has been wiped.

3. If 90 percent of a disk capacity is used for system protection, then only 10 percent is available for storing the current user files. This almost certainly is inadequate. A setting of 40 percent will permit shadow copies to be retained for a reasonable time without interfering significantly with the primary purpose of the disk.

Glossary

A

AppLocker policy A type of policy that can be used on Windows 7 Enterprise and Ultimate editions to restrict the execution of applications based on application identity information.

B

boot image An image that boots a target computer and enables deployment of the install image. Capture and discover images are special types of boot image.

BranchCache A technology that allows files hosted on remote Windows Server 2008 R2 servers to be cached on a branch office LAN.

C

commit In the context of system images, you commit a mounted image when you save the changes you made to it back to the source image.

compatibility fix Also known as shims, compatibility fixes are collected together to create compatibility modes.

compatibility mode A collection of compatibility fixes, also known as shims, that allow programs written for older versions of Windows to run on Windows 7.

connection security rule A rule that determines connection authentication requirements.

D

Data Collector Set (DCS) A DCS is a group of performance counters that you can monitor over a period of time so you can gauge a computer's performance and compare it to values stored in the same set of counters recorded at an earlier time (known as a *baseline*).

Data Recovery Agent (DRA) A data recovery agent is a user account and its associated enrolled certificate that is used for the purposes of data recovery.

default gateway The IP address to which a host on a subnet sends a packet (or IP packet) when the packet's destination IP address is not on the local subnet. The default gateway address is usually an interface belonging to the border router of LAN. In the case of a SOHO or small test network, the default gateway is the static IP address of the WAP or the ICS computer.

defragmentation Files on a hard disk can become fragmented so that they are stored on noncontiguous areas of the disk. Defragmentation addresses this problem by rearranging the disk so files are stored in contiguous areas.

deploy In the context of system images, you deploy an image when you install it on one or more target computers.

DirectAccess Technology that allows clients running Windows 7 to establish an always-on remote IPv6 connection to an organization's internal network.

distribution share A shared network folder that contains a system image to be deployed an all the files, such as unattend answer files, that are part of that deployment.

driver store A protected area on disk that contains the drivers for PnP devices.

dual-boot An action where a computer can start up a different operating system depending on which is selected at boot.

dummy restore This occurs when files and folders are restored to a location other than that in which they were originally stored. You can use dummy restores to check the restore process and to ensure that backed up files and folders are not corrupt.

E

Encrypting File System (EFS) A technology that allows the encryption of individual files and folders to specific user accounts.

event forwarding Event forwarding enables you to transfer events that match specific criteria to an administrative (or collector) computer.

event log An event log stores events that occurred during the operation of the computer system, such as a service or application stopping or starting. Some events store information about normal operations, but others store error indications, such as when an application failed to start a required service. Some events are used to audit access to files and folders, for example.

event subscription An event subscription is a configuration that permits events to be transferred from a source to a collector computer. Subscriptions can be source-initiated or collector-initiated.

G

global address An IPv6 address that identifies a device on the Internet. Global addresses must be unique on the Internet.

H

hash rule A rule that uses a digital fingerprint based on a file's binary properties.

HomeGroup A feature that allows resource sharing on home networks.

I

inbound rule A firewall rule that applies to traffic directed at the host from an external source.

InPrivate Browsing A special mode of Internet Explorer where browsing history, cookies and cache data is not available after the browsing session ends.

InPrivate Filtering A filtering mode that is used to reduce the amount of data sent to third party providers when browsing the Internet.

install image The system image (typically a WIM file) that you deploy to target computers.

IP address (IPv4 or IPv6) A unique address on a computer network that devices use in order to identify and communicate with each other.

IP packet The fundamental unit of information passed across any IP network. An IP packet contains source and destination addresses along with data and a number of fields that define such things as the length of the packet, the header checksum, and flags that indicate whether the packet can be (or has been) fragmented.

L

library A virtualized collection of folders that often contains similar content.

M

mount In the context of system images you mount an image by expanding it into a folder so you can obtain information about it and add or remove features such as drivers, updates, and language packs.

multifactor authentication Two or more different forms of authentication. On Windows 7, this is usually achieved by requiring a smart card and a password.

N

Netbook A small form factor laptop computer. Also known as a *netbook computer*.

O

Offline Files Allows files on specially configured shared folders to be accessed when the computer is not connected to the network.

outbound rule A firewall rule that applies to traffic from the host addressed to an external location.

P

path rule A rule that specifies an application or group of applications by their file location.

performance counter A performance counter indicates the usage of a particular resource, for example the percentage of time a processor is being used or the amount of free RAM that is available.

preferred wireless network A wireless network to which a wireless client attempts to connect and authenticate. Typically, the list of preferred networks contains networks to which the client has previously connected listed in order of preference.

privilege elevation An increase in rights that allows a user to perform a task that require more rights than those assigned to a standard user.

public address An IPv4 address that identifies a device on the Internet (or is allocated to a LAN). Public addresses must be unique on the Internet.

publisher rule A rule that specifies a file or a group of files based on the digital signature the vendor used to sign the file.

R

Redundant Array of Independent Disks (RAID) Volumes that use disk space on several disks to implement volumes that offer increased performance, fault tolerance, or both. Windows 7 supports RAID-0, RAID-1, and RAID-5.

RemoteApp A form of presentation virtualization, where the window of an application that runs on a server is displayed on a client.

restore point A restore point contains information about registry settings and other system information. Windows 7 generates restore points automatically before implementing significant system changes. You can manually create restore points and restore a computer system to a selected restore point.

S

Secure Desktop A special desktop where a user is forced to respond to a UAC prompt before being able to continue using the computer. This works as a security measure to ensure that users are not tricked into providing UAC consent when they do not intend to do so.

shadow copy A shadow copy is a previous version of a file or folder created at the same time as a restore point.

side-by-side migration A process where user data is exported from the original computer to the updated computer.

Software Restriction Policy A type of policy that can be used on all versions of Windows to restrict the execution of applications based on application identity information.

solution accelerator A group of downloads that, in addition to installation files for a major software package, also provides automated tools (if appropriate) and additional guidance files.

staging An administrator can stage a device driver by placing it in the driver store. A non-administrator can then install the device.

subnet An identifiably separate part of an organization's network. Typically, a subnet might represent all the computers at one geographic location, in one building, or on the same LAN. An IPv4 address consists of the address of a subnet (subnet address) combined with the address of a device on the subnet (host address).

subnet mask A number that defines what bits in an IPv4 address represent the subnet address and what bits represent the host address.

system image A disk image file that includes an operating system.

System Image This is a copy of all the files and folders on the system disk (and other specified hard disks) on a computer. You can use a System Image backup to restore the computer to exactly what its configuration was when the System Image backup was created.

system restore A system restore restores a computer system to a selected restore point. System restores do not alter user files.

T

transparent caching The process where files retrieved from remote file servers that exceed a round-trip threshold are cached automatically on the client to speed up access.

Trusted Publisher store A protected area of a hard disk that contains the digital certificates that authenticate signed device drivers.

V

Virtual Hard Disk (VHD) A file with a .vhd extension that acts as if it was a separate hard disk. In previous operating systems, VHDs containing system images were limited to virtualization and the facility was used with Hyper-V, Virtual Server, and Virtual PC software when implementing virtual machines. In Windows 7, you can create and use VHDs on hardware PCs that are not virtual machines.

W

Windows Automated Installation Toolkit (Windows AIK) A collection of tools and documentation designed to help you deploy Windows operating system images to target computers or to a VHD.

Windows Preinstallation Environment (Windows PE) A lightweight version of an operating system (such as Windows 7) that is primarily used for the deployment of client computers.

Windows Remote Shell A tool that allows command-line commands to be executed on a remote computer.

wipe-and-load migration A process where user data is exported and the existing operating system is removed and then replaced with the new operating system. User data is imported.

Index

Symbols and Numbers

About the Authors

IAN MCLEAN, MCSE, MCITP, MCT, has over 40 years of experience in industry, commerce, and education. He started his career as an electronics engineer before going into distance learning and then education as a university professor. Currently, he runs his own consultancy company. Ian has written more than 20 books and many papers and technical articles. He has been working with Microsoft operating systems since 1997.

ORIN THOMAS, is an author and an MCT. He has written more than a dozen certification textbooks for Microsoft Press. He holds many certifications, including several MCSE and MCITP credentials. He is the convener of the Melbourne Security and Infrastructure Interchange and a Microsoft Security MVP. He lives in Melbourne, Australia, with his wife and son and enjoys traveling around the world speaking at technical conferences like Tech.ED.

Get Certified—Windows Server 2008

Ace your preparation for the skills measured by the Microsoft® certification exams—and on the job. With 2-in-1 *Self-Paced Training Kits*, you get an official exam-prep guide + practice tests. Work at your own pace through lessons and real-world case scenarios that cover the exam objectives. Then, assess your skills using practice tests with multiple testing modes—and get a customized learning plan based on your results.

EXAMS 70-640, 70-642, 70-646

MCITP Self-Paced Training Kit: Windows Server® 2008 Server Administrator Core Requirements

ISBN 9780735625082

EXAMS 70-640, 70-642, 70-643, 70-647

MCITP Self-Paced Training Kit: Windows Server 2008 Enterprise Administrator Core Requirements

ISBN 9780735625723

EXAM 70-640

MCTS Self-Paced Training Kit: Configuring Windows Server 2008 Active Directory®

Dan Holme, Nelson Ruest, and Danielle Ruest

ISBN 9780735625136

EXAM 70-647

MCITP Self-Paced Training Kit: Windows® Enterprise Administration

Orin Thomas, et al.

ISBN 9780735625099

EXAM 70-642

MCTS Self-Paced Training Kit: Configuring Windows Server 2008 Network Infrastructure

Tony Northrup, J.C. Mackin

ISBN 9780735625129

ALSO SEE

Windows Server 2008 Administrator's Pocket Consultant
William R. Stanek
ISBN 9780735624375

EXAM 70-643

MCTS Self-Paced Training Kit: Configuring Windows Server 2008 Applications Infrastructure

J.C. Mackin, Anil Desai

ISBN 9780735625112

Windows Server 2008 Administrator's Companion
Charlie Russel, Sharon Crawford
ISBN 9780735625051

Windows Server 2008 Resource Kit
Microsoft MVPs with Windows Server Team
ISBN 9780735623613

EXAM 70-646

MCITP Self-Paced Training Kit: Windows Server Administration

Ian McLean, Orin Thomas

ISBN 9780735625105

Windows Server 2008— Resources for Administrators

Windows Server® 2008 Administrator's Companion
Charlie Russel and Sharon Crawford
ISBN 9780735625051

Your comprehensive, one-volume guide to deployment, administration, and support. Delve into core system capabilities and administration topics, including Active Directory®, security issues, disaster planning/recovery, interoperability, IIS 7.0, virtualization, clustering, and performance tuning.

Windows Server 2008 Administrator's Pocket Consultant
William R. Stanek
ISBN 9780735624375

Portable and precise—with the focused information you need for administering server roles, Active Directory, user/group accounts, rights and permissions, file-system management, TCP/IP, DHCP, DNS, printers, network performance, backup, and restoration.

Windows Server 2008 Resource Kit
Microsoft MVPs with Microsoft Windows Server Team
ISBN 9780735623613

Six volumes! Your definitive resource for deployment and operations—from the experts who know the technology best. Get in-depth technical information on Active Directory, Windows PowerShell™ scripting, advanced administration, networking and network access protection, security administration, IIS, and more—plus an essential toolkit of resources on CD.

Internet Information Services (IIS) 7.0 Administrator's Pocket Consultant
William R. Stanek
ISBN 9780735623644

This pocket-sized guide delivers immediate answers for administering IIS 7.0. Topics include customizing installation; configuration and XML schema; application management; user access and security; Web sites, directories, and content; and performance, backup, and recovery.

Windows PowerShell Step by Step
Ed Wilson
ISBN 9780735623958

Teach yourself the fundamentals of the Windows PowerShell command-line interface and scripting language—one step at a time. Learn to use *cmdlets* and write scripts to manage users, groups, and computers; configure network components; administer Microsoft® Exchange Server 2007; and more. Includes 100+ sample scripts.

ALSO SEE

Windows Server 2008 Hyper-V™ Resource Kit
ISBN 9780735625174

Internet Information Services (IIS) 7.0 Resource Kit
ISBN 9780735624412

Windows® Administration Resource Kit: Productivity Solutions for IT Professionals
ISBN 9780735624313

Windows Server 2008 Security Resource Kit
ISBN 9780735625044

Microsoft® Press

Windows Server 2008 Resource Kit— Your Definitive Resource!

Windows Server® 2008 Resource Kit

Microsoft® MVPs with Microsoft Windows Server Team

ISBN 9780735623613

Your definitive reference for deployment and operations—from the experts who know the technology best. Get in-depth technical information on Active Directory®, Windows PowerShell™ scripting, advanced administration, networking and network access protection, security administration, IIS, and other critical topics—plus an essential toolkit of resources on CD.

ALSO AVAILABLE AS SINGLE VOLUMES

Windows Server 2008 Security Resource Kit

Jesper M. Johansson et al. with Microsoft Security Team

ISBN 9780735625044

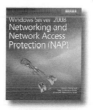

Windows Server 2008 Networking and Network Access Protection (NAP)

Joseph Davies, Tony Northrup, Microsoft Networking Team

ISBN 9780735624221

Windows Server 2008 Active Directory Resource Kit

Stan Reimer et al. with Microsoft Active Directory Team

ISBN 9780735625150

Windows® Administration Resource Kit: Productivity Solutions for IT Professionals

Dan Holme

ISBN 9780735624313

Windows Powershell Scripting Guide

Ed Wilson

ISBN 9780735622791

Internet Information Services (IIS) 7.0 Resource Kit

Mike Volodarsky et al. with Microsoft IIS Team

ISBN 9780735624412

Microsoft®
Press

microsoft.com/mspress